# THE PROCESS OF MANAGEMENT

# William H. Newman
**Director, Strategy Research Center**
**Columbia University**

# E. Kirby Warren
**Samuel Bronfman Professor of Democratic**
**Business Enterprise, Columbia University**

# Jerome E. Schnee
**Professor of Organization Management**
**Rutgers, The State University of New Jersey**

# THE PROCESS OF MANAGEMENT

## STRATEGY, ACTION, RESULTS

5th edition

Prentice-Hall, Inc.
Englewood Cliffs, NJ 07632

**Library of Congress Cataloging in Publication Data**

Newman, William Herman, (date)
  The process of management.

  Includes bibliographies and index.
    1. Industrial management.  I. Warren,
E. Kirby.  II. Schnee, Jerome E., (date)
III. Title.
HD31.N484      1982      658.4      81-11985
ISBN 0-13-723445-7                 AACR2

**THE PROCESS OF MANAGEMENT Strategy, Action, Results, 5th edition.**
William H. Newman, E. Kirby Warren, and Jerome E. Schnee

10  9  8  7  6  5  4  3  2  1

This is a Special Projects book.
Maurine Lewis, director
Susan Adkins, editor
Ray Keating, manufacturing buyer
Olympia Shahbaz, cover design

ISBN 0-13-723445-7

Prentice-Hall International, Inc., *London*
Prentice-Hall of Australia Pty. Limited, *Sydney*
Prentice-Hall of Canada, Ltd., *Toronto*
Prentice-Hall of India Private Limited, *New Delhi*
Prentice-Hall of Japan, Inc., *Tokyo*
Prentice-Hall of Southeast Asia Pte. Ltd., *Singapore*
Whitehall Books Limited, *Wellington, New Zealand*

# Preface

Concern with improving the quality of management continues to accelerate—worldwide. New pressures such as inflation, energy shortages, changes in lifestyles, equal opportunity, and intense international competition keep managers in a central role in our society. And more attention to not-for-profit ventures helps single out managing as a distinct social process.

Fortunately, we are also learning more about the process of managing. Significant research is underway on behavior of people in managerial situations, and actual practice is being scrutinized with a variety of analytical techniques. This research provides insight, sometimes confirming widely held beliefs, sometimes pointing to a needed shift in emphasis. Especially important, it helps us adapt basic concepts to the new situations associated with a changing environment.

The professional manager, the person who must apply these managerial concepts and insights to specific situations, needs a way of thinking about his total task. Of necessity, he is primarily interested in achieving results. And for this purpose the manager wants the concepts stated in an integrated framework directly applicable to his concerns.

The *process* approach provides this practical framework for thinking about managing. It is by far the approach most widely used by business executives. Foreign enterprises and not-for-profit ventures also find the process viewpoint suited to their managerial tasks. An added virtue is that specific techniques such as management-by-objectives, strategy formulation, organization development, job enrichment and the like can be quickly placed in a broader context.

In focusing on the *process of managing,* as we do in this book, we are therefore dealing with concepts that have direct usefulness to persons in managerial positions. Moreover, we are developing an underlying framework that is a basic prerequisite to many advanced techniques and to sensing the relevance of most of the behavioral research in the field.

This edition of the book has been given a new "strategy" orientation. Strategy defines the concrete goals for a company or department. But implementing such a strategy requires management to carefully select an array of more detailed plans, to organize, to lead, and to control. This implementing strategy, the "make happen" character of management, is the primary focus of the book.

Using this strategy/management linkage enables us to stress the following important points:

(a) Managers engage in *purposeful action*. This book is not merely describing social behavior. Instead, it focuses on cooperative activities which are directed toward explicit goals. Achievement of ends is the name of the game.

(b) *Strategy defines the operational goals* of an organization. It is an instrument used by management to mediate between society's needs and the particular mission undertaken by the company or department. And, unless that mission is socially useful, the organization will not survive.

(c) Without implementation, however, missions are no more than good intentions. *Managerial action is necessary* to execute each strategy. A hard look at how managers take this necessary action is the grist of this book.

(d) Effective management—execution of strategy—requires considerable *commitment*. Challenging missions often call for toughness, risk-taking, and difficult trade-offs. Only the manager who can stand up to these pressures is likely to be effective.

(e) Because strategies and environments vary, the kind of managerial action which is appropriate for a particular situation also varies. Considerable insight and skill are required to devise a *managerial design that suits a given strategy*.

This new orientation of the book has required a substantial revision. We have significantly altered the sequence of topics; after introducing the concept of strategy in Chapter 2, we treat planning, decision-making, organizing, motivating, leading, and controlling, in that order in Parts I through VI.

In addition to modifying and updating all chapters, several new chapters have been added. These include

**Chapter 2—Strategy—Defining the Mission.**
Introduces strategy as a powerful management tool for clarifying organizational mission and unifying human effort for achievement of that mission.

**Chapter 8—Quantitative Aids to Decision-Making.**
Treats a wide array of techniques drawn from managerial economics and management science which have potential for improving problem analysis and decision-making.

**Chapter 18—Achieving Personal Leadership**
Recognizes that leading is the "make happen" phase of managing. Examines the functions of leadership and the criteria which guide the choice of an appropriate leadership style.

**Chapter 20—The Art of Giving Orders**
Orders continue to be essential in an organization if work is to proceed in a coordinated manner. This chapter outlines an approach for improving managerial skill in issuing orders.

**Chapter 27—Managing Change**
Because change is an inevitable part of organizational life, managers must be adept in altering the total management system and shifting patterns of behavior within an

enterprise. This chapter suggests guidelines for effectively managing organization change.

All the cases are also new. They include cases from service industries and manufacturing, small firms and large ones, as well as a case contrasting Japanese and American management methods. Because each one is multifaceted, these cases can be used in several ways: case discussion first, followed by the study of concepts; text analysis interwoven with cases; concentration on text and outside readings, the cases being used for review and application. The optimum arrangement will depend on educational objectives, time available, and the background that readers bring to the endeavor.

Most of the questions that follow each chapter have been revised and updated. Bibliographies, also found at the end of each chapter, have brief annotations that will help readers pursue areas in which they are particularly interested. The entire manuscript has been carefully edited and revised to keep the discussion and examples relevant to current issues.

Despite the new orientation and substantial revisions, the basic processes of managing continue to dominate the structure and content of the book. Execution of strategy provides an orientation—a bridge to social purpose—but it does not alter the underlying steps in the management process. And, by moving from company strategy to departmental strategy, the discussion deals with concrete, short-run, management problems.

The concern with achieving results—in contrast to theory building—makes an *eclectic* use of concepts appropriate. Parts IV and V, and Chapter 27, draw heavily on behavioral science. Chapters 8 and 23 stress management science and quantitative techniques. Throughout, viable concepts are drawn from diverse sources. The purpose of the discussion, however, is not to contrast ideas from various sources; rather, it is to develop an integrated framework that will help readers in their professional careers.

A new *Study Guide* has been written to tie into this fifth edition; the availability of the supplement creates wide flexibility in the way this edition can be used.

It is impractical to acknowledge all the helpful comments and suggestions coming from users of the previous edition, literally from every continent of the world. Nevertheless, we do want to note several specific contributions. Harvey W. Wallender III, of Burkholder-Wallender International, made substantial contributions to the Not-for-Profit Notes. We also benefited from thoughtful reviews by Professor Norman Coates, College of Business Administration, University of Rhode Island; Dr. James Gatza, Director of Management Education, American Institute for Property and Liability Underwriters, Malvern, Pennsylvania; Professor Richard Goodman, UCLA; and Professor Borje O. Saxberg, University of Washington.

We are especially indebted to Susan Adkins of Prentice-Hall, Inc, who skillfully edited the manuscript, and to Camilla Koch of Columbia University who put together from three authors a manuscript that could be edited. Joan Daddesa of Rutgers University contributed valuable typing assistance.

The Samuel Bronfman Foundation, through its support of management studies at the Columbia Graduate School of Business, made the writing of this book possible. Close congruence exists between the aims of the Foundation and our interests, and we hope the Foundation trustees are as enthusiastic as we are about this latest aid to management.

WILLIAM H. NEWMAN
E. KIRBY WARREN
JEROME E. SCHNEE

# CONTENTS

## INTRODUCTION

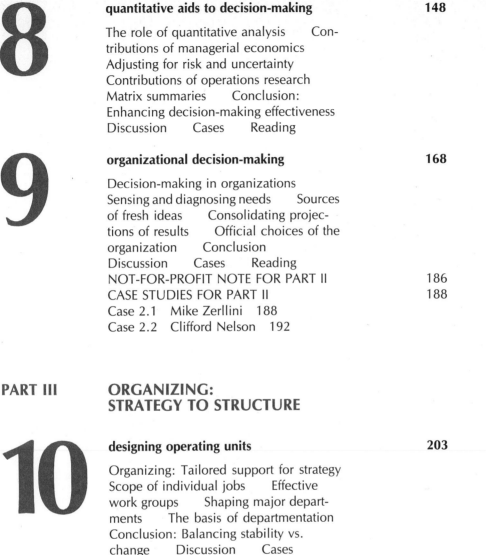

## PART III    ORGANIZING: STRATEGY TO STRUCTURE

**PART V**    **LEADING**

## CONCLUSION   NEED FOR SYNTHESIS

## INDEX

# INTRODUCTION

The ability to manage is one of the most crucial skills in the world today. It is vital to the continued growth of advanced countries, and is an essential element in meeting the aspirations of developing nations.

Of course, some people take a dilettante's view of managing, treating it as an interesting bit of human behavior along with, say, mountain climbing or playing bridge. Others are concerned with managing as a means of attaining personal income and status. Both views are valid; the study of management can be both interesting and rewarding. But the really compelling force that underlies the serious study of management is its profound social value.

Fortunately, our understanding of the process of management has improved significantly in recent years. Although managing is still a considerable way from being a science, analysis of successful practice and of research findings gives us a set of concepts that can add substantially to a person's managerial competence.

These two introductory chapters provide a preview and perspective for the concentrated examination of the management process set forth in subsequent parts of the book.

Chapter 1—Social Role of Managers. The nature of managerial activity is examined in terms of both function and process in this opening chapter. To help grasp several distinct viewpoints of the management process, we sketch briefly the main currents of thought that are now being melded into effective management practice. Then we suggest an approach to individual improvement in managerial ability and explain how the material in this book can be used toward that end.

Chapter 2—Strategy—Defining the Mission. In this chapter we introduce the main strategy theme of the book and describe how strategy enables us to integrate managerial processes in a consistent manner. We examine the several dimensions of strategy in this introductory section because of its value in clarifying the mission of an enterprise and in focusing effort on achieving that mission. Throughout the chapters that follow we shall explain how strategy guides the major management processes and how each process is used to execute strategy.

# social role
# of
# managers

**1**

Learning Objectives

After completing this chapter you should be able to

1. Understand the significance of the role managers play in our society.

2. Describe the external integration and internal integration responsibilities of managers.

3. Explain the influence of personal value systems on the management process.

4. Describe the major schools of management thought.

5. Understand the management process framework and its basis for the design of this book.

6. List and describe the major management processes.

Do-it-yourself may fit a hobby, but in today's world sheer survival calls for the organized cooperation of groups of people. Our capacity to rebuild the slums, to eliminate pollution, to give individuals an opportunity for self-expression, to raise the standard of living, and to achieve our many other social and personal objectives rests on joint activity. If individuals or even whole tribes attempt to be self-sufficient—producing their own food, clothing, and shelter—subsistence is meager at best. But when people join together in various enterprises, pooling their resources and exchanging their outputs, they grasp the means to flourish.

Managers are vital to such cooperative enterprises. They conceive of the service an enterprise can render, mobilize the necessary means of production, coordinate activities both within the enterprise and with the outside world, and inspire people associated with the enterprise to work toward common objectives. *Managers are the activating element.*

Management concepts are being vigorously applied in private firms, but the need for effective managers is just as pressing in nonprofit enterprises such as hospitals, training centers, space agencies, urban transport, and wildlife refuges. Increasing risk, size, inflation, multinational dependence, and the like all intensify the need for able managers.

To understand the significance of managing, let us take a closer look at the role managers play in our society.

**external plus
internal
integration**

One key facet of management is integration. The successful firm must be integrated externally with its environment and internally among its departments.

*External integration*  Every enterprise, be it a university or a steel mill, requires continuing give-and-take relationships with an array of contributors. Consumers provide markets, suppliers provide materials and equipment, investors provide capital, local governments provide functioning communities, and so on. Typically, the relationship with each contributor extends over an indefinite period, and benefits flow both ways—to the contributor and to the firm.[1]

Each of these relationships is dynamic. For instance, the amount, specifications, and delivery schedule that a company desires for its raw materials will change as it adjusts to shifting consumer desires. Likewise, a supplier faces his own shifts in costs, other demands, and capacity. Consequently, continuing mediation is needed to maintain a mutually acceptable flow. Even when the give-and-take between an enterprise and its community or its financial advisor involves intangibles, the need for a sustained exchange of benefits is no less vital.

Management is concerned with more than maintaining good relations with each contributing group separately. In addition, it must make sure that the "price" for cooperation desired by one contributor is compatible with the

---

[1]C. G. Burck, "The Intricate 'Politics' of the Corporation," *Fortune,* April 1975.

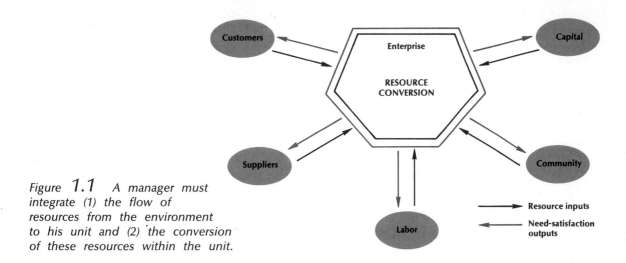

Figure *1.1* *A manager must integrate (1) the flow of resources from the environment to his unit and (2) the conversion of these resources within the unit.*

requirements of *all* the others. For example, before a computer manufacturer can promise a customer equipment of a certain quality at a specific price for delivery on a given date, he must be sure that the supplier of components will not insist on conditions that hinder him from keeping his promises.[2] Similarly, a college dean can't attract students with a program which alumni (or other donors) refuse to finance or which accrediting agencies view as mere play.

Employees pose a dual integration problem for management. (1) They, like other contributors, must receive sufficient benefits to induce them to take the job—but not such high benefits that management is unable to provide necessary inducements to suppliers of materials, capital, services, and other inputs. (2) While they are at work, employees are a volatile element in internal integration—as we shall see in many parts of this book.

Integrating the enterprise externally with its key contributors is a never-ending task. Much more than price negotiations is involved. Dependability, agreement on timing, numerous intangible benefits and inconveniences, adaptability to needs of either party—all enter the picture. Fortunately, many aspects of these relationships are covered by custom or even by legal regulation; without some such stability, the cooperative action of diverse groups would be impossible. But change is sure to be occurring somewhere in the total system, and adjustments to meet this change are likely to impinge on existing arrangements with other contributors.

*Internal integration* If an enterprise is going to fulfill its side of all agreements with contributors, internal operations must be astutely managed. Here, also, integration is vital.[3] The actions of various departments

[2]The English language at times compels the use of the masculine gender for pronouns in the third person singular. Throughout this book, therefore, the use of "he" and "his" should be interpreted as meaning "he or she" and "his or hers," and as referring to women as well as men.

[3]P. R. Lawrence and J. W. Lorsch, *Organization and Environment: Managing Differentiation and Integration* (Homewood, IL: Richard D. Irwin, 1967).

must be synchronized—people must be hired and trained so that they are available when needed, and the like. Balance in allocating resources and in setting priorities must be adjusted in terms of external demands. While such regulating is being pursued, management must also cultivate enthusiasm for achieving the multifold mission of the enterprise.

A vital part of management's task is integrating the efforts of employees, each of whom has his own values and aspirations, into a company program. The program itself reflects the pressures of synchronization and of balancing claims for limited resources (all of which is restrained and shaped by arrangements necessary to keep contributors contributing).

For instance, when General Motors opens a new auto assembly plant in Mexico, local managers must negotiate a host of external relationships. And at the same time, they must design an effective internal system which fits the local people and the input agreements they have made with other groups.

**innovation**

For many years managers were widely regarded as individuals who merely adapted to their situation. If demand for products fell off, they cut back production; if a new source of low-cost raw materials opened up, they switched suppliers; if labor became scarce, they raised wage rates to get the workers they needed. According to this conception, managers performed an essential function—responding to changing conditions—but their actions were dictated by forces beyond their control. The early economists clearly held this view; consequently, they gave scant attention to the problems of management and that blind spot permeates much of economic literature to this day.

Actually, modern managers go well beyond adapting; they exercise a positive influence to make things happen. When they anticipate that the need for their product will drop off, managers seek new products or services in order to maintain employment of the resources they have mobilized; they take the initiative in looking for cheaper sources of energy and promoting their development; they sponsor research for more economical methods of production; they try to anticipate manpower needs and train people to fill them. In short, they are a dynamic, innovating force.[4]

This self-confident, aggressive attitude reflects a deep-seated sense of obligation, or mission. They are not complete masters of their activities, of course; indeed, they must be highly sensitive to a wide range of pressures and restrictions. But managers do more than simply adjust passively. They *initiate* changes in their operating situation and *follow through* with action that, to some extent, makes dreams come true.

**MANAGERIAL VALUE SYSTEMS**     Managers inevitably deal with value issues. They cannot escape them. Any innovative approach to external and internal integration involves trade-offs. Providing more stable employment, for instance, must be balanced against higher inventory risk. For air pollution control, many companies find that control

---

[4]S. Ramo, *The Management of Innovative Technological Corporations* (New York: Wiley, 1980).

devices in chimneys catch eighty percent of unwanted particles whereas a change in production technology would eliminate ninety-five percent. Does the fifteen percent improvement justify a million dollar investment—which will also reduce employment by two jobs? Or, to cite further examples, should a big oak tree be cut down to provide more customer parking space? What restraints should be put on the sale of dangerous products such as dynamite, cigarettes, or pornographic books?

Because managers are expected to take action—to get results—they must make value judgements; they have to make a decision so that action can proceed. In many situations values conflict. The choice may be tough, but decide they must.

To a large extent, the values a manager uses in making choices are based on social norms. Goodwill and continuing acceptability depend on his acting in an acceptable, predictable way.   **society's changing needs**

National priorities are shifting, however. Now management must deal with new emphases, including:

1. *Individual self-expression.* The rising generation of both men and women wants meaningful jobs—as well as the fruits of high productivity.
2. *Racial and urban problems.* Society must make racial equality meaningful; interwoven with this is urban renewal.
3. *Pollution control.* Our material achievements are fast overtaking the finite capacity of our natural environment, as is painfully evident in the energy crisis and in air and water pollution.
4. *Health, education, and welfare.* An ever-increasing share of our natural resources is being directed into such things as medical care, education, public recreation, pensions.
5. *Guns and butter.* Our combined space and military expenditures are already on a scale that challenges our ability to have both guns and butter.
6. *Inflation.* Overriding this array of social aims is control of the crippling effects of inflation.

These new priorities, and others that will undoubtedly emerge, are *additions* to the long-standing goals of a rising standard of living, full employment, national security, etc.; they are not replacements. We want the new benefits without sacrificing any of the old ones.

Unfortunately for a manager, new social goals tend to be vague. No agreement exists as to how much, by what date, and at what cost the new goals are to be achieved. In fact, it is managers who are dealing with specific operations that force realism into the lofty objectives. Managers of necessity confront social reform at the level of concrete action.

Normally, managers feel these shifts in social values through the demands made by resource contributors. Employees ask for more meaningful jobs. Women, blacks, and other minorities insist on equal rights. Communities grant operating permits only if antipollution standards are met. And so on. These new pressures become part of the give-and-take bargaining of external integration that we have already discussed.

The amount of weight (value) that managers give to such pressures depends, in part, upon what competitors are doing. For example, if competing employers offer meaningful jobs then we pay more attention to requests of that sort. If a request is backed up by laws or government orders, it receives even more respect. In addition, as noted under innovation, managers often try to anticipate these pressures and get an advantage by dealing with them early.

The preceding paragraphs suggest how broad social goals get translated into the values used by managers in making concrete decisions. Two other angles should also be considered—the personal values of the manager involved, and organizational values.

**personal value systems**

Individual managers inject their personal values into the decision process. Social values, as we have just seen, are often vague and conflicting; frequently they are promoted by biased special-interest groups. Consequently, in specific situations the manager on the spot has room for his own selection and interpretation.

Each of us has a private value system. It includes, among many facets, enjoyment of or aversion to taking risks; importance attached to people versus things; loyalties to others versus self-gratification; attachment to particular causes or crusades. When confronted with a decision, our response naturally reflects such personal values. The external social forces bearing on the problem are filtered through this personal screen. In the oak tree versus parking lot situation, if the local manager is a conservationist he will probably find some way to save the tree. If he sympathizes with people having parking difficulties the tree is likely to disappear. Similarly, personal feelings about continuing employment for local breadwinners will affect decisions on plant relocation.

**organizational values**

No organization can safely permit its managers to rely solely on their own values. The organization must have coordinated action toward a set of common goals for without such unity the power of joint action is lost. The organization therefore superimposes its values on its managers who accept this necessity and expect it of the enterprise they join.

Establishing organizational values is a delicate process. The organization wants to achieve unified, consistent action and yet give managers considerable freedom. Through selection, education, and participation it hopes to get individual commitment to organizational objectives. Later chapters on planning, decentralizing, staffing, and leading frequently face this issue.

To secure this unity of action, an organization typically adopts policies in such matters as employment of women and blacks. Also, its strategy identifies the dominant objectives regarding services and results. Once established, these become values managers are expected to pursue regardless of their personal preferences. They are the official response of the organization to social needs.

In this way, social aims are melded into selected organizational objectives.[5] The road is bumpy and full of turns, however, and in practice as managers inperpret these aims some very painful value choices must be made.

Managers have a vital, tough job. As already pointed out, managers are expected to be innovative—not merely adaptive—in both external and internal integration. And the more innovative they become, the more difficult will be the value choices they must make. Now what can be learned that will help managers perform their important role better? That question is the focus of this book.

## SCHOOLS OF MANAGEMENT THOUGHT

The act of managing has been studied in several distinct ways. Each approach adds helpful insights, and although a single approach may be incomplete and perhaps biased, we can select good ideas from all of them. Actually, concepts from five major approaches—or schools of thought—are woven into the basic theme of this book. As background for our synthesis, the separate approaches will be described briefly.

**the productivity approach**

The oldest theories of management, indeed the mainstream of ideas, concern productivity. Attention in this approach centers on learning how to *produce in abundance*.

Two supporting ideas are implied when we speak of productivity: (1) A productive operation yields *results*—results in terms of the goods and services sought by society. Here we take a tough and pragmatic stand about whether a specific practice actually produces desired results. (2) A productive operation is *efficient*. The ratio of outputs to inputs is high.

*Scientific management* The first systematic study of management in the United States was made by production engineers. Frederick W. Taylor and his associates shifted an interest in production bonuses to a focus on management, and thus launched what became known in 1910 as *Scientific Management*.[6]

Before bonuses could be set, Taylor insisted, the best conditions and manner of doing a job must be determined. To ensure that machines operated properly, he insisted on preventive maintenance and on keeping tools properly sharpened in a central toolroom. For these methods to work, raw materials could not vary, so he set up raw-material specifications and quality-control checks. Also, to prevent delays due to time lost in giving workers new assignments, careful production scheduling, dispatching, and internal-transport systems were established. Finally, workers suited to the

---

[5]J. E. Ramsey, "A Framework for the Interaction of Corporate Value Objectives and Corporate Strategy," *Journal of Economics and Business,* 28, no. 3, (Summer 1976), pp. 171–80.

[6]F. W. Taylor, *Scientific Management* (New York: Harper & Bros., 1947).

newly designed jobs had to be selected and trained. Only when all of these conditions were met was Taylor ready to use time study to determine a standard day's work.

This sort of approach creates a minor revolution in a shop or hospital that has operated in a haphazard, traditional manner—a revolution in the method of work, in planning and control by management, and in productivity. Nevertheless, these basic concepts, nurtured in a machine shop, have been adapted to all sorts of production operations in plants throughout the world. More important, they have fundamentally altered the way we think about management problems.

*Extensions of the productivity approach* The analytical productivity approach soon moved beyond the plant to all divisions of an enterprise. Notable improvements arose, for example, from systematic arrangements for recruiting, training, promoting, compensating, and providing a variety of fringe benefits to *personnel*. Financial *budgeting* and cost analysis, originally control mechanisms but soon used for planning as well, are now applied to all areas of any kind of enterprise. A steady flow of *mechanization* and automation has transferred from workers to machines a wide array of tasks that can be standardized.

Best known for their use in industrial firms, all these productivity techniques can easily be adapted to nonprofit enterprises that perform large volumes of similar activities.

Many of our modern concepts of planning and control are derived from the productivity approach. Its direct tie between desired results and management methods avoids the abstractions that tend to clutter other approaches. To be sure, we have expanded its scope and time horizon and have added ways to gain flexibility; and especially we have tempered its mechanistic assumptions with insights from behavioral science.

**the behavioral approach**

The behavioral approach to management dates back to 1927–32 where Elton Mayo and Fritz Roethlisberger made a landmark study of the Western Electric Company.[7] In their conclusions they stressed that workers respond to their *total* work situation, and that attitudes toward their work and their social relations constitute an important part of this total. A corollary of such a conclusion is that the early writers on Scientific Management and many people in personnel management had acted on an inadequate notion of worker motivation.

Controlled management experiments in real-life settings, such as those at Western Electric, are rare. It is too costly and complex to experiment with good and bad managerial practice in large, live organizations. Social psychologists, however, experiment with small bits of human behavior under laboratory conditions, and often their findings throw light on a management issue. For instance, we have learned a lot about small-group behavior from

---

[7]E. Mayo, *The Human Problems of an Industrial Civilization* (Boston: Graduate School of Business Administration, Harvard Univesity, 1946) and F. J. Roethlisberger and W. J. Dickson, *Management and the Worker* (Cambridge: Harvard University Press, 1939).

such experiments. Also, an array of psychological studies on individual perception, motivation, learning, and other responses help greatly in designing jobs and methods.

Sociologists rely primarily on field studies. Here, the classic is Max Weber's insightful observation of *bureaucracy* in government, churches, and political parties. For him, pure bureaucracy includes (1) a division of labor with each job clearly defined and filled by a technically qualified person, (2) a well-established hierarchy with clear lines of authority and appropriate staffs and salary for those at each level, and (3) a systematic set of aims and regulations so that actions can be impersonal and coordinated.[8]

Concepts and insights from the behavioral sciences take up a substantial part of this book with parts, chapters, and sections focused predominantly on human behavior. In fact, the entire management process can be seen as conditioning behavior. However, we have not been content to merely summarize behavioral science research data. Since our goal is to improve managerial effectiveness, we have built the book around an operational framework and woven behavioral-science findings into that. In seeking guides for management practice, we have selected those theories and ideas that relate directly to management and have converted them into operational terms.

A third view of management deals only with the way executives make decisions. A political scientist, Graham Allison, and his associates have developed a comprehensive framework for analyzing managerial decisions.[9]

**the decision-making approach**

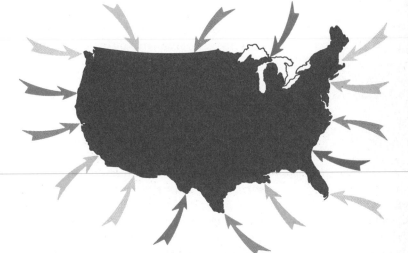

Figure *1.2* As immigrants from many nations have contributed to our national heritage, so have several approaches formed our modern concepts of managerial processes.

[8]M. Weber, *Theory of Social and Economic Organization* (New York: Free Press, 1947).

[9]G. Allison, *Essence of Decision: Explaining the Cuban Missile Crisis* (Boston: Little, Brown, 1971). See also J. G. March and H. A. Simon, *Organizations* (New York: Wiley, 1958); and R. M. Cyert and J. G. March, *A Behavioral Theory of the Firm,* (Englewood Cliffs, NJ: Prentice-Hall, 1963).

They suggest that to understand why a company decides to open an office in Singapore or to fire its president, three kinds of analyses are necessary. The three analyses—or models—are labeled *rational-individual, bureaucratic,* and *political*.

The rational-individual model presumes that decisions are based on thorough analysis, careful weighing of evidence, and logical choice reflecting clear criteria. Here, concepts from microeconomics and mathematic formulae from *operations research* provide refined logical propositions. Although many managerial problems are not specific enough or lack the data needed for such neat quantitative solutions, a formal approach to decision-making does force managers to think more sharply.

The bureaucratic model looks at how decisions are made within an established organization. For major problems, no single person can do all the analysis prescribed for a fully rational choice, so the task is divided into pieces and dispersed throughout the organization. Also it is spread over time. This dispersion and the mechanisms necessary to handle the bits and pieces profoundly change the answers that emerge. Obviously for managers who must rely on the help and decisions of their subordinates, this second view of decision-making is very illuminating.

A political view of decision-making is even further removed from individual rationality than the bureaucratic model. For some people, politics is immoral and therefore they deny its existence. Realists recognize political behavior but have difficulty predicting the decisions that arise from political pressures. Nevertheless, no manager can afford to overlook the way politics conditions the choices that are made.

All three views of decision-making help us design planning mechanisms for a company. When combined, they are far more powerful than the single approaches to decision-making we previously relied upon. Nevertheless, they deal with only part of a manager's job. Making wise choices is obviously important—but organizing, leading, and controlling are also essential.

In Part II we shall examine the ways in which the rational-individual and bureaucratic models of decision-making can be used by managers. The impact of organizational politics on decision-making and behavior will be described in Part V. Our focus is twofold—first to relate the concepts to realistic operating situations faced by managers, and second to place decision-making within the total managerial process so that the decisions themselves are better and their execution is more effective.

**the systems
approach**

The total is greater than the sum of its parts—especially when we are thinking about a total system. Just as a TV set differs from a collection of parts, managing is more than an assembly of plans and reports. The pieces must fit together into a workable system.

Starting from the way a medical doctor must think of the total body, or a telephone engineer must think of all the parts of a communications system, a theory about systems in general has been developed. This theory applies to many complex situations, ranging from space exploration to nursery schools.

The management of a company can be viewed as a system.[10] The various moves that executives make—borrowing capital, controlling quality, hiring black executives—do indeed interact. By relating all these moves in terms of an overall management system, we can develop a much stronger, coordinated force.

In this book we repeatedly stress the benefit of thinking about managing as a total system; we enthusiastically embrace the systems viewpoint. But a systems view is only one dimension. Before we can consider interaction, we must know the nature of the pieces, what purposes they serve, the conditions in which they work well, and their cost. Also we need to know about the resources and requirements of the environment. Conceiving the total system is an essential but insufficient step in good management design.

**the contingency viewpoint**

The contingency viewpoint is a currently fashionable expression of a simple, fundamental idea. There is no single best way to manage in all circumstances; instead, what should be done in any particular situation is contingent upon the needs of that situation.[11] Only a quack doctor prescribes the same medicine to all his patients. The professional first makes a diagnosis; then drawing upon his knowledge of alternative actions and their likely effect, he prescribes for the individual case.

Likewise in management. In our studies—and in this book—we can describe likely issues, suggest alternatives that have worked well in some companies, identify the pros and cons of these alternatives, and propose ways to develop a good fit for a selected alternative. But always the particular course drawn from this background should be carefully fitted to the unique local situation. Managing is too complex, dynamic, and uncertain for pat solutions. Its contingent quality, nevertheless, makes it challenging and rewarding.

**need for an operational framework**

All the streams of thought summarized in this section contribute to the emerging profession of management. Each is making a distinctive contribution, and we shall draw freely on their ideas throughout this book[12] Our quick review noted, however, that none of these approaches gives us a full picture of managing. So we face the task of relating valuable ideas within a workable scheme (and of translating special jargon into simple, understandable terms).

For dealing with this array of ideas, thinking of management as a process has great advantages. Focusing on the process of managing is (1) *operational*, because it expresses ideas in terms of actions a manager must take; (2) *comprehensive*, embracing the major tasks of managing; (3) *univer-*

---

[10]R. H. Miles, *Macro Organizational Behavior* (Santa Monica, CA: Goodyear, 1980), chap. 9.

[11]H. Koontz, "The Management Theory Jungle Revisited," *Academy of Management Review*, 5, no. 2, (April 1980), pp. 175–87.

[12]The *process* view of managing developed in this book provides a broad base for study of more specialized subjects such as the five approaches noted above, and fields like operations research, organization theory, budgetary control, personnel management, behavioral reseach, systems engineering, and the like. Such subjects will become more meaningful and useful when they are seen in relation to the total management process.

*sal*, in that all managers should give some attention to each part of the process; and (4) a key for harnessing executive action to the mission of managers discussed in the beginning of this chapter.

Since the process of management serves as the framework of this book, we should take a close look at its nature and components.

**THE MANAGEMENT PROCESS**    Social processes, of which management is one, are common in civilized society. We worship together, play group games, stand in line while we wait for buses, negotiate contracts, and try people for murder. In each case, because we have an established pattern of what we should do and what we expect others to do, we can achieve a result that would not otherwise be feasible. The particulars of a process may, of course, be changed from time to time. A major college football game has rituals for spectators and players that are quite different from those of the old-fashioned jousting match, and a modern murder trial has changed considerably from legal procedures in the days of Henry VIII. But to understand what is happeing in any social activity—including the management of an enterprise—and, especially, to ensure that what we want to happen does happen, we need a keep appreciation of the social process involved.

Management, like education or government, is a *continuing* process. There are always new mouths to feed, fresh minds to stimulate, and more people to govern. And satisfying today's needs invites higher aspirations for tomorrow. Thus new problems crop up as old ones are solved. For purposes of analysis, of course, we may focus on a single problem, or just one series of actions that lead to a specific end; but in practice, a manager must learn to deal simultaneously with a wide range of problems, each in a different stage of resolution.

Managing is so complex that our minds cannot consider all its facets at the same moment. We need to divide the whole activity into parts in order to grasp the full significance of each, just as we get a clear picture of a company by looking separately at its financial statements, its key personnel, its reputation, its facilities, its policies and organizations, its traditions and social structure. Then we can fit the different aspects into a total system.

The total task of management can be divided into four elements: planning, organizing, leading, and controlling. Although closely interrelated, each of these elements can be analyzed as a subprocess. Each is vital to the success of managers at all levels—from first-line supervisors to presidents. And these four elements are present in managing every kind of enterprise—small and large, manufacuring and selling, partnership and corporation, profit and nonprofit. While looking briefly at these four processes, we shall point out the plan of this book.

**planning**    More and more companies are using strategy as their dominant, overriding plan. Strategy defines the scope of activities, selects a basis for excellence, sets targets, and picks key moves to reach those targets. This central plan then guides more detailed managing.

Because strategy can be such a potent unifying device, it is stressed throughout this book. After describing strategy in the next chapter, we shall repeatedly consider how other managerial devices can contribute to the achievement of strategy.

Specific planning is a crucial step in executing any strategy. Managers consulting with each other and with the people who will carry out the plans set goals for each subdivision. They establish policies and standard methods to guide those who do the work, and they develop schedules to keep the work moving toward the objectives. They readjust plans periodically in light of new information and changes in operating conditions.

Planning can be improved if the basic stages in making a decision rationally are understood: diagnosing the problem, finding good alternative solutions, projecting the results of each alternative, and, finally, selecting the course of action. The way decisions get made within an organization deserves special attention; we shall analyze rational decision-making in detail in Part II.

**organizing**

Once the work of an enterprise grows beyond what a single craftsman can do, organization becomes necessary. We have to assign the various tasks to different people and to coordinate their efforts. As the enterprise expands, this process leads to departments and divisions, each of which has its particular mission. One way to think about the resulting oranization is as a complex machine—say, an airplane designed for transatlantic passenger service. Each part of a plane performs a necessary function—supplying power, pressure, heat, steering, communication, and so forth; *and* the different parts are so carefully balanced and fitted together that changing any one of them often calls for an adjustment in several others.

A manager must also view organization as a social arrangement, because it is composed of people rather than physical objects. The people who are assigned tasks are independent, self-respecting individuals with a variety of motives; informal groups influence the way people respond to managerial action; and the attitudes of all these people are continually shifting and evolving. In organizing, then, we must seek ways of getting the necessary work done as we build a social structure that helps meet the needs of the people doing the work. The technical and behavioral aspects of organizing will be examined in Part III.

**leading**

Planning and organizing set the stage. Then leading triggers action. This "make happen" phase of managing calls for motivating people through personal leadership. All sorts of issues are involved: individual needs, group behavior, informal organization, conflict, internal politics, etc. As explained in Part IV, these forces may either support or work against company plans.

Managers must deal effectively on a person-to-person basis in order to activate plans. Selecting a suitable leadership style, communicating, and giving orders require skills which differ significantly from planning skills. In Part V we advocate a realistic, consistent approach to the problems of dealing with people.

For a ship to reach its destination without sailing far off course, the captain regularly "takes his bearings." A manager, likewise, must measure his progress if he is to reach his objectives. And when he discovers that operations are not proceeding according to plan, he takes corrective action to get back on course or, if this is not feasible, readjusts his plans. This process of measuring progress, comparing it with plans, and taking corrective action is called *control*. As our analysis in Part VI will show, control is not a simple matter. Measuring intangibles such as customer goodwill or executive morale poses difficulties, and devising corrective action that both overcomes an immediate difficulty and creates a favorable climate for future performance calls for ingenuity. Moreover, the dispersal of activities that result from organization creates problems of just who should control what.

**FRAMEWORK RATHER THAN PROCEDURE**

In the following chapters, then, we shall examine each of these four elements—planning, organizing, leading and controlling—in some detail, and we shall divide these major aspects of the overall management process into even narrower subprocesses. Such a systematic view of management provides a convenient device (1) for diagnosing complex management problems and (2) for working on improvements at one stage without losing sight of other stages.

But a framework that helps us think in an orderly fashion is not necessarily a step-by-step procedure that we must follow. Actually, when we deal with a concrete management problem, the available information is not neatly classified and labeled; instead, a great array of facts hits us at once, while some data remains stubbornly hidden. In response to such confusion, our thoughts tend to flit first to one subject and then to another. So the chief purpose of a conceptual framework, such as the systematic examination of the management process in this book, is to help us quickly to place diverse ideas in a useful order.

The framework is more than a series of pigeonholes to tuck ideas in, however; for among the pigeonholes there is a rational relationship that we know in advance. Thus, when we mentally classify a new bit of information as bearing on the long-range objectives of department A, we can immediately relate it to a host of other ideas we have stored in our mind; and, in this relation, the piece of information takes on meaning because it contributes to our comprehension of the total situation. Mankind has advanced from a primitive state largely by developing orderly ways of thinking about problems; in proposing a systematic approach to management, then, we are simply following this time-proved method.

There are, of course, many ways to think about so complicated a subject as management. The approach presented in this book has proved very useful

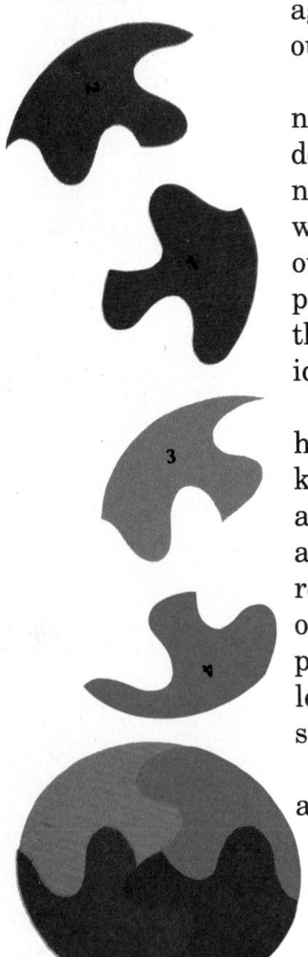

*Figure 1.3 Managing is so complicated that a separate examination of its subprocesses is necessary for a full understanding. But we should never lose sight of the way the processes fit together to form the whole.*

for both practical and theoretical analyses of a wide variety of management situations. So while we should be alert for improvements, we can proceed with confidence that this approach has practical value for anyone in a managerial or staff position or for the researcher who is trying to understand how managers get things done.

One further introductory note: because people with diverse backgrounds talk about management, words are used in different ways. Since this is so, we should clarify our terminology. For ease of discussion, we shall use "manager," "executive," and "administrator" as synonyms. And when we deal with person-to-person relationships, we may use "supervisor" or even "boss" to designate the manager who sits *immediately* above a subordinate in the organizational hierarchy. For these terms, we are simply following common usage. Other words, which have more precise meanings, will be defined as we encounter them.

This book contains two kinds of aids for improving managerial ability: text and cases. The text discussion assists in analyzing the numerous facets of managing and in finding ways to proceed. It provides help in recognizing problems, seeing their interrelationships, conceiving of possible solutions, and developing sensitivity to the advantages and limitations of alternative solutions. Mastery of this mental framework provides a foundation for developing skill.

**design of this book**

At the end of each part, we briefly explore difficulties that may arise in applying to not-for-profit enterprises the management concepts drawn from experience in profit-seeking companies.

Cases then offer an opportunity to start applying the general concepts to specific situations; and a discussion of proposed solutions with other personal will give some check on how well the concepts are being applied. At best, these cases can offer only a beginning in the practice that is necessary for developing managerial proficiency. But this beginning is important, for it *builds a bridge* between general concepts and concrete situations; and we hope it will establish a pattern for going on to the use of concepts in real life.

Careful study of the cases serves three other purposes.

1. They help us overcome the unreal separations that are inevitable in any analytical treatment of an interdependent phenomenon. For example, we shall discuss planning, organizing, and leading, separately. But in actual problems, the plans and policies of a company (Part I), are partly determined by the organization structure (Part III), and vice versa. And the leadership style of an executive (Part V) is influenced somewhat by the organization structure. So, in actuality a manager must solve planning and leading problems *along with* organization problems. Most of our cases present a whole situation; that is, they do not merely illustrate the issues in any one chapter. Instead, they provide a way of seeing the interrelated application of various concepts from all chapters in a realistic, whole-problem sense. They provide a sense of the *system*, while the chapters enable us to concentrate on the parts.

2. They make the ideas in the chapters more *meaningful*. Sometimes we shall find that an idea appears rather simple—even obvious—as explained in the text, and

only when we apply it to a real problem will its full and complex meaning begin to unfold. Applying concepts helps to clarify and reinforce their meaning.

3. They help show that we do not always have facts and concepts that cover all aspects of a complex management problem. As in medicine, management problems often include variables that theory does not explain; there are unique elements in each specific situation. At times, then, all the answers needed to solve a case *neatly* will not be found in the book. This can be very frustrating. Nevertheless, it is a difficulty faced by leaders down through the ages. Actually, it is precisely this need to blend general concepts with the stubborn facts of a practical situation that makes management challenging and fascinating.

## CONCLUSION

Two broad developments have made the study of management timely. (1) In a world where hopes and aspirations are mounting, managers play a crucial role in fulfilling these new goals—and we expect it of them. They initiate growth as well as adapt to dynamic forces. (2) Fortunately, we are learning more about how this important task can be performed effectively. The recognition of management as a distinct social process has led to many studies by researchers and by executives themselves. And from this study has emerged a whole array of insights and percepts that can be put to practical use.

Treating management as a *process* puts our ideas about managing into *operational* terms—that is, in terms that directly relate to executive decisions and actions. And a further division into the subprocesses of planning, organizing, leading, and controlling provides an analytical framework that has proved useful in all kinds of businesses and nonprofit enterprises.

We can improve our management skill by learning about these elements of managing, and by deliberately applying them to concrete situations. Each chapter helps us to learn about managing, and the cases give opportunities to apply the basic concepts.

## FOR FURTHER DISCUSSION

1. "Given the complexities of modern life, the need for effective management of public and private institutions is greater than ever. Yet at the same time, the individual's desire to have a voice in actions affecting him makes managing far more difficult." What do you think of this statement? How should managers deal with these diverse demands?

2. "The primary function of any business is to offer products and/or services to those who can afford them and to do so in a way which is profitable to the firm. Thus the basic goal of a business is profit, its source is in the market, and its components are revenue and cost. The science of economics, which has for hundreds of years been devoted to studying these phenomena, is the major school or discipline for a business manager to draw on. Everything else should be viewed in the context of the economics approach." Do you agree? Explain your position.

3. One of the scarce resources in many developing nations is trained management. Suppose you were given the responsibility for setting up a management course in such a country. Someone else will develop courses in accounting, finance, marketing, and so on. Which of the approaches to management would you draw on in such a course, and why?

4. How will the entrance of more well-educated women into management affect corporate approaches to balancing diverse social needs?

5. "All we needed was tough times to bring us back to basics. Now that we are slipping behind other nations, we can expect much greater emphasis on productivity instead of all that behavioral and systems mumbo-jumbo." Comment.

6. In what ways do you feel that the process of managing a large private corporation (1) differs from and (2) is similar to the process of managing equally large or larger public or nonprofit organizations, such as hospitals, universities, or government agencies?

7. Which of the four elements of management is likely to be most important in a small new business? A large mature business? Discuss.

## CASES

For cases involving issues covered in this chapter, see especially the following. Particularly relevant questions are listed after each case.

Benjo Associates (p. 92), 1, 7, 20
Elizabeth Archer (p. 96), 4, 20, 21
Clifford Nelson (p. 192), 20
Joan Carrier (p. 376), 20
Netsuki Novelty Products Company (p. 451), 9, 10, 11

## FOR FURTHER READING

Hirsch, P. M., "Organizational Effectiveness and the Institutional Environment," *Administrative Science Quarterly,* 20 (1975), pp. 327–44. Comparative study of the strategies used by firms in the ethical pharmaceutical and phonograph-record industries to cope with their external environments.

McGuire, J. W., ed., *Contemporary Management: Issues and Viewpoints.* Englewood Cliffs, NJ: Prentice-Hall, 1974. Valuable set of papers describing schools of management thought, the current status of management thinking, and likely future directions.

Mintzberg, H., "The Manager's Job: Folklore and Fact," *Harvard Business Review*, July-August 1975, pp. 49–61. Fascinating study of how managers spend their time and perform their work.

Newman, W. H., ed., *Managers for the Year 2000*. Englewood Cifts, NJ: Prentice-Hall, 1978. Report of a symposium which previews the year 2000 and the qualities managers will need to cope with future responsibilities.

Osborn, R. N., J. G. Hunt, and L. R. Jauch, *Organizational Theory: An Integrated Approach*. New York: Wiley, 1980, pt. 2. Good elaboration of the contingency viewpoint of management.

Scott, W. G. and D. K. Hart, *Organizational America*. Boston: Houghton Mifflin, 1979. Provacative analysis of how organizational life shapes societal values.

# 2

# strategy—
# defining
# the mission

Learning Objectives

After completing this chapter you should be able to

1. Explain the importance of strategy to an organization.
2. Define strategy and describe its major characteristics.
3. Describe the three major approaches to the determination of strategy.
4. Identify and describe the three sets of data used in the systematic analysis of strategy.
5. Distinguish between corporate, business-unit, and functional strategies and describe their major elements.

Business managers are giving increased attention to company strategy for two reasons (1) Rapid external changes are requiring basic shifts in the way many companies operate. Energy flip-flops, new legislation, social tensions, world instability, unforeseen competition, gyrating costs, material shortages, all create new threats and opportunities. Strategy is the best tool known for adjusting to this stormy setting. (2) Converting a going business to a new strategy is proving to be much more difficult than managers expected. Many parts of the company's managerial system have to be reshaped. Resistance is common. Uncertainty high. Like landing a man on the moon, the goal may be clear but getting from here to there is demanding and complex.

Because execution of strategy is important but so elusive, we shall build bridges to strategy throughout our examination of planning, organizing, leading, and controlling. Carrying out strategy, then, will be a recurring theme.

The strategy theme has another benefit. It helps the reader to see the unity, or wholeness, of a well managed firm. It shows how the various managerial activities can be fitted together to achieve a common goal.

To provide a base for this execution-of-strategy theme, the present chapter analyzes the nature of business strategy. Just what is business strategy? How is it determined? What are the main levels of strategy?

## CONCEPT OF BUSINESS STRATEGY

Broadly speaking, a business strategy is the *choice* of (a) the key services that an organization will perform and (b) the primary bases of distinctiveness in creating and delivering such services, which will (c) enable that organization to obtain a continuing flow of necessary resources.

Here are three illustrations of strategy in quite different fields.

*examples of business strategy*

Digital Equipment Corporation (DEC) established itself in the computer industry by being different. At a time when almost all computer companies were increasing the size and complexity of their products, DEC's strategy was to concentrate on small, simple "mini-computers." Also contrary to industry practice, its early strategy was to provide a minimum of service and to lower its prices repeatedly as experience and redesign permitted. These decisions enabled DEC to become the leader in a niche of the market that is growing faster than the total market; each was based on a belief that the company could best succeed by being distinct from competitors. As the organization expanded its customer focus from scientific users to business firms, it had to add more service. Nevertheless, its internal structure continues to feature low expense. The strategy of consistently focusing on mini-computers for relatively simple uses, on frequent redesign, and on lowering prices to discourage competition, has spurred DEC into becoming a profitable $2 billion enterprise.

Avis follows a very different strategy. It competes head-on with the leader in the car-rental industry—Hertz. It offers the same kind of service, at about the same price, in most of the same locations. The "we try harder"

FIGURE *2.1* *Avis "We try harder" slogan has been instrumental in the company's success.*

Avis

slogan is the key to Avis' survival. Avis seeks to differentiate itself by more pleasant and adaptable relations with customers, and by internal efficiency. By building a competitive enthusiasm based on the idea that the underdog can take on the big buy, Avis makes a me-too strategy work.

Strategy is also needed by not-for-profit enterprises. For example, Pacific Hospital[1] is located in an area with an increasing population of retired people. Consequently, the hospital administrator is pushing a strategy of service to the elderly. This strategy involves discontinuing the maternity and pediatric sections while expanding both staff and facilities for heart problems and geriatric care. Out-patient service is stressed, and a free bus makes daily trips around the community. The administrator is facing resistance by some personnel who contend that a hospital should be prepared to care for all medical needs; however, the strategy of focused service makes possible better care at less cost for the narrower market.

characteristics

Four characteristics of strategy stand out in each of the examples cited. These same qualities are usually present in the strategy of any successful enterprise.

1. The strategy guides the enterprise over a period of years. Time is needed to build momentum and once built, it is hard to change in major ways.
2. The strategy is quite selective in the points it emphasizes. It focuses on key features which are to be important and continuing bases of distinctiveness.
3. The strategy is the dominant guide to action. It provides the overriding operating goals. Ideally, the strategy permeates the entire organization with a sense of mission.
4. The strategy guides the relationship of the enterprise to both its external environment and its internal activities.

These characteristics also suggest what a strategy is *not*. It does not include short-run, tactical moves or the large volume of short-range plans necessary to carry out strategy; it is not comprehensive, covering all external relations and all internal operations; it does not include all the goals and

[1]Disguised name.

values endorsed by the company; it does not always focus on the same group of stakeholders or on the same internal department.

Strategy is valuable as a managerial tool because it is selective, enduring, and priority-setting. It provides a beacon light for the many other essential managerial decisions which must be made. Managers devote most of their effort—as we do in this book—to carrying out strategy and to related activities. By separating out strategy for special attention a manager gets two benefits: (a) he reduces the risk that clear thinking about strategy will be swamped by short-run, expedient action; (b) he can more easily tie the many diverse activities to strategy in a consistent, synergistic manner.

## HOW STRATEGY IS DETERMINED

An enterprise can have a strategy even though no one ever systematically set one forth. For instance, strategy may grow out of a series of decisions regarding immediate problems; similarities in these decisions are gradually identified and accepted as norms which employees are expected to follow. If such emerging norms deal with strategic matters then the enterprise, in fact, does have a strategy which almost everyone follows.[2]

**informal, emerging consensus**

A small, liberal arts college in Ohio—which we'll call Midwest College—had such a strategy. Founded by a church denomination, Midwest had always thought of itself as a "Christian" liberal arts school. Each year the faculty considered changes in courses to be offered, and from these discussions came a strong tradition that Midwest would not offer professional training (except the minimum of education courses necessary to teach in high school and a few music courses). As other denominational schools closed their doors and state-supported universities grew, Midwest increasingly emphasized liberal arts and Christian education in recruiting students and raising funds.

Located in the suburbs of a middle-sized city, Midwest students often found part-time jobs. Then the college added an employment director, and provision for part-time work became an integral feature of the schedule. As a result, Midwest tended to attract students who could not afford to attend the big name colleges. A related aspect was the prevailing seriousness and Protestant work-ethic among students; Midwest did not cater to the playboy type. Tuition was kept somewhat lower than that charged by other private colleges. There were few experimental courses, and academic standards were at least as high as those of the state university (Midwest faculty believes they are higher).

Clearly, Midwest College has a strategy. It caters to a particular segment of the college market. It has developed distinctive appeals, and its teaching technology is adjusted to the special needs of its clientele. The strategy just grew incrementally but commitment to it is strong.

Strategy in some profit-seeking companies evolves in much the same way as it did in Midwest College.

[2]H. Mintzberg, "Strategy Making in Three Modes," *California Management Review,* 16, no. 2 (1973), 44–53.

**intuitive decision by powerful individual**

Henry Ford is a classic example of a domineering enterpreneur who personally sets the strategy for his company.[3] High volume/low price, mass production, standardized products were pillars of the strategy that led to early success. Ford tolerated no deviations. For him, these (and related concepts) were *the* right way. And he had the power to insist that his strategy be followed. Henry Luce, the founder of Time, Inc., played a similar role in the early days of *Time* magazine, and to a lesser extent, at *Fortune* and *Life*.

Usually, such a strong leader does not explore alternatives. Perhaps the directions chosen are merely personal preferences which luckily suit the conditions at the time. Often, though, the person is an astute observer and has a sense of what will, and will not, succeed. The process of picking strategic elements, however, is intuitive; and if early hunches result in success, the confirmed belief becomes "truth."

**systematic analysis**

Reliance on intuition is risky. Only through experience can we tell whether strategy based on intuition is well suited to the prevailing environment. And such past experience is a shaky foundation for further action in a dynamic setting. Few managers in the automobile or magazine industries

[3]For a portrait of Henry Ford and other outstanding American enterpreneurs, see H. C. Livesay, *American Dream* (Boston: Little, Brown, 1980).

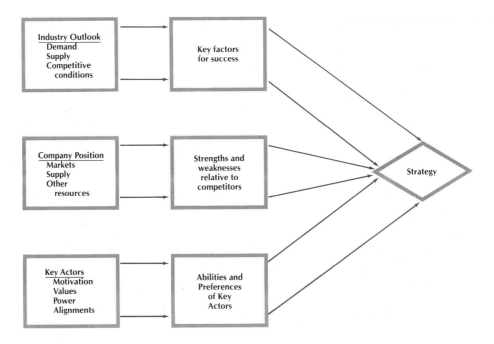

FIGURE 2.2  *The systematic analysis of strategy is based on estimates of the industry outlook, assessments of company strengths and weaknesses, and evaluations of key factors.*

in the 1980s are willing to risk their careers on the intuition of some new Ford or Luce.

Likewise, to hope that a good strategy for the future will somehow grow out of focusing on daily problems is hazardous. Change lurks everywhere. New political and social alignments upset economic trends. Technology based on the computer invades our working habits. So, special attention is needed to ensure that today's actions prepare for tomorrow's world.

Systematic analysis helps to reduce strategy risks. One well-tested approach involves three sets of data and estimates.[4]

A. *Industry outlook.*   By focusing on a single industry the numerous changes in the world at large can be sorted; only those shifts believed to have a major impact on the industry need be studied in detail. The sales volume and profit outlook depend on (1) demand for the services of the industry, (2) supply of these services, and (3) competitive conditions. (We use "service" here to include both physical products and/or intangible values provided by an enterprise.) A further breakdown of factors to consider is laid out in Table 2.1.

The purpose of the industry analysis is to predict future volume and profitability for the entire industry. In addition, *key factors for success* should be identified. These are vital guideposts in designing a company strategy.

B. *Company strengths and limitations.*   Each company (or division) has a history and momentum. It already possesses some strengths, and inevitably will have some weaknesses *relative to its major competition.* Also, it may be in weak or strong position to attract further resources. Naturally, a company will look for a strategy which utilizes its strengths and bypasses its limitations. Important dimensions of a company include (1) its market position, (2) its supply strengths, and (3) its financial and managerial resources. See Table 2.2 for factors to consider in each of these categories.

C. *Key actor analysis.*   Specific organizations with which the company must deal (suppliers, bankers, customers, regulators etc.) will have their own programs and idiosyncrasies; individuals in those organizations will have their personal ambitions and values. Any new strategy will require that at least a few of these persons and organizations adjust their behavior to suit our company. Those whose cooperation is crucial become "key actors."

When studying key actors it is important to predict (1) who will be key actors, (2) their motivations and likely reactions, (3) the power each one has relative to us, and (4) what kinds of alignments are feasible.[5] Information of this sort throws light on the specific help or hindrance which can be expected of other people active in our area. Table 2.3 outlines such an analysis.

Armed with predictions about the industry, company and key actors, we can evaluate strategy proposals. The feasibility of pushing in particular directions can be assessed, and the probable results predicted.

---

[4]C. R. Christensen, K. R. Andrews, and J. L. Bower, *Business Policy,* 4th ed. (Homewood: Irwin, 1978).

[5]W. E. Rothschild, *Putting It All Together* (New York: AMACOM, 1976), chap. 10.

TABLE *2.1*
INDUSTRY
OUTLOOK*

(*Use judgment
to select
factors
important to
specific
industry*)

1. *Future demand for service of the industry:*

| | |
|---|---|
| Long-run growth or decline | Consumer direct need vs. derived demand? Dependent on what life-style or technology? Specialized vs. varied uses? |
| Stability of demand | Substitutes available? Durable vs. consumed when used? Necessity vs. luxury? Government vs. cyclical? Number and size of buyers? |
| Stage in product life-cycle | Still experimental? New, high potential? Mature? Dying? |
| Segments of market | Geography, usage, customer type, associated services, quality level? |

2. *Future supply of such services:*

| | |
|---|---|
| Capacity of industry | Present capacity vs. demand? Ease of entry? Speed of exit? Sunk vs. variable costs? |
| Availability of needed resources | Trained labor? New materials? Energy? Specialized equipment? Number and reliability of sources? Potential substitutes? |
| Volatility of technology | Frequency and degree of product improvement? Of process improvement? Competitive emphasis on R&D? Availability of latecomers? |
| Social constraints | Environmental? Protection? Product safety? Worker welfare? |
| Inflation vulnerability | For costs vs. selling prices. Flexibility up? Down? Timing of changes? Use of replacement costs? |

3. *Competitive conditions in industry:*

| | |
|---|---|
| Structure of industry | Dominance of few competitors? Strong trade association? Cutthroat tradition? |
| Government support and regulation | Subsidies, tariffs and other protections? Restraints on competition? Monopoly regulations? Tax target? |

*Conclusions:*

| | |
|---|---|
| Prospects for volume and profits | Total industry vs. segments? Degree of risk and uncertainty? |
| Key factors for success in industry | Total industry vs. segments? |

*For a discussion of this approach, see W. H. Newman and J. P. Logan, *Strategy, Policy, and Central Management,* 8th ed. (Cincinnati: South-Western Publishing Co., 1981), chap. 3.

TABLE $2.2$
COMPANY
STRENGTHS
AND LIMITATIONS*
(*Use judgment to
select factors
important to
specific company*)

1. *Market position of company:*

   Relation of company sales to total industry
   and to leading competitors

   Past trends? Reasons for change? Opportunities to increase share?

   Relative appeal of company services

   Quality as seen by customer? Product/service leadership? Relative prices? Synergy of marketing mix?

   Relative strength of major markets

   End-use markets? Geographic markets? Relative strength of distribution system?

2. *Supply position of company:*

   Comparative access to resources (availability
   and price)

   Material? Energy? Labor relations? Capital? Government aid? Overall resource costs?

   Unique productivity advantages

   Relative position on learning curve? Location advantage? New vs. old plant? Key patent? Optimum size?

   Comparative R&D strengths

   Creativity tradition? Own work vs. joint ventures? Areas of leadership? "Critical mass"? Capacity to switch emphasis?

3. *Special Competitive Considerations:*

   Relative financial strength

   Current and future cash flow? Relative ability to borrow? To sell equity? Vulnerability to cash squeeze? Future cash commitments?

   Community and government relations

   Reputation in community? Likely target? Ties to government programs? Skill with regulators?

   Abilities and values of managers

   Age/energy? Risk-takers? Adaptability? Demonstrated skills? Dependence on few key people? Doctrinaire?

*Conclusions:*

   Summary of strengths and weakness of company relative to major competitors—in terms of key success factors identified in industry outlook.

*For a discussion of this approach, see W. H. Newman and J. P. Logan, *Strategy, Policy, and Central Management,* 8th ed. (Cincinnati: South-Western Publishing Co., 1981), chap. 3.

*TABLE 2.3*
*KEY ACTOR*
*ANALYSIS\**
*(Significance of each*
*point varies widely,*
*depending on*
*particular situation)*

1. *Who Will be Key Actors?*

| | |
|---|---|
| Vital resource suppliers | Banker? Key material supplier? Large customer? Union leader? Patent owner? |
| Aggressive competitors | Competitors for key resources? Competitors for customers? |
| Regulators | National or local commissions? Permit (license) grantors? Law administrator? Special-interest spokesmen? |

2. *Motivations and Likely Responses of Each Key Actor:*

| | |
|---|---|
| Objectives—driving aims | Status? Growth in selected area? Political power? Security? Reform mission? |
| Patterns of behavior | Established methods and responses? Sources of new information and ideas? Past action leading to success? |
| Other commitments for use of his resources | Announced programs? New opportunities? Pressures on his resources? |

3. *Power Relative to Use of Each Key Actor:*

| | |
|---|---|
| Actor's ability to withhold what we need | His alternatives? His ease of contraction? Impact on others? |
| Our alternative sources | Other customers? Other suppliers? Substitutes? Contraction? |
| Our power over the actor | Dependence on us? Consistent treatment with his competitors? |
| Willingness to use power | Future retaliation? Carryover to other cooperators? Reserve for future use? |

4. *Potential Alignment with Each Key Actor:*

| | |
|---|---|
| One-to-one relationship | Cooperate? Dictate? Accommodate? Fight? |
| Degrees of collaboration | Informal aid? Formal agreements? Joint ventures? Merger? |
| Coalitions | Scope of activities? Members? Common interests? Payoff for each member? |

\*For a discussion of this approach, see W. H. Newman and J. P. Logan, *Strategy, Policy, and Central Management,* 8th ed. (Cincinnati: South-Western Publishing Co., 1981), chap. 4.

Systematic strategy analysis, along the lines just sketched, is common practice in many leading companies. Its chief drawback is that it requires hard work. And when a manager is considering possible thrusts in several different industries, a separate study of each industry is necessary. Nevertheless, objectivity is introduced and risk reduced. Company experience and personal intuition can still be considered, but these inputs are cross-checked and weighed in light of the best analytical data that can be mustered.

**CORPORATE, BUSINESS-UNIT, AND FUNCTIONAL STRATEGIES**

Too often strategy remains just a broadly stated objective. The linking of strategy to actual operations requires explicit and continuing attention. A crucial aid to this linking is to state strategy in operational terms.[6]

Especially useful is to distinguish strategy for three organizational levels: top management of a diversified corporation; business-unit or com-

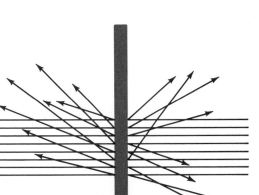

*Figure 2.3   Company strategy gives overall direction to operations and takes priority over the often-diverging interests of various departments.*

pany; and functional departments within a business-unit.[7] Business-units are the primary centers for initiating strategic action. So we shall discuss business-unit strategy first, and then move up to corporate strategy and down to functional strategy.

**the business-unit concept**

A business-unit in its simpler form is an independent, single product-line company such as a bakery, coal mine, or shoe manufacturer. The enterprise could be non-profit, a drug rehabilitation center for example, or it might deal only in services such as public accounting. Each of these business-units has a homogeneous product line, serves a defined group of customers, and manages most of the resources necessary to create its services. Consequently, it can devise a coordinated strategy for its total business.

As a business-unit grows, it may add sales outlets or production plants, but it can still be managed with one central strategy. However, if a firm diversifies into several different kinds of business, we then call it a "diversified *corporation*" and treat each of its self-contained product divisions as a business-unit. For instance, the typewriter division of IBM is a

---

[6]J. M. Hobbs and D. F. Heany, "Coupling Strategy to Operating Plans," *Harvard Business Review,* 55, no. 3 (May–June 1977).

[7]P. Lorange, *Corporate Planning: An Executive Viewpoint* (Englewood Cliffs, N.J.: Prentice-Hall, 1980), chap. 2.

**business-unit
strategy**

business-unit even though legally it is in the same organization as computers. If the shoe manufacturer adds a line of luggage, the corporation would then have two business-units. Incidentally, for ease in reading we may use the terms "company" or "enterprise" as synonyms for "business-unit."

A business-unit, then, is a particular kind of organization. Because it has a distinctive character, we can be more specific about the elements in a good strategy for it.

A business-unit strategy normally should indicate:

1. *Domain sought.* What products or intangible services will the business unit sell to what group of customers? Answering this question requires selection of an industry, and one or more related niches within that industry, in which to operate.[8]

2. *Differential advantages in serving that domain.* On what basis—e.g., access to raw materials, better personnel, new technology, or low costs and prices—will the business-unit seek an advantage over competitors in providing its products or services?

3. *Strategic thrusts necessary and their approximate timing.* To move from where the business-unit now is to where it wants to be what strategic moves will be made early and what can be deferred?

4. *Target results expected.* What financial and other criteria will the business-unit use to measure its success, and what levels of achievement are expected? These are the agreed-upon objectives. Theoretically the objectives could be listed first instead of last; but rarely can the objectives be sharply defined until the *modus operandi* outlined above is settled. For operational purposes, specific targets agreed to by key resource contributors are very useful.

These four dimensions of business-unit strategy are clearly illustrated in Crown Cork & Seal Company. The tin can division of Crown Cork has a remarkable record of growth and profits in spite of maturity and sharp competition in the can industry. Selection of domain is vital. Crown Cork's niche is cans for hard-to-hold products—beer, carbonated beverages, aerosol sprays. Twenty years ago, it withdrew from making ordinary cans, and it has stayed out of bottles, paper, and plastic containers. Within its niche, however, it is the leading producer with sales in the $2 billion range.

Crown Cork seeks a differential advantage over competitors by giving fast, personal service which its less specialized competitors can't match, and by keeping expenses low. Its tough, no-frill operation results in selling and administrative expenses which are less than four percent of sales—significantly lower than competitors.

When Kaiser Aluminum Company introduced an attractive two-piece aluminum can, Crown Cork's leadership was threatened. This led to two strategic thrusts—development (with steel industry R & D) of the tech-

---

[8]D. F. Abell, *Defining the Business* (Englewood Cliffs, N.J.: Prentice-Hall, 1980).

nology to make two-piece steel cans, and rapid investment in equipment to manufacture such cans. The risks were large, the timing crucial; but by moving fast Crown Cork turned a threat into an opportunity.

Target results reflect the values of Crown Cork's president. They are sales growth of about 15% per year while maintaining past profit margins. Incidentally, no dividends have been paid for over twenty-five years.... An outsider may consider Crown Cork's strategy narrow and risky, but the course the company has set for itself is crystal clear.

Too often statements of strategy deal with only a single dimension. A new market or a desired financial return on investment, for instance, may be labeled as "our company strategy." By its narrowness such a goal robs strategy of a needed balanced operational quality. To achieve this balance, all four of the elments just listed should be carefully considered. The resulting strategy will then be an *integrated*, forward-looking plan.

The multidimensions of strategy—domain sought, differential advantage, strategic thrusts, and target results—do not require that a strategy be detailed and comprehensive. Rather, strategy should concentrate on *key* factors necessary for success and on *major* moves to be taken by the particular company at the current stage in its development. The selectivity of key points, and by implication its designation of others as supportive, gives strategy much of its value as a planning device.

**corporate strategy**

Successful business-units often outgrow their original mission. Their market may have matured; they may have strengths that can be applied to related businesses; a broader base may be needed to match competition or spread risk; or assurance of supplies may become critical. For reasons such as these many companies find themselves engaged in several different businesses. Potentially, the federation of units will be stronger than the sum of each business operating independently, but this does not happen automatically. A corporate strategy is needed to yield the benefits of union.[9] Corporate strategy is primarily concerned with building an effective collection of business-units. This requires thoughtful investment (allocation) of resources. Some units will be built up, others liquidated; perhaps new units will be acquired. Because this allocation process is similar to the process by which a financial investment manager changes the composition of securities in his portfolio, the term "portfolio problem" is widely used to identify the distinctive aspects of managing a diversified corporation.[10]

The main elements in a corporate strategy, then, include:

1. The desired portfolio of business-units five to ten years hence.
2. Major moves (thrusts) to get from the present situation to the holdings pictured in (1). Three sub-elements should always be covered:

[9]R. F. Vancil and P. Lorange, "Strategic Planning in Diversified Companies," *Harvard Business Review,* 53 (January–February 1975), 81–93.

[10]H. I. Ansoff and J. C. Leontiades, "Strategic Portfolio Management," *Journal of General Management,* 4, no. 1 (Fall 1976), 13–30.

a) a "charter" for each business-unit to be retained, indicating the domain of the unit, expected results, and resources that the corporation will make available; within these limits, each unit will develop its own business-unit strategy as outlined in the previous section;

b) changes in the portfolio, including desired acquisitions and any sale or liquidation of existing units;

c) consolidated plans for the mobilization and allocation of corporate capital, key personnel and other resources.

3. Target results.

Such a corporate strategy relies on the business-units to be the active, competitive centers. They are the dynamic building-blocks. The main role of the corporation is to help its operating units be effective, and to shift resources to areas where service and result opportunities are the highest.

A successful research-based firm, Coated Optics, Inc., recently faced a corporate strategy problem. The main business involves depositing an extremely thin layer of molecules on telescope lenses, radar receivers, and the like. Most orders are small and often require pioneering technology. Now, a few of the company executives want to use their existing know-how in mass production. One suggestion is to produce fiber optics for use in the next wave of office copier machines ("the successor to Xerox"). However, volume production would require mechanization, automated quality control, new marketing and financial arrangements, etc. The scientist-engineers who now dominate the firm have no interest in such "factory" work.

Coated Optics, Inc. has therefore created a separate business-unit to develop large-volume orders, and the original work has been split between a government division and civilian products division. Each division has its own shop, gets its own business, and is accountable for its results. Thus, the domains are defined. Technical personnel have been assigned. Targets are set. The new fiber optics division is still tooling-up, and is not scheduled to make a profit for three years. During that period, the corporate officers may shift the strategy—expanding or contracting any of the divisions, or perhaps entering still another area.

**functional strategy**     Functional strategy is useful for departments which operate right below the business-unit level.[11] Marketing, for instance, may select a few key approaches which become its persisting, overriding tenets. Personnel, finance, production, or another function which is a major contributor to a particular business, may have its strategy. Of course, such strategy should be compatible with and reinforce the broader business-unit strategy.

The elements typically included in a functional strategy are

---

[11]For a comprehensive discussion of functional strategies and policies, see W. H. Newman and J. P. Logan, *Strategy, Policy, and Central Management,* 8th ed. (Cincinnati: South-Western, 1981), pt. 2.

1. the assigned mission or role within the business-unit;
2. kinds of excellence to be stressed;
3. major moves or "initiatives" to be started in the near future;
4. target results.

A book publishing firm, for example, needs personnel for its expanding output, but in its location skilled workers who do quality work are scarce. One hope is the increasing number of homemakers or hobbyists who want part-time employment. So the firm is trying a personnel strategy of a work week of 20 to 40 hours scheduled largely at employees' convenience. The plan will be tried first in the editorial sections, and if scheduling and work-place arrangements can be developed there, the plan may be extended to accounting and shipping. The targets are a fifty percent increase in output with no increase in turnover rates, and better quality with a stable real cost per unit. Results to date show that some very able people are attracted to the firm, but problems of supervision are rising exponentially.

The Singer Co., to cite an example in marketing, is shifting its selling strategy for consumer sewing machines. For over a century in the U.S., Singer retail stores served as a showroom, training center, and base for field salespeople. Recently, the proportion of homes with a sewing machine has dropped so sharply that many of the 900 stores are no longer economical. At least half will be closed, and Singer will reluctantly follow competitors' practice of selling through department stores. The new thrusts, in addition to slashing distribution costs, include giving Singer's electronic machines a Cadillac image (which will justify its high price). The aim is to maintain Singer prestige and dollar volume while problems elsewhere in the consumer sewing machine division are being resolved.

Note that in both the Singer and the book publishing examples, functional strategy is a prime continuing force but it is subordinate to broader business-unit strategy.

## CONCLUSION: STRATEGY AS AN INTEGRATING TOOL

Every enterprise needs a mission—a specific purpose. Survival depends on it. However, that purpose must be realistic in terms of the desires of society, resources available, competition, and technology. There must be a practical fitting together of hopes and things that work.

Strategy is the best tool yet devised to clarify such a mission and to harness human effort for the achievement of that mission. A well-developed business strategy defines its domain, flags differential advantages sought, lists strategic thrusts, and specifies target results. Once understood, such a strategy provides the focus for joint endeavor. Corporate, business-unit and functional strategy (see Table 2.4) serve a similar purpose for broader and narrower organization units.

*TABLE* 2.4
THREE LEVELS
OF STRATEGY

| | Corporate Strategy | Business-unit Strategy | Functional Strategy |
|---|---|---|---|
| *Scope* | Desired portfolio | Domain: industry & niche | Assigned mission |
| *Sources of Distinction* | Charters for desired business-units | Differential advantage | Kinds of excellence |
| *Initiatives* | Changes in portfolio Resource plans | Strategic thrusts | Major moves |
| *Objectives/ Expected Results* | Target results | Target results | Target results |

For managers and other people working within a company, strategy is an ever-present, potent force. The examples of Avis and Crown Cork illustrate how strategies are translated down to the operating level. Materials are bought and customers served in a way that is consistent with overall explicit strategy. Good strategy leads to action.

Because strategy has an unusual power to unify action, we have introduced the concept early in this book. In following sections we will note how other managerial tools (a) are guided by strategy and (b) can be used to execute strategy. Thus, we are using strategy as an entering wedge into the interdependent, dynamic mechanisms of the total management process.

**FOR FURTHER DISCUSSION**

1. "Strategic planning is by and large an afterthought which has its primary benefit in rationalizing an essentially non-rational process in order to create the illusion that major corporate actions are planned." Comment.

2. "The greatest danger in developing a master strategy is to fail to appraise your key competitors' strengths and weaknesses accurately. Companies constantly over- or under-estimate their competitors." Comment on this observation made by a successful management consultant.

3. Since strategies should guide an enterprise over a period of years, how often should strategies be reviewed to see if modifications are necessary?

4. What can the officers of a company do to increase the objectivity and soundness of its efforts to appraise its strengths and limitations?

5. "Our 'strategy' is to watch what the giants in our industry are doing and then look for crumbs they drop or markets too small for them to bother with." Comment on this statement by the president of a $100 million company in an industry dominated by three $1 billion companies. Contrast his views to those illustrated by the actions of Crown Cork.

6. Can—or should—a not-for-profit organization attempt to develop a long-term strategy when it must seek funding on an annual basis? (Assume that the organization has little in the way of endowments or long-term financial commitments.)

7. Many corporations today have created a position with the title "director of strategic planning." Often the people who have this title report to a top corporate executive and have counterparts at the division level. What should a director of strategic planning do? Explain. How will the nature, rather than the level, of his work differ, depending on whether he is at the corporate or division level? To whom should he report in each case?

## CASES

For cases involving issues covered in this chapter, see especially the following. Particularly relevant questions are listed after each case.

Benjo Associates (p. 92), 1, 7, 20
Elizabeth Archer (p. 96), 1, 7
Mike Zerllini (p. 188), 1
Joe DiMaggio (p. 533), 1
Foster Promotions, Inc. (p. 538), 1

## FOR FURTHER READING

Abell, D. E. and J. S. Hammond, *Strategic Market Planning*. Englewood Cliffs, N.J.: Prentice-Hall, 1979. Comprehensive treatment of concepts and analytical techniques which facilitate strategic planning.

Ansoff, H. I. et. al., eds., *From Strategic Planning to Strategic Management*. New York: Wiley, 1975. Collection of articles which advocate that strategic thinking should permeate the entire management process.

Linneman, R. E., *Shirt-Sleeve Approach to Long-Range Planning*. Englewood Cliffs, N.J.: Prentice-Hall, 1980. Practical advice on the development of strategy in the smaller, growing corporation.

Newman, W. H. and J. P. Logan, *Strategy, Policy, and Central Management,* 8th ed. Cincinnati: South-Western, 1981. Strategy selection (Part 1); policies needed to support strategy (Part 2); organizing and executing strategy (Parts 3 and 4).

Rothschild, W. E., *Putting It All Together*. New York: AMACOM, 1976. Valuable set of guidelines for formulating strategic planning and putting together an overall strategic plan.

Schendel, D. and C. Hofer, eds., *Strategic Management: A New View on Business Policy and Planning*. Boston: Little, Brown, 1979. Good review of major research developments in strategy and planning systems.

# PLANNING: THE EXECUTION OF STRATEGY

## I

Strategy is an instrument used by management to mediate between society's needs and the particular mission undertaken by a company, as noted in Chapter 2. While strategy defines the mission of an organization, missions are only good intentions unless effective implementation occurs. The chapters in Part I examine the development of planning systems for translating strategy into effective decisions.

Planning is a basic management task, one that has a major place in our overall division of management functions along with organizing, controlling, and leading. In every company, managers must decide on a host of issues: production schedules, what services to provide, what prices to charge, how to deal with pressure groups, whom to employ, when to collaborate with the government, and many other matters. Planning is not a manager's only task, but it is certainly an essential one.

Planning systems have a pervasive effect on decision-making in organizations. Because several persons take part in organizational decision-making, ways must be introduced to secure consistency among decisions, coordination of various planning units, and economy in planning effort. We shall look at various types of plans—or planning instruments—used to obtain such consistency, coordination, and economy.

These issues will be considered in the following chapters.

Chapter 3—Sharpening Operating Objectives. In order to convert broad strategy into operating action, the strategy must be recast in terms of specific goals and subgoals. In this chapter, we shall consider how to set up a hierarchy of objectives so that effective action follows.

Chapter 4—Planning Stabilized Behavior. Policies, procedures, and standard methods contribute substantially to consistent and economical decisions. But, as we shall now see, there is a serious question about how far to carry this type of planning.

Chapter 5—Adaptive Programming. A substantial part of every company's planning deals with nonrepetitive situations. Managers must set up programs and decide on tactics to follow. We shall note how such plans must frequently be adapted to new problems and opportunities.

# 3

# sharpening operating objectives

**LEARNING OBJECTIVES**

After completing this chapter you should be able to

1. Explain how objectives are used to formulate a hierarchy of plans.
2. State how short-run objectives relate to long-run goals.
3. Explain the concept of management by objectives (MBO).
4. Describe the principal benefits of management by objectives.
5. Understand the concept of multiple objectives as it applies to organizations and individuals.
6. Describe how managers can adjust emphasis among multiple objectives.

Bridges must be built between strategy (discussed in the previous chapter) and specific objectives that must be carried out next week. Once strategy has been set, operating objectives come into play. Strategy gets translated into effective action only when sharply defined goals for each member of the organization are accepted.

Three kinds of issues arise in setting operating objectives so that a master strategy will become a driving force. First is the translation—the spelling out—of broad goals into smaller and more specific assignments for each part of the organization. Next we make these specific objectives a vital focus in the local managing process; and for this "Management-by-Objectives" (MBO) is a proven instrument. Finally, problems of melding and adjusting operating objectives must be resolved. These are the issues examined in this chapter.

**establishing a
hierarchy of plans**

Strategy, as we use the term, already contains two leads into shorter-range plans. First, strategic thrusts call for a series of actions, such as opening an office in Sao Paulo or selling a public issue of company stock. Each thrust can be subdivided into steps and substeps that are assigned to individuals. This break-down is continued until, to extend the Sao Paulo office example, one person finds the site, another determines the equipment and layout, and a third hires personnel. Note that a hierarchy of assignments emerges with the very specific, immediate steps contributing to an intermediate objective while the intermediate objectives build toward the broader strategic move.

Second, the target results component of strategy is the source of a series of moves necessary to achieve the target. These moves are further divided until tasks of a size suitable to a single person are reached. Again, there is a hierarchy, with each task finding its justification as a contributor to a broader objective.

Much planning effort is necessary to develop operating objectives from strategy. Strategy is selective in the subjects it covers; in contrast, operating objectives should be comprehensive. Current operations as well as strategic changes should be covered. Monthly or even weekly progress, and the development and use of resources, should be spelled out. Because these operating objectives are so crucial to achieving results, we need to look at them more closely.

**diversity of
operating
objectives**

For managerial purposes, it is useful to think of objectives as the results we want to achieve. The words "goal," "aim," and "purpose" also have much the same meaning, because they, too, imply effort directed toward a preselected result.

In this book, we use the word "objectives" broadly. It covers long-range company aims, more specific department goals, and even individual assignments. Thus objectives may pertain to a wide or narrow part of an enterprise, and they may be either long- or short-range. A salesperson may have an immediate objective of clearing up a misunderstanding with a customer, and he may have a five-year objective of cultivating his territory to provide $25,000 in sales each month. Similarly, a company may have a short-term objective of providing stable employment during the next summer and a long-range objective of being a product leader in its industry. These are all results to be achieved.

Often objectives of a particular nature are given a special name. For instance, we may speak of equal-opportunity quotas, expense ratios, budgets, absentee rates, or market positions. The use of such descriptive terms does not remove them from the broad category of objectives.

**meaningful objectives for each job**

Company objectives are always broad and inclusive. Thus, the president of Crown Cork & Seal Company speaks of "$2 billion in sales within five years." Or, an R & D vice-president wants specifications for a low-cost solar water-heater in two years. Such targets are too vague to provide a guide to action for most members of the company. What bearing specific decisions have on the objective is often indirect, and particular activities tend to lose their significance when they are merged into a large, total result. Seeing the broad picture, desirable as it is, does not replace the need for more specific goals for each job. In fact, it is entirely possible for an effective worker to be dedicated to doing his job well and at the same time be indifferent to the broad company objectives.

One task of every manager, then, is to help clarify intermediate objectives for each subordinate. A subgoal may be a dominant market position in a particular city, leadership in salary administration, keeping abreast of new techniques in the industry, or well-kept grounds around the plant. This is the kind of goal a subordinate executive or operator can go to work on.

Care and ingenuity are needed in refining these subobjectives. A total system is involved. All of the contributions to a broad objective—not just one or two—must be assigned to somebody. Often these contributions interact, so that if we change Irene's subgoal it may upset Bob's. Moreover, such jobs always have several subgoals—various aspects of one end result (quantity, quality, cost, etc.) and often several end results (financial reports, management information, protection from fraud for a controller). Tinkering with one of these subgoals may complicate another. Actually, this multidimensional interrelatedness creates so much inertia that it is difficult to adjust operating objectives to support shifts in strategy.

Clarifying objectives and subobjectives is a continuing task. We often like to think that objectives are fixed, but this is only partially true. We shift company strategy to seize a new opportunity; and because the specific objectives assigned to individuals are derived from the broad company goals, a change in strategy is likely to require adjustments in the objectives of several supervisors and operators. In fact, little effective change will occur until assignments down the line are revised. Clearly, defining objectives is neither static nor automatic.

**hopes versus expectations**

An objective may be optimistic, in that the results we hope for will occur if everything works just right—like par on the golf course. Or it may be realistic, a statement of what we actually expect to accomplish—like par plus our handicap. Both types of goals have their uses, but it is important to distinguish between them.

Advocates of optimistic objectives believe that a person will accomplish more with sights set high. If we have the courage to dream great dreams, then we can bend our efforts to make them come true.[1]

Everyone knows of examples of such determination succeeding. The largest transatlantic air-cargo line would never have been more than a small charter carrier without the high objectives of its president. The company spent years obtaining government permission to operate scheduled flights. In the midst of these negotiations, a decision to place a multimillion-dollar order for new jets was made. In this instance, acting on hope rather than on "sound" expectation led to significantly better results.

In all such cases, the aimed-at results are at least possible, with supreme effort, good luck, and favorable operating conditions. Occasionally, even objectives known to be unattainable are used—this, for example: "Give every employee the maximum opportunity to reach his highest potential." This an an ideal to strive for. It provides direction, as stars do for sailors, but it is never reached.

In contrast, we may choose to state objectives in realistic terms, seeking levels that can be achieved without superhuman effort and uncanny luck. Thus reasonable sales quotas can be filled by most sales representatives; with normal diligence, expense ratios can be met by good managers; personnel programs can come up with able workers, if not geniuses; profit targets will bear some resemblance to last year's results. These are goals that management expects to be met. In some areas, performance may surpass the objectives, and this good fortune may help offset lagging performance at other spots.

In business planning, emphasis is generally on tough, but achievable, objectives. There are two reasons for this preference. (1) Frustration or indifference is apt to develop if stated goals are rarely, if ever, achieved. (2) Objectives are used for planning and coordination as well as for motivation; so related activites may go awry if management tries to synchronize them with an objective that proves to be more hope than reasonable prediction.

**short-run objectives as steps toward long-run goals**

A major task becomes more manageable when it is divided into small pieces. This analytical concept is, of course, employed in setting up hierarchies of objectives and in organizing work by departments. Another breakdown is by steps or results to be achieved within a given period of time. This method is commonly used in personal career decisions. For instance, suppose Joan Casey wants to become an executive in a local publishing firm (long-run objective). She may decide that a business education (intermediate objective) will help her achieve this goal. So she takes a course in management as one of several steps toward a formal business education.

---

[1]G. P. Latham and G. A. Yukl, "Review of Research on the Application of Goal Setting in Organizations," *Academy of Management Journal*, December 1975.

©Monroe Pinckard, Rapho Photo Inc.

© 1979, Fred A. Anderson, Photo Researchers, Inc.

Pierre Berger, Photo Researchers, Inc.

Irene Springer

*Figure 3.1* In dealing with so vast an undertaking as an urban-renewal project, it is necessary to break down the project into a series of subobjectives—financing, excavation, construction, and selection of tenants. This practice can be useful on a smaller scale as well.

A step-by-step breakdown is particularly valuable in complicated business projects. The use of satellites in telephonic and TV communication, for example, is a vast and complex undertaking. Receiving and broadcasting stations have to be located on the basis of technical, economic, and political considerations; equipment has to be designed and built, personnel trained, satellites launched, users of the service educated, rates set, and a staggering amount of capital acquired. A job of this sort becomes manageable only when it is broken down into a series of steps. In fact, each major step will be divided and subdivided.

Even relatively simple assignments, such as a political campaign for U.S. senator, may well be divided up into small work units.

The creation of such short-run objectives has several advantages.

1. *It helps make the objective tangible and meaningful.* We all find it easy to project ourselves into the immediate future, whereas the more distant future is filled with uncertainties; besides, we have no compelling reasons to face remote problems now.

2. *Short-run objectives provide a means of bridging the gap between hopes and expectations.* It is entirely possible to have optimistic long-run goals and at the same time be quite realistic about the immediate steps to be taken toward these ends. Working on a tangible, immediate project tends to relieve the frustration that can arise from the magnitude and difficulty of a major objective. This tendency is an asset, provided a manager himself does not become so engrossed with a short-run objective that he loses sight of the existence and nature of the long-run objective.

3. *An outstanding advantage of setting up short-run objectives is that they provide benchmarks for measuring progress.* This advantage is a great aid in motivation and control. When a person sees that he is making progress, he gets a sense of accomplishment even though a job is not yet finished, and he also builds his confidence to tackle the work still ahead.

**MANAGEMENT-BY-OBJECTIVES** Once operating objectives are specified, how do we induce executives and workers to accomplish them? This is largely a matter of motivation and leadership—the subject of Parts IV and V. However, one approach—Management-by-Objectives—is so widespread and so intimately related to the setting of objectives that it should be briefly explained here.[2]

**elements of MBO** MBO represents a whole cluster of management techniques. It combines selected, but by no means all, aspects of planning, organizing, leading, and controlling. Having become a fashionable term, MBO is given personal

[2]G. S. Odiorne, *Management by Objectives* (New York: Pitman, 1965); J. W. Humble, *Management by Objectives* (London: Industrial Education & Research Foundation, 1967); and W. J. Reddin, *Effective Management by Objectives: The 3-D Method* (New York: McGraw-Hill, 1971).

meanings by different writers.[3] Nevertheless, virtually all the definitions stress the following elements:

1. *Agreement.* At regular intervals a manager and each subordinate agree on the *results* (objectives) that the subordinate will try to achieve during the next period (quarter, half-year, or year). The subordinate *participates* actively in spelling out the meaning and feasibility of the assignment he accepts. The broad purpose and the organizational constraints, however, are dictated by the strategy of the enterprise and the mission of the supervisor (as we have explained in the preceding pages). We hope that both the subordinate and supervisor will understand and feel committed to this statement of what will constitute good performance.

2. *Delegation.* The supervisor then makes a high degree of delegation to the subordinate. During this period the main role of the supervisor is to *assist* subordinate(s) in fulfilling the agreement(s). As part of the agreement, the supervisor may be committed to provide certain help, and the subordinate may call for more. But the subordinate is expected to take whatever initiative is necessary to achieve the agreed-upon results.

3. *Evaluation of results.* At the end of the period actual results are measured, and the supervisor and subordinate discuss reasons for success and failure. This evaluation becomes the basis for making another agreement (perhaps at a later meeting) for the next period. And so the cycle continues.

4. *Associated activities.* The evaluation of results often serves as the basis of setting salaries and bonuses and for planning personal development. Also, the negotiation of agreements may lead to modifications in organization, procedures, policies, and controls. But these associated activities are not essential parts of MBO.

The potential benefits from MBO are impressive. Foremost is the greater *personal motivation* of the people who commit themselves to achieve a set of results. Through participation in setting meaningful and realistic targets, and the accompanying delegation of initiative, many individuals internalize their role in meeting company objectives.[4]

**main benefits of MBO**

A sense of accomplishment—of meeting objectives—is wanted by people at all levels. The captain of a ship takes pride in keeping his vessel on schedule; a telephone lineman wants to keep the circuits open; a chief engineer works overtime to make sure that a newly designed product will not break down under operating conditions. Without a recognized objective, none of these people would put forth such effort.

A second benefit of MBO is a *clarification* of the results that will best serve the enterprise. Especially in large organizations, the mission of a

[3]E. C. Schleh prefers the term "Management-by-Results" because the word "results" emphasizes what actually takes place instead of stopping with intentions. See E. C. Schleh, *Management by Results* (New York: McGraw-Hill, 1961). All writers, however, urge that the approach be carried through to measurement and evaluation of results.

[4]J. Bryan and E. Locke, "Goal Setting as a Means of Increasing Motivation," *Journal of Applied Psychology,* 51 (1967), 274–77.

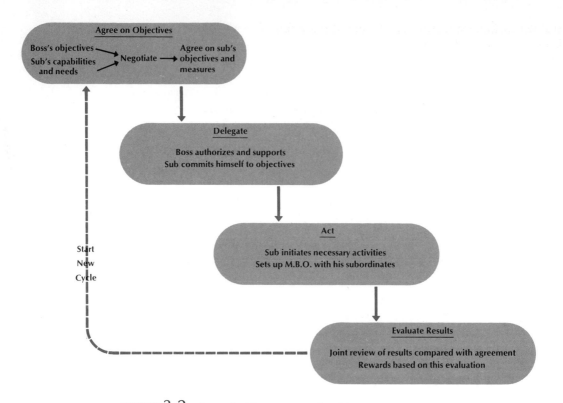

FIGURE *3.2*  *Steps in Management-by-Objectives (MBO).*

particular section often becomes distorted. And as strategy changes over time, the desired results may be blurred even more.

A situation that illustrates unclear objectives arose in the training section of an urban-renewal center. The training director was pushing hard to increase the number of people trained and placed in regular jobs. Consequently he encouraged registration and gave first attention to highly competent people who could be placed quickly. However, these were not people who needed help most. Welfare workers in the area reported that as far as they could detect, the training center was not relieving economic distress. Welfare workers encouraged their clients to sign up for training, but few stayed more than a couple of days, and most said there was no use going there. Only after the objective of the training center was redefined and understood did the coordination between the center and the welfare workers improve.

*Focus* of thought and effort *on results* is a third benefit. All too often mere activity is treated as a goal. Under MBO the activity "call on new customers" is unsatisfactory; instead, a result is stated, such as "firm orders from eight new customers each month." Similarly, "monitor smoke-stack emissions" is unsatisfactory; "hourly stack emissions always within federal standards, and temporary excess never more than five minutes in any hour" is better. The supporting activity may well be necessary, but management's attention is on results.

Personnel evaluation reflects this same emphasis on results. Instead of relying on personality traits, under MBO we assess people in terms of the results they produce. And fresh data is available at the close of each period. Perhaps some personality analysis will help us explain good or bad performance, but we start from the more objective and clearly pertinent comparison of actual results with planned results.

Better response to controls is a fourth benefit of MBO. Both the control standards—the objectives for the period—and the way performance will be measured are part of the agreement between the manager and his subordinate. So the subordinate usually regards the controls as being fair—they are not unexpected or arbitrary. Moreover, with the subordinate personally desiring the objectives, control feedback is helping to achieve personal goals as well as company goals. As we shall see in Chapter 24—"Behavioral Responses to Controls"—such understanding and acceptance alter one's feeling about controls; they become like the gas gauge on your car—aids in reaching a destination instead of instruments of repression.[5]

Finally, MBO has a synergistic effect. The delegation is feasible because of the agreement on objectives; the participation in setting the objectives adds to motivation, as does delegation; and the evaluation based on these same objectives reinforces their significance. Furthermore, in the broader scope, the forward planning for the specific job is consistent with the job duties laid out by organization design; and this job mission has significance and value because its contribution to broader company objectives can be easily traced. The objectivity and impersonality arising from the stress on agreed-upon results reduces feelings of personal dominance and increases the sense of joint endeavor. Each of these features builds upon and reinforces the others; and because they are combined together under the banner of MBO, the psychological effect is synergistic.

**establishing MBO**

Because MBO embraces a cluster of management techniques, it requires hard work to establish. Organizing is involved. Job duties and delegation must be carefully developed, keeping in mind the factors we discuss in part III. Communication and leadership style are also essential aspects; the options and issues in this area are examined in Part V. Controlling, the third phase of the MBO cycle, has its own set of problems, as we shall see in Part VI. And objectives, the take-off pad for MBO, should reflect a rational selection process outlined in Part II. Of course, in a successful *going* enterprise, most of the necessary managerial system will already be operating. So installing MBO calls only for adjustments and refinements. Nevertheless,

[5]A. P. Raia, "Goal Setting and Self-Control," *Journal of Management Studies,* September 1965, pp. 34–53.

any needed changes should be made only after a review of the total situation; MBO provides no easy shortcut.[6]

Defining the operating objectives for each job included in the MBO system is by no means simple. In addition to specific substantive questions, the issue of multiple objectives keeps reappearing.

## MULTIPLE OBJECTIVES FOR ORGANIZATIONS AND INDIVIDUALS

Never does a job, department, or company have a single objective. It may have a dominant mission, but other goals will also demand recognition.

The manager of an airport, for instance, may be charged with making it easy to move planes, people, and freight in and out of his facility. But, among other things, the manager will also be expected to keep operating costs low, use only as much capital for equipment and inventory as is necessary, maintain an efficient work force, and develop employees for promotion to key jobs. Thus he is confronted with diverse, and perhaps competing, goals.

**multiple objectives of a company**

The belief that "the purpose of a business firm is to make a profit" is part of American folklore. It probably started as an *assumption* made to simplify economic theory. Being a half-truth, it proved to be an easy way for even business executives to talk about a complex problem. Then when public accounting made the profit-and-loss statement one of the few universal measures of business performance, the notion became ingrained.

But the suggestion that profits are the sole objective of a company is *misleading*. Obviously a company must earn a profit if it is to continue in existence; earnings are necessary to attract additional capital and to provide a cushion for meeting the risks inherent in business activity. But for survival it is also essential that a company produce goods or services customers want, that its conditions of employment continue to attract competent employees, that it be a desirable customer to the people who supply raw materials, and that it be an acceptable corporate citizen in the community in which it operates. Remove any one of these essentials, and the enterprise might collapse. To argue that profit is the supreme objective is like saying that blood circulation is more important to survival than breathing, digestion, or proper functioning of the nervous system.

Suitable measurement of profit poses an additional drawback. Profit figures reported by existing accounting systems are based on past costs. A new system that attempts to be a common denominator for setting and measuring all company objectives would have to deal with the present worth of future values. This would call for estimates of future conditions and of the influence of intangibles such as morale and customer goodwill; comparability from year to year and between companies would be desirable. The

---

[6]R. Likert and S. M. Fisher, "MBGO: Putting Some Team Spirit into MBO," *Personnel*, January-February 1977.

theoretical and practical difficulties in designing such a system are overwhelming.

In discussing strategy in the preceding chapter, we pointed to the need for multiple criteria for overall company targets. Now, when we are seeking ways to state objectives that have operational relevance, the principle of multiple objectives takes an added significance. For the manager, no enterprise—public or private—has a single objective.[7]

To assist the managers of the enterprise in setting objectives, the General Electric Company has singled out eight "key-result areas".

1. Profitability—in both percentage of sales and return on investment
2. Market position
3. Productivity—improving costs as well as sales
4. Leadership in technological research
5. Development of future employees, both technical or functional and managerial
6. Employee attitudes and relations
7. Public attitudes
8. Balance of long-range and short-range objectives

Several other companies use variations of this format. Note that the list identifies only areas; each firm must fill in specific subjects and levels of achievement that fit its circumstances at a particular time.

Service enterprises likewise should determine their key-result areas. Here is such a list for a public library: circulation (loans and in-library), reference questions answered, cooperation with schools and other libraries, percentage of population using the library, contribution to community cohesiveness, collection of books and reference materials, personnel development, operation within financial budget. As soon as we start dealing with objectives that can readily be translated into action, we are faced with multiple goals.

Each of the objectives of the enterprise will, of course, call forth an array of more specific operating goals, and this fanning out continues through to the detailed objectives for each person in the organization.

**number of objectives for each person**

Having too many objectives can be troublesome. When a company's multiple objectives are subdivided and elaborated into an array of specific, short-term objectives, the work is split up among various people. Nevertheless, one manager may be confronted with thirty or forty identified results that he is expected to achieve—quality output, meeting deadlines, overtime pay, self-development, training of others, aid to other departments, plans for next year, budgeted expense, customer service, and so on.

Such a large array of objectives tends to disperse attention and fails to provide clear direction of effort. Consequently, the number of objectives anyone is expected to focus on should be limited. Some executives feel the

---

[7]P. F. Drucker, *Management: Tasks, Responsibilities, Practices* (New York: Harper & Row, 1974), pp. 95–102.

number should be narrowed to the range of two to five, thereby ensuring concentrated attention; others contend that a person can keep a dozen objectives in mind. In either case, agreement exists that motivation is improved by reducing the number.

Two methods are used to narrow the number of objectives for an individual. First, a distinction is drawn between what Herbert Simon calls satisficing and optimizing.[8] For a variety of results we simply try to achieve a satisfactory standard. Only when results—say, quality, honesty, or maintenance—fail to meet the standard do we give the matter attention. In a sense, these are passive objectives, at least for the time being. Other objectives call for improvement. These are the stimulants to action, and they are fewer in number.

Consolidating several objectives that are means to some higher goals is a second way of limiting the number of key objectives for a job. For example, we might say that the head of the Atlanta office of an accounting firm should obtain ten new accounts next year; embraced in this objective are subgoals regarding speeches, public-service activities, contacts with bankers and other influential people, and visits with potential clients. To be sure, most of the subgoals have to be met if the accountant is to get his ten new clients. Yet focusing on the one net result is easier to deal with, and it encourages delegation of the problem of how to achieve results.

[8]H. A. Simon, *Administrative Behavior,* 3rd ed. (New York: Free Press, 1976).

*FIGURE 3.3* *Too many objectives for one person can be hazardous. In a conventional aircraft, the pilot must contend with a bewildering variety of informational devices. New instruments, such as the contact analog (color, left), condense information about the plane's movement and position and present it to the pilot in forms that can easily be grasped. Deviations from the intended course are thus instantly revealed. Matters related to course—speed, position, and so on—can be ignored until deviation is indicated. The analog demonstrates two ways of reducing the problem of multiple objectives: (1) integrating a variety of elements under a few headings and (2) adopting the "exception principle" of ignoring any given factor as long as it is in a satisfactory range.*

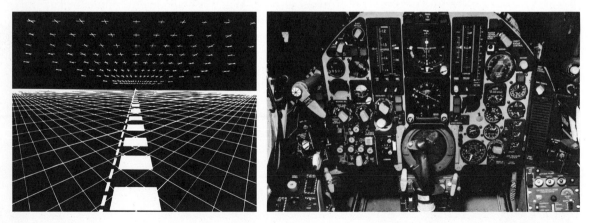

Even half a dozen objectives create difficulties, for emphasis on any one goal tends to reduce attention given to others. The welfare worker urged to process more cases gives less consideration to each problem.

All of us, in planning our own work or in correcting that of others, like to assume that we can give more effort to some goal that is pressing at the moment *without* slackening off on other work. Sometimes we can. Sooner or later, however, a point is reached when attention and effort are simply diverted from one activity to another. More time on football or campus politics means less with the books, and vice versa.

Keeping the emphasis on diverse objectives in balance is hard. A common difficulty is that the tangible, *measurable ends receive undue attention.* It would be easy for a professor to stress the appearance of a report rather than the learning that went into its preparation, simply because the paper itself is so much easier to see. Similarly, in business those results that show up directly in accounting reports often command priority; thus, avoiding overtime expense may be preferred to maintaining quality in advertising copy.

Furthermore, *immediate problems tend to take precedence* over long-run issues. The dilemma of choosing recurs time and again in engineering departments. Customers' orders for immediate delivery have a "here-and-now" quality about them. If he is not careful, an engineer will find himself simply going from one order to the next, always leaving for tomorrow the design of a new product.

The case of *one's own work versus teamwork* may also pose a balancing problem. We all know friendly individuals who are so ready to help with another person's problems that they have difficulty getting their own work done on time. But a self-centered view may also cause trouble. Some results for the company can be created only by teamwork; the task cannot be divided into parts and accountability assigned to separate jobs. Task teams, described in Chapter 10 and the combined work of line and staff are of this nature. So we say that several people are jointly accountable; we measure the result of their combined effort and give each of them credit for the success or failure. But then the problem is this: Smith is a member of a team, and also has several individual objectives. Does he give priority to those results for which he alone is accountable, and let teamwork slide; or does he stress the team project even though other results that are more clearly his may suffer?

According to rational decision theory, we should pursue each of our diverse objectives to the point where added increments of achievement have equal value. Actually, behavioral research suggests, most of us give attention first to one objective and then turn to another, the sequence and direction of effort being determined largely by momentary social pressures.

The desirable balance among objectives shifts over time. With success or failure and with external changes, the incremental values also change. So the wise manager must reappraise preferences. This job is like that of the captain of a large ship who is continually changing speed and direction in relation to the ship's present position, tides, winds, and other conditions.

A regional sales manager of a well-known computer company uses MBO for such a reappraisal on a systematic basis. Every month, he sits down with each branch manager to review past performance; together they agree on three, four, or at most five goals that will be emphasized during the next month. This list may include any of several desirable aims: calling on new customers, pushing the sale of a particular product, recruiting additional salesmen, clearing up customer complaints, or reducing expenses. Sometimes the same item appears on the list for several months. It is generally understood that the branch managers will not completely neglect items missing from the list, but special emphasis will be given to only a few goals. The manager contends that he gets better results by *highlighting* a few items than by talking about many. He is able to maintain an overall balance by the frequent reviews and by shifting from one objective to another as necessary.

The details of this technique are not important here. But we should note several of its desirable features. (1) Any misunderstanding about the quality, timing, or costs of a specific objective can be cleared up at the monthly discussions. (2) Plans are adjusted in light of progress already being made. This practice permits comparison of incremental values. (3) New information and new pressure from headquarters can be promptly incorporated into the action taken at each branch—thus giving recognition to the problems and needs of the many branches, instead of blithely following blanket orders from headquarters. (4) Broad objectives are translated into meaningful and immediately applicable terms for each branch manager.

## CONCLUSION: VITAL ROLE OF OBJECTIVES

Business strategy deals with the company as a whole. It stakes out the role in society that the enterprise wishes to play. Functional strategies likewise set broad guidelines. But these strategies can be achieved only if they have an impact on the behavior of people working in the company. Consequently we have to give close attention to fashioning objectives and subobjectives that are understandable and significant to the executives and other workers affected by them.

These operating objectives are tied to jobs and thus to individual managers and operators who hold these jobs. In terms of "decision-making within organizations," this goal structure is the starting point for diagnosis. Each responsible person predicts potential gaps between his objectives and actual results, and these gaps become the focus of his search, decision, and action.

Since in the hurly-burly of organization life everyone is bombarded by all sorts of information and influences, operating objectives serve the important role of leading to purposeful, consistent action. MBO especially builds this focus; it also encourages commitment and enthusiasm for accomplishing the objectives.

In practice, the definition of clearcut objectives for each job is far from simple. To make operating objectives a vital, energizing managerial tool, we must deal with the following: distinguishing between hopes and expectations, setting short-run objectives as steps toward long-run goals, recognizing the presence of multiple objectives, and adjusting the short-run emphasis on various objectives. Once objectives have been clarified, they provide the guiding, unifying core of company planning.

## FOR FURTHER DISCUSSION

1. The text states, "Strategy gets translated into . . . action . . . when sharply defined goals for each member of the organization are accepted." Who should set these goals—those who develop the strategy or those responsible for developing tactics to carry it out?

2. A standard such as a sales or production quota is of little value unless the assumptions and methods of reaching the quota are spelled out and understood both by the person who is to achieve it and by the person who is to evaluate that person's performance. Comment. Do you agree? Explain.

3. Should a standard or objective that is given to a person be the most reasonable guess about what can be attained? Or should it always be beyond what might be considered the most reasonable expectation? Discuss both sides of this question and indicate what the implications are on coordination and subsequent control.

4. Is the primary purpose of MBO motivational or to improve the quality of planning efforts?

5. In what ways might the demand for clarity and quantification of objectives lead to difficulties when seeking to balance long- and short-run objectives?

6. "Whenever I set joint goals with my subordinates, I begin by stating clearly my expectations and inviting them to change my mind. If they know where I stand, it avoids a lot of game-playing." What do you think of this approach to joint goal-setting?

7. The importance of periodically adjusting objectives is stressed in this chapter. List ways in which a superior may judge whether a subordinate's requests for frequent changes in longer-term objectives are the result of good or poor planning by the subordinate.

8. How should objectives be set and agreed to for meeting the various social and political needs of an enterprise?

## CASES

For cases involving issues covered in this chapter, see especially the following. Particularly relevant questions are listed after each case.

Benjo Associates (p. 92), 2, 5
Scandico (Singapore) (p. 305), 1
Delphi Insurance (p. 369), 2
Joan Carrier (p. 376), 3
Netsuki Novelty Products Company (p. 451), 1, 2
Marathon Plastics (p. 456), 2
Foster Promotions Inc. (p. 538), 3

## FOR FURTHER READING

Beer, M. and R. A. Rub, "Employee Growth Through Performance Management," *Harvard Business Review,* (July–August 1976), pp. 59–66. Good explanation of how the Corning Glass Company links MBO and performance evaluation.

Carroll, S. J. and H. L. Tosi, *Management by Objectives.* New York: Macmillan, 1973. Practical guide to the use of MBO, with an analysis of problems arising in the integration of MBO with budgeting and management development.

Latham, G. P., and E. A. Locke, "Goal Setting—A Motivational Technique That Works," *Organizational Dynamics,* 8, no. 2 (Autumn 1979), pp. 68–80. Summarizes laboratory and field research evidence on the value of goal-setting programs.

McCaskey, M. B., "A Contingency Approach to Planning: Planning with Goals and Planning without Goals," *Academy of Management Journal,* 17, no. 2 (1974), pp. 281–91. Discussion of how an organization's environment shapes its planning process.

Odiorne, G. S., "MBO: A Backward Glance," *Business Horizons,* October 1978. Valuable historical discussion of management-by-objectives programs by an MBO pioneer.

Simon, H. A., *Administrative Behavior,* 3rd ed. New York: Free Press, 1976, chap. 12. Theoretical discussion of multiple organizational goals and the way these are resolved into useful operational goals for personnel action. See also chap. 10.

# planning for stabilized action

**4**

Learning Objectives

After completing this chapter you should be able to

1. Explain the difference between single-use plans and standing plans.
2. Describe the major types of standing plans.
3. Understand the differences between policies, standard methods, and standard operating procedures.
4. Describe three ways of making standing plans more flexible.
5. State the benefits and drawbacks of standing plans.

## CONSISTENT AND ENDURING BEHAVIOR PATTERNS

Objectives, however soundly conceived and clearly communicated, provide only part of the guidance essential to united effort. Even the most highly motivated people need some plan of action, as has become painfully clear in several minority small business development programs where the absence of customary patterns for joint effort has thwarted lofty aims.

Basically, management uses two kinds of plan to direct activities toward established goals: *single-use* plans and *standing* plans. Single-use plans include programs, schedules, and special methods designed for a unique set of circumstances; we shall examine these plans in the next chapter. In this chapter, we shall consider standing plans, a group that includes policies, standard methods, and standing operating procedures, all of which are designed to deal with recurring problems. Each time a particular, but familiar, problem arises, a standing plan provides a ready guide to action.

**need for standing plans**

A wildlife magazine ran into serious difficulties with three firms that bought considerable advertising space in the publication. These firms objected to articles on conservation appearing in the magazine. The editor contended that he was serving readers by reporting on critical conservation issues. The advertising manager argued that there were two sides to every question and that the magazine did not have to join the popular clamor for more regulation. The problem arose because the magazine lacked a clear, well-known editorial policy.

In this instance the editor won. The policy became "Challenging, informative articles that would excite the interest of readers." With this new policy firmly established, the advertising manager had to shift his approach to advertisers; he now says, "You may not like our editorial policy but it builds an audience you would like to reach." The new policy has removed internal conflict; it enables all magazine personnel to work in a consistent direction.

Moreover, procedures have to be adjusted to support policies. This became dramatically evident when the City University of New York adopted an "open-admission" policy. The number of entering freshmen jumped fifty percent, and their academic preparation varied drastically. This change had been anticipated—it was the aim of the new admission policy. But the procedures for registering this heterogeneous group and assigning members to appropriate classes were grossly inadequate. For weeks, students shifted from class to class, and no one was sure who should report where.

If a group of people are to live or work together, they must be able to anticipate one another's actions. There must be some consistency or pattern of behavior. The more interdependent the activities, the more important the ability to anticipate. Without this ability, an individual cannot know what he should do; he is doubtful about what he can depend on from others; and he is unsure whether his own efforts will be helpful or harmful. This is true for a symphony orchestra, football team, diplomatic corps, ship's crew, bank, coffee plantation, or any other working group.

Standing plans are an important means of building predictable patterns of behavior in a business firm. They are especially valuable in the execution of strategy, when managers rely on work being done consistently. In addition, outsiders do business with a firm because of its reliability. Thus, policies and other standing plans buttress strategy by inducing sustained, dependable actions.[1]

## TYPES OF STANDING PLANS

Within the broad category of standing plans, a manager has a choice of several types, notably policies, standard methods, and standard operating procedures. Like formations for a football team, one type of plan may be more useful than another in a certain situation. So a manager needs to know the characteristics of the tools he has to work with if he is to be effective in achieving balanced results. Let us look at the characteristics of the principal types of standing plans.

*policies*

A policy is a general guide to action; it does not tell a person exactly what to do, but it does point out the direction. Familiar policies are summed up in these statements: "We sell only for cash." "We lease, rather than buy, office space." "We insure all property worth more than $10,000 against fire loss." In each instance, an important aspect of a recurring problem has been singled out, and a guide established for dealing with it. When establishing policy the manager has to give considerable attention to these questions: Should a policy give explicit guidance or merely set limits? What kinds of problems should be covered?

Some policies provide only broad guidance. For example, "Our policy is to make college education available to all students graduating from an in-state high school" leaves much leeway as to what is done about classroom space and about keeping up with standards. Similarly a statement that "Preference will be given to goods made by union labor" indicates intent but leaves the purchasing agent free to decide whether the preference comes first or only when all other considerations are equal.

But policies can be much more specific. An investment-banking firm makes this statement on length of vacations.

*Employees shall normally be entitled to vacations according to the following schedule:*
1. On payroll six to twelve months prior to March 1—one week.
2. On payroll thirteen months to five years prior to March 1—two weeks.
3. On payroll five to fifteen years prior to March 1—three weeks.
4. On payroll over fifteen years prior to March 1—four weeks.

What subjects policies should cover and what they should say depends entirely on what will be helpful in solving specific problems. Take customer

---

[1]For an interesting account of the development and evolution of standing plans at Xerox, see D. Hampton, C. E. Summer, and R. Webber, *Organizational Behavior and the Practice of Management,* 3rd ed. (Glenview: Scott, Foresman, 1978), pp. 526–28.

policies. Many companies believe it wise to establish lower, and perhaps upper, limits on the size of the customer they want; location limits are also common. These guides are useful not only to the selling organization, but also to people who must plan production scheduling, warehousing, and shipping. Establishing a policy covering the quality characteristics of customers is more difficult. Credit rating, stability of demand, desire for special service, history on cancellation of orders—all contribute to a definition of "a good firm to do business with." Few companies, however, attempt to incorporate these considerations in a policy, because most customers are good in some respects and weak in others; thus a general guide applicable to many situations is hard to formulate. For guidance on this aspect of selecting customers, certain companies have a policy that simply lists all factors that must be considered in arriving at a decision.

Even when most aspects of a problem do not lend themselves to policy guidance, perhaps one or two aspects do. The complex problem of selecting suppliers of raw materials and parts is a good example. A purchasing agent must make a separate analysis of possible suppliers for each item he buys. Nevertheless, most companies do have a few policies to guide this selection. It may be a policy to buy no more than seventy-five percent of any one product from a single supplier to avoid being dependent on a single source. It may be a policy to secure bids from at least three sources to encourage competition for the company's business. Note that such policies deal only with the number of suppliers, leaving open the selection of specific firms.

A policy, then, may (1) be specific or general in its instruction, (2) deal with one, or many, aspects of a problem, (3) place limits within which action is to be taken, or (4) specify the steps in making a decision. The skill of a manager in using policies lies in how he decides just *what kind of guidance* will be helpful.

For easy reference, policies are often classified by subject, such as sales, production, purchasing, personnel, or finance.[2] Or they may be referred to as *general* policies and *departmental* policies, depending on the scope of activities to which they apply.

**standard methods**     The distinction between a standard method and a policy is one of degree, because both provide guidance about how a problem should be handled. The chief differences relate to viewpoint, completeness, and the attempt to control operating conditions.

*Viewpoint* A standard method deals with detailed activities, whereas a policy is a general guide. But what is general and what is detailed? The answer depends on our point of view. For example, a vice-president in charge of personnel would probably say that a general rule to pay wages comparable to those prevailing in the local community was a policy, whereas job evaluation was simply a method for carrying out this

[2]For a comprehensive discussion of functional policies, see W. H. Newman and J. P. Logan, *Strategy, Policy, and Central Management,* 8th ed. (Cincinnati: South-Western, 1981), pt 2.

policy. But the chief of the wage and salary division would look on a decision to use job evaluation in establishing pay rates as a major policy covering his work; he would consider a particular way of relating one job to another—say, factor comparison—a method. What about still a third person, a job analyst who works for the wage and salary chief? He, too, has his own point of view. He thinks the choice of factor comparison is a policy decision; for him, methods are such things as determining whom to contact and how to conduct interviews in analyzing each job. Clearly, then, whether a particular guide to action is called a policy or a standard method depends on the perspective of the person who is talking.

Still, even such a slippery distinction as this is useful. In planning the work of each job, at whatever level, an executive should think of both the broad framework in which he operates and the more detailed methods he will use. Good policy requires both viewpoints, and we need terms that distinguish between them.

*Completeness*    Standard methods never cover every aspect of an activity, although they do provide fuller guidance than a policy because standard methods apply to a narrower scope of activities. Therefore, it is easier to find general guides that fit most cases. Besides, thanks to Frederick W. Taylor's attempt to plan everything in detail, tradition favors developing detailed methods on the assumption that the more completely a method is planned, the more efficient it will be.

*Control of environment*    The pioneers of Scientific Management— Frank Gilbreth, Taylor, and others—quickly discovered that the conditions surrounding a job often had more influence on output than the performance of the person holding the job.[3] The successful use of standard methods called for standard conditions.

The scientific managers therefore set about to control raw materials, machine maintenance, work flow, tools, training, and other factors that affect output. After such work conditions were controlled, it became reasonable to expect an individual to follow a standard method of work and to achieve a standard output.

Today we can see many applications of this basic idea of controlling conditions so that standard methods will be applicable. An automobile assembly plant is perhaps the most widely known example. In this case, standardized parts reach the assembly line precisely on schedule. Necessary tools are placed within easy reach of the worker. Special instructions for auxiliary equipment are readily available. In fact management has gone to great lengths to make sure that standard methods are applicable to car after car. Although most industries do not go to this extreme, attempts to maintain uniform and effective working conditions are common.

[3]C. S. George, Jr., *The History of Management Thought,* 2nd edition (Englewood Cliffs, NJ: Prentice-Hall, 1972), chap. 6.

Standard methods are essential in the use of electronic computers to make automated decisions. Several conditions are necessary for a computer to "decide"—that is, issue instructions to another machine or to a person about action to be taken. (1) The significant variables in the situation must be measured and this information fed into the machine. (The rest of the environment is assumed to be constant.) (2) Any deviation from acceptable performance flashes a specific cue. (3) Each cue trips a "programmed" response—a standard method for dealing with the situation. All three conditions call for intense standardization. It is clear that unless an operating situation lends itself to a very high use of standard methods, automation is not applicable.

One drawback of developing standard methods and standard working conditions is the cost. Industrial engineers may spend months developing the one best way to perform a single operation. In a large plant, thousands of studies may be needed. Even then, the engineers may be unable to discover a feasible way to control one or two factors. This planning is expensive, and the resulting standard method must apply to a large enough volume of work so that the cost can be recovered through greater efficiency.

A shortcut is to standardize a method already in use, probably the method of the best workers.[4] This approach enables a company to predict processing costs and delivery times. Careful analysis, however, usually reveals places where methods that have simply evolved over the years can be improved. If a company is going to adopt a standard method at all, it pays to adopt a good one.

Standing plans are not always consciously and deliberately established. Some are like common law; they are practices that just grow, become accepted behavior, and are then enforced by those in official positions.

There is no sharp line that divides a company's traditions and customs from its standing plans. From a manager's point of view, we might say that a custom becomes a standing plan when (1) it is clearly enough recognized so that those it affects can describe it, and (2) individuals would be subject to criticism if they disregarded it merely on their own initiative. Other customs and traditions undoubtedly influence behavior, but they can scarcely be considered a part of the planning structure, because they are not sharply enough defined to be enforced.

Standard methods are more difficult to apply to sales and other client contacts than they are to jobs within a plant. These activities are varied, and the diversity of individual behavior is often an important consideration. Consequently, two approaches already mentioned in connection with policies are often used. First, we can standardize certain parts of the total activity—for instance, in sales work, the presenting of merchandise and the writing of sales orders; in a hospital, the handling of admissions, routine tests, and accounting. Second, for some activities we can specify a series of steps, as in conducting an interview or reconciling a bank statement. An

---

[4]The importance of "work simplification" in improving productivity at IBM is described in C. F. Vough, *Productivity* (New York: AMACOM, 1979), chaps. 4 and 5.

executive or operator can use these standard parts in whatever combination seems appropriate for a day's work. This practice permits flexibility while still achieving some of the benefits of standard methods.

A procedure details the *sequence of steps* several individuals must take to achieve a specific purpose. When a procedure for dealing with recurring problems becomes formalized, we call it a standard operating procedure.

standard operating procedures

Company action on even relatively small matters usually requires the work of several individuals. A procedure helps to integrate their bits of work into a meaningful whole. Consider the standard operating procedure set by an insurance company for the employment of exempt personnel (that is, employees not subject to wage-and-hour regulations).

1. A supervisor decides he needs an additional person to help with technical problems.
2. The budget officer must approve the addition unless the supervisor's existing budget has funds available for this purpose (which is unlikely).
3. The supervisor advises the personnel director by phone or in writing of his new need.
4. The personnel director sends a job analyst to the supervisor; the analyst writes a description of job duties and qualifications of the person needed to fill the job, and gets the supervisor's OK.
5. This job description is reviewed by the wage and salary administrator, who classifies the job and thereby sets the salary range for the new job.
6. The employment manager looks for candidates who have the qualifications stated in the job description. He first checks present employees who might be qualified and interested. If necessary, he turns to outside sources. He then picks the two or three most promising candidates.
7. The supervisor interviews the candidates sent to him by the employment manager; he selects the one he prefers or asks for more candidates.
8. The employment manager checks the references and tries to uncover other pertinent information about the leading candidate.
9. This individual is called back for a second interview with the supervisor. They try to reach a tentative understanding about the job duties, salary range, and other matters.
10. The supervisor's boss interviews the candidate.
11. If everything is in order, the supervisor makes a firm offer.
12. The candidate reports to the office of the employment manager, fills in company forms, retirement instructions, and so on. The employment manager gives him background information on the company and its personnel policies.
13. The person takes a medical examination from the company doctor.
14. He reports for duty.
15. The employment manager sends instructions to the payroll clerk about starting date, rate of pay, deductions, and so forth.

Most companies have literally hundreds of such procedures—for grievances, capital expenditures, arranging to use the company car—and most are essential for smooth operation. Picture the confusion if there were no standard procedure for customers' orders. Somehow each order must get immediately from the sales representative to the shipping clerk, the credit manager, and the accounts-receivable clerk; later the persons responsible for billing, inventory records, sales analysis, and sales compensation must be advised. Without a regular routine for handling such matters, customer service would be poor, salespeople would be angry, bills would have errors and become troublesome to collect, and inventory controls would collapse.

Most standing operating procedures apply to the flow of business papers—orders, bills, requests, reports, applications, and so forth. The papers are simply vehicles for information and ideas. But there can be standing procedures with no papers at all; for example, when an exception to a normal price is at issue, the three or four people involved may have a well-established understanding about the steps necessary in making a decision.

Although standard forms are not an essential part of a standard operating procedure, they can be very helpful for a large volume of routine transactions. A well-designed form with space for all essential information aids accuracy of communication, permits rapid handling, and serves as a convenient record.

*Relation to organization*   Formal organization divides the total work of a company into parts, thus permitting concentrated and specialized attention where necessary. Procedures help tie all the parts together. Like an automatic shuttle on a loom passing back and forth through the warp threads, the procedures weave woof threads that bind a firm fabric. Some of the weaving must be done by hand, as we shall see in the next chapter, but a large part of it must become routine and standardized. This is the role of the standing operating procedure.

Clearly, the way a company is organized affects the number and sequence of steps in any procedure.[5] For instance, if each supervisor in the life-insurance company referred to earlier recruited his own technical personnel (as is the case in some companies), at least steps 6, 8, and 10 of the procedure would be changed. Fifty years ago, when there would have been no central personnel department, a supervisor might well have done all the work himself, except for steps 2, 10, and 15. But if the company had more personnel specialists, the procedure might well be more elaborate—as anyone who has been recruited into the Armed Services can testify.

*Keeping procedures simple*   Standing operating procedures tend to become complex and rigid for several reasons. Each unit takes jurisdictional pride in performing its part accurately. Control points are added to avoid difficulties that are often temporary, and these controls then survive like the proverbial cat with nine lives.[6] Executives habitually look for information at

---

[5]Jay describes how the extremely centralized organization within the British Broadcasting Corporation generated procedures with multiple steps. See A. Jay, *Management and Machiavelli* (New York: Holt, Rinehart, 1967), pp. 61–62.

[6]For a discussion of how this problem developed at AT&T, see J. E. Ross and M. J. Kami, *Corporate Management in Crisis: Why the Mighty Fall* (Englewood Cliffs, NJ: Prentice-Hall, 1973), chap. 9.

certain spots, not realizing that it might be more simply compiled elsewhere. Standard forms acquire a sanctity that few dare challenge.

To avoid the choking effect of overelaborate procedures is a continuing task for a manager.[7] A variety of techniques are open to him. He may hire a special procedures-analyst for assistance in this area alone. Among the many possibilities for simplification are mechanical devices for communication and duplication. Perhaps a procedure can be revised so that some steps are taken concurrently. One company found that checking all invoices from vendors was unnecessary; by concentrating on those for over $100, 74 percent of the invoices could be handled more promptly, with a likely annual loss of only $200; furthermore, the work of two clerks was eliminated.

In appraising a standing procedure, a manager wants to ensure that (1) the action each person must take is clear, (2) the information each person requires is provided, (3) the work proceeds promptly, (4) economies are obtained where feasible, (5) control checks are made at strategic points, and (6) necessary records are kept. Meeting these tests and also keeping procedures simple often calls for keen resourcefulness.

## HOW STRICT SHOULD PLANS BE?

There is much double talk about the flexibility of standing plans. An executive may spend ten minutes emphasizing the need for a policy, standard method, or standing operating procedure, and then finish by saying, "Of course, we want to keep it flexible." In a single breath, he has cast out his whole point. How flexible? Flexible in what way? The catch is that the executive has several available courses of action.

One approach is to change standing plans frequently: a policy, method, or procedure remains in effect until a new guide is established, but such revisions are made promptly whenever operating conditions change. Unfortunately, this approach has serious limitations. Many of the advantages of dependability, habitual behavior, customary social relations, and predictable results are lost. Communication about changes in standing plans is difficult, especially if a large number of people are involved; the reasons for the new plan and its full meaning become confused, and loyalty to informal groups encourages resistance to new alignments. Therefore, using frequent change to secure flexibility in standing plans needs to be confined to a few issues—such as a special procedure to handle the Christmas rush—and preferably applied to a small group that understands why the change is necessary.

Another approach to flexibility is to state a standing plan generally, or loosely, in order to permit a wide range of variation within the plan. Or we may list many exceptions to which the plan does not apply. In effect, this simply restricts the scope of the plan; flexibility is achieved by not giving full guidance.

Still a third way is to think of standing plans partly as guides and partly as rules. If we can draw this distinction clearly, the usefulness of

---

[7]For some cynical suggestions on how to avoid this problem, see R. Townsend, *Up the Organization* (New York: Fawcett World Library, 1970), p. 129.

standing plans can be greatly extended. Let us examine this approach more fully.

guides versus rules Some policies are intended to be definite rules having no exceptions. For example, a large pharmaceutical manufacturer has this policy: "All company products, whether prescription or non-prescription drugs, will only be sold in retail pharmacies." This does not mean that the company prefers to distribute only to pharmacies or that only the distribution manager may authorize exceptions; it means just what is says. The company does not want its products carried in non-pharmacy outlets such as supermarkets or discount stores. By restricting distribution to pharmacies, the company believes that its professional image among doctors and pharmacists is enhanced. The policy is also designed to build strong company loyalty among retail pharmacies. Hence the policy is rigidly enforced.

Contrast the distribution policy of the drug firm with the employment policy of a large data processing department in an insurance company: "Individuals added to the computer programming staff should receive a grade of B or better on the programming aptitude test administered by an outside psychological consulting firm." This policy was instituted to ensure that the department's heavy investment in training new programmers was spent wisely. Experience in the insurance company, as well as in other data processing settings, indicated that new hires with a test grade of B or better were very likely to become successful programmers. An analysis of the department after the policy had been in effect for several years showed that 32 percent of the staff had been employed without having taken the programming aptitude test or with a test grade lower than B. What good, then, was the policy? Managers in the insurance company insisted that the policy was very helpful. "It is a distillation of our experience. It reminds us that any time we ignore the test results, we are asking for trouble. However, there are several other factors involved in a selection decision and it has become extremely difficult to hire staff in this field. Consequently, we do not believe that we should be bound by this single consideration. Because of the policy, we are doubly careful when the test results do not measure up." In short, this policy served as a guide but not a rule.

Variations in strictness of application will also be found among standard methods. Even the sales pitch of a Fuller Brush representative is only suggested, and good representatives adapt their sales presentation to individual customers. On the other hand, the methods for running a test in a medical laboratory are usually followed precisely so that the results will be reliable.

Because standing operating procedures always involve several people, less freedom is possible than with standard methods. Each person relies on the other links in the chain. When exceptions to a usual routine are necessary, everyone affected should be notified, for the very existence of the standing procedure creates a presumption that everyone will follow his customary path. Sometimes there is even a standing procedure for making an exception to a standing procedure! Handling rush orders at a plant or

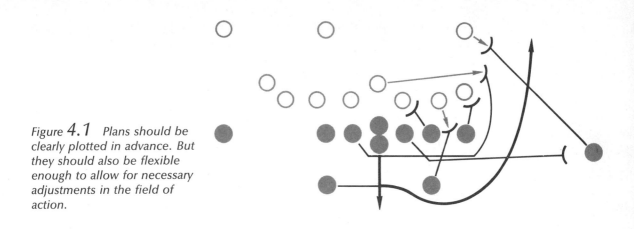

Figure *4.1 Plans should be clearly plotted in advance. But they should also be flexible enough to allow for necessary adjustments in the field of action.*

registering a special student at a university, for instance, may call for this refinement.

Variation in strictness can cause confusion, however. In some cases, the reliability of a standing plan is its virtue. In other instances, rigidity is anything but a virtue. We should recognize the dilemma and deal with it in the following ways.

restrained use of rules

**Make intentions clear** An executive who had built his company from scratch supposedy had a large rubber stamp that read, "And this time I mean it." When he wanted his orders followed precisely, he used the stamp on any documents involved. Modern executives who are otherwise fond of "flexible policies" might well adopt a similar device. Subordinates are often uncertain whether a standing plan is a guide or a rule. Simply making clear how much flexibility is intended will remove much of the confusion.

**Establish rules only for compelling reasons** When we set up a policy, method, or procedure, we often have a strong conviction about the soundness of that plan, and we believe others should follow it to the letter. Our natural tendency is to state it as though it should be strictly observed. But we should remember that a standing plan may remain in effect for a long time. Circumstances may change. Those who apply the plan later may be in a better position to judge its fitness. If they are permitted to treat the policy or method as "recommended practice," they profit by the guidance but are not pushed into an action that fails to accomplish major objectives. Consequently we should have compelling reasons for insisting on strict observance.

Strong reasons for strict observance may indeed exist. *Consistency* of action by several people may be necessary, as in pricing to avoid illegal discrimination. Or consistency over time may be desirable; for instance, accounting reports should be comparable from one year to the next. *Dependability* may be crucial if several people must rely on knowing what others will do, as when a plane lands on an aircraft carrier. *Doers may clearly lack judgment* on the subject covered by a standing plan; most operators of electronic computers do not know enough about the inner mechanism to deviate from standard instructions, nor does the student who is selling magazines to get through college have enough background to adjust subscription rates. In circumstances such as these, standing plans should be strictly observed.

***Use the exception principle***   The so-called "exception principle" simply refers to an understanding an executive may have with his subordinates that so long as operations are proceeding as planned, the subordinates should not bother him. But when exceptions arise, they should consult him. The principle applies to standing plans in this way: subordinates are expected to abide by policies, standard methods, and standing procedures in most instances; but if an unusual condition arises in which a standing plan does not seem suitable, they turn the matter over to a higher authority, who decides whether an exception should be made. Perhaps the "higher authority" will be the executive who established the standing plan in the first place; at other times, permission to make exceptions may be assigned to lower-level executives. Note that in this setup, the standing plans are strict *rules* for operating people, but they are only *guides* for the executives who handle the exceptional cases. Of course, successful operation of the scheme requires that operating people be able to recognize when a situation may merit an exception and demand the attention of the "higher authority."

### WHAT TO COVER AND IN HOW MUCH DETAIL

For what activities should standing plans be established? More specifically: What aspects of such activities? With what type of standing plan—policy, standard method, or standing procedure? In how much detail?

**reasons for standing plans**

Because the ways of using standard plans and the extent to which they are applied always depend upon specific situations, a manager cannot avoid the continuing task of deciding when to add or drop policies, procedures, or standard methods. Here are several reasons why a standing plan may be introduced.

1.   The need for *consistency* and close *coordination* of work, as we have noted, affects the desirability of detailed planning. Where consistency is crucial, as in accounting, pricing, wages, vacations, and the like, the pressure for detailed plans is strong. Where adjustment to local conditions is paramount, detailed plans are apt to get in the way. Similarly if the activities of several persons must interlock (in timing or quality), detailed planning may be necessary. To the extent that work is independent, or coordination is easy to achieve through personal contact, a compelling reason for detailed planning may be lacking.

2.   Higher executives may lighten their work load by using standing plans. Once a policy, method, or procedure is developed, an *executive can delegate* to subordinates the job of applying the plan to specific cases. This delegation relieves him of the need to become personally familiar with each case, while still giving him

confidence that work will proceed according to his wishes. One decision—like a pattern in a foundry or a dress shop—can shape the output of many workers.

3. The *quality* of operating decisions may be improved. Because a standing plan is followed repeatedly, a manager can afford to give careful thought to the formation of the plan. A policy is one means of transmitting the company's heritage of knowledge to many people. The painstaking analysis upon which a standard method is based will benefit many operators when they follow "the one best way."

4. If it uses standing plans extensively, a company may find that it can employ people with less experience or ability to do certain jobs. If so, *payroll economies* should result.

5. Standing plans also lay the *groundwork for control.* By setting up limits within which activities take place, and perhaps by specifying how those activities are to be performed, it is easier to predict results. These predictions can then be translated into control standards (as explained in Chapter 3). In fact, establishing detailed plans encourages tight supervision and control, which may or may not be desirable.

6. A manager should also take heed of the people who do the work as well as of the work itself, in deciding how detailed his plans must be. The greater the dependency of subordinates, the greater the need for detailed plans. Such people want guidance, and they feel ill at ease without it. But if subordinates are highly self-assertive, general rather than detailed plans will be more applicable. Ability also plays a part in deciding on degree of detail. The greater the decision-making talent of most subordinates, and the greater their knowledge about the business, the less detail in planning is necessary.

A manager must remember, however, that these possible benefits are offset by several inherent drawbacks; the more detailed the planning, the greater the drawbacks. Standing plans introduce *rigidity.*[8] Indeed, the *purpose* of plans is to limit and direct action in a prescribed manner, and such plans become ingrained attitudes and habitual behavior. If plans are written down, they tend to be followed until new plans are written and approved. Naturally enough, the executives who develop such plans are inclined to defend them. All this means that it will be hard to change standing plans once they are well accepted. In dynamic situations, where frequent change is desirable, such rigidity is a drawback.

**drawbacks to standing plans**

Planning also involves *expense.* Fully as important as direct outlays for industrial engineering and management research is the time that operating executives devote to analysis, discussion, and decision. Teaching people to understand and follow a new plan also takes effort. Unless particular kinds of problems keep recurring, there is no point in even considering standing plans. The more the repetition, either inherent or contrived, the more useful standing plans will be. But as planning is extended to more areas of business and is increasingly detailed, a point will be reached where the improvements in results do not justify the cost of further planning.

*Time* taken in preparing and installing standard plans—time for analysis, to secure approvals, to develop understanding and skill in their use—

[8]Hampton et al., *Organizational Behavior,* pp. 228–29.

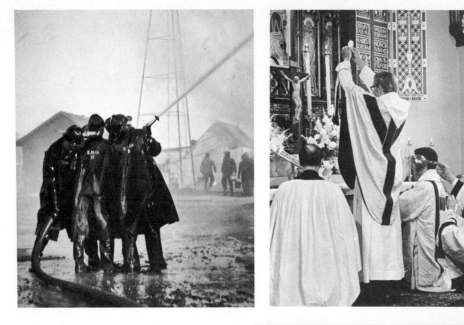

*Figure 4.2   For each position, these questions arise: What aspects of the job should be covered by standing plans? In how much detail? Should these plans be guides or rules?*

may also have strategic value. A customer may want prompt delivery, or the board of directors may want a report next week. In such situations, immediate action may be more important than taking time to discover the best possible method.

Clearly, then, the choice of what a standing plan should cover and how detailed it should be is strongly influenced by the particular work and people involved.[9] Essentially, it is the operating situation, not the personal preference of the manager, that dictates a specific structure of planning. The task of a manager is to identify the salient features of each situation.

## CONCLUSIONS

**freedom versus regulation**

Standing plans are a significant part of a company environment in which workers (managers and operators) make decisions. Policies, standard plans, and standard operating procedures provide decision-makers with limits, alternatives, and other premises. These premises have a double effect: they simplify the task of deciding how a specific problem is to be resolved, and they ensure a degree of consistency, dependability, and quality of decision throughout the company.

Nevertheless, the farther standing plans are extended, the more pressing becomes the dilemma of freedom versus regulation. This is an age-old conflict that men have faced as long as they have participated in joint activities. But urban living and working together in specialized, purposeful organizations accentuates the problem. How much regulation of individual action is desirable? The question takes many forms.

In political philosophy, the conflict is between authority and freedom. Every time a law is enacted, it limits someone's freedom. Yet we must have laws when people live together, so that the actions of one person will not unduly infringe on the actions of others. In psychology and sociology, the conflict is between individual self-expression, initiative, and creativity, and group norms, rules, and customs. Every time a social group derives a customary way of thinking or acting, someone's independence is circumscribed. Yet without such customs the group would disintegrate. In ethics, the conflict is between individual dignity and the common good; and in law, it is a major issue in rendering justice. Finally, in business management, the conflict is expressed as the problem of making plans that coordinate the action of people and regulate their job activities and their communications— but at the same time do not stifle the creativeness and energies of people who are contributing to the group effort.

Unfortunately, no plan is perfect for resolving the conflict between freedom and coordination. In our discussion, we have suggested several key factors a manager should consider in resolving these issues, but his final array of standing plans can be established only on the basis of the specific needs within his organization.

**adjusting standing plans to new strategy**

A change in strategy always requires a modification in at least some of the existing standing plans; since the present policies and procedures were designed to carry out the old strategy, they will not fully support a revision of that strategy. In fact, the difficulty of changing established practices is one of common reason why new strategies fail. Once established, policies, pro-

---

[9]As we shall note in Part III, individual needs change. For a discussion of the changing needs of workers in the workplace of the 1980s, see R. Shrank, "Are Unions An Anachronism?" *Harvard Business Review*, September–October 1979, pp. 107–15.

cedures, and methods become habits; they provide employees with a comfortable feeling of familiarity and security; people develop personal skills—even careers—around them. Consequently, they cannot be changed simply by a memo from the president. Just try, for example, converting a college cafeteria into a gourmet restaurant!

This reluctance to change means that a new strategy takes time and effort to implement. Careful thought must be given to which standing plans will serve the new strategy well and which should be altered. Detailed studies may be required to find the best new patterns, then training and revised rewards are necessary. Experience shows that a strategic change in, say, selling hi-fi equipment directly to retailers instead of through distributors takes at least two years to complete. Automating a large office may take even longer.

The great virtues of stability and predictability which prevailing standing plans provide also retard change. However, this inertia can be redirected, like a gyroscope. If effort is devoted to creating new patterns of behavior—which support a new strategy—then a continuing driving force bolsters the revised strategy.

### FOR FURTHER DISCUSSION

1. "The more detailed the strategy for a business or operating unit, the less the need for methods and procedures, but the greater the need for flexible, detailed policies." Comment.

2. "People like firm, clear rules that let them know what is expected and guide them to better performance. Vague guides are worse than no guides at all." Comment.

3. Consider a fairly significant change in policy that you would like to see implemented in your organization (business, school, class). (a) List other policies affected by this change. (b) List and discuss changes in procedures and methods that would be needed if the policy were implemented.

4. "In a dynamic environment, standing plans are more vital than ever." "In a dynamic environment, standing plans are not only likely to be out-of-date but to be impediments to sound behavior."

With which of these statements do you most agree? Why?

5. "Standing plans are really substitutes for thinking. They are organizational habits formalized to make sure that no one uses his head as long as he can remember what page in the manual the answer is on." Comment on this position.

6. Are standing plans likely to be more important in managing four project teams in a research laboratory or four work gangs on a construction project?

7. "We have a policy which says no employee shall be required to work overtime for more than twelve hours per month, and then only if given one week's notice of need. Yet our supervisors often ask us to put in more than twelve hours and seldom give us more than a day's notice. This has been going on for years. I wish they would either change the policy or follow it." Comment on this statement by a worker in a large electronics plant.

## CASES

For cases involving issues covered in this chapter, see especially the following. Particularly relevant questions are listed after each case.

Benjo Associates (p. 92), 3
Elizabeth Archer (p. 96), 5
Mike Zerllini (p. 188), 2
Clifford Nelson (p. 192), 2
Camden Chemical (p. 298), 3
Scandico (Singapore) (p. 305), 2
Netsuki Novelty Products Company (p. 451), 2

## FOR FURTHER READING

Bower, M., *The Will to Manage*. New York: McGraw-Hill, 1966, chap. 4. Management consultant explains the need for policies and procedures to carry out strategy effectively.

Filley, A. C., R. J. House, and S. Kerr, *Managerial Process and Organizational Behavior,* 2nd ed. Glenview: Scott, Foresman, 1976, chap. 14. Discusses the role of objectives and policies in achieving organizational goals, and examines research evidence on significance of clearly defined goals and policies.

Lawler, E. E., and J. G. Rhode, *Information and Control in Organizations*. Santa Monica, CA: Goodyear, 1976, chap. 6. Incisive discussion of the dysfunctional effects of planning and control systems.

Mockler, R. J., *Business Planning and Policy Formulation*. New York: Appleton-Century-Crofts, 1972, chaps. 5 and 8. Explores the process of establishing policies and procedures, and illustrates their use in specific companies.

Newman, W. H., and J. P. Logan, *Strategy, Policy, and Central Management,* 8th ed. Cincinnati: South-Western, 1981, pt 2. Extensive coverage of the development and use of policies for each major functional area within an enterprise.

# 5 adaptive programming

Learning Objectives

After completing this chapter you should be able to

1. Describe the six basic steps in programming.
2. Explain the relationship among programs, projects, and schedules.
3. Understand the concept of a contingency program.
4. Identify the two major sources of timing errors in single-use plans.
5. Describe the key elements of the PERT approach to scheduling and controlling programs.

In the preceding chapters we examined two broad types of plan: strategy and objectives, which focus on desired results; and standing plans, which establish a structure of customary behavior for achieving these results. Both types of plan are highly useful devices for managerial decision-making, but they do not exhaust the arsenal of weapons a manager can use in attacking problems.

A third type of plan deals with single, rather than repetitive, situations. In such cases, a manager decides in advance what action to take within a given period or what to do to meet a particular problem. Once the time has passed or the problem has been met, a new plan is devised for the next problem. These are called single-use plans.

The basic characteristics of single-use plans can best be explained in terms of programs; other forms, such as schedules and projects, can then be viewed as particular kinds of programs. After examining several types of programs, we shall turn to the more uncertain problems of adjusting programs to a dynamic and uncertain environment. A program lays out the principal steps for accomplishing a mission and sets an approximate time for carrying out each step.

**programming**

A change in strategy always calls for a program to shift from the old to the new. For instance, when General Foods Corporation withdrew from the fast-food business it needed a program for selling off its Burger Chef outlets, dismissing employees, terminating contracts for materials, and recording liquidation losses. Many locations and people were affected, so sub-programs focusing on the various facets (such as the sale of real estate) were drawn up.

The sequence and timing of major moves is often so important that they are included as a component of a new strategy—as suggested in Chapter 2. Each of these moves highlighted in the strategy requires a more detailed program of the steps necessary to advance from the present situation to the target. In addition, getting things done under an established strategy often calls for a program.

Good programming is crucial to smooth and efficient operations. Consider, for instance, the problem faced by an airline in introducing a new type of plane, such as the Boeing 747. Flight crews and ground personnel—literally thousands of people—have to learn new skills. To postpone a re-education program until the planes are delivered would result in chaos. Instead, a company must anticipate by two years the need for competent maintenance people, experienced flight crews, different weather information, and solutions to other new problems. Some personnel need classes of only a few hours; others must spend several months learning complex theories and skills. All this training has to be carried on while regular operations with older planes are maintained.

Only through careful programming can an airline (1) anticipate possible crises and make provisions for them, (2) review the subprograms to be sure that they fit together into a consistent whole, (3) avoid stop-gap decisions in favor of taking sound and economical steps, and (4) use its limited (and expensive) training facilities most effectively.

Skill in programming is a major asset for any operating executive. A personnel director, for instance, needs a program for recruiting more blacks; a treasurer is concerned with a program for selling new bonds; an executive vice-president works out a program for introducing a new product. Programs, in fact, are useful at all levels in a firm: the president may develop a program for merging two companies, and a first-line supervisor may have a program for training Sally to take over Lorraine's job.

## basic steps in programming

Many programming problems can be solved by following six basic steps.[1]

1.  *Divide into steps the activities necessary to achieve the objective.* Dividing work into steps is useful for planning, organizing, and controlling. Planning is improved because concentrated attention can be given to one step at a time. Organizing is facilitated because the steps or projects can be assigned to different persons to effect speedier or more efficient action. Controlling is also enhanced because an executive can watch each step and determine whether progress is satisfactory while work is actually being done, instead of waiting for final results. If the division into parts is to be effective, the purpose of each step should be clearly defined, indicating the kind of work, the quality, and the quantity expected.

2.  *Note the relationships among steps, especially any necessary sequences.* Usually the parts of a program are closely dependent on one another. The amount of work, the specifications, and the time for each step often affect the ease or difficulty of taking the next. Unless these relationships are closely watched, the very process of subdividing the work may cause more inefficiency than it eliminates.

    Necessary sequences are particularly significant relationships. In a drug-addiction program, for example, local counseling centers must be set up and staffed before general publicity is released; otherwise early interest turns into frustration, and the entire effort is regarded as a sham. Necessary sequences have an important bearing on scheduling because they tend to lengthen the overall time required for an operation; since a shorter cycle gives a company more flexibility, the need for delaying one action until another is completed should be carefully checked.

3.  *Decide who is to be responsible for doing each step.* In programming a company's normal operation, the existing organization structure will already have determined who is to perform each activity. But if the program covers an unusual event—merging with another company, for instance—careful attention must be given to deciding who is accountable for each step. These special assignments may create a temporary set of authorizations and obligations. A special team may be formed to carry out the program.

4.  *Determine the resources needed for each step.* For realistic programming, the need for facilities, materials and supplies, and personnel must be recognized. The availability of these necessary resources must be appraised. If any one of them

---

[1]Adapted from a fuller discussion in W. H. Newman and J. P. Logan, *Strategy, Policy, and Central Management,* 8th ed. (Cincinnati: South-Western, 1981), chap. 21.

is not available, another project should be set up to obtain this resource. For example, if a company is short on qualified personnel, it should make plans for hiring and training new employees. Many a program breaks down because the executive who prepares it does not realistically understand what resources will be required.

5. *Estimate the time required for each step.* This act has two aspects: (1) the date when a step can begin and (2) the time required to complete an operation once it is started. Starting time, of course, depends on the availability of the necessary resources: how soon key personnel can be transferred to a new assignment; what work is already scheduled for a machine; the likelihood of getting delivery of materials from suppliers; the possibility of subcontracting part of the work—all have an effect on the time any given steps may begin.

   Processing time, once the activity has begun, is usually estimated on the basis of past experience. In addition, for detailed production operations, time-study data may permit tight scheduling. But for a great many operations, more time is consumed in securing approvals, conveying instructions, and getting people to work than is required for doing the work itself. Unless this "non-productive time" can be eliminated, however, we should include it as part of the estimated time.

6. *Assign definite dates for each part.* An overall schedule is of course based on the sequences noted under step 2 and the timing information assembled under step 5. The resulting schedule should show both the starting date and the completion date for each part of the program.

   A good deal of adjustment may be necessary to make a final schedule realistic, however. A useful procedure is to try working backward and forward from some fixed controlling date. Availability of materials or facilities may set the time around which the rest of the schedule pivots. In sales, a particular selling season, such as Christmas or Easter, may be the fixed point. We must, of course, dovetail any one program with other company commitments. We must also make some allowance for delay. Allowances all along the line are not desirable, because they would encourage inefficient performance, but a few safety allowances are wise so that an unavoidable delay at one point will not throw off an entire schedule.

In summary, a well-conceived program covers all actions necessary to achieve a mission, and indicates who should do what when. Note how all the programming elements arise even in the simple example shown in Figure 5.1. The controller of a pharmaceutical company decided to install a large Xerox duplicating machine to make multiple copies of the many reports his office issued. The Xerox salesperson said, "All you have to do is plug in the machine." But the controller realized that a shift in the office routine was more complicated than this. After some thought he developed the program summarized in Fig. 5.1. With this plan, he was able not only to specify when he wanted the machine delivered but also to prepare both the physical setup and his personnel for the change. He avoided having the office torn up when people were busy with month-end closing, and he had a plan that could easily serve as a control as the work progressed. Most programs are more complicated than this, of course, but their essential nature is the same.

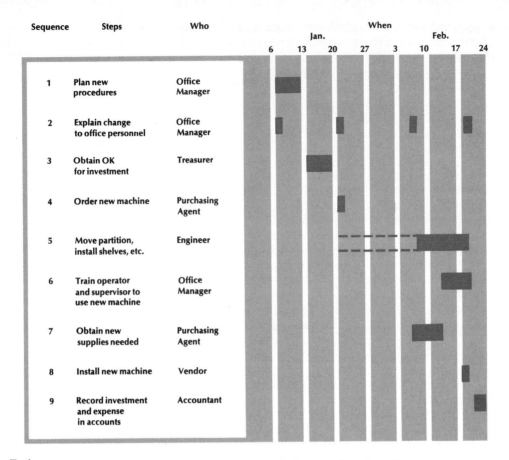

| Sequence | Steps | Who | When |
|---|---|---|---|

*Figure 5.1* A program for installing a new duplicating machine in the controller's office. Starting and completion dates for each step are indicated here by the colored bars. The moving of partitions was delayed so that the office would not be torn up at the end of the month. Training included a visit to see a similar machine in operation in another company. Supplies could be obtained quickly from local jobbers.

**wide use of programming**

*Hierarchy of programs* For some firms, a major program encompasses a large part of company activity. This situation is true in the automobile industry, where annual model changes pace the work of all major manufacturing departments. Lead times are long, because there is a necessary sequence between market and environmental research, functional design, engineering, tooling, and actual production and sales. In fact, in any one year a company must do prepatory work for models that will be sold two, three, and four years later.

Such programming of major steps must necessarily lump together large amounts of work. But each step, in turn, has a program of its own. Thus the stage of providing necessary facilities may be divided into a more detailed schedule showing when building construction and machine purchase must be started and completed. Again, building construction will have its own program, including such steps as defining requirements, selecting a site, getting architectural plans, gaining community approval, completing engineering plans, selecting a chief contractor, and so on. The executive charged with finding a site will probably establish an even more detailed program for his own chore.

Detailed programs are not necessarily connected to successively broader programs; any executive may use them by himself if he wishes. Nevertheless, when the programming approach permeates managerial thinking at all levels, it sets a tone and a pace for the entire company.

*Projects* Often a single step in a program is set up as a "project." Actually, a project is simply a cluster of activities that is relatively separate and clearcut. Building a hospital, designing a new package, soliciting gifts of $500,000 for a college dormitory are examples. A project typically has a distinct mission and a clear termination point—the achievement of the mission.

The task of management is eased when work can be set up in projects. The assignment of duties is sharpened, control is simplified, and the people who do the work can sense their accomplishment. Calling a cluster of work a project does not, of course, change its nature. It may still be part of a broader program, and programming the project itself may be desirable. The chief virtue of a project lies in identifying a nice, neat work package within a bewildering array of objectives, alternatives, and activities.

*Schedules* A schedule specifies the time when each of a series of actions should take place. It is one aspect of programs, as we are using that term. When, as a result of standing plans, the tasks to be done and the persons who must do them are clear, then scheduling may be the only element that needs management's attention. This would be the case, for example, in a frozen-food plant where the line is all set to go, as soon as the manager decides when to start and how many of each size package to produce. Under some conditions, then, planning is simplified by focusing separately on scheduling. In thinking about management broadly, however, the more inclusive concept of programming has wider usefulness.

## STATIC VERSUS ADAPTIVE PROGRAMMING

Our discussion of programming so far has been based on two assumptions that are realistic only part of the time. We have assumed (1) that most of the actions necessary to achieve an objective are subject to direction and manipulation by management, and (2) that management can forecast the time factors—both availability and elapsed time—with considerable accuracy. For a good many problems, notably those that occur chiefly *within* company offices and plants, these assumptions are usually correct.

But when the timing of several important steps is outside management's control and is uncertain, the character of programming changes. Social attitudes, competition, and business cycles are indeed independent variables. When we cannot make such events conform to our master strategy, we need more adaptability, more resourcefulness, and more hedges and retreats. We must still think in terms of major steps, sequences, and timing and duration of each step, but now we must do so creatively rather than perfunctorily as though we were dealing with a routine engineering problem.

**contingency programs**

Typically we draw up a single program; it is the best way we can devise to get from our present position to a stipulated objective. However, we must be aware that external events may not occur as predicted and that the results of our actions may not turn out as anticipated. These unknowns may be serious—perhaps catastrophic. If we stick with our original program, we may get into deep trouble.

The most elaborate way to plan for such uncertain events is to prepare contingency programs. Here we prepare in advance a set of programs. Each is ready to use if a particular circumstance arises. In planning flights to the moon, for instance, a whole array of contingency programs are developed in detail. On the Apollo 13 moon shot, such a contingency plan permitted partial completion of the mission and probably saved the lives of the crew. Contingency planning is also common in military operations.

In contrast, little contingency planning is done by most enterprises.[2] Aside from limited plans for action in the event of fire, we prefer to focus on making our single program work out. Is this disregard of admitted unknowns wise?

The reasons for shunning contingency programs are plain. (1) The effort and expense of preparing such programs is large. Contingencies are many, so the number of programs could quickly multiply. To keep the programs viable, necessary preparations have to be put into effect. (2) Contingency programs are disconcerting. A manager tries hard to develop enthusiastic, committed effort behind the preferred program. Discussing and preparing for a lot of "ifs" adds confusion and distraction. (3) Postponement of planning until the contingency arrives (or can be more reliably forecast) *usually* permits us to get by without very serious losses.

The prudent manager, however, should identify those contingencies whose risks are so large that special programs are justified; and he should ensure that sequential adjustments are promptly made.

**sequential adjustments**

An alternative to setting up contingency programs is making successive modifications in a program as unpredicted (or unassumed) conditions move to center stage.

*Anticipating that feedback data will lead to revisions*    One way to deal with unpredictable and uncontrollable conditions is to ensure a flow of current information as work progresses and to adjust the program when necessary. A surgeon has a general plan of action before an operation starts; a football coach may have a game plan in mind before the kickoff; but each

---

[2]With the growth of strategic planning, more firms are likely to develop contingency programs. See W. E. Rothschild, *Putting It All Together: A Guide to Strategic Thinking* (New York: AMACOM, 1976), chap. 12.

of these specialists expects to be guided more by current developments than by his prediction. An executive-development program is similar—a company may have a tentative ten-year plan for the progression of its outstanding young employees, but everyone expects that the actual performance of these people and the needs of the company will lead to drastic modifications long before the ten years are up.[3]

On the matter of revising plans, the key distinction between static and adaptive programming lies in executive attitude toward change. When a program is regarded as a blueprint, an executive is heavily motivated to make the plan work; changes, he feels, are a confession of partial defeat. But under the adaptive approach, the manager considers some change normal and responds readily when reasons appear for modifying plans.

Long-range programs, used to round out a company's strategy, are almost always revised. This is a prime example of anticipating that feedback data will lead to revision of the program. In other programs the feedback and revision cycle occurs more frequently, perhaps monthly, or when key steps are completed—for example, after test marketing, or when the quality of available funds is firmly established.

*Restricting scheduling to the near future*   When a pharmaceutical company put a new tranquilizer on the market, all executives were confident of a rapid growth in sales; there was talk of enlarging the plant, opening new branch offices, and using profits for additional research. Until the hoped-for sales volume actually developed, however, specific programming was confined to promoting the new product. Timing, and determining the magnitude of other moves, were held in abeyance until sales prospects became more certain.

A manufacturer of women's shoes got into trouble for not following a similar course. The firm opened a new plant in the South; it borrowed money and changed executive personnel on the assumption that most of its production could be transferred to the new plant within two years. Actually, the company had great difficulty in securing quality production from its new plant, and training expenses and spoilage made costs even higher than at the old plant. Consequently, the company was forced to postpone the move and found itself in serious financial difficulty. Had this firm merely scheduled the opening of the new plant, while leaving the time of closing the old factory unspecified, it might have avoided the crisis.

These devices for flexibility—anticipating changes and deferring program commitments except for the near future—sacrifice some of the benefits of a clear, positive program. Preparing for the future is more difficult and some economies may be lost. But these drawbacks are simply the price paid for a somewhat cautious approach to an unpredictable future.

*Adjusting to leads and lags in the flow of goods*   A program for a continuing flow of goods and services differs in important respects from a program for a single event. Procedures and distributors of goods, such as

---

[3]W. H. Newman, *Constructive Control* (Englewood Cliffs, NJ: Prentice-Hall, 1975), chap. 8.

gasoline or aspirin, must think in terms of a *rate* of output for a week or month. Such companies may be affected by seasonal fluctuations in consumption and by the buildup or cutback of inventory in the hands of distributors and perhaps consumers. Thus production must precede seasonal peaks in demand, and if a stable level of operations is desired, a firm must build inventories.

Programs that deal with the flow of goods rarely provide exactly the rate of activity that proves to be needed. The rates of flow must be adjusted, a little here and a little there, as we adjust the hot and cold water in a shower. When a variety of products is involved, this adjusting process becomes complex.[4] Most companies have operating programs for some months ahead, but revise them at least monthly on the basis of feedback information. For perishable products, like bread, adjustments may be made daily.

A program, then, must be suited to the operations it covers, but its essentials remain the same. By anticipating the what, who, how and when, it enables a manager to prepare systematically and carefully for difficulties before they arise.

### IMPORTANCE OF TIMING

Timing deserves special emphasis. Many a strategic program, sound in all other respects, has failed in application because action was taken at the wrong time. A shipping company built a large dock on Lake Erie, anticipating the movement of ocean freight through the St. Lawrence Waterway. The volume of business has been so slow in developing that the dock is now closed down. Perhaps ten years hence the necessary traffic *will* develop, but clearly the construction was premature. On the other hand, many a product has reached its market after the demand has waned—witness the multimillion-dollar loss on the oversized Edsel automobile. There are better and poorer times to ask the boss for a raise, to buy raw materials, to float a bond issue.

Two major sources of timing errors are economic shifts and the moods of key people. Programs inevitably rest on forecasts (or unstated assumptions) about *when* economic and social conditions will be attractive. If the forecast is early or late, the program suffers.

**adjusting to economic conditions**

One strength a company may have, in contrast to an individual decisionmaker, is its own economic forecasting staff. These experts gather data from many sources and make predictions about factors that directly affect company planning.[5] Although forecasters undoubtedly provide useful insights on questions of timing, their occasional errors are conspicuous. The public knows, for instance, that when Dacron fiber was first introduced to the

---

[4]Programming in terms of flow rather than for specific projects is a source of confusion in government planning. The national-income accounts, which reflect flows, are frequently used to express fiscal policy, but Congress makes approprations primarily for a particular project or on an annual-appropriation basis. Aside from Federal Reserve actions, we have few good mechanisms (like hot and cold water taps) to adjust the flows of goods and services.

[5]S. C. Wheelright and S. Makridakis, *Forecasting Methods for Management,* 3rd ed., (New York: Wiley, 1980).

*Figure 5.2  Timing the construction of a major facility calls for adroit adjustment to economic need, to political support or opposition, and to availability of vital supplies and capital. The speed of building the Alaskan pipeline, for example, has required careful balancing of U.S. need for crude oil, political relations with O.P.E.C. countries, strength of popular ecological concern, and conditions in the capital markets.*

market, du Pont built production facilities that far exceeded the demand. As a result, a new eighteen-million-dollar plant was idle for more than two years. The demand eventually developed, but the mistake lay in how fast it should do so.

*Objective appraisal*  A review of a variety of examples of poor timing suggests that executive attitude is more likely to be faulty than the forecasting and programming techniques. As already noted, executives become strongly committed to programs; they believe in them, and desperately want them to succeed. Because of this feeling, it is only natural for them to underrate information that might hint at a need for modification. An executive's unwillingness to face clear trends in the wallpaper industry, for instance, led one company to postpone closing an old and inefficient plant; this decision prevented the company from taking the necessary steps to pull itself out of serious debt.

Prudence requires an objective appraisal. Somehow, either through checking with outsiders or through self-discipline, executives must try to make a detached forecast of when key wants will occur. Moreover, as we will see in Part VI on controlling, key planning assumptions should be monitored as a program gets underway. Objective appraisal will not ensure perfect timing in our fast-moving world, but it will avoid the significant number of problems which can be attributed to rigidity of executive attitude.

*Keeping flexible*  When forecasts are not fully reliable—and few are—a wise executive seeks to *avoid making commitments until necessary*. He tries to distinguish between a bear-by-the-tail situation and one that consists of independent steps. For example, in a marketing program one move, such as national advertising, may necessitate a string of accompanying moves. As in passing a car on a crowded two-lane highway, once we start we have to follow through. But in many research projects, a process may be halted at the end of any of several steps and then begun again without major loss. In the latter situation, because we are not yet committed to subsequent steps, new timing is possible.

A related way to retain flexibility in timing is to *keep two or more alternatives open*. At one stage in its development, Boeing Aircraft had a large military contract that would eventually necessitate a new plant. The time arrived when the firm had to acquire a plant site and begin engineering work if the terms of the military contract were to be met; yet there was sharp disagreement among several parties about the location of the plant. To avoid being caught later in a time squeeze, the company took options on land in both Seattle and San Francisco and hired engineeers to make detailed plans for plants in both localities. More than a year later, but before any building contracts were let, the Seattle location was selected. The company kept two alternatives open until it became clear which one should be followed. Of course, substantial costs were involved in obtaining this flexibility. Boeing had to pay for two land options and two sets of engineering plans, though it knew that only one would eventually be used. Often flexibility can be achieved only at a price.

### anticipating reactions of key people

Among the many forecasts needed for good timing of executive action is a prediction of how key people will react to parts of a program. Temptation is always strong to concentrate on tangible, quantitative elements and slide over the more evasive human factors. Yet the responses of people may make or break a program. Often a proposed action calls for a major effort or readjustment on the part of several individuals or groups, for their behavior patterns, beliefs, and values may be involved. Perhaps political behavior (to be explored in Chapter 21) will also be involved.[6] In timing, we have to judge when the situation is ripe for a new move.

For years a leading Midwestern department store had no blacks in sales positions. The personnel director believed this tradition should be changed, but he anticipated resistance from supervisors and salesclerks. So he waited until there was a shortage of well-qualified salespeople and then hired two blacks, placing them under supervisors who were sympathetic to the change. Actually, these two were noticeably better qualified than most of the whites who could have been employed at the time. Word got around that they were unusually competent, and soon several other supervisors were asking for similar help. Had this change been introduced when well-qualified white applicants were in ample supply and were being turned down, the response might have been quite different.

A large bank installed a long-needed job-evaluation system. Officers and supervisors were pleased with the way the system was working, and the vice-president was anxious to move on to a training program that was also

---

[6]J. Pfeffer and G. R. Salancik, "Organizational Decision Making as a Political Process: The Case of the University Budget," *Administrative Science Quarterly,* June 1974.

badly needed. The president turned down the proposal, explaining that job evaluation had not yet become normal behavior. To introduce a second change on the heels of the first "might give us indigestion." This was the president's judgment on how fast his group could comfortably adapt to a new personnel practice. Not until a year and a half later did he launch the training program.

An executive with a good feel for timing must be socially perceptive as was this bank president. He must know enough about people's needs, hopes, and fears to be able to anticipate their reaction to a proposed plan.

**ADAPTIVE PROGRAMMING TECHNIQUES: PERT**

PERT is a special technique for scheduling and controlling large, complex programs.[7] Originally developed as a planning aid for the design and production of Polaris missiles, PERT (Program Evaluation and Review Technique) has been adapted to a wide variety of undertakings, including new product introductions and the construction of the World Trade Center in New York City.

The design and the production of Polaris missiles involved a staggering number of steps. Specification for thousands of minute parts had to be prepared, the parts had to be manufactured to exact tolerances, and then the entire system had to be assembled into a successful operating weapon. And time was of the essence. The basic steps in programming discussed in the preceding pages were applicable; but the complexity of the project (and the fact that many different subcontractors were involved) called for significant elaboration in the programs.

**recording the network**

As with any programming problem, we start with a plan of action. Suppose our goal is to launch a new product or place a communications satellite in orbit, and we determine the actions that will be necessary to achieve our goal. The first phase of a PERT analysis is to note carefully each of these steps, the sequence in which they must be performed, and the time required for each. This information is recorded in the form of a network—usually on a chart such as those shown in Figs. 5.3 and 5.4.

The chart in Fig. 5.3 is highly simplified so that we can easily grasp its main features. It shows the main steps that an American auto-equipment manufacturer would have to follow to market a new antismog muffler. The manufacturer has purchased a tested European patent so that engineering to domestic requirements is simple; furthermore, he already has a well-organized plant and distribution setup. Arrows on the chart indicate the sequence of events he must follow to get his new product on the market; the numbers on the arrows show the required time for each step.

Essentially, the network is one highly structured approach to recording a "program". This list of events, the sequences, and the elapsed times, are all the data necessary for program planning. The network does not show the

[7]J. D. Wiest and F. K. Levy, *A Management Guide to PERT/CPM,* 2nd ed. (Englewood Cliffs, NJ: Prentice-Hall, 1977)

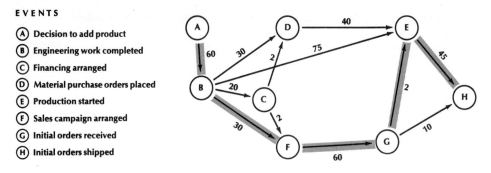

**EVENTS**

- Ⓐ Decision to add product
- Ⓑ Engineering work completed
- Ⓒ Financing arranged
- Ⓓ Material purchase orders placed
- Ⓔ Production started
- Ⓕ Sales campaign arranged
- Ⓖ Initial orders received
- Ⓗ Initial orders shipped

*Figure 5.3   A simplified PERT chart.   Events—that is, the start or completion of a step—are indicated by circles. Arrows show the sequence between events. The time (in days) required to move from one event to another appears on each arrow. The critical path—the longest sequence—is shown in color.*

resources needed for each step, but an understanding of personnel, machines, and money underlies the estimated time for each step. The chief advantage of expressing a program as a network is its emphasis on sequences and interrelationships.

**the critical path**

Because we are focusing here on time, we wish to know where delay, should it occur, would be most serious. The network is very helpful for this purpose. By tracing each necessary sequence and adding the time estimates for each step, we can identify which sequence will require the most time. This is the "critical path." Other sequences will take less time and hence are less critical.

The critical path is especially important in planning and control. Any delay along this path will postpone the completion date of the entire project. On the other hand, by knowing in advance which series of steps are critical, we might be able to replan (allocate more resources, perform part of the work simultaneously, and so on) in order to shorten the total time. In other words, (1) we focus control where it is most essential; (2) we are in a good position to spot potential trouble early; and (3) we can avoid putting pressure on activities that will do nothing to hasten completion.

Moreover, as work progresses, reports on activities that are ahead of, or behind, schedule will enable us to reexamine the timing. Perhaps an unexpected delay has created a new critical path. (For example, if "tooling up"—B to E in Fig. 5.3—required an additional thirty days, a new critical path would be created.) Then corrective action can be shifted to this new sequence in which no slack time exists. In this way PERT becomes a strong control, as well as scheduling, technique.

**uses of PERT**

PERT is typically applied to a much more complicated network than the illustration we have just used; in practice, each of the major steps would be programmed in more detail. The preparation of the sales campaign, for instance, would involve packaging, pricing, sales brochures, installation manuals, training of sales people, placing of advertisements, and the like; and each of these activities should be shown separately in the network. Such delineation improves the chance of catching delays early, and it also spells out the need for coordination at numerous points.

For a complex project, such as the construction of a large plant, the network becomes complicated indeed. A network with 137 events is shown in Figure 5.4. PERT is especially suited to large "single-use" programs having clearcut steps and measurable output. The concepts of an event network and the critical path can be applied to many kinds of situations in which we are interested in getting a job done on time.

**CONCLUSION: DESIGNING PLANNING SYSTEMS**

Having just reviewed in the preceding chapters a whole array of planning methods and problems, we notice that the complexity of the process stands out. The power and benefits tend to be forgotten. Actually, as experience amply demonstrates, using the resources of an organization to do the planning has many potential strengths. Our task as managers is to use this potential skillfully.

To take advantage of the specialized knowledge, ideas, and energies of the various members of an organization, we divide the planning work (as we do other kinds of work) into bits and pieces. Planning in organizations requires many people and much time. This gives us numerous inputs; but we must also develop ways to fit all these pieces together, and to ensure that our farflung planning team is pulling in the same direction.

The best-known mechanisms for achieving such integrated planning have been discussed in the last three chapters. Strategy sets the mission. *Operating objectives* spell out the goals for each executive, and serve as

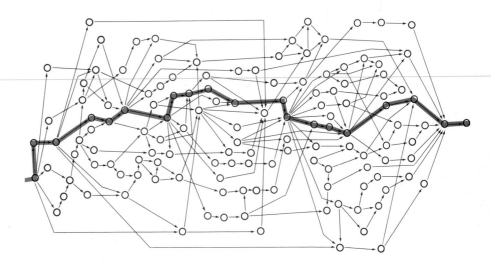

*Figure* **5.4**  *PERT in an actual situation.*

company values in making short-run choices. The strategy and objectives together provide the coordinated direction so essential to purposeful endeavor.

Then, to simplify planning while taking advantage of accumulated wisdom, we create standard patterns—*policies, methods, procedures*— for dealing with recurring problems. Added benefits of this established social behavior are a dependable flow of information and an ability to predict and depend upon the actions of others. And by no means the least of our planning instruments are various programming techniques that tell scattered people how to fit their actions into a united effort.

A recurring theme in planning is that of freedom versus the regulation of individual behavior. As managers, we want unified effort *and* individual initiative, commitment to enterprise objectives *and* fulfillment of personal needs, use of expert judgment *and* creative imagination, coordinated action *and* individual resourcefulness. Fortunately, wise management can provide for some of both. We have indicated explicitly the factors a manager should weigh in deciding when the benefits of giving individuals discretion counterbalance the advantages of regulation. But the choice is not easy, especially in view of changing values and expectations in the contemporary work force.

## FOR FURTHER DISCUSSION

1. "If overall strategies are well conceived and communicated, and good standing plans created, adaptive programming becomes a very simple, mechanistic series of steps that could probably be developed by a computer, trained apes, or some combination of the two." Comment.

2. "Standing plans must be flexible to allow for differences in specific situations, but programs must be very specific and followed to the letter or there is no point in having them." Comment.

3. Good planning is based in large part on good forecasting. Yet areas that are most difficult to forecast are typically most in need of planning. How do you reconcile these statements with the need for, and elements of, good plans?

4. Which of the six basic steps in programming is most important in developing a plan for closing down one of a company's 37 manufacturing plants? Which step would be least important? Which would be most difficult?

5. "If a plan is to be worth the time it takes to write it, there must be full commitment by all who contribute to it to make it work." Comment.

6. How should a manager determine when to develop a contingency program rather than write a more flexible plan that allows those who must implement it to make on-the-spot adjustments if circumstances require?

7. "Since all good programs must sooner or later be stated in budget terms, the controller's office should have primary responsibility for determining the form of the program and overseeing its development." What do you think of this suggestion from the controller of a large multinational company?

## CASES

For cases involving issues covered in this chapter, see especially the following. Particularly relevant questions are listed after each case.

Benjo Associates (p. 92), 6
Elizabeth Archer (p. 96), 5, 7
Joan Carrier, (p. 376), 2
Marathon Plastics (p. 456), 3
Joe DiMaggio (p. 533), 4

## FOR FURTHER READING

Cleland, D. I. and W. R. King, eds., *Systems Analysis and Project Management,* 2nd ed. New York: McGraw-Hill, 1975, chap. 4. Thorough treatment of project management and its role within the organization.

Davis, S. M. and P. R. Lawrence, *Matrix.* Reading, MA: Addison-Wesley, 1977. Useful discussion of the interface between adaptive programming techniques and forms of project organization.

Lorange, P., *Corporate Planning: An Executive Viewpoint.* Englewood Cliffs, NJ: Prentice-Hall, 1980, chaps. 4 and 5. Discusses development of a corporate planning system to implement strategy.

Sayles, L. R. and M. K. Chandler, *Managing Large Systems: Organizations for the Future.* New York: Harper & Row, 1971. Describes innovative management techniques developed and adapted by NASA to manage large projects.

Wiest, J. D. and F. K. Levy, *A Management Guide to PERT/CPM,* 2nd edition. Englewood Cliffs, NJ: Prentice-Hall, 1977. Concise management-oriented introduction to network analysis techniques.

**MANAGING NOT-FOR-PROFIT ENTERPRISES**

Managing not-for-profit ventures is very similar to managing profit-seeking enterprises. Most modern management concepts apply equally well to the not-for-profit group—even though the concepts evolved primarily in business firms.

Nevertheless, as we shall point out repeatedly, each enterprise has its distinctive characteristics, and basic management concepts must be fitted to the particular needs of that firm. In Part I we considered how a planning system can be designed for a specific firm, and the following parts extend this adaptive approach to decision-making, organizing, motivating, leading, and controlling. Not-for-profit enterprises need the same sort of tailor-made management.

The purpose of these notes on not-for-profit enterprises (there is such a note at the end of each part of the book) is to suggest very briefly certain features of not-for-profit ventures that may call for special tailoring.

**WIDE ARRAY OF "INDUSTRIES"**

Thousands of different kinds of nonprofit organizations perform a bewildering range of services. Major groups include those in the table which follows.

Clearly, no single management design will fit such diverse operations. As with business firms, we need an analytical approach that helps us identify key issues and suggests possible solutions. Our discussion in these notes will focus primarily on the first four groups listed above; and within these "industries," we will be concerned with self-contained, self-administered operating units—which we call "enterprises."

| Services Performed | Some Organizations Involved | Services Performed | Some Organizations Involved |
|---|---|---|---|
| HEALTH SERVICES | Hospitals Nursing Homes Clinics | OTHER PRIVATE | Religions Scientific Research Associations Clubs Unions |
| EDUCATION | Universities Schools Trade Institutes | | |

|                     |                  | OTHER<br>GOVERNMENT | Uniformed:<br>Military |
|---------------------|------------------|---------------------|------------------------|
| SOCIAL SERVICES     | Welfare          |                     | Police                 |
|                     | Child-Care       |                     | Fire                   |
|                     | Family Counseling|                     | Civilian:              |
|                     |                  |                     | Regulatory             |
| ARTS                | Orchestras       |                     | Fiscal                 |
| AND CULTURE         | Libraries        |                     | Justice                |
|                     | Museums          |                     |                        |
| COOPERATIVES        | Insurance        |                     |                        |
|                     | Savings Banks    |                     |                        |
|                     | Utilities        |                     |                        |
|                     | Marketing        |                     |                        |

**CHARACTERISTICS REQUIRING SPECIAL TREATMENT**

The planning, organizing, leading, and controlling, approach—outlined in this book—can be readily applied to not-for-profit enterprises. These basic management processes relate to all sorts of purposeful group endeavors. What will be helpful, *in addition,* is to single out those frequent characteristics of not-for-profit enterprises that call for special treatment. When these characteristics are strong, management design should be adjusted to reflect them.

Six characteristics to watch for are these.

1. *Service is intangible,* and hard to measure; this difficulty is often compounded by the existence of *multiple* service objectives.
2. *Customer influence may be weak;* often the enterprise has a local monopoly, and payments by customers may be a secondary source of funds.
3. Strong *employee* commitment to *professions* or a cause may undermine their allegiance to the enterprise.
4. *Intrusion of resource contributors* into internal management—notably fund contributors and government agencies.
5. *Restraints on the use of rewards and punishments,* as a result of 1, 3, and 4 above.
6. Importance of a *charismatic leader* and/or a "mystique" of the enterprise as means of resolving conflict in objectives and overcoming restraints.

These characteristics do not exist in all not-for-profit enterprises (and they may be present in some profit enterprises). But when they are strong, and especially when found in combinations, we know that typical profit management techniques will have to be modified. Examples of the impact of these characteristics on effective management practices will be given in the notes for each part.

The note for each part, then, presents modifications of concepts presented in that part—modifications that may be required to reflect one or more of the characteristics of not-for-profit enterprises.

## PLANNING WITHIN NOT-FOR-PROFIT ENTERPRISES

As not-for-profit enterprises grow, they face the same problems as profit-seeking companies in involving more people in the planning process and in extending the plans to cover more activities. And the same instruments we examined in Part I lie at the heart of their planning process—strategies for adapting to the environment, operating objectives, policies and procedures, programs and schedules.

Multiple goals—that are perhaps vague and hard to measure—may complicate internal planning in a not-for-profit enterprise. Such a mixture of goals tends to muddle the operating objectives of departments, sections, and subsections. Theoretically, the priority among various goals could be resolved by central management so that assignments to an orchestra leader or vocational counselor could be sharply pointed toward specific results. Instead, the multiple ends are too often passed along for subordinate personnel to wrestle with. Thus, *the uncertainty about just what is wanted permeates the entire planning process.*

When goal achievements are hard to measure—as is true in education, welfare, and any other not-for-profit services—operating objectives often shift from results to the activities that we hope will create the desired results. For example, because measuring what students actually learn is difficult, the operating objectives for a teacher are shifted to the number of classes conducted or of reports turned in. Actually, much planning in not-for-profit organizations moves even further back and *focuses on resources allocated for various purposes*—a dollar budget or the assigned personnel—simply assuming that the resources will be used for proper activities, which in turn will produce desired results. In order to improve both planning and final results in the not-for-profit enterprise, ways must be devised to apply the "management-by-objectives" concept to major operations in the enterprise.

The use of standing plans—policies, standard operating procedures, and the like—in not-for-profit enterprises raises the inevitable issues of dependability and simplification versus individual freedom and flexibility. Where professionals hold dominant roles, as in hospitals and schools, many standard methods and procedures are dictated by the professions rather than enterprise management. In fact, professional traditions may be so strong that the enterprise managers have difficulty changing conventional behavior patterns to fit new service missions. The availability of *professional methods and standards* does simplify local planning, but it also imposes rigidity in adjusting to new needs, such as education of hard-core unemployed and modern birth control.

Another potential difference in planning within not-for-profit enterprises arises from the way operating income is obtained. When voluntary contributions or government grants are a prime source of income, the donors may *intrude into the planning process.* For instance, the government may insist on an "affirmative-action program" for the employment of minorities and women. A different kind of impact results if contributions are made only one year ahead; *long-range planning* then faces the added uncertainty about a continuing flow of income—both as to size and the restraints attached to it. Such uncertainty discourages long-range strategic planning.

These characteristics of multiple, hard-to-measure goals, high professionalization, and dependence on financial contributions—to the extent that they exist—complicate planning in not-for-profit enterprises and the ambiguity that they create makes some form of systematic planning even more vital.

These suggestions regarding planning illustrate the approach we recommend for managing a not-for-profit enterprise.

1. Use basic management concepts, since in large measure they apply to both profit-seeking and not-for-profit ventures.
2. Do not assume that all not-for-profit enterprises are alike—they differ even more than profit-seeking companies.
3. Instead, when shaping a structure for a particular enterprise, be alert for the six characteristics above, and adjust for these in the tailoring that must occur in each specific management design.

This approach to managing not-for-profit enterprises will be amplified in notes following each of the next five parts of the book.

Benjo Associates is a small consulting firm founded four years ago by Benjamin Ortiz and Josephine MacMillan. They met in a New Ventures course both took while studying for their MBA's. As part of this course, they worked together with a third student on a project to create and market-test a new business idea.

"We had an idea," Jo MacMillan said, "for a consulting business that would specialize in offering advice to small, professional practitioners. Many doctors, lawyers, architects, optometrists, and other professionals have moved into extended partnerships that now constitute sizable businesses. They can buy data processing services and some halfway decent advice on office practices through existing consultants, but Ben and I saw several niches we felt we could fill. Apparently our instructor thought so, too, and he recommended us for one of the Hutchinson New Venture Initiation grants awarded by the school. When we got the money, Ben and I decided to give it a go. Larry Becker, the third member of our project team, took a job with an advertising agency but owns some stock and now is back with us, running the Dallas office."

The first year was a difficult one for "Benjo," but they grew gradually, and last year acquired a similar firm based in Los Angeles.

"We really took them over from their banks," Ben Ortiz explained. "It was a business very much like ours and had great clients. They had billings for over a million but still managed to lose money. They were overstaffed, had far too much office space, and provided incredible 'perks' to everyone, including a Rolls for the chairman. Their two banks finally called a halt and told them to either sell or they would call their notes. The founders decided to get into another business and we bought them out for a song. We have cut way back on their expenses, reduced their staff by fifty percent, and sent one of our people out to run the office. With half the personnel and much lower costs, we will still do a million and a half this year."

With offices in Chicago and Dallas as well as in Los Angeles, and headquarters in Westchester, Benjo's revenues may soon exceed five million.

"Our core business is still giving *business* advice to professionals," Jo said. "We take care of everything for our clients but we subcontract legal, MIS, and office service work. With laws and views on advertising changing, we have landed several very nice jobs on marketing and promotion recently."

"In addition," Ben noted, "we have picked up several major projects in the entertainment field. We also advise four professional athletes and two professional franchises (different sports from our athletes).

"Jo gets nervous when we move too far away from our original market targets, but I see the common denominator as our ability to give good business advice, particularly on advertising and marketing, to people or groups who have made, or can make, lots of money without having a real business sense. As smart as they may be, many doctors and lawyers are not only naive or uninformed, but absolutely awful business people. Athletes and major league franchise owners are mostly babes-in-the-woods and miss many opportunities to double or triple their incomes.

"I don't want to get into the agent business in a big way, but I do want to expand our base. Funeral homes are a great untouched market for us. Also, we could make a bundle helping small colleges and professional schools, marketing their services and running their shops in a more business-like way; now that the baby boom is almost over, they need help. I have a couple of good-sized travel agents interested in having us come in and help them, but we can't really go after any of these opportunities without more consultants, more space, and more office staff. This must be done carefully and slowly. The key to our success is that we can convince smart people they need us.

"Our strategy is finding individuals, or small groups of professionals, who make lots of revenue through their special talents, but whose talents don't include good business sense. We can help them market and manage their businesses more effectively. We offer nothing more than hundreds of consulting firms, but we know how to reach and work with a special group of professional clients. Above all, they must trust us and feel we are the experts. If we put mediocre consultants in the field or foul up billings, reports, or our own business practices, we have lost credibility and the same word-of-mouth that got us going could kill us. I agree with Jo that we must not chase more business until we have people ready. It's just that suddenly she wants to go *much* more slowly and selectively. When we started, she was the real risk-taker and kept me going when things got rough. I'm a very emotional person and Jo knew when and how to pep me up or calm me down while always moving us ahead. Now, I'm a little worried. At times, she almost seems complacent, like she can't believe it's really happened; like she wants to protect what we have and not look for more.

"I can't do that. With me it's 'go/no go.' I wanted to quit dozens of times and she kept me going. Now that we have the formula, she seems to have developed cold feet and is holding me back. She is the real brains of the business side of our venture; I'm mainly the market developer and talent scout. I try to go along but I wish she would relax and take a few more risks as we did in the beginning."

Jo agrees that she and Ben have had differences of opinion lately, but feels they can be resolved without serious problems for the business.

"Ben's a bachelor," she said; "when I'm angry with him, I tell him he's a bachelor from a long line of bachelors. While he is not a playboy, he loves the ladies and can spend money faster than anyone I know. He gets a good idea and he wants to act on it yesterday but often by tomorrow he has forgotten it or gone off on another tack. He has enormous energy and can work at an incredible pace for sixteen, seventeen hours a day for weeks at a time. Then he 'crashes' for a few days and comes back for more.

"In the beginning, I was very much like him. We took turns picking each other up and tried to time our cycles so they complemented each other and didn't leave us both flat at the same time. Now, I feel we have something that works and we don't have to burn ourselves out. We have a great formula and if we follow it patiently, we can each have a million in ten years. I'm married, my husband has a good job, and I want to take six months off sometime in the next few years to have a baby. But I want to come back and keep developing this business for the next thirty or so years.

"Ben says he hopes to have made enough to retire in ten years. He wants to see us drive faster and further in a much shorter time. He probably won't retire, but I do believe in ten years or less he will be off doing something else and on his own. Since we are incorporated and building a sound organization, the business should be a success without him (or me, for that matter) in a few more years. Right now, though, it needs us both and it needs us pulling in the same direction. Some of our key staff already seem concerned about our differences. They know we are great friends and respect each other but they are not sure where we are headed. If we want to attract and hold good people, we have to offer them clear, consistent signals."

Jo and Ben both agree that these differences are far fewer than the views they hold in common.

"We sometimes get madder than hell at each other and holler and scream," said Ben, "particularly me. Last week, I got so frustrated I smashed a water carafe off the wall of the conference room. Two of our young staff were in there with Jo and me and I thought they were going to dive for cover. There was a deafening silence until Jo's secretary burst through the door. Then Jo just broke up. She pointed at me, laughing like crazy, and said 'The last time you did that was when Irma (my girlfriend) ran off with one of our clients and you didn't want to lose the account.'

"Then *I* cracked up and in a moment everyone else relaxed. I hope they understand we act like that once in a while."

Jo believes that growth should be slower, and limited to clients from their original target segment—doctors, lawyers, and other professionals.

"Both Ben and I know how to reach this group. We know how to win their confidence and what services we can offer. Further, we know how to teach others how to hold that confidence and service those clients. We do virtually all of the early selling and assessment of client need. Others work up proposals but we have final say. Then we are very good at delegating the actual work while maintaining quality control.

"As long as we hold to this approach, we capitalize on our strengths and don't have our staff learn all our tricks and go out on their own to compete with us. Several tried and fell flat on their faces. Only in L.A. have we turned over this key work to someone else. Ben and I handled the N.Y. and Chicago markets, and Larry Becker looks after Dallas. As we get bigger, we will have to turn more over to our staff. One reason I want to go slowly is to have time to figure out how to build in controls so the staff don't mess up or leave with big chunks of business and set up competing firms.

"We have good cost control. We know how long it should take to carry out each step of a dozen or more project categories. We know how many people we need in the field and in support roles. We are learning how long it takes to hire and develop people. These are precious bits of knowledge. A service business is very hard to control because you don't find reliable industry data to guide you. You control by experience because that's the only way to set standards and separate legitimate excuses from wishful thinking.

"We can't do this with entertainers, athletes, sports franchises or, Lord help us, undertakers. We don't know these markets. We have little that is unique to offer them and, worst of all, we don't know how to measure performance in these markets. Perhaps, over time, we can develop the intuition if we go slowly. I don't want to ruin our image, dissipate our energies and have to rely on textbook control systems."

Ben indicates he is willing to go slowly but not as slowly as Jo would like. They have agreed to create a small task force within the firm to consider how they might (1) test their ability to implement their core strategy on new markets, and (2) develop more traditional methods (as opposed to current intuitive guides) of evaluating results, if they should choose to enter new markets or add new services to existing markets.

## FOR DISCUSSION AND REPORT-WRITING

1. What factors did Ben and Jo seem to consider in developing their initial strategy for the business? Evaluate their apparent strategic planning efforts against criteria suggested in Chapter 2.

2. What key managerial choices and operating goals made during the firm's first year might have been significantly affected by Benjo's initial strategy? How did it impact on decisions on scarce resources?

3. Write two or three key new policies that might result from a change in strategy toward Ben's wishes. If Ben's new strategy was accepted, what impact would it have on other standing plans? Illustrate.

4. To what degree may Jo's views on strategy result from differences in her views from Ben's on "developing a strategic sequence"? What other factors may explain her views on strategy?

5. Discuss the pros and cons of introducing MBO into Benjo.

6. To what extent would the need for adaptive programming techniques be affected by the decision to follow Jo's strategy? Ben's strategy?

7. (Summary Report Question, Part I) Apply all applicable techniques discussed in Part I to show how Ben and Jo might decide which strategy makes greater sense at this time.

8.   Draw two means-end chains, one which reflects Ben's views on strategy; the other, Jo's. Show how they may point to a good solution.

9.   What techniques discussed in Chapter 7 should be the most helpful to Ben and Jo in resolving their differences? Why? Which are least helpful? Why?

10.   Illustrate how the ideas on "Consolidating Projections of Results" in Chapter 9 might help Ben and Jo resolve their differences.

11.   What do you think of the way they have organized their company? What factors seem to have been given greatest weight in their decisions on departmentation and delegation?

12.   To what extent does the company appear to be ready to benefit from a matrix-type organization?

13.   What concepts discussed in Chapter 15 would be helpful in developing a better understanding of similarities and differences in Ben's and Jo's motivations?

14.   Is the conflict building between Ben and Jo likely to be constructive, destructive, or both? Explain. What techniques might be used to resolve it?

15.   If Ben's and Jo's differences are not resolved soon, what effect may this have on intraorganizational politics? Explain.

16.   How may the role of leadership change if Ben's views hold sway and the company grows and diversifies rapidly during the next three years?

17.   What communications problems do you see in the current situation? How do you recommend they be corrected?

18.   What do you think of their current division-of-labor actions designed to avoid losing clients to their employees?

19.   How does this approach affect control? What would have to be changed in order for Benjo to create true profit centers? Would you recommend these changes?

summary question
for solution of the
case as a whole

20.   Draw on material from Chapters 2, 26, and 27 and develop a report for Benjo on what changes in strategy *you* recommend and what implications your strategy has on other management processes.

CASE 1.2
ELIZABETH ARCHER

Elizabeth (Liz) Archer and Ned Shilling had been hired at the same time by the Consolidated Instruments Corporation.[1] While they had known each other casually as business majors in college, they became

---

[1]Two different cases drawn from Consolidated Instruments appear in W. H. Newman, C. E. Summer, and E. K. Warren, *The Process of Management*, 3rd ed. Englewood Cliffs, NJ: Prentice-Hall, 1972; they are Consolidated Instruments-A, pp. 571–78 and Consolidated Instruments-B, pp. 674–85.

good friends when participating in a six-week orientation program at CI's Salem headquarters.

"When Ned and I were in college, we had a couple of classes together," Liz said, "but it was such a big school I really didn't get to know him well. We were among four students hired last June by CI and teamed up on several assignments during our orientation course. Ned is a great guy and very sharp. He also loves to look for political and personal motives in business and will spend hours trying to analyze what 'so and so' meant by 'such and such.' It's almost a game with him. Maybe that's why I didn't pay too much attention to his warning last month. Now I'm afraid he may be right and I really don't know what to do. I sure don't feel like doing my Christmas shopping."

After their orientation, Liz and Ned were assigned to different parts of CI. Ned remained in Salem as an analyst in the corporate budget department while Liz was assigned to the Pollution Control Division in Pittsburgh. She works in the planning section of the controller's department and is responsible for checking and consolidating capital requests from the division's other departments for incorporation in the division plan.

CI began as a producer of precision control devices for the petroleum industry. During World War II its president, Homer Peake, successfully developed several important control devices used in aircraft and by 1970, through internal developments and acquisitions, Peake and his successor, David Myers, had broadened CI's market still further. With its most recent acquisition three years ago of the PCD (Pollution Control Devices) Company, CI found itself listed in *Fortune* magazine's list of the five hundred largest corporations in the United States. The company now designs and produces control devices and markets them not only to the oil and chemical industries, but also to the food processing, aircraft, space, and missile industries.

The PCD Division differs from other parts of the CI in that it is the only business that manufactures the end-products in which control devices are used. When acquired, there was considerable debate as to how PCD should be integrated into the existing organization, and it was finally decided to permit it to remain a separate division reporting directly to the president. Given its sales of only $28,000,000, PCD might more properly have been made a part of one of the three existing divisions (see Partial Organization Chart, Exhibit I).

There was a double reason for maintaining PCD's separate identity. First, although PCD sold products in all the markets served by the other divsions, none of the existing divisional general managers wanted to take on the responsibility for the PCD business. Each argued that PCD fit better in another's division. Underlying this disinterest were the low margins and high risks associated with work in pollution-control. Many companies in recent years had sought to establish themselves in the pollution abatement market but despite growing concern by industry and government alike, very few companies were able to earn a profit. When acquired, PCD had shown a

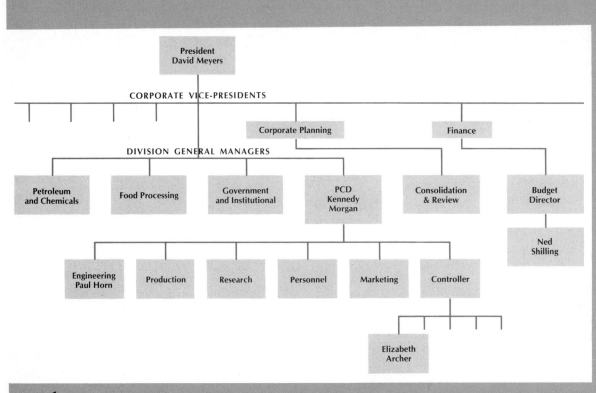

Exibit 1    Partial Organization Chart, Consolidated Instruments

$2,000,000 loss on $28,000,000 sales in its last fiscal year. After three years with CI, sales have risen to $31 million, but after reducing losses somewhat in the first two years, the division reported a $2.3 million loss in its third year.

President Myers' second reason for keeping the PCD company intact as a separate division reporting to him was to facilitate its sale if in five years the division failed to satisfy him that it could meet at least minimum profit standards as well as contribute to technology in other divisions. "I'm eager to do my part to deal with our ecological problems," he told his board, "and we will not expect any miracles from PCD, but within five years it will either be in the black or on the block."

He immediately assigned several capable executives from other divisions of CI to key posts in PCD but kept Joseph MacAllister, PCD's founder and president, as president of the new division. Myers stated:

"MacAllister knows the business. He is only fifty-one, and although he may be a little too much of the Tom Swift inventor-type, he is an adequate coordinator. By backing him up with a new engineering head, a new controller, and two of our good marketing service people, I think we have the makings of a good team. Because MacAllister took most of his equity in PCD in the form of CI stock and options, I'm sure he is as anxious as we are to see things work out.

"Finally, we have assigned one of our best people as his new director of personnel. He will see to it that we bring their salary and benefit programs into line with ours as smoothly as possible, and more important, he will get them working with our management-by-objectives and related programs."

MacAllister received very little direction from Myers during the three years he served as division president.

"I wanted him to feel that he was still in charge," Myers said. "We gave him some good people and replaced most of his debt with CI funds at rates lower than he was paying the banks. I asked him to develop a 'turn-around strategy' and a five-year plan for achieving it. By the end of the first year, he sent it up to us, but it wasn't very good. In essence, it was an extrapolation of his last four years with a log of promises to cut costs. We spent a day reviewing it but I don't think he paid much attention to my suggestions. I told him he needed a clearer strategy. Which customers did he really want? How wide a product range makes sense? I asked him to think through what he felt his niche was in his market.

"At the end of his second year with us, he had sales up to almost $30 million and his losses cut to $400,000. His second crack at a strategic plan was worse than the first. It was filled with sweeping platitudes but no real sense of where they were headed and how they planned to get there. I was very nervous about his seeming inability to think broadly, conceptually, but his sales were up, his losses down, and he promised to show a profit the next year after only three years with us.

"The third year was a disaster, however. While sales were up to $31 million, book losses were $2.3 million. It's worse than that though. This year we will have to write off a great deal of inventory, and incur huge field maintenance and rework costs on products they sold that have not met specifications. A review of their situation indicates that we could have an $8 to $10 million loss and as much as a forty percent drop in sales this year. I have had a talk with MacAllister and we agreed that he step down. He is on a two-year consulting contract and I sent Kennedy Morgan down to see if he can't straighten things out."

C. Kennedy Morgan, at 33, is one of CI's Successful "fast-trackers." He joined the firm six years ago and has had four promotions since. The most recent is as general manager of the PCD Division. Morgan is viewed as a potential superstar by many at CI. One senior executive stated, "Unless he really fouls up, I bet Ken will be heading up a major division within 5 years. If he isn't, I'm sure he will leave us for another company. He is just too good and too ambitious not to make it here or elsewhere."

Morgan took over in February and immediately began to tackle PCD's many problems. In November, he stated: "This is a great challenge. Ever since I got out of school, I have wanted to get into a situation in which I can take something with real potential and bring it from the brink of disaster to a position as a big winner.

"I have made a few personnel changes but no purge was necessary. We have some great people here who know what is necessary and I think they can do it. What they needed was clear, firm direction and a sense of 'can do.' I have always been a real gung-ho type and people say I bring it off without being overbearing. In the eight months I've been here, we have already gotten things turned around. We have all worked very hard, and losses will be high this year and for the first quarter next year. But, then we will start to move and I mean move forward!"

Morgan explained that what had to be done with existing commitments had been cleared up. While incurring heavy costs to make up for past mistakes, those who worked for him praised him for his tough decisive manner, and his ability to motivate. Paul Horn, director of engineering, said:

"I've been around a long time at CI and I've never worked for a better manager. I have only been with this division three years, but he has us all feeling we can really build something. A lot of us figured heads would roll when he arrived. Frankly, I know I made many mistakes and figured I'd be a candidate for early retirement. But he took time to figure out what had happened and told me he needed me. How about that! I figured it was time for Leisure Village and he convinced me I could help him!

"He has done a great job of getting us all to deal with the messy short-term problems that must be dealt with, but he has insisted we begin to think more strategically."

Liz Archer shared this optimism until she had a phone conversation with Ned Shilling.

"I only started here on August 1st," said Liz, "but I love it. Ken—everyone calls him Ken though I still slip and say 'Mr. Morgan'—Ken has really turned things around here. While there are a number of very difficult months ahead, even the old-timers believe they are part of a winning team. People apparently liked Mr. MacAllister and respected him, but felt he wasn't very organized. They lacked any sense of direction or priorities when he was here.

"Ken has worked out a plan for both correcting past mistakes and charting future directions. We don't have any strategic or long-range planning department here. Ken says that is one of his major jobs and he expects all departments to help him. I work in one of the controller's groups—planning it's called—but what we really do is check and put the numbers together. Six weeks ago, we put the finishing touches on the division plan and sent it to Salem a full week ahead of the November 8th due date."

Liz went on to explain that the plan showed the specific steps to be taken next year to correct past problems. It also spelled out an explicit strategy for the division in terms of products, customers and internal technology. As a first step toward implementing this strategy, Morgan has proposed a series of capital investments to reduce costs and redesign products and production facilities. The strategy involved short-term sales drops as part of shifting to fewer, high-volume products produced to higher standards at lower costs. It would involve substantial write-offs and retooling costs as well as six to eight million dollars new investment over the five-year period covered by the plan. Sales would continue to decline for eighteen months, losses would be cut but return on investment would drop until midway into the third year of the plan. By year five Morgan promised to have sales up to $52 million and show at least fourteen percent return on investment.

"While I don't have the background to evaluate the plan," Liz said, "all the department heads feel it is sound. I really felt like I had joined a winner. Then Ned called two weeks ago. After some small talk about Thanksgiving he asked me to swear that if he told me something very important I wouldn't repeat it. He said that if I leaked it, it could cost him his job. I made some joke about as long as it doesn't involve a felony I'd stay silent."

"I don't think Liz believed me when I called," Ned said, "but she called me this morning and made it clear she was wrong to doubt me. I told her last month that I had heard about plans to sell off PCD. The way I heard it, and from a very reliable source, the plan was to really clean it up without any fixed investment and publicize its turnaround and then sell it in two years. I told her I was taking a real risk by telling her, but she is a real nice person and ought to know. When she expressed doubt I told her to watch what happens when Morgan comes up here to review his plan. The way I heard it, Myers himself laughed when he saw Morgan's investment plans. They will try to get him to keep volume up, cut costs, and sound optimistic. He will get a few bucks for product development and sales but not a cent for any fixed investment.

"Liz wanted to know how the finance committee would convince Morgan to go along. I told her they will not level with him but, instead, convince him that he has to wait for new money and get the division looking good first. They will stall and sweet-talk him until he goes along. Next year it will be something else and then whammo!—they sell it right out from under him.

Liz felt, at first, that this was just another example of Ned's tendency to see things as a conspiracy.

"He is not a liar, though," she said. "Even then, I believed him when he said he had heard talk that we might be sold. I figured it may be just one of several options under consideration though, and that they would never send a guy like Ken here just to dress up the turkey. He is much too good and too ambitious for that. Now I don't know what to think. It's even possible, though I think it's very unlikely, that he is in on it."

Liz's reasons for concern stem from the results of the finance committee's review of the division plan. Morgan and his key people spent a day in Salem going over his strategies and operating plans. Upon his return, he met with all department heads and said, "It's back to the drawing board. They like what we propose. Myers was extremely pleased with what we have put together. He even took me aside after the meeting and told me how proud he was of what we are doing. But he explained that for reasons he couldn't disclose he would not be able to invest any sizable sum in this operation *this* year. He asked us to tighten our belts, clean up the remaining problem areas and publicize the hell out of what we plan to do. 'Buy me some time,' he said, 'and give me results and I'll have the capital for you next year or at very worst in eighteen months.' He pointed out that he couldn't allocate fixed capital, with money so tight, until we had really shown we can deliver."

Those attending the meeting, while disappointed, seemed to accept Morgan's explanation and began adjusting their plans. Several complained that what they were doing would make things look better in the short-run but cost much more later.

Paul Horn seemed the most concerned. "We will be doing some things now," he said, "with existing facilities and products that need not be done if we could get started with our new programs. Later, when they do approve the money, it will cost much more and take longer to carry out. Frankly, I don't like the feel of it."

When Ned called to check with Liz and her Christmas plans, he again emphasized that she should not tell anyone about "corporate's plans."

"While he said more people in headquarters now knew about plans for PCD," Liz said, "he emphasized that if I said anything it would be tied to him. He said that he had heard that Myers had really sold Ken a bill of goods. I find that hard to believe but I really don't know what to do.

"Ken has asked me to do most of the cost revisions on our key capital projects on the assumption of both a 12- and 18-month delay. He also wants me to estimate costs on several other projects designed to improve our bottom line this year. I just can't get into it when there is a chance it is all going to be a waste of time. Further, in several places we will be holding out hopes of promotion to people who, instead, may be out of work in two years. They believe us and have turned down other jobs, and invested in bigger homes here. This isn't fair.

"Paul Horn knows Myers from the old days. I'm tempted to tell him what I know and get his advice. He is a neat old guy. He is pushing sixty-three but he dresses and acts like he was thirty. I think I can trust him but for all I know he may be in on the whole thing already. After all, he was sent here by Myers five years ago. Damn! It's like one of those crummy old WW II spy flicks you see on the tube. I don't know what to do or even who to trust."

## FOR DISCUSSION AND REPORT-WRITING

1. What is your assessment of how David Myers dealt with Mac-Allister's strategic planning efforts? What else might Myers have done during the division's first three years as part of CI to insure better planning?

2. What information, assumptions, etc. should Morgan have got from Myers before beginning his planning at PCD?

3. If Myers has decided to try and make PCD look better for sale, should he inform Morgan? Discuss both sides of the question.

4. Assume Morgan knows of the decision. Should others in the division be informed? Why? When?

5. If Myers has decided to sell off PCD and does inform Morgan, which will Morgan (or his successor) need more—good standing plans, single-use plans, or both? Discuss.

6. What should Myers look for in Morgan's one- and five-year plans that would be most influential in deciding whether to continue trying to turn the division's performance around to sell it?

7. (Summary Report Question, Part I) Assume Myers is serious about keeping PCD for at least another two to three years, but cannot invest sizable sums this year, what should be done to develop the best turnaround strategy for the division? Consider both long-term and short-term planning needs.

8. What concepts in Chapter 8 might be most helpful to Elizabeth Archer in making a decision on what action *she* should take?

9. Illustrate how *both* (a) examining the problem in light of higher-level goals, and (b) finding the root cause are vital to Morgan in developing a turnaround plan for PCD.

**part II:**
**planning: elements**
**of rational**
**decision-making**

10. What do you think of the decision to have PCD report, as a separate division, directly to Myers rather than incorporate it in one of the three existing groups? Discuss both pros and cons.

11. Would Morgan be a good choice to head up PCD if Myers had secretely decided to sell it? What factors would you consider, as Myers, in answering this question?

**part III:**
**organizing:**
**strategy to**
**structure**

12. How might we explain Morgan's apparent success in motivating people who have been with PCD for many years? Consider issues raised in Chapter 15.

13. If Myers has decided to sell PCD without informing Morgan, what impact will this have (plus and minus) on Myers' ability to influence the behavior of other key subordinates in the future?

**part IV:**
**motivating:**
**human factors in**
**the organization**

14. How important is leadership to Morgan as compared to developing sound plans and getting enough resources from CI to implement them?

15. In a turnaround situation, such as this, should Morgan be seeking primarily compliance or commitment from his immediate subordinates? What factors should he consider in making his choice?

16. Analyze Elizabeth Archer's dilemma based on key factors from Chapter 21.

**part V: leading**

17.   If Myers doesn't approve key parts of Morgan's turnaround strategy, what must he do to evaluate how well Morgan does during the next year?

18.   If PCD is, in fact, being asked to turn itself around, how would the approach to budgetary controls differ from what would be needed if the division was being readied for sale?

19.   In what ways might better control systems have saved MacAllister's job? Explain.

summary
questions for
solution of the
case as a whole

20.   What specific action would you take if you were in Elizabeth Archer's position?

21.   Assuming you were Kennedy Morgan and learned that the division was probably going to be sold in two or three years, what action would you take?

# PLANNING: ELEMENTS OF RATIONAL DECISION-MAKING

## II

The process of planning covers a wide range of activities, all the way from initially sensing that something needs to be done to deciding firmly who does what, when, and how. Planning is much broader than compiling and analyzing information, or dreaming up new ideas. It also involves more than logic, imagination, or judgment. It is a combination of all these factors that culminates in a decision—a decision about what should be done.

A manager does a lot of mental work before he arrives at a decision requiring company action. This preparation includes selecting pertinent facts, identifying good alternatives, making forecasts, and the like. Each of these steps involves judgment; in a sense, the manager makes a whole array of preliminary decisions. However, when we speak of "decision-making" we refer to the entire process which culminates in commitment to action.

In Part II, our aim is to examine the elements, or phases of the decision-making process. Initially, we shall analyze decision-making as though a single person undertook the whole process alone; at least we set aside for the moment the complications that arise when the process is divided up among many different people. Many plans are, in fact, made largely by a single individual. And if we can discover ways to improve our own decision-making skills, we will be able to make such decisions better, whether alone or with others.

In the concluding chapter of Part II, we alter our focus and consider how decision-making is actually carried out in an organization. We complicate—and add realism to—the rational decision-making process, by noting how the planning system elements described in Part I—objectives, policies, procedures, programs—affect decision-making.

We examine decision-making in the following four chapters.

Chapter 6—Problem Analysis: Diagnosis and Creativity. The first, perhaps the most difficult, and often an overlooked phase in decision-making is a thorough diagnosis of the problem or opportunity to be dealt with. We are also concerned with finding good alternative solutions to the problems identified by diagnosis. Because no company can be a leader by copying what someone else is already doing, we consider how new ideas are born and how to make maximum use of individual creative abilities.

Chapter 7—Choosing a Course of Action. To choose among alternative courses of action, we must predict for each alternative what would happen if we followed that course. We must then compare the different results. Because a projection and comparison of alternatives can become complex, this chapter includes suggestions for simplification.

Chapter 8—Quantitative Aids to Decision-Making. Because risk and uncertainty are inherent in choosing a course of action, we discuss how to adjust alternatives in these situations. We focus on quantitative techniques which can help managers to compare alternatives and make a choice.

Chapter 9—Organizational Decision-Making. Thus far our analysis has assumed that decision-making has been carried on in a single person's mind. In this chapter we shall explore the benefits and difficulties that arise when the elements of decision-making are dispersed throughout an organization.

# problem analysis: diagnosis and creativity

# 6

**Learning Objectives**

After completing this chapter you should be able to

1. Identify the four phases of rational decision-making.
2. Describe the three basic elements involved in sound problem diagnosis.
3. Explain how decision-makers find the root cause of a problem.
4. Understand the concept of means-end analysis.
5. Describe the most common sources of alternatives for solving problems.
6. Identify the most common barriers to creative thought and explain how they might be overcome.

**RATIONAL DECISION-MAKING** Strategy, operating targets, policies, programs, combine to map out action to be taken. They chart a course. In selecting such a course, managers must make many critical decisions. What domain to seek, when to employ women, how fast to move—and a host of similar questions must be decided.

So we turn now to a closer analysis of how to make such decisions wisely. Strategy and its supporting plans will guide the choices. But within these limits alternatives must be found, and benefits compared, for specific situations. Moreover, the choice of strategy itself calls for all the skill in decision-making that an organization can muster.

A manager is more than a decision-maker. He also organizes, controls, and leads. But none of his other activities are more important than making wise decisions. We will be concerned here with managerial planning-decisions—that is, decisions about *actions to be taken* in his department or company. These are crucial.

**use of rational process**

In Western society, with its heavy emphasis on science and utilitarianism, we take for granted that the best decisions are made by *rational* choice. There are alternative ways of selecting a plan—intuition, precedent, voting, divine guidance—but in a purposeful organization such as a business firm, it is the rational decision that is widely believed to be the best.[1]

In spite of this high regard for rationality, in our actual behavior there is a striking failure to follow the basic steps of rational decision-making. Our personal plans typically are not fully rational, and managers often rely on other methods in making their plans. Unfortunately, rational decision-making is hard work; and both skill and wisdom are required in its use. So as a practical matter we use the rational process only for our more important decisions. Even this limited use takes considerable disciplined effort.

Fundamentally, rational decision-making is quite simple. The four essential phases are: (1) diagnosing the problem, (2) searching for the most promising alternative solutions, (3) analyzing and comparing these alternatives, and (4) selecting the best alternative as a plan of action. Before we describe these phases in detail, let us note their general applicability.

*Problem-solving in medicine* A doctor follows all four parts of this procedure in examining a patient to find out what is wrong and in prescribing a course of action. In practice the diagnosis may not be easy, because the same symptoms can result from a number of quite different causes. Special tests may be necessary to identify the underlying cause. Clearly, if the wrong cause is assumed—say, appendicitis instead of gallstones—treatment will be ineffective, even disastrous. Many of the recent advances in medicine deal with better diagnosis.

Having made a sound diagnosis, the doctor then considers possible remedies—such as changes in diet, medication, or surgery. Some remedies will be standard practice, but if the patient has limitations—a weak heart

---

[1]E. F. Harrison, *The Managerial Decision-Making Process* (Boston: Houghton Mifflin, 1975), chap. 2.

or allergies, for instance—other possible treatments must be considered. Next the doctor must weigh the advantages and disadvantages of each possible cure in a specific case. How long will the patient be incapacitated? Are the necessary resources—professional aid, equipment, money—available? Finally, the doctor uses his judgment in selecting what he believes is the best plan, or "prescription." He considers the probability of success and the risk of complications. He may decide to try a simple remedy before taking more drastic measures. Perhaps he considers it wise to do nothing at present, or he may call for an ambulance to rush his patient to the hospital. Every responsible doctor goes through these steps: diagnosis, review of possible remedies, analysis of probable results, and prescription.

The decision-making process often becomes less clear when we tackle organizational problems. Getting agreement on the diagnosis, defining alternatives, obtaining reliable information from specialists on the existing situation, forecasting what will happen, especially in an uncertain environment, and winning enough support to justify positive action are by no means simple. But these difficulties make a firm grasp of the rational process even more valuable. Experience indicates that only a small percentage of people have the insight and self-discipline necessary to apply rational decision-making to muddied "people" problems.

Each of the four phases of rational decision-making will be examined in Part II. We will be concerned in each chapter with (1) helping incumbent and potential managers improve their personal skills, and (2) providing a basis for assessing the way subordinates are making plans. However, the

understanding all
phases

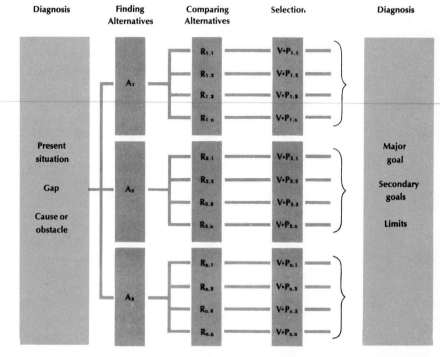

Figure *6.1* *Elements in decision-making. Key to symbols: A alternatives; R results of following an alternative; V value attached to projected result—the values arising from the goals; P probability of the result occurring. Any diagnosis should clarify the items shown in colored boxes.*

four phases build upon one another, as indicated in Figure 6.1; so to solve actual managerial problems, we should bring all four phases to bear. Unusual proficiency in one phase cannot be substituted for neglect in another.

The sequence of our discussion helps in presenting ideas, but it is not intended to be a rigid procedure. Few problems yield to a neat step-by-step procedure: new alternatives may pop up at any time; a problem often needs to be redefined as the analysis proceeds and values are formulated; fact-gathering and judgment permeate the entire process. Therefore, we are considering a mental *framework* rather than a procedure. In a general way, we do work through the phases in the sequence listed, but our minds are apt to jump from one phase to another in a continuing effort to refine our thinking. We bring clear reasoning and focused attention out of such mental rambling only when we have a framework—such as the four phases just outlined—that aids us in relating facts and thoughts in a rational pattern.

## THE CRUCIAL ROLE OF DIAGNOSIS

Accurate diagnosis is the essential first phase of sound decision-making. Unless the diagnosis is correct, subsequent planning will be misdirected and wasteful.[2]

The love of quick action—and perhaps an illusion of omniscience—makes some managers impatient with careful diagnosis and detailed planning. Even if they admit a need for planning, they are confident that they know what their problems are. They are so anxious to get moving that they neglect to take time to check the direction in which they are heading. One impetuous president, for example, pushed through extensive plans for sales promotion, brushing aside any strategy question about who were the right customers. Later, careful diagnosis showed that he was working with a declining segment of the market; even if the sales promotion had been an outstanding success, the recovery of company sales would have been only temporary. The president might just as well have made this correct diagnosis earlier and avoided the wasted sales effort.

Sound diagnosis should cover three basic elements, which are highlighted in the following questions:

1. Just what *gaps* exist between the results we desire and the existing or predicted state of affairs?
2. What are the direct, *root cause* and the intermediate causes of the gaps?
3. Does examination of the problem in the context of higher-level goals place limits within which we must find a satisfactory solution?

We shall first examine the way these three elements can be used in diagnosing a *recognized need;* then we shall consider diagnosing total situations in which attention is not yet focused on a single recognized need.

[2]W. F. Pounds, "The Process of Problem Finding." *Industrial Management Review* (Fall 1969), pp. 1–19.

STATING THE PROBLEM OR
OPPORTUNITY IN TERMS OF
A GAP

111
CHAPTER 6
problem analysis;
diagnosis and creativity

Managerial problems arise in at least two ways. First, actual or predicted results may fall short of the targets included in the strategy or in the more specific operating goals and programs. The planning-control system raises a red flag.

A second kind of triggering is more subtle. A manager may simply *feel* that "things could be better." Perhaps he compares other companies' accomplishments with those of his own firm, or simply desires continuing growth and ever-lower costs. Whatever the source, diagnosis starts with sensing an opportunity for improvement. To go further, however, he must sharpen this intuitive feeling as best as he can into more explicit statements of desired and actual (or predicted) results, so that the felt difficulty or opportunity can be viewed more *precisely* in terms of a gap that must be closed.

When there is a clearcut distinction between say, quality standards and actual or anticipated quality, he can promptly move on to the next element of diagnosis. But many gaps are not so clearly defined. A manager may have only a vague feeling, which he might express as, "Our New England branch should do a lot better," or "I believe Simpson has good potential but is not living up to it." He needs to sharpen these statements before he can proceed with his diagnosis. He might restate his general dissatisfaction with the New England branch thus: "Based on performance of our other branches, and adjusting for differences between branches, New England should get twenty percent more sales without any increase in expenses." This declaration makes the problem a lot clearer. With respect to Simpson it would be more meaningful to say, "Based on aptitude and motivation, Simpson appears to have the capacity to be a regional sales manager in three to five years" (*desired*). "His failure to keep turnover of salesmen to desired levels and his inability to develop new business has produced less than expected results" (*actual*).

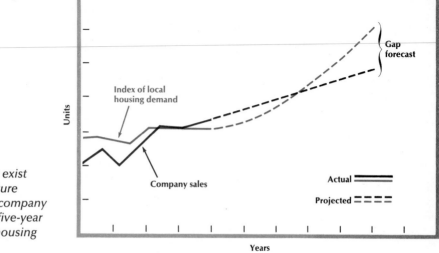

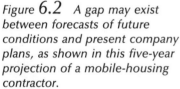

*Figure* 6.2 *A gap may exist between forecasts of future conditions and present company plans, as shown in this five-year projection of a mobile-housing contractor.*

Likewise, a particular event that provokes our attention may not be the problem. Our company's financial statement, for instance, may show a loss for last month. In common speech we might express the problem this way: "What are we going to do about the loss?" By itself, however, this is an incomplete statement of the problem. For management to proceed, this general statement must be refined by indicating what returns are expected and the premises on which the "desired" financial picture is based.

Once a problem or opportunity is identified in terms of a gap between desired and actual or predicted results, many decision-makers move immediately to seek alternative means of closing this gap. We should avoid this temptation, though, because seeking alternatives at this stage is premature for two reasons.

1. Although the gap between desired and actual or predicted results has been brought into focus, for many situations the root cause of the gap is still vague and perhaps incorrectly identified. Until that cause has been defined, alternatives designed to close it are likely to fail or to provide only costly relief of symptoms.

2. Unless the gap is defined in terms of very high-level goals, the objective that we have specified is likely to be merely a *means* of accomplishing one or more higher-level *ends* or goals. Before alternatives to closing the gap are sought, then, these higher-level goals should be identified and tied to strategy. This exploration of the broader situation often uncovers organizational limits on such matters as time, investment, or personnel—limits that must be observed if the solution is to be consistent with the higher-level goals of the organization. Also if the stated gap proves tough to overcome, we may want to consider alternative ways of reaching the higher goal.

**FINDING THE ROOT CAUSE**      As the decision-maker seeks alternatives for closing the gap, he usually does so with some

**search for key obstacle**      notion of its cause. All too often, however, this intuitive and at times subconscious assumption about causality may be only symptomatic of the underlying cause or perhaps not even related to the real cause.

For example, in the early days of frozen foods, manufacturers had a difficult time reaching what they believed to be desirable sales levels. Initially, attempts to close this gap between desired and actual sales were made through consumer advertising. Lack of customer interest in the product seemed a logical cause of low sales. Further, the manufacturers assumed that the source of the indifference was a lack of understanding about the properties and advantages of frozen food. Only after experiencing limited success with advertising designed to educate the consumer did they undertake a more careful quest for the cause.

Studies revealed that, although consumer interest in frozen foods was indeed limited, the major cause of low sales was the reluctance of retailers to stock an adequate supply. The retailers, understandably enough, wished to avoid investing several hundred dollars in refrigerated showcases. Had the manufacturers continued to bombard the consumer, they might have used customer demand to force the retailers to make the investment. This course, however, would have been an expensive way of overcoming the now-obvious obstacle of retailers' reluctance to invest in showcases. But having located the basic impediment, the manufacturers could now devise methods for lending or leasing showcases to hesitant dealers.

At times, then, in searching for a cause or an obstacle, we may have to push deeper and deeper until the *root cause* has been identified. Kepner-Tregoe Associates, management consultants who have focused on diagnosis, suggest two key guides for the identification of causes.[3]

First, in trying to determine why a goal is frustrated, a decision-maker should concentrate on the differences between situations where the desired goal *is* realized and those where *it is not.* Consider, as a simple illustration, the problem faced by a sales manager who is trying to unearth the cause of late field reports from his sales representatives. If some of the representatives get them in on time while others do not, the explanation may be related to the differences in the individuals or their work environment. By exploring these differences, by spelling them out in terms of *what, where,* and *when,* the manager could formulate a number of hypothetical causes. If he found that most of the late reports occurred repeatedly in certain district offices, an elaboration on the differences between district offices might lead to the cause. However, if he discovered that all districts had this problem, then he would have to look for differences in some other factor.

The second Kepner-Tregoe principle stresses the power of *negative thinking* in cause identification. Once a decision-maker has developed hypothetical causes, he should avoid seeking further evidence to support them, endeavoring instead to disprove them or "shoot them down." He should test them against all of the situations in which the problem exists and in which it does not. The logic behind this negative approach is this: although a hundred reasons supporting a hypothetical cause as the real culprit may be found, this positive support can never *prove* guilt; however, if only *one* fact demonstrates that a suspected cause *could not* be the real one, the suspect can be eliminated.

Thus if hypothetical causes are tested against all the distinctions of what, when, and where, most proposals can be eliminated. By this process of elimination, the few candidates that remain, and thus *could* account for the differences, can be subjected to more detailed examination and testing.

**moving from surface to root causes**

Often in seeking the root cause of a problem, we have to move through several levels of causality. Even if the root cause can be found directly, it is well to identify intermediate levels of causality also. Later when looking for a solution, if the root cause cannot be eliminated, we may turn to symptomatic relief by dealing with the more intermediate cause. For example, consider a situation described by a colleague of ours. A friend of his, who was in his late 60s, complained that late in the day he suffered blurred vision and then headaches and dizzy spells. An optometrist told him that his headaches and

[3]C. H. Kepner and B. B. Tregoe, *The Rational Manager* (New York: McGraw-Hill, 1965), chaps. 5–9. Although dealing with business problems, the authors make explicit use of canons of logic expounded by John Stuart Mill over a century ago.

dizzy spells stemmed from moderate deterioration of the eyes, which in turn was the result of old age. Stopping the diagnosis here, the optometrist prescribed bifocal eyeglasses to compensate for the change in vision.

As a result of his difficulty in getting used to wearing his new bifocals, the man tripped on a step and bruised his hip. To be certain that it was just a bruise, he visited a doctor and in the course of his examination mentioned his blurred vision and headaches. The doctor then checked his blood pressure, which proved to be too high, and cited this as the primary cause of the vision and headache problems. To put the doctor's diagnosis in our terms, he had compared the patient's actual condition with a desired state of health and saw the announced symptoms as the cause of the difference. He, like the optometrist, did not stop there but asked, "What's causing the blurred vision and headaches?" The optometrist had assumed the basic cause was old age, but the doctor had gone one step further and had pinpointed high blood pressure as the immediate cause. He then asked, "If high blood pressure is causing the eye trouble, what's causing the high blood pressure?"

Here he made the same mistake as the optometrist and assumed that old age was the direct cause of the high blood pressure. As a result, he prescribed medication and change of diet to provide symptomatic relief for high blood pressure. He, too, treated the symptom because he could not deal with what he felt was the root cause—old age.

Several months later, a routine visit to the dentist revealed that the doctor, like the optometrist, had failed because he had not pushed hard enough in his attempt to correctly identify all the intermediate causes of the problem. The dentist found that the doctor had missed an important link, a molar in which the nerve had died and decay had begun. The impurities introduced into the bloodstream by the decaying tooth were, in fact, the direct cause of the high blood pressure, which in turn was the cause of the eye trouble and headaches and dizziness.

This account illustrates the inadvisability of stopping a diagnosis at a first-level cause. Ask instead, "What's causing the cause?" and then, "What's causing the cause of the cause?" and so on until you have moved to the underlying fundamental cause. In our patient's situation—and the pun is built in—the root cause seems to have been the bad tooth.

The purist may argue that if we follow our own logic, we should not settle for the bad tooth as the root cause, but should ask instead, "What caused the bad tooth?" Then, with the optometrist and the medical doctor, we may point to old age. Even so, what we have accomplished by moving in a step-by-step progression to the most basic cause is to identify all the intermediary causes. This sequence is vital, for if the real root cause, old age, cannot be removed, we should focus on the next cause in the chain—the bad tooth—for it is at this level that symptomatic relief will hit closest to the root cause and hopefully be most effective.

Strictly speaking, unless we deal with the aging process directly, any treatment will be symptomatic. The closer we can come to the root cause, however, the more satisfactory the symptomatic treatment is likely to be.

Unless a problem is defined by very sweeping terms, the recognized need is a *means* of accomplishing a more basic, higher-level *end* or goal. Earlier, in our discussion of "root causes," we described a problem of late sales reports. This problem can be stated as follows:

Desired: Field-sales reports for each month should be filed with district sales offices by the fifth working day of the next month.
Actual: Salespeople repeatedly submit these reports from one to six days late.

Although it is necessary to find the cause of the late reports, in many cases it would be wise to ask also, "Why do I want these reports by the fifth working day of the next month?" (see Figure 6.3).

By asking "Why do I want . . . ," we can put this problem in perspective. Subsequently, when we weigh alternatives, we can do so in light of the higher-order goals. Because getting these reports is only a *means* to an end, we are not interested in ways of reaching the means that conflict with the higher-level end. Any limits or constraints imposed by higher-level goals, then, should be stated specifically.

Suppose the answer to the question is "to provide the manufacturing department with accurate figures on which to base next month's production." Then we can be careful to seek alternative means of getting the reports in on time that are consistent with the need for accuracy. Moreover, for this purpose we are more concerned with product model numbers and

*Figure 6.3  Elementary means-end analysis. Diagnosis of a specific problem.*

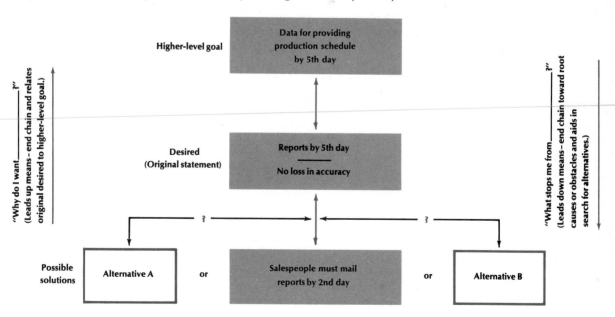

delivery dates than with prices and how sales may tie into future business.

A milk company, to cite a similar example, gave the following instruction to a study team: "Do not submit any proposals unless estimated savings are over half a cent a quart." By knowing that the study aimed at finding a major gain, the team could fully understand this limit on acceptable alternatives. Product engineers often have to design not just a better product but one that is, say, faster than competitors' products or capable of being produced within a cost limit. The existence of such limits is often brought to light by extending the diagnosis of higher-level goals far enough to identify the full dimensions of a satisfactory solution.

## DIAGNOSIS OF THE WHOLE SITUATION

In the preceding discussion, we focused on diagnosis of a recognized need—either a specific difficulty or a known opportunity for improvement. We urged moving directly toward clarifying the gap between the actual and the desired, finding causes, and identifying limits. For most problems, such a diagnosis is all that is necessary.

At other times, though, a broader view may be essential. There are three main reasons why we may need to undertake a diagnosis of the situation. (1) We may wish to redefine a recognized need because we cannot find an acceptable solution to the problem as originally stated. (2) Several problems may be so interdependent that we have to identify all of them and their interrelations before we can put them into a sequence for study and action. (3) We may feel that potential improvements have not been fully grasped by focusing on things piecemeal.

**broadening the definition of the problem**

*Moving up the means-end chain* The late-report problem discussed in the previous section provides a simple illustration of how diagnosis of the whole situation in terms of a means-end chain can be of great help in paving the way for a subsequent search for alternatives. If we are stymied in an attempt to speed up reports, we can seek *alternative* ways of meeting the ends toward which field reports are only one means. Stated another way, if we want these reports primarily to provide accurate information to the manufacturer by the fifth day of the month, and if we have trouble getting them on time, perhaps we should examine alternative ways of scheduling production.

Diagrammatically, this step up a means-end chain, wherein we move from lower- to higher-level goals, is shown in Figure 6.4. It illustrates how we have broadened our inquiry from a diagnosis of a *specific problem*—late reports—to a diagnosis of the *situation* in which the problem exists.

Whether it proves desirable to solve our original problem or to seek ways of getting around it, can be determined after examination of the likely costs and benefits associated with various alternatives. By examining the higher-order goals before seeking alternatives to the problem, however, we open up a set of options that might otherwise have been overlooked. We can either continue to solve the "recognized need" within the context of this higher-level goal, or, if this proves difficult, we can bypass the original

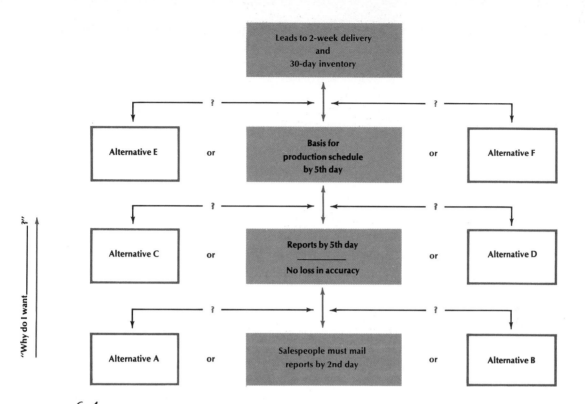

*Figure* 6.4  *Broadened means-end analysis. Analysis moves from diagnosis of a specific problem to diagnosis of the situation in which the problem exists.*

problem and seek alternatives that satisfy the higher-level goals by means other than field reports.

By looking at a means-end diagram, we can see how a more complicated situation might be broken down. This approach permits us to concentrate our analytical talents on each of a number of subparts of a complex problem. We can focus on each part but at the same time be able to see how it fits into the whole scheme. In many problems like the one illustrated here, what originally appears simply as a matter of late sales reports may in fact lead to a recognition of problems and relationships in many other areas of the business. By moving from a diagnosis of the specific problem to a diagnosis of the broader situation in which the problem exists, we pave the way for recognizing and dealing with these interrelationships. Note that a means-end analysis is not sufficient for making a wise choice. All we know is that each means is adequate to meet the higher-level goal; other alternatives may be even more attractive. Moreover, a means-end chain shows only one consequence of a given means; other consequences may sharply affect the desirability of using the means depicted. Therefore, a final decision should be based on all four steps covered in Part II. The chief value of means-end analysis lies in diagnosis.

*Determining how far to go in diagnosing the situation*    An inevitable question is how far we should go in considering ever-higher goals. Two broad guidelines help to answer this question: (1) the extent of the decision-maker's authority, and (2) the time available for analysis.

Take the first point. A district sales manager, asked to tackle the problem of late reports, may lack the perspective or the organizational authority to look farther than the reason for submitting the field reports—accurate information for scheduling. However, if the vice-president of manufacturing were brought into the decision, he might ask, "Why do I want an accurate basis for making production schedules by the fifth day of the month?"

The answer to this question would reveal the next-higher goal in the chain, which might be "to provide for delivery within two weeks of order placement, while maintaining a thirty-day inventory." Perhaps the vice-president of manufacturing will have the authority to search for means of achieving this goal without having an accurate basis for making production schedules by the fifth day of the month.

As a rule, the decision-maker should seek to move as far up the hierarchy of goals as his position and influence in the company permit. If the nature of the problem warrants going farther, he should seek to involve higher-level decision-makers who have the necessary perspective and influence.

When time is pressing, we should go up the means-end chain only as far as is necessary to get a soluble problem. In other words, we don't challenge the entire goal structure of our company each time we encounter a tough problem. Instead we push the analysis to a point at which we feel confident that one or more acceptable alternatives exist. Then we focus on this redefinition of the problem so that a decision can be made promptly and action can be started. Obviously judgment is involved in selecting the point at which prompt action (and low investigation expense) is more valuable than more exploration.

**dealing with interrelated problems**

Problems do not remain isolated—especially in enterprises where internal and external integration (discussed in Chapter 1) is a major element of survival. In these situations, as we diagnose one facet of the business, we soon realize that any proposed action will have impact on several operations not embraced in our initial analysis. Our diagnosis should grasp all these related facets, even though in the end we may decide to deal with them one at a time. Because they are intertwined, the *sequence* of analysis and action is crucial.[4]

Difficulties faced by the Allegheny Electric Company are clearly of this sort. To serve its growing customer demand, the company must substantially expand its generating capacity. In fact, the company already is vulnerable to customer complaints of brownouts and occasional shutdowns. Any solution to this problem must concern plant size (millions of dollars will be

[4]J. L. McKenney, and P. G. W. Keen, "How Managers' Minds Work." *Harvard Business Review* (May 1974), pp. 79–90.

required), timing (five-to-eight-year construction cycle), and type of fuel (nuclear, oil, or coal). But along come antipollution campaigns and interest in ecology; the public's strong fear of radiation leaks has all but eliminated the possibility of erecting a nuclear power plant, and ecological protests have forced the company to give up attempts to secure a favorable location for a coal-operated plant. In the face of all this, the company seeks a rate increase to improve its earnings, claiming that it will not be able to borrow money for the construction of new plants unless its earnings are increased. However, the public concern about pollution and brownouts may pressure the state utility commission to refuse permission for a rate increase.

Obviously, the company has half a dozen major problems, each of which should be carefully diagnosed in terms of gaps, causes and obstacles, and constraints. *In addition,* the total configuration must be analyzed in an attempt to set some kind of sequence for dealing with the related issues.

There is no single answer on how to proceed with such complex diagnoses. If one problem is clearly the most important, it can be studied first; and its tentative solution would set the limits within which related problems are studied. If preliminary analysis shows that acceptable solutions exist for one or more problems, and that the range of solutions will not markedly affect other problems, then these other problems can be temporarily deferred. Another approach is to work on all major needs simultaneously. If this is done, tentative solutions for each need should be quickly provided to the people who are working on related matters so that the anticipated solutions can be used as planning premises in work on other needs and problems. This process is repeated through a series of successive refinements (assuming all the projects progress at about the same rate).

Clearly some sequencing arrangement must be developed. If each problem is diagnosed and studied separately, the opportunities for incompatability, wasted effort, and delay are overwhelming.

## THE QUEST FOR ALTERNATIVES

A thorough diagnosis defines both a specific problem and the situation in which the problem exists. With this definition in mind a decision-maker seeks possible solutions. Rarely does he hit upon only one perfect way to solve his problem. Usually several different approaches might work, but none is completely satisfactory; so he looks for more alternatives, hoping to find a better answer.

Like diagnosis, search for alternatives tends to be shortchanged by busy executives. Finding good alternatives, especially novel ones, calls for a lot of unstructured thinking. Many managers feel uncomfortable with such ambiguous situations, preferring clearcut action along a well-defined path. So they tend to grasp the first alternative that promises a "satisfactory" (though not necessarily the best) result. Theoretical work has been done on how much time and other resources to devote to searching (researching). The rational answer is a function of the probability of finding a better alternative than we already have, the incremental value of such an alternative, and the cost of continuing search in terms of resource inputs and of opportunities foregone during the process. As we note later, since the incremental value depends partly on levels of aspiration, there are sound psychological reasons for continuing the search until an acceptable—or satisfactory—alternative is found (but not much beyond this point).

In practice, the two most common sources of alternatives are the past experience of an executive himself and the practices followed by other executives or other companies.

**building on
relevant
experience**

Faced with a problem, we naturally review our *past experience* for a similar situation that turned out well. With allowances for obvious differences between the former challenge and the present one, the successful action of the past becomes at least an alternative plan for the future.

Much business planning, as well as individual behavior, is built solely on such past experience. This is the simplest approach to a problem, and it is quite adequate in a majority of instances. As long as all goes well, we are likely to repeat past practice. Before long, it becomes habit or tradition. But the catch is that yesterday's solutions may not be adequate for today's problems, as electric-utility executives have discovered when trying to locate new plants.

**selective imitation**

"How does General Motors handle this problem of dealers' inventory?"

"Pete told me he was having the same kind of trouble in collecting from foreign customers. I wonder what he is doing."

Questions such as these are asked every day by executives who scrutinize the practice of other firms or other departments for solutions to their own problems. In fact, a distinctive characteristic of American business, often noted by foreign observers, is the frequency and frankness with which businessmen exchange experiences. Professional papers and trade journals are full of accounts of how the XYZ Company cut its air pollution, boosted sales, or improved quality. Ideas are exchanged at trade association meetings and through intercompany visits. Both the American Management Associations and The Conference Board regularly report business practices of successful firms. In fact, much of what we call "business research" consists of finding out what the person across the street is doing.

Such examinations produce several alternatives that might not occur to executives within the company, and this practice accelerates improvement in business operations throughout the economy. But as with past experience, we should ensure that operations in one company are enough like those in a second to make transferring a practice worthwhile. We should also avoid the danger of too quickly falling in step with another company simply because it is a leader in the industry. Relying on past experience and imitating others produce alternatives that at best merely keep us up with the parade. Nevertheless, we should always consider *selective imitation* as a possible source of alternatives.

Although pressures of time and expense may force a company to plod along conservatively as a follower in part of its activities, it should strive to excel in some respects. In our dynamic and competitive society, at least an occasional spark of creativity is needed if a company hopes to endure. Shifts in customer demand, new technology, increased government regulation, progressive competition, new employee attitudes and mores, and similar changes limit the usefulness of past experience. The uniqueness of each company and the rapid rate of change make imitation hazardous. We need fresh, original, distinctive, and independent thinking to develop alternatives that are copied neither from the past nor from our neighbor, but rather are peculiarly adapted to the circumstances in which we find ourselves.[5]

creativeness

Decisions that add some *new* and useful element are creative. Not all decisions are creative in this sense, of course. Even those that are include much repetition or imitation, but in some important respect a creative decision is different and *original.*

This sort of creativeness is familiar to all of us. Every invention of a product, process, or machine contains some creative element. Sales executives who think up suburban shopping centers or package their merchandise in ready-to-use form are being creative. The person who introduced the "last-in-first-out" method of evaluating inventory was creative. Creativeness is perhaps even more familiar outside the business field and is evident in the great advances of medical science, the development of atomic energy, and in discovery of new forms in the arts.

It is natural to exemplify creativeness by dramatic discoveries such as the Salk vaccine or satellite broadcasting. But close examination will reveal that even everyday activities are shot through with strains of creativeness. A personnel manager may have a creative idea for dealing with the troublesome problem of closing a plant, or a sales clerk may think of an ingenious way to display Idaho potatoes. Every time an executive faces a problem, large or small, he has an opportunity to be creative.

## PSYCHOLOGICAL AIDS TO INDIVIDUAL CREATIVITY

Studies of the creative process and of creative people suggest that creativity is not an exceptional ability within the grasp only of geniuses—anyone with reasonable intelligence may have an original idea; however, a lot of hard mental work is usually required to produce it. The prime requisites for developing creative ability appear to be the Horatio Alger qualities of self-confidence and a will to work. The imagination of a creative person is closely related to the intensity and clarity with which he senses the problems to be solved.

Can we suggest anything more about stimulating creativity? Although psychologists have found no reliable machinery to generate flashes of insight, they have identified a number of common barriers to creative thought.[6] By being alert to these barriers, we can overcome their inter-

[5]G. Zaltman, R. Duncan, and J. Holbek, *Innovation and Organization* (New York: Wiley, 1973).
[6]C. W. Taylor, ed., *Climate for Creativity* (New York: Pergamon, 1972).

ference to some extent. The most common obstacles are cultural and perceptual blocks.

Cultural blocks develop because the push toward social conformity strongly influences our thinking. All of us, consciously or unconsciously, tend to fit in with the modes of living and the attitudes of our associates. Minor exceptions may be acceptable or even desirable, but it is a daring young employee who wears pantaloons or goes barefoot to the office.

This same tendency to follow the crowd—this unwillingness to be different—affects our imagination as well as our actions. Until we are ready to break with current fashions of thought—in a department, in a company, or in society—truly creative ideas will be scarce.

In addition to the barriers that arise from our social background, we often have difficulty with new ideas simply because of the way we perceive things. Psychologists have devised many experiments that demonstrate the importance of perception. In one of the simplest, they place six matchsticks before a person and ask him to make four triangles with the sticks touching each other at the ends. Most people have trouble, and may even give up, because they think only of arranging the matches on a flat surface. Once they conceive of the task as a three-dimensional problem, they quickly form a pyramid.

Transferring habits is one cause of perceptual blocks. The mechanics who built the first automobiles, for instance, were in the habit of thinking of carriages. It was only natural that their early designs for "horseless carriages" merely substituted a motor for a horse. Similarly, in a company where engineering has always been physically and organizationally a part of the plant, executives have a hard time devising a new organization that ties engineering closely to selling. The transfer of past habits to new situations may block out the fresh perception of alternative courses of action.

An additional source of difficulty is that we too readily approach a problem as an "either-or" dilemma and examine only two courses of action. When one medium-sized manufacturing concern, for example, found its

*Figure 6.5  Our perception of things can be an obstacle to creativity, preventing us from seeing the wholeness or diversity of a situation, or even permitting us to see "impossible" objects. Does the silhouette show two profiles or a vase? How many stacked cubes do you count? Why is the third object called "irrational"? New perspectives are often required to enable us to break through our perceptual blocks.*

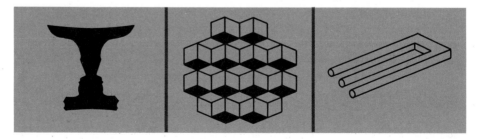

plant running to capacity, its executives wrestled for several weeks with the choice between trying to attract extra capital for building an addition to its plant or giving up plans for future expansion in volume. But these were not the only two courses of action. A third possibility involved subcontracting some of the work, and a fourth one, which the company actually adopted, was the arranging of a "sale and lease-back" deal whereby the company sold its old plant and the new addition to an investor and then leased them back for a long period.

**AIDS TO GROUP CREATIVITY**     Under favorable conditions, a group of people may produce more creative ideas when working together than when working individually. Several different schemes have been devised by business firms to benefit from group stimulation. We shall examine two of the most popular of these schemes, brainstorming and synectics, partly for the techniques themselves but more for the light they throw on the way group activity can contribute to creativity.

You may have been in a group making up a skit to mimic your professors; but even in a more formal group—perhaps a hospital board thinking about ways to gain public support for a new building—the flow of ideas might be similar. One person tosses in an offbeat idea that someone else quickly tops by another. While chuckling over these suggestions, a third person chimes in with a proposal that is really ridiculous, but can in part be salvaged to improve the earlier ideas. The animated spirit of the group is contagious. No one cares whether each idea is practical; just thinking them up is good fun. Out of such a session, an ingenious plan that no group member would have thought of alone is likely to emerge.

**brainstorming**

Alex F. Osborn has used many of the characteristics of group interaction in what he calls "brainstorming."[7] When we are confronted with a problem that calls for an original solution, Osborn recommends that we present the problem to a group of people and ask them to think up as many possible solutions as they can. Important rules for his group procedure are

1. *Rule out judicial judgment.* Criticism of ideas must be withheld till later.
2. *Welcome freewheeling.* The wilder the idea, the better; it is easier to tame down than to think up.
3. *Solicit quantity.* The greater the number of ideas, the more likelihood of winners.
4. *Seek combinations and improvements.* In addition to contributing ideas of their own, participants should suggest how ideas of others can be sharpened or how two or more ideas can be joined together.

Executives have used this technique on a wide variety of problems, including: how to find new uses for glass in autos, how to improve a company newspaper, how to design a new tire-making machine, how to improve highway signs, and how to cut down absenteeism. An hour session is likely to

[7]A. F. Osborn, *Applied Imagination* (New York: Scribner's, 1960).

produce anywhere from 60 to 150 ideas. Most suggestions will be impractical; others will be trite. But a few of the ideas will be worth serious consideration.

Brainstorming seems to work best when a problem is simple and specific. If an issue has too many facets, discussion lacks focus. If a problem is complicated and excessively time-consuming, and if it requires writing out a possible solution, discussion will lose its spontaneity. To overcome these difficulties, careful diagnosis to identify the "real problem" should precede any brainstorming session. Complex issues should be broken up into parts, and perhaps a separate session should be devoted to each important part.

Brainstorming has other limitations. Both the session itself and later evaluation of ideas, many of them worthless, are time-consuming. It also tends to produce superficial answers. To some extent, we can overcome these restrictions by adjusting the way sessions are handled and by selecting as members of the group people who deeply understand at least one aspect of the problem. Many business executives feel that even though brainstorming sessions do not stir up highly useful ideas every time, the stimulating effect of a session carries over into their other work. This stimulation tends to jar people out of routinized habits of thought and to force them to take a fresh look at all their activities.

Controlled experiments by psychologists indicate that during scheduled periods, motivated individuals working independently produce more ideas than when they work in groups. These findings imply that the success of brainstorming may arise largely from ensuring uninterrupted attention, engendering a relaxed and receptive attitude, and stimulating effort. In other words, the conditions surrounding a brainstorming session probably are more significant than the group action per se.

**synectics**　　　　A more formalized approach to creativity through group activity is synectics. The word is drawn from a Greek word meaning "the fitting together of diverse elements." The approach is largely the product of William J. Gordon, chairman and founder of a corporation called Synectics, Inc.[8]

Synectics shares with brainstorming three basic assumptions about creativity: (1) All people possess a greater degree of creativity than they are usually able to tap; (2) in seeking creative ideas, emotional and seemingly irrational elements of thought are as important as the intellectual and rational elements; and (3) the key is to harness the emotional and irrational through methodology and discipline.

Synectics differs from brainstorming in several important respects.

1. As a first step, the problem is thoroughly explored. This step provides a highly analytical treatment both of technical features and of the broad setting. Here the preceding diagnosis is reviewed and questioned. Only after all members of the synectics group are thoroughly oriented to the nature of the problem do they seek novel ideas.

[8]See W. J. Gordon, *Synectics* (New York: Collier, 1968); and G. M. Prince, *The Practice of Creativity* (New York: Macmillan, 1972).

2. Next, the group leader picks a key aspect of the problem and poses this as a general issue or evocative idea.

3. Then explicit devices to "invoke the preconscious mind" are used. These may induce all sorts of fantasies and wild ideas. Typically, all participants are trained in the use of direct and symbolic analogies, impersonations, and other techniques that have proven helpful in developing novel viewpoints and ideas. Thus each participant is well aware of the "method in the madness" of a synectics session.

4. Being skilled in the process, the group can move back and forth from an apparently irrelevant discussion to the real problem. A technical expert within the group assists in appraising the novelty and feasibility of various ideas. So instead of producing a large number of superficial and random ideas as in brainstorming, this group screens ideas frequently.

Because of these characteristics, synectics can deal with much more complex and technical problems than brainstorming, and do so in a sophisticated manner.

What general guides to creativity do techniques like brainstorming and synectics suggest? One crucial characteristic is a permissive atmosphere. Probably the cardinal rule of both approaches is this: postpone the evaluation of ideas. Anyone who says "That won't work" should be quickly squelched, and no one should be afraid to present an idea that is admittedly impractical. Tough, critical, searching analysis is not avoided, but deferred. Withholding judgment is psychologically sound. Social barriers, as we have already noted, tend to make all of us conform to conventional ideas, and in many companies a person who makes a novel suggestion is laughed at or considered peculiar. As a result, new ideas are repressed. In such an atmosphere a person thinks about his ideas carefully and assures himself of their practicality before he dares to express them.

**permissive atmosphere**

In contrast, brainstorming and synectics seek to remove these social barriers for at least a brief period. Because everyone recognizes the dis-

*Figure 6.6  In synectics, an "evocative idea" provides the springboard for creative thought. A food company, for example, is seeking a new airtight plastic bag that can be easily opened and closed. The tough issue is how to hold the bag closed. So, various ways of holding clothing securely together is put forth as the "evocative idea." Starting with the fasteners shown here—but shifting freely to related thoughts—can you "invent" a simple and inexpensive tight seal that someone using crackers, snacks, or breakfast cereal can easily open and close several times?*

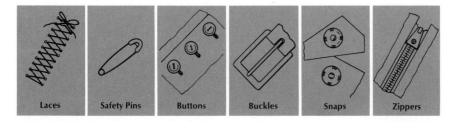

| Laces | Safety Pins | Buttons | Buckles | Snaps | Zippers |

tinction between mentioning an idea and recommending it, a person's reputation for sound judgment is not at stake. The influence of social pressure is reversed. Originality is encouraged, and the desirable member of the group is the person who has a lot of ideas.

Even when no formal technique like brainstorming is used, a permissive atmosphere can go far in encouraging creativity. New ideas are more likely to emerge when they receive a warm welcome. Specifically, in a permissive atmosphere (1) people are free to express ideas even though they are at variance with past practices, group norms, or the views of the leaders; (2) supervisors and colleagues give positive encouragement to a person who wants to try something new and different; and (3) mutual respect for individuality runs deep enough so that a person expresses his creative ideas without worrying about an unfavorable response. The individual who cherishes stability and respects tradition will probably be unhappy in such a permissive atmosphere, but these are the conditions in which creative thinking is most likely to flourish.

**creativity and diagnosis**

Having looked at the creative process, we must now consider a criticism of rational diagnosis relating to its impact on creativity. A few critics contend that the methodical, highly analytical approach suggested for diagnosing a problem inhibits by its nature the decision-maker's creativity. They use the successes produced by brainstorming as evidence to support their position. We strongly believe the opposite to be true.

By clearly and sharply identifying a problem or unrealized opportunity, by clearly homing in on the root cause or obstacle to this problem or opportunity, the decision-maker can utilize his creative talent to the maximum. By looking at the subparts of a complex problem, and at alternative means of realizing higher-level goals, the decision-maker can focus every ounce of his creative talent on seeking ways to solve subproblems for which no satisfactory solution is known. Further, given the nature of a thorough diagnosis, he can do so without losing sight of the relationships among the parts.

Therefore, when we are faced with tough problems, we need keen diagnosis to help channel our creative efforts. The chances that a person who is unaware of a need will think of a novel solution are exceedingly small.

## CONCLUSION: LINKING DECISIONS TO STRATEGY

Managers of all sorts face pressure to reach decisions. While many of these decisions are routine—or can be made so by the devices described in Chapter 4—the pressure is often unique and unstructured.

A quick choice of action in these tougher situations is foolhardy. Such action may be a costly way to get to the wrong place. Before "calling the shot," a manager should (1) clarify the problem, and (2) look for creative alternative ways of solving it. To clarify a problem we have suggested defining the gap between what is likely to happen and what is desired, finding the root cause, and examining the gap in terms of higher level goals and related problems. Then, to flush out good alternatives, past experience can be supplemented by deliberately searching for more creative possibilities.

The search for alternatives may open new angles on the diagnosis; clearly, good diagnosis narrows and speeds the search. So the steps interact. But the two steps combined are the major source of distinctive managerial decision-making.

This proposed diagnostic approach aids strategy implementation by insisting that immediate problems be related to higher goals—and such moving up the means-end chain will lead to strategic goals. Thus, local decisions can be integrated into the strategy program. And in the other direction, strategy aids diagnosis by helping to flag and describe "gaps." In addition, the strategic goals help simplify the search process by setting constraints on alternatives that are worth exploring.

## FOR FURTHER DISCUSSION

1. When should a manager seek to identify a root cause as the key to solving a tough problem, and when should he move to higher-level goals to find an alternative way of getting around the problem?

2. In what ways may participation by lower levels of management in strategic planning affect their ability to do more thorough diagnoses? How may it hinder them?

3. In an effort to stimulate sales, the sales manager of a soap company set up a contest for salespeople in which the one selling the most soap in a one-month period would receive a $200 bonus. During the month sales soared. But during the following months, they fell off sharply, and many customers complained that they had been pressured into overstocking. (1) Draw a means-end chain to illustrate what diagnosis by the sales manager led to a sales contest as a solution. (2) Show how this diagnosis might have been broadened to avoid the undesirable outcome. (3) Explain the advantages and dangers of using a means-end chain in this case.

4. When there is a strong disagreement on the best solution to a technical problem, should a decision-making group move up or down the means-end chain from the gap? Would your answer differ if the group was seeking consensus on a question involving personal values?

5. Can a computer develop creative alternatives to a problem? What similarities are there in the way a computer and the human mind operate in searching for a new idea? What differences are there?

6. To what extent may "change for change's sake" contribute to, or detract from, the likelihood of coming up with a creative approach when it is most necessary?

7. "Creativity is vastly overrated. Do what you know works harder and better than others and you will fare better. In addition to the time and effort involved in the search for creative solutions, any resulting changes make coordinated effort more difficult." Under what conditions would you agree with this statement? Disagree?

8. Should those most closely involved in the diagnostic stage of a decision be expected to play significant roles in the search for alternatives? Discuss.

## CASES

For cases involving issues covered in this chapter, see especially the following. Particularly relevant questions are listed after each case.

Benjo Associates (p. 92), 8
Elizabeth Archer (p. 96), 9
Mike Zerllini (p. 188), 3, 5
Clifford Nelson (p. 192), 4, 5, 6, 7
Camden Chemical (p. 298), 4
Scandico (Singapore) (p. 305), 4
Delphi Insurance (p. 369), 4

## FOR FURTHER READING

Allison, G. T., *Essence of Decision: Explaining the Cuban Missile Crisis*. Boston: Little, Brown, 1971, pp. 1–66. Explains the purpose of this pace-setting book; develops the first of three models—the rational actor; and applies this model to the Cuban missile crisis.

Brown, J. D., *The Human Nature of Organizations*. New York: American Management Associations, 1973, chap. 9. Explores the conformity-versus-creativity issue, especially as it arises in large organizations.

Janis. I., and D. Mann, *Decision Making*. New York: Free Press, 1977. Comprehensive discussion of individual decision-making from a psychological perspective.

MacCrimmon, K. R., "Managerial Decision-Making," in J. W. McGuire, ed., *Contemporary Management: Issues and Viewpoints*. Englewood Cliffs, NJ: Prentice-Hall, 1974, pp. 445–95. Good overview of managerial decision-making.

Stein, M. J., *Stimulating Creativity*. New York: Academic Press, 1974. Explores ways of improving individual creativity.

Taylor, C. W., *Climate for Creativity*. Elmsford: Pergamon, 1972. Reviews guidelines for establishing creative work environments.

# 7

# choosing
# a course of
# action

**Learning Objectives**

After completing this chapter you should be able to

1.  Explain why forecasting is an important part of the decision-making process.

2.  State why managers frequently overlook other consequences and explain how these tendencies may be overcome.

3.  Identify useful approaches for simplifying the comparison of alternatives.

4.  Explain the role of individual and organizational values in choosing a course of action.

5.  Describe the major techniques for testing a choice among alternatives.

## PROJECTION OF ALTERNATIVES

Spotting and diagnosing a problem and then finding attractive alternative solutions is a crucial start. But it leaves us with an unanswered question: which of the alternatives is best? The rational model for making plans, which we are examining in Part II, now stipulates two more steps: for each alternative, we must carefully project the likely results of adopting that course of action, and finally make a wise choice that supports strategy and accounts for the diverse values and uncertainties involved.

Projecting the probable consequences of each alternative—the first subject of this chapter—should be done in a way that helps us compare these possible courses of action. To make this comparison sharp and logical, we must accept the statement of the problem that emerged from our diagnosis, and we must concentrate on our clearly identified alternative ways of dealing with that problem. If we don't maintain this focus, the entire analysis becomes very confused.

**tough versus creative attitudes**

In our discussion of creativity we emphasized such matters as stimulating the imagination, providing a permissive atmosphere, and nurturing screwball ideas. Our purpose was to propose ways to cultivate fresh and original thought.

The comparison of alternatives requires a different frame of mind. Here we want to be as sure as possible that we are right. Therefore we challenge evidence, stick to issues and rule out irrelevant points, prove points logically, and listen to the skeptic. This is a time for tough, critical thinking.[1]

People are usually adept at either creative thinking or tough-minded analysis, but rarely at both. In fact, an individual who excels in one type of thinking is likely to be impatient and scornful of the other. Yet both qualities of mind are needed for decision-making. Every manager should at least be aware of the distinction between creative thought and searching analysis in the planning process, and should understand the contributions different people may make so that he can intelligently seek help where he is weak. In the following sections we shall turn attention to making careful, rigorous comparisons of already identified alternatives.

**focus on the future**

Rational choice relies on predictions. Most of the benefits and costs of any adopted plan arise, not at the moment of decision, but over a period of time afterward. So to make a wise choice, we must *predict* what those benefits and costs will be.

An electric utility's choice of a coal versus an automatic generating plant, for instance, will depend on *predictions* of construction costs, coal prices, atomic-core costs, plant efficiencies, repairs, hazards, pollution regulations, and a variety of other future events. Similarly, the selection of a TV program to use as an advertising medium will rest on forecasts of the rela-

---

[1]C. Jones, "Let There Be Light with Sound Analysis," *Harvard Business Review,* 54 (May–June 1976), 6–7.

tive popularity of that program, the quality characteristics of the audience, and their responsiveness to the message we want to deliver.

Rarely are all the consequences of an alternative certain. Predicting some factors may be very difficult, but we can't escape the task. To consider only history and hard "facts" is a sure path to incomplete analysis.

## FORECASTING CONSEQUENCES

The outcome of any plan of action we select will depend upon both the environment at the time action occurs and the soundness of the plan itself. By environment we mean the whole array of conditions affecting success that cannot be controlled (adjusted) by management. In contrast, the plan (decision) refers to changes—or lack of change—that occur as a direct result of managerial choice. Our predictions must include both sets of variables.

Change is everywhere. Student attitudes, food prices, life styles, wars, medical technology, even church liturgy will change sharply within the next few years. Consequently, we cannot be sure that an action that produced delightful results last month will have similar consequences next year.

**critical factors in the changing environment**

Fortunately we do not have to forecast all the shifts in environment that are likely to occur before we can make a rational decision. Many of these changes will have no noticeable effect on the set of alternatives we are considering, and can safely be disregarded. However, other changes may be critical to success or failure; these variables we must forecast to the best of our ability.[2]

The first move is to select factors in the environment that are critical to the problem at hand—critical because of their potential volatility and because their status will significantly affect the relative attractiveness of our alternatives. In the utility company example mentioned above, construction costs over the five-year span required to build a generating plant might double, with one type of plant rising much faster than the other; relative prices of coal versus atomic cores are even more uncertain; the efficiency of coal-burning plants is quite predictable, whereas atomic-energy technology is still being developed; future pollution regulations may hamper one source of energy and favor another. All these factors are critical to the choice and therefore should be forecast. However, for the selection of a TV program, none of the above factors would be relevant; here, forecasts about audiences for competing programs are critical.

A start on environmental forecasts will have been made as a part of diagnosis, but early forecasts have to be sharpened and expanded to fit the critical factors for the particular set of alternatives we are analyzing. The task would be simplified if we could confidently predict a single level for each critical factor. For instance, it would be helpful to have a simple conclusion

[2]P.T. Terry, "Mechanisms for Environmental Scanning," *Long-Range Planning,* 10 (June 1977), 2–9.

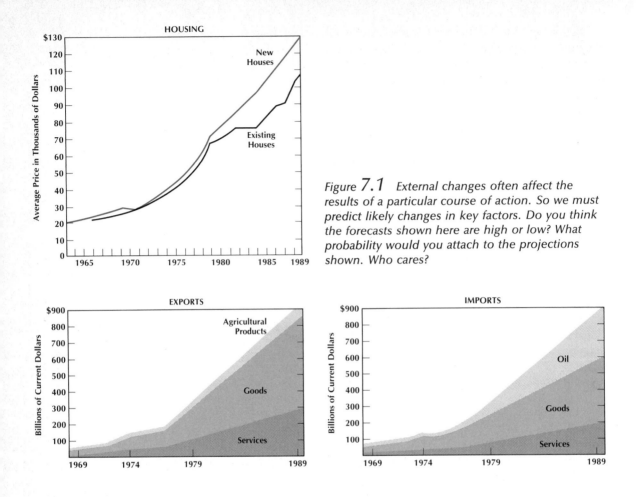

Figure *7.1* *External changes often affect the results of a particular course of action. So we must predict likely changes in key factors. Do you think the forecasts shown here are high or low? What probability would you attach to the projections shown. Who cares?*

that "coal prices will drop twenty-five percent by the time a coal-burning plant can be completed, and will remain stable for the next fifteen years (or rise only as fast as prices we can charge customers)"; or "there will be no additional regulations over radiation hazards of atomic plants." Unfortunately, our forecast will probably show a range of possibilities. For the radiation regulation, we might conclude:

| | |
|---|---|
| No change | 50% probability |
| Significant easing of regulation | 35% probability |
| Sharp increase due to one bad accident | 15% probability |

Such a forecasted array of possible environments is significant. It helps us assess the degree of risk associated with each alternative. It can also be used in "expected values" and in laying out "decision-trees"—discussed later.

A second kind of forecast is also crucial to the analysis of alternatives. predicting impact We must predict what is likely to happen if we take action A, or alternative of proposed action B. Sometimes the tie between a proposed alternative and a result is almost mechanistic, and we can predict outcomes with precision. For example, if we install ten new machines, monthly output can be increased fifteen percent. Most predictions are not so simple. The sales increase resulting from a TV program is by no means certain, even when we know a size and quality of audience. Nor are we sure of the response to a proposed maternity-leave policy for women. So, even with the valuable aid of internal company data, we again face forecasting hurdles and may resort to projecting an array of consequences with probabilities attached to each—as we did for environmental forecasts.[3]

A manager needs thorough acquaintance with an operation and imagination tempered by realism to anticipate fully the consequences of each alternative. Often a wide range of factors is involved. For instance, the sales manager of a manufacturer of power lawn mowers and related equipment recommended that the company establish an assembly shop on the West Coast. He said that this move would lower costs and improve customer service, thereby enabling the company to meet competition of local West Coast manufacturers. At the time, the company had only a sales office and warehouse for finished products in California. Among the questions to which the company sought answers before making a final decision were the following:

1. What will be the difference in cost between shipping parts and shipping assembled products?

2. How much will we have to pay for direct labor in the California plant? How much for indirect labor such as maintenance, janitors, and so on? What reduction, if any, in labor costs will there be at the main plant?

3. How much additional overhead will the California shop require? This includes rent (or, if we own the plant, taxes, depreciation, maintenance, and interest), power, heat, and light. How many clerks and supervisors, at what salaries, will we need for assembly work? Will there be any offsetting reduction in overhead at the main plant?

4. How much additional capital will we have to tie up in West Coast operations if the new shop is opened? This includes capital for equipment, office furniture, and other fixed assets; additional inventory; moving and setup costs; and operating losses during the period when the shop is getting under way.

5. Will the new shop be flexible enough to adjust to seasonal changes in volume of business? What minimum staff will have to be retained during low periods? Would there be greater flexibility at the main plant than at the new shop?

6. Will manufacturing in California subject the company to special state taxes or added liability insurance? Will it be advantageous to establish a separate corporation?

[3]S. C. Wheelright and D. G. Clarke, "Corporate Forecasting: Promise and Reality," *Harvard Busines Review,* November–December 1976, pp. 40–42.

7.  Just what will be the improvement in service to customers? How will local assembly ensure speedier deliveries than warehousing finished products? Will local repair and troubleshooting be feasible, and how much weight will this carry with customers? Will delivery of repair parts be improved?

8.  In addition to actual improvement in customer service, will the "local industry" appeal have a significant effect on sales volume?

9.  Will the quality of the product be as well controlled in California as in the main plant?

10. Will the union at the main plant object to trasferring work to another location? Might jurisdictional problems arise if a different union organizes the West Coast operations?

11. Should the West Coast shop be under the direction of a West Coast sales manager? What responsibility, if any, will the production manager have for West Coast operations? How will accounting and personnel be coordinated with the main plant?

12. How much additional sales volume can be anticipated as a result of establishing a West Coast assembly shop? How much will company profit be increased as a result of this additional volume?

Only after checking into all of these questions was the president of the mower company prepared to make a decision on the proposed West Coast assembly shop. He had a staff assistant assemble financial information and summarize it as shown in Table 7.1.

**weighing "other consequences"**    No managerial action has a single result. Although an action may make an important contribution to a mission, it will also result in some expense or sacrifice. Often we become so intent on one or two challenging objectives that we brush aside other consequences of a plan to meet the objective. For example, Americans who advocate that the United States give surplus wheat to starving people in other parts of the world tend to brush aside the political repercussions in nations whose wheat exports might be curtailed because of our gifts. Similarly, a proposal to increase the proportion of women in executive positions may upset opportunities for blacks, the morale in departments where anticipated promotions will be deferred, and union contract provisions.

The production-planning section of a small company proposed a plan for eliminating overtime. By careful scheduling, and by purchasing a few additional machines and hiring operators for them, the company could cut out overtime, which had been averaging four hours per week for all workers in the shop. But one consequence the proposal did not consider was the 15 percent cut (four hours at time-and-a-half) in take-home pay that the workers would suffer. Labor supply at the time was tight, and the industrial relations director felt sure that such a move would indirectly lead to demands for a higher base rate and perhaps to some turnover of experienced personnel. The possibility of these additional consequences was sufficiently serious that only the scheduling part of the proposal was put into effect; this cut overtime by only one and a half hours, and no conspicuous event like installing machinery called attention to the change.

"Other consequences" tend to be overlooked for several reasons.

TABLE 7.1
RELATIVE
INCOME AND
EXPENDITURES IF
NEW ASSEMBLY
SHOP RESULTS IN
DOUBLING WEST
COAST SALES[1]

| | Main Plant (assembles $200,000 worth of mowers for West Coast sales) | West Coast Shop (assembles $400,000 worth of mowers) | Difference (West Coast minus main plant) |
|---|---|---|---|
| Additions to present investment: | | | |
| Equipment | 0 | $ 30,000 | |
| Starting-up costs | 0 | 10,000 | |
| Parts inventory | 0 | 15,000 | |
| Total | 0 | $ 55,000 | $ 55,000 |
| | | | |
| Annual income and expanses affected: | | | |
| Income (West Coast sales) | $200,000 | $400,000 | $200,000 |
| Expenses: | | | |
| Costs of parts (increments) | 90,000 | 170,000 | |
| Shipping to West Coast: | | | |
| Assembled mowers | 15,000 | | |
| Parts | | 22,000 | |
| Assembly labor: | | | |
| Direct | 12,000 | 24,000 | |
| Indirect | 4,000 | 12,000 | |
| Overhead: | | | |
| Supervision | 0 | 8,000 | |
| Clerical | 0 | 5,000 | |
| Power, heat, light | 200 | 800 | |
| Shop rent | 0 | 7,600 | |
| Depreciation | 0 | 2,000 | |
| Taxes and insurance | 0 | 500 | |
| West Coast sales commissions | 10,000 | 20,000 | |
| Total | $131,200 | $271,900 | $140,700 |

| Net annual gain (sales difference minus expense difference) | | | $ 59,300 |

Rate of return (before income tax):

| | | | |
|---|---|---|---|
| First Year | $59,300 | $55,000 | 108% |
| Average Year[2] | $59,300 | $40,000 | 148% |

[1]Only those accounts affected by the choice of one of the two alternatives are listed. The amounts shown in each column are additional expenditures or income that would occur if that alternative were selected.

[2]Equipment costs will presumably be recovered by depreciation; so the investment in equipment will drop from $30,000 to zero, or average $15,000. Using the $15,000 figure, the total investment would be $40,000 in an average year.

1. Other consequences do not prompt management action. The spur to a decision—the gap we want filled—gets the limelight. The unavoidable extras, whether desirable or undesirable, were not included in our diagnosis and get brushed aside as we concentrate on the major mission.

2. Long-run consequences tend to be undervalued. Pain or pleasure six months or ten years hence is unreal compared with pressure to make this month's expense ratios look good or to quiet an irate customer.

3. The other consequences may not affect us. Even though we conscientiously want to serve the overall good, we are much more sensitive to results that hit us directly. (Social costs pose an issue of this sort.)

4. Unlikely consequences are often disregarded. Attention is absorbed by the most probable outcome, and if a consequence—such as environmental damage—is viewed as a secondary effect and also has only a thirty percent chance of occuring, it may never come up for serious study.

5. Psychologically, most of us tend to perceive acceptable stimuli and to screen out unpleasant ones. So, if a secondary consequence is unattractive, we may be unaware that we are ignoring it.

These tendencies can be overcome and "other consequences" flushed out by asking key executives and other interest-group representatives whether they have a strong preference for one of the alternatives being considered. If the answer is "yes," then attention should be focused on why that plan is preferred; the explanation may reveal other factors that should be considered.

From the preceding discussion, we can see that spelling out the consequences of alternative courses of action is no routine matter. Each managerial situation has its own distinctive characteristics. Because fact-gathering and analysis may become quite elaborate, we need to give special attention to ways of *simplifying the process*. Two useful approaches for simplifying the comparisons are *focusing on differences,* and *narrowing the number of alternatives*. Let us examine each of these.

**FOCUSING ON DIFFERENCES**     This principle is clearly illustrated in the case of the West Coast assembly shop. In choosing between doing *all* assembly in the main plant and doing *part* of it in the West Coast shop, management could ignore the cost of raw materials, which would always be purchased by headquarters at uniform costs. The company could likewise disregard the West Coast sales organization and sales personnel, for no change would be anticipated as a consequence of adopting either alternative. Because the president's salary would not be affected, it too could be passed over.

This principle must be carefully applied, however, for we may be in danger of assuming too many constants. If, for example, further study of the West Coast assembly shop indicates that it would substantially increase sales volume, then management would have to revise its assumption that sales organization and sales personnel would remain unchanged. The cost of shipping finished goods from warehouse to customers presents a similar problem. If establishing the new assembly shop would not alter the pattern

*Figure* $7.2$ *One way to reduce the complexity of having to compare alternatives is to sort out and ignore any common factors. For example, a comparison of the left- and right-hand groups reveals only three distinctive elements in each.*

of final shipment, then shipping costs could be left out of account. But if, on the other hand, the assembly shop is to be moved to a different city, or if management anticipates that sales will jump so much as a result of opening the shop that a more economical method of delivery will be possible, then costs of delivering finished goods should be included as a factor in the decision. In short, there is nothing wrong with disregarding a common element so long as we are positive that the element will, in fact, be unaffected by our choice.

## NARROWING THE NUMBER OF ALTERNATIVES

The energy of managers is limited, and most of us prefer to work on plans that have a good prospect of being carried out; so the quicker we can hit paydirt, the better. To expedite getting at the main alternatives, we can do two things: (1) accept constraint on alternatives, and (2) group similar alternatives during a first screening.

Diagnosis, as described in Chapter 6, often helps develop a list of limits or constraints, against which proposed alternatives can be checked. For instance, one small company, seeking an additional product line, might decide that a new product must be producible on existing equipment because they have unused capacity and lack capital to buy new facilities. Another company might say that a new product must be something its present sales organization could handle; any new product that failed to meet such a basic requirement would be eliminated from further consideration. When alternatives are narrowed down by testing against constraints, close attention can be given to the eligible ones that remain.

In other situations there may be such a large number of alternatives that comparing all of them even on one or two crucial factors would be tedious. To deal with this difficulty, alternatives can be grouped into classes, a representative picked from each class, and a comparison made of these representative proposals. Then concentration can be focused on the class that shows up best. Such a procedure is often used in plant-location studies. First, a region is selected by comparing a city from each region; then cities in the most attractive region are compared; finally, specific sites in one or two of the most desirable cities are given detailed study.

**satisfactory levels
for some factors**

For some factors, it is possible to simplify by setting a satisfactory level of achievement—a level where an objective is met adequately. Any alternative that achieves this level is acceptable. If all proposed courses of action are satisfactory by this standard, there is little or no difference in incremental values. The factor then becomes a minor consideration in making the choice, or may be set aside entirely.

The concept of acceptable achievement ("satisficing") is widely used.[4] Consider production costs. Every manager wants to lower his costs continually—at least, so economists assume. But in practice, we find that a manager keeps his eye on critical levels of cost. When competition is sharp, the production costs of other companies set the critical level; or when a product has a popular price—say, one dollar—the important level is the one that permits a company to get the product on the market at the popular price while maintaining adequate margins to distributors in order to sustain sales volume. Production costs higher than such critical levels are unsatisfactory, and executives will press to reduce costs to the acceptable level. Even lower costs are desirable, to be sure, but the pressure to achieve them is not so great. In other words, the importance of increments in cost savings drops markedly after the critical level is achieved.

Establishing satisfactory levels for quality is also useful. Bringing quality up to a given standard is highly important, but improvements beyond that point, though desirable, are not nearly so valuable. On the other hand, for such matters as accident prevention or sales volume, there is no clear-cut level at which incremental values change sharply.

Where "satisfactory" achievement levels apply, an executive finds that decision-making is simplified. He can reject a proposal if it is unsatisfactory on any account, and thereby narrow the number of alternatives for consideration. If the acceptable standard eliminates all alternatives, he seeks new proposals As the last resort, he lowers his acceptable levels. If two or more proposals meet all the tests of acceptability, then he is back with the problem of choosing but the problem is simpler because fewer proposals are still in the running.

[4] H. A. Simon, *Administrative Behavior,* 3rd ed. (New York: Free Press, 1976).

In any narrowing process, we risk discarding a course of action that, if completely analyzed, would be desirable. Nevertheless, as a practical matter, a complete analysis of all consequences of each alternative is impossible. Using constraints, groupings, and satisfactory levels to narrow down alternatives is as reliable a procedure as you will find.

## MAKING A CHOICE

Decision-making has many facets. Diagnosis defines a difficulty or opportunity in terms of a gap between desired and expected states. It helps pinpoint the obstacles to realizing the desired state, and it focuses attention on any limits that must be observed in seeking alternatives. Past experience and creative thought suggest possible ways of achieving the desired goals. Tough, critical analysis enables us to project and compare the consequences of the most promising ways of meeting the problem. And yet there remains the decisive act— picking one of the alternatives and saying, "That is it."

What emerges from a comparison of alternatives does not constitute a decision. Someone has to decide which set of projected results is best. And to do so, he must apply values.

A college student, in picking an elective course, makes a value judgment. Suppose he has narrowed his choice to either History of the Soviet Union or Corporation Finance. Investigation indicates that the first course would be fun to take—good prof, air-conditioned room, current events; besides, it would be good background for the years ahead. But the finance course is practical stuff that might really pay off, on the job or in personal investments. The finance prof is a good egg, but he piles on the work. Tuition and credit toward a degree can be disregarded because they are the same for each course. The student's projections of the alternatives help him see the implications of each, but he still has to make a choice based on the weights his values place on subjective factors. What weight does he assign to enjoyable experience, cultural background, courses that may "pay off"?

Business decisions, although they include more dollar projections, also involve values. For instance, an American manufacturing firm that wished to enter the Toronto market was considering either using an agent or opening its own branch. Table 7.2 summarizes the chief differences in anticipated results.

TABLE 7.2

| Considerations | Agent | Company Branch |
|---|---|---|
| Investment | 0 | $30,000 |
| Expenses | 5 percent of sales | $12,000 for year |
| Annual sales range[1] | $50,000 to $300,000 | $100,000 to $500,000 |
| Control | Difficult to specify behavior; agent free to quit | Responsive to specific requests; continuity more assured |

[1] Profits at various sales volumes were not computed. High variable costs plus freight and import taxes indicated that gross profit per unit in Toronto would be virtually constant—and low. Hence the emphasis on sales volume and selling expense.

The firm's choice clearly depended on the relative values placed on investment, expenses, sales volume, and control. If sales volume and control were paramount, then a branch operation would be the better selection. But if the firm wished to avoid risking capital and wanted to be sure that expenses were proportionate to capital, then an agent would be the preferred choice. The fact that not all of the factors to be weighed can be summarized into a single dollar measure of "net benefit" requires a balancing of tangible and intangible payoffs. Some kind of value system, in short, is necessary for most key decisions.

**deriving values from strategy**

The first place to look for values is within the company's strategy. Thus the firm that wanted to enter the Toronto market found that its strategy indicated where to put the heavier weight. This was a conservative, management-owned company with limited capital, and its executives chiefly sought a stable operation with assured profits. Consequently, they placed high value on the low risk of a sales agency. But if the strategy of the company had been growth, it is clear that a different set of values would have prevailed, and a sales branch might have been the final choice.

Subsidiary objectives and values are derived from the strategy through a means–end chain. Consider, for example, how the use of an executive-recruiting firm is related to the strategy of long-run growth of a plastics company (as shown in Figure 7.3). Each of the steps had high value to the company. However, the lower steps (subsidiary objectives) had value only by virtue of their relationship to the principal objective through a means–end chain. This particular analysis was helpful to the company's chief engineer when he was confronted with a proposal to install a long-service, versatile mechanic as head of the experimental department. He gave the proposal no value because it was not the best-known means of reaching the ultimate end.

A manager often finds himself working with several means–end chains. He is trying to choose a course of action that will contribute to several objectives, and there will be a means–end chain for each. The strategy itself will usually have several target results—such as a market position target, earnings target, and employment target. Separate means–end chains will be required to achieve each strategic target.

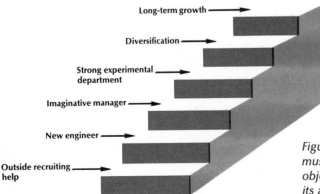

Long-term growth

Diversification

Strong experimental department

Imaginative manager

New engineer

Outside recruiting help

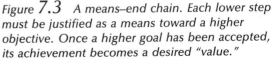

*Figure 7.3 A means–end chain. Each lower step must be justified as a means toward a higher objective. Once a higher goal has been accepted, its achievement becomes a desired "value."*

Multiple goals abound in the external social arena. A quick review of the bills introduced into Congress gives a hint of the diversity of results various groups in society would like to achieve. Enterprises are inevitably caught up in this great swirl of human aspirations, for each firm can survive only if it contributes positively to fulfilling some aspirations and if it avoids serious injury to others. Situations similar to that faced by Consolidated Edison Company of New York are common. Responding to growing demand for electricity and customer complaints of brownouts, the company set an expansion target for its generating capacity. This goal had to be reconciled with environmental objectives; a proposed nuclear plant on Long Island was dropped because of fear of radiation, and expansion of a Hudson River plant ran into thermal-pollution obstacles. Moreover, the company could not overlook profit objectives, which were necessary to support the huge loans that would be necessary when an acceptable plant site could be found. In addition to catering to these service, environment, and profit objectives, the company has goals regarding black employment and urban renewal.

Furthermore, a company's strategy must change because the environment is dynamic. To continue our example, customer service must respond to the summer peak caused by a dramatic rise in air-conditioning, and generating technology must respond by reducing metropolitan air pollution.

The stubborn fact is that the integration process results in a *set* of objectives—not just one.

While objective data can help, making a choice among alternatives clearly involves many subjective judgments and therefore there is a risk that personal desires will substitute for company welfare. Customer A may get prompt delivery of a scarce product because he is the personal friend of a manager, whereas the company good would have been better served by sending the product to customer B. Deliberate mixing of company and personal values does occur, but there is surprisingly little of it in American business. Most managers recognize that, in their roles as company employees, their personal preferences are irrelevant. They must view problems in terms of what is good for the company, and the distinction between business and self is considered a matter of integrity. Ability to make that distinction is an important element in self-respect and is a criterion central management uses in selecting people for responsible positions.[5]

Unconscious bias is more critical than deliberate self-serving. People deal with problems in terms of experience and the pressures that weigh on them. A sales representative is sensitive to sales needs and a production supervisor to plant needs; a person who is fearful of a layoff attaches higher value to stability than one who feels secure; an executive who recalls with nostalgia the days when his company was small—when he didn't have to fuss with so many reports and when "clearance with staff" was not part of his vocabulary—is likely to place more weight on the difficulties of further expansion than a young, aggressive president. Each of these people is trying

[5]B. Taylor, "Conflict of Values—The Central Strategy Problem," *Long-Range Planning,* 8, no. 6 (December 1975), 20–24.

to be objective, but personal values influence his judgment.

It is a fact of life that most of us are good at thinking up logical reasons for doing what we want; we kid ourselves. In making value judgments, it is entirely possible to seek earnestly for the best course for our company and at the same time unconsciously attach values that tend to favor our own interests. We must recognize that the danger of confusing personal desires with sound company values is inherent in choosing among alternatives. To avoid this danger it is important to test choices along the lines we suggest in the next section.

## TESTING A CHOICE

Is there any way a manager can tell when he has arrived at a correct choice among alternatives? Unfortunately, there is no sure test. The most he can do is to reduce the chance of serious error. Over the years, several different ways of checking the soundness of a decision have proved useful. Every manager should be familiar with these techniques so that he can pick those that are appropriate for each specific decision. Urgency of action, what is at stake, and degree of doubt will determine how many checks to use and how far to press them.

**reexamining the analysis and the evidence**

Most people prefer to stick to a line of thinking once it is well drawn in their minds, especially if the ideas are familiar, accepted, and attractive. Consequently a comfortable decision—right or wrong—tends to go unchallenged. To catch errors in such thinking, the following devices are helpful.

*Listen to the "devil's advocate"*   For centuries, the Catholic Church has used the institution of the "devil's advocate" as a way of testing decisions, especially those relating to the canonization of new saints. A person is assigned the task of pointing out weaknesses and errors in proposed action. He assembles the best negative arguments he can. If a proposal cannot withstand such an attack, action is postponed.

In business, a decision-maker himself often makes a deliberate effort to stand aside and think of all the reasons why a proposed action won't work. Before a manager says, "Go ahead," he should take time to calculate everything that may go wrong. But this negative approach may be difficult and unpleasant for an aggressive executive, and if a problem is complicated or involves strong emotions, he should perhaps assign the task to someone else. The role is apt to be unpopular, so a manager should make sure everyone recognizes that the devil's advocate is not passing judgment on a matter, but simply seeing to it that all negative points have been carefully considered.

A decision may be challenged on the basis of evidence, logic, values, or other grounds. At the time of the cross-examination by the devil's advocate, all sorts of embarrassing questions are raised. For example, "If officers need the proposed three-week vacation, why not all employees?" Or, "True, our annual reports do show a high correlation of sales volume and advertising expense, but does this mean that more advertising will increase sales? Maybe the causation runs the other way or does not exist. Remember, the

United States leads India in heart disease and baths per capita, but it does not follow therefore that baths cause heart trouble." A decision is sound only if it can be defended by good answers to such challenges as these.[6]

*Project a decision into detailed plans*    Often we can check on the wisdom and practicability of a decision by spelling out its consequences in more detail. A very large manufacturing company, for example, tested its tentative decision to decentralize into product divisions by using this approach of projecting consequences. It allocated customers, outlined a proposed divisional organization, devised a tentative placement of executives, and estimated the administrative cost of the new setup. This analysis uncovered so many weaknesses and difficulties that the original decentralization plan was abandoned. Not until a year later was a substantially modified reorganization put into effect.

*Reconsider planning premises*    Every management decision is based on assumptions, or planning premises. They may be assumptions supported by sketchy data about future demands for company products; about the availability of raw materials; about the attitudes and future behavior of employees, perhaps based on reports of staff people or hearsay evidence; or about company values that are as much a reflection of personal desires as of company goals. In checking a decision, a manager often finds it useful to ask himself just which assumptions are crucial to the success of a proposed action and to try to obtain futher clarification on these pivotal premises.

All premises cannot be verified, of course. We will always have to contend with incomplete data, errors in perception of facts, and distortion in communication. But an executive should reconsider assumptions so that he at least knows what risks he is taking rather than proceed naïvely.

*Review abruptly discarded alternatives*    Too often an otherwise excellent alternative has been discarded because of a single drawback. In such cases, we should ask whether the assumed drawback is insurmountable.

Consider the following situation: when additional tests were required by the F.D.A., one pharmaceutical firm decided to discontinue its research on a skin-allergy product. The potential market was not great, and the increased—the firm felt unnecessary—investment in testing and launching the product made the investment high. "The potential return is now so low we aren't justified in taking the fifty percent chance of success," said the president. Then the international vice-president proposed that the product be launched in countries where F.D.A. approval is not required—a reversal of the firm's usual practice of first proving products in the U.S. before taking

---

[6]The use of a devil's advocate has been proposed to deal with the decline in objectivity that sometimes occurs in group decision-making situations. See I. Janis, "Groupthink," *Psychology Today* (November 1971), pp. 43–46.

them abroad. Although this revised plan is not very attractive, it does make feasible finishing the R&D effort and removing these uncertainties before trying to satisfy the F.D.A.

Thus, if a critical drawback can be removed, a worthwhile alternative may come back into consideration. The manager may still reject the alternative, but not until he has reexamined the assumed disadvantage.

**securing consensus**

A director of Exxon Corporation has observed, "When a proposal comes before our Board for decision, there is rarely sharp difference of opinion. We try to anticipate problems, and then we discuss possible solutions with everyone directly affected and those who might have useful views. These discussions often seem slow, but by the time we are ready to act, a clear consensus backing the proposal has usually developed."[7]

Most of us use this technique, at least occasionally. We make a tentative decision—whether or not to accept a job—but before taking action, we get the frank opinion of one or two friends; we are testing the decision.

Formal arrangements are sometimes made to get consensus on important decisions. The United States Supreme Court is a notable example. Boards of directors and some company committees presumably provide group review and endorsement of key plans. Some organizations establish special staff units and designate them to provide a second judgment on key decisions. But the use of consensus to test decisions need not be limited to such bodies. Informal advice from individuals may contribute just as much to the wisdom of a decision.

If the assent or dissent of others is to be meaningful, the advisor should be both well informed about a situation and seriously concerned with the soundness of the decision. Neither polite agreement nor logrolling politics nor cavalier advice is desirable.

**pilot runs**

The surest way to test a decision is to try it out. A test will not tell us whether some other decision might work better, but it will tell us whether a proposed plan is at least promising. Sometimes a new product or process can be tried out on a limited scale with custom-made models or equipment. Automobile companies give their new chassis and new engines severe road tests before the products are put into mass production and sold to the public. A chemical company with a new detergent may have its laboratory make up limited quantities for market tests in a restricted area. As these cases show, even if a tentative decision looks good on paper or in the laboratory, a further test under more nearly normal operating conditions is desirable.

Pilot operations have their limitations, of course. They are often costly; they may consume valuable time; and they may not be feasible for some actions (such as floating a bond issue while interest rates are low). Consequently, this test is appropriate for only a few major decisions a manager must make.

---

[7]The important role of consensus in Japanese organizations is described by P. Drucker in "What We Can Learn from Japanese Management," *Harvard Business Review* (March–April 1971), pp. 110–22.

*Figure* 7.4 *Before a new automobile is put into production, specially made trial cars are subjected to severe tests to check the validity of previous engineering estimates.*

Occasionally, we can make a decision one part at a time; when the results of the first part are known, we can use them in deciding the second part; and so on with each succeeding part. Thus we make a series of decisions to solve one main problem.

**sequential decisions**

This form of decision is often used for executive promotions. Suppose a company president has his eye on a salesman named John Baker as a likely replacement for the sales manager who will retire in three years. The president's first step might be to bring Baker into the home office as sales-promotion director. If Baker does that job well, he may be put in charge of sales planning. If his work continues to be effective, he may be named assistant sales manager six months before he is to be moved into the key spot. These successive assignments serve a double purpose. Baker gets experience and learns about home-office operations, and the company can make a *series* of appraisals of his capability to be sales manager. The results of each move provide data used in deciding what the next move should be.

Sequential decisions are in sharp contrast to the bear-by-the-tail decisions familiar in sales promotion campaigns, where it is difficult to discontinue a project after it is launched. Sequential decisions should also be distinguished from the proverbial British habit of "muddling through," whereby one step is taken with the simple faith that some way will open up for the next move. In sequential decisions a tentative plan or a new alternative for dealing with a major problem is in mind from the beginning. The plan is then tested against newly acquired evidence and perhaps revised at each stage.

All these proposed devices for testing decisions have their usefulness. Some fit one situation better than another, but in general, they may be applied in the following order: (1) checking our own thinking by the devil's-advocate approach, projecting detailed plans for implementation, reconsidering assumptions, or reviewing discarded alternatives; (2) securing consensus from other competent people; and then, whenever suitable, (3) making test runs by pilot operation or by sequential decision.

## CONCLUSION: APPLYING RATIONAL DECISION-MAKING

The model for rational decision described in the last two chapters can be applied to all sorts of tough managerial problems—low level or high level, tangible or intangible. Each situation benefits from full diagnosis, creative search for alternatives, careful projection of results, and final choice of action based on strategic and other values. And using the model leads to integrated action *provided* company strategy is employed—as suggested—in both diagnosis and final choice.

Of course, a manager can rarely follow the phases of rational decision-making in the neat order of our discussion. Even if our minds tried to follow such a disciplined path, the trails through the phases would crisscross. In testing a choice, for instance, we may want to get more data, and the added information might suggest new alternatives. Or using a means–end chain to establish values might cause us to revise our diagnosis. Similarly, in discarding alternatives—by setting limits or focusing first on one or two crucial factors—we are in effect making negative choices.

So, we have not mapped a simple procedure. Rather, the model is a highly useful *framework* for putting our thoughts and planning efforts into an orderly, understandable arrangement. With this framework, random thoughts can be put in place, and any necessary backtracking need not confuse us.

The tough task for each of us is, of course, not merely to be acquainted with an approch to decision-making, but rather to master the concept so well that we use it skillfully and perhaps almost unconsciously.

Many managerial decisions are so complex that they defy simple, straightforward analysis. Fortunately, a number of techniques for simplifying and analyzing large-scale decisions have been developed by decision theorists, managerial economists, and management scientists. We consider some of these valuable aids to managerial decision-making in the next chapter.

## FOR FURTHER DISCUSSION

1. Often a manager will develop alternative ways of solving a problem and will find one clearly superior to the others except for one major disadvantage. Before eliminating this alternative, what should the manager do?

2. Should the same people who have developed alternatives play a major role in choosing among them? Discuss both sides of this question.

3. Outside experts often have the greatest "feel" for the occurrence of certain events, but they lack the perspective to evaluate the broader implications of al-

ternatives. How should specialized expertise be utilized in choosing among alternatives?

4. In what ways will (1) the sharpness with which a gap is stated and (2) the degree to which a specific problem is considered in the light of higher-level goals contribute to the process of comparing courses of action?

5. A key to good decision-making by middle managers is a clear knowledge of strategic directions set by higher levels of management. Yet these higher-level strategies may not be communicated to middle levels of the organization for a variety of reasons. How would you deal with such a situation?

6. When should senior level managers require their subordinates to present several options with their recommendations, and when should they request the one option which has support from all their subordinates?

7. Athough a "devil's advocate" may be vital for testing decisions, the unpopularity of people in this role makes them an endangered species in many organizations. How should this dilemma be dealt with?

## CASES

For cases involving issues covered in this chapter, see especially the following. Particularly relevent questions are listed after each case.

Benjo Associates (p. 92), 9
Mike Zerllini (p. 188), 6
Clifford Nelson (p. 192), 9
Delphi Insurance (p. 369), 5
Joe Dimaggio (p. 533), 5

## FOR FURTHER READING

Cleland, D. I. and W. R. King, eds., *Systems Analysis and Project Management,* 2nd ed. New York: McGraw-Hill, 1975, chap. 4. Reviews basic concepts for comparing alternatives and making a rational choice.

Harrison, E. F., *The Managerial Decision-Making Process.* Boston: Houghton Mifflin, 1975. Systematic examination of several aspects of choice.

Leavitt, H. J., "Beyond the Analytic Manager," *California Management Review,* in two parts, Spring 1975 and Summer 1975. Critically reviews the role of analysis in managerial decision making.

Radford, K., *Managerial Decision-Making.* Reston, VA: Reston Publishing, 1975. Treats advanced techniques for solving complex managerial problems.

Simon, H. A., *The New Science of Management Decision,* rev. ed. Englewood Cliffs, NJ: Prentice-Hall, 1979. Classic, concise overview of approaches to structured and unstructured decision problems.

# 8

# quantitative aids
# to decision-making

Learning Objectives

After completing this chapter you should be able to

1. Understand the concept of incremental analysis.
2. Explain the difference between variable and incremental costs.
3. Describe how to simplify the projection of intangible factors.
4. State the difference between risk and uncertainty and explain how to adjust decisions for each condition.
5. Describe the major features of operations-research models.
6. Describe the principal operations research techniques and identify where they are applied.
7. Explain the advantages of matrix summaries.

## THE ROLE OF QUANTITATIVE ANALYSIS

It is hard for any executive to keep in mind all the factors pertinent to a decision and to give each its proper relative weight. One way to reduce the complexity of the job is to introduce quantitative analysis.

The present chapter will examine how basic concepts from managerial economics, decision theory, and management science can assist managers in comparing alternatives and making a final choice. Throughout, we will focus on managerial applications and avoid specialized jargon.

Quantification is a powerful tool for simplifying reality and reducing complex decisions to a more manageable form. However, quantitative techniques pose certain dangers as well. They may invite too much consideration because they are easier to grasp than subjective factors and because they seem more reliable than is warranted by the assumptions on which they are based. Still, for many decisions, the advantages of quantification outweigh the danger that it will be misused.[1]

## CONTRIBUTIONS OF MANAGERIAL ECONOMICS

Quantification of economic factors depends on our ability to use accounting data developed for tax or financial purposes to identify those elements of income, expense, or investment that really change with the alternatives considered. The accounting department, in preparing statements for the Internal Revenue Service, must follow certain conventions. On the other hand, the finance department, in submitting reports to stockholders, creditors, and various governmental agencies, may be required to follow different conventions. When projected in financial terms, it is entirely possible for the same group of alternatives to look quite different depending on which set of conventions is used. As decison-makers, we should be aware of how a decision will look to a tax collector, a stockholder, or a regulatory agency in Washington. But it is probably more important to know how it will look in terms of the real impact on the elements of profit that the firm can control.

The decision-maker must be prepared to take income, expense, or investment figures computed for other purposes and adjust them to reflect the differences among alternatives he is considering. Because this process is so vital, we will outline below concepts from managerial economics that guide decision-makers in carrying out these adjustments.

Incremental analysis is a particular form of the "disregard common elements" concept discussed in Chapter 7. Simply stated, the principle of incremental analysis is: in projecting any relevant revenues, expenses, or investments, seek to identify any *difference* in these flows that will arise from (1) following alternative A compared with flows that will exist by (2) not following alternative A. We disregard those revenues, expenses, or investments that are "sunk"—those that would be incurred or realized in any

*incremental analysis*

[1]D. A. Heenan and R. B. Adelman, "Quantitative Techniques for Today's Decision Makers," *Harvard Business Review,* 54 (May–June 1976), 40–62.

event. Thus we isolate the "incremental" revenues, savings, expenses, or investments that would result from the proposal.

As a first illustration of the incremental concept, consider the case of an international news service that sponsored the design of satellite-communications equipment. After studying the situation closely, management had decided that the undertaking would be profitable if relatively trouble-free equipment could be developed for less than two million dollars in research and development. Research people and engineers assured central management that there was a good chance of success, and the project was authorized. Today, after a few years' work, two million dollars has been spent, but satisfactory equipment has not yet been perfected.

The research people have stated that they have made great progress, even though they have been unsuccessful. They are certain that they can now produce the desired equipment with an additional expenditure of about half a million dollars.

What should management do? Even if the new machine were successfully developed with the additional outlay, the project is still doomed to lose money. As much as three million dollars will have been spent to get savings of a little more than two million dollars. It might appear unwise to spend the additional million—the company officials might be accused of throwing good money after bad. If the most recent cost estimates are correct, however, and unless the news service has much more attractive uses for its money, the expenditure should be made. We can quickly see why if we apply the marginal concept. At this point in time, if the company does nothing, it will recover none of the money already spent on research. This money represents a sunk cost, one already incurred and not affected by the present decision. Therefore, though is may be painful, we disregard it. The question to be asked is, "What additional, or incremental, costs and savings are involved?"

If the present projections are correct, the incremental (additional) costs will be less than one million dollars and the incremental (additional) saving received will be something more than two million dollars. Overall, the company will probably still lose money on this venture, but by continuing the project its loss will be reduced by at least a million dollars—the excess of incremental costs subtracted from incremental saving.

**pitfalls in traditional accounting concepts**

As a further illustration of the incremental concept as applied to cost and revenue, let us look at an abridged case in which we encounter problems arising out of traditional accounting concepts.

The Elton Metal Products Company received an invitation to produce a specially designed pipe fitting to be used in warehouse refrigeration. Elton developed and produced 1,000 fittings at a total cost of $5,500. A large portion of this expense was the cost of developing the fitting and of converting a metal-working machine to make it suitable for manufacturing the piece. Now, on completion of this contract, Elton's sales manager has been offered an additional order from a building contractor for 500 fittings. In setting a price for the second order, the cost statement shown in Table 8.1 has been prepared.

TABLE 8.1

| | Cost for 500 Units |
|---|---|
| Labor | $ 700 |
| Material | 750 |
| Power and materials handling | 50 |
| Research and development | 300 |
| Conversion costs | 400 |
| General overhead | 400 |
| | $2,600 |

The first question we ask is whether some of these costs would be incurred even if Elton turned down the second order.

What of research-and-development costs, conversion costs, and general overhead? Because the research and development has been done, it is a sunk, or nonavoidable, expense. Turning down the order will not reduce this item. Therefore, these certainly are not pertinent costs. Let us assume that the same is true for conversion costs. What of "general overhead"? This entry includes the share of general operating expenses charged to this project— such costs as executive salaries, maintaining the factory, and the like. Again ask the incremental question. Will these costs be reduced if Elton does not produce the additional 500 units, and, if so, by how much? These additional overhead dollars are the crucial costs that should be considered in deciding on this order.

After carefully considering each item shown in the cost statement in Table 8.1, the Elton management has isolated certain items that would *really change* if an additional 500 units were produced (Table 8.2).

Many a cry will be raised at such an estimate because the project is not "carrying its fair share of allocated costs." Strictly speaking, this is true. But what will be accomplished if Elton holds out for a price in excess of $2,600 and does not make the sale? Suppose the top offer is $2,200. If Elton holds out for $2,600 it would be passing up $670 ($2,200–$1,530). Stated in another way, Elton would give up a chance to get incremental revenue of $2,200 while incurring only $1,530 in incremental costs.

TABLE 8.2

| | Added Cost for 500 Units |
|---|---|
| Labor | $ 700 |
| Material | 750 |
| Power and materials handling | 50 |
| General overhead | 30 |
| | $1,530 |

Incremental analysis dictates that unless some alternative use of the facilities represented by $1,070 in sunk costs added more than $670 in additional revenue, Elton would be foolish to turn down this proposal. It should also be noted that Elton would be wise to turn down the proposal if accepting the $2,200 offer would result in losses of more than $670 in *later* price negotiations. However, any future loss that will result from taking this order at a low price is really an incremental cost of the decision. The decision-maker can estimate the amount of "opportunity cost" (that is, income lost in other alternatives or future pricing of this fitting) and compare it with the income gained by taking the order.

**variable versus incremental costs**

We have just faced the first problem encountered in applying the incremental principle of costs—namely, the conventional accounting practice of allocating fixed costs. A second major problem is faced when we attempt to use standard accounting records to forecast costs. A distinction is commonly made between "fixed" and "variable" costs.[2] From our previous observations it would seem that we could arrive at incremental costs by taking only the latter. Unfortunately, the commonly used variable costs are not the same as incremental costs, because they are normally computed as average variable costs. In addition, certain costs that are categorized as fixed in accounting terms may be incremental under other conditions. The following two situations illustrate these problems.

Suppose the Elton company received an order for 5,000 more pipe fittings. Elton would have to buy a second specialized machine to be able to accept this order. The cost of buying the machine, a fixed cost in the usual accounting sense, is an incremental cost in this instance. It is a cost that will be incurred if the proposal is accepted but would not be incurred if the proposal is turned down.

You may ask why we cannot merely add such special fixed costs to the average variable costs computed by the accountant. To see why not, let us leave the Elton example and examine the lists of costs for Millard Stamping Machines in Table 8.3. This table illustrates why variable costs, computed as averages, differ from incremental costs.

As you can see, the difference between average variable costs and incremental costs can be considerable, because average costs are averages of total variable costs, while incremental costs are based only on the variable costs of the additional unit or units being considered.

To illustrate how a wrong decision might be reached if it were based on average variable costs, suppose the best price the twelfth unit could fetch was $11,000. If we were to use average variable costs we would probably turn the offer down since the incremental revenue of $11,000 does not seem to cover the costs of the twelfth unit. The pertinent cost for the twelfth unit, however, is the incremental cost figure, $8,000; using this measure, we see that incremental revenue for the twelfth unit does exceed the increase in costs incurred in producing it.

---

[2]G. A. Welsch, *Budgeting: Profit Planning and Control,* 4th ed. (Englewood Cliffs, NJ: Prentice-Hall, 1976).

TABLE 8.3

| Volume | Total Variable Cost | Average Variable Cost | Incremental Cost |
|--------|---------------------|-----------------------|-------------------|
| 0 | 0 | 0 | 0 |
| 10 | $150,000 | $15,000 | $150,000 (for 10 units) |
| 11 | 160,000 | 14,545 | 10,000 |
| 12 | 168,000 | 14,000 | 8,000 |
| 13 | 176,000 | 13,769 | 8,000 |
| 14 | 185,000 | 13,214 | 9,000 |
| 15 | 200,000 | 13,333 | 15,000 |

By the same token, suppose the best price offered for the fifteenth unit was $14,000. Average variable cost ($13,333) reduces the impact of the high cost of producing this fifteenth unit by averaging it in with the lower costs of the first 14 units. As a result, $14,000 of incremental revenue seems to make this price acceptable. Again, however, the significant measure of the cost of the fifteenth unit is the *additional* cost of producing it—the incremental cost of $15,000. In this case, incremental revenue ($14,000) does not exceed incremental costs ($15,000). Unless there are other reasons for taking a $1,000 loss on this sale, the offer should be turned down.

Alternatives are difficult to compare when one produces large cash income (or requires a substantial outlay) at a much earlier date than others. If we receive cash early, we can use this capital for other purposes; we can lend it at interest if a more attractive use is not available within the company. If, on the other hand, we have to make large outlays early, the capital tied up has a direct or imputed interest cost. To remove this difference caused by *when* cash flows in and out, we can adjust all receipts and disbursements to "present cash value," just as a banker discounts a bond or some other asset that will not turn to cash for several years.[3]

**adjusting for differences in time**

The preceding section has focused on concepts for determining the relevant elements of cost and revenue associated with each alternative. In many complex situations, though, alternatives will also produce drawbacks and benefits that are difficult to translate into dollar costs and dollar revenues. Many of these intangible implications, however, can be stated in dollar terms if we avoid the temptation to evaluate them directly. Consider what happened at Millard Stamping Machines when management faced a decision on whether to accept an offer of $11,000 for one of its machines. Assuming that 11 machines had already been produced and sold for $16,000 and that this sale involves a new customer, what should they do?

**simplifying projection of intangibles**

Based on the tangible and relevant cost and revenue, an incremental outlay of $8,000 will bring in incremental revenue of $11,000. But what about the intangibles? For example, consider just the following two:

[3]J. C. Van Horne, *Financial Management and Policy,* 5th ed. (Englewood Cliffs, NJ: Prentice-Hall, 1980).

1. Possible difficulty in getting the normal $16,000 price from future customers.
2. Possible advantages of getting a foot in the door of the new customer, which may lead to future sales of equipment and parts.

Rather than merely try to weigh apples ($3,000 incremental gain) and oranges (plus and minus the intangibles), we should attempt to put a dollar sign on the intangibles. This is, in effect, what we would do intuitively anyway. So let us identify the elements involved in intangible factors and attempt to express the anticipated effect on these elements in dollar terms. For the first intangible, we should forecast the following:

1. How many future machines are we likely to sell at the $16,000 price if we reject this sale?
2. How many future customers are likely to know what price we charged for the 12 machines?
3. Of those who might know, how many are in a position to demand a price below $16,000?
4. How far below this price will they demand?

Answering any of these questions will indeed involve a great deal of educated guessing. However, we can make these guesses somewhat more easily and accurately then a comprehensive guess about the more general question of "upsetting normal prices."

With the second intangible, the benefits of getting "a foot in the door," the same kind of projections can be attempted.

1. How large is this customer's business?
2. Is he likely to require additional equipment we make? If so, how much?
3. Will he be willing and able to pay normal prices for future purchases?
4. How much future parts-replacement is required, and what is the profit on such replacement?

Again, by taking the elements that determine the nature and magnitude of the intangible and projecting each in dollar terms, we can come closer to developing a dollar projection for the whole intangible factor.

In some cases, to be sure, no matter how hard we try there will be intangible consequences that defy quantification. In the field of operations research, investigators have attempted, through forced-choice comparisons, to develop some valid system for translating the implications of intangibles into dollar terms. However, much remains to be done before such "utility models" (as they are often called) can be widely used.

In summary, we should seek to forecast and quantify as many of the implications of each alternative as possible. Then the remaining, nondollar considerations can be kept to a minimum and presented for final consideration, juxtaposed to the dollar projections. This process does not remove the need for some kind of forecasting theory, nor reduce the desirability of obtaining relevant data, nor make the conclusions less subjective. Its purpose is to put projections into a form that will ease comparisons of alternatives.

One other major consideration in choosing among alternatives is the unpredictability of the environments, which is as much a part of

business life as breathing is of human life. Business cycles, weather, wars and threats of wars, competition, inventions, new laws, and a host of other dynamic situations and events make the future less than certain. Within a business firm, machine breakdown, irregularity in human performance, and failure to maintain standard operating conditions increase our quandary. A manager must be willing to make a decision even when he lacks complete certainty. The same person who takes a tough, challenging attitude toward proposals that are presented to him must be willing to risk making a decision although he is fully aware that the future may play tricks with his present expectations.

Decision-making theorists note that managers can generally make decisions under three possible conditions: *certainty, risk,* and *uncertainty*.[4] As we noted above, conditions of *certainty*, in which managers have enough information to know the outcome of their decisions with perfect accuracy, are rare. *Risk* refers to those situations in which managers know the likelihood of the various possible outcomes associated with a decision. *Uncertainty* exists when managers know the various outcomes associated with a decision but they are unable to estimate the likelihood of these outcomes.

We now turn to techniques for incorporating elements of risk and uncertainty into a choice of action. We begin by examining how statistical probabilities are used to make decisions under risk.

**decision making under risk**

For some events, we have enough statistical evidence to compute the chances that the event will occur. Life insurance provides the classic example. Life-insurance companies know that probably fewer than one percent of men age twenty will die during the ensuing five years, whereas about five percent of the men age fifty will die in the same period. The companies insure enough lives so that these probabilities fit their business. Thus, if an insurance executive were drawing up five-year contracts for twenty-year-olds and fifty-year-olds, he knows that he should get over five times as much income from the latter to make the two policies comparable. Because mortality statistics enable the insurance executive to accurately estimate the probability of each occurrence, he is making his decision under *risk*.

Similarly, if a manager had an investment opportunity with a fifty percent chance of returning $100,000 profit, a forty percent chance of only $20,000 profit, and a ten percent chance of losing $50,000, he could weigh these payoffs by their respecive probabilities and develop an "expected value for the alternative"—in this case, $53,000; that is, ($100,000 × .5) + ($20,000 × .4) − ($50,000 × .1). The "expected value" technique is, in fact, the principal approach for adjusting alternatives to account for *risk*.

Statisticians warn us to be cautious about this simple approach to decision-making under risk. Rarely does a company experience enough of

[4]For a complete discussion of these conditions and appropriate solution techniques see D. W. Miller and M. K. Starr, *Executive Decisions and Operations Research,* 2nd ed. (Englewood Cliffs, NJ: Prentice-Hall, 1969), chap. 5.

the same kinds of event so that losses and gains work out to the most probable result. Because it is likely that actual results will deviate from the average, we should know something about that deviation. Are the actual results of customer acceptance of bids on special jobs likely to be close to our previous twenty-five percent average—between twenty and thirty percent, for example—or is there a good chance that they will range anywhere from five to forty-five percent? The central figure is twenty-five percent in both instances, but in the second case we would be much less certain about future sales.

In only a relatively few decisions can we use statistical probability in a strict sense to adjust for risk. To make precise use of probability techniques, we need data on a large number of similar cases, and we must have a clearly defined sample. Nevertheless, probability theory does give us some useful clues in comparing alternatives. (1) When the alternatives we are considering have different probabilities, we can multiply the appropriate values in each alternative by their respective probabilities and arrive at "expected values"; these values can then be compared, since differences in probabilities have been taken into account. (2) The width of the range within which results are likely to fall (the twenty to thirty percent and the five to forty-five percent in the example above) may be as significant as the average or the single result that is most probable.

**subjective probabilities**

We often infer from limited data the probability of a particular outcome. Such predictions are common in everyday speech. "The Los Angeles Dodgers have one chance in three to win the pennant." "There's only one chance in ten that the UAW will strike at Ford this year." "There's a fifty-fifty likelihood we'll land that government order." "The odds are two-to-one that Smith will turn down the promotion."

Such subjective probabilities help us to deal with decision-making under risk. They at least offer a rough judgment on the likely occurrence of various events. To say, "There's one chance in twenty our Navy contract will be canceled" is much more helpful than "There's a possibility the contract may be canceled."

Occasionally, management can put these probability guesses to more specific use. For instance, a company with annual earnings before taxes of $750,000 was rapidly approaching a stalemate in its union negotiations. The workers wanted a large wage increase that management was not ready to grant. After a long conference with his key executives, the president concluded, "I think there is a twenty-five percent chance of a serious strike. If it comes, our earnings will probably drop $300,000." The controller responded, "Then in comparing costs of various alternatives, we should figure the risk of a strike as a $75,000 cost [$300,000 × .25]." The comments of the president and the controller can be summarized as in Table 8.4.

After more discussion, the president and the controller worked out a probability chart that is more informative because it shows the likelihood of losses ranging from zero to $800,000 (Table 8.5). It also indicates that when a full range of possible consequences is included, the seriousness of a strike threat is somewhat worse than the company first thought.

TABLE 8.4

| Situation | Estimated Loss of Earnings | Subjective Probability | Loss × Probability |
|---|---|---|---|
| No strike | 0 | 75% | 0 |
| Serious strike | $300,000 | 25 | $75,000 |
| | | 100% | |
| | Loss adjusted for probability | | $75,000 |

TABLE 8.5

| Possible Length of Strike | Estimated Loss of Earnings | Subjective Probability | Loss × Probability |
|---|---|---|---|
| 0 days | 0 | 35% | 0 |
| 3-5 days | $ 50,000 | 40 | $ 20,000 |
| 3 weeks | 200,000 | 15 | 30,000 |
| 6 weeks | 400,000 | 7 | 28,000 |
| 10 weeks | 800,000 | 3 | 24,000 |
| | | 100% | |
| | Loss adjusted for probability | | $102,000 |

A similar analysis would be helpful to the president of the power mower company considering a new West Coast assembly shop. Estimates indicate that $19,000 will be lost if the proposed shop handles only the current volume of business in that territory, whereas a net gain of $59,000 will be realized if a local assembly plant doubles sales, as the sales manager predicts. The chief unknown in the picture is sales volume. The president feels the sales manager is overoptimistic. He grants that some increase in volume is likely but he believes that there is only a small chance to achieve the $40,000 volume within a few years. Table 8.6 sharpens these feelings and relates them to estimates of gain for different sales levels.

TABLE 8.6

| Possible Sales Volume (Annual) | Estimated Net Gain | Probability Inferred by President | Net Gain × Probability |
|---|---|---|---|
| $200,000 | $–19,000 | 0 | 0 |
| 250,000 | 600 | 50% | $ 300 |
| 300,000 | 20,100 | 30 | 6,030 |
| 350,000 | 39,700 | 15 | 5,955 |
| 400,000 | 59,300 | 5 | 2,965 |
| | | 100% | |
| | Net gain adjusted for probability | | $15,250 |

Rate of return on initial investment of
$55,000    28% (i.e., $15,250    $55,000)

The president's informed guess is that sales volume will be between $250,000 and $400,000 per year, with the lower volume much more likely. When he adjusts the net-gain estimated by the subjective probabilities, the final value he assigns to the new shop is about $15,000 per year. Although this figure is not so enticing as what the optimistic sales manager would forecast, it still represents an attractive twenty-eight percent return on added investment in West Coast operations.

Unfortunately, these final figures "adjusted for probability"—the $15,250 in the power mower illustration and the $102,000 in the strike example—are quite synthetic. If we want a single value, they are the best we can do. If the companies in these cases had hundreds of similar (though independent) problems, then the average results might be close to the adusted figures. In a single instance, however, the actual outcome is almost certain to differ from the adjusted total. In deciding whether to open a West Coast branch, the president of the power mower company may be equally interested in the fact that there is a fifty-fifty chance that the operation will just break even as he is in the synthetic adjusted total. If he had plenty of capital, he might say "I don't think we'll lose any money, and we might make a handsome profit, so go ahead." On the other hand, if he is short of capital and pressed for earnings, he might decide, "We should allocate our capital and our time to projects where we feel sure of making some profit, even though the potential may not be so high as that in the West Coast operation." In other words, a distribution of probabilities may be as important in making a value judgment as a weighted average.

Similarly, the president of the company confronted with a strike threat may be concerned about the range of chances he is taking. For example, if the company has large payments to make on a bank loan, even a small risk that earnings will be wiped out is serious. But under other circumstances, the company might be quite prepared to take this risk in exchange for other gains. Whenever we face big unknowns, using probabilities—whether by putting them on paper or just estimating them mentally—helps in forming judgments.

**decision-making**
**under uncertainty**

Adjusting decisions for *uncertainty* is more complicated than adjusting for *risk*. The distinction is that under *uncertainty*, a decision-maker has no knowledge of the probabilities of various outcomes and, as a result, no way of calculating the expected value of alternatives, as he does when dealing with decision-making under *risk*.

A number of decision-making criteria—"pessimism," "optimism," or "regret"—can be used to choose among uncertain alternatives. The important point for managers is that, since decision theory provides no one best criterion for selecting an alternative, final choice depends on individual and organizational values. As noted in the previous chapter, these values need to be derived from strategy.

**incomplete data**

Managers often seek to convert a decision-making under *uncertainty* situation into decision-making under *risk* by searching for more complete data thus hoping to find a basis for estimating the probabilities of certain key events which affect their outcomes. Such information-seeking behavior reflects one of a manager's major dilemmas: more information versus more time and expense.[5] When a competitor cuts prices, or an important customer inquires when delivery can be promised, or the still at an oil refinery breaks down, the executive in charge must decide what to do without delay. The costs and risk incurred by delay may be more serious than the probable error inherent in judging on incomplete information.

Overcoming incompleteness of data is a small decision-making problem in itself. Diagnosis, alternatives, projection, and value judgments are needed. Among the ways of increasing the store of information while keeping the expense of obtaining it within bounds, are these: bravely singling out one or two crucial factors and concentrating on gathering facts about them; taking just a sample of the total data we might like to have; and, if feasible, postponing decision until good information becomes available.

Reasonably complete information and prompt decision-making are often hard to combine. The chief hope for conquering this problem is to anticipate the need for such a decision—for instance, guessing that a competitor might cut his prices—and to have pertinent current data already assembled; the military practice of preparing in advance tentative courses of action might even be warranted. Another approach is to split an activity into parts and try to postpone that part where information is weakest. A multiproduct company, for instance, may plan a weekly television program for months ahead, but may defer writing commercials until market conditions reveal which product will benefit most from advertising at a particular time.

When balancing increased accuracy against time and expense, an executive should think in terms of increments, as with other problems. Will the improved accuracy of a decision that arises from additional data be worth the added expense and time to obtain it?

The vast majority of decisions—under *certainty, risk,* or *uncertainty*— must be based in part on evidence that is not fully reliable. Trade-association figures might not be representative of an entire industry; equipment salesmen present their products in the best possible light; social tradition requires that the published statements by company presidents bristle with confidence; market surveys by advertising agencies usually point to the need for more advertising; army generals foresee grave dangers if their appropriate requests are not met in full; and so on. Such data are apt to be only part of the whole truth, and the manner of presentation may be slanted to produce a desired impression.

**unreliable data**

A manager who must make a decision tries to get data that is as reliable as possible, but usually he cannot get the full story from his sources. He has to pick up grains of truth and new insights whenever or wherever he can find them. He can ill afford to disregard the opinions of well-informed persons, even though they may be tarnished with bias.

We are all familiar with unreliable data in our daily lives. We learn a

---

[5]R. H. Gregory and R. L. Van Horn, "Value and Cost of Information," in J. Daniel Couger and R. W. Knapp, *Systems Analysis Techniques* (New York: Wiley, 1974) pp. 473–84.

lot from food advertising without being upset by copywriters' superlatives. When a high school girl pleads, "Everybody is wearing them," parents interpret the remark to mean that three or four of her friends are sporting the style in question. Such information is not as precise as we might like, but we learn to live with it and even to take effective action on it.

Two simple rules are helpful in using unreliable data. (1) Keep aware of the limitations of the information we are working with; label it "suspect," and perhaps adjust it to what we believe is reasonable. (2) Appraise the person supplying the data. What are his interests, ability, judgment, integrity? The more we know of a person, the better able we are to evaluate what he says. We can usually improve accuracy by considering unreliable as well as reliable data, provided we use it with discretion.

## CONTRIBUTIONS OF OPERATIONS RESEARCH

A manager, as we have seen, must often make a choice that involves large numbers of alternatives and unpredictable outcomes. So much complexity is involved that techniques for summarizing and condensing are very helpful. We will briefly describe two: operations research models and matrix summaries.

**operations-research models**

One major contribution of operations research is the concept of a model that summarizes in a few numbers many of the factors involved in a complex choice.[6] Basically, three features are involved in this method of summarizing.

1. Problems are stated in mathematical symbols. Symbols and equations, which make up a convenient shorthand widely used in science, provide a form of expression that is concise and easy for an expert to manipulate.

2. A cardinal rule of the operations researcher is: build a model. The use of physical models is a common practice in industry; for example, aircraft engineers use small models to test new designs in wind tunnels. Such models represent aspects of a real thing. A model of a management problem in mathematical symbols is similar but more abstract. In building a model, the operations research specialist seeks a set of equations that will project consequences, attach values to these consequences, and adjust for risk and uncertainty. The model hopefully presents an orderly picture of the total problem that would otherwise be dealt with unsystematically in the mind of an executive.

3. The third essential feature of operations research is quantitative measurement of the several independent variables and the dependent variables (predicted results) in the equations. Just as a chemist must measure the temperatures, pressures, and other factors he works with, so must the operations reseacher express in quantitative terms the elements in a managerial situation if his model is to be useful in making a choice. This requirement means a tremendous amount of "digging" for facts. It also requires that values be expressed in a uniform scale—usually dollars.

[6]H. M. Wagner, *Principles of Operations Research*, 2nd ed. (Englewood Cliffs, NJ: Prentice-Hall, 1975), chap. 1.

Operations-research models have been applied to a number of complicated management problems.[7] For example, oil companies use them in scheduling refinery runs. Here the problem is determining what proportion of various products to manufacture from a barrel of crude oil. The variables include: different sales prices for gasoline, heating oil, lubricants, asphalt, and other end-products; availability and price of several types of crude oil, each with its own composition and refining characteristics; variations in yield and operating costs of the refinery when a specific crude oil is used to make different proportions of end-products; and costs of storing excess output of specific products during slack seasons. The equations dealing with such refinery-run problems are complex, and electronic computers are necessary to handle the mass of data promptly.

The situations in which operations research has paid off have these characteristics: (1) A problem is so complicated or involves such a mass of data that it cannot be fully grasped by one person's mind yet its parts are so interrelated that dividing it into comprehensible units would not necessarily yield the best answer. (2) The relationships are known, clearcut, and of a type that can be expressed by available mathematical formulas. (3) Statistical data is available for all important variables.

The first of these requirements makes the study worth the trouble, the second is necessary to build a satisfactory model, and the third is a requisite for practical application.

**decision trees**

Some decisions involve a series of steps, the second step depending on the outcome of the first, the third depending on the outcome of the second, and so on. Since there are probabilistic outcomes at each step, we face a sequence of decisions to be made under risk conditions. "Decision trees" are a model to deal with such a problem.[8] Here is an illustration.

Exports from Organic Fibers, Inc., to Australia have been expanding. The local Australian sales agent is now insisting that he be given a ten-year contract, but Organic Fibers' overseas manager recommends opening a company sales office as a first step toward building a plant three or four years later. Decision A is this choice between the sales agent or a sales office. Decision B, to build a plant, will be made only after sales growth has been demonstrated. An alternative to Organic Fibers' building its own plant is to subcontract. In fact, if a sales office is opened and growth is slow, subcontracting would still be an alternative to exporting from the United States; this would be decision C.

To clarify (1) the decisions to be made, (2) the probabilities of key events, and (3) the estimated yields, the decision tree shown in Figure 8.1 was prepared. Laying out on a chart the alternative series of events along with estimates of probabilities and estimated net profit is a very helpful device by itself. To sharpen the choice even more, we should calculate the

---

[7]R. L. Ackoff and P. Rivett, *A Manager's Guide to Operations Research* (New York: Wiley, 1963).
[8]J. F. Magee, "Decision Trees for Decision Making," *Harvard Business Review* (July–August 1964), pp. 126–38.

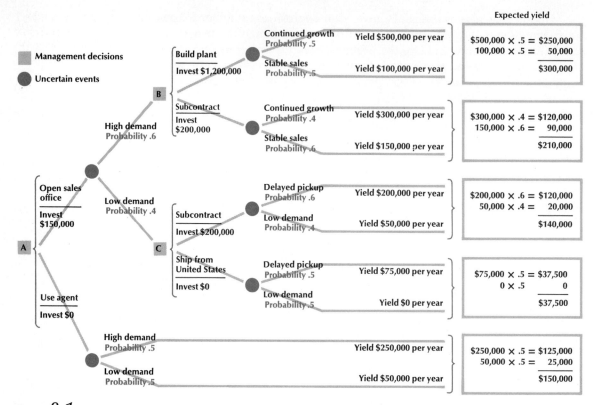

*Figure 8.1* A decision tree for projected Australian expansion. The probabilities and amounts of investments and yields as shown represent management's best estimates on the basis of present knowledge.

"position value" of an established sales office. This can be done by rolling back the expected values as follows:

1. On the basis of our best estimates, *decision B will be to subcontract*. The difference in expected return from the plant and subcontracting ($300,000 − $210,000 = $90,000) is not large enough to justify the difference in additional investment ($1,200,000 − $200,000 = $1,000,000). So we assume the outcome of decision B will be an expected yield of $210,000 and an investment of $200,000.

2. *Decision C will also be to subcontract.* The difference in expected return between subcontracting and exporting ($140,000 − $37,500 = $102,500) is large enough to justify the additional investment of $200,000. So we assume the outcome of decision C will be an expected yield of $140,000 and an investment of $200,000.

3. Using the probabilities of high and low demand, which dictate whether we will be faced with decision B or C, we can compare the two alternatives at decision point A. If the company opens the sales office, the expected yield from decision B is $126,000 ($210,000 × .6), while the yield from decision C is $56,000 ($140,000 × .4). The total expected yield from opening the sales office is therefore $182,000 ($126,000 + $56,000) on a total investment of $350,000 ($150,000 to open the sales office and $200,000 to subcontract). On the other hand if the

162

company uses a sales agent, the total yield that can be expected is $150,000, without any initial investment.

4. *Decision A will be to use the agent.* The difference in expected yield of opening a sales office or using the agent ($182,000 − $150,000 = $32,000) is not large enough to justify the initial investment in the sales office plus the investment necessary to subcontract in Australia ($150,000 + $200,000 = $350,000).

Decision trees can be drawn to fit all sorts of situations, and refinements of the preceding illustration—such as more alternatives, more than two levels of risk, discounting for when income and outflows will occur, and risk of losing the investment—suggest themselves as soon as the problem and premises are explicitly stated. But even this relatively simple illustration points up the inherent complexity and difficulty in making precise quantitative projections.

**computer simulation**

In decision trees and most other operations-research models, we weigh various possible outcomes by their probability to calculate an expected value. Such practice enables us to take account of differences in the chance of success, but the resulting figures are only synthetic scores, not a picture of any result we may actually face. One way to get a better sense of what our world might be like *if* this or that happened is through simulation.[9]

With this technique, a model—admittedly incomplete but the best we can design—is used to project possible results of different alteratives under varying assumptions. Usually the model is programmed into a computer; then we can easily try out all sorts of contingencies—tight money, high demand, and so on—and various actions to deal with such situations. It is like running through football plays on a practice field, knowing that in actual play the situation will be much more complicated. The simulation is helpful in making a choice because it has summarized and condensed at least part of the many considerations.[10]

Unfortunately, in many management situations the factors involved and the relationships between them are not sharp enough for mathematical expression; and if the simulation is oversimplified it loses much of its usefulness.

In conclusion, then, operations-research models are helpful in making a choice in certain types of complex situation. But even where data is available and a useful model can be constructed, we always face the question, "Is it worth the trouble?"; for the myriad relatively simple problems, it is probably not.

## MATRIX SUMMARIES

Many decision-makers want some means, simpler and more flexible than an operations-research model, for summarizing the projections they must weigh in choosing among alternatives. Especially, they need a way to get the intan-

[9]D. B. Hertz, "Risk Analysis in Capital Investments," *Harvard Business Review,* 51, no. 5 (September–October 1979), 169–81.
[10]T. Naylor, *Corporate Planning Models* (Reading, MA: Addison-Wesley, 1979).

gibles into the same focus. Matrix summaries are helpful for this purpose.[11]

Here is an example—one of many variations—of how matrices can be used. The president of a large paper company had to choose a new mill location. He had narrowed his choice to four locations and had consolidated as well as he could the dollar benefits of each into an estimated rate of return on incremental investment. He then identified five other factors that, while they were partially reflected in the dollar figures, had additional intangible implications. For each of these intangibles the president faced two questions.

1.  What *degree of satisfaction* may I expect for each intangible at each mill site?
2.  How *important* is each intangible to me—in the range being considered?

The first question seeks to determine the extent to which a desired intangible need is met by each alternative. The second question recognizes that a favorable position with respect to one intangible may be more important than a favorable position with respect to another.

Because the president could not avoid answering these two questions, at least subjectively, he went one step further and translated his feelings into numbers. He ranked each alternative on a scale from zero to ten for each question, low ranking reflecting low satisfaction or low importance. These evaluations of the intangibles are summarized on the matrix shown in Figure 8.2.

To arrive at a rough indication of the relative significance of intangibles for each site, the degree of satisfaction (in color) in each cell of the matrix has been multiplied by the relative importance (in black). The resulting numbers are a rough index of the relative degree and importance of each intangible for all four sites.

Then, to summarize, the index numbers have been added to show a combined score for each site. This total score had significance only for comparing the alternative sites. Nevertheless, it did help the president make a choice. By concentrating on the last two columns of the matrix, he quickly decided that site 2 was preferable to site 1: the score for the intangibles was about the same, and site 2 had a decided edge in rate of return. After a little thought the president decided that site 3 was preferable to site 4: the significant intangible advantage of site 4 simply could not offset a 50 percent higher rate of return at site 3. That selection left a final choice between sites 2 and 3.

Were the intangible advantages of site 2 worth sacrificing an estimated 1.4 percent difference in rate of return? Looking at the cells in the matrix, the president could see that the chief difference in intangibles was in the favorability of predicted union relations; after further reflection he decided to sacrifice rate of return rather than build a plant where union relations would probably be quite troublesome.

Although this matrix did not give the president an automatic answer, it did two things. First, it forced him to clarify his judgments about the intangibles. Second, it provided a mechanism to help him balance them in

[11]K. Radford, *Managerial Decision-Making* (Reston, VA: Reston Publishing, 1975).

| Alternative Sites | Predicted Availability of Desired Labor/Skill Mix | Predicted Favorable Union Relations | Predicted Favorable Local Legislation and Taxes | Predicted Ability to Hold Capable Mill Managers in This Location | Predicted Unlikelihood of Competitors Moving Nearby | Weighted Total Score for Intangibles | Estimated Incremental Return on Investment Compared with Doing Nothing |
|---|---|---|---|---|---|---|---|
| Site 1 | 6 × 9 = 54 | 5 × 8 = 40 | 6 × 9 = 54 | 9 × 9 = 81 | 4 × 3 = 12 | 241 | 12.1% |
| Site 2 | 5 × 6 = 30 | 8 × 8 = 64 | 6 × 9 = 54 | 9 × 9 = 81 | 3 × 3 = 9 | 238 | 14.7 |
| Site 3 | 5 × 6 = 30 | 1 × 8 = 8 | 8 × 9 = 72 | 5 × 9 = 45 | 4 × 3 = 12 | 167 | 16.1 |
| Site 4 | 10 × 6 = 60 | 6 × 8 = 48 | 8 × 9 = 72 | 8 × 9 = 72 | 5 × 3 = 15 | 267 | 10.8 |

Figure *8.2*   *A matrix for choosing mill locations, showing the president's subjective evaluation of intangibles. Sites below minimum acceptable level on any factor have already been eliminated. The company can easily finance the dollar investment required at any of these locations with an 8 percent bond issue. Quantity and quality of output will not be affected by the choice of site. Key: colored numbers—degree factor is achieved at each site; black numbers—relative importance of a factor; colored underscore—weighted score.*

his mind. Crude though the weightings were, use of the matrix helped integrate the implications of each alternative into a final choice.

All sorts of matrices are possible. Verbal statements instead of numbers may be placed in the cells. Probability estimates may be added. Predictions based on very flimsy evidence may be flagged, weights adjusted for degree of satisfaction, and so on. Basically the matrix is useful because it enables us to summarize a variety of projections in a systematic fashion. Some experienced executives make a tentative decision first and then prepare a matrix with data necessary to justify that decision. Such a practice is not so silly as it first appears, because the executive is testing his intuitive feeling against its logical implications. If the implications appear unsound when they are clearly exposed, he can revise his intuitive judgment.

## CONCLUSION: ENHANCING DECISION-MAKING EFFECTIVENESS

In the last three chapters, we have elaborated on the rational decision-making process. Our focus in this chapter has been on quantitative techniques to assist managers in comparing alternatives and making a choice.

Initially, we considered how quantification simplifies the comparison of alternatives. Because several intangible factors must be dealt with, the challenge is to properly blend quantitative analysis with sound managerial judgment. For many management decisions, solutions will retain a large measure of subjectivity.

Risk and uncertainty are inherent in choosing a course of action and the rational decision-maker must adjust alternatives accordingly. To deal with these complexities, managers must think in terms of probabilities; be sensitive to bias in the opinion of others; and balance the cost of more data against the likely improvement in judgment. Like levees against floods on the Mississippi River, they are helpful primarily as devices for coping with uncertainty rather than for removing it.

Thus far, our approach to decision-making has emphasized rational analysis and choice by a single manager. This rational, individualistic model provides the starting point for studying more complex bureaucratic and political decision-making for the many problems confronting a business enterprise. The joint effort of many people is needed. So, in the next chapter we turn to decision-making in an organization.

## FOR FURTHER DISCUSSION

1. "Any decision that can be made by a computer does not require line management attention. Staff technicians who can identify the factors to be processed by the computer are all that is needed." Do you agree? Discuss your answer.

2. How can a manager determine in any one case whether or not to invest time in securing more data?

3. "The trouble with sophisticated forecasting techniques is that the techniques are so complicated and the predictions so precise that people tend to believe they are accurate." Comment on the several aspects of this somewhat cynical view of forecasting.

4. "Now that more managers have been exposed to quantitative decision-making techniques, we can expect greater use of them in middle-management decisions. Top-level decisions won't change much, though. they will still be largely based on managerial judgment and intuition." Comment on this quote.

5. List and discuss the major pitfalls a decision-maker should consider in seeking to develop and use subjective, numerical estimates of probability. How will your answer differ if the probabilities are to be used in decision trees rather than in a matrix summary of a choice that does *not* involve sequential decisions?

6. The use of simulation techniques for making a choice requires knowledge of computer and mathematical techniques, and practical experience with the elements of the decision to be made. Because few managers are likely to be strong in both areas, how should the different types of expertise and experience be brought together? What problems do you foresee in this effort?

7. Since I know the odds are fifty-fifty in a fair coin-toss, I would gladly bet a dollar if offered a four-to-one payoff if I guessed correctly. Yet I would not bet $20,000 even if assured of a fair toss and given a five-to-one payoff. Am I being non-rational by ignoring expected values in the second case?

8. Under what conditions should the detailed, probabilistic assumptions connected with alternatives be recorded and reviewed after a decision has been made? When might this be unwise?

CASES

For cases involving issues covered in this chapter, see especially the following. Particularly relevant questions are listed after each case.

Mike Zerllini (p. 188), 7, 8, 9
Clifford Nelson (p. 192), 8
Marathon Plastics (p. 456), 6
Joe DiMaggio (p. 533), 6
Foster Promotions Inc. (p. 538), 4

## FOR FURTHER READING

Grayson, C. J. Jr., "Management Science and Business Practice," *Harvard Business Review,* July-August 1973, pp. 41–48. First-person account of the difficulties experienced in applying management science techniques.

Loomba, N. Paul, *Management: A Quantitative Perspective,* New York: Macmillan, 1978. Provides a balanced treatment of how quantitative decision models may be applied to practical problems.

McKenney, J. L. and P. G. W. Keen, "How Managers' Minds Work," *Harvard Business Review,* May-June 1974, pp. 79–90. Suggestions on how to close the gap between the manager and management scientist.

Miller, D. W. and M. K. Starr, *Executive Decisions and Operations Research,* 2nd ed. Englewood Cliffs, NJ: Prentice-Hall, 1969, chap. 4–6. Cogent summary of decision theory and role of operations research.

Starr, M. K., "Management Science and Management," and Hertz, D. B., "The Changing Field of Management Science," in J. W. McGuire, ed., *Contemporary Management: Issues and Viewpoint.* Englewood Cliffs, NJ: Prentice-Hall, 1974, pp. 72–92 and pp. 95–98. Thoughtful discussions of the evolution in management science thinking and practice.

# 9 organizational decision-making

## Learning Objectives

After completing this chapter you should be able to

1. Discuss the major ways in which decision-making in an organization differs from individual decision-making.
2. Explain the concept of organizational distance.
3. Describe how initiators assist with problem diagnosis.
4. Understand the special organizational arrangements required to generate creative ideas.
5. Describe how uncertainty absorption affects the estimates used in decision-making.
6. Explain the concept of a credibility structure and its value in consolidating projections.

In the preceding chapters on decision-making, we explored the basic elements of developing creative and wise solutions to management problems. That analysis was simplified by assuming that the process was being carried on in a single person's mind. Planning in an enterprise is more complicated. Many people take part over an extended period; yet numerous specific decisions must fit together to produce coordinated action. So in this chapter we shall examine ways to deal with this added complexity.

A variety of managerial tools and practices are available to aid decision-making within organizations. In Chapters 3 through 5 we learned how a manager can greatly enlarge his personal decision-making capacity through the design of a total planning system for his organization. Our specific concerns in this chapter will be the strengths and the limitations that organizations inevitably add to the decision-making process.[1]

While reviewing these strengths and limitations, we can also appraise the capacity of organizations to perform each of the elements in rational decision-making. Clearly, if the steps outlined in Chapters 6 through 8 lead to wise decisions by an individual, it is desirable to incorporate those same steps in organization planning. Actually, under the right conditions an organization has a much greater capacity to plan than a single person. To see how and why this jump in capability occurs, we need to link the elements of rational decision-making with organization design.[2] That is, we need to build bridges connecting concepts of individual decision-making with insights about organization (to be discussed in Part III).

Organizations have the potential for making better decisions than an individual because more experts contribute their specialized judgments. This requires, however, that the decision-making is *dispersed* (a) among more people, and (b) over a long period of time. A decision to retreat from a decaying urban location to the suburbs requires inputs from personnel, sales, accounting, finance, legal, office services, and other affected departments. And months, perhaps years, will pass before a clear consensus develops to make the move.

**dispersion of
inputs**

Decision-making in an organization differs from individual decision-making in still another way. The help we get from other people and the guides ("restraints") provided by the enterprise itself rarely come together in a single grand array. Theoretically, if we follow the rationalistic-model approach, we might consolidate all the forecasts and guesses, relate them to selected alternatives, make allowances for time, adjust for risk and uncertainty, apply a formally approved value scale, and emerge with *the* decision. Actually, only in small organizations and for relatively simple decisions can

**succession of
premises**

[1]G. Allison, *Essence of Decision: Explaining the Cuban Missile Crisis* (Boston: Little, Brown, 1971), chaps. 3 and 4.
[2]J. G. March and H. A. Simon, *Organizations* (New York: Wiley, 1958), chap. 6.

we get all the issues and "facts" on the table at the same moment.

Instead, conclusions are reached in *sequence*—often by different individuals—and one conclusion becomes a premise for the next.[3] Thus in diagnosis a district sales manager may conclude that the company's new plastic-base paint is unsuited for the blistering sunshine in his district; the plant engineer, accepting this fact, reports on the technical difficulties of making a special mix for that district; and, on the basis of the engineer's report, the cost accountant prepares some figures on producing two different mixes. These are all preliminary data, but note how one builds on another.

Such interlocking of one conclusion into another is particularly significant in projecting consequences after a problem has been defined and the alternatives identified. Suppose that the difficulty with paint blistering has been diagnosed and we have a proposed second line of "sunproof" paint. The company is now trying to project the results of adding this new line. As general background, the company economist predicts general business conditions and the level of business activity for the next five years. Accepting this forecast, the sales manager predicts sales volume with and without the new line. Then, given these volumes, the chief engineer estimates the new equipment that would be needed and other effects on production; he reports that if the new line is added an automatic grinding mill will be feasible. Now, the purchasing agent, learning from the engineer the kind and quantity of raw materials needed, prepares a cost estimate for raw materials; and the personnel director, using the sales and production forecasts, estimates training and wage costs. With these data, the controller makes a summary estimate of total outlays and receipts.

Note in this illustration that the estimates of each person are built on conclusions of one or more other people. Stated another way, the conclusions of the sales manager become premises for the engineer, the conclusions of the engineer become premises for the purchasing agent, and so forth. Consequently, if we want to be confident that the final decision emerging from this sequence is sound, we must give careful attention to how each premise is set. Personal bias and faulty communication may introduce substantial error in the process. Even officially approved premises need to be reviewed.

**variation in problems**

Problems differ in the number of people who become involved and in the amount of special effort required.[4] The more rare and complex the problem, the more pooling of diverse management talents is necessary. Here are two situations that we shall use as examples throughout the chapter.

The president of Frosty Foods, a successful frozen-food processing company, is aware of the growth in "fast-food" restaurants such as McDonald's Hamburgers. These chains use large quantities of frozen food, and variations of basic products especially designed to fit the fashion trends of this market

---

[3]R. M. Cyert and J. G. March, *A Behavioral Theory of the Firm* (Englewood Cliffs, NJ: Prentice-Hall, 1963), pp. 114–27.

[4]Throughout this discussion we use the term "problem" to include opportunities as well as present and anticipated difficulties.

might increase that volume. Possibly Frosty Foods should buy up a chain of outlets. The move of the Howard Johnson chain to sell food products carrying its name through supermarkets suggests the possibility of synergistic benefits; that is, the combined effect of restaurant and supermarket promotion may be greater than the sum of separate promotion of restaurant and supermarket sales. In other words, the president of Frosty Foods feels that opportunity for some kind of action in the "fast-food" industry exists—even a change in Frosty Foods' strategy—but he is not clear on what action should be taken. We are concerned here with how a plan of action responding to such an opportunity can best be devised in an organization.

Resolution of the situation just described will obviously involve many people. And the manner in which they will work is quite different from that of a food buyer of a motel chain who telephones to request information about frozen meat dishes suitable for cooking in an infrared oven when the regular kitchen crew is off duty.

For these and similar problem situations a manager concerned with the decision-making process should know *who* will do the following: (1) sense and diagnose opportunities, (2) come up with creative alternatives, (3) make projections of probable results, and (4) meld separate projections into a component picture and select one alternative for positive action.

## SENSING AND DIAGNOSING NEEDS

In the diagnosis stage of rational decision-making, an individual starts with his own "felt need" and proceeds to look for causes and limits. But when many people are involved, we face serious risks that important opportunities will pass by unnoticed, or ills be detected too late. "Let purchasing worry about it" is all too easy.

Of course, many managment problems or opportunities will surface in normal operations. The control system (Part VI) flags significant deviations from the plan. A customer, supplier, or other outsider makes a request, as did the motel food buyer mentioned above. Or a conscientious operator or manager has an idea for improving the work he is doing. Some of these wheels will squeak louder than others, but at least the noise is there to be heard.

**discerning new opportunities**

Anticipating obstacles *before* they arise and sensing opportunities in the dynamic environment is more difficult. Managers, such as the president of Frosty Foods, certainly watch major developments, but they also need the help of a mechanism that is alert to all sorts of developments.

*Sensing-units*  Because employees ordinarily give their chief attention to facts and ideas that directly relate to current problems, they often fail to report other facts and ideas to key executives. Perhaps the unreported information deals with a minor but nonetheless significant aspect of the work; perhaps it is an early warning of impending difficulties; or a lead to a great opportunity. Somehow, someone in the communication network

*Figure 9.1* Companies, like nations, must scan their environment to detect threats and opportunities.

should recognize the significance of this bit of information and tell the appropriate executive about it.

To search out just such information, we may assign a person—or perhaps a research unit. He may watch consumer behavior, new patents, employee complaints, proposed legislation, or some other special area. Although he will probably be overimpressed with the significance of his specialty, his purpose is to call attention to valuable information that might go unnoticed.[5]

*Interest-group representatives*   Government agencies, especially, often provide a clear avenue for representatives of various interest groups (labor, small business, environmental protection, and so on) to present information and suggestions. These communication devices bypass the points of routine contact; they enable stimuli from the fringe of the complex to reach decision centers with maximum speed and minimum distortion.

It is hard to keep formal interest-group representation and sensing units alert. After a time they, like managers, tend to accept established institutions and to think in terms of modest changes. Yet we very much need some mechanism to help keep the enterprise relevant to its shifting social, technological, and economic setting. The formal organization is not enough; it must be staffed with perceptive, constructive people.

[5]H. Aldrich and D. Herker, "Boundary Spanning Roles and Organization Structure," *Academy of Management Review*, 2 (1977), 217–30.

Even with such sensing-units, information has to reach someone who perceives its significance, and many bits and pieces of data bear no label as to their relevance. In fact, much information does not flow freely for two reasons.

1. Experience and experiments have shown that people are poor transmitters of ideas. We know, for example, that people who witness the same automobile accident describe it differently. If these descriptions are later passed on orally from Pete to Karen to Joe, the chances are slim that Joe will have an accurate picture of the accident. As information passes through additional intermediaries, the errors of transmission are compounded. Such decay in accuracy is found within businesses as well as outside.

2. Additional distortion occurs when a message passes up or down a channel of command. *Protective screening* tends to intervene between subordinate and superior. A subordinate is apt to tell his boss what the boss likes to hear and will omit or soften what is unpleasant. Perhaps, too, a subordinate will cover up his own weaknesses. We all adopt this procedure, at least mildly, in ordinary conversation with our friends; we do so even more when we talk to a person in a position of power. After two or three successive screenings of this sort, a report is likely to be considerably distorted. Messages coming down the channel are similarly screened. Each supervisor puts his own interpretation on a message, and probably withholds information that he feels his subordinates do not need to know.

The combined result of normal losses in transmission and protective screening is called *organizational distance*.[6] Workers removed from one another by several steps in an organization hierarchy are in serious danger of being estranged. It is difficult for one to know how another really feels and thinks. If they differ in experience, education, and outlook, the inadequacies of communication are further increased.

In face of the diffusion of potentially useful information and the normal communication barriers, we dare not assume that unusual and subtle problems will be recognized.[7] Here we have no predetermined controls nor insistent petitioners. Instead, if the opportunity or potential obstacle is to be identified early, we need an "initiator"—a person who (1) is exposed to the information cues, often through his own initiative, (2) perceives the significance of the cues to company plans and objectives, and (3) insists that careful consideration be given to the perceived problem. An initiator may be a manager or a staff person who has been assigned the duty of discovering problems; or he may be an alert member of the organization with ability to "sense" problems. Rarely is it wise for a manager to rely entirely on himself for this elusive work; so in his staffing (see Chapter 14) he should seek at least a sprinkling of people with this initiating flair.

[6]G. C. Athanassiades, "The Distortion of Upward Communication in Hierarchical Organizations," *Academy of Management Journal*, 16, no. 2 (June 1973), 207–26.

[7]J. D. Thompson, *Organizations in Action* (New York: McGraw-Hill, 1967), pp. 66–79.

Spotting a potential problem is only the start of the diagnosis. Defining the problem in terms of a gap, identifying causes and obstacles, and establishing limits within which a solution must fall—all need attention (as we saw in Chapter 6). Who in the organization performs this part of the diagnosis?

*Complex problems*  For complex and unique problems several people should participate in the diagnosis. The initiator, the manager or managers whose sphere of activities will be affected, and perhaps several other experts or investigators can all contribute. For example, the president of Frosty Foods needs more information about the "fast-food" business: critical factors for success, capital requirements, food-buying practices, and so on. A staff person can dig up this information. The maximum size of an appropriate merger partner should be discussed with the treasurer; the effect of the merger on company sales to other chains should be gone over with the sales manager; antitrust issues, with the company's attorney; and impact on management motivation, with the chairman. These early discussions are very tentative; the whole idea is still very fluid. Actually the discussion will undoubtedly slide over to specific alternatives and rough projections of results, but the main purpose is to sharpen the concept of what is desired and to identify major obstacles early. The whole idea may be dropped at any stage if the prospects for success look dim.

Participation by a number of people serves several purposes. The initiator is needed for his insights and also to keep the idea alive. The experts consulted help clarify the objective and are the major source of information on obstacles. Starting with the premise that the new venture is compatible with company strategy, operating executives define acceptable limits. As we noted in Chapter 6, the senior executive involved shapes the breadth of the study by stipulating how far it should go up the means-end chain and by deciding which company policies are to be regarded as constraints.

At this stage a manager has an exceptional opportunity to guide his organization. He can easily encourage or discourage creative planning in areas he selects. Having endorsed a direction in which a search for improvement should move, he can resort to management by objectives. He can create enthusiasm by having key people participate actively in the formative phases of planning. Because of all these factors, a manager should play an active part in this phase of decision-making and should become as involved here as he does in making the final choice.

*Simple problems*  Diagnosing the more customary and simple case of the motel buyer who requests information on food for off-hours service involves a very different process. The initiator—the buyer—is an outsider. His request is specific and most if not all of the response comes from established decision guides. If Frosty Foods normally carries products that fit the inquiry, the company has only to convince the buyer that he should deal with Frosty Foods; after this, agreement on price and delivery can be sought. Even if the buyer wants a variation from stock items, the problem can be immediately narrowed by company policy toward special orders.

Such simple diagnosis is possible because a whole set of policies and procedures have been designed to resolve promptly just this kind of problem. Obviously if Frosty Foods had just opened its doors and had no standard array of products, product specifications, or sales policies, the inquiry would precipitate a great deal of diagnosis and problem-solving. However, the planning structure, described in Chapter 4, is formulated for the express purpose of avoiding the need for much diagnosis of single transactions. In advance of the specific request, decisions have been made that cover a whole series of similar situations.

*To summarize:* The main questions a manager must answer when thinking about how diagnosis occurs in his organization are these. (1) What provision should he make for scanning both the external environment and internal operation to detect future opportunities and problems? (2) How can he minimize the effect of "organizational distance," so that cues once discovered do not get lost? (3) Who should participate in completing the diagnosis and in revising it as the decision-making process evolves? (4) What role should previously established plans play in simplifying and expediting diagnoses?

The two Frosty Foods illustrations make clear that no single set of answers can be given to these questions. Companies vary in the number of unique and complex problems they face, and so do departments within companies. The provisions for diagnosis should reflect this variation. Even in this first stage of decision-making, we see the benefits and complexities that arise from having several different people participate.

## SOURCES OF FRESH IDEAS

Finding good alternatives is the second basic stage in rational decision-making. Here we certainly expect an organization of many people to have many more good ideas than a single individual. Nevertheless, special arrangements are necessary to stimulate and detect these bright ideas.

Sometimes acceptable alternatives emerge during the diagnosis stage. The people consulted about the problem also know what other firms are doing, and they add ideas of their own. In fact, the cue that triggered the recognition of a problem may have been an action taken by someone else—a proposal by a supplier, or a request by a client.

**relying on operating personnel**

Yet sooner or later, someone has to decide that searching for additional alternatives is not worth the trouble. This decision is often made promptly. When at least one satisfactory alternative is at hand, the person who suggests further search is given the burden of explaining why he thinks a better way might be uncovered.

This tendency to end a search for alternatives too early leads a few wise managers to insist always on serious consideration of at least four alternatives. Such a rule of thumb does not ensure a careful search, but it does avoid the tempting simplicity of an *either* A *or* B formulation. Another tack is to invite suggestions from all key people who would be affected by the contemplated change. Too often this is really an early move to prepare them for an imminent change, and proposals submitted are brushed aside as biased or as ploys to avoid the inevitable. Nevertheless, several fairly good alternatives can often be assembled promptly from such key people.

**separate creative units**

What happens when no acceptable alternative bubbles to the surface? The constraints built into the diagnosis (capital, ownership, time, impact on community, and so on) or a tough obstacle may eliminate all the obvious courses of action. We then turn to creativity.

When the need for creative ideas is predictable and recurs in a known field, we organize to get fresh ideas. Product or process research in a pharmaceutical firm is an example. Specialists are hired and a laboratory is built to create a flow of new, useful drugs, typically within certain predetermined classes. The results are uncertain, but the approach is straightforward. Advertising agencies similarly hire experts to produce fresh themes. A variation occurs in new designs for women's dresses. Small firms often buy designs from an independent designer, but the approach still involves a specialist who creates alternatives for a predicted need. The researchers and creative people may share in short-run diagnosis, but they are primarily a separate group of specialists.

One drawback of relying on specialized people is the possibility of friction. Sharp differences in attitudes and values of personnel in sales and production are often a source of organizational conflict (see Chapter 17). The same type of conflict is often found between "creative guys" and "tough operators." The imaginative person who is ready to entertain all sorts of fanciful notions has an outlook that is very different from that of the operator who carefully distinguishes between fact and fiction, right and wrong, established practicality and daydreaming. Because of this contrast in orientation, we must anticipate friction when two such people are asked to collaborate. To minimize this difficulty, physical separation and relatively few interactions are probably desirable. On the other hand, if we choose to make different types learn to live together, we should use carefully supervised project teams whenever feasible.

**temporary assignment to produce ideas**

The use of specialists is unsuitable when the need for creative alternatives is irregular or unpredictable. Frosty Foods cannot afford to maintain a specialist on mergers with restaurant chains, even if such an expert could be located. Instead, people who have other jobs in the company must temporarily become creators of alternatives.

Conditions that foster creativity were discussed in Chapter 6. A permissive atmosphere, for instance, is conducive to a flow of fresh ideas. Note, however, that the need for alternatives to a unique problem is temporary. We may ask three or four individuals to be creative for a week or only a morning, after which they return to jobs where stress is on analysis and where supervisors tolerate no mistakes. Both the people and their supervisors are asked to shift attitudes and standards for only a brief period. Some of us have this flexibility, but a lot of sophistication about different styles of work is required.

Management consultants can be brought in if the problem is large enough to warrant the cost of the special arrangements. Consultants will have ready-made alternatives for only a few fairly standard problems. These advisors usually work with their client on the entire project—diagnosis, alternatives, projection, and choice—and their chief contribution is typically objective, undivided attention to the project and skill in digging out and arranging facts and ideas. Consultants provide ability much more than specific ideas, for the client personnel who work with them supply many of these. Therefore, company personnel work on a strange and temporary assignment as before; but in this case they are under the skillful guidance of the consultants.

Internal generation of creative alternatives for unique problems should therefore be assigned to people who have considerable flexibility, in addition to the required knowledge of the situation being studied.[8]

Most significant for successful use of any of these arrangements—relying on operating personnel, using separate creative units, or making temporary assignments—is recognition that the mental attitude and surrounding support needed for creativity differs sharply from that needed for projection and choice.

## CONSOLIDATING PROJECTIONS OF RESULTS

What would happen if we follow alternative A? If we follow alternative B? We should predict results for each alternative.

When such projections are made in an organization, people from many departments normally help make them. Also, as we noted at the beginning of this chapter, one forecast often becomes the planning premise of a related forecast; thus a whole succession of estimates may be interdependent. This ability to tap the understanding and judgment of a variety of specialists is a great strength, because it allows organizations to deal intelligently with complex issues that are far beyond the comprehension of a single individual.

The use of different specialists to make projections, however, is not an unmixed blessing. The very fact that each of several individuals contributes a piece of the total picture poses some unique difficulties in consolidating the pieces. We need to appreciate these difficulties and understand what we can do about them, in order to grasp fully the potential benefits to be gained from group projection of results.

All the estimates used in decision-making deal with the future, and all involve some uncertainty. Future sales, for instance, depend on a host of unknowns—competitors' actions, consumer reaction to our tie-in advertising, health of our sales manager, a civil-rights boycott, and the like. When our sales manager makes an estimate of sales for the next five years, he

*"absorbing" uncertainty*

---

[8]*Synectics*—discussed in Chapter 6—is an exception. With this technique only one or two participants have to be qualified to build bridges from fresh ideas to the actual situation.

might hedge his answer with a lot of "ifs"—*if* competitors cut prices by five percent, *if* the advertising plan really clicks, *if* everyone is healthy, *then* sales will probably be around four million or maybe five million.

Such an answer is quite unsatisfactory for the engineer. He says, "I don't have time to guess whether your advertising campaign is any good. Just tell me how much you want, because I have plenty of problems of my own." He prefers a single figure, or at most a narrow range. So the sales manager makes the best guess he can, realizing that his figure may not be accurate. If he is a conservative individual (or experience has taught him that he gets into less trouble when his estimates are low), he picks a low volume. Or, if he is optimistic, does not mind taking a risk, and wants to impress the boss, he picks a higher volume. In any event, he "absorbs" a lot of uncertainty when he finally tells the engineer to assume that sales will be, say, four and a half million.

The engineer is in a similar predicament. Will the refrigeration pumps break down in the near future? Can quality be maintained if a new product line is added? How long will it take to make a changeover to new raw material? And so forth. Again, we do not want an answer full of "ifs." Instead, we ask the engineer to use his judgment, which means that he absorbs uncertainty about a group of factors. Virtually everyone else who provides estimates used in our projection for expanded production will likewise absorb uncertainty.

Such uncertainty absorption is inevitable and desirable.[9] Without it the analysis of problems becomes hopelessly complex. If we attempted to give attention to all the possibilities as one estimate is built on another, the number of possible outcomes would increase at a geometric rate and would soon become incomprehensible. So we accept uncertainty absorption, but try to minimize its dangers.

**recognizing the bias of estimates**

Whenever we depend upon an estimate prepared by someone else, we naturally want to know whether it is reliable. We want to know whether it is optimistic or pessimistic. We want to know of any bias, especially when we are aware that a particular individual has absorbed a lot of uncertainty in a prediction that is used in other estimates.

Bias of some sort is almost inevitable in a set of projections made by different people. Here are four common reasons why one person's projections of results may not be just what the decision-maker needs.

1. *Differences in the perception of objectives.* A manager who is making a decision may have different objectives from the people who are giving him advice.[10] This is most likely when the advisors have strong, professional indoctrination, as in accounting, law, social work, and, to a lesser extent, engineering. The advice and other help such people provide may be strongly influenced by what they believe to be important. If a decision-maker is trying to achieve different objectives, the

[9] R. M. Cyert and J. G. March, *op. cit.*

[10] A. D. Szilagyi, Jr., and M. J. Wallace, Jr., *Organizational Behavior and Performance* (Santa Monica, CA: Goodyear, 1980), pp. 72–77.

sympathetic help he is expecting may turn out to be suggestions leading off on a tangent. The help may still be of some value, but he has to make allowances for its source.

Difference in objectives was found to be an important factor in a study of seventy-four companies' decisions on the use of outside contractors for maintenance work. The study showed that senior executives place high value on stable union relations, whereas maintenance superintendents give greater weight to keeping their costs low and to the number of their employees who might be laid off. We cannot tell from the available information which objectives deserve priority, but clearly the difference in objectives affects the way the two leadership groups respond to this problem.

2. *The "persuasive" advisor.* People vary in their persuasive ability, and it is entirely possible that a person who is making a projection will be unduly swayed by the counsel he receives from an impressive advisor. A review of the role of business economists in twenty firms revealed that the use made of economic forecasts was significantly influenced by personal feeling toward the company economist and by how well he "sold" his conclusions.

Status and company politics are factors here, as well as manner of speech. The treasurer of a food chain served as chairman of its capital-expenditures committee, and his views carried heavy weight in decisions on which division received the largest share of capital for expansion. Partly because of his "power," his recommendations on other matters were seldom challenged. Such influence, again, makes it difficult to reach completely objective decisions.[11]

3. *Special pressure.* Informal groups have a strong influence on the values, beliefs, and socially acceptable actions of their members. All of us are members of several such groups, and we take part of our counsel from these unofficial sources as well as from the advisors and information centers provided in the formal organization. Informal groups, particularly among executives, may strongly support official company objectives and plans—but not necessarily. When we base our planning on numerous personal interchanges, we must be prepared for this reality: social relations cannot be prescribed by an organization manual.

4. *Personal needs.* The aspirations and beliefs, as well as the sweet or bitter experience, of a person making a projection affect his response to the array of help provided by an organization. To be sure, supervisory review keeps reminding the advisor of company objectives and other basic "premises." Nevertheless, there is still room for personal bias to affect the predictions the advisor makes. The fallibility of human nature is simply another source of conflict to bear in mind as we contemplate the organization as a machine for making plans.

When several different projections have to be consolidated, as is necessary to appraise expansion alternatives open to Frosty Foods, the cumulative effect of bias can be substantial.

Faced with uncertainty absorption and likely bias in the estimates he receives from his expert advisors, what can the manager who makes the final choice among alternatives do? He wants to achieve key objectives, and he will be accountable for results; yet he is aware that the projections on which he bases his choice are synthetic and questionable.

**credibility structure**

---

[11]R. Miles, *Macro Organizational Behavior* (Santa Monica, CA: Goodyear, 1980), pp. 132–34.

*Identify reliable projectors*    Among the various people who analyze alternatives and predict outcomes, a few stand out as those whose conclusions can be relied upon. "If Jeanne says it will work, that's good enough for me." "No one really knows for sure, but I'll bet on Philip's estimate." These are highly subjective judgments about specific people. This is the way the manager who has to make the final decision feels about participants in the decision-making process. The "reliable" person might be disliked or perhaps is ineffective in other kinds of work, but his opinion is respected.

Usually we regard a person as reliable on a particular subject, not on everything. One individual has a good feel for labor relations, another for European economic developments, someone else for production feasibility, and so on. One person may possess keen technical insight, whereas another keeps divergent trends in good balance.

Among the qualities that inspire confidence are: knowledge of relevant facts; integrity (not saying things to manipulate other people); sensitivity to a broad range of influences; capacity to visualize change, but not be carried away with one possibility; willingness to accept a given premise and use it as a basis for further thought. A capacity to explain why his projections differ from others is helpful but not essential.

No list of personal qualities, however, substitutes for the judgment of the final decision-maker concerning those on whom he can rely for different kinds of inputs. S. L. Andersen of the Du Pont Company calls this array of dependable advisors the "credibility structure."[12] It is built on an assessment of persons, not on written job descriptions.

*Distinguish credibility structure from formal organization*    A widely held role concept is that the administrative head of a unit (1) provides the official opinions of activities within the scope of the unit, or at least (2) reviews, amends, and communicates the business opinions of anyone within his unit. More specifically, the concept holds that the head of the marketing division makes the official market projections, the chief engineer provides the official engineering projections, and so on. Each one normally consults with his subordinates and may authorize them to speak for his unit, but any projection coming from the unit is subject to the approval of its titular head.

The credibility structure may not agree with the concept just stated. In forecasting the results of a set of alternatives, a respected staff person may have views that differ from those of the operating executives. Perhaps the opinions of a subordinate carry more weight than those of his boss; or an outsider, such as a former division executive, may have the highest credibility. The reason for such a discrepancy between the credibility structure and the administrative organization is that assisting in making projections is only one, perhaps minor, part of the total job of a line manager. The sales manager, for instance, has to plan an annual campaign, maintain good relations with distributors, build and inspire his own sales force, cultivate key customers, exercise control over sales expense, and so on. The optimism,

---

[12]S. L. Andersen, "Venture Analysis," Presentation to the Columbia University Executive Program in Business Administration, August 1969, Arden House, Harriman, New York.

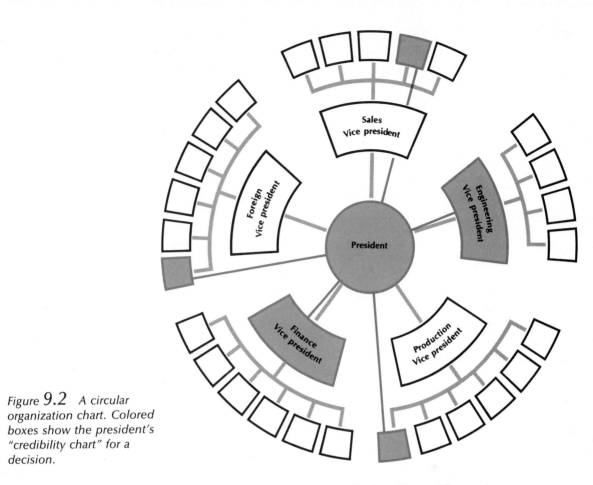

*Figure 9.2 A circular organization chart. Colored boxes show the president's "credibility chart" for a decision.*

enthusiasm, and drive needed for these duties may actually interfere with the objectivity and discernment that contribute to reliable projections. Similarly, a first-rate engineering manager may be a wizard at adapting present plants to variation in the product line, but this does not necessarily mean that he is qualified to predict the cost of building a small plant in New Zealand.

**Dealing with divergence** Strong operating executives have confidence in their own opinions. They do not relish the thought that another's projections are more highly regarded than their own. So when the credibility structure diverges from the administrative structure, we face a delicate relationship. Among the ways to sidestep this kind of embarassment are these.

1. Point out not only the importance but also the difficulty of making a reliable projection in the manager's area; it will follow then that this is one area where expert outside judgment is warranted.
2. If necessary to maintain morale, carry forward two sets of projections, one based on the executive premise and one on the more reliable premise of another person; the difference will be submerged in the total balance.

The important point is never to lose sight of the confidence that can be attached to the projections being consolidated into the final balancing of alternatives.

*Approval of premises*    When one projection becomes the basis of successive estimates, the manager making the final choice may try to control the premises that are fed into the process at early stages. Unless he has confidence in the sales estimates upon which production forecasts are based or in the engineer's reassurance that ecology issues will cause no delay, the entire exercise may have little value. To avoid such fruitless effort, the decision-maker can insist upon his review and approval of conclusions that become premises for the next set of projections.

Control of this sort also may be necessary if a person in the midst of the estimating process finds that he lacks confidence in the premises given to him; in this case he privately makes his own corrections. For instance, if a production manager says, "I know those sales estimates are always twenty-five percent too high" or "The engineers never turn loose a new product when they say they will," and then bases his estimates on a less ambitious assumption, the consolidated projections are not internally consistent. A review and approval of premises at key stages should reduce this need for hidden adjustments. Here again, the control of premises seeks to keep the successive projections in line with the credibility structure.

The whole issue of credibility structure relates especially to complex, unique decisions. For simpler, repetitive decisions the future results of various actions are better known, and there is less use of dubious premises for successive estimates. At Frosty Foods, the credibility structure is highly significant when projecting different merger alternatives; but for the motel inquiry the projections are more reliable and bias is more easily assessed.

**analysis of risk**

In a projection, greater unpredictability can surround some points more than others. For example, in a massive sewage-disposal experiment in western Michigan, the rate of biological decomposition affects the feasibility of the entire scheme, whereas the cost of building a dam can change the total capital outlay by less than one percent. Both events are less than certain, but the risk related to the speed of decomposition is critical because (1) the *range* of possible results is wide—from very slow to fast— and (2) the *effect of variations* will determine the capacity of the entire system. In contrast, building costs of the dam are unlikely to deviate by more than twenty-five percent, and even if they do, this variation has repercussions on only a few aspects of the total venture.

Risk analysis identifies the critical events in a projection—the decomposition rate in the previous example. These points can be identified by careful thought, as was possible for the multimillion-dollar project just cited. If a mathematical model has been prepared to assist in the projection, the critical risk points can be derived from the model.[13]

---

[13]D. B. Hertz, "Risk Analysis in Capital Investment," *Harvard Business Review,* 57, no. 5 (September–October 1979), 169–81.

Having spotted the critical unknowns, a manager can: (1) give close personal attention to the forecasts made for these factors and can probably personally approve premises about these factors; (2) provide for later rechecking as better evidence becomes available; and/or (3) make multiple projections using two or more points on the range. By concentrating only on critical events, multiple projections may become technically feasible.

Most of the objectives of making projections in organizations apply especially to complex, unique problems. To the extent that we can simplify such problems by dividing them into parts and by making the parts less unique, we reduce these difficulties. As noted in Chapters 3 through 5, a company planning structure does just that.

**stabilizing projections**

Explicit difficulties and subobjectives tend to remove bias arising from bureaucratic maneuvering. Policies, standing operating procedures, and standard methods help establish a customary way of dealing with problems. This customary practice provides a historical basis upon which to base projections and creates a stabilized environment in which predictions are more accurate. In addition, consolidation of estimates is easier when each person preparing an estimate visualizes the same consistent manner of operation. These benefits of structured planning were carefully examined in Part II.

*To summarize:* The underlying process of projecting the probable results of different alternatives was explored in Chapter 7. In this chapter we placed that process in an organizational setting. Within an organization a wide variety of expert talent can be drawn upon to round out the projections. Inevitably, we must face uncertainty absorption and biased estimates, but we can reduce the undesirable effects of these factors by recognizing and utilizing the credibility structure, employing risk analysis, and creating a stabilized setting for the projected activities.

## OFFICIAL CHOICES OF THE ORGANIZATION

The final act in decision-making, which follows diagnosis, identification of alternatives, and projection of results for each alternative, is choice of the one alternative to be followed. In organization decision-making, the formal organization design designates who makes this choice.

Fruitless arguments can be held on who *really* makes the decision. Many people may affect the way a problem is formulated or decide which alternatives should receive consideration or which consequences should be forecast. They may influence the values used by the decision-maker in his choice and may block effective execution so that a new decision must be made. But influence is not the official act. In every organized effort, we need a mechanism for decisiveness. If action is to proceed effectively, an official stamp of approval must be provided.

The authority to make decisions, select one alternative and give it official sanction, may be delegated, as we shall see in Chapter 11. The delegation may be surrounded with limitations on scope or with policy constraints. Perhaps decisions will require the endorsement of other executives.

Nevertheless, we continue to look to the formal organization for information on who makes the final choice.

Because the final choice is made in an organizational context rather than by an isolated individual, the decision-maker makes his choices by using a set of values quite different from those that would govern simply a *personal* preference. He is strongly guided (1) by company strategy, departmental objectives, company traditions and norms, and other institutional values; (2) by the company incentive and control system as related to him; and (3) by company politics growing out of conflict within the organization.

## CONCLUSION

When we superimpose the rational decision-making model over the formal organization design, we see that each element—diagnosis, search, projection, and choice—can indeed be carried out in a typical organization. However, bringing to bear the full potential strength of the organization on each element calls for special managerial attention. Clearcut provisions are needed to flag new opportunities, to encourage creative suggestions, to watch for biased estimates, and to clarify who has the authority to make the final choice.

Several new concepts aid in securing rational decisions—sensing units, initiators, uncertainty absorption, credibility structure, and risk analysis.

Even more significant is the cost to the company of making an important, unique decision within its organization. All those involved in the decision use valuable time becoming oriented and making their contribution. In addition, managers must coordinate the many efforts, keep attention focused on dominant objectives, communicate back and forth as the decision evolves, know how uncertainty is resolved, maintain consistency with related decisions, get action before it is too late—all of which absorbs even more effort. Clearly, all decisions made in an active enterprise do not warrant such costs (just as an individual cannot take time to make all his decisions rationally).

Instead, we need simplifying mechanisms that enable the organization to approach the ideal of rational decision-making but do not entail such high costs. We must provide the organization with the type of planning system described in Part I. Such a system encourages consistent and persistent effort, timely action, efficient use of resources, morale among the members—and does all this with a bearable input of managerial time.

## FOR FURTHER DISCUSSION

1. In what ways may increased formalization of the strategic planning process, at the top levels of an organization, affect middle-level managers' ability to sense and diagnose needs?

2. How will the large increase in the number of women entering middle management affect organizational decision-making?

3. A product manager of a food company explained that all major decisions on the group of breakfast foods she was "responsible" for were made not by her but by a product-management committee. She was chairman of the committee, which included the vice-presidents in charge of production,

sales, and research. What advantages do you see to such an arrangement? What potential drawbacks?

4. "One way to increase the soundness of key figures on which I must base decisions is to insist that those who furnish the figures state in writing the assumptions, premises, and techniques used to arrive at them. Although I don't have the time, and in some cases the background, to verify these assumptions, I keep them on file to help sort out reasons for mistakes." What do you think of this approach as described by a vice-president of marketing?

5. "True creativity in organizational decision-making can only be achieved by using outsiders who are protected from political and cultural pressures."

   "True creativity in organiza-

tional decision-making can only be generated by insiders who understand the political and cultural elements of the organization."

   Which statement do you agree with? Discuss.

6. What suggestions can you offer for reducing the negative impact of differences in values placed on the same objectives by participants in a decision? To what extent may these differences prove beneficial? Relate your answers to the material in Part II.

7. What would be the advantages and disadvantages of formalizing the "credibility structure" and printing it along with formal organizational charts?

8. How may the existence of many detailed standing plans affect decision-making in an enterprise?

## CASES

For cases involving issues covered in this chapter, see especially the following. Particularly relevant questions are listed after each case.

Benjo Associates (p. 92), 9
Clifford Nelson (p. 192), 3, 7, 9, 22
Camden Chemical (p. 298), 5
Delphi Insurance (p. 369), 5, 6
Joan Carrier (p. 376), 5, 6
Netsuki Novelty Products Company (p. 451), 4

## FOR FURTHER READING

Allison, G. T., *Essence of Decision: Explaining the Cuban Missile Crisis.* Boston: Little, Brown, 1971, chaps. 3 and 4. Applies a model of the organizational decision-making process to the Cuban missile crisis.

Cyert, R. M. and J. G. March, *A Behavioral Theory of the Firm.* Englewood Cliffs, NJ: Prentice-Hall, 1963. Extends the economic theory of the firm to analysis of the decision-making process in the large, multiproduct firm.

Goldhaber, G., H. Dennis, III, G. R. Richetto, and O. A. Wiio. *Information Strategies: New Patterns to Corporate Power.* Englewood Cliffs, NJ: Prentice-Hall, 1979. Draws on empirical research to recommend managerial strategies for improving information processing, and decision-making in an organization.

Miles, R. H., *Macro Organization Behavior.* Santa Monica: Goodyear, 1980, chap. 11. Good summary discussion of "boundary spanning" units and their role in relating the organization to the external environment.

Simon, H. A., *Administrative Behavior,* 3rd ed. New York: Free Press, 1976. Provides conceptual and theoretical insights into decision-making in organizations. This edition enlarges, but leaves intact, the now-classic formulation of the first edition in 1947.

The underlying steps in making a decision rationally are the same for all sorts of problems and situations. Diagnosis, search for alternatives, comparing courses of action, and choice based on values and uncertainty relate to not-for-profit activities just as much as to profit-seeking ventures. The critical difference arises in the values used in making choices. Multiple and ambiguous goals in not-for-profit enterprises also complicate diagnosis and comparison of courses of action. In diagnosis the limits on acceptable solutions are more difficult to establish, and in comparing alternatives, just which consequences should be carefully projected is unclear. Nevertheless, the crux of the difference between rational decision-making in profit-seeking and not-for-profit enterprises lies in the values used in the final stage of choice. If these key values are established, they can easily be introduced into the earlier phases of the rational model.

In principle, a person making a rational choice in a not-for-profit venture simply derives his values from the service mission of the venture through a means-end chain. In practice, the selection of appropriate values is often complicated. Several factors are likely to add complications.

1. *Divergent goals* often exist within a not-for-profit enterprise. A nursery school, for instance, may aim at day care for children of working mothers, child socialization, a head start on the three R's, creative expression, psychological counsel, or just plain fun. A labor union—to cite a different example—has economic, political, and social goals. And the aims of particular professions within the enterprise may add to this array of goals. Consequently, a decision-maker in such an organization has no single criterion to use in choosing.

2. The concept of whole *sets of values* relating to various dimensions is characteristic of not-for-profit enterprises. Typically, as in nursery schools and unions, several kinds of results are desired simultaneously. There is no recognized priority among these goals, nor is there a common denominator (such as dollars in a profit-making firm) that enables a decision-maker to compare the incremental outputs of diverse results. So he must assess each prepared course of action in terms of several different values simultaneously.

3. Contributors of funds and other resources often have strong feelings about the goals an enterprise should pursue and about the degree of risk that is warranted. Thus, the conservative donor to a college may interject his values into the decision process. A decision-maker who is aware of these *external pressures* must weigh the likelihood and seriousness of antagonizing important resource contributors.

4. A further complication is that the consumer of the service provided—the student, hospital patient, concert-goer, and the like—is in a weaker position than the customer of a typical business firm. Customers of not-for-profit enterprises usually pay only a fraction of the service cost, and often there is a presumption that the producer knows best what the customer should receive. Such *reduced influence of customers* in a not-for-profit enterprise permits the diversity of values noted above to continue without a clear market check.

When we recognize these various influences, it is not surprising that the value pattern in not-for-profit enterprises is often vague and multidimensional. Values in profit-seeking firms are not nearly as simple as economic and mathematic models suggest; but long-run profit does serve as a theoretical basis for resolving conflicts. This convenient criterion is not available for the decision-maker in a not-for-profit venture.

Two main mechanisms are often used in not-for-profit enterprises to provide direction and priority. One is a *charismatic leader*. Especially in new ventures, a dynamic and forceful person often "calls the plays." He has personal convictions about the values to be used in decision-making; and he either has enough power to make important choices himself, or is so influential that his values are accepted by others who make decisions. Field studies indicate that a charismatic leader is even more vital to the success of a not-for-profit enterprise than is an outstanding entrepreneur for a profit-seeking firm.

Another way value conflicts are resolved is through a *mystique* that dominates the enterprise. We use the term "mystique" to describe a strong conviction about the importance of a particular service mission and the unusual capacity of the enterprise to provide that service. The Mayo Clinic, Ford Foundation, Rotary Club, and Red Cross all have an internationally recognized mystique, and many local not-for-profit ventures have a comparable tradition. The mystique establishes the enterprise in a respected role in society. For decision-making it defines the values they are expected to follow.

A charismatic leader and/or a widely accepted mystique help make rational decisions possible by endorsing a particular set of values. With priority of goals known, the entire process of diagnosis–search–projection–choice can be accomplished on a rational basis in profit-seeking and not-for-profit firms alike. But if a charismatic leader or accepted mystique is lacking, rational decision-making in most not-for-profit enterprises is virtually impossible. Instead, decision-making by some kind of consensus, often based on politics, becomes dominant.

CASE 2.1
*MIKE ZERLLINI*

Mike Zerllini put down the letter he had just finished reading for a third time.

"Well," he said, "that's one thing about free advice; you always get your money's worth."

The six page letter was from a friend and former associate of Mike's, Jack Gang. Mike and Jack had worked together for L. P. Harvestvale, a large, prestigious retail chain in California. Both started in sales, moved into buying, and later into merchandising for Harvestvale. Two years ago Gang, a Chinese-American, left to join two brothers who had developed a successful trading company in Hong Kong.

Approximately five months ago, Zerllini took a leave of absence from Harvestvale to join a new venture begun a year ago.

"I was going to resign," he said, "but the personnel director at Harvestvale talked me into the leave of absence. They apparently think very highly of me and felt that if my business venture didn't work out, they could still use me. At the time, I wasn't keen on the leave. I figured that if I was going to try this scheme, I should cut my ties or I wouldn't really give it my full effort. Now, I guess, I'm glad I took the leave since I probably should go back to Harvestvale."

The venture Mike joined five months ago began as a limited partnership set up to publicize and sell merchandise bought in the People's Republic of China.

"A wealthy couple (husband and wife) from L. A., the Coopers," Mike explained, "were really into Chinese art and furnishings. As soon as things opened up with mainland China—I'm sorry, P. R. C.—they went over and not only did a lot of sightseeing but lined up a deal to bring in rugs, jewelry, silk flowers, lots of jade, gold and silver pieces, and other furnishings.

"They got a bank and a few friends to join them in putting up the money and brought in almost $8 million in merchandise. At least that's what they say they paid for it. They ran a few exhibitions in San Diego, L. A., San Francisco, and Seattle and sold some of the most expensive items to dealers, collectors, and even a couple of museums. Apparently they knew their stuff, particularly with regard to jade and gold. They hoped the publicity would allow them to then sell the rest of their goods to retailers and large jobbers. Well, it didn't happen.

"I first heard of them at Harvestvale's and bought some of their Peking rugs and silk flowers. We priced them high, sold some, then moved most of the rest at forty percent off and still had a sixty to seventy percent margin.

"For some reason, however, the Coopers have had trouble with the rest of their goods. Two friends of mine, Bill and Lenore Stern, had met the

Coopers socially and heard of their venture. The Sterns have a very fine antique store in Santa Barbara and bought a few old pieces from the Coopers and talked about how to move the remaining inventory. Then they called me and we worked out a deal."

The Coopers indicated that they did not wish to be involved any longer with the sale of the remaining merchandise and that they would sell it to an intermediary if they could at least break even. They had made a good profit on what had already been sold, but this represented only a third of the dollar value of their purchases. The remaining two-thirds was in a warehouse in San Francisco and nothing had been sold for several months as the Coopers sought a bulk buyer willing to pay $6.3 million or more for the lot. This is what the Coopers figured the value of the merchandise was when they added insurance, storage, and interest charges to their original purchase price.

It was costing them over $100,000 a month to hold the merchandise; their partners had soured, and the banks wanted a plan or their money. At this point, the Coopers were introduced to Zerllini by the Sterns and Mike was brought in to move the merchandise.

"They offered me a base salary of $2,000 a month," Zerllini said, "and agreed to set me up in an office with a secretary and bookkeeper. Since my salary at Harvestvale was $42,500 a year, we worked out a profit-sharing scheme. At Harvestvale, I could earn anywhere from zero to fifty percent bonus, but for the past few years it had averaged around twenty percent or $8,000–$10,000. Thus, if I'd stayed on I probably would have made $50,000–$55,000 this year.

"The deal with the Coopers was that we would fix the inventory value and add ten percent to it to cover their costs for six months. Then, I would get ten percent of every dollar received over this amount. We figured it might take six more months to move the material and when we saw signs that it would start moving, they would go back to China and buy more.

"I would accompany them on the buying trip and be in for twenty-five percent of the profits on any new merchandise. The deal looked good. It was a chance to make it on my own and I figured even if it didn't work out, it would be a good experience. Now, I don't know what to do."

Zerllini and the Coopers' accountant had reviewed the goods in inventory, using several outside appraisers to determine its value. After much debate, the value was set at $6.8 million based on purchase price and costs of duty, shipping, storage and carrying charges already incurred. This meant that with the ten percent add-on Mike had agreed to for his profit-sharing, the merchandise would have to be sold for more than $7.48 million for him to earn a bonus.

"I estimated we could sell the goods for *at least* $8.5 million, so I would earn another $100,000 beyond my base salary for six months' work. Then, on the next batch of goods, I could make a fortune. Well, it just did not work out. The warehouse where they have their inventory is a mess. Security stinks! A number of gold and silver figurines were sitting in crates in an unsecured area. Rugs worth several thousand apiece were stacked like cordwood. Heaven knows what their theft and damage losses will be. They listened to some of my suggestions but I have no authority over the warehouse operation. Their accountant is supposed to oversee it. The more I see of how they run things, the less I like it. The Coopers are nice folks, but lousy business people. Frankly, I think they are in this for a lark, and to finance their hobby and trips to China.

After five months, Mike has sold only half of the inventory for receipts of $4.2 million. Sales proved harder to make than he anticipated and the Coopers were displeased. Mike feels that he was beginning to get into the swing of things and estimates that he could move the remaining merchandise for close to $4.5 million in less than four months.

The Coopers are impatient, however. They are not convinced that Mike can sell the remaining goods in the time or at the revenue level he promises. They have suggested three options to him. Mike might:

1. Resign immediately and receive one month's salary as separation pay.
2. Spend the next month seeking a single buyer to purchase the remaining inventory. The Coopers' accountant feels this inventory now represents a $3,750,000 investment. Mike would receive fifty percent of the proceeds beyond this figure. The Coopers would then end their participation. If no sale was made in 30 days, Mike would be terminated with no additional pay.
3. Purchase within 30 days at least twenty-five percent of the inventory for $937,500, add $62,500 to working capital, and own twenty-five percent of the business. He would then participate, as president, with the Coopers in future deals.

Mike indicates that he might be able to raise a million through friends, loans, etc., but that it would be very difficult in the one month the Coopers have given him. He communicated these facts to his friend, Jack Gang, by letter.

"The purpose of the letter," Mike said, "was primarily to get Jack's advice but, to be honest, I was hoping he might exhibit some interest as a silent partner."

Jack's letter in response began and ended with the same sentence: "This is a very interesting deal, Mike, but my advice is to look for the answer someplace other than in the numbers." Between this opening and closing thought were five and one-half pages of Jack's analysis and suggestions on how to approach the problem. It contained no specific recommendation and no offer by Jack to participate. In several places, however, Jack used the phrase, "I cannot tell how you may value this, but to be of interest to me it would have to exceed . . ."

Mike could not tell if this was a hint of interest on Jack's part or just a way of illustrating the subjectivity of many estimates and what Jack referred to as "opportunity costs." Mike was to meet with several friends and prospective partners the next day and had appointments with representatives of four banks who had indicated a willingness to discuss the situation.

"The Coopers offered me three deals," he said, "but perhaps they would be open to a counter-offer. After I get a feel for what kind of money I might raise, then I will go down to L. A. and meet with them and see if we can't work something out."

## FOR DISCUSSION AND REPORT-WRITING

1. Would the articulation of a clearcut strategy have helped Zerllini decide which option to take at the end of the case? Would it help him develop plans for selling the remaining goods?

2. Would standing plans be useful for a small venture such as this one? What kinds of plans? Why?

*part I: planning: the execution of strategy*

3. How would Zerllini's higher-level goals affect his decision on which offer to pursue?

4. How do you interpret Gang's comment about the decision not really being a function of the numbers? Do you agree?

5. Try to develop at least one additional, creative alternative for Zerllini to counter-propose.

6. What are the most crucial factors for Zerllini to concentrate on in making a choice?

7. How should Zerllini deal with the uncertainties affecting his choice?

8. (Summary Report Question, Part Two) Develop a payoff matrix which would be helpful to Zerllini in first narrowing alternatives and then making the choice.

*part II: planning: elements of rational decision-making*

9. Indicate what the implications on organization structure are for each of Zerllini's current options.

10. If Zerllini becomes a full partner with the Coopers, what authority should he insist on? What should he seek, but be willing to back off on? Explain.

*part III: organizing: strategy to structure*

11. How many differences in the motivation of Zerllini and the Coopers *contribute to* or *detract from* their working together effectively in the future?

12. How might techniques for motivating the person in charge of the warehouse differ from techniques used to motivate someone Zerllini hires to help him sell to small gift shops?

*part IV: motivating: human factors in the organization*

13. What communication barriers are likely to develop between Zerllini and the Coopers in a new joint venture? How may these barriers be overcome?

*part V: leading*

14. What the the key factors to consider in achieving personal leadership in a small organization such as one Zerllini might form if he continues collaborating with the Coopers?

15. Do the Coopers need compliance or commitment from Zerllini if they continue their collaboration on current merchandise? Why? What should they do to ensure the desired response from him?

**part VI:
controlling**

16. How might the Coopers have done a better job of "controlling" Zerllini in order to have a better idea of how good a job he has done for them?

17. How can controls be developed to help determine the degree to which results differed from standards because of environmental changes? Illustrate your answers with factors present in the case.

18. What will be the most crucial controls for Zerllini to establish with regard to warehouse operations, if he continues with this venture?

**summary question
for solution of the
case as a whole**

19. What course of action do you recommend that Zerllini take? Support your choice with both numerical and subjective reasons.

**CASE 2.2
CLIFFORD NELSON**

The Simmons Simulator Corporation[1] is the largest producer of process analysis equipment in the world. Since 1940, Simmons has been a leader in applying advances in data processing technology directly to the monitoring and active control of operating systems.

The company designs and manufactures three main product lines. Of these, the simulator line has been the most profitable for the company. Simmons simulators differ from computer-based simulators in that a Simmons simulator is a small-scale mock-up which physically reproduces the actual operating process, rather than mathematically modelling the process. However, simulator systems do utilize analytical computational capabilities as part of the total simulation process.

Simmons designs and manufactures control devices, instruments, and simulator components, but also purchases these and computer components from other companies. While Simmons holds some key patents, particularly in the simulator component and control device area, the major strength of the company, in attaining its position of market leadership, has been its capacity for developing total systems. Simmons' continued dominance of its industry has been based on a combination of technological innovation with a reputation for reliability and quality service. This combination of product leadership and client service has enabled Simmons to grow rapidly in both

[1] Other Simmons Simulator cases appear in Chapter 28 of W. H. Newman & E. K. Warren, *The Process of Management*, 4th ed. (Englewood Cliffs, NJ: Prentice-Hall, 1977) and as a case simulation developed by T. P. Ference, I. C. MacMillan, and W. Benson.

size, market penetration, and profitability; in the last fiscal year, Simmons realized profits of 600 million dollars on total sales of approximately 3 billion dollars.

H. J. Simmons and the Simmons philosophy

The company was founded in the late 1930s by H. J. Simmons. At the beginning of World War II, Mr. Simmons turned his attention to the development of effective means of controlling total production processes. He recognized the potential of electronic computers as high-speed analytical processors and began developing computer-assisted simulators. By coupling the computer technology with the simulator concept in his emphasis on total process control, Mr. Simmons was able to move his company to a dominant position in the total process control market in the early 1950s.

Simmons employees throughout the organization spoke warmly of Mr. Simmons, and with pride in their contribution to the organization. The "Simmons philosophy"—technical excellence, product innovation, customer service, and employee satisfaction and security—was a real factor in forming decisions and attitudes throughout the company. As Mr. Simmons stated at a recent annual meeting:

"As you know, the success that we have been fortunate enough to enjoy at Simmons has been based on our continued adherence to two basic tenets of good management. (1) The highest purpose of business is to produce quality products to serve today's needs and to be prepared with quality products for tomorrow's needs when they emerge. (2) A Simmons product is a Simmons product while it is being manufactured, when it is sold, and for as long as it is in use by the customer.

"Thus, we will continue to forego short-run profits in the interest of continued investment in product development and product excellence; we will continue to rest our name and reputation on the provision of quality service for all Simmons products at all customer installations; and we will continue to attempt to insulate our employees from fluctuations in the economy or in the levels of business activity through the course of steady employment. We will also continue to honor our obligation to stockholders and to consolidate it through continued improvements in return on investments and realized profits achieved through diligent and demanding management."

the structure of Simmons Simulator Corporation

Although he is approaching 70, H. J. Simmons remains as chairman and president (Exhibit 1). Two executive vice-presidents and the corporate treasurer report directly to Mr. Simmons. One executive vice-president has all staff groups reporting to him. The other has the five operating divisions under him. The operating company is divided into five major divisions, each headed by a division president. The corporate staff is composed of five major groups, each headed by a vice-president. Mr. Simmons, the two executive vice-presidents, the treasurer, and chief counsel serve as the management

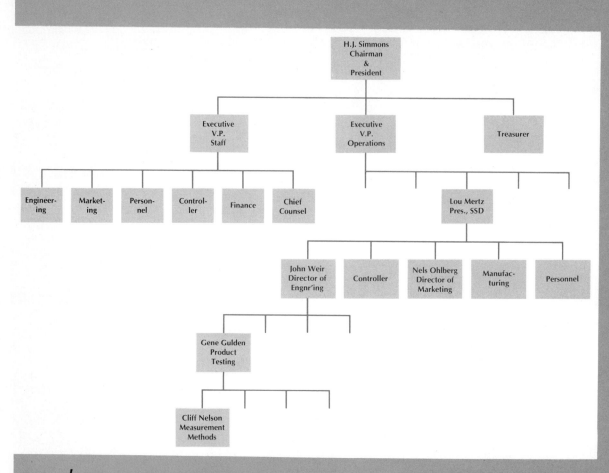

**EXHIBIT I** *PARTIAL ORGANIZATION CHART*

committee. As will be described below, the management committee is the primary mechanism for integrating corporate policy with divisional operations and for the review and approval of divisional operating plans.

The organizational structure reflects two major concerns. (1) The operating divisions have been established to reflect basic product/customer markets. Organizational policies and structure have been developed in an effort to allow divisional presidents maximum flexibility and freedom in day-to-day operations. (2) The corporate staff groups are small, and are intended to reflect technical expertise available to the executive group in determining policy directions and in monitoring the implementation of policy.

The corporate staff groups are located at corporate headquarters in Southern Connecticut. Divisional headquarters are scattered throughout the Northeast.

Corporate planning at Simmons is a combination of a two-year operating plan and a five-year strategic plan, each reviewed and updated annually at both the corporate and division level.

The corporate planning process at Simmons is a year-long effort, repeated annually, and therefore goes on continuously. At the beginning of each planning cycle, each division president receives a detailed statement of the overall strategic plan, and the objectives and needs established at the corporate level. This strategic plan includes an updating of performance against strategic objectives established in previous planning cycles; an identification of specific planning questions which each division is to consider in the present planning cycle; a description of the business environment for the coming year as estimated by the corporate staff; and an identification of special problem areas. The planning document also includes a review of established corporate policies, and, typically, a detailed set of questions and objectives aimed specifically at each of the operating divisions.

With the strategic planning mandate in hand, division management is required to produce an operating plan with three main components.

1. A two-year operating plan to be initiated at the end of the present operating year. This plan should contain, by the end of the planning cycle, projections of sales, costs, resource needs, and staffing plans for all programs, ongoing and new, for the two-year planning period. This two year operating plan should contain detailed responses to all strategic objectives and needs raised by the corporate planning guidelines; should be consistent with corporate resource constraints; and should incorporate all information available from corporate and divisional staff on economic conditions, competitor behavior, and technological developments. The planning process is intended to be an interactive one, reflecting continuous contact between division level planners and corporate staff experts; divisional management is expected to notify relevant corporate staff groups of its plans as they develop in order to elicit useful information, as well as possible instances of corporate nonconcurrence with the divisional plans. Division management is required to make a formal, preliminary submission of its plan to the corporate staff groups at least two months before final review of the plan. Finally, all divisional plans are presented for review and approval to the management committee in the fourth quarter of the planning cycle.

2. In addition to the two-year operating plan, each division is required to produce in each year's planning cycle a detailed, qualitative discussion in its program planning proposals of the opportunities and challenges it faces over the longer period of the five-year strategic plan.

3. Finally, division management is required to present in each planning cycle a detailed response to specific questions raised by the corporate planning guidelines.

Clifford Nelson is in charge of "Product Test: Measurement Methods," a section of the engineering department of SSD. Cliff has been with Simmons for three years, having joined them after completing an engineering degree. His job is to review all testing procedures used to determine whether products and components produced by SSD meet standards set for them.

"I don't determine the standards nor do I conduct the actual tests. My job" explained Nelson, "is to direct and coordinate a group of engineers who develop and evaluate testing procedures. Standards are set elsewhere for everything that has Simmons' name on it. My job is to see to it that we have tests which will assure the division president that those standards are met. It is a very challenging job and I have spent many nights burning the midnight oil working on a technical problem. Up until now I have always had my boss's support."

SSD, the largest of Simmons' divisions, recorded sales of $1.2 billion last year but saw profits challenged by numerous smaller competitors. None could offer the full range of systems and service offered by SSD but several made component elements which matched Simmons in quality and performance. Recently, SSD learned that several smaller companies had begun announcing components which were compatible with Simmons, and competitive systems. These components, which could increase substantially the productivity and flexibility of the total system, were to be available in about six months.

SSD has been working for almost eight years to develop a fully integrated system of its own to offer these features. Nels Ohlberg, division marketing director, stated: "We have the system almost ready to go. It will not only replace most of our existing Series G stuff but will knock out many competitors' ability to sell systems wired together with a hodge-podge of peripherals. Within a year or so, we can offer something better than anything available for less money."

Ohlberg has reason for grave concern. He learned that the new components being announced by competitors were gaining wide praise in the industry. He approached the division president, Lou Mertz, and told him that unless SSD announced its new system within thirty to sixty days, a substantial segment of the market would purchase these peripheral units and tie them into existing systems.

At roughly $100,000 to $150,000 each, these peripherals represent a sizeable investment to the purchasers. Ohlberg fears that once they have bought them and tied them in, they will not be able to justify immediate purchases of Simmons' new system.

"We have waited years to knock out those rag-tag systems made up of some of our equipment and lots of odds-and-ends," Ohlberg said. "At last, we are almost there. We can offer the market a fully integrated system with Simmons' name on it for only a bit more than the Rube Goldberg stuff they have now. If we don't announce, however, before they commit to these latest add-ons, we will face a market which will have to wait at least three or four years to write off their new investment. Our only other option would be to price our new system at levels which would not be profitable and even risk the Justice Department coming in and claiming unfair pricing. We stand to lose millions unless we announce what we have coming in the next two months."

Mertz, the division president, asked for a special report on the matter. All department heads except engineering agree an earlier announcement is needed. The head of manufacturing is certain from prototypes that he can produce what would be promised at costs currently estimated. The division personnel director fears that failure to announce could lead to major sales loss and threaten layoffs. The division controller confirms that not announcing in the next sixty days would cost the division millions in lost profits.

Engineering has indicated that they are confident the new system they have designed will pass all tests and can be produced in volume at cost and quality levels currently forecast.

"The only reservation I have," said John Weir, director of engineering, " is that several key components have not met final test standards and thus the whole system cannot be said to have passed final tests. Corporate has made it very clear in the past that they will not even look at a new product announcement until all final tests have been passed. Since this is a very important new system, standards have been set very high and our tests are designed to not only meet high confidence levels but they are layered in a manner that offers even higher degrees of certainty. If we use the tests as currently set up, it could be a year before standards are met. I have asked Cliff Nelson's boss, Gene Gulden (director of product test), to have him find a way around our dilemma."

Gulden made it clear to Nelson that everyone was counting on him. "Cliff is the best we have," Gulden said. "No one knows more about this area than he. At first he told me the problem could not be solved by changing the tests, but when I relayed this up the line I got blasted. Ohlberg was almost apoplectic.

"'No third-level technician is going to hold us up,' he bellowed. 'You tell that narrow-minded provincial jerk that if he can't see the big picture you'll find someone who will!' Of course, I had to tell Ohlberg not to give me orders; that I would handle my own people. But basically I agree with him. Cliff just wants to play it extra safe. If there are problems later, he is afraid he will be blamed. I have told him not to worry."

Cliff is worried nonetheless. He feels that he could alter certain tests and by shifting their sequence probably squeak through final tests in the time requested.

"But," he says, "we would be cutting all kinds of corners. Anyone looking at these changes compared to normal division practices would know we really twisted this one. My boss, Gene Gulden, has told me not to worry; that, while the division president said he wants to hear all sides of this issue, he knows he can't afford to be late. Therefore, they say no one will question our changes. I'm not sure. Normally, when all departments agree and the division plan meets corporate guidelines, it sails through corporate review. But what happens if corporate engineering staff or even legal get wind of this? They might not concur, and if they force debate I could be in trouble. I hate to seem like a narrow technician who can't see what is best for the division but, damn it, the tests they want would be shoddy and could easily be misleading even if applied rigorously."

## FOR DISCUSSION AND REPORT-WRITING

1. In what ways should major strategic decisions made at Simmons influence this decision on announcing the new system?

2. In what ways may standing plans prove to be important in dealing with this situation? What are their limitations or drawbacks?

3. Should this decision be escalated to the president or be resolved at the division level? Why?

4. Why might the "problem" on the announcement be stated differently by Nelson? Ohlberg? Mertz? Simmons? How would each state it?

5. Develop a means-end diagram which shows how one might *link up* the several problems as defined by Nelson, Ohlberg, Mertz, and Simmons.

6. From Nelson's perspective, is it more important for him to push toward root causes of his gap or move toward higher-level goals by asking "Why?" Explain.

7. What higher-level constraints need to be considered by the company? Which ones would not affect this decision if it were being made in a smaller company? How can H. J. Simmons be assured that higher-level constraints will be brought to bear on this decision?

8. In what ways may subjective probabilities be useful in making this decision? Who should estimate these probabilities?

9. (Summary Report Question, Part II) Assume you are H. J. Simmons. Using this case to illustrate your answer, indicate (a) the key steps that should be taken, (b) the people (management levels or positions) who should make the decision, and (c) the checks built into the system to ensure that this kind of decision is made well.

10. In what ways does Simmons' organization structure contribute toward making a decision in this case which is consistent with overall corporate strategy? In what ways may the structure detract from the decision being made in a corporate, strategic context?

11. Who should have what kinds of authority in making a decision on when to announce?

12. Discuss the role(s) that (a) division and (b) corporate staff should play in decisions such as this. What authority should each level have?

13. When or how would conflict be desirable (healthy) in this situation? When and how would it be destructive?

14. What should H. J. Simmons do to increase the chances of desirable conflict emerging and being resolved satisfactorily?

part IV: motivating: human factors in the organization

15. Should Ohlberg seek compliance or commitment from Nelson in this situation? Why? Should H. J. Simmons hope for compliance or commitment from Nelson with regard to his strategic guidelines? Why?

16. In what ways may political factors (a) *enhance* or (b) *detract* from the likelihood of this announcement decision being made in a manner which is best for the entire company?

17. How may H. J. Simmons' personal leadership style affect the quality of the decision on this announcement?

part V: leading

18. What should be included in corporate level controls to ensure that divisional decisions on situations like this are made in the context of corporate strategy?

19. Would broad corporate controls suffice to ensure a good decision at division level in this case or are detailed corporate controls needed? Explain.

20. How should corporate staff be used in "controlling" divisions in situations such as this?

part VI: controlling

21. What action would you take if you were Cliff Nelson? Be specific as to *how* you would carry it out. If you were the division head (Mertz), what action would you take once you learned of Nelson's decision?

22. Based in part on your answer to question 15, what changes might you make, as Simmons, to increase the chances of this kind of decision being made well?

summary questions for solution of the case as a whole

# ORGANIZING: STRATEGY TO STRUCTURE

**III**

Company strategy has a profound effect on organization structure. Indeed, organization design must be properly matched to strategy in order to ensure effective execution. A key step in strategy implementation is translating strategy into the managerial and operating work to be done.

Organizing helps a manager unite the work of different people in order to achieve goals. Whether the number of people be only a few or thousands, their effective cooperation requires organization. Two elements are invariably present in organizing: dividing the work into jobs and, simultaneously, ensuring that these separate clusters of work are linked together into a team effort. We can see these two elements in a football team, in a hospital, or in a government bureau, as well as in business firms. The success of any of these enterprises depends significantly upon how skillfully their managers assign individual tasks so that they combine into integrated, purposeful action. The organizing process will be discussed in the following chapters.

Chapter 10—Designing Operating Units. Here we focus on merging simple operating tasks into jobs; linking such jobs into work groups, and then combining work groups into major operating departments and service divisions of the enterprise. The aim is to find those combinations that will bring forth the most effective cooperative effort.

Chapter 11—Designing the Hierarchy: Delegating and Decentralizing. The work of managing must be allocated. This involves delegating and redelegating to successively lower levels of supervision. In this chapter, we shall see that the scope and degree of decentralization are critical features in this dispersing of authority.

Chapter 12—Staff-Line Roles in Strategic Action. In this chapter we explore how staff assists in the execution of strategy. As enterprises grow, the task of managing them becomes more complex; thus, we consider the ways staff can lighten the burden of key executives.

Chapter 13—Matching Strategy and Structure. The overall structure of a company must be adjusted as the firm expands. In this chapter, we see how organizations can be adapted to three basic stages of development: single entrepreneur, departmentalized company, and multiple-mission company.

Chapter 14—Staffing to Execute Missions. In this chapter we explore approaches for obtaining an effective match between the organization structure and the human resources in an enterprise. After pointing out variation in individual abilities, we shall consider how far the organization design should be changed to suit personal strengths and weaknesses.

All the chapters in this part deal with "formal" organization—formal in that the patterns of division of work and of personal relationships are deliberately set up and are clearly recognized and discussed by those concerned. The primary interest is to achieve goals of the enterprise; thus our analysis is based largely on the "productivity approach." The more informal aspects of organization which arise out of social relationships will be examined in Part IV.

# designing operating units

**10**

Learning Objectives

After completing this chapter you should be able to

1. Discuss how to determine the desired division of labor.
2. Explain the differences between functional groups and compound groups.
3. Identify the five principal bases of departmentation.
4. Describe the key factors which affect the choice of departmentation.
5. Discuss the strengths and weaknesses of each form of departmentation.

## ORGANIZING: TAILORED SUPPORT FOR STRATEGY

In Part I and II we explored the contribution of sound planning and rational decision-making to effective strategy. Now in Part III we turn to organizing, another crucial managerial process that bears on the success of every enterprise.

The tie between corporate organization and strategy has long been recognized. Over twenty years ago, A. D. Chandler traced the impact of strategy on the structure of General Motors, du Pont, Exxon, Sears Roebuck, and other large firms.[1] We shall review this line of analysis in Chapter 13. Also well known is the interplay between strategy and key managerial personnel—a topic dealt with in Chapter 14. The interdepedence of strategy and organization within business-units is less well understood. Yet, in view of the vital role we see for business-units, their organization is a potential source of major improvements in productivity. That's where most of us build our careers. The next three chapters deal with the organization of effective business-units.

In each business-unit, the strategy and its supporting plans call for action of many sorts. People don't run machines, sell, devise computer programs, etc., just to look busy; each task arises because it contributes directly or indirectly to the company mission. Questions of emphasis, priority, and coordination are always present, strategy and its supporting plans providing the basis for official answers. Organizing deals with the way numerous activities are combined into jobs and departments; it combines activities into a team effort.

Organizing is a creative process. The form that any particular organization takes depends on the kinds of activities involved, and on the results called for in the specific strategy. The emerging organization is a tailormade instrument designed for a specific situation and purpose.[2] When the situation or purpose change, the organization should also be changed. In the next three chapters, therefore, we don't present predetermined organization types. Instead, we examine elements, alternatives, and factors to consider in designing unique structures.

**harnessing specialized effort**

Organizing starts by assigning basic operations—such as baking bread or teaching class—to different individuals. Then, to aid in coordinating this work, several of these jobs are combined into sections, sections into departments, and so on until all operations of the enterprise are covered. We may choose to add a variety of advisors and helpers, but it is the operating work that generates the actual flow of services to consumers.

---

[1] A. D. Chandler, *Strategy and Structure* (Cambridge: MIT Press, 1962).

[2] In stressing a model where influence runs from (a) strategy and plans to (b) activities, and through activities to (c) organization, we are not denying the possibility of a reverse flow in which existing organization helps shape (constrain) strategy. See D. J. Hall and M. A. Saias, "Strategy Follows Structure!" *Strategic Management Journal,* 1, no. 2 (April 1980). However, for the manager who is concerned with achieving target results, then the predominant influence flows in the direction presented in the text. See also the discussion of strategy, technology, and management design in Chapter 26.

This grouping of operating activities into jobs, sections, and departments—"departmentation" in technical jargon—should be done carefully. For example, the kind of service customers get in a department store or medical office depends greatly on how work is divided. Or to cite production examples, the effectiveness of textile mills in India and electronic plants in the United States has been sharply improved by changing the basis for *combining* operations into sections and departments.

Also, the way work is structured affects the kinds of people who are qualified to be hired and promoted. After a job is established, employees often guard their roles jealously; in fact, companies and even whole industries have been shut down by jurisdictional disputes.

To emphasize the significance of first-level operations, we focus first on the combining of operating tasks into individual *jobs*. Next we consider grouping jobs into effective *work groups*. Only then do we treat the consolidation of work groups into *departments*. By starting with the simplest units and moving to more complex ones, we can keep the beguiling issues of grand design for an entire enterprise in proper perspective.

**SCOPE OF INDIVIDUAL JOBS**    How many different tasks can a single person perform well? In practice we find jobs ranging from the nut-tightener on an assembly line to the cabinet-maker who does everything from selecting his raw wood to polishing his finished product. These are extremes. Let us examine several other examples for keys to how much division of labor is desirable.

Flying a small plane in Alaska, a bush pilot fuels, loads, navigates, communicates with the ground, calms his passengers, and makes minor repairs. In the operation of a 747 jet, however, these tasks are divided among dozens of people, each of whom has a limited number of clearly specified things to do. Why the difference?

how much division of labor?

The explanation lies partly in the volume of work required to operate a 747. Also, each person must be highly skilled in his particular task, and able to give it adequate attention. Moreover, the larger payload can support the expense of a multiple crew; so this example suggests that a greater division of labor is desirable if it can be afforded.

In the medical field, general practitioners are now hard to find. Doctors are specialists, and the patient spends a lot of time reaching the particular doctor who treats his specific ailment. Again, there is benefit from a high degree of skill and knowledge. But when we extend this approach to insurance sales representatives, doubts begin to arise. Should we specialize our sales force—one for annuities, another for estate planning, separate people for fire and liability insurance? And a more recent issue, should another specialist sell mutual funds? Several companies have concluded that such specialization is unwarranted. Instead, they argue that a single relationship with each customer provides a coordinated service at less expense, and that these benefits offset gains from high specialization.

The design of jobs in a filling station illustrates another consideration. One worker might only pump gasoline, a second grease cars, and a third serve as cashier. The catch here is providing enough work to keep each person busy. The volume of work fluctuates, and some jobs take longer than others. So specialization is eliminated in order to ensure full-time jobs.

College teaching is an area in which high division of labor along functional lines has been resisted. The tasks of course design, instruction, and testing could be allocated to separate specialists. However, most college professors resent any interference with "their" courses. In fact, professors are urged to do research and still perform the whole gamut of teaching tasks. The rationale for such a broad job scope includes the ease of coordinating the various phases of teaching and a belief that a person cannot be good at one teaching task without being proficient in all the others. Students themselves undoubtedly have an opinion about the effectiveness of this arrangement!

The question of job *scope*—the number of different tasks one is expected to carry out—arises in every walk of life. Because of the way jobs are structured, people quit jobs, professions are built, unions call jurisdictional strikes, psychological security is found and lost, companies prosper or languish.

striking a balance

As the preceding examples show, effective job structure requires a careful assessment of what the physical circumstances permit and of the primary benefits sought. Factors that usually deserve attention include the following.

*Benefits of functional specialization*   By narrowing the scope of a job, full utilization can be made of any distinctive skill an individual possesses.[3] As a person concentrates on a limited range of duties, he can learn these very well and give them full attention. Wage economies may also arise; instead of paying a premium for a versatile "triple-threat man" for all positions, the more routine tasks can often be assigned to less experienced and less expensive employees. Furthermore, whenever a sufficient volume of routine work is isolated, mechanization becomes a possibility; for example, use of computers for office work.

*Need for coordination*   Often several tasks should be closely synchronized or coordinated—as in labor negotiations—and one person can do this more easily than several. When information about a specific situation has to be pooled in a single spot, the difficulty of communicating bits of information from person to person may more than offset benefits of specialization. Relevant here is the rule that tasks should be separated only where there is a clean break, as between lunch and dinner but not during a meal.

[3]For a comprehensive discussion of the benefits of specialization, see F. W. Taylor, *The Principles of Scientific Management* (New York: Harper & Row, 1947).

*Morale of the operator*    How the operator feels about the scope of his job may be vital.[4] The employee's pride in his work and work suited to professional dignity are positive factors. On the other hand, monotony is depressing for most people. Sometimes monotony can be partially relieved by rotating people from job to job or by allowing the worker to deviate from his set routine. But, if a *wide variety* of choices must be made, some operators feel that the job is unreasonably complex. This broad area of human response to organization is explored more fully in Part IV.

Rarely will any single job design be all good or all bad. Some potential benefits of specialization may have to be sacrificed for better coordination and employee morale, or vice versa. That choice depends primarily on values derived from the strategy of the enterprise.

Three restraints on designing individual jobs should not be overlooked. (1) The volume of work always places a limit on the division of labor. We do not want a specialist to sit around most of the day waiting to do his part. (2) One technology may be so superior for some kinds of work that we have little choice in job design. Operating a taxicab, playing first violin in a symphony orchestra, and removing bark by means of a hydraulic machine in a lumber mill are situations of this type. (3) It takes effort not only to design a sophisticated system of work but also to have the workers adopt it as a normal way of doing things. Such investment is warranted only when the system will have repeated use.

## EFFECTIVE WORK GROUPS

To have well-designed jobs is not enough. The complexities of modern production require the combined efforts of a variety of people. After tasks are grouped into jobs, the next step is to combine jobs into work groups. By work groups we mean a set of people who see each other on the job almost daily, whose work is usually interdependent in some respects, and whose output is viewed by outsiders as a single achievement. How should these groups be formed?

Whenever several similar jobs exist, they can be put in the same section as suggested in the upper part of Figure 10.1. On the other hand, when several different skills are needed to complete a block of work, jobs can be grouped as indicated in the lower part of the diagram. For example, a salesman, repairman, and bookkeeper could be placed together in the branch office of an office-equipment company. The former grouping we call "functional," the latter "compound."

Under some circumstances, the use of compound groups permits us to take advantage of a combination of several benefits that are sought in the design of jobs. Individual members of the group can be specialists in different fields, and coordination is achieved by interaction within the group. Furthermore, close personal relations and a sense of group achievement contribute

**benefits of compound groups**

---

[4]For a comprehensive treatment of the relationship between job design and motivation see J. R. Hackman and G. R. Oldham, *Work Redesign* (Reading, MA: Addison-Wesley, 1980).

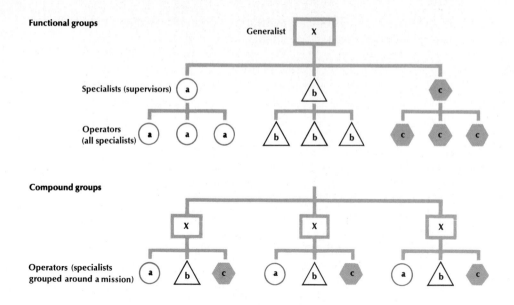

**Functional groups**

Generalist   X

Specialists (supervisors)   a   b   c

Operators (all specialists)   a a a   b b b   c c c

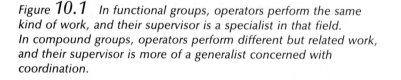

**Compound groups**

X   X   X

Operators (specialists grouped around a mission)   a b c   a b c   a b c

*Figure* **10.1**   *In functional groups, operators perform the same kind of work, and their supervisor is a specialist in that field. In compound groups, operators perform different but related work, and their supervisor is more of a generalist concerned with coordination.*

to morale. Small branches of a bank, a 747 airplane crew, and other geographically separated units often have these characteristics. Compound work groups may also be formed around a product or service, such as a maternity ward in a hospital.

A crew of workers operating a highly automated chemical plant or power station is usually a compound group of specialists. In fact the operators on a single assembly line can be viewed as a compound group, although here the design and pace of the equipment carry most of the burden of coordination.

Compound groups should be used when local coordination is vital.[5] An industrial-equipment company, for instance, might combine sales, repair service, and parts warehousing in each of its local offices in an effort to provide distinctive customer service. Local coordination is even more vital for a surgical team composed of a surgeon, assisting doctor, anesthetist, and nurses. Here as in the previous examples, a clear-cut block of work calls for the effort of several specialists.

[5]For a discussion of coordination techniques in work units, see A. H. Van de Ven, A. L. Delbecq, and R. Koenig, "Determinants of Coordination Modes Within Organizations," *American Sociological Review*, 41, (1976), 334–35.

Attractive though compound groups may be, functional grouping of operations is actually more prevalent. Why so?

Functional grouping usually makes full-time jobs easier to arrange. While a compound group may consist of six sales representatives, two repairmen, and one accountant, it cannot readily be made up of six sales representatives, one and two-thirds repairmen, and five-sixths of an accountant. With the latter workload the spare time of the repairman and the acountant is usually lost. Also the need for different specialists is any one compound group may be high today and low tomorrow. Functional grouping, with interchangeable people in the same group, allows a manager to balance these partial and irregular workloads more efficiently.

When each specialist requires high-cost equipment, the expenses of idle time are even greater. The operator of a multimillion-dollar wind tunnel used in aircraft engineering is an extreme example, but even the office space and company car of a field investigator can be expensive.

Technical supervision is often desirable. Unless the operators themselves possess high professional competence, their manager will normally need substantial technical knowledge. Even when plans are made centrally, the supervisor must interpret policies, resolve on-the-spot problems, coach new employees, and relay to his bosses the information they need. This kind of supervisory work can be done with greater expertise within a functional group. A supervisor need not be the only source of technical guidance, as we shall see in Chapter 12, "Staff-Line Roles in Strategic Action." But his expert understanding of the work is essential.

Compatibility within a group and with the supervisor is more likely to exist in a fuctional group than in a compound group. Our feeling of compatibility with fellow workers rests heavily on similar attitudes and values—for example, attitudes toward risk-taking, meeting deadlines, short-run versus long-run achievements, and the importance of people versus things. In these terms we can achieve greater compatibility by putting, say, caseworkers together, researchers together, accountants together, and so forth. It is true that such a group tends to reinforce each other's biases and as a result may be less cooperative with other functional groups. But the social satisfactions they derive from their work will also be enhanced.

The design of work groups, then, involves at least broadly a set of considerations similar to those used in the formation of individual jobs; benefits of specialization, need for coordination, effect on operators' morale, and expense repeatedly claim attention.

As we shall see in Part IV, work groups tend to become close-knit social groups. Once jelled, they tend to resist change. They can be a great source of strength for an enterprise or a seriously retarding influence; they should be composed with care.

## SHAPING MAJOR DEPARTMENTS

To achieve unified action, work groups must be combined into departments. At this level, organization designers shift attention from an array of very specific operations to a broad grouping of activities that will

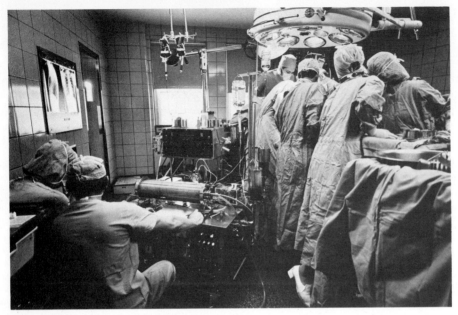

*Figure 10.2  A surgical team illustrates (1) clear division of labor within the group and (2) responsive interaction of the group to achieve a coordinated result.*

facilitate central management. The work groups become building blocks to be arranged so that the major missions of the enterprise receive proper emphasis, while the various operating groups are supported in performing their respective tasks. As the enterprise adusts to its changing environment, the shape of these major departments may have to be altered.

Growth forced a small manufacturer of instruments to recast his basic organization structure. A resourceful instrument maker and a chemistry instructor had teamed up to make high-quality instruments for laboratories, and the business grew around specially designed equipment. The organization consisted of a production shop, a sales manager, and an office that handled all finance and clerical work. Then the company designed a machine for testing water pollution and found a potential market for hundreds of identical instruments. Sales jumped, and the shop was swamped with work.

The new business called for a major reorganization. Instead of merely expanding the three existing departments, the company established a separate department for each product line. While overhead expense is higher in the new setup, the prospect for preserving the strength of a close-knit, responsive laboratory-instrument business while opening the way for unfettered growth in the pollution-control field offsets this extra cost. Note that the choice of departmentation in this example depends on where coordination and specialized attention are most needed, and on the impact of technology.

Designing jobs or work groups cannot be done well without taking the major departments into consideration. Contrariwise, the scope of departments depends partly on what makes a good work group. Design choices are interdependent. A final decision at one level is held back until thought has been given to its impact elsewhere in the structure.

The principal options for organizing work in a major department include groupings by *function, product, process, territory, and customer.*

*Function*   Under this arrangement, operations are divided into major functions. For example, firms concentrating on automobile insurance usually have departments for sales, underwriting, claims, finance, investment, and legal. A stereo equipment manufacturer will probably have research and development, production, marketing, and finance as basic departments. As noted in the previous section, such functional departments become expert in their particular area, give adequate attention to an activity that otherwise might receive hurried treatment, and act consistently on matters that require uniform, organization-wide treatment.

*Products*   The work of a purchasing department is often divided by products—permitting each buyer to become expert in his dealings with certain supplying industries and companies. In department-store merchandising, specialized knowledge about product lines such as hosiery, jewelry, furniture, and men's suits is essential in selecting goods to sell, in pricing, and in sales promotion. Product subunits are often introduced within an engineering department to help aquire detailed knowledge about the diverse aspects of a product.

Such product subdivisions are used when the products handled differ significantly from each other, and when those differences are important in gaining a relative advantage over competitors.

*Process*   Manufacturers—and government offices—often perform several distinct processes that may serve as the basis for organization within a production department. In steel production we usually find separate shops for coke ovens, blast furnaces, open-hearth furnaces, hot-rolling mills, cold-rolling mills, and the like. Each process is performed in a separate location and involves a distinct technology.

The grouping of activities by process tends to promote efficiency through specialization. All the key people in each unit become expert in dealing with their aspect of the business. On the other hand, process classification increases problems of coordination. Scheduling the movement of work from unit to unit becomes somewhat complex; and, since no unit has full responsibility for a customer's order, a process unit may not be as diligent in meeting time requirements and other specifications as a group of people who think in terms of the total finished product and their customers.

The conflict between the desire to increase skill in performance through specialization and mechanization, and the need for coordination to secure balanced effort, recurs time and again in organization studies. Insurance companies, hospitals, and even consulting firms face the same issue.

*Territory*   Companies with salespeople who travel over a large area almost always use territorial organization within their sales departments. Large companies will have several regions, each subdivided into districts, with a further breakdown of territories for individual sales representatives. Airlines, finance companies with local offices, and motel chains all have widely dispersed activities and consequently use territorial organization to some degree.

The primary issues with territorial organization are three.

1.  What related activity should be physically dispersed along with those which by their nature are local? For example, should a company with a national salesforce also have local warehousing, assembling, advertising, credit and accounting, and personnel? And how far should the dispersion occur—to the regional level or to the district level? Typically, whenever such related activities are dispersed, they are all combined into a territorial organization unit.
2.  How much authority to make decisions should be decentralized to these various territorial units? In other words, how much of the planning and control work should go along with the actual performance?
3.  What will be the relationship between the home-office service and staff units, and these various territorial divisions?

The major advantage of territorial organization is that it provides supervision near the point of performance. Local conditions vary and emergencies do arise. People distantly located will have difficulty grasping the true nature of a situation, and valuable time is often lost before an adjustment can be made. Consequently, when adjustment to local conditions and quick decisions are important, territorial organization is desirable. On the other hand, if many local units are established, some of the benefits of a large-scale operation may be lost. The local unit will probably be comparatively small; consequently the degree of specialization and mechanization will likewise be limited.

*Customers*   A company that sells to customers of distinctly different types may establish a separate unit of organization for selling to, and serving, each. A manufacturer of men's shoes, for instance, sells to both independent retail stores and chain stores. The chain-store buyers are very sophisticated and may prepare their own specifications; consequently, any salespeople calling on them must have an intimate knowledge of shoe construction and of the capacity of their company's plant. In contrast, sales representatives who call on retailers must be able to think in terms of retailing problems and be able to show how their products will fit into the customer's business. Few sales representatives can work effectively with both; thus, the shoe manufacturer has a separate division in its sales organization for each group.

Commercial banks, to cite another example, often have lending officers for different types of customers—railroads, manufacturing concerns, stockbrokers, consumer loans, and the like. These people recognize the needs of their own group of customers, and are in a good position to appraise their credit worthiness.

Ordinarily, customer groups include only selling and direct-service activities. Anyone who has been shunted around to five or six offices trying to get an adjustment on a bill or a promise on a delivery will appreciate the satisfaction of dealing with one person who understands the problem and knows how to get action within the company. On the other hand, this form of organization may be expensive, and a customer-oriented employee may commit the company to actions that other departments find hard to carry out.

This description of functional, product, process, territory, and customer departmentation indicates that many variations are possible when organizing within a major department. We now consider the key factors involved in choosing a basis of departmentation.

Several key factors are found in almost every departmentation problem, regardless of level, so typically an optimum arrangement of the various factors is sought instead of reliance on a single consideration. The following paragraphs provide a useful summary of factors already noted and add new dimensions to several of them.

key factors in departmentation

*Take advantage of specialization*   A division of labor that permits specialization in certain kinds of work should be considered. Such concentration enables people to become experts and, assuming appropriate placement of personnel, allows a company to make full use of the distinctive abilities of its operators.

Usually specialization is thought of by function, but the possibility that an employee may become an expert on a product or on a particular type of customer should not be overlooked. In other words, "What is the focus on the person's specialty?" The question forces consideration of whether a particular body of knowledge and skill is important for getting a job done. The more crucial such knowledge and skill is to the success of the enterprise, the stronger will be the pull to set up a division or a job built on that specialty.

*Aid coordination*   Even though certain activities are dissimilar, they may be put under a single executive because they need close coordination.[6] Buying and selling women's dresses in a department store, for

---

[6]For a discussion of the trade-off between specialization and coordination, and a review of alternative coordinating (or "integrating") devices, see P. Lawrence and J. Lorsch, *Organization and Environment* (Boston: Harvard Business School, 1967).

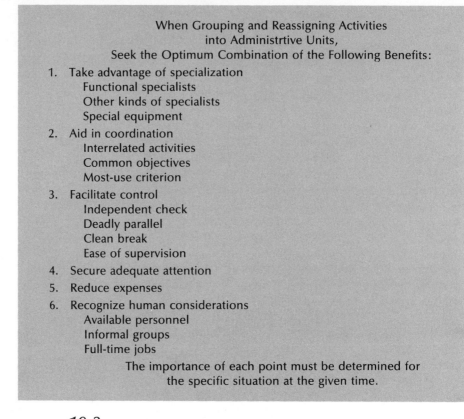

When Grouping and Reassigning Activities
into Administrtive Units,
Seek the Optimum Combination of the Following Benefits:

1. Take advantage of specialization
    Functional specialists
    Other kinds of specialists
    Special equipment
2. Aid in coordination
    Interrelated activities
    Common objectives
    Most-use criterion
3. Facilitate control
    Independent check
    Deadly parallel
    Clean break
    Ease of supervision
4. Secure adequate attention
5. Reduce expenses
6. Recognize human considerations
    Available personnel
    Informal groups
    Full-time jobs
        The importance of each point must be determined for
        the specific situation at the given time.

*Figure 10.3* *Basic factors in departmentation.*

example, may be the responsibility of a single executive because he can sense style trends and customer reactions and can time changes accordingly.

A clearly recognized *common objective* is important in securing coordination. The type of decentralization stressed by duPont, General Electric, and many other companies splits up engineering, production, and selling among product divisions. This arrangement enables the management of each division to coordinate these diverse functions because the dominant objective of each unit is to make a success of its particular product line.

Coordination may be a factor when placing miscellaneous activities, as well as when grouping major functions. In any organization, there are a number of "orphan operations"—receptionists, chauffeurs, telephone operators—and no compelling reason may exist for putting them in a particular place. They can be assigned to the department that makes the *most use* of their work. This solution at least simplifies coordination between a service and its major user.

*Facilitate control*   The way activities are apportioned has a marked effect on control in an organization. Clearly, if one activity is to serve as an *independent check* on another—as accounting on disbursement of cash or inspection on quality of production—these activities should be separated.

Departmentation, which makes it easier for management to measure performance and to hold people accountable for results, is a real aid to control. Thus it is desirable to make a *clean break* between the duties of one department and those of another. Oil companies, for example, often place all the work done by a refinery under a single manager because the line between what is inside and what is outside the refinery is a fairly clear one and also because all work within the refinery is so interrelated that a neat separation into two or more divisions would be difficult to establish.

Those companies whose volume and technology justify two or more operating units may use the *deadly parallel* as an aid to control. This means that operating units are made as nearly identical as possible so that their respective expenses and productivity can be directly compared. Chain stores, telephone companies, government bureaus, and even schools find that the deadly parallel provides performance standards that bring inefficient operations into sharp focus.

Control of actual operations is always simplified if an *immediate supervisor is on the spot* where he can see what goes on and can talk to workers frequently during the day. For this reason, a firm may place final assembly operations in a branch warehouse under the control of the sales department, even though the work seems logically part of production.

*Secure adequate attention*    A principle reason for placing an activity high up in an organization structure is to ensure that this operation receives full consideration from top administrators. Similarly, auxiliary services are sometimes separate from primary operations in order to obtain adequate attention for all phases of work that should be done.

"Adequate attention," however, is a difficult guide to use in departmentation. If an executive pays heed to all demands for attention, he may be inclined to break up an otherwise neat pattern that works well most of the time. Therefore an executive must decide not only how important an activity is at a given moment but also how important it will be in the future.

*Reduce expenses*    The pattern of departmentation may directly affect expenses in two ways. First, a new unit—say, a purchasing department or a central training service—may require additional executives. These new executives will add to salaries, traveling expenses, secretarial work, telephone and other services. In addition to these identifiable costs, the people in a new unit inevitably use up some of the time of other executives by talking with them and writing memoranda that have to be read and answered. Perhaps the addition of a single person will make no marked difference, but if an array of specialists all press for attention from busy line managers, the total burden on the line managers can become quite heavy.

A second expense consideration is the rate of pay needed for different kinds of jobs. An industrial sales department, for instance, might require that all sales representatives have engineering training plus five years experience with company products. But another organization might reserve such high-paid positions only for special assignments, using lower-paid people for routine sales work. Obviously, no company will want to incur additional payroll expense unless by doing so it will benefit significantly from improved effectiveness.

***Recognize human considerations*** In Part IV we shall give careful attention to the human-relations aspects of organization structure. There are a number of reasons why we may have to modify the coldly logical and emotionally detached organization plans we are discussing here in Part III. Among the reasons are availability of personnel, the existence of informal groups, traditions within an enterprise, and prevailing attitudes toward different forms of organization. We mention these points here simply as a reminder that human factors must be brought into consideration before a final decision is reached.

## CONCLUSION: BALANCING STABILITY VS. CHANGE

In this chapter we have been concerned with the way operating activities are assigned to people. The grouping of operating work has been analyzed by using a bottom-up approach that consists of three phases: (1) the grouping of operating tasks into individual jobs; (2) the combining of jobs into effective work groups; and (3) the combining of work groups into departments.

The overriding consideration at each of the three levels of organization design is strategy and the plans which elaborate that strategy. These plans determine the nature of the work to be done; then organization translates the work into jobs, groups, and major departments.

In choosing a basis for departmentation we attempt to do six things: (1) take advantage of specialization, (2) aid coordination, (3) facilitate control, (4) secure adequate attention, (5) reduce expenses, and (6) recognize human considerations. No single organization design provides us with the desired level of each of these six features. In essence, departmentation is the subtle task of selecting the proper compromise among these features.

Organization structure should contribute to the stability of working relationships. It enables each person to know the particular part he is expected to play in the total activities of his company. And from it he also learns what he can expect others to do. For these reasons, duties should not be shuffled among people each time a new idea strikes. On the other hand, dynamic pressures in society and within a company require the modern manager to be constantly alert to the need for readjusting the way he has divided work among his subordinates. In enterprises generally, *thoughtful* changes in departmentation are made too infrequently rather than too often.

## FOR FURTHER DISCUSSION

1. How do decisions on the division of work influence the effectiveness of an organization?

2. In designing an organizational structure, is it better to *start* at the bottom and organize around the work done there and then build up to higher-level departmentation, or vice versa? Discuss.

3. What factors make it difficult for a modern corporation to adapt to the type of external change that necessi-

tates departmental rearrangement? How did businesses adapt to such changes during the early stages of industrial development?

4. Indicate which material in Chapter 10 you feel is most relevant for determining how much division of labor is appropriate.

5. Would you expect the number of standing plans written for compound groups to be more or less numerous than those for functional groups?

6. "We used to have a great safety record in this plant," said a firstline foreman. "That is," he went on, "until we set up a separate safety department in the plant personnel office. In the year and a half since this group was set up, accidents have gone up almost twenty percent." How would you explain this phenomenon?

7. Arrangements have just been completed to transfer the franchise of a minor league baseball team to your hometown. A ballpark is being built to seat 12,000, and the owners of the team have offered you the job of organizing and managing the refreshments concession. They will provide any capital and facilities you may require.

1. Describe the operating work that would have to be carried out in running the concession.

2. What alternative means of organizing this work are plausible? What factors influence the desirability of each alternative?

3. In dividing the operating work, did you use the "top-down" or "bottom-up" approach, or did you trace the steps of the operation? What are the arguments for each of these approaches?

8. "Whatever the organization structure, it should be changed significantly every five to ten years just to shake things up." Comment on this statement by the president of a large bank.

## CASES

For cases involving issues covered in this chapter, see especially the following. Particularly relevant questions are listed after each case.

## FOR FURTHER READING

Child, J., *Organization: A Guide for Managers and Administrators*. New York: Harper & Row, 1977. Useful managerial overview of organization design ideas, and techniques for applying these ideas.

Filley, A. C., R. J. House, and S. Kerr., *Managerial Process and Organizational Behavior,* 2nd ed., Glenview: Scott Foresman, 1976, chap. 15 and 16. Summarizes research evidence on behavioral effects of division of labor, and on product vs. functional departmentation.

Gulick, L., "Notes on the Theory of Organization," in *Papers on the Science of Administration,* eds. L. Gulick and L. Urwick. New York: Institute of Public Administration. Columbia University, 1937, pp. 3–45. A classic that is fully applicable today.

Litterer, J. A., *The Analysis of Organizations,* 2nd ed. New York: Wiley, 1973, chaps. 15 and 16. Good discussion of elements involved in division of work at operating level.

Lorsch, J. W. and P. R. Lawrence, *Studies in Organization Design.* Homewood:

Irwin-Dorsey, 1970. A volume of eleven articles based on separate field studies of various structural dimensions.

Miles, R. H., *Macro Oranizational Behavior*. Santa Monica, CA: Goodyear, 1980, chaps. 2, 3, and 4. Good summary of the major studies exploring the relationship between technology and structure.

# designing the hierarchy: delegating and decentralizing

# 11

Learning Objectives

After completing this chapter you should be able to

1. Understand the three inevitable features of delegation.
2. Contrast the main differences between centralized and decentralized planning.
3. Identify the seven guidelines for determining the degree of decentralization.
4. Explain the concept of profit decentralization.
5. Describe the benefits and limitations of profit decentralization.

## DIVIDING MANAGERIAL WORK

Growth invariably leads to a management hierarchy. As a firm becomes larger, more levels of managers are needed to ensure co-ordinated planning, direction, and control. Centralization–decentralization—the focus of this chapter—concerns the vertical allocation of management action along this hierarchy, whereas departmentation—discussed in the previous chapter—involves a horizontal allocation of operating work.[1]

**persistence of the problem**

The question of how much work the chief executive should do himself and how much he should reassign to his subordinates has bothered administrators for centuries. One of the earliest references to this dilemma is found in the Book of Exodus, where there is a report of Moses' experience.

Moses sat to judge the people; and the people stood about Moses from the morning unto the evening. And when Moses' father-in-law saw all that he did . . . he said unto him: "The thing that thou doest is not good. Thou wilt surely wear away, both thou and this people with thee; for the thing is too heavy for thee—thou art not able to perform it thyself alone.

"Hearken now unto my voice. . . . Be thou for the people Godward, and bring thou the causes unto God. [Then] thou shalt teach [the people] the statutes and the laws, and shalt show them the way wherein they must walk, and the work that they must do.

"Moreover thou shalt provide out of all the people able men, such as fear God, men of truth, hating unjust gain; and place such over them, to be rulers of thousands, rulers of hundreds, rulers of fifties, and rulers of tens; and let them judge the people at all seasons. And it shall be that every great matter they shall bring unto thee, but every small matter they shall judge themselves. So shall it be easier for thyself, and they shall bear the burden with thee."

The fundamental problem Moses faced is still with us. The burden on executives is especially acute in enterprises that are changing and growing. As product lines are diversified and new employees added, executives find that they can no longer give proper attention to all the management problems that cross their desks. Unless they decentralize, they find that they, like Moses, are unable to cope with the job by themselves.

The allocation of managerial work is one of the most subtle aspects of the organizing process. The degree of decentralization may vary from department to department within a single company. The sales department, for example, may be highly decentralized. But the controller may retain direction over a great deal of planning, organizing, and motivating of the operations under his direction.

For insight into this web of relationships we shall first examine the delegation process and then consider factors determining the degree of decentralization that is desirable in a specific situation. The chapter closes with a penetrating look at profit-decentralization—an organizational arrangement well suited to a dynamic society.

[1]*Operating* work, as noted in Chapter 10, embraces the basic activities necessary to create goods and services—the selling, machine-running, bookkeeping, and engineering in a manufacturing plant; the copywriting, art work, media selection, and campaign scheduling in an advertising agency; or the arranging for temporary care of children, locating foster homes, making actual placements, raising funds, and keeping records in a child-placement agency. *Managerial* work refers to the guidance of other people, and includes the activities of all levels of supervisors from first-line foreman to president.

**THREE INEVITABLE FEATURES
OF DELEGATING**
Delegation is familiar to anyone in a supervisory position; it simply means entrusting
part of the work of operations or manage-
ment to others. A filling station owner delegates car greasing to Bill and
pump tending to Charlie. The president of Republic Aircraft Corporation
entrusts financial matters to Ms. MacGregor, the treasurer. Such delegations give rise to what we commonly call a boss-subordinate relationship.

Every time a manager delegates work to a subordinate—say, a president to a marketing manager, or a first-line supervisor to an operator—three
actions are either expressed or implied.

1.  The manager assigns *duties*. The person who is delegating indicates what work
    the subordinate is to do.
2.  He grants *authority*. Along with permission to proceed with the assigned work,
    he will probably transfer to the subordinate certain rights, such as the right to
    spend money, to direct the work of others, to use raw materials, to represent the
    company to outsiders, or to take other steps necessary to fulfill the new duties.
3.  He creates an *obligation*. In accepting an assignment, a subordinate takes on an
    obligation to his boss to complete the job.

These attributes of delegation are like a three-legged stool; each depends on the others for support, and no two can stand alone.

Duties can be described in two ways. First, we can think of them in    **duties**
terms of an activity. For instance, we may say that Turner's duties are either
to run a turret lathe, to sell in Oshkosh, to direct an employment office, to
discover and analyze facts about the money market and trends in interest
rates, or to measure distribution costs. According to this view, delegating is
the process by which we assign activities to individuals.

Second, we can describe duties in terms of the results we want to
achieve. Following this approach, we would say that in the first two examples, Turner's duties are to turn on his lathe a certain number of pieces per
day according to engineering specifications, or to build customer goodwill
and secure a prescribed number of orders in the Oshkosh territory. Here we
are talking about objectives. We define the duties in terms of accomplishment.

Because of differences in jobs, such goals may be stated as either long-
run or short-run results. They may represent overoptimism or realistic expectation. Nevertheless, if the delegation of duties is phrased in terms of
goals, a subordinate is likely to get psychological satisfaction from his work,
and he will have advance notice of the criteria on which his performance will
be judged. A person's duties will be clear to him only if he knows what
activities he must undertake *and* what missions he must fulfill.

If a person is assigned duties to perform, is it not obvious he must be    **authority**
given all necessary authority to carry them out? An advertising manager
needs authority to buy space, hire a copywriter, and take other necessary

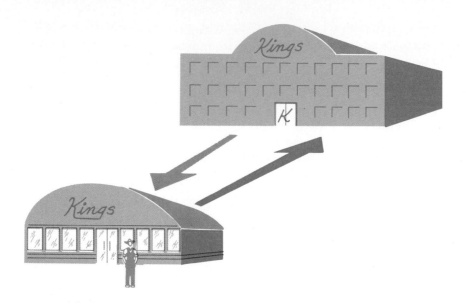

*Figure 11.1 In a fast-food chain, carefully defined duties and limited authority are delegated from headquarters to the manager of each retail outlet. The manager, in turn, has an obligation to the executive who assigned the duties and authority.*

steps if he is to gain his assigned objective of building customer demand for company products.

Unfortunately, assigning authority is not simple. We should understand exactly what kind of authority is within the power of a manager to grant; typically, several restrictions fence in the authority a manager has at his disposal.

Administrative authority consists of certain permissions or rights: the right to act for the company in specified areas (to buy raw material, accept orders from customers, issue press releases, admit people into a plant); the right as spokesperson for the company to request other employees to perform activities of various kinds; and the right to impose sanctions and discipline if a subordinate disregards his instructions. These rights are vested in the head of an enterprise by law and custom, and they are supported by the moral approval of society. They stem partly from concepts of private-property rights, partly from acknowledged authority of the political state, and particularly from the long-established human habit of looking to hierarchical leadership in cooperative undertakings. Because of this background, employees, and in fact our whole society, accept the idea that the head of an enterprise—whoever he may be—has certain rights of authority and that he may reassign these rights.[2]

[2] For a discussion of the conditions under which a person will comply with higher authority, see C. I. Barnard, *The Functions of the Executive,* 30th anniversary edition (Cambridge: Harvard University Press, 1968), pp. 165–66.

When an employee takes a job, he also (1) expects to take orders from someone designated by the company; (2) looks to management for permission to use company property or to act as an official representative of the enterprise; and (3) expects a superior to review his work and bring pressure on him to improve if it is unsatisfactory.[3] Such socially accepted rights constitute formal authority, and management can assign these rights when it erects a formal organization.

Authority is an essential element of any modern enterprise, but we must not confuse it with unlimited power. Not even a company president or section manager has the power to force customers to sign orders or suppliers to sell raw materials, or the power to compel the *enthusiastic* cooperation of associates and subordinates. The rights that an administrator may transfer are more akin to authorization than they are to power.

In addition to inherent limitations on the authority that an executive can delegate, virtually every company imposes limitations of its own. Typically, an executive is permitted to act strictly "within company policy" and "in accordance with established procedures." A manager may in theory have formal authority to hire and fire people in his division, but in fact he must adhere to a myriad restrictive procedures that require him, for example, to refer job descriptions to the planning department before he can fill a new position, to satisfy the personnel department that no capable person is available within the company before he can hire an outsider, to set salaries within an established range for each job classification, and to refrain from discharging anyone without two prior warnings at least a month apart. Another department head may have to endure comparable restrictions surrounding purchases of raw materials and, especially, of new equipment.

Because of these various limitations on authority, when a task is delegated, the rights associated with it must be specified.

By obligation—the third inevitable feature of delegation—we mean the moral compulsion felt by a subordinate to accomplish his assigned duties.[4] When duties are delegated to him, a subordinate is not free either to do the work or leave it as suits his convenience. A price checker is derelict in his duty if, on Friday afternoon, he mails out a batch of unaudited bids to customers merely because his work had piled up and salesmen were anxious to get the bids to their customers. Similarly, a clerk assigned to unlock the office in the morning fails in his obligation when he shows up two hours late with the excuse that his brother had unexpectedly stopped overnight for a visit.

Although agreement is usually implied rather than expressed, when a subordinate accepts an assignment he in effect gives his promise to do his

**obligation**

[3]Simon uses the concept of "area of acceptance" to describe the individual's inclination to accept most orders. See H. A. Simon, *Administrative Behavior* (New York: Macmillan, 1961), pp. 133–34.
[4]N. R. F. Maier, "The Subordinate's Role in the Delegation Process," *Personnel Psychology,* 21 (1968), 179–91.

best in carrying out his duties. Having taken a job, he is morally bound to try to complete it and can be held accountable for results. A sense of obligation, then, is primarily an attitude of the person to whom duties are delegated. Dependability rests on the sense of obligation, and without it cooperative business enterprises would collapse.[5]

### APPLYING CONCEPTS OF DELEGATION

**should duties and obligations extend beyond authority?**

A common saying in popular management literature declares that "authority and accountability should always be equal." Behind this statement lies the conviction that if a person is assigned duties, he ought to be furnished with enough authority—no more and no less— to carry them out; and if given authority, he has a corresponding obligation to use it wisely. Although there is an element of truth here, it is unfortunately an oversimplification. Let us see why.

The first difficulty is the word "equal." Duties are concerned with objectives and activities, authority with rights, and obligations with attitudes. Although these three concepts are indeed related, it is hard to find a common denominator for measuring equality among them. Also, as we have seen in our discussion of formal authority, there are only certain kinds of rights that an enterprise can pass along to its managers, and there are usually very substantial restrictions on how even these rights may be used. To permit anyone to charge into action without constraints would lead to chaos. Frequently a person must try to achieve objectives with authority far short of what he feels he needs.

It is more nearly accurate, though not so pat, to say to the boss—the person doing the delegating—"Duties, authority, and obligation depend on each other and you should therefore correlate them thoughtfully"; and to the subordinate—the person receiving the delegation—"You are obligated to fulfill your duties to the maximum extent that is feasible in light of your authority and the conditions under which you have to work."

**an obligation cannot be delegated**

What happens when duties and authority are redelegated? Does this redelegation relieve the executive who makes it of *his* obligation? Suppose the treasurer of the Omaha Chemical Company delegates to the chief accountant the task of maintaining an accounts-payable ledger. The chief accountant, being too busy to maintain the records himself, assigns the job to a clerk.

The redelegation of the job by the chief accountant to the clerk does not at all change the initial relationship between the treasurer and the chief accountant. The chief accountant still has the same duties and as much

[5]In delineating the chief features of delegating, we have avoided using the word "responsibility" because it means different things to different people. Some use it as a synonym for duty, whereas others think its meaning is identical with obligation. From time to time, however, we shall use the idea of accountability as a synonym for obligation.

authority, and even though he has turned over the major parts of these to the clerk, he can reclaim them if he wishes. More importantly, the chief accountant still has the same obligations to the treasurer. The additional obligation between the clerk and the chief accountant in no way relieves the chief accountant of his obligation. It is as though the treasurer lent ten dollars to the chief accountant, and the chief accountant in turn lent the money to the clerk; the chief accountant cannot satisfy his obligation to the controller by giving him the clerk's IOU.

If we were to abandon the principle that one cannot delegate obligation, there would be no way of knowing who was accountable for what.[6]

An issue faced over and over in delegating is whether each person should have only one boss. On this point, formal organization theory is clear. A worker—operator or manager— may have relationships with many people, but he needs one supervisor whose guidance can be regarded as final. What are the reasons supporting this concept of a single chain of command?

**dual subordination**

All executives and all subordinate employees respond to a variety of influences, not just to those emanating from their line bosses. Nevertheless, the evidence indicates that as important as other people may be in influencing the behavior of an employee, the line boss is usually far more significant. Reasons for the overriding influence of the line boss are not hard to find. Normally the boss trains and directs an employee and explains what he should do; the boss authorizes what the subordinate may do; he assists in getting necessary materials and tools and often represents "his" people throughout the organization; he checks results and initiates corrective action when necessary; he praises, blames, disciplines, promotes, recommends changes in pay, and otherwise motivates his subordinates. These activities are closely interrelated, and if they are to have their greatest impact, they should spring, integrated, from one source.

When two bosses try to share the fundamental role of immediate supervisor, their actions are likely to be inconsistent. One may praise, whereas the other may suggest improvements; the first may urge speed and initiative, whereas the second may withhold authority; they may make assignments that conflict. People can and do get along with two bosses, just as a child accepts guidance from two teachers; but unless the two bosses have a very close working relationship, they may find many opportunities for maneuvering for advantage and may tend to be unjust to the subordinate. When there is one boss, the likelihood of a consistent pattern of supervision is greatly increased. The experience of managers over the years indicates that it is wise to have one supervisor who resolves conflicting demands and has final say on priorities.

---

[6]P. D. Weisse, "What A Chief- or Group-Executive Cannot Delegate," *Management Review,* May 1975.

Clear-cut duties and authorities do not imply that everyone should work in his own isolated corner. Instead, in most delegations, managers make it very clear that a subordinate should consult with others and keep them informed as he proceeds with his own duties.

Furthermore, a few assignments are specifically joint undertakings. Some companies emphasize their concern with cooperation by saying that a person is accountable for both work and teamwork, and they are dissatisfied with the person's performance unless he measures up well on both counts. Cooperation is definitely part of a job and should be as clear as other duties.

Relations between supervisors and subordinates are subject to continual readjustment. We should modify delegations as the work to be done and the people who do it change. Nevertheless, the vast number of relationships are stable—at least for some period of time. This stability is important. A worker learns what to expect of his boss; the boss learns how much he can depend on each of his subordinates; people doing related work learn how to deal with an established hierarchy. Such patterns of expectation are essential if we are to get day-to-day work done smoothly and quickly. If the delegating has not been done well, and if boss-subordinate relationships are unclear and become sources of friction, the company unity will be lacking.

## HOW MUCH DECENTRALIZATION?

The preceding discussion centered on the process of delegating. Now we turn to the extent and content of such delegation.

Experience has shown that *planning*—that is, identifying problems and deciding what action to take—is usually the most crucial element in thinking about decentralization. Organizing, leading, and controlling are also important, but assigning those activities to various executives typically depends on how we have allocated planning duties. When we look more closely later on at leadership and control, we shall trace the interplay of these phases of management with decisions concerning decentralization.

There are several ways to divide the work of planning among executives, and these are important for describing varying degrees of decentralization.[7]

**By subject**  This is the simplest way to divide planning. An executive normally makes decisions only for the operations that he also directs. However, when an operation affects several related departments, as does pricing or inventory control, he may stipulate that certain other persons are to be consulted before binding decisions are made.

Dividing planning by subject is especially useful in situations where there is a senior executive and a lower executive who reports to him. A chief accountant, for example, might say to his office manager: "I'll decide what

[7]For a thoughtful historical perspective on the centralization vs. decentralization debate, see A. Jay, *Management and Machiavelli* (New York: Bantam Books, 1974).

226

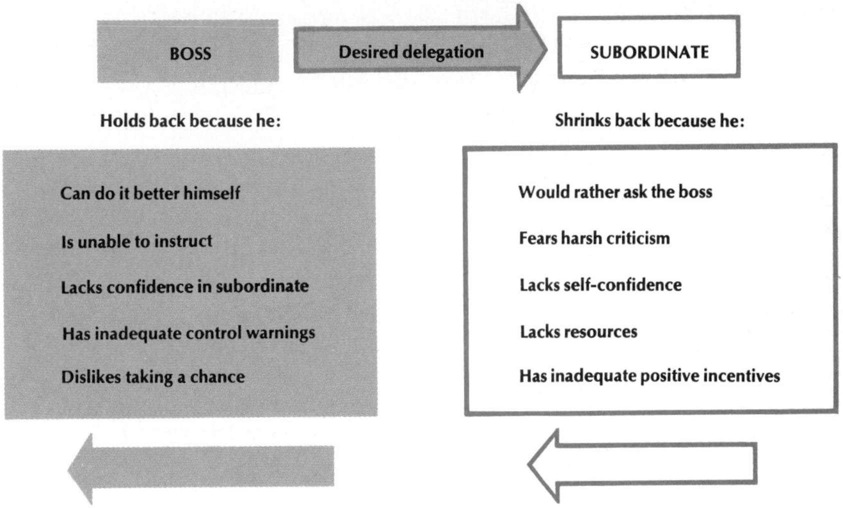

| BOSS | Desired delegation → | SUBORDINATE |

**Holds back because he:**

Can do it better himself

Is unable to instruct

Lacks confidence in subordinate

Has inadequate control warnings

Dislikes taking a chance

**Shrinks back because he:**

Would rather ask the boss

Fears harsh criticism

Lacks self-confidence

Lacks resources

Has inadequate positive incentives

*Figure 11.2 Personal obstacles to effective delegation. Even when organizational design calls for delegation, personal factors may obstruct the transfer.*

accounts to keep and where different types of items should be charged—that is, I'll set up the accounting system. But I want you to schedule the flow of work through the office, determine the number and types of people we need, and figure out whether it would pay us to get more automatic equipment." Or the vice-president in charge of sales might select the markets to be cultivated and then assign his sales manager the detailed planning of direct-mail publicity, personal contacts, and other activities designed to secure orders from the customers within these markets. Note that in each of these examples certain subjects are decided by the senior person and other subjects by his subordinate.

*By type of plan* Often a sharp division of administrative work by subject is not feasible. A senior executive may want some say in the way a particular type of situation is handled, and yet lack time to make daily decisions on individual problems. This partial involvement can be accomplished by relying on the various parameters of a planning system, as described in Part I. For example, an executive can establish *objectives* and *policies* to set the direction and limits of action. Subordinates can then make decisions on specific cases within this guiding framework. For instance, the president of a telephone company can say, "No employee with more than two years of service is to be discharged as a result of installation of automatic-dialing equipment." The managers of local branches must act within this limit and plan for the transfer or retraining of any displaced workers with a two-year service record.

Sometimes a senior executive wishes to be more specific. If so, he can lay out a step-by-step *procedure* (Chapter 4) to be followed, or a *schedule* (Chapter 5) of dates by which specific action is to be completed. Thus an advertising manager often sets deadlines for drawings, magazine copy, radio scripts, and other parts of his promotion campaign. His subordinates are free to make detailed schedules for their own work provided the master schedule is met.

227

In still other situations an executive may announce that certain *premises* (Chapter 9) are to be adopted when plans are made for the future. For example, he tells the production manager to prepare his budget on the assumption that there will be a twenty percent increase in sales volume for the following year.

From the point of view of decentralization, the questions are *to what extent* these different types of plan should be used and *who* should set them up. Clearly, the more management circumsubscribes or regiments work by means of objectives, policies, and so forth, the more highly centralized the organization will be.

**By phase of planning**   Planning is not typically an isolated activity performed by a single person insulated from his associates. In fact, the more important the plan, the more likely that several people will participate in formulating it. As we noted in Chapter 9, planning consists of several identifiable phases: diagnosing and identifying a problem, finding possible solutions to the problem, gathering facts, projecting the results of each alternative, and, finally, choosing one alternative as the course of action to be followed. In practice, the work of each of these phases may be performed by different persons.

Except for final decision-making, none of these phases need be regarded as the exclusive domain of a particular person. Anyone who spots a trouble area that needs to be cleaned up or has evidence that will contribute to the sound analysis of a problem should be encouraged to volunteer his ideas. Eliciting such voluntary assistance, however, is not enough in itself. Someone must still be responsible for ensuring that each phase of the planning process is properly performed.

Just how these phases are actually handled depends a great deal on the atmosphere that prevails within each company. In one company it might be presumptuous for a first-line supervisor to suggest a change in personnel policies, whereas in another company the supervisor might get fired if he failed to spot potential trouble and recommend a plan for avoiding it. When a possible change is being studied, some companies expect a lower-level supervisor to provide only the information he is asked for, whereas others expect him to speak his mind on anything he believes pertinent and, perhaps, to come up with counterproposals. These are all examples of how the burden of planning may be allocated in terms of phases or steps in the planning process.

**Summary**   To decide who should do what about planning, we need to ask ourselves these questions.

1.  What is the subject?
2.  Is a *single* problem being decided, or is a *general* guide being established—such as an objective, policy, procedure, schedule, or premise?
3.  Do we want several executives to participate in the decision? If so, which phase of the decision-making process is each expected to take on?

Decentralization is concerned with how much of this complex planning activity should be assigned to each executive, from the president down to first-line supervisors.

**229**
CHAPTER 11
*designing
the hierarchy*

degrees of
decentralization

How are these concepts put into practice? The following two examples (illustrated in Figure 11.3) help answer this question. To make it easier to compare the degrees of decentralization, both examples concern sales activities.

*Decentralized planning*    A company that manufactures materials-handling equipment has a field force of twenty-four representatives. Six are branch managers, and each has one to four sales representatives. The branch managers spend at least half of their time in actual selling. Because industrial equipment is purchased at irregular intervals, the sales people have to follow new sales leads; they cannot depend on a regular flow of repeat business from established customers.

The management of this company thinks it has a highly decentralized sales operation. However, two important areas are definitely centralized: products and prices. Product-planning is handled by the engineering department in the main office. A variety of standard equipment is described in a product book, and sales representatives sell this equipment whenever it is suited to the customer's needs. If special equipment is required, the sales representatives simply gather the operating data and submit these facts to the home office. The engineering department then decides what to recommend to the customer and prepares the necessary sketches. The setting of prices is also centralized. Prices of standard items and special orders are set by the sales manager. In making these decisions, the sales manager draws on field information on customers, cost figures from the estimating department, and his knowledge of the competitive situation.

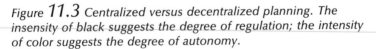

*Figure 11.3 Centralized versus decentralized planning. The intensity of black suggests the degree of regulation; the intensity of color suggests the degree of autonomy.*

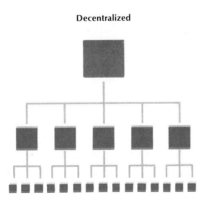

Decentralized

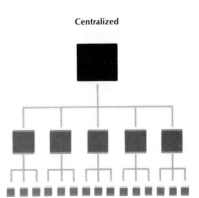

Centralized

Except for product-planning and price-setting, people in the field have almost complete freedom. Which customers to call on, what selling methods to use, which conventions and trade association meetings to attend, when a long-distance phone call is worth its cost—all are determined locally. The branch manager is the key person in many of these decisions, but he may rely on an experienced sales representative to do his own planning.

The home office provides a variety of descriptive circulars, prospect lists, technical advice, and other services. Nevertheless, it is up to the branch manager and the sales representatives to decide what use, if any, they will make of these services.

Notice that the planning of sales is rather sharply divided by subject. The chief engineer decides what products will be sold, the sales manager sets the prices, the branch managers select the customers. Only limited use is made of policies and standing procedures. There is considerable cooperation in the planning process, particularly through the exchange of ideas and information. This exchange has not been formalized, however, to a point where the executive making the decision feels relieved of the preliminary phases of planning (except for the preparation of cost estimates used in pricing).

Not everyone in the company is convinced that the present method of dividing up the sales planning work is the best. One manager advocates much more centralized planning and direction; he insists that sales quotas should be established, that sales representatives should be directed to specific prospects, and that direct-mail advertising should be tied in closely with sales calls. However, most executives believe that the local people can judge what will produce on-the-spot results better than anyone sitting in the home office.

*Centralized planning*　　A quite different way of dividing sales planning work is followed by a successful Midwestern oil company. Each of the forty-two branch managers has a fuel-oil and industrial-sales manager, a gasoline sales manager who concentrates on sales through filling stations, and a branch engineer who leases, staffs, builds, and exercises financial control over company-owned filling stations.

Most sales planning is done in the main office. The marketing vice-president sets general prices and establishes policies covering any price reduction to meet local competition. Advertising is planned and executed at headquarters. Sales promotion, keyed in with the advertising program, is planned in detail at the home office and includes decisions on the color stations are to be painted and on the design of signs. A variety of training aids for station operators are also planned centrally: instructions for waiting on customers, care of washrooms, methods of car greasing, and the like.

The branch managers, then, are primarily concerned with carrying out plans that have already been made. They hire, train, pay, direct, and motivate the key people in the branch office—all in accordance with company policy and other plans. If a price war breaks out, they adjust local prices in accordance with policy or, if necessary, request the home office to adjust them. They take care of the innumerable little problems that inevitably arise in the sale of a substantial dollar-volume of product. Often they pass new ideas for sales promotion along to the main office. Their principal duty, however, is to carry out the sales program as effectively as possible rather than to propose new ideas. The executives of this oil company would strongly resist any proposal to give branch managers the freedom in planning permitted by the manufacturer described above.

These two examples illustrate not only the general difference between a centralized and decentralized organization, but also the need to think specifically about each type of problem (for instance, pricing in the industrial-equipment company) even though a general pattern has been established. In practice, an endless variation in degrees of delegation exists, and properly so. Each company operates in its own unique circumstances of size, reputation, competitive strategy, existing equipment, abilities of key executives, and other factors. Each manager must figure out what allocation of executive duties best fits his needs. We can, however, identify certain factors that will help a manager make that allocation wisely.

The following seven factors should be carefully weighed when choosing the best place in the executive hierarchy for each category of decision-making.[8]

guides to
"how much
decentralization?"

1. *Who knows the facts on which the decision will be based, or who can get them together most readily?*

   Sometimes a single individual—salesperson, advertising manager, purchasing agent—is in constant command, through the normal course of his work, of all the facts needed to make a given type of decision, Such a person alone is naturally best equipped for decision-making on the issue. Many decisions, however, require information from several different sources—a decision whether or not to buy a new machine, for example, requires data on production methods, plant layout, future colume, availability of capital, workers' attitudes, and so forth. Channels of communication must be established to funnel all this information to a single point; the question, then, is whether it will be easier to pass general information down the line or specific information up the line. This raises considerations of the accuracy, time, and cost of such communication.

2. *Who has the capacity to make sound decisions?*

   Clearly, if people at lower levels—engineers, office supervisors, branch managers—lack the ability and experience needed to make a wise decision, there is a compelling reason to withhold decision-making authority from them. Such capacity, however, is usually a relative matter. Perhaps the president can make a very wise decision about granting credit, but the branch manager can make one that is almost as effective. Since we want to save the president's energies for more important matters, and the branch manager's judgment on this subject is satisfactory, we should lodge the planning for extending credit with the branch manager.

3. *Must speedy, on-the-spot decisions be made to meet local conditions?*

   The repair of airplane breakdowns or the buying of fruit at wholesale auctions obviously requires that someone with authority be at the scene of

---

[8]R. J. Cordiner, *New Frontiers for Professional Managers* (New York: McGraw-Hill, 1956).

action. A similar, though less dramatic, need for prompt action occurs in negotiating contracts, employing personnel to meet unexpected work loads, or adjusting the complaints of irate customers.

4. *Must the local activity be carefully coordinated with other activities?*

Sometimes *uniformity* of action is so important that all decisions must be made centrally—for example, ensuring that all customers in a single area are charged the same prices, or determining the length of vacation for all employees in the same plant. Other decisions, such as determining a weekly production schedule or laying out a national sales-promotion program, require that activities in several areas be closely *synchronized;* here, at least some central planning is called for.

5. *How significant is the decision?*

A relatively minor decision—one that will increase or decrease profits only by a dollar or two, for example—clearly should be left to a junior executive or operator. The expense of communication up and down the channel of command and of the time required for the senior executive to handle the problem, would be far greater than any savings that might result from his judgment. On the other hand, any decision that will have a major effect on the total operation—either a single transaction or a basic policy—should be approved at least by a senior executive.

6. *How busy are the executives who might be assigned planning tasks?*

In dividing up work among executives, overloads must be avoided. A top executive may already have so many duties that he will have to shirk additional responsibility for planning; or a plant superintendent may lack the time for careful analysis and thoughtful decision. If a busy executive has a distinctive contribution that only he can make, perhaps he can be brought in on one phase of the planning, while the rest of the chore is assigned to someone else.

7. *Will initiative and morale be significantly improved by decentralization?*

Decentralization typically builds initiative and good morale in lower-level executives. We should be sure, however, that such feelings will be generated, and that they are desirable, in each specific situation. Companies that are faced with frequent shifts in consumer demand, in technology, or in the competitive situation must actively promote adaptability and initiative among their workers. In other enterprises, such as many public utilities, where the rate of change is much slower, too much originality and initiative among junior executives may actually create discontent and lower morale. Similar sharp differences in the need for initiative are also found in various departments of a single company.

In using these factors as guides to the degree of decentralization that is appropriate in a specific situation, a manager must determine how much weight to attach to each. Often the factors pull in opposite directions—the need for speed may suggest greater decentralization, while the desire for coordination may dictate greater centralization. Clearly, each factor must be carefully balanced against the others. Allowance must also be made both for traditional behavior and for growth in the abilities of individuals. So we see again that the managerial task of organizing calls for a high order of judgment.

**PROFIT DECENTRALIZATION**     There is one form of decentralization that is highly important to larger companies: profit decentralization. Under this plan, we split a company into business-units (discussed in Chapter 2), each of which is responsible for its own profit or loss.[9]

Two characteristics lie at the heart of the plan. (1) All the major operations necessary to make a profit are grouped under the manager of a *self-sufficient* unit. This, of course, is a matter of departmentation (discussed in Chapter 10). Typically, several such self-sufficient, self-contained units are established in a company. (2) The management of these units is so highly decentralized that each of them becomes *semiautonomous*. In effect, we have a series of little businesses operating within the parent corporation. The manager of each unit has virtually the same resources and freedom of action that he would enjoy if he were president of an independent company. He is expected to formulate his own strategy and to take whatever steps are necessary to ensure that his "little business" will make a profit.

> self-sufficient, semiautonomous units

Though profit decentralization is the key concept in organizing large concerns like General Motors Corporation, it is by no means confined to industrial giants. Smaller companies such as Research-Cottrell and Dana Corporation have found it admirably suited to their needs.

Ordinarily the business-units are built around product lines, and the engineering, production, and sales of each line are placed within the decentralized division. The same idea, however, has been applied to department-store chains, which place all their operations in each *region* on a profit-decentralization basis. In fact, this form of organization has become so successful and popular that most diversified companies use it in at least a modified form.

A major advantage of profit decentralization is its stimulating effect on the *morale* of the key people in each of these self-sufficient, semiautonomous divisions. Executives are able to see the results of their own methods, to take the action they believe best, and to feel that they are playing an important role. The resulting enthusiasm and devotion to the success of their division tend to spread to employees at all levels.

> benefits

Because business-units established under profit decentralization are of a *manageable size*, fewer people have to exchange information, and they can communicate with one another swiftly and effectively. Thus, executives find it easier to comprehend the information that is funneled to them.

Situations requiring administrative action are more likely to receive *adequate attention* under profit decentralization. In a large-scale enterprise, it is all too easy to neglect a product or an operation that contributes only a minor part to the total sales volume. In a smaller business-unit, however, such problems become relatively more important, and executives are much more likely to take the necessary corrective action.

The smaller size of the business-units and the heightened ease of communication also lead to improved *coordination*, particularly in the critically

---

[9]The effect of diversification on the need for decentralization is described in R. A. Pitts, "Diversification Strategies and Organizational Policies of Large Diversified Firms," *Journal of Economics and Business,* 28. no. 3 (Summer 1976), 181–88.

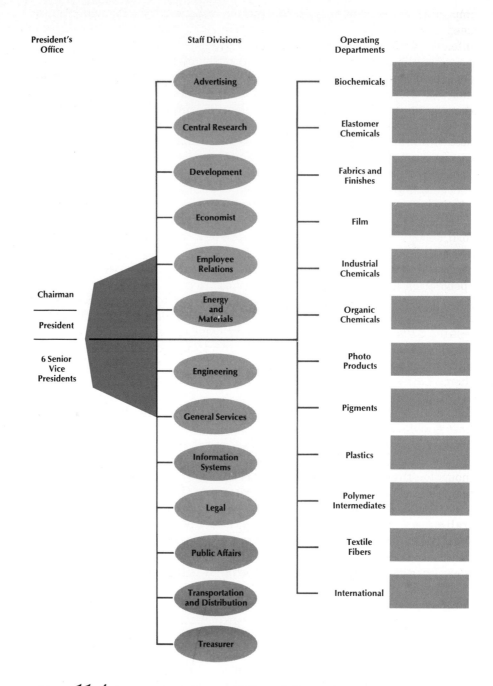

| President's Office | Staff Divisions | Operating Departments |
|---|---|---|

**President's Office**

Chairman

President

6 Senior Vice Presidents

**Staff Divisions**

Advertising

Central Research

Development

Economist

Employee Relations

Energy and Materials

Engineering

General Services

Information Systems

Legal

Public Affairs

Transportation and Distribution

Treasurer

**Operating Departments**

Biochemicals

Elastomer Chemicals

Fabrics and Finishes

Film

Industrial Chemicals

Organic Chemicals

Photo Products

Pigments

Plastics

Polymer Intermediates

Textile Fibers

International

*Figure 11.4 Organization of a multi-billion dollar company. Each operating unit is a self-contained business with its own engineering, production, marketing, and finance activities. The staff divisions provide services to the departments and to the president's office.*

234

important areas of serving customers, matching production and sales, and keeping costs in line with income. Bureaucratic attitudes are less likely to interfere with voluntary cooperation.

By making both measurement and accountability more clear cut, profit decentralization promotes more effective *control*. The profit-and-loss statement of each business-unit provides a significant measure of results, and there is less need to make arbitrary allocation of costs. Moreover, because a self-sufficient division is also semiautonomous, its manager can be held accountable for resulting profit or loss. If the results are poor, he can be required to take corrective action; if they are good, he can be, and often is, generously rewarded.

**limitations and difficulties**

If profit decentralization contributes all these impressive advantages, why is it that all large enterprises are not organized in this fashion? Unfortunately, certain distinct limitations and problems are inherent in its use.

For one thing, not all companies can be *divided neatly* into self-contained business-units. Technology may make it impossible for a large operation to be broken up into several smaller ones. A steel mill, for example, cannot be split down the middle. On the other hand, in operations such as wholesaling or retailing, which involve a large number of products, sales volume of any one product may be insufficient to support the expense of a separate management and a staff of specialists. One of the limitations of profit decentralization, then, is that the operations of the company must lend themselves to being divided into self-sufficient units of manageable size.

A related problem springs from the auxiliary-service activities that the company must perform for the business-units. Will a single, central *service unit,* such as purchasing or plant engineering, be really *responsive* to the needs of each of several business-units? If so, what happens to their presumed autonomy and accountability for profits? These are not insurmountable problems, but they do emphasize that profit decentralization brings in its wake a series of potentially troublesome issues.

Although we have referred to this type of organization as profit decentralization, we must remember that profits, though important, may be an *inadequate measure* of the performance of a business-unit, at least in the short run. A business-unit may decide, with the full approval of top management, to spend money on advertising to improve its market position; for two or three years it may spend large sums developing a new product. In other words, the unit may be achieving its objectives even though it is showing a relatively small profit. Conversely, by keeping down expenses for non-recurring or deferable items, a business-unit may make a good profit showing even though it is slipping in customer goodwill or development of potential executives. This means that the use of profits for purposes of control is valid only if it is interpreted with a full understanding of what is happening within the business.

Perhaps the greatest difficulty in the use of profit decentralization is to find executives with the *capacity and willingness* to work effectively within the system. The business-unit managers must be prepared to take the initiative on any matter that affects the long-run success of their units. They must be aware of the direct and indirect results of their own actions, instead of trying to rely on someone in the home office to keep them out of trouble. In other words, they must act as responsible stewards of the resources put under their direction.

Top administrative officials in the company, in turn, must accept their obligation to maintain a "hands-off" attitude toward the decentralized business. As the president of a successfully decentralized company put it, "This calls for confidence in the capabilities of other people, a belief in teaching rather than telling, patience while others are learning—perhaps through their own mistakes—and a willingness to let others stand out in the public eye."

And yet we must remember that many executives of business-units have been trained to concentrate on a particular specialty rather than to take an overall view of an integrated business and that the top executives of many corporations have achieved their position through positive, aggressive action. This experience makes the behavior described in the two preceding paragraphs difficult to achieve in practice. The key managers in a company that adopts profit decentralization must have a realistic understanding of their new roles and must be flexible enough to adjust their behavior accordingly.

**restrictions on autonomy**

Clearly, there are many areas in which business-units are *not* autonomous. Everyone agrees that corporate management should retain some influence over the separate businesses. In consultation with the business-unit managers, corporate management should (1) set business-unit strategy and annual goals, (2) establish the broad policies within which the units are to operate, (3) approve the selection of key executives within the unit, (4) approve major capital expenditures (which in effect means approving any major expansion), and (5) review any single transaction that might entail a major change in the profit or loss of the unit. In addition, the headquarters office might want (6) to establish certain procedures for accounting, personnel, or purchasing to ensure consistent action throughout the corporation. Furthermore, corporate management can interpret all these limitations so broadly that it may retain the right to interfere with the business-unit operations almost anywhere it wants to.

The use of policies, procedures, programs, and other types of plans have already been examined in Part I. Parts IV, V, and VI will discuss means for securing motivation, leadership, and control. The point here is that the manner in which these processes are performed can either support or vitiate the underlying concept of profit decentralization. Therefore, if we organize along profit-decentralization lines, we must also plan, control, and lead in a manner compatible with profit decentralization.

## CONCLUSION: FOCUS ON PLANNING

In this chapter, we discussed first the process of delegating and then related this to the allocation of managerial work, especially its assignment to executives at different levels, from first-line supervisors to the president. Planning—that is, making decisions about actions to be taken—stands out as the crucial activity in managerial decentralization; once it has been decided who should do what planning, then other aspects of managerial work can be adjusted to fit into the pattern. Each manager has to allocate planning work among his subordinates, and we have identified several factors that can help him design a pattern of decentralization suited to the particular conditions he faces.

One special type of allocation, especially appealing to diversified companies, is "profit decentralization." Analysis of profit decentralization highlights the intimate connection between the way a company is departmentalized and the forms of decentralization that are desirable. We shall return to this interrelationship in the chapters on overall organization structure. But first we need to consider, in the next chapter, how staff can be fitted into the total allocation of managerial work.

## FOR FURTHER DISCUSSION

1. In what ways would you expect the degree and type of decentralization that takes place in a conglomerate with sales of $200 million to differ from the degree and type of decentralization practiced in an equally large farm-equipment producer?

2. "Phyllis Mason isn't my boss, but she is clearly the brightest, most experienced person in our lab. My boss is a great scientist but a poor manager. Therefore, most of the people in the group look to Phyllis for direction." Comment on the benefits and drawbacks implied by this statement.

3. "We do a great deal of delegating in order to increase accountability for results but we reserve the right to overrule lower levels of management on decisions in certain areas." Should the areas referred to by a senior vice-president of a small plumbing supply company be spelled out in detail or just described in broad terms?

4. "When I delegate a portion of my job, I inevitably *add to* rather than reduce my duties and obligations." How do you interpret this statement made by a department head?

5. It is important in delegating work to differentiate clearly between accountability for strategic vs. tactical decisions. Can such distinctions be made? Should they?

6. The chief accountant of the Chicago division of a company reports to the general manager of that division. Accounting forms, regulations, and procedures, however, are designed by the corporate controller and must be followed by the division chief accountant. (1) Who is the chief accountant's boss? (2) What is the nature of his obligation to the division general manager? To the controller? (3) How, by wise delegation, might potential friction be avoided? (4) How does this situation relate to bypassed supervision?

7. How can the decision-making techniques discussed in Part II be used in choosing the desired degree of decentralization?

## CASES

For cases involving issues covered in this chapter, see especially the following. Particularly relevant questions are listed after each case.

Mike Zerllini (p. 188), 10
Clifford Nelson (p. 192), 11

## FOR FURTHER READING

Chandler, A. D., Jr., *Strategy and Structure.* Cambridge: MIT Press, 1962. Traces the development of the decentralized, multi-division structure in American industry.

Drucker, P. F., *Management: Tasks, Responsibilities, Practice.* New York: Harper & Row, 1974, chaps. 41–48. Insightful discussion of the relationship between decentralization and organizational effectiveness.

Greenwood, R. G., *Managerial Decentralization.* New York: D. C. Heath, 1974. Description of General Electric Company's move to a highly decentralized organization.

Ross, J. E. and M. J. Kami, *Corporate Management in Crisis: Why the Mighty Fall.* Englewood Cliffs, NJ: Prentice-Hall, 1973, chaps. 12 and 19. Concise summary of centralization vs. decentralization debate supported by case studies of actual company experience.

Stewart, R., *The Reality of Organizations: A Guide for Managers.* London: Macmillan, 1970, chaps. 5–8. A useful short statement, written for managers, on delegation and other relationships within organizations.

Vancil, R. F., *Decentralization: Managerial Ambiguity by Design.* New York: Financial Executives Research Foundation, 1979. Contemporary treatment of the managerial trade-offs associated with decentralized organizations.

# staff-line roles in strategic action

# 12

Learning Objectives

After completing this chapter you should be able to

1. Understand the similarities and differences between specialized staff and general staff.
2. Describe the central features of completed staff work.
3. Discuss the most important prerequisites for successful line-staff relationships.
4. Describe the various ways in which staff may exert influence within the chain of command.
5. Identify four common problems associated with the use of staff.

## THE CONCEPT OF STAFF

After a manager has decided on major departments and has settled on a degree of decentralization, he is ready to consider what staff units he wants and where he should place them in the organization structure.

Staff is a key device managers can use to cope with pressures from our increasingly complex world. It is a special way of sharing the total managerial load—a device that supplements decentralization.

**definition of staff**

Staff work is that part of managerial work that an executive assigns to someone outside the chain of command. If an executive wants to relieve himself of some of his administrative burden, he may assign it to a staff assistant instead of delegating it to subordinates who would also be accountable for operations.

As we explained in Chapter 11, a manager always reserves some of the duties of planning, motivating, and controlling when he delegates operating duties to a line subordinate. If he uses staff help, he simply assigns part of this reserved administration to a third person.

A president or the head of a large department may use several staff people for different phases of his total management task. Some of these staff assistants may even have several subordinates of their own who form a staff section. Whatever the number and size of staff sections, the aim of staff work remains the same—to help an executive manage.

**examples of staff**

The concept of staff comes from military organization, but the business world uses the term more loosely.[1] Practices vary widely from company to company and from job to job, with the result that we find widespread confusion about what a staff person is supposed to do. Because there is no single pattern, managers must design each staff position individually, as they do other jobs, deciding what activities they can advantageously assign to each position. Three examples will indicate the range of possibilities.

*Specialized staff*  Market research illustrates *specialized* staff work. A typical market-research unit gathers a wide variety of information about consumer habits, economic trends, competitors' actions, and marketing practices. The unit carefully analyzes this information and gives operating executives advice on marketing problems. For example, market researchers can suggest sales potentials to use in setting quotas for individual salespeople, and can test customer response to product change. Operating executives do not have time to gather such information themselves, and they hesitate to ask their sales force to do the work for several reasons: specialized skills are required, objectivity is essential, and sales people should spend their time getting orders from customers.[2]

---

[1]J. D. Hittle, *The Military Staff: Its History and Development.* (Harrisburg: Stackpole Books, 1961).

[2]W. French and D. Henning, "The Authority-Influence Role of the Functional Specialist in Management," *Journal of the Academy of Management,* 9, no. 3 (September 1966), 187–203.

An industrial engineer is a good illustration of a staff person in the production area. Typically he not only gathers information but also goes further than the market researcher in preparing specific plans. Layout of plant equipment, production methods, operating standards based on time studies, incentive plans, systems for production scheduling, quality-control techniques, preventive maintenance—these are among the problems an industrial engineer often tackles. Solution of such problems requires concentrated attention and may involve more technical knowledge than a production manager has.

*General staff*   Not all staff people concentrate on a specific type of work. Sometimes a manager wants an assistant to whom he can turn over a wide variety of problems. The assistant's duties can vary all the way from functioning as a first-class secretary to serving as an alter ego to the boss in delicate negotiations. The staff person with such unspecified duties is often called "assistant to the _____."

On different days, we might find an assistant to the president gathering information on the national economic outlook, editing a statement for the president to make before a Congressional committee, investigating a complaint about company service, or meeting with a group of long-service employees who urge the company to advance the compulsory retirement age to seventy.

*Corporate services*   Very large companies sometimes attach to the central headquarters staff units that work primarily as consultants to operating divisions. In the General Electric company, for instance, one corporate "service" unit focuses on community relations, another on operations research, and so on. Each "service" is charged with anticipating external developments, advancing the state of the art in its particular field, organizing training courses to pass these advanced techniques on to executives and staff people in the business-units, and being available as consultants on the invitation of the business-units. Service is stressed. And to encourage operating people to use this service, senior executives at General Electric do *not* use these units for evaluation and control.

Some corporations have a few staff people who concentrate on strategic planning. Typically, this staff makes studies in areas outside the domains of existing business-units for the purpose of locating areas or even companies that are attractive expansion possibilities. A more controversial and less common assignment is independent evaluation of strategies recommended by existing business-units. A third potential duty of strategic planning staff is to devise planning procedures to be used throughout the corporation, and to expedite the flow of paperwork and information that aids strategic decisions. However, the main responsibility for strategic planning remains with line executives; staff merely helps.

In these examples of staff and in the many others that will appear in this book, we find a delegation of managerial work to people who do not supervise operations. These delegations, like all delegations, carry with

241

CHAPTER 12
*staff-line roles
in strategic action*

them duties, authority, and obligation. But the duties do not entail direct supervision over executives or operators.

**when to use staff** Since staff complicates an organization, we should examine carefully the need for staff assistants.[3] Generally speaking, a manager can justify assigning duties to staff when he is overburdened or lacks a necessary technical skill. Managers may hesitate to delegate more work to operating subordinates for any of the following reasons:

1. *Operating subordinates would not give an activity adequate attention.* For instance, a vice president of personnel may be appointed if department managers are skeptical of modern techniques and central management fears they will slight this activty.

2. *The work requires an expert.* Most managers, for instance, lack knowledge of real estate and the law, so staff assistants may be provided in these areas.

3. *The company needs coordinated and consistent action among several operating units.* The need for consistency in fair-employment practices or in pricing may prompt a staff appointment. Or, coordination of a national advertising campaign with local sales promotion may need concentrated attention.

4. *The manager wants help in controlling the operating departments.* Keeping track of local operations is especially difficult when activities are dispersed in many geographical locations.

5. *The manager seeks aid in analyzing problems.* Any manager may become so busy with pressing short-run problems that he needs an assistant who can help him think through basic questions.

## SCOPE OF STAFF WORK

We can define the work of a staff person in terms of both the subjects or problems he covers and what he does about them. Unless a staff person, his boss, and everyone he works with understands the scope of his work, his efforts may cause more trouble than help. It is not enough, for example, to say that a personnel director should handle staff services in the field of personnel relations. Rather it is more constructive to list the types of problems in the field and then decide how far we expect a staff person to go in dealing with the problem. Figure 12.1 indicates this general approach.

**clarifying assigned duties**

This chart reveals that the role of a personnel director may differ in various areas. In dealing with unions, for example, he is likely to serve principally as an advisor. On the other hand, no appointment to vacancies can be made without the concurrence of the personnel director.

The chart also suggests that for some activities, such as recruiting employees, handling pension plans, or sponsoring company athletic teams, a firm may grant its personnel director operating authority; in these areas he ceases to be staff and becomes a supervisor of auxiliary services.

[3]J. A. Belasco and J. A. Alluto, "Line and Staff Conflicts: Some Empirical Insights," *Academy of Management Journal*, 12, no. 1 (1969), 469–77.

| Activities | Subjects | | | | | | | |
|---|---|---|---|---|---|---|---|---|
| | Recruiting | Selecting Employees | Training | Compensation | Benefit Plans | Health and Recreation | Union Relations | Employee Records |
| **1. OPERATING WORK** | | | | | | | | |
| Supervises service operations | ■ | | | | ■ | ■ | | ■ |
| **2. STAFF WORK** | | | | | | | | |
| Influences actions outside own department; to do so, he: | | | | | | | | |
| A. Advises boss | | | | | | | | |
| 1. Identifies areas that need improvement | | | | ■ | | | ■ | |
| 2. Finds likely solutions | | | | ■ | | | ■ | |
| 3. Gathers and analyzes data bearing on choice of solution | | | | ■ | | | ■ | |
| 4. Gets concurrence or objections of people affected | | | | ■ | | | ■ | |
| 5. Recommends tentative solution | | | ■ | ■ | | | ■ | |
| B. Advises associates (mostly operating executives under his boss) | | | | | | | | |
| 1. Identifies areas that need improvement | | | ■ | | | | ■ | |
| 2. Finds likely solutions | | ■ | ■ | | | | ■ | |
| 3. Gathers and analyzes data bearing on choice of solution | | ■ | ■ | | | | ■ | |
| 4. Gets concurrence or objections of people affected | | | ■ | | | | ■ | |
| 5. Recommends tentative solution | | ■ | ■ | | | | ■ | |
| C. Prepares documents putting plans into effect | | ■ | | ■ | | | ■ | |
| D. Interprets and sells established plans | ■ | | | | | | | |
| E. Reports compliance to associates | | | ■ | ■ | | | | |
| F. Reports compliance to boss | | | ■ | | | | | |
| G. Concurs on specific acts | | ■ | | ■ | | | | |
| H. Sets policies and systems | | | ■ | | | | | |

*Figure 12.1  Chart for analyzing the duties of a personnel director.*

Each check mark on a chart such as this represents careful thought about the functions of a particular staff person in a specific company. The chart is of course only a summary. For many duties under the heading of Subjects, we must think through several subtopics. "Training," for instance, includes by implication considerations of what should be done for executive personnel, orientation of new employees, training on the job, personal-development plans, and so forth. All this detail cannot be shown on a single chart, but the same kind of analysis applies to each subdivision.

The same approach should be followed when we determine the duties of each staff position. The principal task of the market researcher is to gather and analyze data for his boss and other operating executives—A.3 and B.3 on the chart. The industrial engineer, on the other hand, is likely to undertake all duties listed under A to F on the chart. An internal auditor is predominantly concerned simply with reporting compliance to his associates and his boss—items E and F on the chart. If we analyze duties in this manner, we will go a long way toward eliminating misunderstandings about the use of staff.

**completed staff work**

Some people feel that the ideal staff arrangement results in "completed staff work," a concept that General Archer H. Lerch has described as follows:

Completed Staff Work is the study of a problem, and presentation of a solution, by a staff officer, in such form that all that remains to be done on the part of the head of the staff division, or the commander, is to indicate his approval or disapproval of the completed action. The words "completed action" are emphasized because the more difficult the problem is, the more the tendency is to present the problem to the chief in piecemeal fashion. It is your duty as a staff officer to work out the details. You should not consult your chief in the determination of these details, no matter how perplexing they may be. You may and should consult other staff officers. The product, whether it involves the pronouncement of a new policy or affects an established one, should, when presented to the chief for approval or disapproval, be worked out in finished form.

. . . It is your job to advise your chief what he ought to do, not to ask him what you ought to do. He needs answers, not questions. Your job is to study, write, restudy and rewrite until you have evolved a single proposed action—the best one of all you have considered. Your chief merely approves or disapproves.

Do not worry your chief with long explanations and memoranda. . . . In most instances, completed staff work results in a single document, prepared for the signature of the chief without accompanying comment. If the proper result is reached, the chief will usually recognize it at once. If he wants comment or explanation, he will ask for it.

The theory of completed staff work does not preclude a "rough draft" but the rough draft must not be a half-baked idea. It must be complete in every respect except that it lacks the requisite number of copies and need not be neat. . . .

The completed staff work theory may result in more work for the staff officer, but it results in more freedom for the chief. This is as it should be. Further, it accomplishes two things.

1. The chief is protected from half-baked ideas, voluminous memoranda, and immature oral presentations.
2. The staff officer who has a real idea to sell is enabled more readily to find a market.

When you have finished your "completed staff work" the final test is this: if you were the chief would you be willing to sign the paper you have prepared, and stake your professional reputation on its being right? If the answer is in the negative, take it back and work it over, because it is not yet completed staff work.

Although there is room for argument about some details of this proposal, such as the heavy use of written documents and the infrequency of personal discussions between a staff person and his boss, the central theme has much to recommend it. All too often, a staff person is willing to toss in ideas or information without thinking a matter through to a practical conclusion.

245
CHAPTER 12
*staff-line roles
in strategic action*

Useful as completed staff work may be, it is not ideal for all situations. It is expensive in terms of both the quality and the number of staff people needed. An additional expense is the interference with busy supervisors and operators involved in preparing a completed recommendation. Not many management posts warrant such extensive assistance.

Still another drawback in some companies is the tendency for a strong staff to undermine decentralization. A staff person may initially emphasize help to managers in lower echelons, but if cooperation is not immediately forthcoming, he then turns to completed staff work and urges the big boss to issue an order. If the boss does so, of course, the center of decision-making moves higher in the chain of command.

In view of these possible objections, we may find ourselves saying, "It's a good idea when used in the right place." To return to our previous examples, we can conclude that completed staff work would be an approach well suited to an industrial engineer but not to a market-researcher or an internal auditor.

## RELATIONSHIPS BETWEEN STAFF AND MANAGERS

**normal staff relationships**

The relationship between a staff member and the operating executive with whom he works depends in part on the staff duties we discussed on the preceding pages. A person who only gathers facts or only checks on performance, for instance, will have relations with his superior that differ from those of an assistant who has concurring authority. Nevertheless, we can identify several features that characterize almost all successful staff relationships.

1. A staff person is primarily a representative of his boss. He does things that the boss would do if he had the necessary time and ability. He is an extension of the boss's personality—advising, investigating, imagining, encouraging, following up on matters in his particular sphere. A staff person's position gives him stature and imposes an obligation *not to misrepresent* the boss. If occasionally he declares his own views, which may be at variance with those of his boss, he should be careful to make the distinction clear, for people normally presume that a staff representative is sufficiently close to his boss to be able to reflect accurately the thinking of his superior. Let us note in passing that a boss has an obligation to spend enough time with each of his staff assistants so that they can, in fact, establish a consistent point of view.

2. A staff person must *rely largely on persuasion* to get his ideas put into effect. Lacking the power of command, he must build confidence in his opinions and must be sufficiently sensitive to the problems of those he would influence to win their acceptance of his proposals. The staff person who cannot accomplish all, or at least most of, the things he wants done by winning voluntary cooperation had better look for another job.

3. A staff person must be prepared to *submerge his own personality* and his own desire for glory. He must be an ardent teamworker, recognizing that his boss or

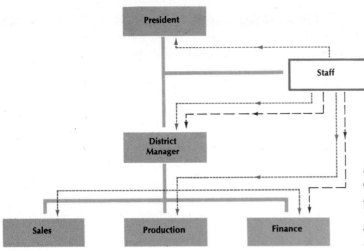

Figure *12.2*  *Typical relationships of central finance staff with managers in the regular line of command. The dotted line (color) indicates advice and assistance. The dashed line indicates functional authority.*

some other operating executive will get credit for carrying the ball. To achieve improved results, he must be prepared to see others receive recognition for ideas that he may have subtly planted several months earlier.

These three characteristics of staff work, when consistently maintained, go far in overcoming the inevitable friction that arises when a third party is interposed in what is naturally a close relationship between a line supervisor and his subordinate.

We usually speak as though a staff person performed his job by himself. But in larger companies he may in fact have several assistants. Multiplication of people does not, however, change the relationship between staff and operating executives. *Within* a staff unit, there are the usual subordinate-boss, or "line," relationships. Just as any boss delegates—setting up duties, authority, and obligation—so the head of a staff unit builds a series of line relationships between himself and others within his group. We call these people "staff" because of their work, not because they are in any way absolved from the customary subordinate-boss relationship.

**staff influence within the chain of command**

A staff person charged with bringing about improvements in a particular area has two courses of action open to him: he may make a recommendation to an operating executive who is directly or indirectly his boss and then rely on the executive to issue the necessary orders to put the plan into effect, *or* he may try to secure voluntary acceptance of his ideas without the support of formal orders transmitted down the chain of command. The second, or voluntary, approach is very common, because a top operating executive is either too busy to bother with an issue, or he does not want to upset a pattern of decentralization.

In such circumstances, how does a staff person accomplish a mission? Let us say a senior operating executive has delegated a task to his West Coast superintendent; he has assigned duties and granted authority, and the

247

*CHAPTER 12*
*staff-line roles*
*in strategic action*

superintendent has a sense of obligation to him. Because of the direct relationship with the senior executive, the superintendent is free (except as we will note below) to accept or reject the counsel of a staff person. Why then can a staff person expect to exert any significant influence?

For one reason, people are inclined to accept the advice of a staff person because they regard him as a *technical expert*. Engineer, statistician, repair mechanic, or lawyer—each has a specialized field in which his word is likely to be taken as authoritative.

For a second reason, when a staff person has an impressive title, reports high up in the organization hierarchy, and has an office that exhibits the symbols of importance, he enjoys exalted *status*. His views will be taken seriously by reason of his status alone.

*Skill in presenting ideas*, as we mentioned earlier, is still another reason why staff people are likely to be influential.

A perhaps more subtle source of influence is *potential backing* by a senior operating executive. If people down the line believe that advice they have rejected is bound to return as a command, they often conclude that it is wiser to take the advice in the first place. (Conversely, a staff person soon learns when and how far he can push a particular point.)

Finally, if a staff person's views may significantly *influence* an employee's salary increases or promotions, that employee will probably accord the staff person's recommendations more than just polite acknowledgment. This inclination is especially strong for employees away from the seat of a company—for example, a branch personnel officer or a branch accountant who aspires to transfer within his functional field, perhaps to the home office.

In summary, then, even though a staff person may have no command authority whatsoever, he may still get his recommendations accepted if he is intelligent, persuasive, impressive, and influential. Obviously, the potency of influence depends on each individual and each situation.

Despite all the influence he can muster, a staff person may find himself on the sidelines watching the real action taking place without his participation. In a healthy organization, operating executives are strong-minded, vigorous individuals. Not infrequently, such executives welcome staff assistance only on highly technical matters or when it suits their convenience. To counteract this tendency, some companies follow a practice of compulsory staff consultation. Under this arrangement, a staff person *must* be consulted before action is taken. For example, department heads cannot confront a pesonnel manager with salary increases already promised or promotions already made; they must instead consult with him before they act. In other cases, a lawyer must have a chance to read a contract before a vice-president signs it. Under this plan an operating executive is not blocked from proceeding as he thinks best, but he is required to stop and listen to advice from another point of view.

**compulsory staff consultation**

Compulsory consultation supplements a more general requirement for successful staff work, the requirement that a staff should have access to any information that relates to its field of interest. No mere directive, of course, can ensure that a staff person will gain access to underlying motives that are often important for complete understanding of a problem; he can obtain such information only when he shares with others mutual respect and confidence. Nevertheless, it is helpful for management to make clear to employees that they are to keep the staff fully informed.

A related practice that some firms follow is to require each staff unit to make a semiannual or annual report on any weak spots it has uncovered in its field. This requirement may put a staff person in the delicate position of revealing a weakness that an operating executive at a low level wants to conceal from senior administrators. The staff person finds himself playing detective and risks not being welcomed back later. On the other hand, the inevitability of the report may prod the operating executive into taking corrective measures, presumably with the help of staff, so that the latter can mention constructive steps along with unfavorable conditions. Fundamentally, what each company needs is a climate that nourishes bold statements of fact to anyone concerned, coupled with sympathetic and constructive efforts to help improve deteriorated conditions. Covering up facts because of fear of criticism is not healthy. Managers and staff people can count on a free flow of pertinent information on troublesome situations only if operating personnel are confident that they will receive constructive help in return.

**concurring authority**

Under some circumstances, a manager may desire to further strengthen the hand of his staff. If control over certain operations is very important, staff may be granted concurring authority so that no action can be taken until a designated staff person agrees to it.[4] Such concurring authority is probably most familiar in quality control, where an inspector usually must pass on raw materials or semifinished parts before they move to the next stage of production. Other examples include required legal approval before signing a contract, or the personnel manager's o.k. before making a promotion.

Whenever we grant concurring authority to staff, we realize that a senior administrator wants to ensure that the staff viewpoint is incorporated into operating decisions. It is a "safe" arrangement, because operating executives cannot take heedless action. On the other hand, it slows down action, for if the staff and operating people do not agree, someone must appeal up the administrative line, perhaps even to a senior executive who is boss of all operations and staff. In addition, although management can hold both a staff and an operating person accountable for any actions they *do* take, both have plenty of opportunity for passing the buck when they do *not* take action.

These considerations suggest that we should grant concurring authority only when the point of view represented by a staff person is particularly important, and when possible delay in action, while agreement is being ironed out, will not be serious.

[4]For an innovative use of concurring authority in long-range planning, see E. K. Warren, *Long-Range Planning: The Executive Viewpoint* (Englewood Cliffs, NJ: Prentice-Hall, 1966).

**249**
CHAPTER 12
*staff-line roles
in strategic action*

Even when these conditions are met, it is important that we carefully define the grounds on which a staff may withhold its approval of a proposal. For instance, it is one thing for a controller to block a capital expenditure because of lack of funds, and quite another if he blocks it because of his personal disapproval of a plan. An inspector may delay a shipment of goods because they do not come up to standard, but his company should not permit him to take over the engineer's function of deciding how a product should be redesigned. Dynamic action would be difficult under such a system.

**functional authority**

The most extreme formal technique for extending staff influence is the granting of functional authority. This means that a staff person can give direct orders to operating personnel in his own name instead of making recommendations to his boss or to other operating executives. His instructions then have the same force as those that come down the channel of command. As in direct-line relationships, a staff person probably consults with whomever he instructs; and the person receiving the instructions may point out difficulties in execution to the staff and to the line boss. But until orders are rescinded or revised, the company expects the worker to carry them out.

Naturally, we give a staff functional authority only over those areas in which its technical competence is recognized and its opinion would probably be accepted anyway. Thus a chief accountant may have functional authority over accounting forms and systems, a medical officer over physical examinations, and a legal counsel over responses to any legal suits against the company. On such matters, the word of a staff officer will be followed in at least 99 percent of the cases; it is simpler to have it clearly understood that his word is final.

The trouble with functional authority is that it is tempting in its apparent simplicity. For example, it is too easy merely to say that a personnel director will have functional authority over all personnel matters, a sales promotion director over sales promotion activities, and a controller over all expenses. Such sweeping assignments can wreak havoc in an organization. For if the personnel director can issue instructions that cover the selection, training, and motivation of all employees, he is virtually in a position to dominate all operations. And since expenses are fundamental to nearly every company decision, the controller with functional authority over such matters becomes tantamount to a general manager. In addition, wide use of functional authority may burden operating managers with conflicting orders; it tends to undermine the status of supervisors, and it complicates accountability. These difficulties arise from the indiscriminate use of a delicate arrangement.

What then are the circumstances in which we may use functional authority? The following three conditions are desirable, and at least two should always be present before we grant a staff person such authority:

1. *Only a minor aspect of the total operating job is covered.* Accounting forms and Blue Cross contracts, for instance, are only incidental to most operating jobs. Although these matters should receive the thoughtful attention of somebody, the plans adopted do not substantially affect the bulk of operations.

2. *Technical or specialized knowledge of a type not possessed by operating executives is needed.* If a sales manager or a production superintendent is going to accept the advice of, say, a tax expert or a medical director anyway, we can simplify decision-making by granting functional authority to such specialists.

3. *Uniformity, or at least consistency, of action in several operating units is essential.* For instance, pension rights of employees who are transferred among several divisions of a company should be treated consistently, as should credit terms extended to customers. A staff unit with functional authority is more likely to deal consistently with such matters than the divisions acting separately.

**a composite pattern**

Of the various means we have considered for strengthening the influence of staff, functional authority moves farthest from the purely assisting and counseling relationship first described. Compulsory consultation and concurring authority are intermediate positions. For reasons already noted, we should move cautiously from establishing an easy, simply helpful relationship toward insisting that a staff person must be heeded. Briefly stated, as staff is made more powerful, its scope should be confined.

In practice we often provide a different kind of relationship for different duties of a single position. A company attorney, for instance, might cover the whole range. On most matters he just *gives advice*, but in one or two areas *consultation* is compulsory; for a limited group of decisions his *concurrence* is required; and possibly over a few technical matters he has *functional authority*. But such a composite set of relationships is apt to be confusing. We will court the least trouble by keeping staff people in *advisory roles*.

**EXTERNAL, INDEPENDENT STAFF**

A few large corporations use a special type of staff to doublecheck those strategic decisions which require huge commitments of resources. Atomic power, new automobile engines, the Alaska oil pipeline, a new family of computers, and similar large-scale programs call for unprecedented levels of investment.

In contrast to the staff discussed earlier in this chapter, this external group is not expected to collaborate with operating managers in the initial preparation of plans. Instead it provides an independent check.

Six significant features stand out in this design for staff work as it has been developed by a large computer manufacturer.

1. Each business-unit has its own highly competent staff that provides technical and coordinating assistance in the usual fashion. The external staff is not regarded as a substitute for this kind of help. Nevertheless, top management does want assurance that the multimillion-dollar decisions embraced in operating plans are wise, and that no major opportunities for improvement are overlooked. The magnitude of commitments and the unpredictable environment faced by this company call for extraordinary efforts to ensure that the right action is taken.

2. The external staff is judged on the basis of the success of the business-units. If results are good, previous staff work is considered to be good even though the external staff did no more than endorse business-unit proposals. However, when business-unit results do not come up to par, the external staff person who ap-

proved the plans may be in deep trouble along with executives of the business-unit. Clear evidence of bungled execution reduces staff accountability somewhat. But the basic doctrine is: "If the patient is well, the doctor gets a good fee. If the patient gets sick, the doctor may find himself even sicker." This means that both the external staff and the business-units are evaluated by the same standard—good results.

251
CHAPTER 12
*staff-line roles
in strategic action*

To make this accountability stick, the cause of any large difficulty is traced back to major decisions, and the staff person is penalized if he concurred with a poor decision made perhaps two to five years earlier.

3. The external staff reviews the strategies and annual plans of the business-units before central management's endorsement. If the staff believes the plans are good it concurs in writing. The plan may, and often does, involve substantial risks, but these risks should be fully explored and potential losses minimized.

4. When the staff does not concur, it must develop an alternative proposal. Mere "viewing with alarm" is not enough. The external staff must seek, and the business-unit must provide, data that permits the staff to formulate a positive plan to eliminate its objections to the unit's proposals. The staff has to be realistic and prepared to defend its alternative.

5. Often differences between the proposals of the business-unit and the staff are ironed out voluntarily. One group convinces the other, or an even better third plan emerges. Both parties, however, are committed. Pressure from either side is no excuse. When sincere differences in judgment arise, these are presented to one or more senior executives to "umpire" the decision. Such umpiring is necessary to get on with the game—to prevent positive, aggressive action from being stalled.

6. To ensure that staff focuses on major issues and to prevent the entire planning mechanism from being bogged down with nonconcurrences, the size of the external staff is limited. With only a few people to investigate and to prepare alternative plans, the external staff must be very selective in the issues it tackles.

The external-staff concept has strong supporters. The chief benefit is an independent check on major planning decisions. Alfred Sloan sought a similar independent judgment throughout General Motors through his "finance" staff, but he placed them inside each division; they were internal rather than external staff.

In thinking about when to use external, independent staff, one should also recognize some limitations. A comprehensive, explicit, forward-looking procedure must be in use if the external staff is to grow with the plans and exercise a constructive influence. The scheme is expensive in terms of both talented personnel and the energies of many executives involved in the duplicate planning effort. The vital accountability concept requires careful evaluations delving back several years and a willingness to censure an executive for his actions that far in the past. Attitudes about external interference with planning have to be modified to tolerate two or more competitive proposals. In addition, but by no means least important, a new type of resilient, farsighted staff has to be located and trained; unless such individuals have practical wisdom about the industry they serve, the entire procedure is only an added burden.

**PROBLEMS IN USING STAFF**     Throughout our discussion, we have implied many difficulties that arise in connection with staff.[5] A summary of four common areas of trouble may be helpful to those who will either use staff or serve in staff positions.

**vague definition of duties and authority**     Time and again, we find friction between operating executives and staff people simply because the role of staff is misunderstood.[6] The word "staff" provides no formula for resolving questions of what the duties should be. Some people within an enterprise may assume that a staff person is merely a fact-gatherer or, at most, an advisor to his own boss. A boss may want a staff assistant to make suggestions to people throughout the organization; and the staff person himself may be so zealous about his areas that he believes he should control as well as plan. With three such disparate views in competition, sooner or later we can expect a clash and perhaps hard feeling.

A common source of confusion is strengthening the influence of staff to meet a specific problem—through either required consultation, concurring authority, or functional authority—but failure to delineate the scope of this additional authority. For instance, during an energy shortage the chief engineer may be given "concurring authority over new uses of power." Trouble will arise unless everyone concerned recognizes that the new authority extends only to adding power-consuming equipment.

What is needed to overcome these problems is mutual understanding by all principal parties of the duties and authority of each staff person and, even more importantly, a working relationship built out of experience that translates the general understanding into smooth work habits and attitudes.

**scarcity of good staff**     All too often, we can trace a staff failure back to a selection of wrong people for staff positions. A staff person needs both competence in his specialty and skill in staff work. Without technical competence, of course, he is hardly worth the nuisance he is to other executives. But technical competence alone is not enough. He must be affable, sensitive, discreet, and honest so that he may earn the confidence of other people; he must be articulate and persuasive so that he may win genuine acceptance of his proposals; he must be patient but persistent (rather than resort to commands) in his efforts to get results; he must find satisfaction in good team results rather than in personal glory; he must have a high sense of loyalty to his boss and of obligation to duty, even in the face of the frustration of highly circumscribed authority. Unfortunately, we do not often find a person with this combination of abilities and attitudes coupled with technical competence.

---

[5]P. Browne and R. T. Golembiewski, "The Line-Staff Concepts Revisited: An Empirical Study of Organizational Images," *Academy of Management Journal,* 17 (September 1974), 406–16.
[6]G. Dessler, *Organization and Management: A Contingency Approach* (Englewood Cliffs, NJ: Prentice-Hall, 1976), pp. 139–41.

253
*CHAPTER 12*
*staff-line roles*
*in strategic action*

Sometimes a company uses a staff job as a training post for future operating executives, but also occasionally as a dumping ground or pasture for an unwanted operating executive. If such a person is a misfit in his staff position, the company creates a new problem in trying to solve an old one. Staff work, by its very nature, creates delicate relationships, and if a company has only unqualified people available, it had better sharply curtail staff jobs in scope or eliminate them entirely.

**mixing staff and operating duties**

It is not always practical to completely separate staff duties and operating duties into different jobs. We noted, for example, that a controller typically supervises corporate accounting directly and also has staff duties in connection with budgets and analysis of expenses of other departments.

Small companies that can afford only a limited number of executives may ask a single individual to fill two positions. For instance, a sales-promotion mnager may also supervise selling in one district. Or a company with one large plant and two or three small assembly plants may have its production superintendent run the main plant and also maintain an undefined staff relationship with the assembly plants.

Still a third type of mixture of staff and operating duties—one which we find in both large and small companies—is to have senior operating executives serve as staff to the president on companywide problems. A large operating department may follow a comparable arrangement by having key executives wear two hats: one when they run their own divisions and an other when they act as advisors on whatever problems face the whole department.

Theoretically, such a combination of duties should cause no difficulty so long as the executive and the people he works with understand which role he is playing at any one time. The practical difficulty is that this distinction is hard to maintain. The executive himself may be unable to shift gears from being a hard-driving operating executive to being a reflective staff counselor. Even when it is clear in his own mind, he may fail to tell others which role he is playing. When we compound this difficulty by failing to clearly define duties and authority in each kind of work, we wind up with a "staff" that has a vague assignment to dabble in other people's problems.[7]

The remedy lies in real understanding of what staff work is, agreement on what each person should do, and care in assigning individuals who are both technically and temperamentally qualified.

**disregard of staff by the boss**

A fourth source of staff difficulties may be the very manager who has created staff positions in the first place. He undoubtedly finds his total administrative burdens more than he himself can carry and sets up one or more staff positions to relieve him of part of the load. But if he falsely

---

[7]Because the lines between staff and line often becomes blurred, some observers call for a redefinition of the staff concept. See G. G. Fisch, "Line-Staff is Obsolete," *Harvard Business Review* (September-October 1961) pp. 67–79.

assumes that he has solved his difficulties and can forget about them he is certainly sowing seeds of future woe.

A boss must maintain close enough and frequent enough contact with a staff person to enable the latter to serve effectively as an extension of the eyes, ears, and mind of his superior. It is by no means necessary for a specialized staff person to see his boss daily. What is essential is that the two maintain sufficient contact to ensure their general accord on approaches and values.

Even more devastating to confidence than lack of contact is the willingness of some executives to make decisions in an area assigned to a staff person without ever consulting him. Suppose a senior executive specifically

*Figure* 12.3 *A senior executive, by his treatment of suggestions, strongly affects the influence of staff throughout the organization. In this chart, the color shading represents degrees of the staff person's participation; the black shading represents degrees of the senior executive's response.*

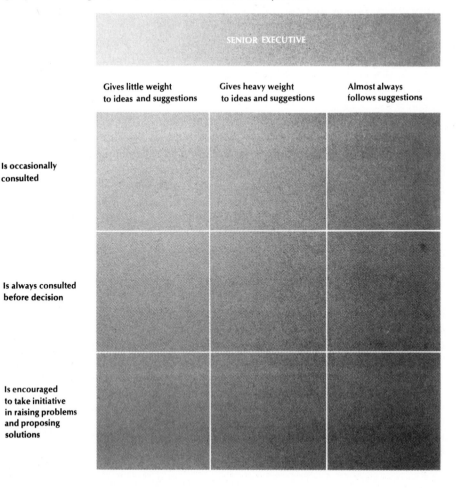

SENIOR EXECUTIVE

| | Gives little weight to ideas and suggestions | Gives heavy weight to ideas and suggestions | Almost always follows suggestions |
|---|---|---|---|
| Is occasionally consulted | | | |
| Is always consulted before decision | | | |
| Is encouraged to take initiative in raising problems and proposing solutions | | | |

STAFF MAN

charges his budget director with preparing capital-expenditure budgets. But later, when an operating subordinate presses him, the senior executive approves a large expenditure without first talking to the budget director. The next time the operating executive needs capital, he will probably again bypass the budget director and go directly to the senior executive. Soon the budget director will be a useless adjunct.

In contrast, the budget director will have greater status if the senior executive insists that his operating executives talk through all matters of capital expenditure with the budget director before bringing any request to him. Soon the operating people will learn that to get approval for capital expenditures, they must work with the budget director. In short, when an executive creates a staff position, he must be prepared to discipline *himself* to use the staff if he expects others to do so.

255
CHAPTER 12
staff-line roles
in strategic action

## CONCLUSION

The concept of staff is appealing, for it permits an executive to extend his capacity. The staff assistant performs managerial work that the executive is too busy to do or for which he may lack technical competence. However, the arrangement is easily abused. Unless mutual understanding exists regarding the subjects covered and the action expected of the staff, relations between supervisors and subordinates may become confused.

Moreover, anything as delicate as staff relationships rarely continues on an even keel. Somebody will undoubtedly become too aggressive, one person will step on another's toes, people will observe consultations in the letter rather than in the spirit, jealousies will creep in. To keep emotional flare-ups at a minimum and to maintain relationships between staff and operators as he desires, a manager must take time to provide continuing coordination and guidance. He must know whether his staff has become autocratic or lazy, whether their assistance is constructive, whether they are persuasive of their viewpoint, and whether operating people are too submissive or too independent.

In other words, by creating a staff an executive may facilitate his total job, but he also imposes upon himself new burdens: contact with staff, supervision of relations between staff and operating executives, and self-restraint to the point where he too uses the staff according to his prescription.

## FOR FURTHER DISCUSSION

1. "Staff/line distinctions are obsolete in today's complex organizations," said a professor of management at a recent professional meeting. What might have prompted him to say this? To what degree is he right? Wrong?

2. How may increased concern about failure to implement strategic plans effectively influence the role of staff in (1) strategy formulation and (2) strategy implementation?

3. A regional sales manager (line position) who has authority to change prices in his region consults with the corporate director of market research (staff position) and is given several "pieces of data" that the market-research manager feels would dictate a price reduction. If the regional manager accepts this advice and later finds his revenue

was adversely affected, who should accept the obligation for this loss?

4. Assume you have been appointed public relations director for a college; your task is not only to issue press releases and other public statements but also to "help the college conduct all its activities so as to create a favorable public image." What kind of authority should the president of the college grant to you so that you could be most effective in your job?

5. Which of the four common problems in using staff are likely to be most serious with regard to a company's strategic planning efforts?

6. Consider the following two statements:
1. The more heterogeneous a company's products, markets, and technologies, the less the potential for effective functional staff groups at the corporate level.

2. The more heterogeneous a company's products, markets, and technologies, the greater the need for effective functional staff groups at the corporate level.
How do you reconcile these two statements?

7. What should be the major differences between the work of a corporate staff group in marketing, research, and other similar activities and divisional counterpart staff groups? How will their work (corporate and divisional staffs) complement each other? How may they conflict?

8. "Our company plans to hire more female MBA's and engineers and place them in staff positions. These women are bright, articulate, self-effacing, and able to compromise. If we could just hire some that are also independently wealthy, we would have perfect staff candidates." Discuss.

## CASES

For cases involving issues covered in this chapter, see especially the following. Particularly relevant questions are listed after each case.

Clifford Nelson (p. 192), 12
Camdem Chemical (p. 298), 14, 24
Scandico (Singapore) (p. 305), 5
Marathon Plastics (p. 456)

## FOR FURTHER READING

Burns, T. S., *Tales of ITT: An Insider's Report*. Boston: Houghton Mifflin, 1974, pp. 59–68. A provocative discussion of the special role played by corporate staff within the ITT Corporation.

Dubin, R., *Human Relations in Administration*, 4th ed. Englewood Cliffs, NJ: Prentice-Hall, 1974, chap. 10. Behavioral views on the role of staff specialist.

Litterer, J. A., *Analysis of Organizations*, 2nd ed. New York: Wiley, 1973, chap.

23 and 24. Clear review of various roles of staff in business, and of line-staff relationships in business organizations.

Rhenman, E., L. Stromberg, and G. Westerlund, *Conflict and Cooperation in Business Organizations*. New York: Wiley, 1970. Penetrating analysis of difficulties with traditional line-staff concepts, as revealed in Swedish companies.

Sayles, L. R., *Managerial Behavior*. New York: McGraw-Hill, 1965. Useful discussion of how lateral relationships, including line-staff roles, develop in an organization.

# 13

# matching strategy and structure

Learning Objectives

After completing this chapter you should be able to

1. Explain the principal features of the three major types of overall organization designs.

2. Describe the major factors which determine the span of supervision.

3. Explain the distinctive characteristics of conglomerate organization.

4. Describe matrix organization and identify its benefits and drawbacks.

5. Explain why large enterprises have established an office of the president.

Departmentation, decentralization, and staff can be analyzed as separate issues—as we have done in the three preceding chapters. In an active firm, however, they are closely interrelated. Just as in the design of an airplane, the relative size and weight of each component, and the ways the components are related to one another affect the performance capabilities, so it is with the structure of an enterprise. The components must be melded together.

Typically we give close attention to this integration into an overall structure when a company adopts a new strategy. If we neglect to change the structure to fit the new strategy, tensions and bottlenecks will force us to make tardy adjustments.

Initially in this chapter, we shall explore the effect of a company's size and complexity on the overall structure best suited to its needs. If the company's strategy calls for growth and more product diversity, its old organization will be strained. Especially critical are shifts in strategy which push the firm into another of the three basic stages of growth.

The second part of the chapter deals with even more complex arrangements. As corporations struggle to take advantage of environmental changes, seeking adaptability and flexibility in their strategic response, they may resort to more involved set-ups.[1] We will explore these in terms of conglomerate organization, matrix organization, and an "office of the president."

**stages in growth**

Overall organization for any company is strongly influenced by its size and complexity. Smaller firms with simple activities operate very well with an elementary organization. But as a firm grows in size and its activities become more diversified, it needs a more elaborate structure to fit the new strategy.[2] The simplest form of organization is the *single entrepreneur* where one key individual functions with a group of helpers. Organizational growth will strain the capacity of this design and necessitate a transition to a *departmentalized firm*. Continued growth and diversification may require the conversion of a departmentalized firm into a *multiple-mission company*.

These organization designs highlight key stages in the development of an organization. The transition from one stage to the next may be gradual and many firms may, in, fact, never be forced to move to the more complex forms. By recognizing the major features of each design, strategy and structure can be more soundly matched.[3]

**THE SINGLE ENTREPRENEUR**   As the central figure in the organization, the single entrepreneur is aware of operating details and personally gives instructions to the helpers. Of course, the assis-

---

[1]T. Burns and G.M. Stalker, *The Management of Innovation* (London: Tavistock, 1961).

[2]For a pioneering study of the link between strategy and structure, see A. D. Chandler, Jr., *Strategy and Structure* (Cambridge: MIT Press, 1962).

[3]For a more comprehensive discussion of these issues, see Chapter 17 of W. H. Newman and J. P. Logan, *Strategy, Policy, and Central Management,* 8th ed. (Cincinnati: South-Western, 1981).

tants learn the routines of repetitive activities and can proceed with minimum guidance. And they may become specialized in their normal assignments—such as, accounting, dealing with customers, or making repairs. But changes from customary patterns, and initiatives toward moving in new directions rest with the boss.

Basically, the division of labor among the operators depends upon the type and volume of work. Delegation is simple. There is no formal staff, although experienced personnel often guide newcomers; and when several people do similar work one of them may become the informal leader.

A typical single-leader organization is the diner and twenty-room motel run by G. P. Olsen in eastern Minnesota. The diner was Olsen's first venture, and recently he added an adjoining motel unit. Olsen continues to be very active in the daily operation of both the diner and the motel, and he closely supervises the work of persons indicated in Figure 13.1.

Figure *13.1*   Organization of Olsen's diner and motel.

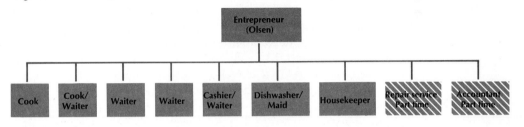

Many other small businesses—dress shops, drugstores, filling stations—are operated in this fashion, often with remarkable success. The key individual normally has high energy and skill, doing part of the work himself as necessary. Even though the business may be legally a corporation, action pivots around the moving spirit.

The limitation of this simple organization form is the capacity of the single entrepreneur (or two individuals if it is run as a partnership). He can add helpers as the business grows, but each new subordinate requires some supervision. Sooner or later the coordinating head can no longer keep track of what each person is doing; motivation and control slip; and planning lacks careful backup investigation. The manager must find some way to free himself from normal day-to-day operations, especially when the business involves nonroutine activities and frequent emergencies.

**THE DEPARTMENTALIZED COMPANY**

A shift in organization from the single-leader form to a departmentalized structure opens up opportunity for great expansion. First, a change must take place in the way the senior executive sees his role. This is crucial. Next a *series* of departments is established, each organized

**reliance on
functional
departments**

to suit growing needs. As the total volume increases, staff positions may also be added. Having escaped from the restraint of the supervisory capacity of a single person, the company can multiply its activities many fold.

Delegation to strong department managers provides relief for the over-burdened entrepreneur. Typically a manager is appointed for each major function—sales, production, finance, and the like. These people (or *their* helpers), take charge of day-to-day operations: they schedule, expedite, and watch inputs and outputs. And because they focus on a narrower span of work than the entrepreneur, they become more sensitive to particular needs and opportunities.

With such help, the behavior of the senior executive should differ sharply from that of the single entrepreneur. Because the senior executive must be willing to delegate, he no longer knows what is happening day by day and he accepts decisions that are not quite the way he would have made them. A cardinal purpose of creating functional departments is to give the senior executive time to focus on interdepartmental coordination and on policy and strategy issues. Many entrepreneurs find this required change in their personal behavior very difficult and sometimes impossible.

The contrast between an entrepreneur who runs the show single-handedly and a departmentalized set-up is made clear by a comparison of Figures 13.1 and 13.2. The organization for a three-hundred-room motel shown in Figure 13.2 leaves the general manager free to coordinate, deal with emergencies, be active in community relations, and give more attention to long-range planning. His job differs sharply from that of G. P. Olsen.

Most departmentalized companies focus on a single product/market objective. For such firms, dividing operations into major functions is usually the best method of primary departmentation. As we noted in Chapter 10, such functional departments become expert in their particular area, give adequate attention to an activity that otherwise might receive hurried treatment, and act in a consistent fashion on organizational matters.

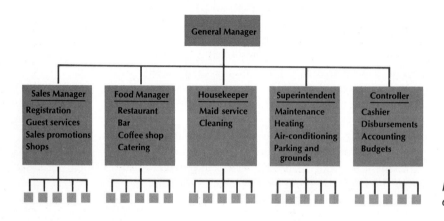

*Figure 13.2 Organization of a large motel.*

Once the critical transition from a personal, closely supervised organization to a series of departments has been made, a whole array of possibilities are available for further expansion. Each department can organize for its own growth. While it is important for each department to be strong and dependable, there is also a need for overall organizational balance; an outstanding research division can wreck a company if it creates new products faster than the finance department can find money to pay for both research and product development.[4] As departments and managerial work are placed in a total structure, the emphasis and balance that is most needed by a specific company in its current setting must be considered.

An enterprise should establish as separate, major departments those activities that are most likely to affect its success. The heads of these departments should report directly to the chief executive so that he can be in close touch with crucial activities.

What work is emphasized will depend on the nature of the industry and the way a particular firm seeks to be distinctive. Some department stores, for example, believe that advertising is a primary key to success, and so they are likely to set up a separate advertising department that reports directly to the president. On the other hand, a company that sells industrial supplies and raw materials, a business in which advertising is much less important, will probably make the advertising department a service division within its sales department.

Developing new and efficient products is vital to the success of a chemical company, and so in the organization chart of the Colonial Chemical Company (Figure 13.3), the research and development department reports directly to the president. In contrast, a company that is principally concerned with processing established products — such as a dairy or a textile mill — usually relegates research or engineering to a subordinate role in the production department.

To discover how much emphasis a department deserves in an organization structure, we cannot simply count the number of its employees or the dollar volume of its transactions. In a commercial bank, for instance, we shall probably find many more employees who maintain the building or sort checks or keep customers' accounts than members of the credit department who analyze the soundness of loans. The former activities, however, are relatively routine, whereas the granting of credit calls for delicate judgment. Consequently, loan experts typically work directly under the bank president, whereas bookkeepers, check-sorters, and janitors are customarily grouped together, reporting to an executive in charge of "internal operations."

The strategic importance of a department's function, product, or area may shift with the passage of time. A clear illustration of this point is the changing status of industrial relations. Prior to the increase of union

[4]Examples of how this imbalance can affect the fortunes of a company are contained in J. E. Ross and M. J. Kami, *Corporate Management in Crisis: Why the Mighty Fall* (Englewood Cliffs, NJ: Prentice-Hall, 1973).

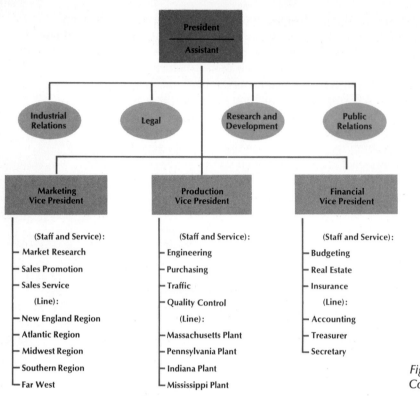

(Staff and Service):
- Market Research
- Sales Promotion
- Sales Service

  (Line):
- New England Region
- Atlantic Region
- Midwest Region
- Southern Region
- Far West

(Staff and Service):
- Engineering
- Purchasing
- Traffic
- Quality Control

  (Line):
- Massachusetts Plant
- Pennsylvania Plant
- Indiana Plant
- Mississippi Plant

(Staff and Service):
- Budgeting
- Real Estate
- Insurance

  (Line):
- Accounting
- Treasurer
- Secretary

*Figure 13.3* *Organization of Colonial Chemical Company.*

power, industrial relations and personnel matters in most firms were handled by a subordinate unit in the department with the largest number of employees. Now almost all large companies have a vice-president in charge of personnel and industrial relations who reports directly to the chief executive. Chemical production in the oil industry, variable committees in insurance companies, and family planning in welfare agencies are other examples of activities that have similarly risen in strategic importance and hence in organizational status.

A successful departmentalized company may become quite large. Some such firms — for example, in the life insurance, paper, and pharmaceutical industries — have sales or assets of several hundred million dollars. The growth of a departmentalized company and the elaboration of the structure does not alter the basic process. The firm starts with a sharply focused product/market mission, and then establishes specialized departments, each of which has a different though important contribution to make to that mission. The work of these departments is interdependent, so the entire operation has to be managed as an integrated whole.[5] The role of the general

[5]The critical need for coordination of these interdependent parts is treated by P. R. Lawrence and J. W. Lorsch, *Organization and Environment* (Homewood: Irwin, 1967); and J. R. Galbraith, *Designing Complex Organizations* (Reading: Addison-Wesley, 1973).

manager of such an organization is to find department managers who will be responsible for day-to-day operations while he concentrates on coordination and longer-run strategy and policy issues.

**span of supervision**

A recurring issue in overall organization design, especially as a firm grows, is the workload of each executive. How many immediate subordinates should each executive have? This topic has been the subject of much debate, particularly since behavioral scientists discovered what every practical manager knows: no single number is the correct answer in all cases.[6]

Very real limits do exist in any person's capacity to supervise. His time and energy are limited, and if he has too many subordinates he cannot provide good personal leadership to all. It takes time to assign tasks, to answer questions, to motivate subordinates, to mediate arguments, to coordinate work within the unit and with other departments, to make sure that necessary supplies are on hand, and to perform the many other duties of a supervisor.

The question of limits on the span of supervision is important in designing an organization structure, for it directly affects the number of executives needed. The narrower the average span, the more supervisors needed, and that adds to payroll expense. Another drawback is that additional layers of supervisors complicate communications from the chief executive down to operators and back up the line.[7]

The personal energy of an executive influences to some extent the number of people he can supervise effectively. The following factors also affect what spans are feasible in a specific situation:

[6]L. F. Urwick, "V. A. Graicunas and the Span of Control," *Academy of Management Journal,* June 1974, pp. 349-54.
[7]G. Dessler, *Organization and Management: A Contingency Approach* (Englewood Cliffs, NJ.: Prentice-Hall, 1976), pp. 125-27.

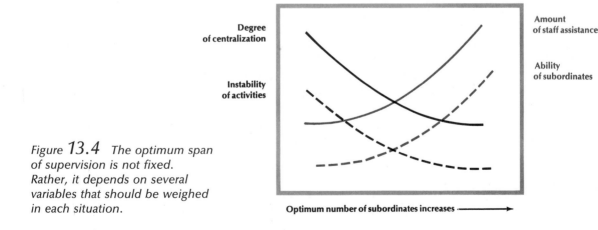

Figure *13.4* The optimum span of supervision is not fixed. Rather, it depends on several variables that should be weighed in each situation.

1. *Time devoted to supervision.* All supervisors spend part of their time personally doing operations. Foremen serve as relief men; sales managers call on important customers; company presidents testify before Congressional committees. In addition, nearly all executives participate in company planning, serve on company committees, and plead for new personnel and equipment. Both types of work reduce the time an executive can devote to supervision.

2. *Variety and importance of activities being supervised.* A manager who is confronted with complex issues needs more time to dispose of them than an executive who deals with routine, one-person problems.

3. *Repetitiveness of activities.* New and different problems take more time to handle than those we have faced many times before.

4. *Ability of subordinates.* Green, inexperienced help takes more of a supervisor's time than well-trained persons who have good judgment and initiative.

5. *Degree of decentralization.* An executive who personally makes many decisions is able to supervise fewer people than one who must merely provide occasional coaching and encouragement.

6. *Staff assistants provided.* When subordinates get from staff people much of their guidance on methods, schedules, personnel problems, quality standards, and perhaps other aspects of their work, they need less contact with their line supervisor.

For these reasons the span of supervision should be tailored to each executive position. And such optimum spans relate directly to the number of departments and divisions that can be placed under each executive.[8] Span of supervision, then, is another interdependent factor to be included in the balancing of an overall structure. When growth strains a span of supervision, relief must be sought: increase decentralization, add a supervisory layer, increase staff, simplify activities—or perhaps move to a multiple-mission design.

**THE MULTIPLE-MISSION COMPANY**

Successful enterprises outgrow a departmental organization. As they grow from fewer than a hundred to over a thousand employees, communications become more formal, standard procedures prevent quick adjustments, the convenience of each department receives more consideration than company goals, and people feel insignificant in terms of total results. Careful management can diminish these tendencies, but sooner or later sheer size saps vigor and effectiveness.

Successful companies take advantage of opportunities to diversify product lines, to develop new sources of materials, and to provide new services in response to changing social needs; this new strategy adds complexity. But large functional departments often give only secondary attention to such opportunities; they are too busy doing their established tasks well. So the new developments fail to receive the attention and the coordinated effort they deserve.

[8]H. Stieglitz, "Optimizing Span of Control," *Management Record,* 24 (September 1962), 25-29.

Unless a company makes a deliberate strategic decision to stay relatively small and clearly focused on a particular mission—a strategic option few American companies elect—a shift in organization becomes necessary.

**semi-independent divisions**

The basic remedy for oversize is to split up into a series of small businesses within the larger company. Typically these divisions, or "business-units," are based on separate product lines. The section of marketing that deals with the particular product is transferred from the marketing department to the business-unit; similarly production, engineering, and perhaps other functions are transferred. Ideally each unit has within it all the key activities necessary to run independently — it is *self-sufficient.* Moreover, the management of the newly created business-unit is given a high degree of authority, making the unit *semiautonomous.* The general manager of such a unit then has virtually the same resources and freedom of action as the president of an independent company, and is expected to take the necessary steps to make the "little business" successful.

This form of organization we called "profit decentralization" in Chapter 11 — stressing the need for initiative and a feeling of full accountability by business-unit managers, matched with loose-rein supervision by central managers. The main advantage of setting up such self-contained business-units are ease in management, better morale, adequate attention, faster coordination, and sharper control.

Even when it is practical to place within a business-unit all of its own marketing and production activities, some central services are retained by the company. Obtaining capital, exploratory research, and staff assistance on labor relations, law, and market research, for example, usually can be performed more economically in one place for all divisions of the corporation. Such central assistance gives internal business-units an advantage over fully independent companies.

A company may have anywhere from two to a hundred such product divisions. Profit decentralization, however, has been applied by department-store chains on a territorial basis; and large metal fabricators place their mining and transportation activities ("process units") in self-contained business-units.

The drawbacks are of two types. Overhead expenses are increased because of the larger number of high-ranking executives and associated cost of more headquarters personnel. Unless a reasonably large and sustained volume of business can be developed for each business-unit, this increased expense may even offset the benefits. The second kind of limitation is technological: can the major departments be split up and still remain relatively efficient? We need to take a closer look at this second issue.

**difficulties with optimum size**

When shifting an organization to small, self-contained business-units, we soon discover that functional departments often cannot be neatly divided. Technology and other forces dictate an *optimum size* for various activities. For instance, an oil refinery to serve Salt Lake City alone would be much too small to be efficient. On the other hand, the task of increasing employment of minorities can readily be handled within separate product or territorial divisions.

The optimum-size issue is complicated because a desirable volume for one function may be undesirable for another. A men's-clothing firm, for instance, found that plants with two to three hundred employees could achieve virtually all economies of scale in production and that larger plants caused more personnel problems. However, the output of one such plant would be far too small for marketing purposes. National advertising and promotion were the key to the firm's marketing success, and the sales volume needed to support national distribution was six times the output of a single plant.

These differences in optimum size affect the number of self-contained business-units we establish. In an aluminum company, for instance, marketing considerations call for a dozen separate divisions, each focused on a product/market-type target. Production technology, however, dictates that almost all end-products come out of a few large plants. These plants cannot be split up by product lines. So twelve self-contained product divisions are impractical.

A review of self-contained business-units in a wide variety of industries indicates that most of them have a volume of work that is below the optimum size for one or two functions and above the optimum size for other functions. The aim, of course, is to build units that are optimum in size for critically important functions, even though this results in some diseconomies in other areas.

**compromise arrangements**

Companies often try to get most of the benefits of self-contained business-units and also keep functional operations at optimum levels. For example, one paper company leaves production in a single functional department, but it breaks product engineering and marketing down into strong product divisions. The division managers are expected to act like "independent businessmen," except that they must contract for their supply of products from the production department.

A comparable arrangement is used by a food processor, except that here it is selling rather than production that is centralized in one department. Each product division does its own product design, engineering, buying, production, merchandising, and pricing, but it utilizes the sales department to contact customers. The rationale here is that a single field organization can cover the country more effectively for all divisions than each could do separately.

Whenever a product division has to rely on an outside department for a key activity, problems of adequate attention, coordination, and control become more difficult. Occasions for bickering jump dramatically. Central management has to judge whether the harm done by restricting self-sufficiency is offset by the benefits of the large-scale activities in the functional department.

The concept of a series of self-sufficient, semiautonomous business-units is an appealing answer to the problems of growth. It is particularly suited to those increases in volume that are based on diverse markets or additions of related products. However, designing divisions that are of optimal size is not a simple task.

## NOVEL NEEDS, NOVEL SOLUTIONS

Organization is an instrument—a powerful tool—designed to fill specific strategic needs. As strategy changes, the company must seek new ways to organize suited to the new conditions. We now examine three organizational designs that have evolved in response to new business strategies.

1. *Conglomerate organization* has evolved in response to the strategic initiatives of some large, complex enterprises.
2. Rapid technological change and complexity are fostering *matrix organizations*.
3. Increasing involvement in social issues accentuates the need for an *office of the president*.

These three developments are not the only forces calling for new approaches in design, but they illustrate the way environmental change impinges on an organization and show how a basic social institution such as managerial organization is adapted rather than scrapped.

## CONGLOMERATE ORGANIZATION

Typically, conglomerate organizations are built of previously independent companies, each with its own traditions and a full complement of central services. Moreover, these companies are not expected to contribute to each other's business. So there is little to be gained from "coordination" and from overall service units. A conglomerate is truly a collection of disassociated businesses.[9]

The primary activity at the headquarters of a conglomerate is financing—raising and allocating capital. This may be done by public issue of securities or by an ingenious array of mergers, spin-offs, and subsidiary financing. However, the number of employees directly involved is small. "Corporate planning" in the majority of conglomerates consists entirely of looking for attractive acquisitions and does not deal with businesses already in the fold. The presumption is that each operating unit will do its own strategic planning—except for major questions on sources and uses of capital.

**focus on financing**

Since the interactions between the central office and the operating companies in a conglomerate are largely limited to finance, the basic organization structure can be simple. The chief executive in each operating company reports to the president or a group vice-president in the central

---

[9]N. A. Berg, "What's Different About Conglomerate Management?" *Harvard Business Review,* November-December 1969, pp. 112-20.

office. In addition, there will be the usual transfer of funds and upward flow of financial reports. This is all that's needed.

Of course, each operating company has its own organization; this may be a single entrepreneur, a departmentalized company, or a multiple-mission organization or any variation that best suits its needs. Incidentally, the legal status of the operating company is not significant from the viewpoint of managerial organization. Each operating unit will be treated as a separate company even though its corporate identity may be washed out for financial reasons.

**strengthening
subsidiary boards
of directors**

In addition to financing, conglomerates can perform a significant role in directing and controlling their subsidiaries. The conglomerate's role is to provide able "outside directors" to serve on the subsidiary's board of directors.

Obtaining good outside directors is a chronic and serious problem in American industry. A conglomerate, however, has sufficient stake in the success of its operating companies to locate and employ individuals who are fully qualified to be good outside directors. Such a person should devote full time to serving as a member or head of the board of perhaps half a dozen operating companies. By ensuring that major decisions are wisely made, insisting that unpleasant action be taken promptly, and providing counsel on future possibilities, a strong director can stimulate operating executives. Thus, by aiding with finance and by identifying talented outside directors, conglomerates help strengthen their operating companies while leaving them to handle their own central-management functions.

## MATRIX ORGANIZATION

Landing a man on the moon was largely a scientific achievement. It also required *managing* a huge, highly complex, interrelated, and uncertain development and production undertaking. Matrix organization was used in this effort, and part of the "fall-out" of the space program has been more careful analysis of this organizational form. Actually, matrix organization did not originate in the space program, and it has applications in a wide variety of enterprises.[10]

**need for
coordinated,
focused action**

A drawback of the typical organization with its functional departments is that unusual, complex projects often get shunted about, progress slowly, and are the cause of endless meetings of key departmental executives. The more innovative and complicated the project, the more likely is fumbling to occur.

Matrix organization strives to (1) ensure the coordinated, focused attention that such projects require and (2) retain at the same time the benefits of specialized expertise and capabilities that only functional departments

---

[10]J. R. Galbraith, "Matrix Organization Designs: How to Combine Functional and Project Forms," *Business Horizons,* February 1971, pp. 29-46; and L. R. Sayles, "Matrix Management: The Structure With a Future," *Organizational Dynamics,* Autumn 1976, pp. 2-17.

can provide. For example, the production of reactors for nuclear power plants calls for unusual engineering, materials and parts with heat-resistance far beyond any previously fabricated, scientific knowledge concerning reactor design, a special and very large assembly operation, and a whole array of new inspection techniques. Production is complicated by high uncertainty about how to achieve required quality and safety margins, by a desire to keep costs low enough to allow nuclear power to compete with coal- and oil-generating stations, and by the pressure to complete such units in time to overcome national electric-power shortages.

Companies making nuclear reactors do have departments that are expert in science, engineering, purchasing, fabrication, and inspection, but each of these departments has twenty to a hundred different orders to work on at one time. Also, they do not have standard answers for dealing with nuclear reactors, and do not know what related decisions other departments may make for a specific order. Many conferences within and between departments become necessary. Disagreement on design or manufacture is likely to arise. Production falls behind schedule, and costs rise. To overcome these typical difficulties on an important piece of business, some mechanism is needed to channel part of the company's store of talent into the specific project and to ensure open communications on interrelated issues and prompt agreement on action to be taken.

This kind of situation is not peculiar to heavy-equipment manufacturers. An advertising agency, to pick an example far removed from physical hardware, is in the same predicament. It has departments staffed with experts in market research, copywriting, art work, television shows, media selection, and other functions—all useful to various clients. Client A wants a specific advertising mission accomplished, one suited to its particular situation. The organization problem is how to draw on the outstanding capabilities of the functional departments and at the same time get an imaginative, tailored program for client A when he needs it. Comparable situations in management-consulting firms and in large building-construction firms are easy to visualize.

The matrix-organization answer to the problems just posed is to appoint a project manager for each clear-cut mission and then to assign from each of the functional departments the talent needed to complete the mission. Figure 13.5 indicates the arrangement for the nuclear-reactor order.

**project managers of cross-functional teams**

During the time a functional specialist is working on the project, he looks to the project manager for direction; he is "out on loan." When the project is finished, or when he is no longer needed, each specialist returns to his functional department for assignment to other duties. The project manager must rely heavily on these assigned people for counsel and decisions in their respective areas. If the team is small, its members will have frequent contact with one another and will be fully informed of the current status of the project. In these circumstances most of the coordination will be voluntary. From time to time, tough, trade-off decisions (sacrificing in one place to gain in another) may be necessary, and these will be made by the project manager.

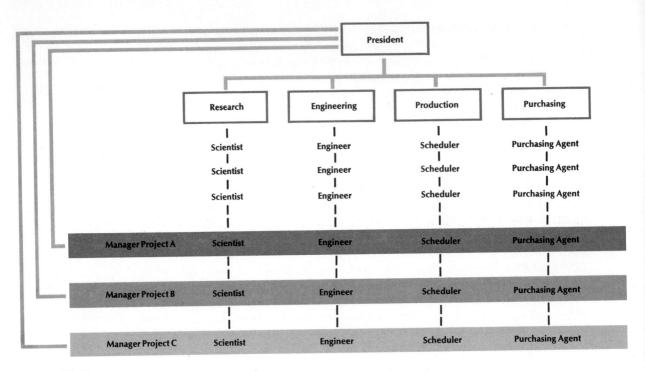

*Figure* $13.5$   *Matrix organization. Each project manager is boss for his project, borrowing the talent he needs temporarily from the functional departments. The heads of functional departments develop capable people—and perhaps other services—but do not supervise them while they are assigned to the project team.*

The personal relations within a project team are delicate.[11] Although the project manager is the nominal boss, each member of his team is on temporary assignment and will return to his functional department, where his long-run career is primarily determined. To draw the best from his group, the project manager must therefore rely on both the challenge of the job and on his personal leadership. Because of this heavy reliance on voluntary cooperation, project teams work best on projects for which the quality of the finished product or service, its deadline, and its costs are clearly specified.

**service role of functional departments**

Usually a functional department does more than supply the project team with its members. It also provides backup service. The project engineer may want drafting help and advice on technical matters; and perhaps at some stages a whole crew of additional engineers will be needed. Similarly, the market-research man calls on personnel in his home department when he needs specialized assistance. When actual production is begun, the work will be done in the company shops (or subcontractors' shops), which are supervised by the department head. Only in the case of large projects lasting

[11]P. R. Lawrence, H. Kolodny, and S. M. Davis, "The Human Side of the Matrix," *Organizational Dynamics,* Summer 1977.

several years, or when work is performed on a remote site (as in construction), are the people who do this backup work transferred to the project. Instead, the functional department performs backup work according to requests from the project team in the same way an outside subcontractor might take on a specified task.

Thus, the project manager calls each move, watches progress, and decides on the next moves. His success, however, depends largely on the capabilities that the functional departments place at his disposal. In the short run, the project manager supplies the initiative; then he and his team provide the coordinated, positive direction that is hard to obtain in a purely functional setup. In the long run, however, the quality and training of the specialists, and the operating capabilities of the functional departments, determine the kind and volume of projects a company can handle effectively.

Obviously this kind of interdependence is hard to keep in balance. Members of the project team, in their push to get specific results, tend to take over line supervision and stir up the resentment of those who are being pushed around. Furthermore, the service that a functional department can provide is rarely performed as fully, as well, or as quickly as project managers would like. Especially when progress is poor, tension arises over who is failing to do all that he should.

In the construction and space industries, and occasionally in other situations suited to matrix organization, the job we have been describing for a functional department may be performed by a subcontractor. For instance, an advertising agency may use an outside creator of television commercials rather than maintain a department for this purpose within its own firm. This increases the negotiating aspects of the project manager's job, but basically the respective roles are not altered by the multiplication of legal entities.

Project managers and teams can also be used for special, one-time, cross-organizational changes, such as moving to a new location, absorbing a small company, or opening a foreign plant. Here the arrangement is clearly temporary and does not create any continuing modifications in organization design.

**priorities and trade offs**

The strong position given project managers creates difficulties in scheduling work within functional departments. Each project has its own timetable. Also, not all projects will use any one service to the same extent. The resulting irregular call for service is likely to conflict with the requirements of other projects, and each project manager will think that his work should have priority. Even when an advanced plan for all services is neatly dovetailed, the inherent uncertainties connected with such projects results in some being late and in others wanting greater use of needed specialists or facilities than was originally requested. The manager of a late project naturally feels it is important to catch up, and the manager who has struggled to stay on target strenuously objects to being penalized for another project's tardiness. Someone must decide who gets served first.

The head of a functional department is rarely the right person to set priorities. Naturally an even flow of work is wanted, and what is convenient is not necessarily best for the overall enterprise. Incidentally, periods of peak demand are often followed by little or no work, and the functional head is then seeking business to justify retaining trained personnel. Perhaps a bottleneck can be relieved by working overtime, but who decides when the overtime premium is warranted and which project is assessed the additional cost? Priority squabbles are eventually resolved, partly by give-and-take and partly by improved scheduling methods (as discussed in Chapter 5). But a residual set of priority and trade-off decisions will have to be made by a senior executive who can attach weights in light of total company values.

Because a matrix organization is both delicate and complicated, it should be used only when simpler organization designs are inadequate to cope with the dynamic nature of the work to be done.

**product managers**    Matrix organizations should be distinguished from organizations that use product managers. Theoretically, a company organized on a functional basis but with several different products could have a manager for each product. Each product manager would work very much like the project managers we have just described and would shepherd his product through the functional departments from research to customer delivery. But there is a difference between projects and products. A product is expected to generate repetitive sales and become part of the line. Most of the activities relating to it become a normal part of operations. Only occasionally, or in limited areas such as seasonal sales promotions or competitive pricing, does the product need more attention than the functional departments provide.

Therefore, a product manager typically needs less power than a project manager. He serves in a *staff* capacity, making sure that his product does not get lost, calling attention to unexpected opportunities, bringing together people from two or more departments when agreement on coordinated action is needed, suggesting ways to improve results, and the like. Usually the final decisions about the product are made by departmental executives, although in the case of highly competitive consumer goods a product manager sometimes decides on pricing, sales promotion, and inventory. Primarily, however, the product manager aids and stimulates the functional departments to do their jobs well, whereas the project manager carries the initiative and accountability while departments act in a service capacity.

Both project and product managers are organizational members who secure alert, responsive action in a milieu of rapid change. At the same time, both rely on the technical competence and efficient operations of functional departments. All sorts of variations are possible. Personal relationships are delicate; conflicts can be sharp. But we have here the possibilities for flexible, sophisticated action.

**OFFICE OF THE PRESIDENT**    The modern chief executive of every large enterprise is under severe pressure. The demands placed on his time by external and internal problems, by nonbusiness as well as business affairs, by both long-range and short-range planning cannot possibly be met by one human being. Relief must be found.

The intensity of the pressure is growing, but the problem is not new. For years chief executives have had a few personal assistants to relieve them of minor tasks and to expedite their numerous conferences, public appearances, and problem analyses. In a relatively stable situation, a whole array of corporate staff units may be created. Although these staff units normally provide service to their associates and to others throughout the organization, they are also available to assist the chief executive directly.

Decentralization, especially profit decentralization, is a second way to relieve the harried chief executive. As we have seen, a variety of factors affect the wisdom of decentralizing, and so this alternative may not be attractive. Furthermore, even after decentralizing the remaining tasks for central management are very heavy.

A third alternative, practiced by a few companies including du Pont and Exxon Corporation, is to have some (though not necessarily all) full-time members of the board of directors. Such board members are full-time employees who have been relieved of supervision of their part of the enterprise. They devote their full energies to central-management tasks. Some allocation of work among the board members is made, and channels of communication are established. However, all regular board members are available to give undivided attention to new problems and future opportunities. Two drawbacks make this arrangement unattractive to most enterprises. First, a full-time board of highly succesful executives is expensive; few companies can afford it. Second, the benefits of an independent, objective check on company actions by outside directors who are not judging their own decisions, are lost.

Recently the concept of a "president's office" is becoming more widely used and, as is the case with the office of President in our federal government, the president's office is viewed as a distinct unit of the organization. It has its own internal structure as well as its relations with other separate units and departments. Various staff aides and communication flows are part of the design, but the key feature is a team of two to five senior executives who share the central-management tasks.

The division of duties among the senior officers depends on their own capabilities and the currently pressing problems. One executive might deal with external relations—with customer groups, governmental bodies, industry associations, and the like—while another concentrates on internal operations. Three other executives might handle technological questions, legal matters, and finance. But the essence of the concept is synthesized action rather than specialization along any line. Regardless of how the work is shared, an intimate and frequent interchange is essential so that the office functions like a close-knit partnership. The office is expected to repond to numerous external and internal integration needs (discussed in Chapter 1) in a way that provides a consistent and unified posture for the company.

The success of this arrangement rests predominantly on the personalities of the executives involved. At the top level they are sure to be strong individuals; yet a president's office requires a high degree of sharing and mutual support. Not all strong people are willing to play the game this way. Other features of organization design may depend on the characteristics of persons in key positions, but this dependency is never so great as in the case of the president's office.

We should note in passing that the concept of a "president's office" might also be applied to the management of any large, complex unit. Certainly dual executives are not unique. In this case a manager typically has an alter ego who shares with him the duties of the position. For this arrangement to be effective there must be a proper blending of personalities, and the managers must have experience in working together. The senior person must have complete confidence in his associate because, as in a legal partnership, either partner can usually speak for the office. The relationship is so highly personal and potentially unstable that it should be avoided if some other provision is practical.

## CONCLUSION: EVOLVING ORGANIZATIONAL FORMS

The examples of new emphases in organization discussed in the latter part of this chapter illustrate again how organization design needs to be adapted to the technological, economic, and social environment in which the enterprise operates. The basic elements of managerial organization have persisted for centuries, but designing a specific structure is the neverending task of adjusting to current opportunities.

As a company succeeds and grows, it must change its organization. Many variations and compromises are essential if the organization is to fit the specific technology, optimum size, resources, and other features of a specific firm. A cardinal aim in developing such variations should be to strengthen the company in those areas in which it has chosen to build a strategic distinction. In this way, organization gives potency to the unique service the company wants to provide.

In each of these diverse overall structures, the elements of organization examined in Chapters 10, 11, and 12—departmentation, decentralization, and staff—are the bricks and mortar. The way they are combined and interwoven differs. But the underlying processes of combining activities into operating and managerial jobs, of mapping relationships between these jobs, and of adding supplementary services reappear over and over again. Although the stages of organization growth suggest ways of adjusting to size and complexity, the structure for each specific company must be a unique application of the elementary organizing concepts. The opportunity, indeed the necessity, for creative adaptation arises in every structural design.

## FOR FURTHER DISCUSSION

1. "One of the major omissions in most strategic planning efforts is the failure to consider fully the structural changes required as strategy shifts. Usually the strategy is developed and *acted on* and then people start thinking about what changes in structure are needed. This is wrong!" Comment on this statement by a leading management consultant.

2. Other things being equal, does greater diversification of product, technology, or markets lead you to favor more or less decentralization than you would favor in a more homogenous company? Discuss.

3. How can tracing the horizontal flow of a complete action—such as buying a new batch of raw material, designing and placing into production a new product, or employing and training a new worker—aid in designing an organization structure?

4. "The six factors given as affecting the proper span of supervision omit the

single most important one." What factor do you think the person who made this statement had in mind?

5. To what extent may serious organization problems arise as a company grows and shifts its strategy from skimming new products and markets to servicing more mature products and markets? How might these problems be dealt with?

6. Why do few companies elect to stay relatively small and clearly focused on a single mission, since to do so would probably make organization simpler and more efficient?

7. "We have been using a matrix organization for years. We just didn't realize it so we called it a 'gang' or 'crew.'" Comment on this observation by the president of a construction company.

8. What factors would be most important in determining whether to deal with pressures caused by the size and complexity of a business by (1) decentralizing more or (2) creating an office of the president?

## CASES

For cases involving issues covered in this chapter, see especially the following. Particularly relevant questions are listed after each case.

Benjo Associates (p. 92), 12.
Elizabeth Archer (p. 96), 10
Camden Chemical (p. 298), 10, 13, 14, 24
Scandico (Singapore) (p. 305), 6
Joan Carrier (p. 376), 5
Netsuki Novelty Product Company (p. 451), 7
Foster Promotions Inc. (p. 538), 8

## FOR FURTHER READING

Corey, E. R. and S. H. Star, *Organization Strategy: A Marketing Approach.* Boston: Harvard Business School, 1971, chap. 1–5. These summary chapters highlight the natural conflict between product/market program management and "resource" management.

Davis, S. M. and P. R. Lawrence, *Matrix.* Reading: Addison-Wesley, 1977. Concise review of matrix organization and its diffusion among companies in the U.S. and abroad.

Drucker, P. F. "New Templates for Today's Organizations." *Harvard Business Review,* 52 (January-February 1974), 45-53. The author advocates new patterns of organization design to cope with increased complexity.

Kilmann, R. H., L. R. Pondy, and D. P. Steven, *The Management of Organizational Design.* Amsterdam, The Netherlands: Elsevier, 1976. Comprehensive examination of all phases of organization structure.

Leontiades, M., *Strategies for Diversification and Change.* (Boston: Little, Brown, 1980), chaps. 2 and 6. Insightful analysis of the stages of corporate growth and the impact of growth on organization structure.

Miles, R. E. and C. C. Snow, *Organizational Strategy, Structure and Process.* New York: McGraw-Hill, 1978. Innovative study of organizational adaptation to the environment.

# 14

# staffing
# to execute
# missions

Learning Objectives

After completing this chapter you should be able to

1. Identify the characteristics of job descriptions which are important for preparing person specifications.

2. Describe the three principal ways of stating person specifications.

3. Discuss the personality characteristics of managers which should be considered in staffing decisions.

4. Identify the principal methods used to assess individuals.

5. Discuss the major alternatives for dealing with weak incumbents.

6. Describe the three major steps in long-run personnel planning.

## ADJUSTING FOR PERSONAL DIFFERENCES

In the preceding four chapters, we have considered how the organizing process aids in achieving the master strategy of an enterprise. However, an effective organization design is not sufficient; the sound execution of strategy requires that each structural arrangement be staffed with the appropriate people.

Each specific job within an organization must be filled by a specific person, but that person may not fit the job neatly. Individuals differ in ability, learning, and, as we shall see in Chapter 15, in attitudes and behavior. Moreover, the same person changes over time as he gains experience and as his interests shift. If we find ourselves trying to fit a square peg into a round hold, we must fix either the peg or the hole or both.

Changes in strategy create staffing problems. A manager well suited to rapid expansion, for instance, may lack the caution and concern for detail that is needed when strategy shifts emphasis from growth to generation of cash. One airline company had to "kick upstairs" its outstanding promoter and then try two other presidents before getting a good match with its new earnings-focused strategy. Similarly, labor unions often find that an aggressive union president, suited to a period of organizing, is too restless and unbending after union recognition is well established.

## PREPARING INDIVIDUAL SPECIFICATIONS

The overall process of matching jobs and individuals resolves itself into the following subproblems: What kind of a person is needed for each job? What are the abilities of the people now in the organization? How can individuals and jobs be best matched in the short run? Should the individual be trained or replaced, or should the job be adjusted? How can people be obtained to match long-run needs?

**clarifying job specifications**

The first step in matching jobs and individuals takes up where organizational analysis left off. If an organization is designed properly, a series of *job descriptions* is available. A job description sets forth the objectives, duties, relationships, and results expected of a person in the job. A controller's job description, for instance, might include this duty: "Prepare monthly profit-and-loss statement." A hospital administrator's description might include statements such as, "Coordinate all community relations" and "Promote outpatient services so as to relieve pressure on bed facilities."

In order to match jobs and individuals, job descriptions must be more explicit and concrete. The declaration that a controller should prepare a monthly profit-and-loss statement, for example, does not say whether he personally must compute the state, local, and national taxes, or whether he can delegate this task to an expert. The hospital administrator may be in charge of all community relations, but does this duty involve delivering speeches, appearing before medical boards, or conducting health programs for school children?

The *relationships required* by a position must also be made explicit. Does the job require a lot of talking with many different people, or is it

*Figure* $14.1$ *For some jobs, candidates can be examined during a trial period. But where long training is required, we put people to the test in "real-game" situations, in hopes that their full potential will be realized. Or we analyze their past performance with the assumption that it will predict future achievement.*

NASA

independent, calling for only short, terse communication? With what kinds of people must an incumbent deal? Are they sharp traders or indifferent, uneducated operators? Will they interpret "democratic" advice-seeking as a weakness, or have they learned to be independent and to resent orders? Do they want friendship mixed up with their work relationships, or would they prefer to keep their contacts at work matter-of-fact and impersonal?

Perhaps a job description will have to be amplified in other ways, so that it spells out, for instance, how much decentralization is intended, what frequency of innovation is expected, or what managerial techniques are to be used. In clarifying job descriptions, thoughts need not necessarily be put in writing, but they should be clearly in the minds of everyone involved in the delicate task of matching specific individuals with specific jobs. The central point is to think through the nature of a job completely and carefully.

**translation to individual specifications**

The second major step in matching jobs and individuals is translating the duties in the amplified job description into "individual specifications." A statement of duties often does not tell specifically what to look for in appraising an incumbent or a candidate for a position. Suppose a controller is being sought for a large company, and one of his duties is to "report any critical developments, as shown by accounting records, to the board of directors." How is it possible to tell whether a person is skilled at this work? If a plant manager must "coordinate sixteen foremen," how can a person who can do so be recognized?

Of course in appraising an individual already in a position, past performance, compared with the behavior and results desired, will be the main evidence used. But when a new candidate is being considered or a position changed, a list of the crucial characteristics of a person in that job is needed.

Specifications should not be so closely tied to those exhibited by previous successful executives that people with different experience and personality are automatically excluded. In particular, highly qualified women and members of minority groups must be kept in the talent pool used to fill vacancies.

Actually, three quite different ways of stating individual specifications are in common use.

1.  Certain standardized tasks can be *tested directly*. Candidates for a lifesaving job can be run through a series of tests in a pool; prospective typists can be asked to type a sample passage; often an aspirant can be observed on an actual job for a brief period. Unfortunately, such standards cannot be applied to complicated and unusual tasks (which are typical of many executive jobs), and they tell little about how a person will fit into a working group. So additional specifications, especially for executive positions are needed.

2.  Past *work experience and accomplishment* may be useful as an indication of ability to do similar work in the future. For example, a large chemical company specified that its vice-president of finance "should have served as chief financial officer for a medium or large chemical-processing company for a period of eight years; should have been responsible for tax accounting in a medium-sized company for at least two years; should have had at least fifty people reporting to him." A water company specified that its plant manager should have demonstrated ability to "reduce costs, develop subordinate personnel, and avoid stoppages and breakdowns."

3.  Specifications may include a list of *personality characteristics* that are stated either in the technical jargon of behavioral scientists or in more general terms, such as "friendly temperament" and "apparent energy and ambition." The reason for resorting to personality characteristics is that experience may be an inadequate indication of the qualities needed for a position. A job may be so unusual that few candidates have pertinent experience, and experience may fail to demonstrate clearly all the qualities that might be needed for success in a new situation.

In practice, most statements of individual specifications for executive and staff jobs include a combination of desirable experience and personality characteristics stated in lay terms.[1] The use of scientific phrasing is limited, expensive, and complex, requiring people with formal training to prepare and judge them. Besides, the behavioral sciences have not yet reached a high degree of accuracy; hence, a solid record of experience, supplemented by intuitive judgments of personality, may be just as reliable for predicting managerial ability as the more intricate methods of the social scientists.

Preparing the experience section of an individual specification is relatively simple and grows directly from analyzing the duties of a particular job. We fully recognize the value of experience specifications and urge that they be used whenever appropriate. That much of the discussion on the following pages deals with personality characteristics means not that such characteristics are more important than experience, but merely that personality specifications are more difficult to prepare and that the opportunity is greater for managers to improve this aspect of individual specifications.

[1]T. W. Harrell, *Managers' Performance and Personality* (Cincinnati: South–Western, 1961).

## IMPORTANT PERSONALITY CHARACTERISTICS OF MANAGERS

Psychologists, psychiatrists, sociologists, and cultural anthropologists have identified and classified hundreds of human characteristics. None of the classifications is "right" or "wrong." Some are useful in studying individuals in the family, others in dealing with the mentally ill, still others in analyzing small work groups. In this discussion, we have selected from both science and business practice certain characteristics that, in our opinion, are most *useful to managers* in writing individual specifications, in appraising people, and in planning personnel development.[2] For convenience, we shall discuss these under five headings: knowledge, decision-making talent, self-reliance and self-assertion, social sensitivity, and emotional stability.

**knowledge**

In matching an individual with a job, an inevitable question is, "What does he need to know?" The knowledge an aspirant to an executive position should have can often be specified in terms of specialty, depth, coordination, and management. Every managerial position calls for specialized knowledge of, say, selling methods, water pollution, petroleum economics, or bond discounts. Some jobs require knowledge in depth, whereas others demand only general acquaintance with a field. The president of a company, for instance, may need some general knowledge of public relations, but the public relations manager should have thorough knowledge of sociology, politics, communications media, and kindred subjects.

Then, it must be considered what coordinating knowledge a manager will need to tie in his activities with related jobs; such knowledge includes an understanding of operations—facts, technology, and problems—and of the people whose work is related to their area of the company. Managerial knowledge is a grasp of management principles and techniques applicable to a variety of situations. Of course other kinds of knowledge may be necessary for specific decisions, but consideration of specialty, depth, coordination, and management provide a good start in identifying knowledge requirements for a particular job.

**decision-making talent**

Jobs differ in the complexity and novelty of problems that must be solved. The president of a large aerospace firm needs a different order of decision-making ability from that needed by the head of a motel chain. Let us note several of the personality factors that contribute to decision-making talent.

*Analytical ability*  This ability enables a person to break a problem into parts, identify relevant facts, interpret the meaning of facts, and project the consequences of a decision. Because so many facts bear on a typical management problem, an executive needs what might be called an intuitive analytical sense in order to select key facts and eliminate the rest.

[2]E. E. Ghiselli, *Explorations in Managerial Talent* (Pacific Palisades: Goodyear, 1971).

*Conceptual-logical ability*   To get meaning from a vast array of facts, they must be assembled under large concepts. For instance, an executive may take a chart that shows declining sales, information from competing companies, and reports on the activities of the company's own sales representatives, and pull them all together into one concept—"Poor customer service." Synthesizing facts involves both inventing concepts and using logic to connect concepts in casual relationships.

*Creativity*   Tough problems usually cannot be resolved by known methods. A fresh approach, a new twist, a novel arrangement of recognized parts, or the addition of a different material or system is often necessary to find an acceptable solution.[3] Preferably, an executive can create original ideas himself; at a minimum he needs acumen in spotting the good ideas of others.

*Intuitive judgment*   This resembles the "hunch." Up to a point a decision-maker looks at a problem analytically and logically and then suddenly seems to "know what to do." Even though the process is only partially systematic and conscious, a decision does emerge. Intuitive judgment is particularly important when all facts cannot be gathered, when conceptual and logical arguments are fuzzy, or when immediate action is required without waiting for long, rational analysis.

*Judgmental courage*   Unlike a scientist, an executive must often act without careful research and foolproof logic to back up his decision. Psychologists associate ability to do so with a person's *tolerance of ambiguity* (his capacity to deal with uncertainties without breaking down) and with *frustration tolerance* (his ability to deal continually with difficulties without becoming discouraged). Courage is needed to make decisions when confronted by uncertainties and frustrations.

*Open-mindedness*   The sixth component of decision-making talent, particularly important in individual specifications, is receptivity to new ideas. Does a person conscientiously listen to others and try to determine the relevance of their ideas in solving current problems?

In summary, we can say that although decision-making talent is difficult to pin down, some of its elements can be identified. An executive who is analytical, logical, creative, open-minded, intuitive, and courageous is more likely to make useful decisions than a person who is weak in these qualities.

---

[3]G. M. Prince, *The Practice of Creativity* (New York: Harper & Row, 1970).

**self-reliance and self-assertion**

In satisfying needs and solving problems, people differ in how much they rely on themselves and how much on others. Jobs, too, differ in what they require of a person in the way of taking initiative, asserting ideas with persistence over those of others, and presenting ideas forcefully and energetically.

Psychologists have studied this trait and describe degrees of self-reliance—or lack of it—in terms of a range between extremes. Some talk of dominant ⟷ submissive characteristics; others speak of independent ⟷ dependent or of active ⟷ passive behavior. Practical business executives often use the expressions "initiative," "drive," or "self-starting ability" to identify the same quality, at least for the end of the continuum they are most interested in.

This trait is one that is revealed in everyday activities. To check yourself on this quality, observe what you do when you wake up in the small hours of the night because you are cold. Do you try pulling the covers closer around your neck hoping the chilly air will go away? Or do you face the problem, climb out of bed, and get another blanket? Many executive jobs need the type of person who gets another blanket.

Closely allied with self-reliance is ambition, or "achievement motivation." Having mastered one problem, most persons set higher goals for themselves and start working toward them. Individuals differ, however, in how much they advance their aspirations. Some aspire to make "big jumps," whereas others are content with modest progress.

**social sensitivity**

Some people react to a problem largely in terms of the feelings of those involved. They have a high capacity for *empathy*—the ability to project imaginatively into the thoughts, feelings, and probable reactions of another. A socially sensitive manager might empathize with an auditor or a salesperson in Alaska without necessarily approving of their feelings and behavior; but because the manager really senses their reactions, he is likely to be sympathetic to, or at least understanding of, their points of view.

Social sensitivity may be helpful, of course, in almost any job, but it is of critical importance for most selling, staff, and executive positions.[4]

**emotional stability**

Emotional stability indicates a good adjustment to life. People who are emotionally stable tend to act in the following ways: (1) they accept different people, including those they do not like, calmly and objectively; (2) they react to obstacles by steadily increasing their efforts or finding new ways to achieve their desires, rather than by denying that the obstacles exist, becoming overly depressed, lashing out aggressively, or rationalizing their inabilities; (3) they know when they cannot achieve a given goal, and shrug their shoulders and turn their attention to other matters that interest them;

[4]W. R. Dill, T. L. Hilton, and W. R. Reitman, *The New Managers* (Englewood Cliffs, NJ: Prentice-Hall, 1962).

(4) they react happily to moments of success but remain objective, without experiencing childlike exhilaration and becoming overly optimistic; (5) they behave simply and naturally without artificiality or straining for effect.

The test of a person's emotional stability comes, of course, when he is subjected to conflict and tension; and some jobs test a person more than others. For instance, the tension experienced by the sales manager of a newly formed pharmaceutical company is likely to be greater than that felt by the chief accountant in a savings bank. So a higher degree of emotional stability would be needed in the sales job than in the accounting job.

**perceptive use of personality factors**

The personality factors we have been talking about will be of greatest usefulness if a list of specifications is prepared for each job. The following examples suggest how a manager should tailor specifications to a job.

It is a good idea to provide complementary abilities in an executive and his key subordinates. Thus an executive who has intuition, courage, and a penchant for fast action might want an assistant who has analytical skill and a predisposition for research and fact-finding. If a new supervisor is to be appointed over a group of subordinates who are highly dependent, he will need considerable self-reliance and self-assertion.

The position of production scheduler presents a different problem. His work must interlock frequently and closely with that of a wide variety of people—perhaps a dozen shop supervisors, inventory clerks, purchasing agents, maintenance people, sales representatives, and others. Anyone appointed to such a job should have considerable emotional stability if he is to remain problem-centered and get along with everyone.

In contrast, the jobs of researcher and development engineer typically require persons with specialized knowledge and keen decision-making talent. Social sensitivity and emotional stability, although desirable, would not be so essential for such jobs as for a production scheduler. The position of sales representative calls for still different abilities—social sensitivity and self-reliance ranking at the top of the list.

Executives need considerable courage and self-assertiveness when a company is making frequent changes to adapt to new competition or rapid changes in technology. A high degree of emotional stability is also desirable, as major changes mean stress for everyone whose job is affected by new practices.

A final remark about individual specifications. All the preceding discussion has been couched in terms of fixed and set working environments, including a stable array of subordinates, associates, and social structure. This approach implies that an individual must adjust to fit a position. But sometimes adjustment may run in the other direction. A job may be shaped, at least to some extent, to fit the person. A manager must always think closely about both the job—however it may be revised—and the characteristics of a person who could fill such a job well. Also, jobs change over time. If a new strategy is likely to be adopted, then the qualities needed in the people who are to meet the revised priorities should be specified.

Job analysis and individual specifications are not ends in themselves; they are vital preparations for a third step—assessing specific individuals to see how well they match the jobs created by an organization design. Specifications provide standards, and the manager must now evaluate people in terms of those standards.

**appraising experience**

Measuring what a person has done is relatively simple and direct. For example, if the specifications for a vice president in charge of production state that, "He should have ten years of experience as head of manufacturing in a medium-sized company," matching his work record to the specifications is all that is necessary. The same is true if experience specifications are stated in terms of *results* rather than years; for instance, "He should have increased the sales in his territory significantly during his tenure as branch manager." But when the specified results are intangible—such as having developed good subordinates or maintained goodwill with suppliers—there are measurement problems. Often, in a complex situation, it is difficult to know how much the person being appraised influenced the outcome, and how much of the outcome was caused by other forces. On such matters it may be desirable to pool the subjective judgments of several people.

Appraisal of experience is somewhat analogous to what a statistician does when he predicts the gross national product by fitting a trend line to the experience of the past ten or twenty years. He is not sure of the precise values and weights of all underlying forces; hence, without knowing the forces, he simply projects a line that is the result of all of them. Similarly, it is often possible to use past achievement to predict a person's likely future success, without being sure which personal abilities determined success. Although such prediction is admittedly risky, it is often the best way to size up an individual. The method does have two attractive advantages—it is inexpensive and can be used by executives who lack technical training in psychology.

The reliability of an appraisal based on experience depends partly on the *relevance* of past experience to the new job. If a person is being evaluated in his present position, naturally the pertinent issue is whether current results are satisfactory. But when a person is being considered for transfer or promotion, his past experience must be related to a job with different specifications. And if the candidate's background does not quite fit the new specifications, is the fit close enough? In this event, past experience is probably used as evidence about personality factors, and judgment may be improved if it is recognized that a shift has been made from one kind of criterion to another.

A common safeguard in making promotions in many companies is a policy of testing a person in several different jobs. These assignments are useful *both* for training and for appraisal. If there is any doubt about Claire's or Pete's ability to get work out on schedule, we can assign them a task in which they can gain experience and their development can be watched closely.

A job may be unique or so new that no previous work closely resembles it; it is useless to insist on full experience in this case, and the appraisal must be made on the basis of a person's ability and personality. Executives are rarely skilled psychologists, yet they must and do appraise personality. For years, managers have depended on their intuitive judgment in selecting personnel. Because such selection is so crucial, measures that can improve the quality of judgment should be adopted. Here are three practical rules that are applicable to large and small companies. **personality appraisal by executives**

1. Make individual judgments on sophisticated grounds. Instead of resorting to vague terms like "personality" or "a good worker," define specifically the qualities needed in a job. By doing so, an appraiser can detect his own biases and cultivate objectivity, which will enable him to judge people realistically.
2. Use group judgment. In order to prevent mistakes in perception and judgment, many companies insist that three or four executives appraise a person on each specification.
3. Maintain a file of key incidents in each person's performance. Recent events tend to be remembered and overemphasized. A more balanced appraisal can be made with the help of a systematic record that includes revealing incidents about the person over a period of years. Such a record should denote both strengths and weaknesses, and it may indicate the directions in which an individual is developing (perhaps he has overcome earlier knowledge deficiencies, and he may be showing more—or less—self-reliance).

Personality and aptitude tests provide quite useful information for certain types of well-defined positions, such as salesperson, computer programmer, and routine production worker. Clinical interviews by skilled psychologists are also useful when simpler methods do not clearly indicate certain characteristics, for example, emotional stability. As our knowledge about human behavior in work situations increases, the value of such tests should also improve. **tests and clinical interviews**

Unfortunately, in our present state of knowledge, psychological tests have only limited value as predictors of success in specific jobs.[5] The diversity of job specifications, along with the complexity of individual motivation and behavior, makes the design of a reliable test extremely difficult. Tests may be invalid for minority candidates. Furthermore, only the largest companies can afford the great expense of designing and giving tests that are adapted to specific jobs. Except for preliminary screening of a large number of raw recruits, psychological tests and clinical interviews will probably continue to be used largely as supplements to managerial judgment. For executive posts especially, the chief value of tests lies in corroborating or questioning personal estimates. Assessing people on the basis of experience and observable personality characteristics will endure as an important management duty for a long, long time.

[5]J. P. Campbell, et. al., *Managerial Behavior, Performance, and Effectiveness* (New York: McGraw-Hill, 1970).

**assessment centers**  The assessment center is a relatively new concept for identifying managerial potential.[6] In an assessment center, candidates participate in several performance simulations while trained observers evaluate their behavior.

One widely used assessment device is the "in-basket exercise," in which participants are asked to deal with a realistic set of messages, telephone calls, letters, and reports. Assessors evaluate the candidate's decisions with respect to such abilities as willingness to take action, organizing ability, memory and ability to interrelate events, and ability to delegate. Similarly, leaderless group discussions are employed to assess a candidate's persuasiveness, flexibility, self-confidence, and aggressiveness. As more and more firms have introduced assessment centers, simulation exercises have been customized to fit the firm's particular situation. Thus, in the assessment center operated by a large department store chain, an assessor places an "irate customer phone call" in order to rate the candidate's ability to control emotions, demonstrate tact, and satisfy the complainer.

Some assessment centers have achieved impressive accuracy in predicting which candidates will advance to higher managerial ranks. There are, however, some disadvantages which offset this predictive capability. Since an assessment typically involves a number of assessors working with a small group of candidates over a number of days, assessment centers are very costly. Care and sensitivity are required to manage the stress situations created by the competitive aspects of assessment center simulations. In addition, low assessment center ratings may demotivate personnel who are competent in their present positions.

**SHORT-RUN PERSONNEL PLANNING**  Present personnel will seldom match completely the specifications prepared for existing positions. An appraisal of personnel typically reveals that some people have less ability than desired whereas others have unused talents. What can a manager do to improve this match of human resources and organization needs? Both short-run and long-run adjustments are necessary. In the short run concentration on present employees and present jobs is necessary. The long run allows much more flexibility, as we shall discuss later.

**the weak incumbent**  Probably the most difficult and unpleasant short-run problem arises when an individual already in a job fails to measure up. In such cases, there are three alternatives for improving the congruence of person and job.

1. Change the job. This procedure is a matter of "tinkering" with the organization structure. Three examples of such tinkering are withdrawing a duty from one position and assigning it to another, adjusting the degree of decentralization, and providing additional assistance where a person is weak.[7]

[6]A. Howard, "An Assessment of Assessment Centers," *Academy of Management Journal,* 17, no. 1 (March 1978), 115–34.

[7]F. Fiedler, "Engineering the Job to Fit the Manager," *Harvard Business Review,* September-October 1965.

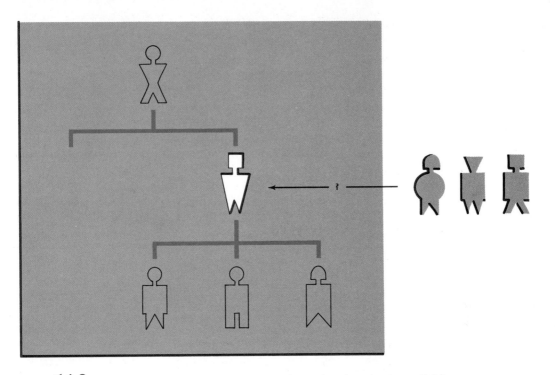

*Figure 14.2*  *Short-run personnel planning. Neither subordinates nor available candidates outside the company are able to fill effectively a gap that has occurred in the company organization. There is a mismatch between the job as now conceived and the qualifications of candidates who are available to fill it.*

2. Change the incumbent. Perhaps through counseling and training, the employee may overcome the gap between his present performance and what the company desires.
3. Remove the incumbent. If a person cannot be expected to become competent in a reasonable time or if the job cannot be changed to fit him, it may be necessary to transfer or dismiss him and fill the position with someone who more nearly fits the individual specifications.

Action in such situations is often painful because it upsets both expectations and established behavior. But procrastination may undercut the effectiveness of a whole department or company.

In deciding on which of the three methods to follow in matching person and job, several questions should be answered carefully.

**deciding on a matching method**

*How closely does the job interlock with other positions?*  The degree of interdependence between a given job and other jobs directly affects the ease or difficulty of changing the organization to fit a person. For example, the Montana sales representative of a Midwestern paint company may be ineffective without upsetting the work of others; the company simply has a somewhat reduced volume of business, and might cut the incumbent's territory or have him concentrate on a limited number of customers, so that his duties match his abilities. But poor performance by a billing clerk may have far-reaching repercussions. Customers may get too many items of one color and not enough of another; the accounts-receivable clerk may spend extra time trying to straighten out invoice difficulties; salespeople may have trouble with customers; inventory records may be snarled up; and so on. To adjust the billing job to fit the capacities of the present clerk is not practical as it would set off a chain reaction that would alter several other positions.

***Will training make the person acceptable?*** Some personal deficiences can be corrected fairly promptly, whereas others can be altered little if at all. For instance, product knowledge or specific company knowledge can often be quickly acquired, but conceptual-logical abilities require native capacity plus many years to develop. This distinction is important, because it is tempting to keep a person in a position because he is familiar with current facts and routines, even though he lacks the imagination and drive to do a really satisfactory job over a period of time.

***Is a good replacement available?*** One small firm had a chief engineer who was cantankerous, uncompromising, and slow. But the company retained him because his technical knowledge of the product line was far superior to that of any subordinate or of engineers in other firms who might be attracted by the salary the company could afford to pay. Eventually, it was hoped, one of the younger engineers could take on responsibility for contacts with the sales department, production department, and customers, thereby permitting the current chief to concentrate on developing new products. Pending the event, however, the president took over some of the duties that ideally should have been the chief engineer's; the assistant production superintendent was assigned the task of expediting plans for new products; and a coordinating committee that met weekly was formed. In this instance, the organization was changed to fit an individual because a good replacement was unavailable.

In thinking about promotions and transfers, the manager must be wary of chain reactions. Perhaps the Canadian branch manager is well qualified to replace an ailing vice-president, but how will the work of the Canadian branch be carried on? Although analysis starts with matching a particular candidate to a specific job, it can lead to thought about the best arrangement of the whole structure of jobs and people.

***How long will the person remain on the job?*** If an unsatisfactory incumbent is within a few years of retirement, or can be transferred soon, then temporary and expedient adjustments in work assignments may be warranted.

***Is superior performance urgent?*** The president of a large soap company, which was heavily dependent on advertising to compete with such companies as Lever Brothers and Procter & Gamble, was saddled with "a grand old man" as advertising manager. He was not up-to-date on advertising research, use of television, and other new developments in sales promotion. The pressure of competition forced the company to bring in a competent advertising manager in short order, despite the consequences for the old man. Urgency, in terms of time and importance, required such a course.

Most cases are not so clearcut. Just how important is it to have a job filled exactly according to specifications in the organization plan? What obligations does a company owe a person who has given long and perhaps distinguished service? Should any weight be given to long personal friendships? Must the need for change be clearly evident, or can changes be made on the basis of uncertain estimates of the future? Because answers to such questions of value tend to be personal and subjective, an executive should check his judgments with two or three associates.

***How will removal affect morale?*** Removing a widely known, well-liked individual may cause other employees to say, "Don't go to work for this company—they fire people at the drop of a hat." Even if everyone else remains in his job, a pervasive feeling of insecurity may be created in a department by the removal of one popular individual. Negative effects on morale can be lessened by letting it be generally known that the person dismissed was given a fair chance to demonstrate his ability, that he was offered a transfer with dignity to another position, and that he was given a dismissal benefit for early retirement.

Sometimes, on the other hand, morale is improved by the removal of a person from a position for which he is not qualified. If employees see that someone is kept on a job even though his performance is mediocre, they may develop the general attitude expressed by the question, "Why push yourself?" And many a competent young person has been discouraged to find his advancement blocked by a series of inadequate people in key posts. In such situations, removal of a weak incumbent will be a signal that management is prepared to distinguish between good and poor performance, and this will boost morale among the more able employees.

The foregoing list of questions certainly indicate that no universal answer can tell a manager whether he should fit his organization to people or find people to fit the organization. Because a manager has an obligation to carry out company strategy, we urge that he give independent and detailed study to the design of an organization that is well suited to that strategy. But in the short run, a manager must clearly meld this ideal design—as reflected in person specifications—with the abilities of available personnel.

Resignation, death, or unanticipated transfer may create a vacancy with little warning, and the empty position needs to be filled as soon as possible. In such cases, there is usually a choice of replacements, but rarely will any of the candidates completely match the specifications for the vacant position. Again we face the question of how much a job should be modified to fit an individual.

**an unexpected vacancy**

Consider the sudden death of your professor or the manager of a local supermarket. Ths issues to be faced in seeking a successor are similar to those already discussed. Must the job be done so that it readily interlocks with other positions? What requirements for the job can be learned after the person is appointed, and what qualities must he already possess? How will the position vacated by the new appointee be filled? Is top performance immediately important, or is gradual learning and adjustment feasible? If duties are to be reassigned, what will be the impact on morale? Does this unanticipated event present an opportunity to correct previous faults in the organization or to move toward a long-range organization plan?

Expedient, compromise steps—such as having one executive cover two jobs—may be unavoidable when an unanticipated vacancy first occurs. But these moves should be clearly announced as temporary. Then prompt action should be taken to work out a more satisfactory arrangement. The danger, of course, is that the expedient action may be allowed to continue for so long that later adjustments will not be made; or if they are, people will be upset by what they regard as another reorganization.

**the strong incumbent**

Some people in every organization will have greater ability than their jobs call for. A familiar question arises: Should the job be adjusted to fit the person? In fact, such adjustment tends to happen. There are four common situations that call for it. (1) If the work that interlocks with a person's regular duties is poorly performed, a capable individual often gives advice and checks on performance that lies beyond his assigned sphere; by doing so, he sets the stage for having duties transferred to him. (2) When a special problem arises, a capable person is often asked to help with its solution. Repeated assignments to such special projects may lead to his having additional duties as a regular part of his job. (3) Further, to paraphrase an old rule of science, "Organization abhors a vacuum"; if important activities are not being taken care of at all, the most capable person around often steps into the breach. (4) Finally, quite aside from assigned duties, the influence of a strong individual is apt to extend beyond his prescribed area.

Such natural, if unplanned, expansion of a job creates no difficulties until the person becomes so involved in unofficial activities that he neglects his regular duties, or until he gets promoted. The first danger can be avoided if the supervisor insists that the individual keep his main assignments in clear perspective. Promotion, however, is likely to cause a more severe jolt. The shock is like that on a football team built around a backfield star who leaves the game with an injury. Weaknesses formerly covered up suddenly become serious. A wise manager, therefore, should keep abreast of how work is actually getting done and should use his outstanding subordinates for special assignments or in other ways that do not make his organization vulnerable to serious upsets when the exceptional performer moves on to another job.

A final observation applies to all shifts of personnel, whether initiated by a manager or by a worker leaving his job. No two persons are identical; each has his own strengths and limitations. Consequently, when a person takes a new position, he will—and should—perform the work in ways that are somewhat different from those of his predecessor. At first, he may not be prepared to carry the full load, but later he will probably take on some duties that were not assigned to his predecesor; on the other hand, other duties may be more fully delegated or initiative for them transferred to staff advisors. Inevitably, then, at least minor adjustments will occur in the assignments of duties and in social structure. During this transition, while people are learning new relationships, a manager has an opportunity to make alterations in organization without treating them as special problems. Such a period is also a natural occasion to introduce features of a long-range organization plan. For all these reasons, *placing an individual should be considered in terms of organization* as well as from a strictly personnel viewpoint.

## LONG-RUN PERSONNEL PLANNING

Personnel planning for the long run differs in several particulars from the short-run problems just discussed. It is concerned with all jobs and all employees at once, with matching a complete roster of personnel to total job requirements; it is concerned with filling future vacancies rather than existing jobs; and it allows time for long-term learning, especially through rotation of personnel.[8] Three major steps are involved in the process of long-run personnel planning: (1) projecting the organization structure and the personnel that are required to operate that structure, (2) matching the projected personnel requirements with present employees, and (3) planning for individual development so that people will be qualified when job openings occur.

**projecting personnel requirements**

The first essential step in long-run personnel planning is to forecast the organization structure that will best meet the future needs of the company. The environment of any company is constantly changing—new products are introduced, existing products are modified, production processes altered, automation is introduced, advertising policies shift, and so on. Public-service enterprises are changing even more rapidly. The whole job structure should keep pace with such changes. Adding positions because of growth and new activities may be necessary, and existing positions may be assigned quite different duties ten years hence.

With this future organization structure as a basis, specifications for each position can be prepared. Naturally, some aspects, such as personality characteristics to complement people in related jobs, cannot be included in these early individual specifications. Nevertheless the main elements of each job should be thought through. The aim is to develop a clear understanding of what future personnel requirements will be.

[8]E. H. Burack and J. W. Walker, eds., *Manpower Planning and Programming* (Boston: Allyn and Bacon, 1972).

**matching people with requirements**

The second step in long-range personnel planning starts with appraising all key personnel and cataloging their characteristics without reference to specifications for a particular position. This *inventory of talent* should include, in addition to present executives, younger men and women (including members of minority groups). For even if these younger members are not yet in key spots, a good deal of positional shifting will undoubtedly occur during the following three to ten years.

With a list of individual specifications for jobs and an inventory of talent, jobs can be matched to individuals. First consideration for any position similar to a present job goes, of course, to the incumbent. Does he have the abilities that will be needed in the future? He may be highly qualified; perhaps he needs further development; possibly he should be replaced. His age must also be considered. If he will retire within the period covered by the long-range plan, obviously a replacement should be found. As an analytical device, some companies draw up an organization chart with colored bands around the boxes; red, say, to denote a vacancy within three years, amber for five years, and purple for ten.

From the preceding steps the initial set of vacancies have been spotted—new jobs, jobs where the incumbent should be replaced, and jobs that will be vacated by retirement. The individual specifications for each of these vacancies, plus the inventory of talent will identify the *most probable* candidates to fill the vacancies. Some companies pick a single candidate for each post; others pick two or even three (at least for the major positions) because they are not certain which candidate will be best qualified by the time the vacancy opens up.

A second set of probable vacancies is created as soon as people have been identified as candidates for promotion. Are there employees qualified to

*Figure 14.3 Long-run personnel planning. To prepare for an anticipated future need, the organization guides the development of candidates, so that when the vacancy occurs, one or more individuals wil have qualifications that match the requirements of the vacated position.*

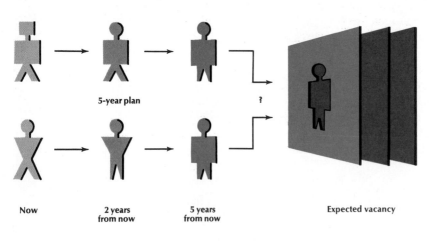

Now | 2 years from now | 5 years from now | Expected vacancy

5-year plan | ?

move into the present positions held by these candidates? Again, a list of most-probable candidates can be prepared by comparing individual specifications with the inventory of talent. Theoretically, a third set of vacancies could be studied to find replacements for the replacements, and so on. In practice, complete plans for replacements are rarely carried beyond the second set; because so many uncertainties exist, such a projection is unwarranted. Instead, division managers simply recognize that some turnover will undoubtedly occur; consequently they develop—often with the help of the central staff—junior people for promotion without knowing just who will move where.

The important result of this analysis is that management foresees, several years in advance, both its need for people to fill certain key vacancies and the most promising individuals for those jobs.

**planning individual development**

Few if any candidates will have all the essential characteristics for the positions to which they might move. To overcome these deficiencies, management must determine what experience is needed and what capabilities should be developed. Some companies call the forms on which this information is listed "gap sheets."[9]

At this stage of planning, any major difficulties in staffing the projected organization will become apparent. It may turn out to be so hard to fill certain positions with satisfactory executives that a firm will have to reconsider its organization design, at least at those points. In small firms, whose owners will undoubtedly continue to occupy key posts, adjustments may be necessary because of the owners' strengths and limitations. A three-year program, of course, is more likely to require adjustment of organization to personnel than a ten-year program, for there is obviously more opportunity to acquire and develop suitable personnel during the longer period.

Once a decision has been made on the gaps—the improvement and abilities a person needs to qualify for promotion—individual-development can begin. Management can help in individual-development, especially in providing needed experience. For example, a sales representative who is a candidate for branch manager might first be placed in a home-office staff position for two years. This service would broaden his perspective and acquaint him thoroughly with home-office activities and people. Executives who need broader perspective can be offered an opportunity to take part in a university's executive-development program.[10]

Most of the individual-development, however, will depend on the person himself. He will have to choose, at several points in his development, a career path—looking toward more intensive specialization, overseas assignments, managerial tasks, or other alternatives. Probably he will not be told exactly what management plans for him, but an ambitious person will guess

[9]F. J. Staszak and N. J. Mathys, "Organization Gap: Implications for Manpower Planning," *California Management Review,* 17, no. 3 (Spring 1975), 32-38.
[10]R. J. House, *Management Development: Design Evaluation and Implementation* (Ann Arbor: University of Michigan Press, 1967).

and will act on any suggestions about where he should try to improve.

Long-run personnel plans, like any other long-range plans, should be revised periodically. With the passage of time, forecasts of operating conditions and concepts of an ideal organization for the company will change. Assessments of people will change, too, because some will develop faster and others more slowly than anticipated. In addition, resignations may require a revision of proposals for replacements. Nevertheless, if the whole process of long-range personnel planning successfully serves its purpose, qualified people will be available to fill vacancies as they arise, and short-run organization adjustments made necessary by inadequate personnel will occur less often.

## CONCLUSION: ORGANIZING—A CONTINUOUS PROCESS

Matching individuals and jobs, as we have set it forth in this chapter, consists of rather sharply defined steps: clarifying jobs, preparing individual specifications, appraising personnel, making short-run adjustments, and planning long-run development of people to fit predicted organization needs. This step-by-step presentation is a useful approach to a dynamic problem. But the approach is not intended to provide a blueprint that should remain fixed once it is drawn.

Organizations are never completely established. Even the best plan soon becomes outdated by changes in work and personnel. The need for adjustment —often minor, occasionally major—is continual. Instead of being a static machine, an organization is an evolving social system.

In Part III, we have been principally concerned with designing a system for getting work done. Clearly, such a plan is essential in order to achieve the mission of any enterprise. But emphasizing work alone tends to be too mechanistic. The wise manager conceives of an organization as a social system, not simply as a machine. Consequently, we devote our full attention in Part IV to the stuff of which an organization is made—people. In the chapters that follow we will examine how a manager builds a set of individual roles and interpersonal relationships that is congruent with the structure of work provided by a formal organization.

## FOR FURTHER DISCUSSION

1. Gil Bennett has been with your company for twenty-seven years; during the last twelve years he has been assistant purchasing agent. With the death of the chief purchasing agent this man is promoted to that job. After several months, it appears that although he was a good assistant, his former boss had never really developed his initiative, and he is barely adequate in the top purchasing position. As his supervisor, what action might you take? What factors would influence your action?

2. How may recent efforts to develop different strategies for different divisions of the same company affect staffing decisions for key divisional positions?

3. What role, if any, should a candidate's sex have in key staffing decisions?

4. As a hedge against being caught without competent personnel, one company adheres to a policy of having at

least two people capable of filling each key position. Aside from the cost of such a policy, how else might this be impractical? How else might fear of key personnel shortages be allayed?

5. "Person specifications should be developed only in very general terms. As long as I have a rough idea of what I'm looking for, I select the best person for the company. If he doesn't fit the job I hired him for, but is good enough, we'll find him another job in the company. There are just too many ways to 'skin a cat' for me to write detailed person specifications." Comment on this statement made by the vice-president of marketing of a large consumer goods company. Would your views

change if the person quoted were head of a state governmental agency?

6. "Position descriptions should be written by experienced personnel officers after interviewing the line managers affected. This is critical to get objectivity and skill in written descriptions." Discuss.

7. Since jobs will change over time, how much obligation has a company for helping an individual change and how much of the obligation should lie with the individual?

8. Discuss the benefits and drawbacks of having assessment-center feedback go only to the person assessed and not made a part of his personnel file.

## CASES

For cases involving issues covered in this chapter, see especially the following. Particularly relevant questions are listed after each case.

## FOR FURTHER READING

Bray, D. W., R. J. Campbell, and D. L. Grant, *Formative Years in Business: A Long-Term AT&T Study of Managerial Lives.* New York: Wiley, 1974. Describes AT&T's pioneering efforts in assessing managers.

Dinsmore, F. W., *Developing Tomorrow's Managers Today.* New York: AMACOM, 1975. A businessman focuses his long experience on the process of developing managers.

Mahler, W. R. and W. F. Wrightnour, *Executive Continuity: How to Build and Retain an Effective Management Team.* Homewood: Dow Jones-Irwin, 1973. Practical guide to executive development, based on extensive experience.

Shaeffer, R. G., *Staffing Systems: Managerial and Professional Jobs.* New York: The Conference Board, Report 558, 1972. Describes the process of filling managerial jobs in a systematic and planned manner. Four company systems are discussed in detail.

Schneider, B., *Staffing Organizations.* Santa Monica: Goodyear, 1976. Good overview of personnel selection and staffing from a psychological perspective.

**ORGANIZING
NOT-FOR-PROFIT
ENTERPRISES**

*Decentralization* should be given special attention in not-for-profit enterprises. If employees have strong professional training and standards—as do most medical doctors and teachers—then decisions about work embraced within the professional code can be safely decentralized. In fact, the professionals will probably insist that they make their own local decisions.

In contrast, for intangible, hard-to-measure services not covered by clear professional standards—ranging from art selection to zoo-keeping—important decisions must be centralized. For such matters, senior executives have difficulty communicating to subordinates the meaning of enterprise objectives, and consequently do not dare make broad delegations. Moreover, full delegation may be obstructed by two other characteristics often present in not-for-profit enterprises.

1.  Because judgment about good or poor performance is necessarily subjective, the use of rewards and punishments tends to be restricted. Sales and productivity bonuses—or their equivalent—are simply not feasible. Instead, promotion, discharges, and the like are traditionally made on the basis of external training or seniority. This separation of rewards from performance of assigned tasks weakens the influence of managers on subordinates, and—lacking confidence that their instructions will be carried out—the managers are reluctant to delegate.
2.  Private donors, government agencies, and other suppliers of resources to not-for-profit enterprises often impose special conditions on their continuing support. Senior managers must always be alert to how action of the enterprise will be viewed by these outside interest groups. This leads to "defensive centralization": managers retain decision-making authority so that they can avoid actions that outside interest groups find objectionable.

When deciding how much decentralization is appropriate in a specific not-for-profit enterprise, clearly these factors of professionalization, clarity and measurability of objectives, traditions of rewards and punishments, and vulnerability to outside criticism should be considered—in addition to the more general factors discussed in Chapter 11.

A second distinctive issue in organizing not-for-profit enterprises is providing links with contributors of funds and other resources. Often special jobs or sections for this purpose must be created. Quite obvious is the need for a donation-raising organization in a venture heavily dependent on private contributions, or for a government contract unit in a venture supported by public grants. The critical task, however, is integration. The interests and values of contributors may differ sharply from those of scientists, prima donnas, and doctors who actually create the services of the enterprise. As

Paul Lawrence and Jay Lorsch point out, the orientation of such special groups makes even communication between them difficult.[1] Consequently, we need people to fill buffer roles, who can relate to both inside and outside groups and can promote agreement on actions to be taken. This integrating task is especially difficult in those not-for-profit enterprises in which the service is intangible and objectives are multiple and shifting. A good organization will recognize this need.

A third and more general aspect of organizing not-for-profit enterprises is the care required in shifting from the single entrepreneur stage to a departmentalized structure. As noted in the Note accompanying Part II, most small not-for-profit organizations have a strong "mystique" about the importance of their service mission and the unique contribution being made by their enterprise. These beliefs encourage informal relationships, flexible work assignments, and widespread commitment to enterprise goals. But when growth leads to a departmentalized organization, with more specialized jobs and layers of supervision, worker reaction is likely to be much more negative than in similar transition in a profitmaking concern. The mystique loses its charm for all but élite occupations, and entrenched executives neither recognize a need nor have skills for managing in a more formal manner. Recent alienation and unionization of hospital workers and stagehands illustrate this problem. Whenever possible, then, a move to a departmentalized organization should be gradual and accompanied by planning, training, measuring, and rewarding on a sophisticated basis.

Another impact of professionalization, especially when it is reinforced by traditions transferred from government civil service, is hindrance to promotion from within. In Chapter 14 we have assumed that individuals adapt and grow as they gain experience. We also stressed that organizations change and that this change provides opportunities for people to expand the scope of their activities. In private enterprise, many of our personnel-development practices are built around such promotion from within.

This kind of personal career building based on the internal dynamics of an enterprise is difficult when employees are tied to a profession. Of course, some internal movement occurs. But we have to look harder for people who are willing to step outside their professional roles and adjust their activities to the particular needs of the enterprise. To develop managers requires extra attention, for job rotation is difficult and executives who do not come from one or two élite professions have trouble gaining respect. Only recently have doctors learned to respect a hospital administrator who does not have an M.D., and college professors are even more skeptical of a dean without a Ph.D.

As in private enterprise, personal and social factors in the not-for-profit enterprise require call for modifications in the organization structure. The impact of these human factors will be examined in Part IV.

---

[1]See Chapter 1 of their *Studies in Organization Design* (Homewood, IL: Richard D. Irwin, Inc., 1970) for a brief statement of this proposition.

The Camden Chemicals Company was founded in 1880 by George Parker Longview. For more than sixty years it remained a small, specialty chemicals company doing business primarily along the eastern seaboard. Buying much of its raw material from the large chemical companies in the Wilmington area, Camden sought and developed markets which were too small for the giants to pursue.

During World War II, Camden developed several patents which allowed it to grow rapidly and profitably after the war. Under the direction of G. P. Longview (great-nephew of the founder), the company grew from $8 million to over $600 million in sales in the last forty years. Camden's growth came initially in sales to paint, dye, and ink companies and later to the food industry. All sales were bulk chemical shipments, usually under one-year contracts, to these industrial users. Camden's profits, particularly during the 1950s, were tops in the specialty chemical industry.

Before the company's patents expired, they sought to assure good margins by investing in modern production facilities and by acquiring a number of small companies selling to the consumer market. The bulk of the modernization was completed ten years ago, and the acquisitions began soon after.

**plant modernization**

The modernization of Camden's production facilities began fifteen years ago under the direction of a bright young engineer, Donald Sherwood. Commenting on this period Mr. Sherwood said:

"Mr. Longview gave me responsibility for planning and carrying out the construction of our Linden Plant. This was then the biggest and most modern facility in the industry. I brought that project in six months ahead of schedule at eighty-five percent of our budget and within one year it was operating at efficiency levels thirty percent higher than estimated. After that, I had responsibilty for planning and building eight other facilities. All but one have proven to be more than we hoped for in terms of site choice, capacity, and efficiency.

I was only thirty-two years old when he gave me the Linden project and Mr. Longview seldom gambled on young people. When he promoted me to vice-president of Industrial Products Production four years ago, I was the only vice-president in the company under fifty. Mr. Longview was a very strong-minded individual and even with sales doubling every two or three years he continued to make all of the key decisions—until he had his heart attack."

Four years ago, G. P. Longview suffered a mild heart attack and was forced to consider a major reorganization of the company. Up until this time the company was organized on a functional basis. There were nine vice-presidents who dealt primarily with industrial products. They all reported directly to Longview. In addition, Camden had acquired twelve chemical companies selling consumer goods. Each was headed, initially, by a general manager (usually the president of the company prior to acquisition). Several of these companies subsequently were sold or consolidated into another acquisition. At one time, however, Longview had as many as ten consumer division managers reporting to him, as well as nine functional vice-presidents. As a result of divestiture and consolidation, six such consumer product divisions remained at the time of the reorganization, and each was headed by a general manager. All six of these general managers reported to Longview.

George Ebbert, a senior partner of a major management consulting firm, commented on the organization at that time in this way:

"You would not believe it possible for a company that large to be managed as it was. Including special assistants, Longview had over twenty people reporting to him. With regard to the company's traditional industrial products, he made *all* of the key decisions and they were carried out by nine functional vice-presidents. He ran this part of the business in a highly centralized, autocratic manner. As for the consumer products divisions, he virtually abdicated all operating responsibilities to the division general managers.

"All of his acquisitions in the consumer market were made through exchange of Camden stock. The general managers were paid a modest salary but offered a profit-sharing program tied primarily to their divisions' results.

"Longview insisted that the consumer products divisions buy internally all raw materials that could be supplied by Camden's industrial product plants. Whenever possible, these internal sales were made at market price. When conflicts arose, Longview personally arbitrated and set the transfer price. For other than these pricing issues and major capital budgeting decisions, however, the consumer product 'companies' were highly autonomous. Longview claimed to have no 'feel' for the consumer business so he simply looked at results. If he was unhappy he gave the division general manager three to twelve months to improve results or he replaced him or sold the division.

"When he had his first heart attack, he called on us for help. Like so many real entrepreneurs, Mr. Longview had so dominated most of his subordinates that he had no one we really felt he could groom as his replacement. We went through the candidates one by one, over and over, and failed to find someone who satisfied us both. Don't get me wrong—he had many very able people but they tended to be functional 'doers' who depended on Longview to provide overall direction and coordination. Only among the consumer products general managers did we feel he had several possible successors. Since at that time all the consumer product sales contributed only twenty percent of volume and less than ten percent of profits, Mr. Longview vetoed these candidates."

After several months of study, Longview agreed to a reorganization (see Exhibit I) but delayed its announcement for another month until he decided to name John F. McDonald as president.

**John F. (Jack) McDonald**

After ruling out all inside candidates for the job of president, Longview selected Jack McDonald for the post and named himself chairman and chief executive officer. McDonald, a lawyer and partner with a major law firm, had been in charge of the Camden Chemicals account for six years. During this time, he supervised specialists from his law firm who handled tax, patent, and major acquisition matters for Camden Chemicals.

"I picked Jack because he is the smartest man I've ever met," said Longview. "He was first in his class at law school, has a C.P.A., and can absorb even highly technical data like a sponge. He was young (forty-four), ambitious, and gained people's respect very quickly."

It was Longview's expectation that over five or six years, he would bring McDonald along and name him chief executive officer sometime prior to the time when Longview, at seventy, would have reached mandatory retirement age. Unfortunately, after only two and a half years a second heart attack struck Longivew and he died several months later.

"Quite apart from our personal loss," McDonald said, "Mr. Longview's death was a major loss to the business. While I learned a great deal working

Exhibit *I*  *Partial Organization Chart*

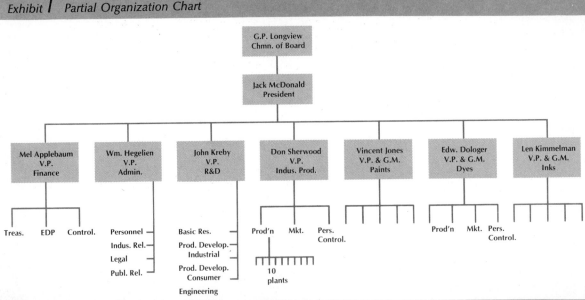

for him, he still made all the tough decisions and frequently found it hard to communicate to me the criteria he used. With another year or two under his tutelage, I think I could have run this company with its current organization and a few changes in personnel. For about a year now, I have tried but I am having trouble getting my arms around the business, given its current structure. I'm not at all sure I know what to watch, besides profits, that will give me early signals of where there may be trouble ahead. I have turned to George Ebbert for advice but I'm not sure I agree with either of the proposals he has made."

Ebbert has reviewed the situation and initially made the recommendation not to make any structural changes.

Ebbert's first
proposal

"Having done such a complete study for Mr. Longview several years ago, I have a real feel for this organization and its people. It would have helped for McDonald to have had another year or so to get used to the organization and it to him, but he can do the job nonetheless. Our recommendation is that he merely make a few personnel changes to build more of his own 'team', improve his measurement and control systems, and delay any structural changes for a year or two."

The personnel changes Ebbert proposed would have involved replacing three of the seven vice-presidents now reporting to McDonald.

"Don Sherwood simply is not a general manager," said Ebbert. "He is not even a good operations manager. He was an excellent engineer and project manager who I would hire tomorrow to build plants and get them started. He just does not know how to manage an ongoing operation. He gets bored and then neglects details. He has no real feel for marketing and never could tie the commercial side of the business into production. As vice-president of Industrial Products, he is a fish out of water. When Mr. Longview was alive it didn't matter because he really ran the industrial products business for Sherwood. McDonald cannot do this and needs a strong general manager to pull it together.

We recommended that he replace Sherwood with Bob Topeka (director of Marketing, Industrial Products Division)."

The other two personnel changes recommended by Ebbert were to replace Edward Dologer as general manager of the Consumer Dyes Division and to ask John Kreby, vice-president of Research & Development, to take early retirement in three months.

McDonald asked Ebbert to suggest an alternative structure to the present one.

Ebbert's second
proposal

"I am not happy trying to coordinate the work of seven vice-presidents and, in effect, run four businesses (Industrial plus three consumer companies)," McDonald said. "Within a year or two," he added, "we will go over a billion dollars in sales. Mr. Longview virtually ran our industrial business by himself up to the time of his death and he was happy to let others run the consumer businesses. I cannot do either! I have trouble operating in the highly centralized way he ran Industrial Products, and the highly decentralized way he ran Consumer Products. I would like to decentralize all planning and centralize control. I can go along with replacing Dologer and perhaps ask Kreby to retire early, but I refuse to dump Sherwood. Ebbert is right—Sherwood is not a general manager, but he always did everything he was asked to do and he helped build this company. Though he is in his early fifties and could probably still find a good position elsewhere, I don't want to lose either his loyalty or his experience. Further, I would prefer a structure which is more consistent in terms of centralization or decentralization."

In response to McDonald's comments, Ebbert recommended the organization shown in Exhibit II.

"This structure," Ebbert said, "will make things easier for Mcdonald. It gives him two product groups to coordinate and two senior staff people to help him. Under this scheme, both Applebaum (vice-president, Finance) and Hegelian (vice-president, Administration) would have the same functions reporting to them as at present but those functions would have only twenty-two percent to thirty percent the number of people they now have. The rest would form the nuclei of group staffs reporting to the two group vice-presidents. When Kreby retires, he would disband corporate R & D and reassign his people to the group vice-presidents.

"This structure will be a bit top heavy at first with regard to staff and it pushes profit responsibility further down the line, but it will work. As the company, grows, it will be a better structure than the present one. I would have preferred waiting a year or two to install it, but it will work now if

Exhibit II

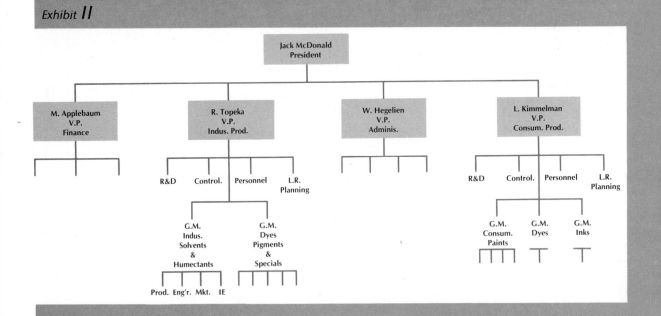

McDonald is willing to replace Sherwood with Topeka. I don't know why he wants to keep Sherwood. He just does not fit the business at his current level without a Longview to do most of his work for him."

"I have great respect for George Ebbert," said McDonald. "As a consultant, he has helped hundreds of companies, and after all, it was he who tipped the balance in my favor when Mr. Longview was looking for a successor. Nonetheless, I am not completely happy with either of his proposals. I have already explained my concerns with the first, but I would consider it if I didn't have to replace Sherwood. His second proposal seems to me much sounder in terms of offering a more consistent structure, but it may well result in too much decentralization before I really feel I have taken command or can build control systems that give me more indicators and bases for learning the business. All I get now are data that tell me what happened in financial terms. Whether results are good or bad, I'm never quite sure *why*. I must have a system which lets me learn more and still not fall apart in the interim."

As a result of his concerns, McDonald has developed a third alternative (see Exhibit III). "I am not at all certain that my plan makes more sense than Ebbert's. It just seems like a cleaner break in accountability, with fewer key decisions made down the line. It is a structure that will allow me to learn the business faster and find out more about my key people. After I have done both, then I would be more comfortable with the set-up in Ebbert's second proposal (Exhibit II)."

*Exhibit III*

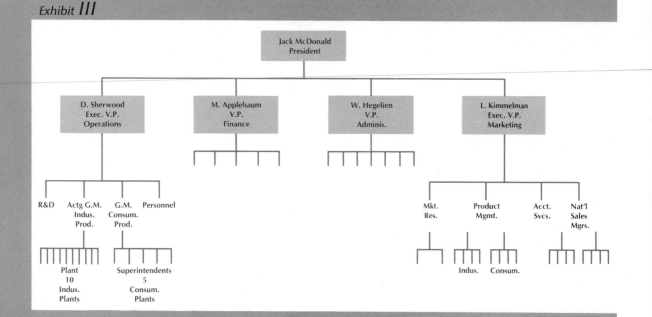

McDonald has communicated his thoughts to Ebbert by telephone and mailed him a copy of his suggested organization structure. Ebbert has considered this proposal and asked to meet with McDonald tomorrow morning at 10:00 a.m. to discuss all three alternatives. McDonald agreed and concluded, "I am not going to insist on my proposal. I will keep an open mind until I hear Ebbert's response. Perhaps he will convince me to go with one of his two plans, or perhaps we can come up with another approach that will be better than any of the three we now have before us."

## FOR DISCUSSION AND REPORT-WRITING

1. How should McDonald go about evaluating whether Camden has developed sound strategies for each of its major businesses?

2. Would instituting an MBO system at this point in time be easier in the industrial products divisions or the consumer products divisions? Explain.

3. Which of the several organization structures under consideration would require the largest number of corporate and standing plans? Why? What kind of standing plans would be required?

4. Ebbert and McDonald have developed different solutions to the problem of organization design. How do the differences in solutions result from differences in how each would define the problem (gap), as opposed to differences in their views on higher-level goals ("ends")?

5. Would participation of the current senior executives in reorganizational plans be useful? Consider both pluses and minuses, and how McDonald might deal with the minuses to gain the benefits of participation.

6. Evaluate each of the proposals against "Key Factors in Departmentation."

7. How will each option affect the need for both specialization and coordination?

8. Consider the issues raised in Chapter 14 which might be most important in deciding what to do about Don Sherwood.

9. How should "Guidelines for Choosing the Degree of Decentralization" affect the choice McDonald faces?

10. Could McDonald organize the industrial products group in a different manner than consumer products? Recall that Longview did this for years.

11. What are the major personnel factors to consider in choosing among the alternative structures? Which should be given greatest weight? Why?

12. To what degree should the structure be modified as a result of concern for one person such as Sherwood?

13. How should the strategies for industrial and consumer groups affect the choice of organizational structure?

14. (Summary report question, Part III) List the major advantages and disadvantages of each of the current proposals. If limited to these options, which do you recommend?

part IV:
motivating: human
factors in the
organization

15. Which of the suggested organization structures is likely to have the best and worst impact on custom and tradition? On motivation and morale?

16. What steps might McDonald take to increase constructive conflict? How would decisions on organization design bear on your answer?

part V: leading

17. Given McDonald's concerns about not yet being fully prepared to fill Longview's shoes, what should he look for in terms of political behavior within the organization?

18. How may the shift in leadership style from Longview to McDonald affect the need for, and appropriateness of, a contingency approach to leadership?

19. In what way did the old organization match Longview's leadership style?

20. What changes in communication from the president to his *current key subordinates* may be necessary to match McDonald's (as opposed to Longview's) leadership style?

part VI:
controlling

21. How should the control process change if McDonald accepts Ebbert's recommended change in structure? How should it change if his (McDonald's) recommendations are followed?

22. Comment on the kind of control system Longview probably used with the consumer products divisions. Would this system be more or less appropriate to Mcdonald if he did not change the structure?

23. Which factors presented in Chapter 24 should have the most impact on McDonald's decision on organization design? Explain.

summary question
for solution of the
case as a whole

24. Develop detailed recommendations on organization structure, staffing, and control based on your assessment of the situation.

## CASE 3.2
## SCANDICO (SINGAPORE)

Nels Engberg is managing director of Scandico (Singapore), a wholly owned subsidiary of Scandico, Ltd., a large Swedish shipping company. He has had this position for almost four years after having been hired away from a competing shipping company. Scandico, Ltd., with headquarters in Stockholm, owns and operates a large fleet of commercial vessels (freighters, tankers) which produce over seventy percent of the company's revenues and profits. Most of the remaining revenue comes from its freight service division which handles a variety of transit services for large industrial customers. Wherever possible, the transit service group seeks to use Scandico vessels but they are not limited to them as means of transport.

Scandico has offices in more than a hundred locations. The large offices are headed by a managing director who typically will have two general managers reporting to him. One integrates all shipping activities, while the other looks after transit services. While there is a great deal of direct contact between these two general managers, it is the responsibility of the managing director to coordinate these two groups to assure greatest benefit not just to his office but Scandico's international operations.

Scandico (Singapore) is a large operation with almost eighty-five percent of its volume managed by Axel Lindt, general manager of shipping. Profits have been very good recently and headquarters management feel this is due to Engberg's knowledge of the market and skills as a negotiator. While Lindt is regarded as an excellent administrator, Engberg is seen as the key to the office's successful maintenance of high margins.

Michael Day, who is forty, came to Singapore about two years ago as general manager of Services, after serving for several years as shipping manager in Sao Paulo, Brazil. Prior to that he had worked in various positions for another shipping company. His performance in Brazil was regarded by corporate management as acceptable, but not outstanding.

"His biggest problem as head of a shipping operation was his lack of skill in negotiating with large customers," said Peter Alstrop, Scandico's president. "He just didn't seem capable of driving a tough bargain. He generated a good bit of business and maintained the clients he took over, but our margins were almost always lower than we felt they should be. When we called him on the margins negotiated he always had a good reason for getting less than we thought he should get. We had real trouble pinpointing where he was 'wrong' given the distance, but his overall results, though acceptable, just weren't up to what we thought they should be. Day is a charming, bright man and knows shipping well. He just doesn't seem to have the skills to negotiate the few extra points that spell the difference between acceptable and good margins. In other respects, he appears to be an excellent manager and developer of people. We transferred him to Singapore with high hopes. He is a manager we feel has the potential to head up one of our large operations and we have told him so. By having him work for Engberg, we hoped he would develop the skills and toughness he needs. Engberg was not anxious to have him. He has produced good results recently and did not feel he needed Day.

"We couldn't convince him to take Day on as general manager of shipping, but he did agree to name him as general manager of services if we promoted his current general manager of services to a key job in Australia. Engberg drives a hard bargain even with us, but we went along with him with the understanding that while Day would manage services, Engberg would include him in negotiations with large Chinese customers. The Chinese are among the best and toughest bargainers in the world. We felt Day would learn a lot by watching and gradually helping Engberg negotiate with them. We felt he could do this and still manage our service operation there since it is small and runs very smoothly."

After Day's first year, he was evaluated by Engberg and the appraisal, along with Day's responses, were forwarded to the company's personnel office in Stockholm. Walter Nielsen, corporate director of personnel, indicated he was "a bit unhappy" with what he deduced from the forms.

"Overall," Nielsen said, "Engberg has given him a satisfactory rating, but has criticized him for not paying enough attention to details in his services group. Engberg's feels that Day wants to avoid the nitty-gritty and let his subordinates handle details which he should get into himself."

Day, in his comments on his appraisal, in diplomatic terms according to Nielsen, says that "he isn't getting what he came to Singapore for, namely, experience in negotiating." Day feels he can give his subordinates the freedom he does, that it is good for their development, and that he doesn't let them make any serious mistakes. He has asked Engberg to include him in more big projects and to let him take on a few small negotiations on his own.

"Since we sent Day over to learn," Nielsen said, "and Engberg knows this, Day's requests seem reasonable. Besides, we hoped Day could show Engberg a few things on how to delegate and develop his subordinates. Engberg needs to develop this talent if he is to manage a larger operation."

Nielsen communicated these views in a long letter to Engberg and indicated that he had discussed the situation with Peter Alstrop, the company's president, and Mark Hammersmith, vice-president, Far East, Engberg's direct superior. Both, according to Nielsen, agreed with Nielsen's views.

Reluctantly, Engberg began to bring Day into several large projects and over the next year gave him three small projects involving negotiations to manage himself. When Day received his second appraisal from Engberg, he again was given an acceptable overall rating but was strongly criticized on two counts.

"Day is a smart man," says Engberg, "but he can't or won't face up to conflict. He doesn't want to hear about problems unless they are purely technical problems. These he dives into and solves well. People problems, particularly conflicts among people, seem beyond him. He will either walk away from them or give in and compromise *his* goals to try to get others to come to agreement.

"This means he often neglects important details in running his service division. He will give good technical advice but if two or more of his subordinates can't agree on something, they have learned not to come to Day, but to solve it themselves. This would be all right except they often lack the perspective to come to good decisions.

"My second concern is more serious. With his desire to avoid conflict, he just cannot handle tough negotiations. He gives away too much. This not only costs us in the specific deal he is working on but has ramifications on many other current or future deals.

"In short, I do not believe he will ever make a good negotiator or a good manager. He is a walking encyclopedia, though, and could make a fine staff resource and I have tried to encourage him to take this route, but he won't listen. For some reason, he thinks I don't like him and that I am undercutting him with the people here and in headquarters. As a result of this, despite my efforts to correct this impression, he has started politicking and trying to line up allies here and at headquarters. While I was away for two weeks of meetings in Stockholm, he wheedled his way into several negotiations and we ended up with deals I do not like. I have reprimanded Lindt, the general manager of shipping, for not keeping Day out of these deals. Lindt said he was under the impression that Day had important friends at headquarters who wanted him to get as much exposure as possible to negotiations. I asked Lindt where he got this idea and he said it came from comments Day had made and from a cable he had received from Nielsen (corporate director of personnel), requesting that he, Lindt, give personal attention to Day's development in shipping.

"When I heard this," said Engberg, "I hit the ceiling. I had never seen this cable. I regard Nielsen's actions as most inappropriate and I fired off a telegram to him telling him how I felt and demanding that Day be transferred as soon as possible to another location. We do not need what he has to offer in Singapore, and his presence here is becoming increasingly disruptive to my operations.

"Nielsen's response completely ignored my protest of his high-handed behavior and invited me to come to Stockholm to discuss this matter. I'll be damned if I see the value of traveling so far to discuss this matter and I wired Nielsen to this effect, repeating my request that Day be transferred. I sent copies of all correspondence on this matter to my boss, Hammersmith. In the past he has always been very supportive but in this case, he seems to be passing the buck. A week passed and I received an invitation from Peter Alstrop (president) to come to Stockholm and discuss the Day case and 'other related issues.' I really don't understand this and I'm tempted to ask Alstrop for clarification but this may not be wise. I called Hammersmith and he suggested that perhaps I should go and find out what Nielsen's been up to. The rumor mill has been very active here lately and for the first time since I've been here, I see signs of polarization. If Day isn't moved, he may well build a following among my weaker people who like his 'laissez faire, don't-make-waves' approach to things. Day has been telling them, I'm sure, that I am too tough and by always trying for the extra points, he says I am creating good short-term results but not developing an organization or customer relationships which can stand up over time. Rubbish! I have produced good results here for three straight years. Hammersmith says I'm his best producer, but he has an enormous geographic area to oversee and I don't see him more than two or three times a year. Frankly, I don't expect much help from him. I'll probably have to straighten this out myself."

1. To what degree might Engberg's differences with Day have been caused by failure to set proper operating objectives?

2. Should an operation like Scandico (Singapore) operate within a large or small number of standing plans developed in headquarters? What kind of standing plans would be most helpful? Least helpful?

3. List what you feel are four or five different problems (gaps) present in this case. Develop a means-end network which shows the relationships among these problems. Which should Engberg tackle first? Which should the president, Alstrop, tackle first?

4. What do you think of Nielsen's statement, "Since we sent Day over to learn . . . Besides, we hoped Day could show Engberg how to delegate and develop his subordinates"? To what degree might these dual objectives be complementary? Contradictory?

5. Assess Nielsen's actions against concepts of corporate staff presented in Chapter 12. Consider both good and bad aspects of his behavior.

6. To what degree might a matrix organization be appropriate to Scandico? If it were in place, how would it affect Day's situation in Singapore?

7. How good a match of structure and people appears to exist with respect to Engberg and his position in the company? With respect to Day?

8. How adequate do you feel Engberg's appraisal of Day is? What might Nielsen do (have done) to assure that a sound appraisal of Day was carried out?

9. How should Engberg's performance be appraised and his career development planned?

10. (Summary report question, Part III) Do you believe Day can learn to be a better negotiator? What specific action steps should be taken to determine whether he can improve and, if so, how to help him?

11. Assuming that Day remains in Singapore, what steps should Engberg take to deal with his concerns about polarizing the group?

12. Does the conflict which appears to be building in Singapore have any potential benefits to the organization or is it likely to be only destructive?

13. How should Nielsen and/or Alstrop have sought to motivate Engberg to train and develop Day? Is it still possible for them to motivate him to carry out this task? How?

14. Do you think it possible for two such apparently different leadership styles as Engberg's and Day's to function in the Singapore division?

15.    What steps might Engberg take to "channel political behavior" if Day remains in Singapore? What steps might Nielsen take?

16.    How might controls be developed which help headquarters assess the degree to which Engberg may be building or detracting from longer-term results?

17.    To what degree may the large number of offices make control of individual offices easier than if there were ten offices? Harder?

18.    What role(s) should headquarters staff play in control of the hundred offices?

summary
questions for
solution of the
case as a whole

19.    What recommendations would you give to Engberg? What specific action steps should he take?

20.    Assuming Alstrop wanted Day in Singapore for his career development only, what action should he take now?

# MOTIVATING: HUMAN FACTORS IN THE ORGANIZATION

The planning and organizing of work was the center of our attention in Parts I, II, and III. Although we often talked about the people who do the work we focused on how planning systems and organization design could be used to further the goals of an enterprise. In these earlier discussions we assumed that organization members would do what they were told, that higher levels of management could assign goals, and that in general managers and operators would adapt their behavior to the needs of an enterprise.

Although planning systems and organization structure are important influences on the behavior of people, knowledge of these formal dimensions is not sufficient for understanding and predicting human behavior. Both individual motivation and the informal relationships that develop within an organization modify the formal structure and influence organizational effectiveness.

People are the chief resources used by a manager; he depends on their actions to achieve results. Consequently, it is important for a manager to understand the full range of factors, formal and otherwise, which influence the "motivation" of organization members. In Part IV we shall draw on current concepts in psychology, sociology, anthropology, and political science to improve our understanding of human behavior in organizations.

Chapter 15—Individual Needs and Work. Here we consider basic human needs and the ways in which formal organization motivates people by helping them to fulfill these needs.

Chapter 16—Group Behavior and Informal Organization. This chapter deals with the pressures of culture and of informal groups that may strongly affect what workers do in their jobs. Then we examine the importance of committees in organizational life and explore ways to harmonize formal and informal organization.

Chapter 17—Managing Organizational Conflict. Some conflict in organizations, like friction in machines, is unavoidable. Here we explore sources of such clashes of interest, the distinctions between destructive and constructive conflict, and how we can organize to deal with conflict.

# individual needs and work

Learning Objectives

After completing this chapter you should be able to

1. Classify the human needs that can be satisfied by working in an organization.

2. Explain the relationship between an individual's level of aspiration and the potency of a particular need.

3. Distinguish between on-the-job satisfactions and off-the-job satisfactions.

4. Understand how organization design can be used to increase need satisfaction.

5. Describe the role of pay in satisfying human needs.

## NEEDS SATISFIED THROUGH WORK

Revamping strategy and organization structure, or elaborating the grand design into detailed plans and job descriptions, are activities vital to the success of a company. But they do not actually get the work done; they rest on the assumption that individuals throughout the organization will do the tasks assigned to them. So fundamental is this assumption that we will examine it in this and the next three chapters.

Since people are the chief resource used by a manager, and he is so dependent on their actions to achieve results, it is vital for him to understand why people behave as they do.

Formal organization is one means of guiding the behavior of people. But we have to appreciate the full range of influences, formal and otherwise, on the behavior of organizational members. Both personal drives and group pressures spur action. In this chapter we focus on the social and cultural motivation of individuals, and then we will look at an organization's internal social systems in Chapter 16.

The purpose of this chapter is threefold.

1. To present a way of thinking about human needs—an approach that will be useful throughout the rest of the book as well as here;
2. To consider ways formal organization can help meet human needs;
3. To discuss how salaries can be related both to needs and to formal organization.

The term "needs" is sometimes used to refer only to essential requirements for survival. Here, however, we shall follow the practice of psychologists and adopt a much broader meaning. Need includes both what a person must have and what he merely wants. Psychologists say that as long as a person wants something, he has a psychological need for it, regardless of what someone else may think of the justification for this desire. With this usage, we avoid making subjective judgments—for example, whether it is a matter of necessity or desire for a college student to have a car on campus.

Needs vary widely among individuals, but this variation is largely a matter of degree and of different ways of satisfying needs. There is enough similarity in the basic aspirations of most people so that we can talk of general human needs.

Many classifications of needs have been made. We shall confine our attention to those that can be satisfied to a significant degree by working in a business enterprise, for these are the needs a manager may be able to do something about. Drawing on A. H. Maslow's classic analysis, these job-related needs include: physical needs, security needs, social needs, and self-expression needs.[1]

physical needs

All human beings have needs that pertain to survival and physiological maintenance of the body. The objects of these needs include such things as food, drink, shelter, rest, and exercise. Until such needs are reasonably well

---

[1]A. Maslow, "A Theory of Human Motivation," *Psychological Review,* 50 (1943), 370-96. See also A. Maslow, *Motivation and Personality* (New York: Harper & Bros., 1954).

satisfied, they are strong, driving forces. Our society is sufficiently prosperous, however, that the minimum physiological requirements can be met. Management has devoted a good deal of attention to providing adequate ventilation, heat, and light to ensure working conditions that make a workplace physically satisfactory—even attractive.

**security needs**

In an age when our entire Western society seems to have an obsession with security, we all quickly recognize needs in this area. We all want the satisfactions we now enjoy to continue and hope that no misfortune will cross our path. Guarantees are impossible, particularly in a dynamic society, and we must couch our hopes for security in realistic terms. Both economic and psychological security are involved.

With respect to work, most of the attention of social reformers has been focused on *economic security*. People worry about steady employment, provisions for old age, and insurance against catastrophes that might call for large financial outlays. Private enterprise and government have both sought

Figure *15.1* *Jobs differ
sharply in the degree to
which they provide
physical, social and
self-expression satisfactions.*

ways of providing at least minimum financial protection against these risks. Discussions of pensions, unemployment insurance, health insurance, and similar plans have made all of us sensitive to economic security.

A more subtle matter is the need for *psychological security*. This need relates to a person's confidence in dealing with the problems that confront him. His ability to meet future job requirements, the fairness of present and future supervisors, the balance of benefits and losses that result from economic and technological changes—all conjure up hopes and fears. Everyone needs assurance that he will be able to adjust satisfactorily to such new conditions.

One source of psychological security is knowing the rules of the game. For example, the student who at the beginning of a course wants to know what the final grade will be based on or how long research papers should be is trying to remove an irritating uncertainty. Uneasiness about the effect of a rumored reorganization on one's job can lead to high anxiety because the rules of the game may change. Somehow we have to develop confidence that we shall be able to cope with new situations successfully.

**social needs**

Social needs are satisfied through relations with other people, and in most of us the desire for *sociability* is strong. We need contacts with informal groups as well as with close friends. Such contacts include friendly greetings, casual conversations, and amusing luncheons that a person—whether he is a mimeograph operator, foreman, or vice-president—engages in with his associates at the office or plant. Companies have found that when employees have friendly relationships on the job, absenteeism tends to be low. In fact, people often go to their jobs or to a social function despite a headache or a lack of interest in the activity itself, just to associate with other people.

Closely related to sociability is a sense of *belonging*. Everyone wants to feel that he is a recognized member of a group; that he will be included in group plans and will share informal information, both gossip and fact; that others will help him in trouble and will expect him to help them.

A third social need is desire for *status*. In a business, status depends on the value of a position in the eyes of others. Status always implies a ranking along some kind of scale, and the hierarchy of a formal organization is one of the commonly accepted gauges. In addition, occupations differ in status value in various companies and communities. For example, being an actuary at the Metropolitan Life Insurance Company may command much more respect in "nice" suburbs than being a pier boss at an ocean dock, even though the pier boss is paid more. Within companies, distinctions may be drawn between machinists and pipefitters, between locomotive engineers and firemen, or between sales clerks and cashiers. Status distinctions are drawn within classes of occupation. Everyone in a company usually knows who is the top person, the fastest typist, or the manager of the most profitable branch. Status inevitably implies competition, and competition is especially vigorous in the United States, where most people seek to improve their status. But perhaps even more pronounced than the desire to rise is the desire not to lose status. A lathe operator may refuse to sweep around his machine or an executive may refuse to answer his own telephone—even though to do so might be the simplest way to get work done—merely to maintain his status in the eyes of those about him.

Aside from what others may think, each person is concerned with his private aspirations, and in this matter he measures himself. He asks, "Does this job permit me to do what *I* would like to do, to be what *I* want to be?" In brief, everyone needs to express himself. At the nucleus of the cluster of needs for self-expression we find self-assertion, power, personal accomplishment, and personal growth. Let us look more closely at each of these four needs.

**self-expression needs**

Every mature adult wants to assert himself, to be independent at least to some extent. As we grow from childhood to adulthood, we rely less and less on other people to help us survive, to make decisions for us, and to show us how to behave and act. We want increasing control over our own destiny. In short, as we mature we progress from dependence toward independence.

By the time a person reaches maturity, he attains a level of *self-assertion*—we might say independence or initiative—that he must maintain if he is to stay happy. Being independent makes life more pleasant for him than taking advice from others. Although this drive for self-assertion varies in intensity from person to person, nearly everyone has at least some need to be independent and to exercise initiative.

In some persons, desire for self-assertion slips over into a strong urge for *power*. Like the thrill a youngster gets from driving a car, the ability to make things or persons respond to one's own will can be a strong motive.

Most of us also desire a feeling of personal *accomplishment*. Craftsmen take pride in their work, whether it be a neatly typed letter, a difficult surgical operation, or a welded joint that may never be seen by the public eye. Some people feel deeply about educating children, making highways safer, or otherwise contributing to the general welfare. For them, satisfaction comes from knowing that they have done a worthwhile job well; regardless of public acclaim or the size of tasks, they enjoy an inner sense of accomplishment. Few people, in fact, can do their best work unless they feel satisfaction of this sort.

In addition, people normally want an opportunity for *growth*. Satisfaction comes from the *process of achieving* as much as from the accomplishment itself. A college graduate in accounting may be happy while he first learns a small part of a company's cost accounting, but after he has solved problems there, he wants to move on to something else. He at least wants variety, but he probably also wants a task calling for greater skill. Individuals vary greatly in the kind and amount of growth to which they aspire. Psychologist David McClelland gives us impressive evidence that even the growth of nations is closely tied to their peoples' need for achievement.[2] We can anticipate that with increasing education, travel, and tech-

[2]D. C. McClelland, "Business Drive and National Achievement," *Harvard Business Review* (July-August 1962). See also D. C. McClelland, *The Achieving Society* (Princeton: Van Nostrand, 1961).

nological change, the desire for growth opportunities will become even more pressing than it has been in the past.

**potency of needs**

The total array of human needs seems overwhelming.[3] Even those needs related to work—physical, security (economic, psychological), social (sociability, belonging, status), and self-expression (self-assertion, accomplishment, growth)—make us wonder, "Can human beings ever be satisfied? Part of the answer lies in the relative potency of these various desires. In this connection, we shall consider marginal values, aspiration levels, and emotional factors.

**marginal values**

How intensely an individual wants more of a thing—say, food, social recognition, or job security—depends partly on how much he already has. What is an additional, or *marginal,* unit worth to him?[4] He might sell his birthright for air to breathe if he were suffocating, but when fresh air is in plentiful supply, it loses its marginal value. In times of earthquake or war,

[3]Note that psychologists have proposed alternative frameworks of human needs. For example, Alderfer contends that most people only distinguish between three kinds of needs. See C. P. Alderfer, *Existence, Relatedness and Growth: Human Needs in Organizational Settings* (New York: Free Press, 1972).

[4]The "expectancy theory" of motivation formulates this question in a much more elaborate manner. This theory is centered around three variables: "valence," or strength of needs; "instrumentality," or the likelihood that desired goods or pleasures will satisfy needs; and "expectancy," or the probability that effort expended will produce desired outcome. See V. Vroom, *Work and Motivation* (New York: Wiley, 1964).

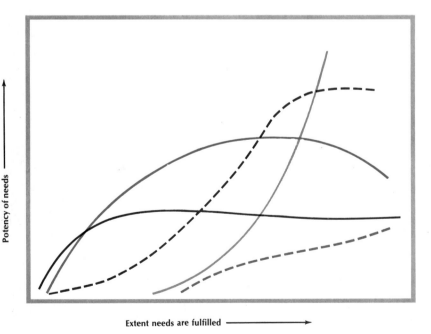

*Figure 15.2 Marginal potency of needs varies with fulfillment. Some needs, such as physical protection from weather, are fully satisfied and drop off; others, like esteem of friends, keep expanding. The shapes of these curves differ among individuals, and even for the same individual over time.*

starving people have traded diamonds for food; once adequately fed, however, these same people become more interested in security and self-expression.

At a given moment, each person has a hierarchy of needs, ranging from those that seem urgent to those that are faint. As the most basic needs become satisfied—that is, when a person has sufficient water, shelter, and so on—the next most important needs such as job security and good supervision become the real governors of his behavior. Some needs become dormant then, but others, such as a drive toward personal achievement or desire for social recognition, tend to keep expanding. Frederick Herzberg applies the term "hygiene factor" to those needs that do not expand—they may cause great distress when not met but provide little drive once they are. The other needs, which keep growing, are called the "motivating factors" by Herzberg.[5]

Whether a need continues to be potent as a person derives increased satisfaction depends largely on his levels of aspiration and on his ability to draw qualitative distinctions rationally.

**aspiration levels**

The potency of a need depends on whether a person expects the need to be met. A desire to become company president, for instance, is not a strong motive for one who says to himself, "I know I'll never make it." On the other hand, a design engineer who expects ample opportunity for self-expression will be very dissatisfied if he is assigned routine drafting. To understand human needs, then, we should not only identify each need and note how well it is already being met, but also consider how much more satisfaction of each type of need a person really aspires to attain.

Incidentally, many workers—especially those on routine jobs—do not expect great things from their work. A majority are satisfied with their present jobs—mainly because their aspirations are not very high. We are kidding ourselves if we assume most of these people want tough, varied, and ever-expanding jobs. Nevertheless, a large minority would welcome more meaningful work, and this number will probably rise as education levels go up and as women and minorities shift their expectations.[6]

A person's self-image strongly influences his aspiration levels; that is, what he believes his abilities are, and what he thinks his role should be. If he regards himself as the best salesperson in a company, he will work harder to achieve top ranking than someone who considers himself a plodder, "about as good as the average." Similarly, the executive who views himself as a natural leader will be highly concerned about social approval of his ideas. Of course self-images change over time. Repeated failures to achieve an expected satisfaction normally lead to a downward adjustment in aspiration, whereas successes encourage new dreams of glory, especially if one's

---

[5]F. Herzberg, "One More Time: How Do You Motivate Employees?" *Harvard Business Review*, January-February 1968, pp. 53-62. See also F. Herzberg, *Work and the Nature of Man* (New York: World Publishing, 1966).

[6]L. Porter, E. Lawler III, and J. R. Hackman, *Behavior in Organizations* (New York: McGraw-Hill, 1975), p. 47.

friends are experiencing similar failures or successes. A person typically makes these adjustments in his self-image quite slowly, however.

Social scientists have observed three things about aspiration levels that are especially pertinent for a business manager.[7]

1. Change in the extent of need fulfillment—either up or down—is especially potent. For instance, a drop below a level that has become accepted is felt as a severe deprivation.

2. For many needs, people expect improvement from year to year. Indeed, the improvement is often more important than the absolute standard. (Perhaps this is why our forefathers spoke about "life, liberty, and the *pursuit* of happiness.")

3. Operators and managers recognize that in every firm there is a certain amount of dirty, routine, and otherwise unattractive work to be done. Performing such tasks satisfies few human desires directly; it is simply necessary work. Nevertheless, most people realistically expect to do some unattractive but necessary work as part of their jobs. Even though it does not contribute directly to meeting needs, it may be consistent with levels of expectation. Throughout life, everyone learns to mix the bitter with the sweet; we are simply seeking to devise a more pleasant mixture.

**rational vs. emotional factors**

Rarely do we calculate marginal values and aspiration levels systematically and logically; the potency of a need is more often based on our feelings. Even the person who wants to act logically is confronted with a formidable task. Our list of work-related needs is already complex, but there are still others, connected with family, religion, and other aspects of life, that also demand satisfaction. There are many ways to satisfy each of these needs, especially when we recognize *degrees* of satisfaction. For instance, we may use numerous foods of varying quality to satisfy the hunger need; we may satisfy social needs by a wide range of activities, from going to parties to working in an office together. For any given need, we may select from numerous alternative goals to fulfill it. Furthermore, we may adopt any of several alternative actions to attain each goal. We are therefore confronted with almost unbelievably complex decisions about what to do at any one time—or *would be* if we logically determined each action. We cannot carefully calculate all the pros and cons and so we rely chiefly on habits, attitudes, and emotional response.

No one can prove that as much as ninety-five percent of people's actions are uncalculated, but this is a useful approximation for a manager. It warns him that attempts to change people's behavior by logical argument will meet with limited success. Instead he must try to learn which needs have high potency for his subordinates and then try to create a work situation in which each subordinate finds his satisfactions by helping to achieve company goals.

[7]K. Lewin, "Psychology of Success and Failure," in T. W. Costello and S. S. Zalkind, *Psychology in Administration* (Englewood Cliffs, NJ: Prentice-Hall, 1963), pp. 67-72.

## SATISFYING NEEDS ON THE JOB

In our discussion of human needs, we have concentrated on those desires that can be met, at least to some degree, by working at a job. Such satisfactions, however, may arise either directly or indirectly from the work; this distinction has an important bearing on how a manager seeks to motivate his subordinates.

Work itself can be satisfying. A sense of achievement, for instance, arises from doing a job well. When a person performs an assigned task and at the same time satisfies his basic needs, we say he enjoys "direct," or "on-the-job," satisfactions. In such a case, it is the work itself and the normal relations with other people at work that provide satisfying experiences.

In contrast, there may be rewards for work that are not generated as an aspect of work activity. Familiar forms of this kind of reward are pay, vacations, and pensions. Let us note that the satisfactions that arise from such rewards take place *outside* the management system or work situation, and mostly outside the company. Work is simply a means of obtaining satisfaction at a later time and place. We shall refer to these as "indirect," or "off-the-job," satisfactions.

When these distinctions are applied to the human needs discussed early in this chapter, we may be surprised to note how important on-the-job satisfactions are in the total picture (see Table 15.1). Most of the literature in economics and scientific management stresses financial, or off-the-job, compensation. But behavioral scientists have insisted—and this is one of their major contributions—that on-the-job satisfactions are also highly important.

| Needs | Direct, On-the-Job Satisfactions | Indirect, Off-the-Job Satisfactions |
|---|---|---|
| Physical needs | "Working conditions" | Money to buy necessities of life |
| Security needs | Psychological security | Economic security |
| Social needs | Sociability, belonging | Money to attain social status |
| | Status within company | Recognized title in reputable company |
| Self-expression needs | Self-assertion, power, sense of accomplishment, growth possibilities | Improved ability to engage in hobbies |
| | | Money to seek power |

TABLE 15.1
HUMAN NEEDS RELATED TO WORK

In our society off-the-job satisfactions from work depend largely on money. We use pay to buy things that satisfy physical needs and contribute toward social status. Economic security during old age or in time of catastrophe is also assured by money. But the lack of direct association between work and such satisfactions has a serious drawback—it too often leads to this familiar attitude; "I don't care about the job as long as the pay keeps rolling in."

Not all off-the-job satisfactions come through money, however. Employment with a well-known company and a good title contribute to social status away from work. Some people would rather be vice-president of a local bank than sales representastive for Chilean Nitrates at a higher salary, simply because the bank job carries more prestige among their friends.

Companies may provide housing, recreation, and other off-the-job benefits. During recent years, however, most companies have withdrawn such forms of compensation because of worker resistance to "paternalism." Because of a desire for independence, which we have already discussed in connection with self-assertion, most employees prefer that their employer keep out of their private affairs. They are likely to resent even a generous program if management clearly expects them to be appreciative of the good things bestowed on them. A company can and should help build a wholesome community, provided it maintains the independence and self-respect of the citizens.

Many social, self-expression, and security needs must be fulfilled on the job if they are to be satisfied through work. But providing on-the-job satisfactions is not a simple matter for two reasons. First, the principal difficulty lies in meeting needs for social contact, self-expression, and psychological security. Fulfilling each of these needs call for the active participation and often the initiative of a worker himself. A manager cannot *force* a worker to enjoy his associates, be independent, take pride in his work, and be confident of the future; a manager can only create an environment in which such feelings can flourish. For a manager who is accustomed to moving equipment, shaping raw materials, and otherwise achieving goals by positive action, an approach limited to facilitating action by others may seem slow. Yet all he can do is encourage growth and foster independence.

Second, on-the-job satisfactions should arise only while *people are doing the work that is necessary to meet company goals*. The sequence of events is not that a manager first assures worker satisfaction and then hopes that the happy workers will decide to do the tasks assigned to them; as we observed in our discussion of potency, a satisfied need does not motivate behavior. Nor does a benevolent boss parcel out satisfactions as rewards. Rather, actually doing a task that leads to company success must, at the same time, be what workers derive their satisfactions from. Both parties to the transaction benefit, just as a bee in the process of making honey from a blossom fertilizes the potential fruit.

Because work must be done if an enterprise is to remain in existence, a manager may prefer to organize work purely on the basis of technology;

then, as a separate issue, use "indirect" incentives to stimulate good worker performance. However, if he expects his subordinates to be self-reliant, eager, and dependable instead of apathetic, indifferent, and lazy, he must try to set up the work in ways that offer people substantial, direct, on-the-job satisfactions.

## MEETING HUMAN NEEDS THROUGH ORGANIZATION

The structure of a company defines an environment of formal rules, job descriptions, and communication networks in which people live during working hours. This environment can satisfy needs or block them; it can develop good attitudes or bad; and it can determine, in part, what people think and learn. Therefore, structure—as well as planning, face-to-face leadership, and control—is highly important in getting results.

In the following paragraphs, we shall present a variety of ways in which organization structure may contribute to, or detract from, the satisfaction of human needs. There may be other more compelling considerations in making the final choice of an organization pattern, but our purpose here is merely to point out some ways that organization alone can affect the satisfactions of the people in it.

*creating small units*

When many workers are required for an operation, the social satisfactions will be greater if we can assign the workers to small groups of, say, three to ten. For instance, an insurance-company typing pool of perhaps sixty typists is too large to serve as a social group. The typists would form small, informal friendship groups, of course, but their socializing would probably be a thing apart from their work. On the other hand, if we could organize the work into small units, the typists could, to some extent, serve their sociability needs *while doing assigned work*. Moreover, a sense of *belonging* would probably be stronger in the smaller unit, and if we could measure the group output, we might find that the small groups engendered a sense of personal achievement.[8]

*avoiding organizational isolation*

Taking social needs into account in organizing should make us wary of carrying to the extreme the process of cutting down the size of work groups. We should not isolate an individual.[9]

The personal secretary to the president of one of the country's largest corporations once remarked that in many ways she was not as happy as when her boss was a lower executive. "This office is beautifully furnished and has the latest equipment, and I do have prestige as the president's secretary. But it is quiet in here, and the door is always closed. We're so busy I never have a minute to get out and talk with Jean and Betty and Ken like I used to." This woman was isolated by space and walls, but we can produce

[8]P. Gyllenhammer, "How Volvo Adapts Work to People," *Harvard Business Review,* July-August 1977, pp. 102-11.
[9]T. Rotondi, Jr., "Organizational Identification and Group Involvement," *Academy of Management Journal,* 18, no. 4 (December 1975), 892-96.

the same result by breaking down work into such *extremely specialized and independent parts* that a person lacks opportunity to interact with fellow workers while performing his work. We might call this *organizational isolation.*

Consider a roomful of design engineers. We might assign one engineer to a small, specialized project with which no other engineers are concerned. Day in and day out, he designs perhaps only pipelines, whereas all other engineers collaborate in designing chemical-processing units. Because he has little reason to discuss his work with others, he must either sacrifice social satisfaction during his working hours or steal time from the company to have conversations on other matters that are either partly or wholly irrelevant to the job of designing pipelines.

As an alternative, we could include this person in a unit of engineers who design processing units and pipelines at the same time. Both his enjoyment of work and the amount he does might increase. He would derive social satisfaction in discussion problems with his colleagues and from talking to construction supervisors who come into the drafting room to seek advice on construction operations. Such "socializing" is inherent in the position and does not involve serious interruption of assigned work.

**job enrichment**

In addition to inhibiting social interaction, narrow specialization takes a toll on worker satisfaction. The assembly-line worker who spends day after day tightening a single bolt has become a classic example of a person who has a routine, monotonous job. Although many workers do not object to such work because of off-the-job satisfactions, they enjoy little pride of accomplishment.

Dividing work up into highly specialized jobs may also affect a person's opportunity for growth. To take a simple example from office work, a large oil company meticulously divided up work in its billing department among four employees: one typist listed in separate columns on an invoice all types and quantities of products from customer orders; a second clerk entered prices next to the products typed in the list; a calculator operator multiplied quantity by price and entered the total for each product; finally, a fourth clerk added up product totals, adjusted for special transportation charges, and entered the total amounts customers owed. With each person doing such small tasks, each one found little room for growth on the job; only by being promoted was there hope for growth. The company, however, changed the organization of this operation. Instead of restricting each person to a specialized task, management divided up the work so that each operator completed a whole invoice from typing to totaling. Output went up and the number of errors down.

Other companies have found that similar job redesign has improved results.[10] Part of the benefit comes from technical improvements. Coordi-

---

[10]For examples of job enrichment at A.T.&T., see R. N. Ford, *Motivation Through the Work Itself* (New York: American Management Associations, 1969). For examples of job enrichment at Texas Instruments, see W. J. Roche and N. L. MacKinnon, "Motivating People with Meaningful Work," *Harvard Business Review,* May-June 1970, pp. 97-110.

nation is simplified, less time is wasted in moving work from one step to another, and only one person has to give attention to each piece of work—as with the invoice in the preceding example. Another benefit is increased worker satisfaction. A job becomes more challenging than under the former step; a worker becomes aware of a natural completeness, or wholeness, to his task, and this affords him a greater sense of accomplishment. A worker on an enriched job also becomes better prepared for other assignments.

**rearranging work
flows**

In order for a person to satisfy his social needs, his relationships with others must be *reciprocal*. We do not enjoy always giving and never receiving, any more than we enjoy a one-way conversation. For a high degree of satisfaction, the initiation of contacts and the exchange of information should be roughly equal and reciprocal.[11]

An easy give-and-take is hard to establish when a staff expert with functional authority simply tells other people what to do. Relationships in such a case tend to run in one direction. Similarly, companies often set up controls so that information flows only upward from the operating level to a staff person who measures and analyzes results. Either arrangement may accomplish its primary purpose, but it would not provide for satisfying social relationships.

The General Hardware Manufacturing Company had an organization that illustrates this point. A staff engineer who reported to the president was assigned the duty of operating a research department to plan new products and new uses for existing products. After top management approved product innovations, this product-planning director was expected to help the president convey and clarify instructions to the plant and sales managers. This one-way flow of decisions did not provide opportunity, especially for the plant manager, to enter into give-and-take discussion with the product-planning director about the work itself. Physical separation and the status of "an expert from the head office" contributed to the difficulty of establishing reciprocal relationships. The same company also located in the home office a cost expert who watched over all expenditures—labor, overhead, and manufacture of specific products. His principal duty was to request data and explanations from plant managers and pass an analysis of this information on to the president. Again, the flow was one-way, as indicated in Figure 15.3. As we might expect, the plant managers did not look forward to their meetings with either the product-planning director or the cost analyst; similarly dealing with plant managers was just one of the crosses the central staff had to bear.

If the company would modify the work structure so that the people concerned with product development, plant operation, and cost analysis could come together in frequent discussions of how to operate each plant in order to contribute most to company profits, the feelings and social satisfactions would be different. One organizational change that might bring this

---

[11]G. Strauss, "Tactics of Lateral Relationship: The Purchasing Agent," *Administrative Science Quarterly,* 7 (1962), 161-86.

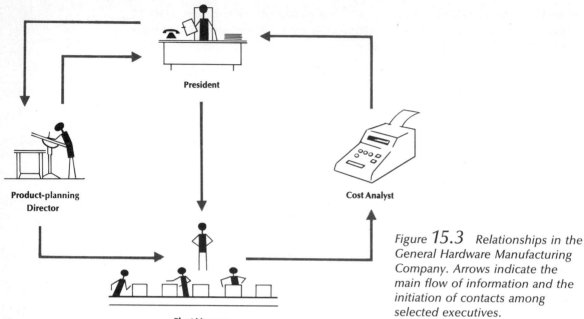

**Product-planning Director**

**President**

**Cost Analyst**

**Plant Manager**

*Figure 15.3  Relationships in the General Hardware Manufacturing Company. Arrows indicate the main flow of information and the initiation of contacts among selected executives.*

about would be to combine all three functions under a single executive—a plant manager with expanded duties. Another possibility would be to locate cost analysts physically in each plant, where they could serve the plant manager as well as prepare reports for the president. Even shifting greater responsibility for product development to each plant manager, with the result that he would make suggestions and ask for help from the central research group, would encourage reciprocal relations. The company would have to make any such modification with its total situation in view, but the alternatives mentioned indicate how the organization could be restructured to meet social needs more effectively.

**splitting up established roles**

Some jobs become firmly structured and embrace a fixed range of duties, particularly when a long period of formal training is required and when professional associations are active in the field. In hospitals, for instance, the roles of doctor, graduate nurse, and dietitian are sharply defined by tradition. Similarly, in a manufacturing concern, a first-class machinist or mechanical engineer may have a clear self-image of what he should and should not do. He has a "professional" pride in his job and the way he performs it.

Occasionally efficiency suggests reshaping such a role. Perhaps a draftsman can take over some duties that for years have been done only by engineers; or perhaps—this would be even more devastating to the engineers' pride—some aspects of design work might be shifted to salespeople. Part of the price of any such change will be a loss of self-esteem by the people whose "professional" job is being split up. The probable resistance may be strong enough to cause management to doubt whether a new organization is worth the rumpus. One large electronics firm, for instance, delayed a major reorganization because it would hurt the status and pride of its electrical engineers; at the time, good engineers were hard to recruit and hold, and the firm felt it had to provide a full range of satisfactions to retain key people.

Most people take pride in reporting to a high-level executive. It enhances their status, even though the executive may be too busy to see them frequently. Indirectly, it may also give independence—if the executive has many people who report to him, he *must* grant considerable freedom of action. Perhaps pride of place in an organization's hierarchy explains why over one hundred important officials report directly to the President of the United States.

Adding a supervisory level in an organization structure cuts into satisfactions from status, especially of those who report to the newly established supervisor. In one advertising agency, for instance, two department managers resigned when they discovered that they would no longer report directly to a vice president. The people in their departments felt demoted, even though no one would have suffered a reduction in pay or a change in duties.

Related to the matter of place in the hierarchy is the question of titles. Titles provide significant status satisfactions both within and outside a company. Theoretically, titles (or rank in military establishments) could be assigned on individual merit, irrespective of job duties or position in an organization hierarchy. But because titles are important in helping people understand a formal organization, they should describe where a job fits into a total organization structure. Even within this limit, however, managerial ingenuity in devising attractive titles can make substantial differences in employee satisfaction. "Let's give the guy a title instead of a raise" is not just a wisecrack; the right title may increase a person's satisfaction with his job.

**organizational status**

By its very definition, decentralization means increasing a subordinate's freedom of action. This freedom naturally affects the fulfillment of self-expression needs. At one extreme a job description for a sales representative might simply specify, "Call on all customers in the Norfolk territory at least once a month and present company products that appear to offer most appeal at that time." At the other extreme, the guides and rules defining the same job might spell out exactly how the representative should approach customers—for instance, by presenting samples first and mentioning price only incidentally, or even by spouting a canned sales talk that he has memorized from the company manual. In the first case, a person could give his initiative free rein, but in the latter circumstance, he would have much less opportunity for independent self-assertion.

The issue of opportunity for independence is also of concern to managers throughout a company. The supervisor of a cost-accounting department in a factory, for example, may have either a high or low degree of delegation from the plant controller. He may or may not be free to work out his own methods for gathering data from heads of operating units; he may or may not be allowed to plan the vacation schedule for employees in his department; he may or may not be permitted to determine the schedule for sending summary reports to the controller.

**decentralization**

The higher the degree of decentralization—that is, the greater freedom allowed—the more satisfaction a subordinate can expect from asserting his own ideas. Moreover, the more a person feels he is "running his own show," the more he will enjoy satisfactions of achievement. With a greater decentralization, a person has more chance to grow in his position and, in so doing, to prepare himself for more complex assignments. Clearly, decentralization ministers to self-expression needs by providing opportunities to satisfy them; but as we noted earlier, fostering opportunity is as far as management can go in satisfying this class of human need.

Organization of self-contained, semiautonomous divisions has already been described in Chapter 11 as a special form of decentralization. The separate divisions of the General Electric Company and the Du Pont Company are well-known examples of such profit decentralization. This arrangement offers the managers of such divisions unusual chances for self-assertion and growth. In fact, a recognized benefit of profit decentralization lies in the strong appeal of challenging experience it offers the managers of each division. Here, indeed, organization structure ministers to human needs.

"Task teams" also require decentralization, as we will note in the next chapter. Moreover, they are small units, and easy two-way communication becomes normal. In these respects they contribute significantly to personal needs of the members. Resistance may be encountered when they are first established, however, if a technical specialist on the team feels that his role is being fractured (he may have to leave his office and live where "the shooting is going on") and that his status is downgraded.

## freedom versus order

A recurring issue in matching personal needs with an organization's is how to balance individual freedom against established order. Today nonconformity is fashionable, and many young people regard fitting into any regulated system as a sacrifice. The issue calls for sensitive balance.

One cluster of basic human needs, as we discussed, hinges on security. A known, orderly way of working together is an important source of such security. Established roles, normal procedures, and planned change all help members of an organization to feel psychologically secure. They know what to expect, and they have a recognized place in the total activities. People also want opportunities for self-expression, but no one can enjoy freedom in a completely unstructured, unpredictable environment. But, as we have already noted, after the need for security is fairly well satisfied, it drops in importance. The practical questions, then, deal with *marginal increments* of security and self-expression.

Our reaction to orderliness depends substantially on our feeling about the necessity for it. Musicians, artists, and researchers voluntarily submit to all kinds of disciplined behavior—with no sense of lost freedom—if they regard the drill as necessary to their personal expression. Similarly, when we are committed to an objective, we accept all sorts of necessary guidance in reaching our end.

For centuries most people have satisfied their self-expression needs off the job, and now the dramatic reduction in the work week provides increasing freedom for the pursuit of independent personal interests. People neither want nor expect to depend solely on their jobs for opportunities for self-expression.

So we don't face a simple trade-off between the orderliness required by technology or economics on the one hand and individual freedom on the other. Nevertheless, rising living standards, increased mass education, and higher aspirations raise the marginal value attached to individual self-expression. Perhaps as a general guide, we should start with the assumption that organization designers tend to overdo systems and formal assignments. This means that we should look for opportunities to leave discretion with individual operators and managers and should be ready to modify existing organization to keep it relevant to current social moods.

## INTEGRATING PAY, NEEDS, AND ORGANIZATION

Although to say that "people work for a paycheck" is a gross over-simplification (as our preceding discussion has shown), financial compensation is a vital source of satisfaction. The size of a paycheck *does* matter to virtually every worker, from president to office boy.

The real question is how pay fits into the relationship between jobs and need satisfaction.[12] To be sure, pay enables workers to meet their physical needs and those of their families. If a paycheck is large enough, they may have steak instead of hamburgers, two cars instead of one, or a color television set in the bedroom. But a paycheck means more than just what it buys. It is a symbol of status, a source of self-respect, an avenue to security. These primarily non-economic aspects of the paycheck often have more impact on how a person behaves in his job than its purchasing power.

Several of these "indirect" influences of pay on behavior are closely related to organization design. They also intertwine with on-the-job satisfactions. Because an alert manager will want to give attention to such interrelations, we now turn to several key issues in this area: Can we substitute money for other kinds of satisfaction? How should a pay system be related to formal organization? Can we use pay to reinforce the influence of staff and of executives? How should individual raises be related to assigned duties and company objectives? What burdens does the use of incentive pay place on organization structure?

Can a company pay high salaries and wages and disregard security, social, and self-expression satisfactions? For instance, provided pay is high, will a capable individual work as a subordinate for a supervisor who is highly critical, makes even minor decisions, and gives no opportunity for growth in the job? Experience answers, "Money isn't everything." Competent people shift to other jobs where the work is more attractive even if the pay is lower. Those who do stay on an unpleasant job are likely to develop negative attitudes toward their work and the company, to show little ini-

**pay instead of other satisfactions**

[12]For a more comprehensive discussion of the issues discussed in this section, see E. E. Lawler III, "Reward Systems," in J. R. Hackman and J. L. Suttle, *Improving Life at Work: Behavioral Science Approaches to Organization Change* (Santa Monica: Goodyear, 1977).

tiative, and perhaps even to restrict their output. Even though high pay may attract a worker, it does not win his emotional support if his job is low in direct satisfactions.

However, a job so brimful of direct satisfactions that it is actually fun still requires reasonable pay. The pay cannot be much below the prevailing rate for comparable work because of the psychological aspect of pay. The amount of compensation reflects the importance a company attaches to the work; it is a symbol recognized by other people inside and outside the company. Even though a person likes a job, he also wants others to think well of him and of the job. We can conclude, then, that a wise manager must consider *both* direct and indirect satisfactions. Most people are willing to substitute one for the other only to a limited extent. We can apply the principle of marginal value to both situations: extra-high pay cannot compensate for the reduction of on-the-job satisfactions below a commonly accepted level, *and* a high degree of job satisfaction will not keep a person working if his pay significantly degrades his self-respect or social standing.

Exceptions to this general proposition can be found, of course. Some jobs, such as preaching or teaching, carry enough social prestige and ego satisfaction to attract people, even though business pays for comparable ability at a significantly higher rate. We can also fill dirty or risky jobs by paying premium rates. In general, however, both fair pay and satisfying work are necessary to attract and motivate good people.

**relating pay to formal organization**

This conclusion still leaves us with the question of what compensation is "reasonable" for specific jobs in a specific company. One important guide for both a manager and those who receive the pay is this: A pay rate should reflect the difficulty of a job. Jobs that require more skill, longer training, or more obligation should command higher pay. We should note that this guide is based on formal organization, for job descriptions specify duties and, at least by implication, the abilities needed to fill each position. Any pay system that is inconsistent with formally asigned duties may lead to discontent.

Status is the chief issue. A difficult or important job should have a high status. Because pay level (along with title and place in the official hierarchy) is the most conspicuous evidence of status, we should take great care in matching duties and pay. Employees at all levels are sensitive to this point. Strikes have been called over the amount of difference in wages between, say, electricians and machinists, not because of a few cents per hour, but because of what the difference meant in relative status. On the executive level, a vice-president of a certain department store was quite satisfied with a $45,000 salary until he learned that another vice-president, whose job he considered no more important than his own, was earning $50,000; immediately, he felt insulted, downgraded, and discriminated against.

Management usually dovetails salaries and duties by a procedure called "job evaluation."[13] Steps in an evaluation include: (1) comparing all

[13]E. B. Flippo, *Principles of Personnel Management,* 4th ed. (New York: McGraw-Hill, 1976), pp. 109–29.

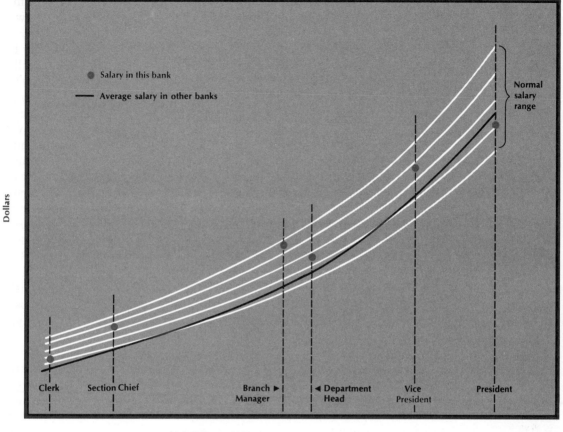

Figure *15.4* *A possible salary structure for a small bank. The structure reflects the difficulties, duties, and status of jobs, the rates paid by other firms, and the possibilities for salary increases in any given position.*

jobs on many counts—such as scope of duties, skills, and working conditions—and placing the jobs in a series of grades; (2) establishing a general salary level for each grade based on going rates for comparable work among other firms; and (3) creating a salary range for each grade that will permit increases from minimum to maximum as an individual progresses from beginner to expert in any one job.

No matter how elaborate the job-evaluation technique we use for our pay system, it will not be successful unless it is *accepted* by the employees to whom it applies. They must believe that it fairly reflects differences in jobs; the grades assigned must coincide with the relative standing of various roles as the workers conceive of them. Without such acceptance, the status and self-esteem of some workers will suffer, and the pay system will have a negative effect on their eagerness to do their work.

Management has a further reason to be concerned with the relative pay level of people in supervisory and staff positions. The feeling is common in American society that we should respect the opinions of persons who earn more money than we do, whereas the opinions of persons earning less are open to challenge. The simple assumption is that earnings are a measure of the soundness of a person's views. Although this is an unwarranted assumption, it exists whether we like it or not.

Because of this feeling, a low-paid staff person will have more difficulty winning acceptance for his ideas. An operating executive may say to himself, "Why should I take that fellow's advice? He doesn't earn half as much as I do." Thus if management wants to increase the influence of a particular individual, one way to achieve its aim is to give him the prestige of a high salary. Similarly, a supervisor should get paid more than his highest-paid subordinate.

Raising a person's salary is not the only way to build his influence, but we should not overlook the impact of salary on an individual's ability to operate within an organization.

How a company grants merit increases has a direct influence on behavior in the organization. To an individual himself, an increase is a sign of his personal progress; he will try to continue behaving in the way that he thinks led to his raise. His colleagues are likewise alert. They know who gets raises more often, and who gets none at all, and they take their cues accordingly. At the same time, workers typically have strong opinions of what they feel is "fair"—that is, who deserves a raise.

Consequently, management should be careful to grant increases to those who are, in fact, improving their effectiveness and should try to get everyone to agree that the policy on giving raises is reasonable and fair. In this matter, as with most others, management's actions speak far louder than its words. Playing favorites or being soft and giving everybody a small increase just to avoid arguments will undermine appeals to do a better job. On the other hand, if management consistently matches merit increases with known contributions toward company strategy, it reinforces the whole structure of formal plans and organization.

If merit increases should go to people who perform their assignments well, how about extending the idea to incentive pay, which varies directly and immediately with performance? Commissions for salespeople and piece rates for factory workers are common examples of incentive pay; at the managerial level, we find executive bonuses based on profits, on actual results compared with budgets, or on other quantified measures of results. Occasionally, when a whole group of people must cooperate to achieve results, a firm will offer a group bonus.

Desire for security has become so intense that today few employees on any level—president, sales supervisor, or machine operator—subsist entirely on incentive pay. Instead companies assure a degree of security either by guaranteeing minimum earnings regardless of results or by paying a base salary and adding incentive pay as a bonus. Even though incentive pay may be a small percentage of total compensation, it focuses attention on the particular achievements that management uses in determining the amount of bonus.

Incentive pay introduces several requirements in organization design. We must sharply define the mission—the end result—of a job eligible for a bonus, and the results must be measurable. Many jobs, such as that of chief accountant or personnel director, cannot be defined in this manner. Even the work of a sales representative is not simple to describe. His primary task may be to obtain orders, but in addition he is expected to cultivate new customers, obtain information on new products, deal with complaints, and keep his own expenses low. If his bonus is based solely on new orders, he is likely to slight his other duties.

For an organization, this means one of two things. Either (1) authority should be highly decentralized—for instance, we might authorize the manager of a division to change prices, hire people, and take other action that is necessary to achieve profits, on which his bonus is based—or (2) management should standardize and control the work conditions that affect output—for a production worker who is paid a piece rate, this means that material should be readily available, machinery in good operating condition, helpers adequately trained, power and light dependable, and so forth. In both instances, the location and adequacy of staff and service work are important to the person who receives incentive pay. Again, we see that an organization pattern and a salary system are closely interrelated. If we use incentive pay, we get into questions of delegating authority, providing service and staff, and defining duties so that they conform to the bases of bonuses.

## CONCLUSION: MOTIVATING PEOPLE AT WORK

In this chapter, we have focused our attention on the personal needs of managers and operators—especially on their physical, security, social, and self-expression needs, because these can be met to a significant extent through working in an enterprise. A manager should not only identify the specific needs of the people he directs, but also be sensitive to the relative potency of these various desires. Such an understanding provides a manager with a foundation for deciding how to act to motivate his people.

A manager should be alert to the connection between on-the-job satisfactions and organization. Often he can adjust his organization to increase the direct satisfactions of his subordinates. By tying the amount of pay to the importance and influence he wishes to give various jobs, he increases the chances that the organization will actually work as he wants. The objective should be to design a structure in which on-the-job satisfactions are enhanced at the same time company aims are furthered.

We have been primarily concerned with how a manager utilizes organization, task design, and pay to develop a motivating work environment. In the next chapter we consider the powerful influences of groups and informal social systems on the satisfaction of individual needs. Later, in Part V, we will examine the vital role of leadership in contributing to, or detracting from, the fulfillment of needs.

## FOR FURTHER DISCUSSION

1. How may a clear understanding of the strategy of a business-unit affect the ability to motivate key employees?

2. "Our organization has made a practice of hiring and promoting people whose needs are largely unfilled. This sure makes it easier to motivate them." Discuss.

3. There seems to be much greater concern today than there was fifty years ago with the need to devote more of our resources to dealing with problems such as ecological abuses, racial injustice, war, and so on. How would you explain this concern? How may it affect business?

4. "Our company works very hard to provide people with the opportunity to achieve status in the eyes of their fellow employees. One of the keys to making this possible is our concerted effort to eliminate status symbols." How do you interpret this statement made by the president of a successful firm?

5. How may the increasing number of dual-career families affect management's ability to motivate such employees? Assume both do not work for the same organization.

6. What do you consider the most significant changes in America over the last two or three decades that are likely to influence the attitudes of people toward work as a means of satisfying their potent needs? Consider your answer to the first part of this question in terms of the age of the people you have in mind. Would the changes you consider significant have as much, more, or different kinds of influence on people under twenty-five than they would on those over thirty?

7. "I have no use for all this job-enrichment stuff that is supposed to fulfill me. I get all the fulfillment I need as a mother, wife, member of the school board, and as a Sunday School teacher. I work because I'm bored between 7:30 a.m. and 3:30 p.m. and we can use the extra money. I wish these unfulfilled psychologists who keep running around the plant would leave me and my job alone." Consider this statement from a forty-year-old woman.

8. It is generally agreed that rewards are very strong motivators when they are closely linked to the specific performance of an individual. How does this affect the ability of an organization to motivate its people toward achieving strategic objectives?

## CASES

For cases involving issues covered in this chapter, see especially the following. Particularly relevant questions are listed after each case.

Hackman, J. R., "Work Design," in J. R. Hackman and J. L. Suttle, eds., *Improving Life at Work: Behavioral Science Approaches to Organizational Change.* Santa Monica: Goodyear, 1977, pp. 92-162. Clear review of concepts and research findings on worker satisfaction, motivation, and the effect of job enrichment.

Lawler, E. E. III, *Pay and Organizational Effectiveness.* New York: McGraw-Hill, 1971. Comprehensive discussion of the pschological dimensions of financial motivation.

Meyer, H., "The Pay-for-Performance Dilemma," *Organizational Dynamics,* Winter 1975, pp. 39-50. Provocative analysis of the problems associated with most pay systems.

Staw, B., ed., *Psychological Foundations of Organizational Behavior,* Parts I-IV. Santa Monica: Goodyear, 1977. Excellent series of articles on motivation and individual behavior in organizations.

Steers, R. and L. W. Porter, *Motivation and Work Behavior,* 2nd ed. Santa Monica: Goodyear, 1978. Articles present a wide array of behavioral studies relating individual behavior to the characteristics of the work being done and especially to the job design.

Walton, R., "The Diffusion of New Work Structures: Explaining Why Success Doesn't Work," *Organizational Dynamics,* Winter 1975, pp. 3-22. Important study exploring the fate of job enrichment experiments within several companies which pioneered in this area.

# 16

# group behavior and informal organization

**Learning Objectives**

After completing this chapter you should be able to

1. Understand how customs and roles develop within an organization.

2. Explain how group norms and group cohesiveness develop.

3. State the benefits and drawbacks of using committees.

4. Describe the major approaches for harmonizing social groups and formal organization.

5. Discuss the major guidelines for the formation of integrated task teams.

**THE INFORMAL**
**ORGANIZATION**

337
*CHAPTER 16*
*group behavior and*
*informal organization*

The official plans and formal organization that describe duties and specify relationships provide only one set of external pressures to which people respond. An organization structure that carries official approval is a strong influence, but there are many other pressures, and a wise manager will try to design his organization so that these other influences support, rather than detract from, desired results.

One important set of influences arises from a simple and obvious characteristic of human behavior. People live and work together. Their relationships soon result in patterns of behavior and belief, which social scientists call "cultures." Within the broader national culture, every enterprise develops its own "subculture"—that is, the beliefs and patterns of conduct that are associated with living and working together in that company. Two aspects of a business subculture of particular concern to a manager are the following:

1. The *customs,* habits, and ways of working together that develop informally in an expanding enterprise. These customs, which grow up around normal company activities, elaborate and extend, or perhaps modify, formal organization.
2. The informal *social groups* among employees that strongly influence their attitudes, beliefs, and behavior. These informal groups often (though not necessarily) center on personal interests and noncompany objectives.

Research on human relations in established organizations clearly demonstrates that informal social relationships influence how people respond to managerial action and have a direct bearing on effectiveness and efficiency.[1]

Striking examples of the effect of cultural attitudes and customs arise in international business.[2] American executives have often tried to transplant to a foreign country a management system that worked well in the United States. The results have often been confusion or sabotage—and an added bit of resentment of Yankee enterprise. Unfamiliarity with the concept of staff guidance, reluctance to mix people from different social strata in informal work groups, reverence for red tape, skepticism of numerical evaluation schemes, and similar reactions have prevented superbly designed organizations from operating as they were intended.

Although social traditions and informal relationships can be annoying to an executive, they are essential for getting a day's work accomplished smoothly. Like fire, the force is destructive when improperly handled; but once one understands how to work with a force, it can be employed for constructive purposes. A manager cannot manipulate social behavior in any way he pleases, but he can attempt to design work structures in such a way that social pressures and formal organization tend to support each other.

In the present chapter, then, we shall seek answers to the following questions: How do customs and traditional roles develop in a business enter-

[1]I. D. Steiner, *Group Process and Productivity* (New York: Academic Press, 1972).
[2]A. Pizzam and A. Reichel, "Cultural Determinants of Managerial Behavior," *Management International Review,* 17, no 2 (1977), pp. 65–72.

**how customs
develop**

prise? Can formal organization and informal customs be made more compatible? How do informal social groups affect the behavior of workers? What can we do to encourage such group pressure to support company objectives?

**CUSTOMS AND ROLES**      Only a small fraction of our behavior is deliberately chosen. During any day, we take part in many activities, and it would be impossible to analyze each separate movement or remark before we act. Such a pattern of behavior is not irrational; it is essential. Because purely intuitive or emotional responses are likely to get us into trouble and deliberate choices are not feasible, we rely heavily on custom and habit to direct our behavior.

Reliance on customary behavior applies to our business activities, as well as to our private lives. When a person buys a car, the dealer has a customary way of recording the sale, arranging for financing, and preparing the car for delivery. Similarly, when a company hires a new employee, it follows customary practices in arranging a medical examination, entering the person's name on the payroll, and introducing him to his new assignment and to his fellow workers. Often a situation will have unique features that call for thought—for instance, the new employee may have a physical handicap—but it is possible to give attention to these unique features because in handling the situation so much can be based on customary ways of doing business.

Once established, a customary way of doing business looks "natural." But many minority small-business development programs, for example, have floundered and sometimes failed because social networks for performing new tasks were lacking. Often a deep-seated suspicion of procedures used in the traditional business establishment has contributed to the problem. It takes time to learn how to work together.

New strategy upsets old customs. The Acme Auto Parts Company for years sold only to repair shops and other "professionals." When it decided to serve do-it-yourself car owners as well, changes were needed in advice to customers, pricing, credit, etc. Many existing employees resented taking "all the trouble" with these greenhorns; usual ways of dealing with customers no longer fit.

Customs become established, or learned, principally through personal experience. Some guidance may be provided by company planning—an organization structure assigns duties to various positions, and a company manual formally states policies and procedures. Nevertheless, only when people actually work can a custom become established. Moreover, formal plans almost never cover all aspects of a job. Any employee—be he president or janitor—acts on a problem in a way he hopes will be satisfactory. If the results are poor, he will probably try some other solution the next time he meets a similar problem. Once he finds an acceptable solution, he will probably repeat it each time a similar problem arises. As the same solution is applied over and over again, customary behavior begins to emerge.

Our emphasis on behavior based on experience should be a warning to anyone who thinks of managing purely through formal organization and written plans.[3] Before formal instructions become customary behavior, they have to be accepted in actual use. What an employee considers "acceptable" is determined by a variety of factors, such as favorable reaction of other employees, approval by his immediate supervisor, contribution to company goals, and personal satisfaction from doing the work.

If an immediate supervisor does not insist that workers follow official plans, then other considerations are likely to determine the particular work pattern that becomes customary. For example, if employees can disregard a "no smoking" rule without serious consequences, they are likely to adopt smoking on the job as customary conduct. Similarly, if a branch manager finds that he can hire new employees without following company instructions to consult with the personnel director at headquarters, the formal plan for hiring loses its significance. On the other hand, if a branch manager consistently consults with his vice-president in charge of sales before changing sales territories even though formal organization does not require it, the practice becomes embedded in the company structure as customary behavior. Formal plans can have their full impact only when they become an integral part of custom.

Work customs are especially important when several different people work together. Each person learns to rely on the others to perform their parts of the total task in a customary manner. A hospital dietician, for instance, may assume that her order clerk will place rush orders on the top of each batch of meal requests she sends to the kitchen; if the clerk overlooks this little custom, a rush order may not get the attention it deserves. To cite an illustration from a Midwestern hardware firm, the production manager normally consulted with the sales manager before authorizing unusually long runs of a product. Once, when the sales manager was away on a trip, the production manager had to decide whether to schedule a long run of chain hoists, so he overlooked the usual cross-check. Actually, it turned out that the sales manager planned to curtail his selling efforts on this model, and only by accident was the prospect of an unusually slow-moving inventory discovered two weeks later and the order cancelled before actual production commenced. These examples show how one person may depend on the customary behavior of another—much as players on a good doubles team in tennis depend on each other to cover different parts of the court.

When each person learns what to expect of others with whom his work interlocks, coordinated effort is greatly simplified. And conversely, deviations from usual behavior call for special warnings to other people if we are to avoid confusion that might damage efficiency.

**expected roles**

As we have seen, some customs spring from the habitual actions of particular people. But, in addition, jobs often require traditional roles. People have preconceived ideas of how a person appointed as, say, credit manager, supervisor, or baseball umpire, should behave. In other words, each

[3]W. E. Reif, R. M. Monczka, and J. W. Newstrom, "Perceptions of Formal and Informal Organizations," *Academy of Management Journal*, 16, no. 3 (1973), pp. 389–403.

Courtesy Bill Mark

*Figure* **16.1** *When a person assumes a given role, his duties and authority and sometimes even his gestures and clothing are well defined.*

established role strongly influences the behavior that is expected of anyone who fills that role. Established roles are common throughout society. We expect ministers to epitomize virtue, ship captains to be stern disciplinarians, and football coaches to be hard-driving authoritarians whose consuming interest in life is winning games.

In business, and especially within a single enterprise, the role for any given position may be firmly established. For instance, what a cost accountant should—and should not—undertake and what his attitude toward traditional accounting should be may be clearly defined in the minds of all people who work with him. The existence of such definite roles gives a stability to relationships in business; at least we predict from them how a person will fill a given position.

We run into difficulty, however, when complete agreement is lacking on all features of a role. Top executives may be inclined to think of a job in terms of a formal organization plan that is embellished with details contributing to company objectives. An incumbent himself may have a somewhat different point of view based on his own preferences and experiences. His subordinates may attach importance to still other features of the job, and his associates may be concerned with how his position interrelates with their work. Such lack of "role congruence" causes incompatible expectations about how a key person will behave and complaints about weak performance.[4]

[4]D. Hampton, C. Summer, and R. Webber, *Organizational Behavior and the Practice of Management,* 3rd ed, (Glenview, IL: Scott, Foresman, 1978), pp. 193–200.

One of the best-known examples of such variation in conception of a role is the job of foreman. Top management thinks of a foreman as dedicated to getting quality production on schedule at low cost. His subordinates, on the other hand, expect him to be friendly, fair, and helpful, to represent them in dealings with higher management, and to be sympathetic to actual work difficulties. If a foreman himself tries to live up to both sets of expectations, he gets "caught in the middle." If he accepts either the labor view or the managerial view, he will be subjected to pressure from the other group.

Ideally, the job description that stems from formal organization *and* the other sets of expectations should merge into a single, consistent concept of a job. But, as we noted in Chapter 14, we can accomplish this only if (1) the job description is realistic in terms of both the technological and human resources available; (2) there is full communication and agreement by everyone concerned on what a person in the job is expected to do; and (3) the person actually on the job performs as anticipated. It is when these three conditions are fulfilled that a formal organization becomes a vital reality.

An additional reason why managers need to pay attention to socially accepted roles is summed up in the sociologists' concept of "legitimacy."[5] Every complex organization is laced with a maze of contacts between different positions—requests for information, suggestions and countersuggestions, and inspection of results. Employees regard some of these contacts as entirely legitimate and deeply resent others. Their response to a suggestion or to a request is determined largely by whether it is an accepted, legitimate part of a role. If everyone expects a person occupying a particular position to become involved in the work of other people, then everyone thinks his action is legitimate. On the other hand, if he steps outside the bounds of customary behavior, he is thought to be "poking his nose into other people's affairs," and the result is sure to be friction.

## INFORMAL GROUPS

Small social groups significantly affect the way a formal organization actually works. Informal groups of from three to perhaps a dozen members spring up naturally whenever people work together. They are common among college students and in large government offices as well as in business firms. Members of such groups see each other frequently on the job, at lunch, or riding home from work. They discover common interests and exchange ideas. A group thus forms spontaneously. If one or two members tend to be leaders, their position arises naturally out of the situation rather than from formal selection.

*social groups within organizations*

Most people get many of their day-to-day satisfactions from such groups.[6] Among the "rewards" for belonging to such a group are sociability, a sense of belonging (which contributes to feelings of inner security and

---

[5]J. R. P. French and B. H. Raven, "The Bases of Social Power," in D. Cartwright, ed., *Studies in Social Power* (Ann Arbor: University of Michigan Press, 1959).

[6]D. Roy, "Banana Time: Job Satisfaction and Informal Interaction," *Human Organization*, 18, (1960), 158–68.

personal worth), a sympathetic ear for troubles, aid on the job (both information and occasional direct assistance), and some protection through a united stand against pressure from a boss or outside force.

Small-group rewards are especially prized by people who work in large organizations, where, too often, the work itself provides few satisfactions. If the work is fragmented and remote objectives are not felt to be significant, then the social satisfactions derived from subgroups become a major force in behavior on the job.

A small informal group—whether composed of lathe operators, members of a vice president's staff, or senior executives in an electrical-engineering department—falls into routines for its activities. Members sit together in the lunchroom; Mary stops to chat with Steve before going home in the evening. When the members work near to one another, interchange may take place from time to time thoughout the day. Sometimes a pattern of contact is extended to include off-the-job activities, such as bowling, golf, bridge, or union meetings. In addition, a group tends to evolve a pattern of attitudes, at least toward subjects of common interest. Members frequently discuss their feelings toward their boss, company, rates of output, "young squirts from college," or the accounting office; often, they all hold similar views on such subjects.

Each person normally belongs to several small informal groups. One may be founded on physical proximity at work, another on a common interest in baseball, and a third on an interest in a professional society—for example, the Society for Advancement of Management. A political-protest group draws together quite a diverse collection of people. Some of these groups may be fairly inactive, and people may drift in and out of them. But those based on daily work relationships are likely to be the strongest and most enduring.

**effect of social group norms,** group norms,
**groups on worker** group norms,
**behavior**

It is typical of social groups to put pressure on members *to conform to group norms,* which are standards and expectations governing behavior. This push to conformity is, of course, common throughout life. A school child gets teased by his classmates if his clothing is too fancy. Young couples who move to suburbia match their neighbors by selling the motorcycle and buying a sportscar. Even the nonconformist in college expresses his defiance in ways endorsed by his fellow nonconformists—for instance, new polished shoes must *not* be worn even if the owner has to go to a lot of trouble to get them dirty and scuffed up. Of course, the particular matters on which to conform vary from group to group and from time to time.

In addition to such standards of conduct, groups also *provide many beliefs and values* to the individual. Joe or Kathy may believe that the personnel director is a "good guy" and that the advertising director is a "screwball"—not from any personal observation or conviction, but merely because these are the sentiments passed on to them by their group. They may believe that all senior executives draw fabulous salaries, that only a Stanford graduate can get ahead in the firm, that their company has the best

Irene Springer

*Figure 16.2  As group members work together over time, group cohesive-
ness develops. A cohesive group is likely to exert pressure on a member
who disagrees with the majority.*

engineering department in the industry, and many other articles of faith,
because they are strongly held by their social group. A group can also
influence feelings about such matters as pilfering, accuracy in keeping reports, importance of efficient control of quality, or service to customers.

Employee groups may strongly support the company strategy, as has
been the tradition at IBM, or they may be indifferent or even opposed to it.

Even when an individual has direct evidence contrary to group senti-
ment, he may accept group judgment. In a series of experiments with groups
of college students, all persons except one in each group were instructed to
give incorrect answers to a simple question about which of several lines was
longest. As different sets of lines were flashed on a screen, the exception in
each group found his judgment consistently at odds with that of half a dozen
other people in the same room; eventually he began to distrust his own
perception and started giving the group answer.[7] At work, when facts are
less clearcut, and group pressure is even greater, the temptation to accept
group opinion is strong. Fortunately there continues to be a good sprinkling
of rugged individualists who maintain their independence of judgment.
Even these people, however, are likely simply to remain silent rather than
challenge some cherished bit of lore.

[7]S. E. Asch, "Effects of Group Pressure Upon the Modification and Distortion of Judgments," in
H. Guetzkow, ed., *Groups, Leadership and Men* (Pittsburgh: Carnegie Press, 1951).

The pressure of a group on its members is substantial, for (as we noted earlier) an individual gets many of his satisfactions in his job through group responses. If he deviates too far from group standards, other members may no longer want to associate with him and may treat him as though he were an oddball, if not a traitor. Group influence is particularly strong in *cohesive* groups. The members of a cohesive group strongly identify with group norms; the close attachment to common beliefs and to other group members produces high group solidarity.

The member of a cohesive group who deviates from an accepted norm will be subjected to severe social censure.[8] For this reason, cohesive groups exert considerable control over the output of individual members. If a group of production operators agrees to restrict daily output to an accepted group standard, low productivity will result. On the other hand, if group norms favor high output, a highly cohesive group can be very productive. Low performers are likely to be considered outcasts in such high-producing groups.

Behavioral research has found one further characteristic of group behavior that is of direct interest to management. A group will probably *resist any change* that upsets its normal activities, especially if the change is initiated by an outsider. A new method, a change in office layout, or a reassignment of duties modifies established patterns of social relationships. Social groups may be broken up, and this disruption means loss of known satisfactions in exchange for an unknown future. Consciously or unconsciously, people resist such changes, even when offsetting advantages may benefit individual members of a group, and new groups may replace old ones. Managers should thus anticipate resistance when they upset social patterns.

## HARMONIZING SOCIAL GROUPS AND FORMAL ORGANIZATION

The behavior of small groups has an impact on many facets of management, as we shall note especially in our later discussion of leadership. In the present chapter, we are particularly interested in their impact on formal organization structure. What can we do to harmonize social groups and formal organization?

**adopting group practice**

Many times people in a company think up new ways of doing things that are not only more satisfying to their group, but also better for company efficiency. For example, job descriptions in a plumbing-equipment company indicated that the sales department was simply to refer all complaints about product design to the engineering manager, so that he or his representative could talk with customers about their specific difficulties. The sales manager, however, had trouble getting minor changes made that he felt were necessary for overcoming the complaints of big customers. So the sales manager developed a habit of obtaining from these customers full information on

---

[8]J. R. Hackman, "Group Influences on Individuals in Organizations," in *Handbook of Industrial and Organizational Psychology,* M. D. Dunnette, ed. (Chicago: Rand McNally, 1976).

what they wanted. Then after an engineer had been assigned to investigate the complaint, the sales manager talked at length with the engineer about what changes could be made. Actually, the engineers found that their job was simplified, and in time they began to rely heavily on the sales manager for customer data. Sometimes salespeople would provide information directly to the engineers, and on troublesome cases a meeting of salespeople, sales manager, engineer, and engineering manager would be held.

As new complaints arose, members of the sales department frequently contacted the engineers and pushed hard for changes they wanted made. At this stage, the vice-president in charge of research and engineering protested to the president. He said the salespeople were taking up too much of the engineers' time, interrupting the engineering work schedule, and "high-pressuring" his people to make too many changes. "They are violating the organization structure," he said, "and ought to be stopped."

After thorough investigation, the president decided that the company's product development was being significantly improved by the role the salespeople had assumed in modifying products. So the president had the job descriptions rewritten to provide a new duty for the sales manager—that of visiting customers who complained of product design and then holding conferences with the engineering manager. The president worked closely with both executives to be sure the new statement of duties was feasible and acceptable. *Now,* even the vice-president in charge of research and engineering says that the new organization is best for the company.

Such cases indicate that our first step in dealing with informal group actions that do not "fit" the formal structure should be at least to entertain the hypothesis that the group standards and behavior are beneficial. We need not accept the group behavior, of course. After investigation, we may decide that the informal action must be changed to meet company requirements. But we should always be alert to the possibility that behavior that develops informally serves the company well and should be incorporated into the formal structure.

**form integrated task teams**

A second possibility of harmonizing small-group practice with formal organization lies in the design itself. Formal organization—that is, how workers are grouped together and what the specified relationships are—provides the setting for many informal groups. Can we design a formal organization structure so as to encourage social groups that are inclined to support, rather than conflict with, the aims of an enterprise?

Organization studies in several countries—in textile mills, loading docks, sales offices, and coal mines—strongly support the formation of integrated task teams.[9]

Three guides for organization design help foster such informal groups sympathetic to company goals.

---

[9]T. G. Cummings and S. Srivastva, *Management of Work: A Sociotechnical Systems Approach* (Kent, OH: Kent State University Press, 1977).

*Figure* $16.3$  In an integrated task team, each member has an assigned role, but it is the immediate task itself that calls for action and voluntary coordination of effort.

***1. Combine related tasks into clusters—or blocks—so that each cluster produces a "meaningful" end product.***   First, we should identify blocks of work that have a natural unity, whose end result we can clearly visualize. Such a block may be all activities that pertain to securing a customer's order, or to making a particular product or part. Second, we should place authority for doing such a specific, complete block of work squarely on a small group of people. These people will constitute a team, and it is up to them to complete the effort. One person may be captain, but the assignment belongs to the entire *task team*.

This proposal is in sharp contrast with the practice, encouraged by scientific management, of dividing work into highly specialized pieces and, when volume permits, of creating a specialized department to perform each narrow task. Under this latter system, detailed, centralized planning is encouraged, and supervisors are primarily concerned with seeing that operators do not deviate from the program. Such a work structure promotes informal groups that are uninterested in company goals.

By assigning meaningful jobs to a task team, we hope that a social group will form that is interested in achieving end-results. In fact, there is considerable evidence to indicate that indifference to company goals and restrictions on output will be less under the task-team organization than under a highly functionalized organization.

These behavioral-science conclusions relate directly to the forming of work groups (see Chapter 10).

***2. Place people with all skills necessary to complete the assigned task as close as possible to the point of action.***   The best arrangement is to have people with the necessary skills within the task team itself. Thus a self-contained sales team might include a sales representative, a service engineer, a delivery person and a clerk-secretary in the office. Each person would understand how the total unit functions and could easily make direct personal contact with any other member of the unit.

Unfortunately, such an integrated unit is uneconomical for many tasks. The need in a single task team for a particular skill may be insufficient in volume or may occur at such irregular intervals that the inclusion of a qualified full-time worker on the team is unwarranted. An alternative arrangement, then, is to assign a staff or service person to work with *several* operating units and to locate him in close proximity to all units. By locating him where he can have frequent face-to-face contacts with people on the various task teams, we encourage his becoming a member—albeit a part-time one—of their respective social groups.[10]

Still another arrangement is to form a task-team for a specific project. We note here that the behavioral concept of a task-team reinforces the idea of project management explained in connection with matrix organization in Chapter 13.

In each of these arrangements, individuals with specialized skills are placed close to the scene of action, where they can form informal groups associated with the end-result rather than with their specialties.

***3. Supply each task team with full facts on its work.*** An operating unit, such as we have been describing, should be self-regulating. Since it is close to its work, a team will readily have available much control information. For example, if one part of the work falls behind—or gets ahead of—related activities, all members of the team will know it promptly and can adjust their efforts accordingly; or if a customer changes the specifications on his order, the whole team can quickly readjust to the new requirements. In other words, each member of the team, because he has personal contact with what is happening, knows whether all phases of the operation are proceeding as planned. Armed with such information, the team itself regulates its efforts to achieve desired results.

If control information, not obvious to the team members, becomes available elsewhere, this too should be fed back quickly to the operating unit. Data on laboratory tests or costs of materials, for instance, may first be recorded at a point remote from actual operations; this information needs to be communicated immediately to the persons who can take corrective action. Because the task group promptly receives data on its efficiency and progress and has full delegation to make changes, it may become so engrossed with results that it will avoid sparring matches with supervisors. Furthermore, the abundance of available statistical data will allow the group to base its work-related beliefs on fact rather than fiction.

These guides for organizing around task teams come to us from research on small groups that usually do operating work.[11] Practical application of these guides has been worked out for such tasks as running an

---

[10]The effect of proximity on the ease of joining social groups has long been recognized in the auditing field. But in this instance, to ensure independence of an audit, management wishes to *prevent* close friendships, so it deliberately moves auditors from place to place before loyalties to a social group can become strong.

[11]E. J. Poza and M. L. Markus, "Success Story: The Team Approach to Work Restructuring," *Organizational Dynamics,* 8, no. 3 (Winter 1980), pp. 2–25.

open-hearth steel furnace, assembling typewriters, and handling customer orders in an office. Use of the basic ideas, however, need not be confined to operating work. We can also create task teams to do managerial work. The best-known examples in this field are from companies using profit decentralization. Here, as with task teams doing operating work, tasks are assigned in blocks that have a natural unity; people with the needed skills are placed within the group; and the team is self-regulating to a high degree. Very little research has been done on social group behavior among executives, yet here lies great opportunity to discover new ways of applying insights on group action to managerial work. The applicability of the task-team concept to both managerial and operating work illustrates the feasibility of adjusting organization design so as to capture benefits from typical group behavior.

## USES OF COMMITTEES

A committee is a group of people specifically designated to perform a managerial act. Both its strengths and its weaknesses arise from assigning the task to a group rather than to one or more individuals. Typically, members devote only part of their time to committee work because they have other major duties.

Committees are particularly useful in situations where group judgment aids in improving the quality of decisions.[12] Group judgment, for example, is the principal reason for the new products committee in the Grayson Pharmaceutical Company. On this committee are representatives from the research, production, marketing, and finance departments. The research representative reports on new products that look promising, and his marketing colleague predicts the potential demand for such products. When these people agree on an item that seems likely to succeed, the production person gives counsel on the costs of manufacturing the new product. The financial member of the team brings all these figures together and compares the anticipated profit rate with that on alternative uses of the company's capital.

All this collective wisdom is used in recommendations by the committee to the president about new products that should be developed. Conceivably, the president could get the same information by talking separately to the representatives who serve on the committee. But, as we noted in our discussion of creativity in Chapter 6, the exchange of ideas in a group provides greater stimulation than an interaction of only two minds at a time. A chain reaction of thought—enhanced by the diverse knowledge and decision-making talents of group members—occurs. John's comment sparks an idea in Betty's mind; Betty's idea may not be useful but it may start Norma on a new line of thought that, when combined with some facts Mark presents, points the way to a solution that no one had thought of before.

[12]A. C. Filley, "Committee Management: Guidelines from Social Science Research," *California Management Review,* 13, no. 1 (1970), pp. 13–21.

Thus, the use of a committee can provide new thoughts and uncover weak points, thereby improving the quality of final recommendations. These benefits from group decision-making will occur, however, only if we develop a permissive atmosphere in which all members of the group freely express their thoughts without being concerned about making an impression on their colleagues or their boss.

A committee can also be a powerful coordinating device for arriving at an integrated decision. By this we mean a decision that takes into account the needs of the various divisions of the company and one that each participant personally accepts as the best that can be worked out in the circumstances. Coordination results because everyone present—manager and subordinates—is influenced by the facts, information, and feelings of everyone else.

This use of a committee to achieve coordination is illustrated by the management committee at Redondo Steel Corporation. The president and all vice-presidents are members, and meetings are devoted largely to reports on current problems. In this way, all vice-presidents are kept informed of one another's activities. Often a coordinated plan is agreed to in a meeting—say, a program for dealing with a strike in one of the divisions—and a background is laid for subsequent person-to-person contacts on special issues, because each member of the committee is informed about the total company.

Both of our illustrations of committee work happen to be top-level committees. In other companies, we might find at lower levels a need for group judgment or coordination that would justify setting up a committee covering a narrow scope of company operations. Occasionally, committees are also established to provide a safe and/or acceptable decision—for instance, a salary committee to ensure that personal bias does not determine who gets a raise or a bonus.

In addition to the possibilities of higher-quality decisions and improved coordination, the use of committees can engender greater acceptance of decisions. If they are fully involved in formulating plans or choosing alternatives, committee members are more likely to support committee decisions and assist in their implementation. By consulting with a committee, instead of one person at a time, a manager can stimulate group cohesion. As friendships and mutual understandings develop among committee members, there will be increased pressure to conform to group standards. For example, a group of office supervisors in a casualty insurance company helped their office manager develop a clerical training program and a procedure for transferring clerks to meet peak loads. Later, when one of the group disregarded the plans, he was sharply criticized by the others. Typical remarks were: "You helped make up the procedure, so why don't you follow it?" and "If you weren't ready to do some training, why didn't you say so?" Had the plans been developed by the office manager with only individual consultation, group pressure to abide by them would not have been nearly so strong.

Committees suffer from some inherent disadvantages[13]—notably (1) the slowness of getting committee members to meet and arrive at a conclusion, (2) the expensive man-hours required for committee meetings, and (3) the possibility that motivational deadlocks will lead to mediocre decisions.

*Slowness* A major risk in using committees is the tendency for committee members to delay decision-making by prolonging the number and length of meetings. In extreme cases, a committee's decision may come too late for strategic effectiveness. For example, the president of a rapidly expanding midwestern bank became concerned with the sharp rate of increase in the bank's operating costs and overhead costs. He established a committee made up of one manager from each of the bank's seven branches to suggest ways for the bank to lower, or at least hold the line on, costs. The committee's mandate was to "examine alternatives for utilizing bank buildings and equipment, and personnel more effectively."

While the committee members attacked their task with zeal, it took eighteen months for their committee to provide a final report. This comprehensive document which was supported by 800 pages of research data and reasoning proposed seventeen recommendations covering such matters as central purchasing policies, equipment standardization, and uniform salary scales. Despite the soundness of some proposals, the considerable delay in managerial action raised doubts within the bank and in the outside financial community about the bank president's real commitment to controlling costs. Moreover, the bank's costs continued to escalate during the committee's eighteen months of deliberation; by the time the final report was available, the overall financial condition of the bank had become precarious.

*Expense* A second disadvantage of committees is the time and cost associated with committee meetings. There are a whole host of situations where the possible gains from the use of a committee are too small to warrant this elaborate a decision-making process. Deciding what plane to take to Denver, how to turn down the request of a vendor's salesman for an interview, or what kind of stationery to buy at the Buffalo branch are typical examples. Of course, if a decision would apply not to a single instance, but would establish a standard method or standing operating procedure, then the use of a committee may be justified.

A manager may, of course, prefer to use committees to *save his time*. By talking with several people at once, and by immediately ironing out any differences in the suggestions they make, the manager may be able to arrive at a decision promptly. Besides, the manager will probably devote less total time to the committee than he would by talking to all the participants separately.

For the other committee participants, however, time will be saved only if they are concerned with all phases of a problem. Otherwise, they may

---

[13]G. E. Manners, Jr., "Another Look at Group Size, Group Problem Solving, and Member Consensus," *Academy of Management Journal,* 18, no. 4 (December 1975), pp. 715–24.

spend hours listening to other people talk about matters on which they can contribute little or nothing. In a meeting called to draw up a schedule for product shipments, for instance, the main issue may be to forecast customers' orders; if so, a plant manager who has been invited to the meeting merely waits until the discussion finally gets around to questions of production capacity and economical runs. Unfortunately, too many executives like to have all their key people present to answer possible questions or make suggestions if needed; so they call a meeting without thinking about the question of who can really contribute and without having regard for the interruption in the activities of their subordinates.

*Deadlocks* If the personal interests of committee members conflict with organizational objectives, motivational deadlocks are likely to occur. Such deadlocks will inhibit committee decision-making and produce unsatisfactory compromises. A regional office equipment manufacturer encountered such difficulties when the president established a committee to develop a system for allocating salesmen to territories more effectively. The members of the committee were the director of marketing, director of administration, and one person from each of the four sales territories. Once it became apparent that the committee's analysis would suggest considerable shifting of people among territories, the salesforce members on the committee became solely concerned about their own geographical preferences. Much foot-dragging ensued with calls for reconsideration of the committee's objectives and reassessment of the committee's analytic approach to the problem. Because the committee was unable to arrive at a consensus recommendation, the president found it necessary to disband the committee and to defer indefinitely decisions on reassigning the salesforce.

## CONCLUSION: THE DYNAMICS OF INFORMAL ORGANIZATION

In this chapter we have emphasized the importance of understanding the informal social systems that develop within an organization.

In a business firm, as in a city government or a local P.T.A., we learn a great deal from organization charts, definition of duties, and other formal statements of how the enterprise is expected to work. Nevertheless, to get a full understanding of an organization, we also need to know which members have the most influence on accepted beliefs, what the prevailing attitude is toward the role of the various officers and executives, what small groups exist and what their influence is, and whether strong cliques are at work.

The social relationships in an organization do not remain static. Because the competition of social groups shifts with time and with changes in personnel, relationships evolve. With these shifting social relationships formal job descriptions and organization manuals tend to become obsolete.

When he includes social dimensions in the total picture, a manager may modify his organization design. Perhaps task teams or some other arrangement that recognizes social behavior in his group will be introduced;

or while thinking about changes in assigned duties, he may give attention to the tugs and pulls of learning new social relationships.

Nothing we have said in this chapter diminishes the need for a formal organization structure to get work done effectively. Our emphasis on social behavior simply indicates that organizing is a more delicate task than it appears when our attention is focused only on the work to be done. By viewing the organization as a social unit rather than as a work-producing machine, a manager can be more skillful in designing the formal structure and in his planning, leading, and controlling.

## FOR FURTHER DISCUSSION

1. Discuss the relationships between matrix management concepts (discussed in Chapter 13) and the need for clarifying expected roles.

2. What steps can management take to shape informal groups so as to facilitate congruence with the organization's goals?

3. How do you account for the fact that the same people may belong to many different kinds of groups?

4. In what ways should decisions on delegation (discussed in Chapter 11) be based on knowledge of the existing informal organization?

5. One of the real dangers of clarifying expected roles is that it can easily lead to stereotyping. What is the difference between clearly defined roles and stereotyping, and why is the latter regarded as a danger?

6. How may the proper use of committees contribute to tying the informal to the formal organization structure?

7. Identify one of your habits. Think of a habitual response that is a relatively *unimportant* aspect of your behavior. Perhaps it is a speech habit or a tendency to walk from one place to another along a prescribed route. Do *not* select a habit that affects you in a *major* way, such as smoking. Having identified such a habit, try to break it. If possible, ask a friend to help by calling it to your attention. How do you feel when this unimportant habit is challenged? How do you explain this feeling?

8. Are strongly held customs and habits likely to be more of a problem when changing strategic directions? Or when revising standing plans?

9. In what ways is the significant increase of women moving into managerial ranks likely to affect the informal organization?

## CASES

For cases involving issues covered in this chapter, see especially the following. Particularly relevant questions are listed after each case.

Elizabeth Archer (p. 96), 12
Camden Chemical (p. 298), 15
Scandico (Singapore) (p. 305), 11
Delphi Insurance (p. 369), 13, 14, 15, 16
Marathon Plastics (p. 456), 10, 11

Aram, J. D., *Dilemmas of Administrative Behavior.* Englewood Cliffs, NJ: Prentice-Hall, 1976, chaps. 5 and 6. Discusses the management dilemma of reconciling individual preferences with group norms.

Gyllenhammer, P., *People at Work.* Reading, MA: Addison-Wesley, 1977. A detailed look at Volvo's innovations in work redesign and the resulting changes in the social system of a plant.

Hackman, J. R., "Group Influences on Individuals," in *Handbook of Industrial and Organizational Psychology,* edited by M. D. Dunnette. Chicago: Rand McNally, 1976. Insightful description of the impact of work groups on individual behavior.

Janis, I., *Victims of Groupthink.* Boston: Houghton Mifflin, 1972. Provocative description of how group processes affected a number of famous and infamous political decisions.

Maier, N., ed., *Problem Solving in Individuals and Groups.* Belmont: Brooks Cole, 1970. Includes articles on group problem solving and decision-making.

Shaw, M. E., *Group Dynamics: The Psychology of Small Group Behavior.* New York: McGraw-Hill, 1971. Good source of behavioral science findings relating to behavior in groups.

# 17

# managing organizational conflict

Learning Objectives

After completing this chapter you should be able to

1. Identify the major sources of intraorganizational conflict.
2. Distinguish between constructive and destructive conflict.
3. Describe the major ways of organizing to deal with conflict.
4. Understand why organizations create desired conflict.
5. Explain the concept of an umpiring system.

Conflict, in the sense of a clash of interests or incompatible desires, is all around us. We do not want our rustic countryside to be spoiled by civilization, and yet growing population forces us to build suburban homes connected by webs of power and telephone lines. We want full employment and at the same time no inflation. We want neighborhood schools and also integrated schools. We want freedom to drive as we please and no petroleum imports. The list goes on and on.

Similarly, within an organization some people will want assurance of jobs and stability, others the excitement of growth and modernization, and still others more pay for a selected few (including themselves). Life is not a grand harmony. Conflict exists. We have to learn how to live with it, how to use it constructively, and how to minimize its destructive aspects.

In this chapter we shall focus on *intraorganizational* conflict. For instance, when Jones's successful pursuit of his purposes would prevent Smith from carrying out his plans, management faces a conflict situation. Because both people cannot fully succeed, a lot of jockeying and infighting may arise. In fact, more effort may be devoted to internal competition than to end results. Such intraorganizational conflict often grows out of divergent goals; however, it is through clash over action—or over proposed action—rather than through a difference in motives that conflict becomes apparent.

Intraorganizational conflict poses four broad questions that are particularly significant to a manager.

1. What are the *sources* of such conflict in organizations?
2. How can we distinguish between *constructive* and *destructive* conflict?
3. How can we *organize* to increase the chances that conflict will be constructive?
4. How can we conduct our *interpersonal relations* to reconcile conflict that cannot be relieved by organization means? This issue is considered in Part V.

**SOURCES OF CONFLICT**   To deal constructively with conflict in his organization, a manager must be sensitive to where the conflict is likely to arise. Let us look at five typical sources.

Committed people want the resources with which to achieve their goals. The researcher looking for new products, the regional manager providing service to New England customers, and the guard charged with protecting the plant—all want equipment, personnel, supplies, and other resources. The total of such requests from all parts of the enterprise usually far exceeds the quantity of resources obtainable, and the resulting scramble is the cause of a lot of action and reaction throughout the organization.[1]

**competition for scarce resources**

Capital budgeting—the allocation of funds for long-run investment—often becomes a focal point for this kind of conflict.[2] We have sophisticated

[1] L. R. Pondy, "Organizational Conflict: Concepts and Models," *Administrative Science Quarterly,* 12, no. 2 (1967), 296–330.
[2] J. L. Bower, *Managing the Resource Allocation Process.* (Boston: Harvard Graduate School of Business Administration, 1970).

techniques for making quantitative comparisons of budget requests, but these do not remove the underlying conflict. Too often the kind of rituals that characterize collective bargaining with labor unions are also present: exaggerated requests, one-sided evidence, bluffing, catering to the personal status of the bargainers, preoccupation with precedent, drawn-out negotiations. If we are not careful, this process can degenerate until both motives and honesty are distorted.

Capital is not the only scarce resource. It is often difficult to expand a company's marketing capability. If product A is given more attention, then product B gets less. This generates tension among those concerned with different products, a tension similar to that found among college department chairmen who are agitating for more courses in their respective fields. Although each chairman recognizes that only so many courses can be added, each feels that the expansion of his department should not be fettered.

Personnel is often scarce, so competition may arise over the allocation of people. In government offices and others, the number of qualified workers sharply affects the ability of a division to expand. So when employment ceilings exist, a scramble to get workers normally ensues.

Competition for scarce resources is such a pervasive feature of organization that managers devote substantial planning and control effort to wise allocations (see parts I and VI). More than technology and economics are involved. If a company allocates resources to a group of employees or to a division, it in effect endorses that group's activities. Thus, allocation of scarce resources for some purposes and not for others is a concrete expression of what the company's strategy really is.

**built-in conflicts**

A second normal source of conflict is deliberately created. In the process of organizing, jobs that breed conflict are designed. Many staff jobs have this characteristic. An industrial engineer, for instance, may be assigned the task of finding more economical methods of making portable cassettes. His new, efficient methods often complicate life for the manager supervising cassette production: workers may resist change because their previous social relations have been upset; quality will be hard to maintain while the new method is being introduced; and schedules must be revised. For the production manager, lower costs are only one of his goals. He is concerned also with the smooth integration of employee attitudes, quality, equipment maintenance, and so on. Consequently he tends to be cautious about new methods, and we are thus likely to find the staff person zealously pushing his special assignment while the line manager drags his feet.[3]

This kind of conflict is aggravated when the staff person is a cocky young college graduate and the line manager is someone who has come up from the ranks and who responds intuitively rather than analytically. Furthermore, the two people will be responding to different criteria of success.

---

[3] J. A. Belasco and J. A. Allutto, "Line and Staff Conflicts: Some Empirical Insights," *Academy of Management Journal*, 12, no. 1 (1969), 469–77.

Then if the change is made successfully, the question of who gets credit is another potential sore point.[4]

Note that staff jobs are frequently established with the express purpose of ensuring adequate attention to an aspect of a total operation that line managers for some reason slight. Moreover, several different staff people often make demands on the same manager—personnel, quality, cost, public relations, safety, to name but a few. By design, each of these has his own ax to grind.

Managers know in advance that the separation of control from operations will occasionally produce conflict. The people concerned with operations are certainly not opposed to dependable quality, fast service, low cost, or other features for which separate control jobs are often established. But the total operating assignment and the conditions under which the work is done are such that independent checks are necessary, and when an independent-control person raises an objection, the operating manager is annoyed.

The very reason for the creation of such staff units and special-purpose operating units is to get more attention for the particular purposes of these units. Managers with other important assignments will be too preoccupied with their own focused objectives. So units that will challenge normal tendencies are built in. From the conflict will come a better-balanced, overall result.

**conflict arising from differences in work characteristics**

The best way to run department A does not necessarily fit smoothly with the best way to run department B. Each type of work has its own optimum technology, and vigorous pursuit of one specialty may make work more difficult for people in related activities.[5]

Friction between production and marketing provides a common illustration of this conflict over optimum technology. Most production will benefit from long runs, standardized products, limited variety, and predictable levels of activity. On the other hand, marketing benefits from a variety of products, special adaptations that fit customer desires, fast changes, and prompt delivery. Under these circumstances, the marketing manager may make requests of production that the production manager feels will hinder him from doing his job well, and vice versa.

A research director, to note another common conflict, seeks unique products or processes and insists on high quality. Long lead times are needed for experimentation, and output is limited to the test tube or pilot plant; hence a research director's priorities differ from those of a production chief or marketing manager.

Differences in technology prevail in all kinds of enterprises. Of course, steps are taken to mediate such conflicts. To achieve overall organization

---

[4]R. H. Miles, "Role Requirements as Sources of Organizational Stress," *Journal of Applied Psychology,* 61 (1976), 172–79.

[5]J. A. Seiler, "Diagnosing Interdepartmental Conflict," *Harvard Business Review,* 41 (September-October 1963), 121–32.

goals, some departments must deviate from practices that are optimum when each department is considered separately. Our point here is that people who know that their job could be done better if they did not have to cater to an alien activity find it hard to accept these compromises.

**divergent personal values and aims**

Paul R. Lawrence and Jay W. Lorsch point to a further reason for conflict between functional departments.[6] The personal values of the type of person who is attracted, say, to research differ sharply from those of a person in production. The researcher is usually intrigued with the unknown, places a high value on scientific "truth," is prepared to wait weeks or months to get an answer, and thinks other people should act as rationally as *he* does. In contrast, the usual production worker prefers to deal with known phenomena, has a practical and intuitive sense of what is right, wants prompt and positive action, and is more comfortable with authoritarian relationships. The typical sales executive has still another set of values, ways of dealing with people, and time span within which he wants to see results. When people with such different orientations try to solve a mutual problem, they quickly find that they don't talk the same language.

Divergence of personal values often comes to the surface in government agencies. One person may advocate a cause (better jobs for blacks or equal rights for women), another may want to follow a strict interpretation of established law, and a third may stress current responsiveness to the electorate or party leaders. They will agree on some matters but sooner or later will find themselves in conflict.

Two people seeking the same job have a clear conflict in aims. A system of promotion-from-within on the basis of merit deliberately places people in competition for more attractive jobs. There are traditions governing appropriate methods of competition—like the medieval codes of chivalry in combat—but ambitious people sometimes resort to sharp internal politics, aggressive bids for recognition, and adroit maneuvering. Even when promotion is not at stake, some compete aggressively for recognition and status.

**ambiguous organization**

Another common source of conflict in organization is lack of agreement on who should do what. For instance, in one company the president thought

[6] P. R. Lawrence and J. W. Lorsch, *Organization and Environment: Managing Differentiation and Integration* (Boston: Harvard Graduate School of Business Administration, 1967).

*Figure 17.1 Divergent values lead to intergroup conflict, especially when each group holds strong views about the use of a limited resource, such as land. Within an enterprise, too, managers and supervisors vie with one another for a share of available personnel, equipment, supplies, and funds.*

the controller's job was to establish accurate accounting records, to compare actual expenses with the budget, and to point out deviations to all executives directly concerned. The controller himself thought that he should press executives to avoid budget overruns and should report only unresolved deviations to the president. A newly appointed operations-research director thought the controller's task was only to maintain accounting records and to make accounting information available on request from other executives. The ill will that grew out of this role ambiguity lasted far beyond the three months required to reach a formal agreement.

Jurisdictional squabbles can arise anywhere, from the senior level down to the operating level, where, for instance, it may not be clear who can commit the company to deliver a special order on Sunday. Job scope is not a trifling matter, as nationwide strikes over jurisdictional lines demonstrate. Many firms prepare written job descriptions only irregularly, and even when more systematic attention is given, such descriptions can never be complete and are soon outdated. The more dynamic the company, the more likely are conflicts to arise from ambiguous organization.

Unclear strategy also invites personal or informal group conflict. People may differ sharply on how the company should proceed. For instance, in the early 1980s executives within the American Motors Company disagreed on the importance of forming a partnership with a foreign auto company. Until that issue was firmly resolved, various factions were jockeying for influence and power.

## CONSTRUCTIVE AND DESTRUCTIVE CONFLICT

Conflict within organizations can be constructive or destructive, as the preceding review of likely sources indicates. Although destructive conflict captures more attention, the positive effects can be substantial if we keep the pressures within bounds.

**constructive conflict**

Built-in conflict, as we have observed, deliberately seeks the benefits of an *additional viewpoint* or an *extra check*. Staff positions frequently are created to ensure that a particular aspect of operations—quality control, product development, personnel training, public relations, and the like—gets adequate attention. The external staff described in Chapter 12 improves the quality of major decisions, and the very existence of controls, though sometimes irritating, leads to careful performance of operations that will be evaluated.

Self-satisfied, complacent personnel are less likely to be found where some conflict serves as a prod. When challenge to improve is lacking, companies, like nations, tend to become soft and cater to the convenience of those in charge. Rivalry and competition call forth extra effort. As in athletic competition, recognition, status, and the sheer fun of winning stimulate people to try harder. Within organizations, conflict stirs people to think up new alternatives, to make sure results exceed standard, to anticipate trouble, and to alter their usual patterns. The manager's aim, of course, is to see that this extra effort is focused on company objectives.

**destructive conflict**

In contrast to the potential benefits just discussed, conflict inevitably produces emotional stress. We can all stand some degree of stress; research even suggests that a little stress serves as a tonic. But when stress goes beyond the invigorating stage, it becomes debilitating.

Furthermore, conflict pressed too energetically carries some activities beyond a useful service. The hospital clerk is overly concerned with his subgoal if he places his need for tidy files above a patient's desire to return home and keeps that patient sitting until all records are neat. Likewise, an airline-ramp service director charged with cleaning planes sometimes insists on completing his task meticulously even when his thorough cleaning of rugs conflicts with getting planes off on schedule. In terms of balanced customer service, the clerk and the service director are "suboptimizing." That is, by pursuing their subgoals to an optimum point, they are detracting so much from other desirable results that the overall service is hurt. A similar danger exists for almost all staff services.

The most detrimental effect of conflict is goal distortion. In the budgeting process, for example, if the marketing department must request double the appropriation it needs in order to end up with the correct amount, the integrity of communication becomes suspect. Likewise, legal or personnel needs may be overstated in anticipation of watering down, at the approval stage or in practice, in response to conflicting pressures. One way of describing this behavior is to say that people start "playing games"—perhaps bitter personal games—instead of pursuing their assigned mission.

**escalation of conflict**

Any internal conflict, either constructive or destructive in its original form, becomes very destructive if it is carried too far. When a conflict gets out of control, a variety of behaviors are likely. Adversaries suspect each other's motives and read sinister intent into almost any action. With suspicions aroused, each makes stronger demands on the other. Any failure to achieve outstanding results is blamed on the other party, and one's own behavior is defended—often in an emotional and nonrational manner. At this stage, information is withheld and distorted; so what actually happens, and why,

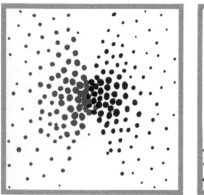 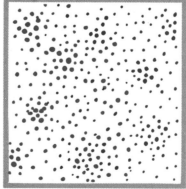

*Figure 17.2 Polarization and depolarization of conflict. At left, lines of conflict are clearly defined, the clash is sharp, and all elements rally on either side of the issue. At right, vague clusters hint at potential issues, but there is some mingling of feelings; and the cluster that is forming in the center at the bottom suggests a genuine coalition.*

is unknown. Soon there is deliberate sabotage of the adversary's moves. To "win" is now much more important than to accomplish any original operational goal.

In international affairs we can read accounts of such behavior in the daily papers. Within companies, an escalated conflict rarely surfaces. But unfortunately many of the same responses occur under a superficial politeness. Clearly we need mechanisms that forestall this sort of escalation.

## ORGANIZING TO DEAL WITH CONFLICT

Behavioral-science writers have for many years assumed that conflict was undesirable and concentrated on ways of minimizing it. Primary attention was on individual attitudes and interpersonal responses. Recent writing, however, has shifted to channeling and harnessing constructive conflict.[7] Actually, conflict is such a pervasive aspect of organized action that a manager has to consider it in all phases of management—planning, organizing, leading, and controlling.

At this point in our analysis, we are pulling out for special emphasis some of the ways a manager can use *organization* to create, restrain, or eliminate conflict. Earlier, in Part II, we discussed approaches for reconciling conflict and securing consensus in organizational decision-making; additional ways of dealing with conflict will be considered in Parts V and VI.

**create desired conflict**

First, we reemphasize that some forms of conflict are useful and may be deliberately created. For instance, to secure adequate, expert, independent attention to a special aspect of an operation, a manager can establish a separate staff unit. Recently, to cite a specific activity, some company presidents have set up units to promote the employment of blacks. In addition to providing counsel and special-training facilities, such a unit prods supervisors to put forth extra effort to accommodate the new worker.

Separate control units are also commonly used. In order to permit independent action, such things as inspection, audit, and cost control are set apart from the operations they control. Such independence and divergence of objectives promote conflict, but the net effect on overall results justifies the separation.

Competition can be introduced by setting up a series of similar operating units and making regular comparisons of their results—the deadly parallel. Retail outlets, bank branches, national forests, social-security offices, and TV stations are only a few of the many activities in which this concept can be applied. When units operate at separate locations, conflict between them centers largely on status and allocation of scarce resources, so cooperation is not vital.

These examples indicate that conflict, like fire, can be a useful force when properly directed.

---

[7] K. Thomas, "Conflict and Conflict Management," in *Handbook of Industrial and Organizational Psychology,* edited by M. D. Dunnette, (Chicago: Rand McNally, 1976).

**establish an
umpiring system**

Whenever conflict units are deliberately set up—and in many other situations when units compete for scarce resources—a mechanism for guiding the conflict is necessary.[8] Formally established strategy and other plans set the framework within which conflict is to occur; and points in the organization are designated to make the inevitable choices.

To prevent such conflicts from escalating, an agency is needed to settle the matter quickly, an *umpire* who will "call the play" promptly according to a set of known criteria so that the game can go on. Not everyone may like the decision, but the issue ceases to be an open invitation for strife, and all people concerned can proceed to more constructive activities. Because the criteria for judging are known, conflicting parties can often anticipate the decisions of the umpire and adjust their behavior accordingly, thus solving the conflict even before it is necessary to arbitrate.

The usual "umpire" is the boss—the executive who directly or through intermediaries supervises the conflicting parties. In small enterprises and within single departments, the senior executive normally knows both the

[8] R. E. Walton and J. M. Dutton, "The Management of Interdepartmental Conflict: A Model and Review," *Administrative Science Quarterly,* 14 (1968), 73–84.

*Figure 17.3* *When conflict is deliberately built in to an organization, safeguards are needed to prevent the escalation of conflict. One useful device is an "umpire" to "call the plays" promptly.*

UPI

local facts and general objectives well enough to allocate funds and resources wisely. In addition he can maintain the desired balance between line and staff.

For more complex operations, however, the careful evaluation of the alternative uses of resources is a major task in itself. Here it is best to designate an individual or committee to make the allocation. In addition, a procedure specifying the information and opinions supporting a request for resources should be clearly stated. Such a setup is fairly common for capital allocation and for financial budgets, but the mechanisms for resolving other kinds of bargaining conflicts often require special designs.

The use of a committee for allocation purposes creates another organization problem. Who should be on the committee? A committee composed of competing parties merely provides a forum for continued conflict, and its decisions are likely to reflect logrolling rather than company objectives. So if group judgment is desired, a committee of objective members is clearly preferable.

A provision for appeals is common. Typically an appeal moves up the rungs of the management hierarchy. If a manager feels that a resource allocation will cause great harm, or if either line or staff people feel that their scope has been unwisely confined, a request for modification is made. Here again, decisions by senior umpires usually become precedents—as in common law—and influence the way future choices will be made by lower-level umpires. By explicitly relating the bases for such choices to company strategy, the umpires guide conflict behavior toward desired action.

**design integrated units**

When conflict resolution calls for frequent and varied adjustment in the activities of several people or several units, an umpire system becomes slow and unwieldy. In these circumstances, grouping together the interrelated activities may be the best way to localize the conflict. Three examples of this arrangement have already been discussed.

1.  In Chapter 10 we noted that compound groups rather than functional groups enable operators to adjust their own efforts so that a completed piece of work is produced. An airplane crew and a surgical team are classic examples. The conflicting pressures are still present, for we have retained specialists with their inevitable differences in perspective and values. However, the compound group is small enough so that the need for coordination is evident and personal face-to-face communication is natural. Social pressure promotes self-coordination.

2.  The concept of self-sufficient operating units, which we discussed under "profit decentralization" in Chapter 11, also encourages localized resolution of conflicts. Here again the persons whose work pulls them toward conflicting positions are placed in the same organization unit. Hopefully, the central mission becomes the overriding objective, and frequent personal contacts provide the occasions to iron out conflicts. Furthermore, a senior executive is on the spot to umpire when needed.

3.  Project teams in matrix organizations, described in Chapter 13, utilize the same principle. The association of specialists needed for the project is temporary, but the hope is that these persons will be able to adapt their respective professional

orientations to the task at hand. Usually this happens. If conflict arises, it typically is not within the project team but between the project team and the service departments and usually concerns the allocation of resources.

Integrated units, such as those just cited, can be very helpful in avoiding destructive conflict. Unfortunately this arrangement is not always practical. The cost of pulling a small piece of a functional unit away from the major department may be high and may result in intense disturbance. Technology may prevent the separation, or the departments may lack people with sufficient competence to exercise the decentralized authority needed in an integrated team. A piece of computer cannot be split off, nor can a fraction of an advertising executive. Integrated units are a useful approach but not a panacea.

**separate the contestants**

A design that is the opposite of an integrated unit may be necessary in some circumstances. If we conclude that the conflicting parties simply cannot work together, then organizational separation *plus* a liaison mechanism can be a useful alternative.

A classic example of this approach is reported in W. F. Whyte's study of restaurant operations.[9] The cooks—the skilled élite in a restaurant—strongly dislike taking orders from waitresses or runners who have less status. The waitresses, under pressure from customers, are persistent in their requests, and all too often the conflict over priorities and quality escalates into personal feuds with disastrous results to customer service. In this situation a mechanical system for communicating customer wants to the cooks removes the personal interaction initiated by the waitresses. The status of cooks, the evidence shows, is not hurt by receiving a sequence of inert written requests, and the waitresses learn to wait outside the kitchen until the number of their order is flashed on a screen. The opportunity for cooks and waitresses to get into a hassle is eliminated.

A comparable separation is used by successful plastics companies. In this field, frequent changes in technology and in customer requirements put pressure on relationships between research, production, and marketing. But differences in the attitudes of people in these departments, and of costs, quality, and personal behavior, are so great that they have difficulty communicating. Therefore they are kept apart, and an integrating unit serves as a liaison. The liaison person can talk the language of each department and so becomes an influential mediator of inherent conflict.

Incidentally, a go-between is often used in Eastern cultures. To avoid the embarrassment of an open disagreement or conflict, a third person serves as an intermediary until a mutually acceptable course of action is identified. Not until then do the principals directly discuss the proposition. Most Westerners prefer direct confrontation. But if status differences or other sources of incompatibility are major irritants, we may find that separation and the use of an intermediary are useful.

[9] W. F. Whyte, *Men At Work* (Homewood, IL: Irwin, 1961), chap. 8.

All the preceding suggestions for dealing with conflict assume that it will continue to be present. However, some destructive conflict is avoidable. Confusion about the approved organization, for instance, can be cleared up by managerial action. Perhaps formal job definitions have to be interpreted, and the words have to be backed up by action consistent with them. This can be done.

More complicated but also desirable is making sure that procedures, information flows, and especially control standards and evaluations match the organization design. If a set of clear, consistent roles is understood and accepted, one unnecessary source of conflict is removed.

Even after these steps are taken, some conflict will remain—the tension built in to get its benefits, and the friction that is a by-product of meeting other organizational needs. Managing this remaining conflict will be considered in Part V.

## CONCLUSION: CONFLICT AND GROWTH

In this chapter we have considered conflict that arises in relatively stable situations. Growth or a shift in company or corporate strategy further complicates the picture. By upsetting established relationships, by introducing new priorities for allocating resources, and by increasing uncertainty, a whole array of latent conflicts flare anew.

The basic sources of conflict, its nature, and its potential usefulness and costs are still the same. but company growth means that a manager must work out a revised set of mechanisms and ground rules. The organizational arrangements just discussed will probably have to be adapted to the new situation. Even more demanding of managerial time will be controlling and leading during the transition. A manager's skill in two-way communication and in gaining acceptance of new objectives will strongly affect the type of conflict that emerges during this unsettled period. We will return to these aspects of the manager's job in Part V.

## FOR FURTHER DISCUSSION

1. How may the increase of women in executive positions affect (1) levels of conflict and (2) the likelihood of constructive resolution of conflict?

2. What effect may a large number of standing plans have on levels and forms of conflict? Consider both positive and negative effects.

3. Discuss the relative merits and drawbacks of using go-betweens to aid in conflict resolution as compared with the direct confrontation approach. Consider criteria that would serve as useful guides in deciding when one approach is more appropriate than the other.

4. Is conflict more or less likely in implementing strategic decisions than tactical ones? When is constructive conflict more important for strategic or tactical decisions?

5. "I not only believe conflict, when it arises, to be potentially valuable, but in many situations I will seek to create conflict between evenly matched individuals or departments. There's nothing like a little competition to help find the fittest." What is your opinion of this statement by an advocate of "managerial Darwinism"?

6. Assume that a situation exists in which conflict arises from differences in objectives and in which outcomes are relatively certain. How may discussion of higher-level objectives (broader ends for which the conflicting objectives may be seen as means) aid in resolving such conflict?

7. In what ways may decisions on decentralization affect the potential for creating and identifying conflict? Relate your answers to the material in Chapters 11 and 13.

8. How do group behavior and informal organizational factors (discussed in Chapter 16) affect (1) levels of conflict, (2) forms of conflict, and (3) likelihood of successful resolution?

## CASES

For cases involving issues covered in this chapter, see especially the following. Particularly relevant questions are listed after each case.

## FOR FURTHER READING

Filley, A. C., *Interpersonal Conflict Resolution.* Glenview: Scott, Foresman, 1975. Useful guidelines and suggestions for resolving interpersonal conflict.

Miles, R. H., *Macro Organizational Behavior.* Santa Monica: Goodyear Publishing Co., 1980, chap. 5. Good summary of sources of conflict and strategies for managing conflict.

Nightingale, D., "Conflict and Conflict Resolution," *Organizational Behavior, Research and Issues,* G. Strauss, et al., eds. Madison: Industrial Relations Research Association, 1974. Clear statement of the nature of conflict as seen by (a) human relationists and (b) pluralists, and the proposals of each group for conflict resolution. Very useful framework for sorting out diverse views about conflict in many areas of management.

Robbins, S. P., *Managing Organizational Conflict.* Englewood Cliffs, NJ: Prentice-Hall, 1974. Explains why and how intra-organization conflict should be managed, including the possibility of making constructive use of conflict.

Thomas, K., "Conflict and Conflict Management," in *Handbook of Industrial and Organizational Psychology,* M. D. Dunnette, ed. Chicago: Rand McNally, 1976. Develops a valuable framework for analyzing individual conflict-management styles.

# not-for-profit note for part IV

**MOTIVATING IN NOT-FOR-PROFIT ENTERPRISES**

The personal and social pressures that we have been examining in Part IV bear similarly on not-for-profit enterprises. Personal needs, group behavior, and intergroup conflict call for similar modifications in the organization structure of every kind of joint venture. And the task of matching designed jobs and individuals arises in all organizations.

Certain characteristics that are strong in some—although not all—not-for-profit enterprises do, however, complicate the process of refining the organization structure.

A large number of "professionals," for example, make job enlargement and job enrichment difficult. In medicine, education, social work, and elsewhere we see increasingly narrow specialization—neurologists, psychiatrists, pediatricians, vocational counselors, music teachers, speech therapists, choreographers, anesthetists, and numerous other specialists. Each field requires special training, and most have rigid qualification examinations. Such professions develop their own code of conduct, values, and beliefs; and they have rather sharp ideas about what activities are—and are not—within their province.

One or more of these professions often play a crucial role in a hospital, school, welfare agency, or other not-for-profit enterprise. In fact, members of an established profession view the enterprise in which they work largely as a place for them to practice their profession. But for the enterprise manager, such high professional orientation adds rigidity. The manager runs into resistance if he tries to modify traditional boundaries of professions. In hospitals, for instance, the use of paramedics is typically regarded as unethical. On the other hand, expanding job content—commonly called job enrichment—often encounters, "That's not my specialty; it is not what I was hired to do." To a large extent, where professionals predominate, a manager must design his organization to appeal to prevailing professional norms.

The dominance of professionals in not-for-profit organizations may also limit the way in which a manager can motivate subordinates. Professional groups have actively supported tenure in educational organizations, "civil service" rules in government, and seniority rules in union contracts. These rules originate to prevent abuses of managerial power—to protect academic freedom, to guard against the "political-spoils" system, to stop a boss from favoring only his friends. But in addition to preventing abuses, the rules also sharply restrict managers' power to promote legitimate goals of the enterprise. Although restraints on the use of managerial power are also found in profit-making ventures, they are more common in the not-for-profit group. Such shackles on managerial power invite insubordination.

Fortunately, *commitment to enterprise goals* is often strong among workers in libraries, clinics, child-care centers, and many other not-for-profit enterprises. Even though a manager's power may be limited this impotence is not serious *if* satisfactions from the work itself provide the motivation to accept instructions.

Commitment to service goals, however, is often qualified for the following reasons. First, as an enterprise grows and the work is subdivided the persons doing routine tasks may have difficulty relating their task to the lofty service goal. Especially when some elite group of actors, doctors, or curators dominates the planning and the limelight, the lesser folk (stagehands, orderlies, and caretakers) may feel that "commitment to the cause" has a hollow ring.

Second, a person's predominant commitment may be to personally performing a service, and he supports the enterprise only as a means of doing his thing. Thus, a devoted teacher who has taught generations of students English grammar may be quite uncommitted to a new educational objective of social adjustment. The very fact that a person is committed—to any goal—means that he is less adaptable to shifts in goals of his employer.

These considerations indicate that managers in not-for-profit enterprises cannot assume that all employees will have strong commitment to enterprise goals. The not-for-profit manager is, in fact, continually challenged to create the type of work environment which increases the likelihood of commitment.

Unhealthy conflict is perhaps a greater danger within not-for-profit enterprises than in profit-seeking companies. A combination of two factors may produce sharp conflict. The main creators of services—such as opera singers, research scientists, or kindergarten teachers—are likely to have aspirations and values that differ sharply from those of the financial manager of the enterprise for which they work. The football coach has aims that don't match those of the history professor, and so on. Often compounding such divergence in personal aims is the absence of a clear, overriding enterprise objective that can be used to arbitrate disagreements among the functional specialists. Many not-for-profit enterprises have multiple goals—for example, most universities promote research, teaching, community service and the glory of alma mater. The combination of differing personal values and ambiguous enterprise goals opens the way for destructive infighting.

Each not-for-profit enterprise has its own characteristics. It may or may not have unusual difficulty with job enlargement, or internal conflict as briefly outlined in this note. As cues to potential problems along these lines, we should look carefully at professionalization among employees, and at multiple or ambiguous goals that open the way for internal bickering.

"During the next ten years, we will find out who the best managers are," said George Hankinson, chairman of Delphi Insurance. "There just aren't that many 'tricks' in this business. Most of the industry leaders, by now, have evolved a strategy and determined which niches to go after. The companies which come out on top are going to be the ones who implement well . . . who can make it happen, and that means management."

Hankinson was addressing the top twenty-four executives at Delphi. As the first speaker, he set the theme for a three-day meeting held at the Spring Vale Country Club. He had called this meeting to consider how to (1) identify, (2) develop, and (3) utilize more fully middle management talent.

"This company has already moved into the top five in our industry. I want Delphi to be number one in profits, if not in volume, in the next ten years and we are going to do it through better management and more highly motivated personnel. While I hope for new services, new markets, new wrinkles, we are not going to count on them as the key to our continued growth. We are going to get there primarily by doing the same basic things our competition does but doing them better and doing them for less. Through motivation and management, we will get there. We must get more from *fewer* people, not so much to reduce payroll costs, but to improve effectiveness by challenging people with more demanding jobs.

"Ladies and gentlemen, I am proud of you! I believe that the group in this room includes the finest top executives in this industry. I also believe that we have at the bottom of this organization tens of thousands of outstanding hourly producers. Our agents, actuaries, underwriters, analysts, etc. are, in my judgment, the best group in the world.

"But—ladies and gentlemen, our *middle* is flabby and very, very mediocre! We are a company whose success stems from two dozen geniuses at the top and thousands of highly competent, well-motivated producers at the bottom, but our middle management ranks are overstaffed in terms of numbers and layers, and understaffed in terms of ability. We have too many mediocre people shuffling papers and keeping each other busy. We undoubtedly also have in these layers too many good, once-good, could-be-good, managers being suffocated by the absence of challenge and our continued acceptance of mediocre performance on their part and that of their peers.

"This will change! I want us to develop plans to reduce the number of layers, combine jobs, and do whatever is necessary to develop *fewer, more challenging* positions. Then, through attrition and dismissal, we will thin the ranks and shift to the new structure. Simultaneously, we must develop systems to find those who want to grow, to help them grow, and to give them *bigger* jobs though not necessarily *higher-level* jobs. The purpose of this meeting is to work through what has to be done, *this year,* to move quickly in these directions."

Leroy Carthage, a senior vice-president and a man of considerable independent income, was the first to respond to Hankinson's statements.

"George," he said, "I have been part of Delphi for almost forty years now. In four or five more, I'll collect my clock and retire, so I don't care much whether we try out your notion or not, but frankly I think you're making a big mistake.

"You are dead right in your description of what *is* right now. I don't know about that genius stuff but you have twenty-four of the best senior vice-presidents in this industry. You are also right when you describe our lower-level people as outstanding individual contributors. Finally, you are dead right in describing our middle management ranks as 'havens for hacks.' But George, I truly believe you are wrong to try to change it. Most of those middle management jobs require detail-oriented bureaucrats to somehow get all the papers shuffled properly. They are dull, routine, uninspiring, nongrowth supervisory and middle management positions but they are *necessary.*

"If you put really good high-potential people in those jobs, they will go nuts in a year. Face it George, there are lots of dull, boring jobs that just have to be done. I don't think you can change these jobs. Let's just be grateful that there are enough dull, boring people to do them."

"You were born two hundred years too late, Leroy," Hankinson quipped. "You could have been a great Louis XIV or at least Marie Antoinette's baker. If we don't try to strengthen the quality of people by creating more demanding jobs, where will we find replacements for those in this room when the time comes?"

"This group can be replaced," said Leroy, "the same way it was built. There will always be a few people with talent who want *so badly* to escape the mediocrity of middle management they will somehow rise above it. If we don't find someone at the right time, we will do just what we did with Jeb and Franklyn"—pointing to the corporate counsel and executive vice-president of finance. "We'll go hunting at IBM or Exxon or G. E. George, all you are going to do is raise a lot of people's expectations and ultimately disappoint them when we can't keep delivering new challenges. It's better that you just let them write notes to each other and snooze a bit. Finally, George, if you do try to change things, you are going to have one hell of a transition. What do we do with several thousand long-service, middle managers who are very well suited to their current jobs but can't handle a bigger one and won't accept a smaller one?"

The other senior officers remained silent throughout this exchange. Some looked uncomfortable, several smiled and exchanged winks.

"I hear you, Leroy," said Hankinson, "loud and clear, but we *will* change things. Do you realize that with 'assistant to's' and 'deputy this and that's' there are seven levels of management between you and the hourly people in your division? I'm not singling you out as the worst offender, either. This is, to me, totally unacceptable. I want fewer layers, better people, and probably fewer people. We have sound strategies for our several businesses. In fact, they were sound five years ago, but by the time things creak up and down this pyramid, we waste millions of dollars and many opportunities. We must get fewer, better, more self-motivated managers *throughout* this organization.

"I heard Leroy's views. What do the rest of you think? We *will* get started; the question is how."

## CASE 4.1b
## DELPHI INSURANCE

Roger Whitehall, executive vice-president of corporate affairs, sat at his desk reviewing material on his task force assignment. Following George Hankinson's remarks at what came to be known as "Spring Vale, One," all who attended considered means of meeting the chairman's challenge. Ultimately, task forces made up of participants in "Spring Vale, One" were formed to examine major elements of Hankinson's objectives. Whitehall had been asked to coordinate the work of several groups looking for ways to reduce the number of layers of management throughout the corporation. By way of getting started, he decided to look at his own areas of responsibility and had requested information on any efforts which had been made recently to "flatten the pyramid" (reduce layers) in his area.

One project attempted by an accounts payable group caught his eye. The organization hierarchy from Whitehall to this group is shown in Exhibit 1. Almost two years ago, Ted Gotlieb, a department manager, had attempted an experiment with the six sections reporting to him at the time. Four sections he left as they were but he combined the work of the remaining two sections reporting to him. This new "experimental section," which came to be known as the "can do" section, was organized quite differently from any of the remaining twenty-eight sections reporting, through department managers to assistant vice-president, Virginia Ebberly. These twenty-eight other sections typically consisted of a section head, four shift supervisors (most sections worked a three-shift, seven-day week schedule), four technical assistants, and twenty-five to thirty clerks. The "can do" section was recruited from personnel throughout the controller's division. A series of tests were developed and used to select approximately two dozen candidates for positions in this section. After six months of training, carried out part-time, eighteen people qualified for the "can do" section. It was hoped that they would be able to accomplish equal or higher productivity than other

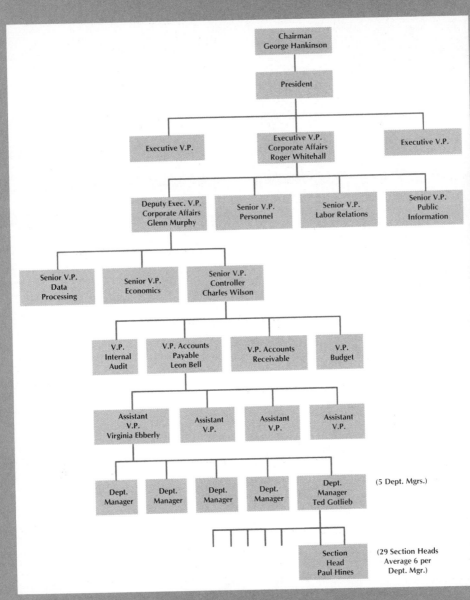

Chairman
George Hankinson

President

Executive V.P.

Executive V.P.
Corporate Affairs
Roger Whitehall

Executive V.P.

Deputy Exec. V.P.
Corporate Affairs
Glenn Murphy

Senior V.P.
Personnel

Senior V.P.
Labor Relations

Senior V.P.
Public
Information

Senior V.P.
Data
Processing

Senior V.P.
Economics

Senior V.P.
Controller
Charles Wilson

V.P.
Internal
Audit

V.P. Accounts
Payable
Leon Bell

V.P. Accounts
Receivable

V.P.
Budget

Assistant
V.P.
Virginia Ebberly

Assistant
V.P.

Assistant
V.P.

Assistant
V.P.

Dept.
Manager

Dept.
Manager

Dept.
Manager

Dept.
Manager

Dept.
Manager
Ted Gotlieb

(5 Dept. Mgrs.)

Section
Head
Paul Hines

(29 Section Heads
Average 6 per
Dept. Mgr.)

*Exhibit I*

sections typically having thirty-three to thirty-seven people. Much greater knowledge and use of data processing, more highly trained personnel, very high esprit-de-corps characterized this group. One year after the department began its work, this group was maintaining an average output forty per cent higher than other sections with half the staff. In addition, error rates were significantly lower than in any other section. Even given slightly higher salaries for the clerical people, the section's total payroll cost was thirty percent lower than other sections.

During the next five months, however, the experiment seemed to sour. Paul Hines, the young section head, reported a surprising drop in motivation, output, and quality of work.

"The first signs of trouble showed up about five months ago," Hines said. "I reviewed the shift supervisor's appraisals and talked personally with all personnel. Given their outstanding performance record and their excellent performance reviews, I thought this would be a real pleasure. I had kind words and raises for everyone. While they seemed pleased, I was surprised to pick up an undercurrent of dissatisfaction. Some were at least a little upset with what they considered 'sniping' and 'teasing' directed at them by members of other sections. Most accepted my explanation of this as jealousy but were still upset by it.

"More troublesome to me was an even more common phenomenon. At least a dozen, while pleased with their results, asked me, in effect, what comes next? Here they are doing much more important, much more difficult work than any other section and getting paid and recognized for it, and after only one year they are asking for more."

In an effort to deal with what Hines considered potentially dangerous symptoms, he instituted a number of changes. In collaboration with three other sections, he began training part-time clerks in these sections to handle the more complex work of his section.

"My plan was to get another nine people trained and then rotate the twenty-seven between my eighteen positions and nine slots in other sections," Hines explained.

"I hoped this would help me in four ways. *First,* it would give me some back-up. With only eighteen people, I'd be in trouble if I lost two or three at one time. With some of my original eighteen starting to show prima donna signs, I wanted to be ready. *Second,* since all of my eighteen eventually would spend one-third of their time in other sections, they would be reminded how much better off they are with me. *Third,* the rotation gives me a chance to share the wealth a bit and might reduce inter-section jealousy. *Fourth,* and finally, this arrangement gives me flexibility and protection at minimum cost. While I would have to maintain all twenty-seven at a slightly higher pay grade, even when they are doing easier work in other sections, the cost is minimal and I can justify it on the basis of their versatility.

"Once word got out as to what we had in mind, I had a delegation of my original eighteen, strongly protesting this 'further dilution of their work.' Further? Where do they come off with 'further'? I was so upset with the arrogance of the delegation I had to bite my tongue. Since then—three months ago—output is down, absenteeism and error rates are up. I have just about gotten the new nine ready but I'm not certain whether to begin the rotation. I have asked my boss, Ted Gotlieb, for advice. He has bucked it up to Virginia Ebberly who took it to Leon Bell, the big boss. From what I heard,

Bell has taken this one up even higher because of some studies going on at corporate. Originally, we hoped if this experiment worked we might overhaul at least all of Gotlieb's sections or even try it throughout accounts payable. Now, I'm not sure it makes sense. Our original improvements just may not be sustainable. The old Hawthorne Effect[1] may account for the short-term improvement and we may have caused more problems than it is worth."

Roger Whitehall has heard the essence of Hines' views through intermediaries who tend to be even more pessimistic about the experiment than Hines.

"Maybe this is a case we should discuss in one of our task forces," said Whitehall. "If this is indicative of what we may run into when we try it at managerial levels, we ought to know it. On the other hand, this is only one situation and after all, they were only clerks so perhaps we would get different results with managers and senior professionals. Since we may kick this around for months, I'd better get word out to handle this at local levels. If they wait for us to get the implications of this one fleshed out at my level, they could have a mess on their hands."

## FOR DISCUSSION AND REPORT-WRITING

part I: planning:
the execution of
strategy

1. What do you think of Hankinson's "strategy" to concentrate on implementation of existing strategies rather than seek to modify or add to them in any significant manner?

2. Hankinson seems to place a great deal of emphasis on the role of managers in bringing about improved results. How appropriate do you feel his optimism is for a company such as this in the insurance industry?

3. If Hankinson succeeds in reducing the number of layers of management and increasing the quality of middle management personnel, how *should* that affect the need for, and types of, standing plans?

4. Hankinson and Carthage apparently disagree on *means* of improving productivity, not *ends*. How might a good diagnosis of the whole situation help them reconcile their differences?

5. How should Hankinson test his choice of the best way to improve company results before making major changes in the organization? Might the current task forces help? What are their other roles?

6. How appropriate, in your opinion, is Hankinson's participative approach to implementing his decisions? In what ways might it be better or worse to have involved only a few key people and developed more detailed plans before informing or involving others?

[1] Studies of Western Electric's Hawthorne plant indicated that productivity improvements may result more from the *attention* given an experimental group than from basic changes in their work. Such improvements tend to disappear as attention and the novelty decline.

7. Estimate the likely impact of Hankinson's plans, if they are successfully implemented, on each of the six key factors in departmentation.

part III:
organizing:
strategy to
structure

8. How might an educated outside analyst determine whether Hines has decentralized too much to his "can do" section?

9. How might Hankinson test the validity of Carthage's statement, "If you put good . . . people in those jobs, they will go nuts in a year"? Does Hines' experiment confirm Carthage's assertion? Why? Why not?

10. What will be needed in Delphi to meet short-run and long-run personnel planning needs if Hankinson's decisions are to be implemented effectively?

11. Comment on Carthage's comment that "There are lots of dull, boring jobs that just have to be done. I don't think you can change these jobs. Let's just be grateful that there are enough dull, boring people to do them."

part IV:
motivating: human
factors in the
organization

12. How do *you* account for the initial improvement in results and the apparent subsequent decline in motivation?

13. Why do you think Hines' recent efforts to deal with "unhealthy symptoms" have had the impact they have on the motivation of the original eighteen members of his section?

14. What responses do you forecast from Hines' section (all twenty-seven) if he goes ahead with his plans?

15. Hankinson's plans will have a major impact on informal groups, customs, and roles in middle management levels. What steps should be taken to deal with this impact?

16. (Summary Report Question, Part IV) Suppose Hines was involved in an automobile accident and will be away for a long time. You are his replacement. What specific steps would you take with regard to the "can do" section?

17. How would you characterize Hankinson's leadership style based on his approach to senior management at "Spring Vale, One"?

part V: leading

18. How important a role will internal politics play in affecting the implementation of Hankinson's decision? What might he do to channel political behavior in a constructive direction?

19. Should Hankinson seek compliance or commitment from his top vice-presidents in carrying out his decision? Discuss.

20. What effects would a significant movement toward Hankinson's goals have on control systems used by and for middle management?

part VI:
controlling

21. What kinds of controls might be most helpful in assessing more fully the results of the "can do" section?

22. Review the materials presented in Chapters 26 and 27 and select those points most important to Hankinson's desire to change the organization. Illustrate your grasp of these materials by showing how they would affect his decision and the steps necessary to implement it.

summary question
for solution of the
case as a whole

Joan felt more embarrassed than nervous as she waited for her interview with Fred Means, Dean of Placement. She had gotten to know and respect Fred during her two years as an MBA. In fact, it was Fred's recommendation which, she was told, tipped the balance and got her an offer from Metropolitan Trust three and a half years ago.

Metropolitan Trust is a leading lending institution in a medium-sized midwestern city. During the 1950s, it moved to a form of statewide banking by buying a number of small banks located throughout the state.

By the mid-1970s, Metropolitan had virtually given up competing with its much larger domestic and foreign competitors in many markets. Losses also piled up in Real Estate and Corporate Banking but while Metropolitan's Retail and Trust activities continued to grow and contribute profits, total results were very poor.

Five years ago, a major shake-up in the bank's senior management took place. The chairman, president, and three vice-presidents of the headquarters bank retired or resigned and their positions were filled by younger executives from other leading banks. Changes were also made in the affiliate banks around the state. Much turmoil resulted from these changes and last year, the "new" president, several of the new senior vice-presidents, and several more long-service executives left under pressure from the board. This time all but two of the positions were filled from within, including that of president and chief operating officer.

Elwood Monroe, sixty-one, chairman, named Edward "Chip" Joyce as president and indicated that he saw no further changes in the bank's senior management for the next four or five years.

"When I retire," Monroe said, "I expect Chip to move up. He is only forty-two now and should have many years to continue modifying and strengthening his team. When I came in five years ago we had to make many changes because the bank was simply too hidebound. The average age of the senior v.p.'s was fifty-six and they had been here since Adam learned to farm. The organization was far too conservative for the world of modern banking. Why, even our middle management ranks averaged almost thirty years with the bank.

'Now we have a good mix of age at the senior level and, while we still have a layer below them of older v.p.'s, our assistant v.p.'s and junior officers are young, bright, and aggressive. Chip will have some pruning to do but his toughest job will be to hang on to those fast-trackers three to four levels below him and make sure we keep and utilize the best of them."

Joyce agreed this would be a challenge.

"The demographics of this bank are interesting," he said. "We really cleaned house at the top five years ago and more selectively last year. Now we have a great mixture of very capable, experienced bankers and younger executives. Just below this top-level group of, say, fifteen senior vice-presidents, we have perhaps 150 to 200 people who make up the next two levels of management. They tend to be long-service people who survived all the recent turmoil. Many are outstanding bankers but quite a few are either 'semi-retired' or spend more time on bank politics than business. I can't afford to shake things up any more for a while, though, because our younger people, at their level or below them, are just not ready to move up and I can't afford to make any more wholesale moves from other banks.

"I have requested, from personnel, a thorough overhaul of our evaluation, development, and job rotation programs. We have added some real pros to personnel and in a year or two should be better able to identify, groom and, if necessary, 'protect' our real high potentials."

Among the areas which have faced dramatic change in the past five years is the retail division. A major consulting firm was brought in to review what was needed by way of reorganization. When they began their study the bank had sixty branches. Thirty-two were metropolitan branches and twenty-eight "branches" were scattered around the state. The metropolitan branches reported through seven area heads to one retail vice-president. The twenty-eight branches around the state reported to a second vice-president through six area heads. The two vice-presidents reported to the senior retail vice-president.

Following the consultants' recommendations, the retail group was trimmed to forty-nine branches. Twenty-four metropolitan branches now report through five assistant vice-presidents (area heads) to the vice-president, Retail Banking: Metropolitan Division. A smaller consolidation in statewide branches, sees twenty-five branches reporting through five area heads to the vice-president, Retail Banking: State Division. The metropolitan and state division vice-presidents report to a senior vice-president, Retail, in headquarters. All of the metropolitan and most of the state branches no longer handle customer loans, trust, or other services. These activities are now centralized in the ten area offices or, for some services, in other divisions of the bank. Most branches are thus limited to checking and savings accounts and act as referral sources for other services to either a retail area manager or other divisions of the bank.

The ten area heads are a mixed group. One of the bank's non-retail vice-presidents described them as follows: "I would guess that two or three of the area heads are 'on the shelf.' They are long-service people whose performance as branch managers was good. After the reorganization one or two were too good to leave in a branch. The reorganization took all the real banking and most 'relationship work' out of a branch. The branch manager today is not a banker but a personnel type who has to somehow manage the characters in the branches. He is also a referral source who steers branch customers to the right division for other services.

"Most of the oldtimers who headed up branches retired or were pushed out. Some went to division-level staff jobs and a few became area heads. Most who went the area route are just putting in time and trying not to make waves. A few were really ticked off by all the changes at the branch and were determined to maintain their drive as area heads. Most of them are gone or neutered by now. The rest of the area heads are kids 'on the make.' They know they are on high-potential lists and must serve eighteen to twenty-four months in the field before getting another promotion. The retail division v.p.'s (metropolitan and statewide) really have a tough time with the eleven area managers. Neither of the two retail division v.p.'s is likely to go any higher and they know that one of their young hot-shots is likely to be their boss in four or five years. What a zoo!"

The metropolitan retail division vice-president is Sam Stebbens. Sam has thirty-three years with the organization, having started as a teller while still in high school.

"Sam is a real gem, if a bit of a diamond in the rough," said Edward Joyce. "When I was named president, I personally visited all of our offices. When Sam heard I wanted to visit the five area offices and twenty-four branches in his division, he insisted on coming with me. He literally held my arm on several occasions as we entered a branch. I felt like a high school kid being taken by 'Uncle Sam' to visit 'his bank.' Yet I couldn't get angry. He knows everyone by name and they all know him. While I heard some remarks about him being old-fashioned and out-of-touch, they seem to love him at the branches. He is a very strong man, and has an excellent record with the bank."

Joan Carrier has a somewhat different view of Sam Stebbens. She was trying to think how to describe him when she was jarred from her thoughts by a booming voice.

"Come on in, Joan! How are you?" asked Dean Means as he enveloped Joan in a bear-like arm and almost carried her into his office.

"So, you're in the market, huh?" And, without waiting for an answer, Means added, "I have heard a lot about changes at Metropolitan. From what I hear, the new team at the top is outstanding but you may have to put up with a lot before you leapfrog over the 'walking wounded.' Are you definite about leaving or just shopping around?"

"If you have some time, Fred," Joan said, "I'd like to explain what's happening and perhaps you can give me some advice."

Fred nodded, put his feet up on the desk, and listened without interrupting for the ten minutes it took Joan to lay out her concerns.

Joan had spent her first several months in credit training and then became a junior lending officer. She was told informally that she was on a "high potential" list and likely to move around the bank rapidly. Move she did. After eight months, she was assigned to an asset-based finance task force responsible for recommending bank policy in this market to the bank's executive committee. Four months later, she became assistant to the senior vice-president of national accounts. After one year in this position, as a result of a strong recommendation from the senior vice-president, she was assigned to the statewide banking group and asked to head up a study team working on recommendations for the bank's statewide strategy. Her first five months on this assignment involved a great deal of travel and meetings with senior officers all over the state.

Joan was shocked when in the midst of this assignment, she was called in and told she was being removed from the post and assigned to the retail group.

"They told me," Joan said, "that I hadn't done anything wrong and that this was a key move for me since I needed line experience. As an area vice-president in retail, they said I would get that experience under a real old pro—Sam Stebbens. If I didn't take it, they said I couldn't count on getting another chance like it when my statewide assignment was complete.

"On the surface, it sounded plausible but I wanted to complete the job and show I was right about an issue that got some of the old-timers in the affiliate banks upset with me. I just did not have time to support my case before they got me."

Joan felt that her transfer to the retail area, while perhaps part of an overall development plan, had been hastened by pressure from senior people in the affiliates who felt she was steering her committee toward unsound recommendations.

"I'd love to see my personnel file," Joan told Fred. "I'll bet there now is one bad mark and if I hang in with Sam, there may be two. This is a small bank, despite the dollar volumes. With two bad marks against me in this organization, I might as well start packing."

Joan had been an assistant vice-president and area manager for ten months when she called and asked to meet with Fred.

"I just can't figure Sam out," she explained to Fred. "I respect him and admire him but he is suffocating me. Our styles are as different as day and night! He is extremely autocratic and worries about the smallest details. He has policies and procedures for everything under the sun and there are only two ways to do things—his way and the wrong way.

"When I arrived, he couldn't have been nicer. He told me he knew I might only be with him for two years but he hoped to teach me about retail banking and get me ready for my next job. I quickly learned that most of what he wanted to teach me, I could learn from other area people and the best of my branch managers. Since I considered this assignment a test of my line management skills, I worked hard to earn their respect and build a real team in my area. Some of the other area heads and even one or two of my branch people thought I was nuts to worry and risk offending Sam, but now they have joined the rest and tell me that we are really building a much stronger group. I'm not here so much to learn retail banking as how to manage other line executives. Sam has these priorities reversed.

"One area manager said, 'Look, kid. You had better remember why you are here and that is to get Sam's blessing. This isn't one of those giant banks. A person like Sam has tremendous clout. You don't need to worry about improving retail or winning friends in the branches. That's not going to help you. You are headed up the ladder if you get Sam's backing. Even the president listens to his advice.'

"I have tried to please Sam," said Joan, "but I can't seem to satisfy him without giving up and becoming his puppet. Last week he called me in and adopting his most fatherly manner said, 'Joan, you are such a bright young woman. Why don't you stop fighting and let me help you. You try so hard and waste so much energy that you're exhausting me trying to keep you out of trouble. You have two months until I have to file your annual appraisal and I would hate to spoil such a promising career by having to state that you continue to act in a headstrong way and insist on exposing us to problems by failing to coordinate your activities through me.'

"Frankly, Fred, I don't think I can change his views and if he writes me up using those descriptions, I've had it. If I ask for a transfer now, I know he will clobber me so I have considered looking elsewhere. What do you think?"

"What would you have to do to please him?" Fred asked.

"I'm not even sure, Fred. He accepts—he says—the fact that I have a much more participative style, but he has told me not to 'waste' so much time in meetings and visiting the branches. When I insist this is the only way I can learn what is going on, he just lays that patronizing smile on me and says, 'Read the reports or ask Sam.' I can't get a feel for things from those damn reports, Fred. He can because he reads *between* the lines. Further, I can't direct my people through memos and calls.

"Finally, I got him to loosen up and let me try it my way but he insists that I go over the agenda for all meetings with him in advance. Then he tells me where to end up on each item and how to 'read' and manipulate the people present.

"I tried to explain why this violates the purpose of the meetings and blocks team-building but he just laughs. So help me, yesterday he casually got up in the middle of a discussion, put his arm around me with a huge hug and a frown said, 'Let's try it Sam's way for the next two months.' I think I ought to split but I hate to give up. I'm no quitter, Fred, but I just don't see how I can turn things around. If he were a younger man with a feel for modern banking, I could work with him but he is so set in his ways, I can't reach him."

## FOR DISCUSSION AND REPORT-WRITING

*part I: planning: the execution of strategy*

1. In what ways are changes in Metropolitan Trust's retail strategy linked to changes in their structure?

2. How good an "adaptive programming" job does it appear was done in shifting both strategy and structure at Metropolitan Trust?

3. How should operating objectives for the metropolitan retail branches differ from those established for the branches around the state?

4. Given the apparent changes in the nature of retail branches, how appropriate is it for Joan to encourage greater participation from branch managers in decisions she must make?

part II: planning: elements of rational decision-making

5. Would matrix management have been more or less appropriate to the retail branches before the scope of their operations was reduced and many services centralized?

part III: organizing: strategy to structure

6. As part of her long-run career development, should Joan Carrier have been told if indeed she was removed from her prior assignment primarily for the reasons she suspects?

7. Was this a good choice of jobs (supervisor) to give her at this time in her career? Discuss pros and cons.

8. How does Sam Stebbens appear to be motivating Joan Carrier at present? Can he increase her motivation and still get her to do things his way? How?

part IV: motivating: human factors in the organization

9. How might Joan Carrier deal more effectively with her boss so as to satisfy his needs and still accomplish her objectives?

10. What do you think of Joan Carrier's apparent means of dealing with the conflict she is facing?

11. What appears to have helped and hindered efforts, in recent years, to change customs and roles within the bank?

12. (Summary Report Question, Part IV) What specific steps should be taken to increase the likelihood of maintaining the motivation and performance of both capable, older, long-service employees and younger, newer professionals such as Joan Carrier?

13. If Sam Stebbens could accept Joan Carrier's leadership style, but not change his, what effect might their differences in style have on her subordinates?

part V: leading

14. What impact may differences in leadership styles have on creativity in the retail branches? How important is creativity in the retail branches?

15. What are the pluses and minuses of Joan Carrier engaging in political behavior to try and improve her current situation?

16. At this point in time, should Sam Stebbens be seeking commitment or should he settle for ambivalent compliance with respect to Joan Carrier doing things his way?

17. What effect, if any, do you feel Joan's sex has on both her situation and her present options?

18. How may control systems used to evaluate the metropolitan branches differ from or be similar to those used in branches around the state?

part VI: controlling

summary question
for solution of the
case as a whole

19. In what ways would the number and kinds of controls appropriate to branches supervised by Joan Carrier have to change if she is allowed to manage in her highly participative way? Would setting up very detailed controls be a way for her to allay her boss's concerns?

20. If you were Joan Carrier, what would you do? List at least three detailed alternatives she should consider and explain your choice.

# LEADING

# V

If a sound planning system, effective organization, and ability to motivate were sufficient to ensure managerial success, we could end this book right here. But managers must put plans, organization and motivated personnel *into action*. They must make day-to-day interpretations and elaborations of plans, communicate the plans to workers, watch results and appraise feedback; they must make continual organizational changes to fit new conditions; they must use their knowledge of individual motives to predict the most likely response to managerial requests. Only when these additional tasks, which we discuss in Parts V and VI, are performed will the process of managing be complete.

Leading is the process by which a manager directly and personally influences the behavior of subordinates. It is a two-way relationship; subordinates in turn feed back information—ranging from highly subjective, personal responses to data on operating conditions—that is vital to the manager in his subsequent actions.

Leading is the "make happen" phase of managing. Wise managers predict how their subordinates will respond to their requests, based on the prevailing set of conditions. If the expected responses are inadequate, we then seek means of changing them. Building commitments to shared goals, providing additional rewards, removing objections, or using power may all be tried. The leadership style selected must be suited to the specific situation and the need for prompt action. We shall examine the leadership process in the following chapters.

Chapter 18—Achieving Personal Leadership. Here we shall look closely at the functions of leadership and at several attitudes that help an executive fulfill these functions. We shall pay particular attention to the criteria used to select an appropriate leadership style.

Chapter 19—Communicating. Good person-to-person communication is vital to a manager in order to develop the kind of superior-subordinate relationship proposed in the previous chapter. This chapter explores the art of listening and of conveying meaning to others.

Chapter 20—The Art of Giving Orders. In this chapter we draw upon the behavioral concepts introduced in Part IV and the leadership framework elaborated in Chapter 18 to examine how managers issue orders.

Chapter 21—Political Behavior Within Organizations. Some of the talents helpful in leading also apply to the proper channeling of political behavior within an organization. In order to keep a company on course we must link political motives and company strategy.

Clearly, in thinking about leading, we make use of an array of behavioral concepts—many of which we have already encountered. Personal needs, group norms, conflict, rewards, and perception are all involved in the motivation we are seeking. A main feature of Part V, however, is the framework that enables a manager to relate these forces to executing his specific plans.

# achieving
# personal
# leadership

# 18

## Learning Objectives

After completing this chapter you should be able to

1. Explain the role of leadership in management.
2. Identify the structural prerequisites to developing voluntary co-operation.
3. Describe the contingency approach to leadership style.
4. Discuss the factors which influence the choice of a leadership style.
5. Explain how leadership attitudes contribute to good leadership.

**GAP BETWEEN DECISION AND ACTION**

John F. Kennedy was at the peak of his career in 1962 when he ordered the removal of U.S. missiles from their locations in Turkey. His decision was taken after careful review of the alternative plans prepared by many layers of different organizations. The Joint Chiefs of Staff, the State Department, and the National Security Council had carefully coordinated these data and added their recommendations. When President Kennedy decided on the removal, clear written directions began their spiral path from the Oval Room in the White House toward the silos in Turkey.

Yet, months later, during the height of the Cuban missile crisis, Kennedy learned that his decision had not been carried out.[1] In his famous confrontations with Soviet Premier Nikita Khrushchev, Kennedy was told that the Russians would withdraw their missiles from Cuba if we would remove ours from Turkey. President Kennedy was shocked to discover that his decision had not been executed and that his control systems had failed to keep him as well informed as was his competitor about the status of his decision.

What went wrong? Is it possible that those responsible for carrying out this decision did not understand what they were to do? Were they unwilling to comply with the decision? Or did they lack the commitment necessary to execute the decision when confronted by obstacles? If this could happen to one of the two or three most powerful executives in the world, imagine how much more likely it is to happen to the average manager.

Although many forms of human effort are required to build organizations, develop plans, and design control systems, they are all for naught unless their outcomes are put into action.[2] A construction superintendent has to convert blueprints into a power dam. A football coach has to transform plays that look foolproof on paper into touchdowns on the field. A director has to turn a Gilbert and Sullivan score and libretto into a lively stage production. Such a conversion of ideas into results is an essential element in every manager's job, and how skillfully he does it profoundly affects the return from all other phases of management.

**THE ROLE OF LEADERSHIP IN MANAGEMENT**

Broadly speaking, leadership deals with the steps that a manager takes personally to get subordinates and others to carry out plans. It bridges the gap between managerial decisions and actual execution by other people.

Other phases of managing, especially motivating (discussed in Part IV), also help to close that gap; they are entwined with leadership. But here in Part V we will focus on *personal* leadership; that is, on human relationships between the leader and the led in which the distinct personalities build mutual understanding and trust.

---

[1]For a comprehensive description of the Cuban missile crisis, see G.T. Allison, *Essence of Decision: Explaining the Cuban Missile Crisis* (Boston: Little, Brown, 1971).

[2]G. Odiorne, *How Managers Make Things Happen* (Englewood Cliffs, NJ: Prentice-Hall, 1962).

Effective leadership generates close person-to-person relationships. It is rooted in the feelings and attitudes that have grown up between people over the entire time they have worked together. It is a never-ending process, with actions and reactions flowing both ways. Feedback is essential—so much so that the next chapter is completely devoted to two-way communication.

Such personal, active leadership serves two broad purposes. One stems from the impact of the leader on others—he cultivates cooperation and commitment.[3] The second results from the impact of the others on the leader—they give him information and responses that modify his behavior and future plans.[4] This is a two-way interchange.

## ELEMENTS OF PERSONAL LEADERSHIP

Behavioral science studies have confirmed a variety of managerial actions which help a leader develop cooperative attitudes. We will briefly review these, and then in the next section consider situational factors that affect their use.

*structural prerequisites to voluntary cooperation*

The total process of managing must be reasonably well performed for voluntary cooperation to flourish. We cannot do a poor job of organizing, planning, and controlling, and then expect a kindly leader to miraculously pull us out of our troubles.

Managerial leadership operates within a structure—a structure of plans, organization, and controls. And on the basis of this formally designed structure, a social structure develops—as we have seen earlier in the book. Many of the habits and persistent feelings of workers (both managers and operators) arise from the formal and social structures we create as a part of managing, and these feelings affect workers' responses to a leader's request. Major points at which structural design may have a significant bearing on the responses of workers follow.

***Clear organization*** When a person has known duties—and corresponding authority—he can develop a pride in his work, a recognized status, and a sense of inner security. By making clear the role of staff, we avoid a source of confusion and perhaps conflicting obligations.

***Individuals well matched with jobs*** A person's feeling about his work also depends on whether his job is suited to his abilities. Through personnel planning we try to make full use of an individual's abilities, but at the same time we try not to put him in a spot where he becomes discouraged and defensive because he cannot meet his obligations. Minor modifications in organization structure are often made, either enlarging or con-

---

[3]E.P. Hollander, *Leadership Dynamics: A Practical Guide to Effective Relationships*. (New York: Free Press, 1978).

[4]For evidence of the vital role of communication in the leadership process, see H. Mintzberg, "The Manager's Job: Folklore and Fact," *Harvard Business Reivew*, July-August 1975, pp. 49–61.

tracting an assignment, so that the person and his job are well matched. Such matching fosters a cooperative feeling.

*Effective communication networks*   With each person necessarily doing only a piece of the total work in a company, we must design systems that provide him with the information he needs, promptly and accurately. If he is kept well informed, his work can proceed smoothly and he can take pride in his accomplishment; whereas poor communication leads to confusion, frustration, and negative attitudes toward meeting company goals.

*Sound objectives*   To create personal satisfactions, broad goals should be translated into specific aims that are meaningful to each employee, and then reasonable levels of achievement should be agreed on. Such specific goals can become the basis for a great deal of voluntary cooperation, and achieving them can give a worker a significant sense of accomplishment.

*Workable policies, methods, and procedures*   A structure of plans for handling repetitive problems creates a necessary stability and a pattern of behavior that make work more satisfying to most employees. For aside from an occasional rebel, most people derive a sense of security from an established, known set of norms. A good body of standing plans also eases the task of performing work. In addition, if some flexibility can be introduced by using many of the plans as guides rather than as fixed rules, employee attitudes are likely to be even more cooperative.

*Balanced control systems*   In Part VI we shall see that control systems too can be designed in a way that minimizes the usual negative reaction to controls and provides constructive help to people in meeting their accepted goals. To achieve this, it is necessary to select the right criteria of performance, set reasonable standards, measure output reliably, and provide prompt and direct feedback. A poorly designed control system, in contrast, can give rise to a good deal of discontent and make a manager's job of developing voluntary cooperation difficult.

*Progressive off-the-job benefits*   The most conspicuous way to cultivate cooperation is to be progressive (generous) with off-the-job benefits. In addition to paying relatively high salaries (see Chapter 14), a company may be a leader in cutting hours of work, granting holidays, providing paid vacations, giving liberal pensions, guaranteeing employment, arranging for health and other insurance, sponsoring recreational activities, and providing still other fringe benefits.

Such added compensation obviously increases the attractiveness of employment by a progressive company. Here again the way employees feel about what they are receiving is crucial. To create positive sentiments, a benefit must (a) be generous relative to historical patterns and (b) be at least as good as benefits provided by other well-known employers. Thus there is a built-in escalation in the costs of such provisions and a risk that even slowing down on increases will lead to disappointment because worker expectations have not been fulfilled.

All the preceding ideas are examined more thoroughly in other parts of the book. The purpose of this quick review is merely to refresh our memories on how often the feelings of employees and the design of plans, organization, and controls are intertwined. In the following discussion of personal actions by a manager that help develop voluntary cooperation, we are assuming that the total management structure is conducive to effective person-to-person leadership. The entire structure may not be completely to everyone's liking, of course, but on balance it must be favorably regarded by subordinates if through personal behavior a leader is to generate enthusiasm in them for carrying out company plans.

What can a supervisor do in his person-to-person relations with subordinates to build a sustained feeling of cooperativeness? The following pages examine a series of managerial actions that nourish a cooperative work climate.

**thoughtful supervision**

*Friendliness and approval*   The kind of friendliness we are concerned with here runs deeper than mere cordiality and politeness. A subordinate is dependent on his supervisor for a variety of things—job assignments, information, help in overcoming problems, and the like—and he wants assurance of *approval* from this strategic person. Being friendly is one way a supervisor can convey approval.

*Consistency and fairness*   Inconsistent treatment by a manager in a few key areas of a job can anger people to a point where they become disgusted with their entire job. The president of a medium-sized import-export company, for instance, was so unpredictable in his demands that his chief accountant resigned. The accountant explained: "I can't live with a guy like that. One day he's hounding you for figures—'guesstimates' if necessary. The next day accuracy is all important, right down to the last penny. The Dr. Jekyll–Mr. Hyde act was driving me nuts." Consistent supervision enables subordinates to develop normal patterns of behavior. Knowing what to expect and how to respond, they feel more secure and self-confident.

Even more important to a spirit of cooperation than consistency over time is consistency—or fairness—of treatment among subordinates. A feeling among people that management plays favorites ("Pete gets all the soft assignments; he can take a day off and nobody kicks.") can quickly reduce voluntary cooperation to zero.

Here we get into difficulty in determining just what is fair. The principle of equal treatment clashes with another strong belief. Every person should be treated as an individual. If Joe has thirty years of service with the company, or his leg is in a cast because of an automobile accident, or he is going to be sent abroad in six months, should he be given special consideration?

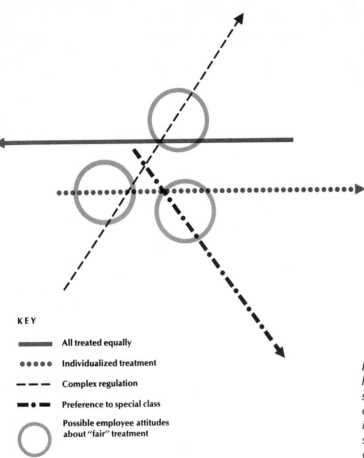

*Figure 18.1   Attitudes differ about how managers should treat subordinates. Four possible patterns of treatment are shown. Circles indicate which methods three separate groups of subordinates consider "fair."*

To build a spirit of cooperation, we must give rewards and punishments and perform other supervisory acts in a manner that *subordinates feel* is consistent or at least reasonable. Equal treatment is only a starting point. Many exceptions to strict equality are regarded as fair. Joe can be given special treatment—because of his long service, or accident, or future job—if the reason is known and accepted as legitimate and if subordinates believe that future exceptions will be made consistently for others in a similar situation. Among many employees, in fact, fairness actually requires that those with long service or in poor health be given special treatment.

***Support for subordinates***   A manager can provide a wide range of supports for his subordinates. One is simply to help in getting a job done. For example, machines may need repairing, tough customers may need to be impressed by an executive from the home office, letters should be answered while a subordinate is in bed with the flu, and so on. A subordinate will feel more secure and confident if he knows he can get help from his boss *if and when* he asks for it.

A supervisor may also support his people outside the department. He may vigorously seek every salary increase his people deserve; he may try to keep work flowing to his people at a steady pace—that is, avoid critical demands one week and layoffs the next; he may negotiate frictions with related departments—perhaps getting engineers to modify unworkable specifications or answering complaints from customer-service people; he may push for better offices or equipment; and he may keep his people informed about changes that affect them. When subordinates know their boss is representing their needs with a fair measure of success, they are inclined to follow his lead.

*Law of the situation*   Whenever possible, a supervisor should let the facts of a situation tell his subordinates what should be done—rather than to say, in effect, "Do this because *I* tell you to." An American manufacturer of electrical equipment lost a big order to a foreign competitor who quoted an appreciably lower price, and the domestic firm faced the prospect of losing substantially more business for the same reason. The general manager might well have issued a lot of edicts about cutting costs. Instead, he laid the full facts before his engineers and production people, announcing, "We have a problem." The situation rather than the general manager issued the order to cut costs.

Similar reliance on the law of the situation can be used for small problems as well as large ones. For instance, a customer's complaint about an error in billing or the illness of a key person in a department obviously requires some kind of action. A manager may in the end decide precisely what is to be done, but the *need* for action is accepted by subordinates not because he says so, but because they recognize an objective to be met. When people respond to a situation rather than to an order, they have a sense of self-expression. Their identification with the desired result fosters a willingness to cooperate with a program of action.

*Prompt settlement of grievances*   Over time a manager can expect subordinates to have occasional work-related grievances. Most of these will be *minor:* a fifty-cent error on a paycheck, a chair that snags stockings, lost telephone messages, failure to announce a new title, and the like. Any minor grievance by itself is not particularly important, but until it is settled, it is a continuing source of annoyance. By prompt attention to such matters, a manager not only removes the irritation but also shows concern for the feelings of subordinates. Even if a grievance cannot be resolved in just the way the subordinate wishes, the manager clearly demonstrates that even minor needs are worthy of respect.

The leadership concepts just listed fit so many situations that we can regard them as constants. With rare exceptions, *any* manager will be a more effective leader if he utilizes the precepts of friendliness and approval, consistency and fairness, support for subordinates, law of the situation, and prompt settlement of grievances. In contrast, the next two concepts— participation and permissive supervision—should be treated as variables. The *degree* to which each can be wisely employed varies with the situation.

**use of particpation**

Participation in decision-making should be regarded primarily as a means of arriving at better decisions.[5] But if participation is justified as a method for improving decisions, we can also anticipate a strengthening of the motivation of those who participate. A simple case will suggest the difference in the way subordinates feel when participation is and is not used.

Al Harrison, a young man recently graduated from business school, has a job as a trainee in a medium-sized factory that makes automobile wheels for sale to large companies. After a year with this company, he has now been in the production control department six months, where he reports to Mr. Baker, the department supervisor. At this point, Baker could treat him in two ways.

| High Participation | Low Participation |
|---|---|
| *Almost every day Baker comes over to Al's desk and asks him for some kind of advice. One day it may be whether a large order can be run in between the two small ones on Al's list; the next it may be what Al thinks ought to be done about a bottleneck in the buffing department. Over the six months, Al has seen Baker's real interest in his ideas, and about 30 percent of them put into effect.* | *Al thinks that Baker likes him as a person. Baker is always courteous, he shares jokes with Al, and even invited him to dinner a couple of times. When it comes to actual work in the department, Baker is tough but fair. He tells Al what to do, lets him do his job, but expects Al to keep his mind off departmental problems. He does not believe that anyone in the department should take care of problems that are rightly assigned to him as supervisor.* |

If we compare these two ways of treating Al, we see that the high-participation approach (left column) gives Al more opportunity for self-expression; he probably enjoys his work more and feels surer of Baker's approval. With such treatment, Al undoubtedly feels more closely identified with results in the entire plant, and will spontaneously cooperate in overcoming plantwide problems.

As a general proposition, the higher the degree of participation (that is, the more the initiative, the wider the scope, and the greater the influence of a subordinate) the stronger will be the resulting inclination to cooperate with company plans.

However, the participation must be genuine. The manager must really want contributions of knowledge, diverse viewpoints, or decision-making skill from his subordinates and must be prepared to devote the time required to obtain their counsel. If he is merely putting on an act, his subordinates will soon detect his insincerity. Then, asking for participation is likely to do more harm than good. As one realistic, autocratic manager put it, "My people already know I am an S.O.B., and I don't want them to think I'm a hypocrite too."

[5]V.H. Vroom and P.W. Yetton, *Leadership and Decision Making* (Pittsburgh: University of Pittsburgh Press, 1973).

An operation is closely supervised when a boss frequently observes it and makes suggestions to the worker. The boss in such situations acts much like a backseat driver who calls attention to things the driver has already observed, is free with suggestions about just how the car should be driven, and plays "Monday-morning quarterback" for every minor mistake. We often hear people say of this sort of person, "He's a good boss in a way, but he's always needling those who work for him." The most disconcerting action of such a boss is to transfer an assignment before a subordinate has an opportunity to finish it.

**closeness of supervision**

Such interruptions of a previously assigned task tend to have adverse effects on a subordinate's cooperative attitude. The boss may well be trying to be helpful, but the subordinate is likely to interpret the boss's actions as lack of confidence or as a reflection on his ability. Even if the subordinate overcomes his discomfort and impatience with the interruptions, he is apt to feel like an automaton and to become quite indifferent about his work.

In contrast, when assignments are made in terms of results to be achieved and a supervisor becomes involved in the actual performance of the work only on the request of a worker, a feeling of self-reliance is encouraged. The subordinate can rightfully take more pride in his work, and he has clear evidence of his boss's confidence in him. During a training period, close supervision is normally expected, but an experienced worker—from vice-president to janitor—finds close supervision somewhat insulting. If close supervision is continued after reasonable training, a worker develops neither the inclination nor the work habits to take the initiative voluntarily in meeting new problems.

## CONTINGENCY APPROACH TO LEADERSHIP STYLE

Throughout this book we urge that managers select the type of planning, the particular form of organization, and the system of control that best suits the specific problems confronted. There is no universal solution; instead, a wise manager looks at his needs and available resources, then charts his course to fit that contingency. In each part, our discussion of issues, various options, and factors affecting final design provides guidelines for adjusting the way of managing to a particular set of circumstances.

Leading should also be shaped by a contingency approach.[6] The measures adopted should be suited to the situation. This concept is not always accepted. Instead, we find advocates for Theory-Y, management-by-objectives, self-actualization, and a variety of other motivational techniques.[7] The originators, or more likely some of their disciples, have missionary zeal for what they believe to be the "one best way." Such single-

---

[6]F.E. Fiedler, *A Theory of Leadership Effectiveness* (New York: McGraw-Hill, 1967).

[7]Many writers in this area advocate a single, "ideal" leadership style. Well-known examples are: R. Likert, *The Human Organization* (New York: McGraw-Hill, 1967); D. McGregor, *The Human Side of Enterprise* (New York: McGraw-Hill, 1960); and R.R. Blake and J.S. Mouton, *The Managerial Grid* (Houston: Gulf Publishing, 1964). Actually all these writers are well aware of the total circumstances necessary to make their proposals work. In this respect, we are different from them in that we are more concerned with the total management job. The manager

393

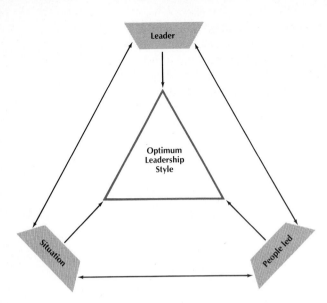

*Figure 18.2   In order to determine the best leadership style, three factors must be considered: (1) the leader; (2) the people who are led; and (3) the situation in which leadership is necessary.*

**adjusting to the situation**

mindedness can perhaps be explained because (a) advocating a single technique is simpler, or (b) the technique fosters some human values that appeal to the advocate. Usually such techniques have considerable merit when used in the proper setting; but they may waste time and actually be harmful when the necessary support for them is lacking.

A key to finding the right combination of leadership actions—often called "leadership style"—is to consider carefully (1) the situation in which the leading takes place, (2) the people being led, and (3) the personal characteristics of the leader himself.[8] Because differences occur in all three of these factors, we can expect significant variation in leadership styles all of which are effective. (See Figure 18.2.)

The situation in which a manager is striving to get action often constrains or encourages the leadership style he uses—that is, the extent to which he uses participation, shares information, is permissive, and supervises only in general terms.

Two factors which affect the choice of a leadership style are the amount of discretion permitted by the technology and the practicality of close supervision. In any organization, there are numerous tasks where technology provides workers with limited discretion. Because an assembly line is de-

---

has to deal with external and internal integration and in doing so he becomes involved with organizing, planning, and controlling, as well as with leading. He is forced to balance diverse pressures. Some of his most difficult decisions concern how far he should push a particular form of planning, or organizing, or controlling. We feel that it is useful for a manager to view participative leadership in the same light.

[8]R. Tannenbaum and W.H. Schmidt, "How to Choose a Leadership Pattern," *Harvard Business Review*, May-June 1973.

signed to control as much of the environment as possible, the opportunities for participation in decision-making and permissive supervision are reduced. One might argue that such mechanistic tasks that require minimal flexibility and creativity should be eliminated. Clearly, much of the job-enrichment literature strives to make that point. If a careful analysis of an individual's or group's total tasks leads to the decision to reorganize the job, then indeed a new leadership style may be practical. Until such a change in duties takes place, however, close supervision is an acceptable means of achieving these tasks.

The practicality of close supervision and strong control must be considered when selecting a leadership style. The service people who maintain complex computers are subject to close supervision and control when they are being trained. As they learn their trade in the classroom, or under the eye of an experienced person, they can be closely supervised. But when that service engineer goes out in the field, close supervision and control become too costly. How well he performs now is much more a function of his skills and his motivation. An assembly-line operator, on the other hand, is almost continuously subjected to close supervision and tight controls. Because of technological constraints, close supervision and control are necessary.

In the examples shown in Figure 18.3 we see the desirability of matching a leader's permissiveness to the degree of discretion permitted by technology and the practicality of close supervision, as well as other situational factors such as the need for fast action, risks involved, and creativity desired. Theoretically, congruence between leadership style and a situation can be achieved either by the leader's adjusting his style to suit the situation or by our changing the situation to fit the leader (or by a little of both). In the examples given in the first column, changing the situation would be difficult, so, at least in these instances, most of the adaptation should come in the behavior of the leader.

*Figure 18.3  The impact of the situation on leadership style. Activities that are similar may dictate a high or low degree of permissiveness and participation. Although the activities in the box at left are similar to those at right, permissiveness and participation vary.*

| Low Degree of Permissiveness | Determining Factor in Situation | High Degree of Permissiveness |
| --- | --- | --- |
| Running a subway train | Degree of discretion technology permits | Running a sightseeing bus |
| Overcoming a blackout due to power failure | Need for speed | Locating a new power plant |
| Operating sanitation equipment (garbage truck) | Satisfactions built into job | Finding ways to reduce water pollution |
| Flying a passenger airplane | Risks involved | Teaching history in college |
| Operating TV broadcasting equipment | Creativity desired | Producing a TV show |

Participative, permissive leadership affects the behavior of some subordinates more than others. One simple distinction is the rate of turnover. On some jobs employees are not around long enough to grasp, and have an interest in, the ramifications of their job. Similarly routine work often attracts workers who do not expect or want their jobs to be too demanding; they get their kicks elsewhere. In terms of our discussion in Chapter 15, such employees do not look to their job for fulfillment of self-expression needs. We are not suggesting that these employees will have a negative response to, say, minor participation. Rather the point is that we cannot assume that such people welcome deep involvement, nor do they relish the self-discipline that is entailed under a permissive leader who expects subordinates to set their own high goals and regulate their behavior to achieve the goals. On the other hand, if the group to be led consists of energetic, ambitious people who expect to be with the company a long time and hope to find personal challenge and self-expression in their work, participative, permissive leadership is called for.

Different types of work naturally attract different types of people. College professors differ from maintenance men; locomotive engineers differ from security analysts; and so forth. The difference in values and orientation of production, research, and marketing men reported by Paul Lawrence and Jay Lorsch have already been noted in Chapter 17 as a potential source of conflict.[9] This suggests a different leadership style for various departments partly because the work situation calls for different kinds of behavior and partly because the people to be led differ. In other words, from the viewpoint of leadership, the situation and the type of people to be led may be mutually reinforcing factors.

A third factor to be considered in picking an effective leadership style is the leader himself. From experience, and under many other influences, each of us develops a set of attitudes, values, beliefs, and habitual ways of coping with our environment. This set of personal characteristics may make it easy for some managers to be highly permissive and participative. Such managers have a strong respect for other people, believe that virtually everyone has high potential, take a keen interest in helping people reach their potential, and are willing to take personal risks on the success of other people. They are said to be *people-oriented*.

Other managers are less sure of the capacity of their fellows. They prefer to put their trust in system, law and order, and checks and balances. These managers are not antisocial, but when they have heavy obligations and want to be sure to accomplish a mission, they tend to rely on facts and figures, regulations, cross-checks, and their own direct involvement. Let us say that they are *system-oriented*. These managers have difficulty when there is a high degree of permissiveness, participation, and sharing; they tend to supervise closely.

[9]P. Lawrence and J. Lorsch, *Organization and Environment: Managing Differentiation and Integration* (Boston: Harvard Graduate School of Business Administration, 1967).

In the hurly-burly of running an enterprise mismatches occur. A situation plus the people to be led may call for a people-oriented leader but the actual manager may be system-oriented—or vice versa. Behavioral scientists have given much attention to this predicament. They are especially concerned about a shortage of people-oriented managers.[10] This preoccupation reflects (1) higher expectations of workers regarding job satisfactions, (2) a high degree of voluntary cooperation required by more jobs, and (3) the personal values of many behavioral scientists. The emphasis is in tune with the times, but we should not overlook the possibility that some managers need conversion in the other direction—toward a systems orientation.

When we face a mismatch we can (1) try to adjust the situation and subordinates to fit the leadership style suited to the present manager, (2) replace the manager, or (3) convert the manager. This first alternative may be unattractive because the adjustment of subordinates either through a job transfer or through training efforts, can be very disruptive. Similarly, the adjustment of the situation may result in a less-than-optimum organization design.[11](Actually, Sears, Roebuck did just this because good overall store managers were scarce, and the loss due to a less-than-optimum organization structure was smaller than the cost of trying to force the managers to use a style unsuited to them.) The alternative of replacing managers is rarely used because an equally effective replacement in all managerial functions (never mind a better one) is hard to find. Therefore, most effort goes to converting systems-oriented managers to people-oriented managers.

Conversion of mature managers is tricky. Intellectual reasoning is not enough; a person's beliefs and attitudes have a deep emotional basis. Only when we can achieve a propitious match of the situation, the led, and the leader will the fullest degree of participation and permissiveness be feasible. Many managers may conclude that some lesser degree of participation and/or permissiveness is more suitable in the particular circumstance they face. Such a choice does not, of course, preclude the substantial amount of cooperation attainable through the other leadership concepts outlined earlier in this chapter.

Up to this point we have clearly suggested that leadership style be adapted to individual situations. A manager's desire for varying permissiveness and participation in dealing with the same individual is, in fact, quite common. Both parties expect different leadership styles to be employed. This mutual expectation that some aspects of work will be treated differently from others has a parallel in planning and in decentralizing which vary from subject to subject as we noted in Chapters 4 and 11. Leadership styles are normally adjusted to these variations in planning and decentralizing.

**compatibility among leadership styles**

---

[10]Blake and Mouton, *Managerial Grid*.

[11]For some interesting suggestions on methods of adjusting the situation see F.E. Fiedler, "The Leadership Game: Matching the Man to the Situation," *Organizational Dynamics*, Winter 1976, pp. 6–16.

A final aspect of using different leadership styles is the need for consistency in the eyes of subordinates. As noted, varying leadership styles are normal and expected. But unpredictable shifting from one to another can be very disturbing. If a manager employees high participation one month, then next month permits only limited participation, subordinates will not only be confused; they will also question their boss's integrity. The key here is communication. If a manager chooses to modify his previous leadership style, subordinates should be told about the change and given the reasons for it.[12]

**LEADERSHIP ATTITUDES**     Our review of managerial leadership has emphasized the key part personal relations play in this process. Managers are dealing with the reactions of individual personalities to one another. To improve their ability to lead, then, they have to be perceptive about people.[13] Most will never become trained psychologists, but can develop an awareness of the more obvious factors that might confront them in a given situation. Even such an awareness, however, requires a set of attitudes that often need cultivating: *empathy*, *self-awareness*, and *objectivity*.

Knowing about the importance of these attitudes will not ensure their development, of course—just as knowing we should not get mad and actually controlling our anger are quite different matters. Still, by understanding which attitudes contribute to good leadership, problems can be better diagnosed and managers may discover where they personally should try to improve.

**empathy**     Empathy is the ability to look at things from another person's point of view. If a leader is to guide, motivate, and get information from others he needs the capacity to project himself into that person's position. How does that person feel about the company and his job? What values does he attach to friendships, security, titles, and the many other things affected by his work? How will he interpret the words and actions of his boss, his associates, and his subordinates? What are his hopes and aspirations? What difficulties are bothering him at the moment? Whom does he trust, and whom does he fear? Note that empathy is not a case of asking, "What would *I* do if I were in your position?" because any one of us might bring to the position quite different knowledge and feelings. We are empathetic only when we can sense and feel, almost intuitively, *how another person reacts* to a given situation.

An executive may set up a new vacation policy or make some other change he intends as an aid to his subordinates, but if he thinks of the change in terms of how *he* would like it rather than how the people affected will like it, the move is likely to misfire. To be empathetic we need *respect* for the other person as an individual. We may disagree sharply with his

---

[12]W.A. Hill, "Leadership Style: Rigid or Flexible," *Organizational Behavior and Human Performance*, 9 (1973), 35–47.

[13]W.E. Zierden, "Leading Through the Follower's Point of View," *Organizational Dynamics*, 8, no.4 (Spring 1980), pp. 27–46.

values and consider his reasoning false, but we should still recognize that his feelings and beliefs seem just as valid to him as ours do to us. A salesperson, for instance, often finds he needs such attitudes; if he is a good salesperson he has a lot of empathy for his customer, but he does not necessarily endorse the customer's behavior or beliefs.

**self-awareness**

Knowing oneself ranks with empathy as a requisite for leadership. An executive needs to be *aware* of the particular impact he makes. He should know his own predilections for, say, taking action hastily, being brusque with people who don't understand instructions the first time, getting so involved in specific problems that he bypasses supervisors in resolving them, and so forth.[14]

Moreover, a leader should know how he appears to other people. Many of us have an image of ourselves that differs from the way others see us. A manager may think of himself as fair and objective, for example, but some of his subordinates may consider him to be biased in favor of young men with college degrees. Regardless of which view is correct, the manager may have difficulty in motivating and communicating with a subordinate who is convinced he is biased unless he knows that the subordinate thinks so. Finally, with an awareness of his own preferences, weaknesses, and habits, and of what others think of him, a manager should learn what impression his actions make on other people. One high-ranking executive, for instance, growled over the telephone at the secretaries and assistants of his immediate subordinates when the latter were "not in." In so doing, he unwittingly created morale problems for his subordinates and virtually cut himself off from any voluntary help from lower-level personnel. But this executive, whose manner with his immediate subordinates was much less gruff, was unaware that by expressing his displeasure to secretaries he was creating difficulties.

**objectivity**

A third quality that is crucial to good leadership is objectivity in person-to-person relations. Something causes everyone to behave as he does. To identify the influences on Joe Jones's actions, is to take an important step toward guiding his behavior. Instead of getting angry with Joe for resisting a new method, for instance, his response should be recognized and an attempt made to find out what caused it. Or if a salesperson is unusually energetic, understanding what motivates him suggests a way to induce similar behavior in other salespersons.

Such detachment may not be easy to maintain. We commonly react to the behavior of others emotionally instead of coolly and analytically. Besides, a manager is often deeply concerned with the outcome of his subordinate's activities and therefore lets his intense feelings cloud his objectivity.

In addition, empathy fosters sympathy and personal identification with other people; yet a good leader should be both objective and empathetic. The viewpoint of a physician is similar to what a leader needs to reconcile these

[14]P. Hersey and K.H. Blanchard, "So You Want to Know Your Leadership Style?" *Training and Development Journal*, 28, no. 2 (1974), 22–37.

two attitudes. A good physician understands his patients' feelings—he is empathetic in a high degree; but his *own emotional involvement* with his patients must be limited if he is to make an objective diagnosis and perhaps take action that he knows involves substantial risk. He is well aware of the problems of his patients as individual personalities, and at the same time he deals with such problems in a detached, scientific manner. A good manager, likewise, understands the feelings and problems of his subordinates; yet he keeps enough psychological distance to be fair, just, and constructively concerned with performance.

Many qualities contribute to a manager's ability to lead. We cannot make a complete and unassailable list of such qualities, partly because they vary with the people being led and with the circumstances in which the leading takes place. Nevertheless these three qualities—empathy, self-awareness, and objectivity—are needed in the vast majority of cases.

## CONCLUSION

Managerial leadership is primarily concerned with converting plans into action, and in an enterprise this involves highly personal, person-to-person interaction between each manager and his subordinates. In his role as a leader the manager is in a particularly tight spot. He must act within the constraints imposed by technology and his environment, must fulfill company objectives, and at the same time must be responsive to the individualized needs of his subordinates.

To be an effective leader, a manager must understand the feelings and problems of his individual subordinates. Such feelings change, partly as a result of the behavior of the manager himself, and problems change with the ebb and flow of events. To keep in tune with these personal "facts," the manager needs empathy, self-awareness, and an objectivity about behavior.

A manager is concerned with both productivity and the personal satisfaction of his associates. Such a merger is not easily accomplished. We have noted that it is built upon a wisely designed managerial structure, a prerequisite for effective leadership. Then an objective, empathetic manager can work with his subordinates in a manner that gives each individual the continuing support and encouragement he needs. The various guides that we have suggested give no formula, but they do point to the quality of relationships that build sustained cooperative attitudes.

Leading is an endless process for a manager. Not only do the problems and plans of an enterprise keep changing, thereby creating new issues calling for leadership, but individuals also change. One important skill needed in developing constructive leader-follower relationships is two-way communication, a process we consider in the next chapter.

## FOR FURTHER DISCUSSION

1. Assume a division of a large company shifts from a strategy of aggressive pursuit of market share to one of seeking less growth but more stable profits. How would such a shift in strategy affect the leadership style needed by the division's general manager?

2. Identify the key factors which will determine the leadership effectiveness of

women moving into senior management positions.

3. "For a supervisor to exhibit true leadership over subordinates is virtually impossible in a business setting. This is so because the needs and values of the subordinates are not only different from, but often conflict with, the needs and values of the organization which the supervisor must seek to satisfy." Do you agree? Discuss.

4. Is it possible for the appointed leader of a department to enjoy some of the benefits of informal leadership by using a member of the group who is recognized as an informal leader? What are the pros and cons of such an arrangement?

5. A recognized authority on leadership entitled an article "Engineering the Job to Fit the Manager." Is this author likely to advocate the contingency theory of leadership?

6. "I'm continually amazed," said a national sales manager of a company selling office equipment, "at the failure of many outstanding salespeople to become effective leaders when appointed to branch management posts. A good salesperson has very little power over customers. Sales are made with good products and the attributes of a leader. Why can't those same attributes be used to lead the branch when the salesperson is put in charge?" What do you think of this observation?

7. What is the distinction between *paternalism* (which is strongly criticized by both unions and human relations experts) and measures for securing voluntary cooperation discussed in this chapter? Is paternalism wise in other countries such as Japan or India, but not in the United States? Why?

8. Is it likely to be easier or more difficult for a senior vice-president to lead a number of vice-presidents reporting to him or for a first-line supervisor to lead a group of hourly workers reporting to him? Discuss.

## CASES

For cases involving issues covered in this chapter, see especially the following. Particularly relevant questions are listed after each case.

Benjo Associates (p. 92), 16
Mike Zerllini (p. 188), 14
Camden Chemical (p. 298), 18, 19, 20
Scandico (Singapore) (p. 305), 14
Netsuki Novelty Products Company (p. 451), 13, 14, 15, 17
Marathon Plastics (p. 456), 12, 18

## FOR FURTHER READING

Burns, J.M., *Leadership*. New York: Harper & Row, 1979. A distinguished political scientist analyzes the place of leadership in the American social, political, and economic system.

Fiedler, F.E. and M.M. Chemers, *Leadership and Effective Management*. Glenview: Scott, Foresman, 1974. Surveys various leadership theories, then develops a "contingency model" for selecting leadership behavior.

Hersey, P. and K.H. Blanchard, *Management of Organizational Behavior*, 3rd ed. Englewood Cliffs, NJ: Prentice-Hall, 1977. Concise summary of major theories of leadership.

Jennings, E.E., *An Anatomy of Leadership*. New York: McGraw-Hill, 1972. Examines the need for courageous and innovative leadership in the modern corporation.

Sayles, L., *Leadership*. New York: McGraw-Hill, 1979. Useful set of guidelines for practicing effective leadership.

# communicating

# 19

After completing this chapter you should be able to

1. Identify the major obstacles to effective personal communication.

2. Summarize the major guides for empathetic listening.

3. Understand when to use empathetic listening.

4. Describe how a manager can improve his ability to convey meaning to others.

5. Explain the concept of feedback confirmation.

## PERSONAL COMMUNICATION: FOUNDATION FOR LEADING

Mutual understanding is essential to lasting leadership. Throughout our discussion of leadership, we have assumed that the manager understands his subordinates and that they understand him. In practice, deficiencies in such understanding are a major stumbling block.

The critical element here is an ability to communicate person-to-person. A manager must learn from his subordinate the latter's thoughts, feelings, and motivations. He must also clearly convey his explicit and implicit instructions, along with their significance and the feeling that lies behind them. Because skill in such interpersonal communication is so vital, it is the focus of this chapter.

Many other forms of communication are important in managing an enterprise. As we have seen in Parts I and II, both planning and decision-making depend on a vast flow of data. Division of labor, decentralization, staff, and other features of organization—analyzed in Part III—create the need for management information systems. But this kind of information flow does not provide the highly personal understandings that underlie leadership.

To improve one's ability to communicate person-to-person, one should: (1) be aware of common obstacles to gaining understanding, (2) understand the process of empathetic listening, (3) convey meaning to others, and (4) get feedback confirmation by testing the signals. Throughout our discussion of these topics, however, we should think of their relevance and suitability to each of the leadership styles explored in Chapter 18. In person-to-person communication, as in virtually all other areas of managing, the value of a concept or technique depends upon the situation to which it is being applied.

## OBSTACLES TO UNDERSTANDING

One reason communicating is not easy lies in the different point of view of receiver and sender. Let us take an example. Joan Brown

*differences in viewpoints*

is sales manager for one of the leading American manufacturers of men's and women's apparel; her salesman in the Atlanta territory is Al Williams. Brown has always gotten along with Williams, enjoys talking with him, and likes to help Williams when she can. Recently Brown has been looking at figures on population and buying power; these indicate that the Atlanta district has greatly increased in both categories. So on a visit to the Atlanta office, Brown said to Williams, "I've been wondering if the Atlanta territory is the right size for one person to cover."

In making this apparently simple observation, Brown meant to imply that the work load in Atlanta has apparently increased, and that some arrangement must be made to keep the company growing and profitable in relation to its competitors. She is also trying to convey a feeling toward Williams that she likes him and is concerned about his satisfaction with his job.

Al Williams, however, has just returned from 300 miles of travel on a July day with temperatures over ninety degrees, a trip that included sixty

*Figure 19.1* *The diagnosis of breakdowns in communication networks is a major challenge!*

miles of a dusty unpaved road. Before his boss came in, he read his mail and found a routine communication from New York asking him to fill out a complete set of forms on forecasting purchases by each customer and to "get these back to us next week if possible." Williams knows that he will have to work a couple of nights to finish the forms in time. In addition, Brown is the first woman Williams has ever worked for. So when Brown says, "I've been wondering if the Atlanta territory is about the right size for one person to cover," this series of thoughts runs through Williams' mind: "Brown has never been over the back part of the territory; she doesn't know what the territory is really like; she thinks of it as a big smooth map; now she thinks I'm not working hard enough so she's asking why I'm not producing more sales."

Situations like this occur in industry every day. An executive makes a seemingly simple statement, and a responsible subordinate who gets along well with his boss receives quite a different communication. Why was Brown's communication ineffective?

First, we should note that to Brown and Williams the word "territory" means different things on the factual level. Williams has seen thirty towns in the back part of the territory, known forty-five customers in those towns, traversed thirty roads connecting them, and experienced how much time it took to talk to Al Jackson in Marietta compared with the time it took to talk to Jack Freeman in Valdosta. These 107 facts, along with hundreds of others, he has lumped together in his head, into a construct called the "territory." From literally thousands of things he has heard and seen, Williams has abstracted a "territory." It has *meaning* to him. Brown, on the other hand, has looked at many maps, reviewed statistics on the number and names of customers, measured distances, looked at population and buying-power statistics, and has lumped all these facts together into something *she* calls a "territory"; the word clearly has another meaning for her.

In addition to such differences in factual content, the feelings a person intends to transmit may not correspond to those that are received. Joan Brown, when she spoke, actually felt friendly toward Al Williams; but Al did not receive that impression. He may generally feel that Brown likes him, but this statement did not reinforce that feeling. At this point, then, just as each person is thinking of different intellectual abstractions, so each one is feeling different emotions.

If Al Williams is to understand Joan Brown, the latter must find some way to overcome this semantic barrier, a barrier created by both the difference between her own factual experience and that of Williams and the differences in her feelings and his.

Incidentally, Brown will gain very little by asking Williams, "You know what I mean by the Atlanta territory, don't you?" Williams can really only answer, "Yes." If he says anything else, his boss is likely to think that he is not too bright. Furthermore, if by saying "Yes" Williams really believes that he does understand, he can only mean, "I understand what *I* heard," not "I understand what you heard yourself say."

**organizational distance**

Any subordinate naturally wants to look good in his boss's eyes. Consequently he selects the information he passes up the line so as to create a good impression, and he holds back information that makes him look bad. In organization jargon, he protectively screens the information that he transmits. A boss likewise, may feel that, because of his position, he should not be completely candid with his subordinate. Individuals differ, of course, in the extent to which they permit a status discrepancy to interfere with a free exchange of ideas and feelings, and in extreme instances organizational distance blocks all except formal communication.[1]

**perfunctory attention**

Often in our conversations with others, we only half-listen to what they say. We are so busy with our own thoughts that we tend to give attention only to those ideas we expect to hear. When an accountant talks to the controller, the controller may pay attention only to how work is progressing and may disregard clues on morale or friction with staff. In fact, psychological studies show that many of us ignore information that conflicts with our established patterns of thought; we simply do not believe that Steve is serious about quitting or that a key customer would buy foreign-made equipment, because such thoughts do not conform with the ideas we already hold. Especially if we are deeply committed to, or emotionally involved in, some matter, we prefer to pay no more attention to bad news than Hitler did to reports of inadequate supplies during the latter part of his regime. We tend

[1]K. Roberts and C. A. O'Reilly, "Information Filtration in Organizations," *Organizational Behavior and Human Performance* (1974) pp. 253-65.

to retain our private concept of the world by saying to ourselves, "I just don't believe——is so."

A manager is especially likely to give perfunctory attention to incoming communications when he is very busy with other matters. He simply has so many other distractions that he selects those parts of a total communication that can be readily used. Novel and irreconcilable bits of information or unexpected feelings get brushed aside. Under some circumstances, an executive may be justified in such cursory treatment of mesages, but he pays a price in being superficially informed.[2]

Western culture stresses "objective evidence," "full knowledge of the facts," and "exchange of information." But at the same time we are taught to hide our emotions. Unlike a small child whose feelings are openly expressed, a mature adult is expected to moderate his emotions—or at least *appear* to moderate them. Likewise, our culture encourages us not to publicly recognize emotions in others. Except with one's closest friends, it isn't polite to discuss strong feelings.

**repressed feelings**

A result of this repression of feelings is that we are inept in communicating them. Of course, there are such cues as body language.[3] But particularly in a business or other organizational setting, special effort is required to detect how people feel, and we rarely find an opportunity to verify our guesses directly.

Still another difficulty faced in developing a clear, mutual understanding with a boss or a subordinate is the meaning—or interpretation—given a message.[4] We do—and should—consider the source of a message: The sender may be biased, he may draw his ideas from an unrepresentative sample, or he may deliberately twist the evidence. But trouble is caused by lumping everyone in broad classes—for example, assuming all salespeople exaggerate. True, the typical salesperson tends to be too optimistic, but that doesn't mean that everything he says is unreliable. Moreover, hopes may lead us to infer a meaning that was never intended; for example, a friendly talk with the boss does not necessarily mean we are in line for a promotion.

**inferred meanings**

Then, too, the particular situation at the time a message is received may *accidentally* affect the meaning attached to it. If Al Williams had been working over his prospect list instead of just returning from a hot, dusty trip, the meaning he drew from Joan Brown's comment about the size of the Atlanta territory might have been quite different. To take a similar example from another company, a plant superintendent was talking with one of his foremen about the high cost of certain products on the same day that the company controller distributed a bulletin on keeping time cards posted accu-

[2]H. Mintzberg, *The Nature of Managerial Work* (New York: Harper & Row, 1973).
[3]A. Scheflen, *Body Language and Social Order* (Englewood Cliffs, NJ: Prentice-Hall, 1972.)
[4]J. C. Athanassiades, "The Distortion of Upward Communication in Hierarchical Organization," *Academy of Management Journal*, 16, (June 1973), 207-26.

rately. The foreman inferred that the superintendent thought he was faking his time reports. Actually, the superintendent had no such idea in mind; the arrival of the two messages on the same day was a pure accident.

Sensitivity to these common difficulties with person-to-person communication within organizations helps managers to spot misunderstandings. They may not be able to correct the difficulties—most are imbedded in our social customs—but they can sharpen their communicating skills so as to work around them.

## EMPATHETIC LISTENING

The kind of communication we are exploring in this chapter requires the mutual exchange of ideas and feelings between manager and subordinate. The manager must *listen* and he must also *impart* facts and feelings. But for the interchange to be most effective, he should emphasize listening. If he starts by giving his views to a subordinate, as many managers are inclined to do, he is likely to stifle upward communication because of his status and latent power. Of course, a manager does give directions, as we shall soon note; but the form of communication we are examining here builds understandings and relationships that underlie and greatly simplify his task of directing.

**what empathetic listening involves**

When listening empathetically, a person opens the way for another to talk freely about his ideas and feelings without having to justify each statement he makes. The listener reserves his own views and preconceived ideas, while giving close attention to what the other person is trying to express. The listener is simply trying to gain insight into what is "on the other fellow's mind." This is a valuable skill at all levels, but probably most valuable to the high-level manager who, because of his status, has difficulty getting subordinates to give him their "whole message."

Empathetic listening makes use of certain techniques employed in psychiatry where a patient first expresses his feelings, then recognizes the facts of his problem, and finally develops a workable adjustment of these facts. A manager, of course, is not about to undertake psychotherapy, but he can use some of its concepts to nurture a mutual understanding of day-to-day problems at work. The manager can listen sympathetically, without injecting his own views, to a subordinate's attitudes and emotions about his job; and in so doing, the manager may help the other to gain a more objective appreciation of the total situation.

For a manager, this kind of nondirected interview may be the only way he can learn the full feelings and operating problems of his subordinates. Without such an understanding, a manager is in a poor position to predict responses to requests or to energize forces to shift those responses.

**example of empathetic listening**

An illustration of empathetic listening will give concreteness to the technique we have been discussing in general terms. Let us compare the way two different executives approach the same situation. The following facts were presented to executives at a management-development program; then members of the group interviewed a person who knew the full story and who responded as Tony Flynn probably would have.[5]

Tony Flynn works in the assembly department of a company that manufactures television-broadcasting equipment. The operation requires that people work in teams. Tony has been employed by the company six years. During the first two years he showed aptitude for the job, but his attendance record was so irregular he was warned twice that he would be dismissed unless he got to work steadily. For the past four years he has a good attendance record and is a competent, experienced workman. Although Tony gets along with his fellow workers, he has always been very quiet and reserved, and company records do not contain any explanation of his early absences. Three days ago (Monday) Tony did not show up for work, nor did he phone that he was sick—which company rules require a person to do in cases of illness. Tuesday the same thing hapened, and the employment manager got no answer when he tried to call Tony's home. Again, on Wednesday, no Tony. This morning Tony appeared on time, but looking a bit disheveled and glum. The superintendent of the assembly department asked the supervisor under whom Tony works to send him to his office.

## One interview with Tony developed as follows:

SUPT.: Hello, Tony, it's good to see you. Sit down a minute.

TONY: *(Taking chair beside desk)* Thanks.

SUPT.: Tony, we've missed you the last few days.

TONY: *(Half to himself)* Yeah, been out all week, until this morning.

SUPT.: That's right, I'm sorry to say, and you know how one man out upsets your crew. We didn't have a substitute most of the time.

TONY: *(Pause)* Yeah, afraid I caused some trouble.

SUPT.: And not calling in, Tony, that made matters worse because we didn't know what to plan on. You've been here long enough to know how important it is to keep full crews in assembly.

TONY: *(Again, half to himself)* Should have called in, that's right.

SUPT.: Tell me, when you realize how important it is, how could you just disappear for three days? We couldn't even get an answer at your home.

TONY: I just couldn't make it, and been too messed up to call in. Sorry I caused so much trouble.

SUPT.: Tony, I've looked over your record. The last four years have been fine. We need good men like you. A few years back the absences were pretty serious, and I sure hope we're not going to slide back to that trouble again. Yet, the recent record looks real good. *(Pause)* What do you think, Tony, can you keep that record as clean as it has been the last couple of years?

TONY; I'd sure like to. I've been trying. *(Pause)*

SUPT.: We need good men like you. You know the work, and you pitch in when we have to get work out in a rush. But we have to be able to depend on the men we keep

---

[5]Professor Alex Bavelas assumed the role of Tony in both of the "role-playing" views digested here. The persons who took the position of superintendent were given only the facts known to management before the interivew; they were free to conduct the interview as they chose and did not listen to anyone else before their turn. The two interviews selected represent contrasting approaches. The conversations have been condensed to conserve space.

in your spot. If you think this won't happen again, we're mighty glad to have you back.

TONY: Well, I need my job, and I'll do the best I can.

**Another executive took a different tack with Tony.**

SUPT.: Hello, Tony, we've been missing you. Sit down and let's talk about it.

TONY: *(Taking chair beside desk)* Thanks.

SUPT.: You been under the weather, Tony?

TONY: I'm all right, I guess.

SUPT.: Gee, Tony, the way you say that, you don't sound very sure.

TONY: *(Half to himself)* Well, I've got to feel all right.

SUPT.: Hmm?

TONY: *(Pause)* I just gotta keep going somehow.

SUPT.: It takes some real push, sometimes.

TONY: Lost three days' pay already. Not sure I can stay awake today.

SUPT.: Been losing sleep?

TONY: Can't sleep even when I get to bed. *(Pause)* Took Mary to the hospital Sunday—no, that would be Monday—about 2 a.m. She darned near died that morning. Went home to see about Patsy that evening. She was bawling to see her mother, but I left her with the neighbors anyway. Spent most of the night at the hospital. Tuesday, Mary at least knew who I was. Tuesday night I took Patsy home—the neighbors got kids of their own—and she cried and fussed most of the night. Last night I tried to give her supper. It was awful. Mary's getting better, they say, but she still looks like a ghost. Well, I figured I had to get back to work this morning.

SUPT.: No wonder you look bushed. Think you can keep going?

TONY: Guess I can get through to the weekend. The neighbors will keep Patsy in the day and a high school girl is coming to sit with her in the evening so I can go see Mary. But we can't keep this up forever, and I don't know how to pay the doctor's bills and blood transfusions and all that. (Pause) Guess I'd better take Patsy down to Mary's sister's. Could do that Sunday without losing any more pay.

SUPT.: Tony, you don't have to settle everything right away. You say your wife is getting better, and that's most important. If you can get Patsy taken care of for a couple of weeks, maybe the public-nursing service can help your wife get back on her feet. The personnel department could tell you about that.

TONY: Sure, we might make out that way for a while.

SUPT.: I'll phone Joe [Tony's supervisor] to find a few minutes you can talk with the personnel people today. And if you do have to take time off, be sure to phone us, Tony. You know how important it is to make up a full crew.

TONY: *(Leaving)* Yeah, thanks. I'll call in if I have to be out any more, but I don't think it will be necessary.

In the first conversation the superintendent was not unfriendly, but he was so preoccupied with the problems of staffing his department that he failed to get information from Tony that was needed in dealing with the situation constructively. In the second interview, the superintendent said very little until Tony had talked about *his* problems. Then the superintendent was in a much better position to take action that would avoid future absences.

From studies in clinical psychology and psychiatry, and experience **guides for listening** with nondirected interviewing in industry, have come a series of guides for empathetic listening.[6] For a manager the most useful of these guides are

1. Listen patiently to what the other person has to say, even though you may believe it is wrong or irrelevant. Indicate simple acceptance (not necessarily agreement) by nodding, lighting your pipe, or perhaps interjecting an occasional "Um-hm," or "I see."

2. Try to understand the feeling the person is expressing, as well as the factual content. Most of us have difficulty talking clearly about our feelings, so careful attention is required.

3. Restate the person's feelings, briefly but accurately. At this stage, you simply serve as a mirror and encourage the other person to continue talking. Occasionally, make summary responses such as, "You think you're in a dead-end job," or, "You feel the manager is playing favorites"; but in doing so, keep your tone neutral and try not to lead the person to your pet conclusions.

4. Allow time for the discussion to continue without interruption, and try to separate the conversation from more official communication of company plans. That is, do not make the conversation any more "authoritative" than it already is by virtue of your position in the organization.

5. Avoid direct questions and arguments about facts; refrain from saying, "That just is not so," "Hold on a minute, let's look at the facts," or "Prove it." You may want to review evidence later, but a review is irrelevant to how the person feels now.

6. When the other person touches on a point you want to know more about, simply repeat his statement as a question. For instance, if he remarks, "Nobody can break even on his expense account," you can probe by replying, "You say no one breaks even on expenses?" With this encouragement he will probably develop his previous statement.

7. Listen for what is *not* said—evasions of pertinent points or perhaps too-ready agreement with clichés. Such an omission may be a clue to a bothersome fact the person wishes were not true.

8. If the other person appears genuinely to want your viewpoint, be honest in your reply. But in the listening stage, try to limit the expression of your views, for these may condition or repress what he says.

9. Do not get emotionally involved yourself. Try simply to understand first, and defer evaluation until later.

A great deal of practice and self-awareness are needed before most managers can follow these guides for listening. Much of the time, a manager must assume a positive, self-confident role, making decisions and giving orders. Clearly, empathetic listening calls for a sharp change in pace. But unless he can develop the self-discipline and humility to listen respectfully, a manager is likely to lose touch with the reality of others.

[6]R. Hopper, *Human Message Systems* (New York: Harper & Row, 1976).

The process of listening we have just described will be effective only under several necessary conditions. One requirement is *time*. The kind of conversation we have considered takes more than a minute or two. An executive must be willing and able to give his subordinate uninterrupted private attention for fifteen minutes, half an hour, or perhaps longer—just for listening. With other demands on his time, an executive must value highly the benefits of listening before he will take such a block of time out of his busy day. Moreover, he must be willing to listen when a subordinate wants to talk.

Another requirement is recognizing the unique qualities of each subordinate. We cannot understand the feelings and problems of another person unless we *respect his individuality*. R. L. Katz has pointed out that each person has his own values, which

stem from his previous experiences (his expectations of how other people behave), his sentiments (the loyalties, prejudices, likes and dislikes which he has built up over a long period of time), his attitudes about himself (what kind of a person he is—or would like to be), the obligations he feels towards others (what he thinks others expect of him), his ideals (the ways he thinks people should behave and how things ought to be done), his objectives and goals (what he is trying to achieve in a given situation), and perhaps many other things.[7]

For empathetic listening to be successful, we do not have to know everything about an individual, but we must be prepared to respect individual differences in personalities.

The *personal discipline* of the executive is a third requirement. All of us are inclined to respond emotionally to what others say. We normally approve, challenge, get angry, or react in other ways. Yet for empathetic listening, we must remain objective, and objectivity calls for practiced self-discipline.

Finally, a passive, nondirected approach by a manager presumes that his *subordinate has feelings or problems he wants to talk about*. Perhaps the subordinate is disturbed by something that has happened, or he may have a strong response to a proposal his boss or some other executive has made. But when a person is content with—or indifferent to—his work, then "Um-hm" tactics by his boss will result in a fruitless conversation indeed.

Empathetic listening is a valuable process, but it should be used only when a manager can devote the necessary time, remain objective, and respect the individuality of the person he is talking to, and when that person apparently has repressed feelings that the manager wants to understand.

## CONVEYING MEANING TO OTHERS

Listening deals with one direction in two-way communication. A manager also has to *transmit* his ideas to subordinates. Here again, the aim is to develop a mutual understanding of ideas, problems, and feelings; and again, the difficulty is that each party—the manager and his

[7]R. L. Katz, "Skills of an Effective Administrator," *Harvard Business Review,* September-October 1974, pp. 90-102.

subordinate—may assume the other assigns the same meaning to a message that he does.

A simple model, used in analyzing electronic communications such as television or bouncing messages off satellites, may help us identify the reasons why B does not always understand just what A meant to say. Figure 19.2 shows the basic elements.[8]

**technical communication model**

In electronic communication, the message usually consists of words or physical forms; encoding and decoding involve converting the message to and from electric impulses; and major difficulties of distortion and noise may arise in the channel. In face-to-face communication, we have fewer channel difficulties, but in encoding and decoding we run into many subtle, psychological problems.

Many of the concepts we have used to analyze listening apply equally well to the job of imparting ideas. The meaning of words, for instance, enters directly into encoding and decoding, and the effect of emotions on what we give attention to can garble the meaning of a message as it flows in either direction. In the following suggestions for improving the transmission of ideas from supervisor to subordinate, then, we shall review insights about the kind of behavior that should permeate a leadership relation.

When an executive has a message he wants to get across to a subordinate, he should take time to reflect on the attitudes and interests of that person. The subordinate will probably be preoccupied with other matters that seem important to him, and he will be inclined to pay attention primarily to those ideas that are related to his personal needs. Moreover, his emotional state will affect his receptiveness to new messages.

**the world of the receiver**

Consequently, if a manager wants to get across an important idea, a new meaning—not just routine information—he must be sensitive to the world of the person who will receive the message. How that person perceives it will depend as much on what is already in him as on the content of the

[8]H. Leavitt, *Managerial Psychology,* 4th ed. (Chicago: University of Chicago Press, 1978), chap. 10.

Figure *19.2* A simple technical communication model.

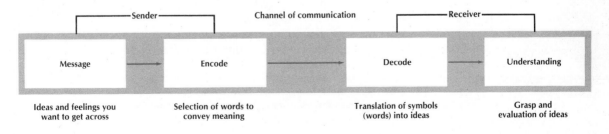

| Message | Encode | Decode | Understanding |
|---------|--------|--------|---------------|
| Ideas and feelings you want to get across | Selection of words to convey meaning | Translation of symbols (words) into ideas | Grasp and evaluation of ideas |

message. If the manager has a close relationship with him, based on previous empathetic listening, he will know something of his world and how he is likely to interpret the new message. Of one point the manager can be sure: "logical" arguments will not go far if the message requires the subordinate to alter his values. Therefore, as a sound starting point, the manager should consider the personality of the person to whom he wishes to convey a meaningful mesage. In addition, he should ask himself: How will the idea look to him? Can anything be done to prepare him for the point to be transmitted.

**meaningful language**

As we have seen, words—even ordinary terms like "territory"—may mean different things to the sender and the receiver of a message.To get meaning across, we must try to use words in the sense that the receiver will take them. Long and technical words, although perhaps more precise, often have to be discarded in favor of short terms that are easily grasped. Maybe the other person *should* be smart enough to understand our language, but our aim is to reach a mutual understanding—not to test his literacy.[9]

Some repetition helps in most learning—assuming that the learner is trying to understand. So a message may be repeated, preferably in different words or with new examples. It is even more effective to draw attention to an idea by relating it to a current experience of the subordinate; he then sees the meaning of the words in terms of his personal behavior.

**free, face-to-face interchange**

It takes a while for us to assimilate an important idea, to get used to it. We have to roll it around in our minds and savor its implications. When trying to communicate a significant message to a subordinate, a manager should provide him the time for such assimilation. One way to do so is simply to exchange thoughts with him about the message, to talk it over. The subordinate may think out loud, "Wow, that new product would louse up our production schedule . . . . We could promote a couple of those young engineers who are getting restive . . . . How would the shipping department handle it? . . . ," and so forth. The executive may also express his thoughts—both pro and con—about the proposition. This interchange is highly informal, and neither person states firm conclusions.

During such a give-and-take discussion, many doubts and misunderstandings come into the open. If the executive is skillful at listening, he can probe long enough to uncover misunderstandings and then restate his meaning or intention. Frequently the executive himself has not thought through all aspects of an idea, and a discussion of this sort may result in clarification—and perhaps modification—in his own mind.

Note that during this assimilation stage, authority is set aside while both people seek a mutual understanding. Mutual respect and trust are necessary, because each person is exposing his tentative, speculative, unconsidered reactions. If the conversation has rambled, the executive may well

[9]M. Rosenberg, "Words Can Be Windows on Walls," in W. Nord, ed., *Concepts and Controversy in Organizational Behavior,* 2nd ed. (Santa Monica, CA: Goodyear, 1976), pp. 485-90.

summarize the message as it has been redefined at the end, but the free, face-to-face interchange should have clarified the meaning substantially.

One of the best ways an executive can give meaning to a message is to behave himself as he asks others to do.[10] The new president of a sugar refinery wanted to break a tradition that pay increases and promotions for executives depended primarily on long, loyal service. He stated on several occasions that raises would be made only on the basis of demonstrated improvement in performance. Most executives let the statement slip by as just another part of a pep talk. But at the end of the year, a good many executives (including the president's son) did not get raises even though they had worked hard; a few people who could show significant improvement in results received good bonuses. The grapevine spread the word, and at this point the president's message took on meaning.

communicating through behavior

In contrast, the vice-president in charge of sales of another company became worried about low gross-profit volumes and told each of his district managers not to grant special discounts to large—or tough—customers. Within a few weeks, however, the vice-president himself made several concessions to two customers he handled personally. This action changed the meaning of his "no special discount" statement to "no special discounts except by the vice-president." It created resentment on the part of the district managers because they felt the vice-president was inconsistent in what he said and did.

Subordinates sense quickly the presence, or lack, of consistency in their boss's words, spirit, and action. In fact, subtle feelings and values may be conveyed better by example than by words, although there is no reason for not using both. The poet Emerson put it this way: "What you are (do) thunders so loud I cannot hear what you say."

## FEEDBACK CONFIRMATION

These general guides—recognizing the interests and attitudes of the person receiving a message, expressing the message in terms that are meaningful to him, having a face-to-face discussion of the idea, and accompanying the words with consistent action—aid the manager to convey meaning to subordinates. But how can he be sure they actually receive a message as he intends it? We have already noted that merely asking a man whether he understands provides scant assurance.

To confirm that our communication has resulted in mutual understanding, we need to keep alert to any feedback that is available. The simplest check is to observe whether the subordinate behaves in accordance with the message. When direct observation is not practical, as is often true for an executive, he can watch various reports and results for cues. And for more intangible or subtle messages, the listening process described earlier

[10]O. W. Baskin and C. E. Aronoff, *Interpersonal Communication in Organizations* (Santa Monica, CA: Goodyear, 1980), pp. 74-76.

in this chapter may be the most reliable feedback. If a manager has developed a close leadership relation with a subordinate—the kind we are exploring throughout Part V of this book—he should have enough frank interchange of ideas and feelings to provide indications of how well he has communicated.

## CONCLUSION

In this chapter we have been examining communication, not as a routine or a procedure, but as one of the essential elements in leading. Both facts and feelings need to be transmitted between a leader and each subordinate. For this purpose, we have explored what is necessary for a manager to listen empathetically to subordinates.

Far more significant than technique, however, is the kind of relationship developed. Mutual understanding, mutual respect, confidence and trust that permit frank discussion of personal feelings and problems, integrity in matching action with words—all these reflect leadership at its best. We may not achieve such two-way personal communication with all our subordinates all the time, but our effectiveness as leaders will be enhanced to the extent that we succeed in doing so.

## FOR FURTHER DISCUSSION

1. "While I have been accepted by my peers and feel our communication is open, I must be missing something. We sit for hours in executive committee meetings and I think I am following the flow of ideas and contributing. Then, a day later, I hear of actions 'recommended' by the committee which don't jibe with my understanding of our conclusions. Either I miss something when they all head for the men's room or I still don't understand the culture of this group."

   What do you make of this comment by the first woman appointed to the position of senior vice-president and member of the executive committee of a small chemical company?

2. As an experiment in empathetic listening, try the following. Have one participant play the role of a top-notch young executive who has just informed his boss that he is thinking about taking another position. Have a second participant play the role of the boss. The young executive, while being honest with his boss, should be somewhat reticent about revealing his real reasons for quitting. With the person who is to take the role of the boss out of the room, agree on the real reasons for his quitting; for example, you might select any of the following: fear that nepotism will block his advancement; his feeling that the company president is stubborn and not very bright; desire to move away from his mother-in-law who is a close friend of the boss's wife; belief—based on grapevine information from a source that cannot be revealed—that the company will be sold to a much larger firm; or you might think up some other reasons. Then have a role-playing talk between the boss and his subordinate. See if the boss can uncover his subordinate's reasons for leaving by using the guides for empathetic listening. Following the role-play, write down illustrations of (1) where the superior succeeded in employing these guides, (2) where he failed, and (3) how a different approach might have been more successful.

3. How does the degree of delegation affect the nature and importance of communication? Consider both horizontal and vertical communication.

4. An expert on communication has suggested that the term "co-perception" would be a better word to describe what is needed to bring about true communication. What do you think he means by this? Relate your answer to the material in Part IV on human needs.

5. "I have just one question for those who advocate empathy and understanding of subordinates' problems. To whom do I go for treatment when I get through? Am I supposed to sit and listen to a lot of silly mistakes, alibis, and complaints, and just say, 'Uh-huh—you're late because you resent your mother's domination'? It seems a lot better for their performance and my psychological well-being that, when there is something wrong and I know what to do about it, I come right out and speak my piece." Comment on this statement.

6. In general, participation in planning not only achieves positive responses to managerial influence but contributes, even more, to good two-way personal communication. How may highly participative planning systems occasionally *interfere* with good two-way communication?

7. What factors should a manager consider in deciding when to follow up an oral communication with a written summary?

8. In what ways may custom and tradition as discussed in Chapter 16 aid with good two-way communication? How may they interfere?

## CASES

For cases involving issues covered in this chapter, see especially the following. Particularly relevant questions are listed after each case.

Benjo Associates (p. 92), 17
Mike Zerllini (p. 188), 13
Camden Chemical (p. 298), 20
Marathon Plastics (p. 456), 13
Netsuki Novelty Products Company (p. 451), 17
Foster Promotions Inc. (p. 538), 14

## FOR FURTHER READING

Baskin, O. and C. Aronoff, *Interpersonal Communication in Organizations.* Santa Monica: Goodyear, 1980. Explores basic communication relationships in organizations and their impact on organizational efficiency.

Davis, K., ed., *Organizational Behavior: A Book of Readings,* 5th ed. New York: McGraw-Hill, 1977, chap. 12. Reviews studies of communications barriers, especially at the first level of supervision.

Hall, J., "Communications Revisited," *California Management Review,* Spring 1973. Penetrating discussion of person-to-person communication. Argues that each of us can learn to adjust our interpersonal style.

Haney, W. V. *Communication and Organizational Behavior,* 3rd ed. Homewood: Irwin, 1973. Comprehensive discussion of communication and its impact on behavior in organizations.

Johnson, B., *Communication: The Process of Organizing.* Boston: Allyn and Bacon, 1977. Innovative treatment of communication from an organizational perspective.

Knapp, M. L., *Nonverbal Communication in Human Interaction.* New York: Holt, Rinehart and Winston, 1972. Useful introduction to the study of nonverbal communication.

# 20

# the art of giving orders

Learning Objectives

After completing this chapter you should be able to

1. Identify the range of responses to managerial orders.

2. Identify a manager's three major options for shifting the responses of subordinates to managerial orders.

3. Understand the drawbacks of using coercion in modern organizations.

4. Explain the two principal ways in which a manager can develop compromise.

5. Describe how a manager may establish congruence between his aims and those of his subordinates.

"You don't have to like it, just do it!" This command certainly echoed along the Nile as pyramids were built, and quite likely the medieval monastic scribe heard it from the head monk. And the power of the overseer was strong enough to get obedience.

Not so today. In our world of growing affluence and desire to protect individual freedom, "Why should I?" has become a legitimate question. In a modern enterprise, the response to a manager can range anywhere from enthusiastic, committed behavior to opposition and refusal to carry out orders.

Nevertheless, orders continue to be essential. In every organization, for work to proceed in a coordinated manner, the persons designated as managers must give the official word as to what is to be done. Sooner or later—after the planning, organizing, motivating and communicating which we have been discussing—each boss says to each of his subordinates, "This is what I want you to do." The manager's task of leading is not complete until that message, in one form or another, is sent.

The wise manager, however, is very careful about the orders he issues. His aim is to prompt action, to achieve results. And he is aware that a subordinate may not respond in the desired way.

In this chapter we outline an approach, to improving one's skill in issuing orders. The approach builds on insights and techniques for motivation and leadership that we have explored in Chapters 15 to 19. The basic concept, in simple terms, is this.

Setting: A manager wishes to request (order) a subordinate to take some action or accomplish some result. Both individuals recognize that the request springs from their manager/subordinate relationship which has been created by the formal organization.

Steps for manager:
1. Predict response of subordinate to the request.
2. Decide whether that response is acceptable.
3. If not, select an activating mode to shift the predicted response.
4. Repeat cycle: predict revised response, etc.

Prediction, gap analysis, and corrective action are all parts of the process.

**POTENTIAL RESPONSES TO MANAGERIAL ORDERS**

To guide behavior, a manager must predict how his subordinates and other people involved will respond to his requests in each situation. Will they simply refuse to comply (mutiny), or grasp the opportunity for action like a charged-up runner (fanaticism), or do something in between?

A useful way to think about possible responses to a manager's order is suggested in Table 20.1. This diagram shows a range of *feelings* and a corresponding range of *actions*, moving from a strong negative response, through ambivalence and indifference, to positive, internalized commit-

TABLE 20.1
RANGE OF
RESPONSES
TO A
MANAGER'S
ORDER

| | Negative Sentiment | | Ambivalence | |
|---|---|---|---|---|
| | Strong | Mild | *I don't feel like it but . . . .* | |
| | negative | negative | *I'll try* | *I'll* |
| Range | feeling | feeling | | *do it* |
| of Feelings | toward | toward | | |
| | request | request | | |

| | Opposition | | Ambivalent Compliance | |
|---|---|---|---|---|
| | Fight | Deceit | Minimum | Full |
| | or | Avoidance | compliance | compliance |
| Range | flight | | Inertia | Momentum |
| of Actions | | | As long as external pressure is maintained | |

ment.[1] For convenience the diagram is divided into four stages, although in practice responses may fall anywhere along the continuum. The four stages are opposition, ambivalent compliance, indifferent compliance, and commitment.

**opposition**

Refusal to carry out instructions does occur. The person receiving the request may believe that the task is too dangerous, that it is outside the kind of work he was hired to perform, that it is demeaning or will subject him to ridicule. He may object to dirty assignments or to work in cold or wet locations—"I don't have to put up with that." Tasks he feels are unethical or nonprofessional may be refused. An assignment that means moving his family to an undesired location ("Siberia"), or travel that interferes with a cherished hobby can create opposition. Unfair allocation of tough and easy jobs may stir up revolt.

Strong negative feelings from causes such as these may lead to one of several actions by the individual who receives the request. If he feels very strongly, he may insist that he will quit the job unless the instruction is changed. Or if resignation is untenable, he can object, appeal, and seek support of colleagues for his case—and meanwhile refuse to comply.

Mild negative feelings are likelier to result in more subtle responses. Instead of open opposition, the assignment may just not get done. Some excuse is found for successive postponement—necessary supplies or outside help is for some mysterious reason not available when needed; papers get lost; other more important work interferes; illness occurs. If necessary a bit of deceit about what actually has been done avoids a confrontation.

[1]M. H. Jones, *Executive Decision Making* (Homewood, IL: Irwin, 1957), p. 130.

420

| Indifference | | Positive Sentiment | |
| --- | --- | --- | --- |
| Why should I? | Why shouldn't I? | Mild internalized positive feelings | Strong internalized positive feelings |

| Indifferent Compliance | | Commitment | |
| --- | --- | --- | --- |
| Minimum compliance | Full compliance | Minimum commitment | Full commitment |
| Inertia | Momentum | | |
| As long as no counter pressure exists | | | |

Whenever a manager predicts such opposition behavior, he clearly should either modify his request or take steps to modify the response. A maxim in political science says, "Never pass a law that cannot be enforced." Applied to management this suggests, "Never issue an order unless you predict it will be acceptable or unless you are prepared to take steps to ensure its acceptance."

Any time someone carries out another's request, we might say that he is "complying." As we will use the term, however, compliance signifies actions that result from either ambivalance or indifference.

**ambivalent compliance**

Ambivalence—both negative and positive feelings—are often present when someone complies with an order. The prevailing mood is likely to be, "I don't want to do it but considering the advantages, I will." The ambivalence arises because negative feelings—such as those listed directly under "Opposition," or perhaps merely dislike of the work—are coupled with positive inducements—such as pay, economic security, fellowship with peers, respect of outsiders, and the like. The single action of complying with the manager's request results in a mixture of feelings.

In ambivalent compliance that borders on opposition, most of the positive feelings come from external sources—from other people who want the request to be acted upon. The actor himself has no direct interest in the outcome, but he does respond to the pressures (rewards or punishments) that these other concerned people place upon him. The external pressures may stem from any of the following or, usually, from some combination: (1) a hierarchical superior, (2) peers, (3) subordinates, (4) spouse, friends, family, (5) general societal values or perceived expectations.

In the absence of these *external* pressures, the individual would not comply. Mild pressure brings minimal compliance. Greater pressure may produce full compliance. The moment that pressure disappears or is avoided, however, effort will probably slacken or cease.

**indifferent compliance**

Individuals may also *comply* with a request without experiencing either ambivalence or commitment. They are simply indifferent to the request, and compliance may be achieved with only the slightest push. This is the "zone of indifference" that Chester I. Barnard wrote about several decades ago.[2]

One of the authors recalls an incident that took place during the stormy period of campus protests. Shortly after one major demonstration, the author approached an elevator with an armload of books. Two students stood chatting near the elevator and the author asked one, "Would you please push the 'up' button for me?" The student in a calm but defiant tone answered, "Why should I?"

Taken aback and at a loss for a suitable retort to this rude rebel, the author blurted out, "Why not?" Then it was the student who blinked and, after a moment's hesitation, said, "Sure, why not?" as he pushed the button. In this encounter, as in many other situations, the "Why not?" may be as difficult to answer as the "Why?" In an era in which everything from soap to virtue is "sold" or at least legitimized as "relevant" or "meaningful," we are likely to forget that many responses are positive simply because there is no real reason for not complying with a request.

Most of us expect to accept instructions when we take a job. Such a response is part of our role. Especially when the overall work situation is pleasant, we are quite prepared to give passive compliance to requests that fit within prevailing work patterns.

Of course, if bare compliance is inadequate to achieve company goals, or falls so far short of what people want from their jobs, a manager will have to seek commitment, and moving people from compliance to commitment requires special managerial effort, much as shifting from opposition to compliance. But first we have to decide whether expending the effort to encourage such a shift is necessary.

**commitment**

Still another response to a manager's request is commitment (see Table 20.1). Commitment connotes a positive, welcoming feeling about the requested performance. The more positive the feeling, the greater the commitment. In addition, this feeling comes from *inside* the individual. He reacts favorably because the task is something he wants to do; it helps him serve directly one or several of his own "needs."[3]

All sorts of people engage in committed action. A mail carrier, for instance, may feel that delivering mail accurately, promptly, and without damage is a satisfying activity; he does the job well, not to avoid punishment, but because he believes this is the right way to do an important job.

[2]C. H. Barnard, *Functions of the Executive* (Cambridge, MA: Harvard University Press, 1938).
[3]B. Buchanan, "To Walk an Extra Mile: The What, Whens, and Whys of Organizational Commitment," *Organizational Dynamics* (Spring 1975), pp. 67–80.

*Figure 20.1  To guide behavior, a manager must predict worker's responses. The actual inscription carved in stone on the face of the New York Post Office is: "Neither snow, nor rain, nor heat, nor gloom of night stays these couriers from the swift completion of their appointed rounds." Drawing by Handelsman; © 1976 The New Yorker Magazine, Inc.*

The inscription in the drawing reads: "NEITHER LETHARGY, INDIFFERENCE, NOR THE GENERAL COLLAPSE OF STANDARDS WILL PREVENT THESE COURIERS FROM EVENTUALLY DELIVERING SOME OF YOUR MAIL"

Similarly, a life-insurance counselor usually feels that he is really helping his clients by selling them large policies; he is pleased each time another breadwinner protects his family from a severe catastrophe. Likewise, the superintendent of a telephone exchange may want his to be the lowest cost unit in the company—as a matter of pride and personal satisfaction.

The reasons a person feels committed toward a particular goal vary widely. As we saw in Chapter 15, motivation varies not only among individuals but within the same individual in different situations. The person may believe that his work is making a significant contribution toward a social objective that he strongly endorses. Or, often the person holds a view of how a job or task should be performed—say, a firstclass truck driver or a surgeon—and takes pride in performing work that meets such a standard. A game spirit may be invoked—being better than a competitor or exceeding self-imposed standards. But whatever the underlying motivation, the important feature from a manager's viewpoint is that the individual derives personal satisfactions from an activity that is also helping to meet company goals.

In full commitment, the pressure to carry out the task must be *internal*. The actor seeks to carry out the task, not because his boss or peers or friends exert influence, but rather because *he* himself feels that he should. In contrast to compliance, the primary pressure to act is no longer external.[4]

[4]F. Luthans and T. Davis, "Behavioral Self-Management—the Missing Link in Managerial Effectiveness," *Organizational Dynamics* (Summer 1979), pp. 42–60.

In stressing the internal aspect of commitment, we are not saying that fair treatment, bonuses, and other rewards that a manager makes to a committed worker have no influence. A favorable climate and overall satisfying job certainly pave the way for commitment. However, when commitment is present, these highly acceptable rewards have merged with other motivations in such a way that the task itself takes on positive value for the individual. No longer does the individual perform the task, as in ambivalent compliance, merely as a means of obtaining some payoffs. Instead, the internalized values—of the mail carrier, the life-insurance counselor, the telephone company superintendent—are now congruent with company goals. And with commitment comes energetic, flexible, creative effort to achieve those goals.

## DECIDING UPON A DESIRED RESPONSE

Our review of potential responses to managerial orders—opposition, ambivalent compliance, indifferent compliance, commitment—points to several alternative ways that managers can shift such a response. The choice begins with forecasting how subordinates will respond to the manager's order. The manager must decide whether this response is acceptable, and if it is not, choose one of the methods of altering undesirable responses.

Opposition is obviously unacceptable. If opposition is predicted, the manager must immediately devise steps to shift the expected response to the right on the scale shown in Table 20.1—at least to ambivalent compliance or, theoretically, all the way to commitment. Or he must alter his request.

Both compliance and commitment, however, may get the desired work done. So here a manager has a choice. He faces a question for each action to be executed: which would be preferable—compliance or commitment? Furthermore, if the preferred response does not match the predicted reaction, what can be done to bring the two together?

seek compliance

Why might a manager accept compliance in certain situations? First, if he has just been confronted with opposition, even ambivalent compliance may be a great improvement—and to strive for more in the press of getting things done may involve too much delay and expense. Second, for many activities compliance is quite adequate. Routine activities often call for no more than dependable performance—filing expense reports, keeping the car greased, sending out sales literature. Even more significant activities like maintaining standard temperature on a refinery still may require little judgment. Every position from president to janitor contains substantial amounts of such work—for which compliant action produces acceptable results.

Mere compliance, however, has limitations. External pressure must be always present, and supervision close. More seriously, it fails to bring out much latent energy, initiative, or individual adaptability.

Committed workers can ease a manager's burdens in several ways. A person with commitment to a task works more energetically and with more imagination. He is his own "energy source" and requires less close control.

The behavioral scientists build an even stronger argument for commitment. Writers with humanistic values like McGregor, Argyris, McClelland, and Myers contend that in today's society we should appeal to such higher-order needs as self-expression (see the discussion of individuals' needs in the early part of Chapter 15). Rising expectations, they say, will make more and more people dissatisfied if their work serves only their physical and security needs. Instead, the illness of alienation can and should be cured by commitment. Incidentally, research findings show a closer link between what we call commitment and worker satisfaction than between commitment and productivity. F. Herzberg's distinction between hygienic and motivating needs, explained briefly in Chapter 15, provides a more direct tie to company productivity. Commitment contributes primarily to not-fully-satisfied motivating needs, and this in Herzberg's scheme builds productivity.

By relying on commitment, then, a manager serves two objectives—greater effort toward company tasks and greater satisfaction of employee higher-order needs.

But not all situations lend themselves to this ideal solution. One kind of limitation is technological. Some work, such as operating a paper-making machine or collecting tolls on a bridge, has so little opportunity for variation that the strongly committed worker may feel constrained and frustrated. Another limitation is the cost of establishing commitment relative to its benefits in particular settings. Normally, shifting a response from compliance to commitment entails significant costs. The manager of a gasoline station, for example, would certainly prefer committed attendants who are responsive to each customer's needs. But the cost and difficulty of obtaining such commitment may be so high that the manager decides to settle for indifferent compliance. A similar dilemma often confronts the manager of bargain-price chain-store outlets.

Always the manager must invest a lot of his own effort. Changes in work structure or technology may be necessary. Perhaps some new personnel will have to be brought in and indifferent workers retired. A new group morale will be needed. And all this takes time.

The manager must estimate (1) how strong a sense of commitment he can create by these steps, and (2) how beneficial will be the resulting additional effort, self-control, flexibility, and initiative.

## CHOOSING AN ACTIVATING MODE

The perceptive manager can predict how subordinates will respond to his requests in specific situations. Often this expected response will be quite acceptable, but when it is not, there are three broad ways to influence subordinates to act in a more acceptable way. We call these "activating modes"

1. coercion,
2. compromise, and
3. seeking congruence.

Each of these approaches has distinct strengths and limitations, and consequently must be carefully chosen.

The most likely situation calling for each activating mode is indicated in Figure 20.2. In actual practice, the steps taken to change a response must be finely turned to the specific setting; but the chart does introduce us to the normal relationship between the range of responses to a manager's order and each method for bringing about a change.

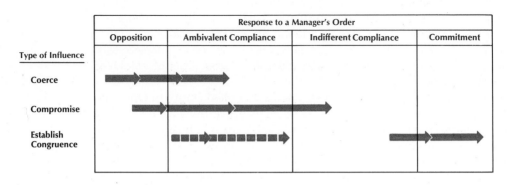

Figure *20.2*  *Situations in which various activating modes are used to shift response to a manager's order.*

## USE OF COERCION TO SECURE COMPLIANCE

Throughout history coercion has been used to secure obedience. Here we are concerned with a manager's use of coercion to overcome opposition and shift that response to at least minimum compliance.[5]

**what coercion is**

Coercion involves the imposition by one individual or group of *its goals* on another. If you have been coerced, you have *not* been led to alter your basic goals or your feelings toward the goals of the coercer. You pursue his goals (with varying degrees of effort) without accepting them because you see such pursuit as the lesser of several evils. Thus, coercion can only move responses from negative toward ambivalent compliance.

In the pure form of coercion, the coercer disregards the needs and wishes of the weaker one, and pursues only his own ends. If compliance is not forthcoming, increased pressure is exerted until the subordinate gives

[5]J. A. Lee, "Leader Power for Managing Change," *Academy of Management Review,* 2 (1977), 73–80.

in. Rarely, however, can coercion be used in such an unrestrained fashion in a modern corporation.

use of coercion to shift responses

Coercion has its principal effect in its potential use, rather than in its actual use. We can see this most clearly in the use of penalties.[6] An actual demotion or a withdrawal of a challenging assignment, for example, contributes little directly toward meeting an objective of either employee or firm; indeed, the immediate effect may even be a drop in output. What is important is fearful *anticipation* of such a penalty, for it motivates an employee to behave as the company wants.

The actual use of a penalty is, of course, significant—not because it gives a person "what is coming to him," but because it makes clear what will happen if there are further digressions. A two-week layoff for repeated tardiness, for instance, benefits a company only if the fear of future layoffs leads to punctuality.

Rewards work similarly. Fear of missing a raise in pay or a transfer to a more interesting job—sometime in the future—stimulates effort now. But a policy of making promotions and pay increases routinely, on the basis of length of service or seniority, provides little power to secure obedience because a person gets his reward even though he fails to obey instructions conscientiously.

Because of some inherent disadvantages, coercion tends to be used sparingly in modern organizations. A principal drawback is its tendency to increase negative feelings on the part of those being coerced. Even though it may bring compliance, it increases the reservoir of resentment toward future managerial influence, and although we achieve compliance, we may undermine the possibility of building commitment.

## USE OF COMPROMISE

A second basic way to shift responses to a request is compromise. To compromise, according to Webster, is "to settle by mutual concessions." In leadership, compromise requires that both the manager and his subordinates modify or give up part of what they want. Neither party is completely satisfied, so we have ambivalent compliance.

Those captains of industry—and of ships—who like to think that they have absolute power balk at the idea of compromising. They feel that compromise invades their managerial prerogatives. A modern manager, however, is well aware that he has no divine right to command. Instead, he has to consider objectively how best he can obtain adequate responses to his requests—and compromise is one of the means. Compromise in the meaning used here is a normal fact of life, and we believe it should be treated as such.

A manager typically arrives at a compromise either by (1) initiating the compromise himself, thus voluntarily composing the terms, or (2) by bargaining.

[6]R. D. Arvey and J. M. Ivancevich, "Punishment in Organizations: A Review, Propositions, and Research Suggestions", *Academy of Management Review,* January 1980, pp. 123–32.

A manager turns to compromise when (1) the predicted response to his request is unsatisfactory, (2) prompt action is desired, and (3) the cost and possible failure of other activating modes are high. We often find ourselves in such a situation.

Sensing the need for a compromise, the astute manager may try to think of one that is likely to be acceptable to all parties, and then try to initiate this proposal. By anticipating the need for mutual concessions, he hopes to avoid the rancor of bargaining and also to maintain his formal power. For example, if his subordinates are becoming increasingly annoyed with computer print-outs and the barrage of accompanying requests, he may decide (or arrange with the controller) to discontinue several existing reports. Then when he announces a newly devised "computer aid," he can simultaneously tell of relief from other pressure.

Whereas the power to coerce has its principal effect in its potential rather than actual use, compromise is most effective in shifting behavior toward compliance when it is actively used. In fact, compromise may make its most significant contribution toward eliciting positive responses when it is used by a manager who has the power to coerce. The manager who is able to coerce or exact a lopsided compromise (in his favor), but who refrains from doing so, may create a climate favorable to future cases in which he must compromise or seek commitment.

The use of compromise involves three dangers.

1. It may be perceived as a sign of weakness, and thereby invite opposition to later requests.
2. It may create embarrassing precedents.
3. It may be an "easy" treatment of a situation in which a more difficult congruent resolution would give more lasting benefits.

All three of these dangers were faced by the supervisor of seven draftsmen in an engineering consulting firm. The prevailing practice for overtime pay was quite flexible: when work was slack, the draftsmen left the office early with no loss in pay; in exchange, when rush projects required overtime, they worked up to an extra ten hours per week with no additional pay; beyond the ten hours, they received overtime pay at their regular hourly rate. This arrangement was quite acceptable until a union organizer started preaching "time-and-a-half for all hours over the regular thirty-five-hour week."

The supervisor predicted that the draftsmen would neither quit nor join the union in the near future even though he insisted on continuing the past practice. However, the draftsmen clearly felt that they should get time-and-a-half for all extra hours beyond ten per week. Rather than say no, which he had the power to do, he devised a compromise that still was simple and flexible. "I told them that instead of making an issue in the personnel department, I would handle it informally. I promised to get them some extra money by approving payment for one and one-half hours for every overtime hour over ten. It worked well because they trust me to do right by them and I trust them not to drag their feet. I told my boss and he liked it too."

"Now," the supervisor continued, "I have another touchy one. For this summer we just got several big projects we hadn't planned on. Normally our summers are our slow times. To get these projects our salespeople submitted very low bids. To complete the work on time, I will have to ask our people to give up a total of five weeks' vacation. Four of my people get three weeks of vacation, two get four weeks, and one gets two weeks. I'm sure we can get them to allocate this time among themselves. I don't want to have to hire someone else to do the work. My problem is that while I can pay them for the vacation time they give up, these low-margin projects will not permit me to pay them the equivalent of time and one-half. I'm sure that most of them won't like the idea of giving up vacation time with no bonus involved."

To illustrate the three possible dangers of compromise, consider first how the draftsmen perceived their superior's prior actions. If they see a pattern of compromise on his part (in the decision on added pay for overtime) stemming from his fear of a union, they may interpret that decision as a sign of weakness and thus might resist his request for giving up vacations with no bonus.

With respect to the second danger, the supervisor developed the overtime compromise at least in part to avoid "changing our compensation practices every time a problem comes up." In the process, however, he created a potentially dangerous precedent with his compromise if, this time, he must say no and his people do not accept his reasons.

To illustrate the third danger, he may again work out an acceptable compromise and move their expected response from opposition to ambivalent or indifferent compliance. By so doing, however, is he missing an opportunity to review the entire work-compensation area and develop a longer-term, flexible program that is more congruent with the company's goals and those of his people? Developing such a program may take time, and creativity has its risks. A rational appraisal might lead him to invest the time and take the risks in light of potentially greater commitment from his people. But the ease of another compromise may well lead him away from a better long-run approach.

**bargaining**

Many compromises are reached through bargaining—rather than being composed almost entirely by the manager. Collective bargaining with labor unions is required by law, but informal bargaining between a manager and single subordinate or group of subordinates is even more widespread.

In the bargaining process, each party indicates (with varying degrees of candor) what he would like; he listens to the other person; and he expects some give-and-take in reaching a compromise agreement.

The style of bargaining varies. One style is showmanship and bluffing —so common in union negotiations that it has become a ritual. Quite different is open, candid confrontation—all cards on the table; this style is often used in person-to-person bargaining. But perhaps even more prevalent is submerged bargaining, in which the demands and threats and even the proposed concessions are not openly stated but are nonetheless recognized as part of a negotiation.

Both parties in manager-employee bargaining should recognize that more than a single, immediate request for action is involved. More important is developing a sound basis for *continuing* cooperative efforts. Also, the potential use of power by either party is always in the background—both the amount of power and the willingness to use it; this inevitably affects the concessions made and agreements reached.

The choice of whether or not to use bargaining to reach a compromise, and of the style of bargaining, is made by subordinates as well as managers. If subordinates insist on bargaining, their manager must join in the process.

An advantage of open bargaining is that subordinates' needs will be more accurately known—the compromise will not be based on what a manager guesses someone else wants. Moreover, because each person decides the concessions he will make, the compromise will lessen his regret. In this regard, during the bargaining process we should look for changes in the work situation that are of high value to one party and of little or no significance to the other. Bargaining is not entirely a "You win, I lose" affair; a creative solution more attractive to all parties may be found.

The great disadvantage of bargaining, of course, is its strong emphasis on conflict.[7] Areas of disagreement are stressed, perhaps magnified out of proportion to their real significance. In formalized collective bargaining we even have specialists whose positions depend on uncovering and increasing sensitivity to sources of discontent. Such emphasis on conflicting goals makes ambivalent compliance the best response that a manager can hope to achieve.

Fortunately, bargaining need not take center stage. For some issues, such as level of pay, it is possible to agree on criteria for adjustments (cost of living, prevailing rates in the labor market, or matching a leading company). A permanent arbitrator can establish a "common law" pattern for resolving other kinds of disputes, or a company by its own actions may build such a tradition. Open communication (discussed in Chapter 19) can lead to quick resolution of conflicts that do arise. And, long-term agreements, formal and informal, can make bargaining only an occasional affair.

Avoiding frequent discussion of conflicting goals is especially important to the manager who seeks commitment. Bargaining that involves acrimony and bluffing is especially injurious to feelings of trust and confidence that accompany commitment. Some conflict is inevitable, and means for resolving it—perhaps through bargaining—must be found. But if we seek commitment, this resolution must be made promptly and adroitly to establish a climate favorable to positive, enthusiastic action.

## CONGRUENCE: GATEWAY TO COMMITMENT

The ways of shifting predicted responses to a managerial order already discussed—coercion or compromise—lead to ambivalent or indifferent compliance. They may (or may not) also help set the stage for

[7]A. Filley, *Interpersonal Conflict Resolution* (Glenview, IL: Scott Foresman, 1975).

commitment. But to switch subordinates to a committed response requires that a manager resort to another kind of influence.

Commitment involves a subordinate's desire to carry out the request *for his own satisfaction*. This is an internal, emotional feeling. For instance, if you are the West Coast manager and your marketing vice-president asks you to increase the company's share of the market from ten to twelve percent, ideally your response should be one of strong commitment to that goal. The goal becomes a personal challenge you are committed to. You believe your company should have even more of the market; you'll have fun showing other managers how strong your district is; customers on the West Coast really need your product; building up the territory carries with it more recognition in headquarters and a good bonus; and you have a lot of ideas about how the job can be done. On the other hand, if you regard the request as unfair—the vice-president often asks you for too much and gives too little—your boss will be lucky to get even compliant effort from you toward the new market share goal.

The primary way a manager can encourage such feelings of commitment is to establish *congruence* between his aims and those of his subordinates. Congruence is the gateway to commitment. It exists when both the manager and those he seeks to influence believe the request will meet their perhaps different but desired goals.

A useful way for a manager to develop congruence is to encourage subordinates to embrace general company objectives. Frequently employees identify themselves closely with their company. They genuinely feel, for example, that "What's good for General Motors is good for me." Even more common is identification with a division or a department just as a professor wants his department to be successful and well respected. If, in addition to such identification, the employee feels that his work contributes to the strength of his department or company, then his work takes on a special significance for him. He is contributing to a cause.

A separate factor is the feeling of being "on the team"—especially on a successful team. When an individual feels that he is making perhaps a small yet significant contribution to group accomplishment, and he is recognized for that contribution, he tends to identify with the group and its goals. The group achievement represents a projection of his own achievement. And when he feels that he has had some participation in setting group goals, the group (company or departmental) objectives become even more his own. By helping people sense the importance of the roles they play, a manager nourishes this feeling of group affiliation.[8]

Embracing company or departmental objectives is one path to congruence; but, while always desirable, it is not the only means. Congruence can also arise from the specific work a person is asked to do. The work that Sue Smith does, for example, results in beautiful sales-promotion brochures that the company likes, and it also gives her an opportunity to use her flair for

[8]R. N. Ford, "Job Enrichment Lessons from AT&T," *Harvard Business Review,* May–June 1970, pp. 97–110.

*Figure* $20.3$ *When an individual contributes to the success of a winning team, there is likely to be congruence between individual aims and organizational objectives.*

artistic photography. Sue observes, "Sure, what my supervisor asks me to do is a means of reaching his own and company ends. Though I don't care as much as he or the president about such ends, they aren't in conflict with my own goals or values. And, if I do what he asks, I get to achieve my ends in a way I would choose for myself if I were my own boss. I'm far from indifferent, because I want the same results as he wants—but for different reasons [ends]."

Sue is not ambivalent or indifferent toward her work; she loves it but for reasons which differ from her manager's goals. She is more than compliant as she is committed to satisfying her goals.

Productive work may provide many kinds of satisfactions. Pride in the output, sense of creativity, self-expression, and demonstration of professional skill are among the psychological rewards of a job well done. Although we usually think of such satisfactions in connection with crafts, professions, or other individualistic work, managers and team workers may get the same sort of elation from the results of group effort.[9]

With care a manager can design his organization so that there is opportunity for people to get these satisfactions from their particular work—as we recommended in Chapter 15. Job enlargement (more activities) and job enrichment (more decentralization) are ways of expanding the scope of a position so that the incumbent finds his work more rewarding. Of course, it

[9]J. R. Hackman, "The Design of Work in the 1980s," *Organizational Dynamics* (Summer 1978), pp. 3–17.

is necessary to assign an individual to a job that provides opportunities for work satisfactions that appeal to him.

Through this process of skillfully designing jobs and matching people to them, a manager can build congruence. Then if he actively assists and supports people in those positions in achieving their immediate goals, a high degree of commitment normally follows.

## CONCLUSION

Giving orders is an inescapable, vital part of the process of managing. More systematic attention to how it is done, we believe, can often significantly improve a manager's effectiveness.

A constructive approach to giving orders is to recognize that a manager's request of a subordinate may receive opposition, ambivalent compliance, indifferent compliance, or commitment. Using this framework, a manager should predict the probable response to his exercise of authority and compare that predicted response with an acceptable (optimum) response for that task in the existing setting. When there is a good match between the predicted and acceptable response, the request is made and action proceeds. But when a mismatch is predicted—when the likely response will be inadequate—the manager then must consider what he can do to shift the response or perhaps modify the request.

Commitment is an "ideal" response. Many situations arise, however, for which compliance is both normal and acceptable. So, making a realistic choice among these responses in specific situations is a recurring task for every manager. These choices are not secondary issues; they affect the entire tone and effectiveness of a company's operations.

The tough stage in giving orders, of course, is overcoming mismatches between a desired response and the predicted behavior. When a manager forecasts an unsatisfactory response—opposition when he wants compliance, or compliance when he wants commitment—he must immediately consider what he can do to shift that response. Coercion, compromise, and establishing congruence are all possible means he can try to bring about a different response.

## FOR FURTHER DISCUSSION

1. Do external economic conditions have a greater effect on a manager's ability to issue orders today than they did between 1950 and 1970?

2. In what ways may it be better to change orders if opposition is forecast? When might it be wise to give the orders even though strong opposition is forecast and the orders well may have to be modified?

3. Give a personal example in which someone with formal authority over you gave you orders that elicited a strong negative feeling, and in which, further, you managed to avoid doing it without punishment.

4. When trying to influence behavior toward achieving a strategic objective, would a manager be more or less likely to accept compliance than when pursuing a tactical objective? Identify other variables which might be critical.

5. The text suggests that it is not only necessary but also desirable to seek, from the same individual, compliance to some requests and commitment to

others. Consider the desirability of seeking or accepting different responses to the *same request* from several members of a group who must share in carrying it out. What should be considered before accepting this situation? What are the dangers? Might there be advantages?

6. Which is a better response—ambivalent or indifferent compliance?

7. "Frequently, when I predict a negative reaction to an order I have to give, I will ask for something my subordinates will like even less. Then after a certain amount of debate, I back off and 'settle' for what I originally wanted. Invariably I get a better reception than I would have otherwise." Comment on this use of compromise by a magazine editor.

## CASES

For cases involving issues covered in this chapter, see especially the following. Particularly relevant questions are listed after each case.

## FOR FURTHER READING

Filley, A., *Interpersonal Conflict Resolution*. Glenview, IL: Scott Foresman, 1975. Discusses conflict resolution techniques for dealing with opposition to managerial requests.

Kreitner, R. and F. Luthans, *Organizational Behavior Modification*. Glenview, IL: Scott Foresman, 1975. Describes how behavioral modification programs may be used to shift responses to managerial requests.

Milgram, S., *Obedience to Authority: An Experimental View*. New York: Harper & Row, 1974. Controversial experiment on the obedience of individuals to malevolent authority. Important reading.

Schleh, E. C., *The Management Tactician*. New York: McGraw-Hill, 1974. Successful consultant explains how total job relationships may be restructured so as to make commitment likely.

Staw, B., ed., *Psychological Foundations of Organization Behavior*. Santa Monica, CA: Goodyear, 1977, pt. 4. Good collection of articles describing the exercise of power in organizations.

Willcoxon, S. R. and C. J. Brocato, "Improving Results Through an Integrated Management System: A Case Study." *Management Review*, February and March 1976. Report of AT&T long-lines program aimed at setting goals and gaining commitment to them.

# political behavior within organizations

# 21

## Learning Objectives

After completing this chapter you should be able to

1. Identify the distinguishing features of internal company politics.

2. Discuss how individuals develop political power within an organization.

3. Describe why coalitions form within organizations.

4. Explain the relationship between political behavior and organizational decision-making.

5. Describe the benefits and drawbacks of political behavior within organizations.

6. Understand how a manager can effectively channel political behavior.

## POLITICAL BEHAVIOR

Understanding intraorganizational politics is an essential skill for all managers. We discuss this non-traditional subject here because some of the talents helpful in leading are also useful in grappling with politics—empathy, objectivity, creating informal loyalties among individuals, recognizing individualistic wants. Company politics can be well understood only after one has a good grasp of planning, organizing, and the informal social structure of a company. It is important to recognize, however, that this chapter does *not* deal with leading (as we have defined it). Leading focuses on manager-subordinate relationships; intraorganizational politics is concerned with a special set of relationships among members of the organization outside the channel of command.

For some writers, "politics" is a dirty word. E. E. Jennings, for instance, implies that company politics are "devious, indirect, and underhanded."[1] Political action is often treated as a negative influence on morale and productivity within an organization.[2] In contrast, for a political scientist, political behavior is a normal, essential element in "winning the consent of the governed."

We regard politics as necessary and unavoidable, and consequently we must deal with it. From the viewpoint of effective management, political action can have both good and bad effects, so this behavior should be guided into those areas where it is a constructive influence.

Since our concern here is with behavior within an organization, we will focus on the pursuit of individually held objectives *by doing reciprocal favors* and *by using power to reward or to punish*. This use, or definition, of "politics" sets aside the politics of external relationships—an important subject but beyond the scope of this book. To be able to harness intracompany political behavior, a manager must understand

1. the distinguishing features of internal politics,
2. the relationship between "causes" and coalitions,
3. the role of politics in organizational decision-making, and
4. the need to channel political behavior effectively.

## DISTINGUISHING FEATURES OF INTERNAL POLITICS

exchange of favors

Politics starts with the exchange of favors.[3] As in the pioneer days when neighbors helped each other when in need, mutual assistance with a rush order or filling in for a sick coworker is normal social

---

[1]E.E. Jennings, *The Mobile Manager: A Study of the New Generation of Top Executives* (Ann Arbor: University of Michigan Press, 1967).

[2]See A.J. DuBrin, *Fundamentals of Organizational Behavior: An Applied Perspective* (New York: Pergamon, 1974).

[3]B. Mayes and R. Allen, "Toward a Definition of Organizational Politics," *Academy of Management Review*, 2 (1977), 672–77.

Figure *21.1*  *The exchange of favors in business is usually unspecified. Here, setting budgets and handling rush orders are presumably handled in a purely objective fashion. But if a production manager receives kindly treatment in his budget request, he is likely to ensure that the rush order of interest to the budget officer gets prompt attention; or perhaps the sequence is reversed. The favors may consist of prompt attention and sympathetic attitudes.*

behavior within any organization. In this process, implied obligations arise. If a person has helped you several times you are expected to help him when the opportunity occurs. Typically, in this elementary form, no attempt is made to precisely balance the good turns done; in fact, a statement that any direct return was expected would probably be emphatically denied. Rather, the practice is one of mutual helpfulness.

Whatever etiquette may require us to say, however, a person is expected to help his friend. Thus, if I have upset my normal shipping schedules several times to help you placate customers, I do expect your support in a negotiation with central personnel about a revised job evaluation. The subtlety here is the extent, if any, to which either you or I deviate from official instructions or professional conduct. Clearly, I can get things done faster and better if I have friends at key points where help is needed.

There is nothing inherently sinister about this kind of behavior, as critics of politics imply. Much voluntary coordination is achieved through trading of favors, and deep personal satisfactions arise from mutual helping. It is the amplification of the practice that *may* lead to negative complications.

**variations in political behavior**

Each organization member has the opportunity, if not the necessity, to play one or more political games. In our jobs we all have some discretion to allocate our effort and to set priorities; and in many managerial jobs a person has great latitude in deciding what his organization unit will do. The way a person allocates his energies can assist some fellow workers and perhaps hurt others. His action or inaction, therefore, has political implications. Everyone from receptionist to chairman of the board has this political dimension to his behavior, for he is inevitably helping some people more than others.

People vary in the degree to which they act with political motives in mind. (Also, those affected vary in the extent to which they perceive an act as a personal favor or disfavor.) Some individuals concentrate on objective results and appear to be quite insensitive to who may be helped or hurt, while others become preoccupied with how their actions will be viewed by influential persons. Most of us are in between. A "company politician" is an organization member who chooses his actions primarily on the basis of who will be helped and who will be hurt.

**use of power**

The possession of power greatly adds to a person's political strength.[4] Here we use "power" to mean the ability to supply or withhold something another person wants. For example, the receptionist has power to help (or hinder) a visiting salesperson who wants to see the purchasing agent; the chairman of the board has power to make capital appropriations and to appoint people to attractive jobs. The ability to inflict penalties—such as restrictions on the scope of freedom or loss of a job—is the negative form of power. Clearly, if a person has power and is willing to use it in exchange for favors, he can generate strong support for moves he would like to see made. Even an advisor to someone with power has political strength.

Power is so important to political effectiveness that its acquisition becomes part of the game. The politically motivated person does things he hopes will place him in a powerful position; and once in such a position, he has added capacity—by granting or withholding favors—to increase his power even more. Consequently, the sources of power and the way it is used within an organization deserve very careful attention.

**sources of power**

Individuals can develop political power in an organization in a variety of ways. The more common ways include

1. Formal appointment to a line position that by tradition or design gives the incumbent authority to make key decisions. For instance, the appointment enables one to add or withdraw products, select locations, grant discounts, appoint executives, promote and pay bonuses, select vendors, and the like. Clearly the more options the incumbent has—that is, the more decentralized and less constrained his job—the more power he possesses.

2. Opportunity to review and veto plans. Typical examples are a controller's authority to review budgets, a legal counsel's authority to review contracts, an environmental advisor's authority to examine ecological impact.

3. Direct supervision of the resources necessary to carry out essential steps in the plan.[5] The person who supervises the troops in the field, the computer, the plant, or even the mimeograph room can help get a project done quickly and well, or his opposition can add to delays and mistakes. Personal indispensability is even more effective. A government official once remarked, "Let them pass all the laws they want as long as I administer them."

[4]V.E. Schein, "Individual Power and Political Behavior in Organizations: An Inadequately Explored Reality," *Academy of Management Review*, 2 (1977), 64–72.
[5]J. Pfeffer, "Power and Resource Allocation in Organizations," in *New Directions in Organizational Behavior*, B. Staw and G. Salancik, eds. (Chicago: St. Clair, 1977), pp. 235–66.

4. Access to, and especially control over, the flow of information that is needed to identify opportunities or problems, and/or information that tells what actually is being implemented.[6] With this knowledge a person can easily pass tips to his friends and embarrass his competitor.

5. Quick, direct access to persons with power, coupled with ability to influence them—a "power behind the throne." Usually this influential advisor status arises through personal friendship and confidence; or it may reflect the advisor's active or latent ability to rally support from a pressure group—union, banks, or college alumni.

If a person with power from such sources as these elects to take care of his friends and punish his enemies, he can muster considerable support for programs he wants to sponsor. Rarely is the power used blatantly; it is usually clothed with plausible rationalization, and may take the form of expediting or foot-dragging rather than open support or opposition. For instance, an announcement will explain, "This appointment is an exception based on unusual need," or "The proposal for a new plant is being sent back for further studies because of unexpected technological problems." Nevertheless, the political message comes through to those who live in the company society.

We should note that there are restraints on the use of power for political purposes.

1. The formal managerial structure places limits on the use of power—as we shall see in the closing section of this chapter.

2. Favoring one person often deprives another, and an individual in power soon faces the dilemma of whom to help. The "art" of politics lies in aiding as many people as possible in ways they feel important without seriously antagonizing anyone.

3. Several persons are active in any political game, and in many situations they tend to check one another (though not necessarily in a way that benefits the enterprise).

Summarizing briefly, the distinguishing characteristics of political behavior within organizations are (1) the exchange of favors, (2) choices based on who will be helped or hurt, and (3) the acquisition and use of power to reinforce this "you scratch my back and I'll scratch yours" process. Innumerable variations in scope, method, and effectiveness arise, but these features will be found at the heart of all internal politics.

**CAUSES AND COALITIONS**   Thus far we have discussed political behavior without reference to the motives of the politicians. Although a few company politicians are interested in power alone, most are strong supporters of a cause. The cause is an ideal or goal—or set of these—to which the person is dedicated. In public life a cause may be better housing for blacks or tariff protection for local industry; within a company it may be higher-rank jobs for women, increased use of computers,

**political objectives**

[6]A. Pettigrew, "Information Control as a Power Resource," *Sociology*, 6 (1972), 187–204.

keeping production concentrated in the Toledo plant, or a larger market share than the XYZ Company. Often the cause is tied to loyalty to one's department or profession. Also, alternative strategies are typically causes for some executives.

With such a commitment the politician can proceed with zeal. The distinction between his personal benefit and the cause becomes fuzzy—if it

*TABLE 21.1*
*CAUSES THAT MAY*
*LEAD TO INTERNAL*
*COALITIONS*

| Type of Organization | Examples |
| --- | --- |
| Military | Nuclear submarines |
| | Women in command posts |
| Church | Ecumenical movement |
| | Medical missionaries |
| Local government | Lotteries to support schools |
| | Family-planning clinics |
| Private business | Geographical dispersion of offices |
| | Addition of low-priced brand |
| | Retention of all production in U.S.A. |

is drawn at all. He is still exchanging favors, making choices based on who is helped or hurt, and seeking power. But the criterion for whom to help and how to use the power is tied to the cause.

Protecting one's career and advancing a cause are especially likely to be entwined. A person may demonstrate ability while advocating a cause; thus his career prospects are improved by successful promotion of the cause. Drawbacks arise, however. Powerful people may disagree with the cause, and any advocate may be damned—currently or in the future—along with the cause. Of course, one may support a cause only temporarily, vacillating according to an assessment of the feelings of executives who affect careers. Carried to the extreme this attempt to curry favor with those in power will be interpreted as purely opportunistic and as lacking character and integrity. So, the person concerned about building his career has to select his causes thoughtfully and sincerely.

Moreover, devotion to a cause may be shared by other members who prefer not to take political initiative. These people become supporters of a political leader who espouses their cause. Although such support is normally passive, it does provide voluntary service and also potentially active backing, which the political leader can arouse in case of a showdown. Clearly this latent support strengthens the political potency of the leader who champions a popular cause.[7]

[7]For an early discussion of this phenomenon in public affairs, see H.D. Lasswell, *Politics: Who Gets What, When, How* (New York: McGraw-Hill Book Company, 1936).

A popular cause is often joined by other politicians. In fact, support from a variety of directions is essential for any complex endeavor. So *coalitions* are formed. People whose main interests may be quite diverse join such a temporary alliance to support the cause. Members of a coalition do not give up their independence, and they may continue to differ sharply on some issues; but they do agree on joint action with respect to the cause.[8]

For several years the marketing manager of a furniture company had been recommending adding an upholstered line—but other executives were preoccupied with the expanding volume of dining and bedroom furniture. Then, when sales dropped, both the personnel and manufacturing managers joined the cause—the personnel manager to provide promotion opportunities for trainees, and the manufacturing manager to use the space and service facilities of a new plant. With this support, a decision to add upholstered furniture was made.

Coalitions are easier to form in opposition to a proposed change or to a person than for a positive action. Among people with diverse goals, we are more likely to agree on what we don't like. The dean of a school of architecture, for example, became intrigued with matrix organization. However, several of his department heads viewed the proposal as a threat to their domains and decided to buck it. Each kept raising problems and drawbacks to such an extent that the plan became surrounded by doubt and was finally dropped.

In a coalition, each member contributes his influence—and if necessary uses his power—to bring about the desired results. Most coalitions in companies are quite informal and spontaneous, although on major controversial issues the coalition leaders may systematically seek support and modify the proposed plan to obtain crucial backing. By participating in coalitions an individual can extend the scope and impact of his political behavior.

## POLITICS IN ORGANIZATIONAL DECISION-MAKING

We find political activity within organizations partly because neither the purely rational nor the organizational approaches to decision-making provide complete guidance for action. Gaps in explicit plans open the way for the trading of favors.

The rational decision-making concept (discussed in Part II) runs into difficulty when it is applied to a dynamic, multidimension enterprise. Multiple objectives, at least at the operating level, replace the single overriding goal; even a single objective may have different dimensions, such as jobs that are both secure *and* challenging. So the criteria for making a choice are not clearcut. Also, although a means—end chain does tie a specific action to a general objective, there may be alternative routes that receive scant atten-

---

[8]This definition of coalition differs from that of R.M. Cyert and J.G. March in their *Behavioral Theory of the Firm* (Englewood Cliffs, NJ: Prentice-Hall, 1963) in its more limited scope and uncertain duration. Thus in our terminology, senior executives make a much stronger commitment to their company than merely joining a coalition.

tion. And often uncertainty about the future environment or long-run results is so high that we must act on faith. All this leaves room for debate about the optimum decision, for plausible arguments can be advanced for several. And with strong-minded executives in a growing enterprise, timely resolution of such a debate may require a "political" action.

Nor does the organizational decision-making structure give full guidance on how members are to act. Everything cannot be planned; expense, rigidity, and external changes impose limits on the extent of planning. Moreover, delegating some authority helps build commitment and fulfills personal needs (see Chapters 11 and 15). To secure prompt action, management deliberately creates several local power centers and then finds that it cannot measure the use of that power against specified goals—at least in the short run. In addition, managers often deliberately build conflict into an organization and then encounter difficulty keeping specialized units focused on some larger goal (see Chapter 17). Again, the absence of clear guidance opens the way for politics.

These practical limitations on the customary approaches to organizational decision-making create the arena for political behavior.[9] Frequently, whether we like it or not, a single right decision is by no means obvious. Necessarily, you and I and a lot of our coworkers have some freedom in the choices we make. And in this gray, unspecified area politics will color, if not determine, the shape of company action.

**motivational benefits of politics**

The exchange of favors in its elementary form is a necessary ingredient of voluntary coordination. Such reciprocal give-and-take facilitates all sorts of helpful operating adjustments that are impractical to plan in advance. And in addition, although we may prefer to think that our colleagues are generous with their help whenever opportunity arises, reinforcement for that generosity comes from a recognition that failure to join in mutual help can have serious personal consequences of a political nature.

The credit analysts in a Chicago commercial bank, for instance, each follow a separate set of customers, but they frequently exchange industry and company data to help each other. If requested, an analyst will make a great effort to get information wanted by a coworker. However, one analyst chose to stick to his own accounts; he felt that he had all he could do watching his own customers, and could not take time doing someone else's research. As a consequence, this analyst not only failed to get cues and supporting data from other analysts, but his suggestions for improving procedures in the department were resisted—"We had fun shooting down all his bright ideas," explained another analyst—and he was socially isolated. After two years in the credit department he left the bank.

Politics also engenders other kinds of motivation. For instance, commitment to causes can create great enthusiasm and drive. Personal loyalty is likewise a practical motivator, and often satisfies a psychological need. Polit-

---

[9]M.L. Tushman, "A Political Approach to Organization: A Review and Rationale," *Academy of Management Review*, 2 (1977), 206–16.

ical behavior is by no means the only way to generate such feelings, but we should recognize this potential energizing force. Obviously, directing such energy toward constructive ends is essential.

Since political behavior is, as we have noted, one of the facts of organizational life it would be a mistake to overlook the positive contributions such behavior can provide.

Unless it is very carefully channeled, however, intraorganization politics can undermine the effectiveness of an enterprise. Four influences call for specific attention.

**debilitating effects of political behavior**

1. Pursuit of the personal goals of politicians (either self-selected causes or personal drive for power or promotion) usually detracts from the central strategy of the enterprise. To the extent that political action succeeds in diverting resources from and/or blocking efforts toward target results, effectiveness suffers.

2. If internal politics escalate into a major power struggle, a substantial amount of attention and energy is devoted to the internecine warfare itself. "We spend more time outmaneuvering each other than we do serving the customer," one disillusioned executive remarked.

3. The company incentive mechanisms directed toward company strategy may be undermined by the rewards and punishments meted out by those with political power. And the more imprecise the company measurement-and-reward system, the more vulnerable it will be to counterproductive internal political pressures.

4. Politics often focuses on short-run tradeoffs. In this process long-run programs tend to be sacrificed because both the measurements and payoffs from long-range programs occur well into the future.

## CHANNELING POLITICAL BEHAVIOR

The preceding analysis indicates that, although some features of political behavior can be beneficial, there is serious danger that it can dissipate the concerted effort that organization is intended to deliver. Needed, then, are ways to harness and direct the energies of people who have a bent for politics. The following measures will move us a long way toward this end.

Troubles start when political pressures pull away from the central strategy of an enterprise. Consequently, the results sought by the enterprise (or department) and the balance between them should be clear and agreed upon. Then numerous supporting activities (and political maneuvering) can be evaluated in terms of their contribution toward achieving these strategic goals.[10]

**sharpen strategy of the enterprise**

Such sharpening of strategy is easier to propose than to do. Strategic thrusts are multiple and sometimes competing; they shift over time; the optimum way of attaining them is always uncertain; and in subdividing necessary work we often create conflicting subobjectives. Nevertheless,

[10]J.P. Kotter, "Power Dependence and Effective Management," *Harvard Business Review*, July-August 1977, pp. 125–36.

mechanisms exist in an organization (that is, in a well-organized bureaucracy!) for identifying the strategy which, for a given period, carries official
endorsement. This must be articulated if undesirable political activity is to
be flagged and checked. With approved thrusts and targets known, the
company can hope that political efforts will be directed toward their achievement. What is wanted is congruence in the results sought by politicians and
by the enterprise.

**tie resource
allocations and
rewards to
strategy**

The capacity to give or withhold resources and rewards is a foundation
of political power. The key modification that management must introduce
here is to structure the allocation and reward processes so that the best
payoffs clearly go to people who are actively contributing to achievement of
official goals—and not to mere political allies. Note that again the ideal
arrangement is one in which political payoffs and rewards—as well as company rewards—support the enterprise's strategy because the same results
are being sought.

To tie approved strategy into resource allocations and rewards, these
procedures and criteria must be carefully watched.

1. For standard, repetitive situations the steps to be taken to obtain resources and
   rewards and the criteria that will be used in allocating them should be known in
   advance. Thus, the procedures and the standards used in extending customer
   credit or in granting an extra week's vacation should be explicitly stated. Then
   individual discretion—aside from assessing the facts in each case—is reduced to
   a minimum. And there is little occasion for intramural politics.

2. Budget allocations, promotions, assignment to high-potential project teams, provision of R & D support, personnel quotas, and the like cannot be treated in the
   "programmed" manner as just suggested in (1). The possible alternatives and the
   criteria used to choose among them are too numerous and shifting to fit a single
   model. However, decisions on such matters, can be made jointly and openly—
   that is, several executives and/or staff people should participate, opportunities
   for suggestions from even more people should be provided, and final approval
   should be given by a senior executive after he is informed of the disagreements
   or doubts of qualified people. Such open consultation provides opportunities to
   check political maneuvering and to test the compatibility of proposed action with
   approved strategy. In those situations where conflict has been deliberately built
   into the organization decisions on resource allocations and rewards must be
   approved at least by a common superior who is aware of the inherent potential
   for "politicking."

3. Even more subtle is tying rewards to informal cooperation in achieving company
   goals. Cooperation here refers to the flow of key information, the energy applied
   to unexpected problems, a willingness to make changes that primarily aid some
   other division, the provision of minor but necessary services such as duplication
   and supplies, and the like. The measurement of such cooperation or the lack of
   it is difficult, and no specific decision warrants the kind of review suggested in
   (2) above. So a formal measurement-and-reward system is unwarranted. Nevertheless, persons who can grant or withhold such aid may use this power politically. Whenever possible, procedures and jobs that give people power to interrupt
   communication and work flows should be avoided, even at some extra expense,

thereby reducing the potential for a strong political base. However, if power positions are unavoidable, then such jobs should be filled by individuals who are loyal to overall company strategy.

The underlying aim of these various arrangements is to create a situation in which virtue is rewarded and crime does not pay—"virtue" being decisions contributing to target results and "crime" being decisions calculated to enhance political strength even though they are dysfunctional.

This is a secondary step. The primary way to avoid undesirable political activity is to create a setting in which the desired results are known and the major sources of power are administered in support of those goals—as recommended above. However, in spite of these positive influences, some individuals will occasionally become so obsessed with promoting their private goals that they resort to politics that run contrary to company interests. Specifically, they reward and punish and start building coalitions for actions inconsistent with recognized company strategy.

**punish deviant power-seekers**

When such behavior is discovered, it should be promptly and openly reprimanded; if continued it should be punished by more severe measures—such as transfer to a powerless position or by dismissal. Every organization develops a climate—a set of traditions, values, and standards—that subtly shape behavior. Tolerance or intolerance toward independent power bases is part of this climate. And if a company wishes to avoid becoming infested with petty power-players, the practice must be explicitly frowned upon. Just as people sense (and anticipate in their decisions) the existence of political pressures, so too will they sense firm disapproval of private politics contrary to company interests.

Every company must attract a variety of resource suppliers—people of different skills, capital, materials and services, government support, customers, and the like. Although these groups find association with the company beneficial, there is inevitably some bargaining over the terms of cooperation. And this bargaining is very similar to the political process we have been examining—an exchange of favors and mutual help, the development of relative power positions, and perhaps informal coalitions in concluding agreements.

**isolate resource acquisition from internal operations**

If this external bargaining with resource suppliers gets mixed up with internal decision-making, the likelihood of deviant internal politics jumps sharply. For instance, if a banker is given a veto on expenditures or a union leader controls work assignments, each becomes a member of the decision-making apparatus; then, if either pushes for the parochial interest of the bank or union when decisions are being made within the organization, we find ourselves in the same fix as with a self-centered politician.

An examination of numerous institutional arrangements for bargaining with resource contributors is not the primary focus of this chapter. Broadly speaking, to keep internal politics adequately channeled, arrangements for resource inputs should be set for a year or more; and once set, team behavior should be expected. After ground rules for contributing the resource have been established, integrated company action takes over. The concept of "no divided interest" becomes paramount. This does not mean that company decisions are indifferent to the need to reach future agreements with resource contributors; it does mean that the two categories of decisions are separate.

## CONCLUSION: MANAGING INTRAORGANIZATION POLITICS

This set of proposals (see Figure 21.2) for channeling intraorganization politics proposes bureaucratic devices to prevent political behavior from upsetting the organizational model. We give priority to the organizational approach because, as far as business is concerned, the political model lacks any modus operandi for securing concerted group effort toward common goals. Neither theoretically nor practically does it guide decision-making in a manner that would permit enterprises to survive and serve their strategic and social ends.

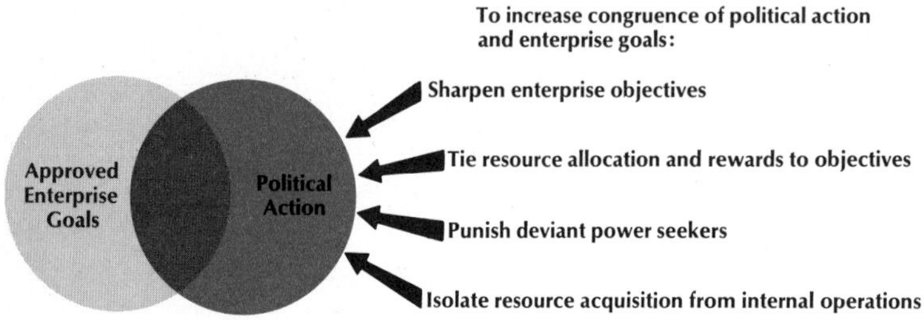

Figure 21.2  Ways to harmonize political and company goals.

Using political analysis as a tool, a manager can channel intraorganization politics, thus preventing political behavior from interfering with the attainment of organizational objectives. It is imperative that potential deviant behavior be harnessed. Some political motivations may be turned to constructive purposes if the manager is able to identify them with organizational objectives being pursued.

We conclude that a manager should view intraorganization politics as an added dimension to the planning, organizing, and motivating systems. The harnessing of political behavior calls for an understanding of, and a commitment to, company strategy, and for the kind of measurement and control which we consider in Part VI. So again the interdependence of various parts of managing stands out. The challenge for each manager is to put all these parts together in a way that best suits his own opportunities.

## FOR FURTHER DISCUSSION

1. Is a knowledge of politics more important to the president of a company when he is seeking to *formulate* new strategic directions or after they have been formulated and he seeks effective

implementation of new strategies? Discuss.

2. "Politics is essentially the art of the *practical*. Managers, since they don't have to get elected, should be less concerned about what is practical and

more concerned about what is *best*. I don't want politics in my bank." Comment on this from the president of a large bank.

3. Would politics be more or less useful in a matrix organization than in a centralized functional structure?

4. "I have great respect for the women we have moved into senior management but they just do not seem to understand the importance of doing a little 'politicking' from time to time. Because they try so hard to use only logic and their personal power, they get less done." Comment on this observation from a corporate executive.

5. "A politician's power stems less from what he legally can force others to do than it does from using his skills as a 'broker' to get others with more power

than he has to join him." To what extent does this comment, made by an early nineteenth century American statesman apply to today's governmental politicians? How about today's corporate politicians?

6. In general, do you feel that effective use of organization politics is more important at high management levels or among first-line supervisors?

7. How may the role(s) played by staff managers affect the amount and form of political behavior they should engage in?

8. How does a coalition differ from a tightly knit group which contributes greatly to an organization's objectives? Are coalitions usually good or bad in terms of their impact on an organization's effectiveness?

## CASES

For cases involving issues covered in this chapter, see especially the following. Particularly relevant questions are listed after each case.

## FOR FURTHER READING

Allison, G.T., *Essence of Decision: Explaining the Cuban Missile Crisis*. Boston: Little, Brown, 1971, chaps. 5 and 6. Develops the third of three models used by Allison in his pace-setting study—government politics; and applies this model to the Cuban missile crisis.

Du Brin, A.J., *Fundamentals of Organizational Behavior*. New York: Pergamon Press, 1974, chap. 5. Describes various forms of political maneuvering in organizations.

Korda, M., *Power*. New York: Random House, 1976. An experienced executive's perspective on obtaining and using power.

Pettigrew, A.M., *The Politics of Organizational Decision-Making*. London: Tavistock, 1973. Detailed study of the power and politics involved in selecting computer equipment in a large British firm.

Swingle, P.G., *The Management of Power*. New York: Wiley, 1976. Strategies for managing political behavior within organizations.

Pfeffer, J., *Power and Politics in Organizations*. New York: Pitman, 1980. Examines the relationship between formal structure, informal organization, and organizational politics.

# not-for-profit note for part V

Leading is likely to be a delicate task for not-for-profit managers. Their use of rewards and punishments is often circumscribed, but this may be offset by greater commitment of subordinates to enterprise goals. Both of these tendencies, however, must be carefully appraised in each situation.

As he starts to convert plans into action, a manager in a not-for-profit enterprise should be aware of how much power he can muster if it is needed. Of course, a leader's power does not disappear just because the goals of an enterprise are other than profit. College football coaches, church sextons, and co-op managers occasionally are fired; some labor unions and some symphony orchestras are run by powerful autocrats. Nevertheless, in a large majority of not-for-profit ventures, *a manager's ability to give bonuses and other rewards for good performance, and to impose penalties for poor performance or insubordination, is quite restricted*—as compared with the pressure available to managers in profit-making firms.

One reason for this restraint on the use of power is the difficulty of evaluating performance. If output is intangible and goals ambiguous—as previous notes have suggested—a manager lacks a clear-cut basis for giving rewards or punishment. And in the absence of standards that both he and his subordinate understand, rewarding or punishing is apt to appear capricious. So in many not-for-profit enterprises, we find strong traditions against managers making rewards or imposing penalties based on an individual's performance. Furthermore, as discussed in the note for Part IV, in fields such as education and government, these restraints are formalized.

Securing voluntary cooperation from specialized personnel becomes harder as a not-for-profit enterprise grows. In a departmentalized organization, the gap between the dominant occupations—usually professionalized—and lay workers becomes wider. In large hospitals, for instance, many lay workers no longer feel the same commitment as the élite professionals to a service mission. So they unionize and press for their own ends.

It becomes much easier to obtain voluntary cooperation if the supervisor who translates broad goals into specific assignments is accepted as a legitimate spokesman. Professionals such as doctors and professors may resent an intervening executive who is not a qualified member of their own "guild." In fact, workers who feel that their supervisor is incompetent may be even more critical of him when they are concerned about end results than they would be if they were indifferent. Such an "unqualified" supervisor may fail to secure voluntary cooperation even though the worker agrees with the overall objective.

Before issuing orders the wise not-for-profit manager will first predict his subordinates' response, as proposed in Chapter 20. If this expected response is less enthusiastic than desired, the manager then considers possible ways of changing the response. At this stage our not-for-profit manager may realize anew that he lacks power to coerce. So he must rely on trying to win commitment, on creating conditions favorable to indifferent compliance, or on some sort of compromise.

In the note accompanying Part I, we observed that internal planning in not-for-profit enterprises is complicated by the existence of vague and hard-to-measure goals. When fuzzy objectives are combined with the restraints imposed by professionalization, operating executives have considerable leeway in what they actually do. And such leeway permits *political maneuvering* for personal ends. It is a tribute to thousands of lower-level managers in not-for-profit enterprises that the potential for maneuvering is not often abused and that results in most instances are reasonably satisfactory. Nevertheless not-for-profit executives face the continual challenge of properly channeling political behavior and retaining a focus on the pursuit of organizational objectives.

A leader in a not-for-profit enterprise faces formidable obstacles. As a result, in vigorous not-for-profit enterprises, we often find that the available energizing forces must be supplemented by charismatic leadership or institutional mystique.

The Netsuki (pronounced 'Netski' in the U.S.) Novelty Products Company is a wholly owned subsidiary of the Kono Group, a large Japanese conglomerate. For many years, the Netsuki Company (Japan) has exported large quantities of electronic toys and games to the United States. In addition, components were sold to U.S. toy and game manufacturers. In the late 1970s, after almost two years of study, the Kono Group purchased some seventy acres of land in Hartung, Wisconsin, and built a large modern facility for assembling the most popular of its products sold in the U.S.

Shegie Tanaka, general manager of U.S. operations, explained his company's reasoning.

"It is a great honor," he said, "to locate here in America's heartland. Your resources are so abundant, your people so strong and appealing. We most sincerely hope we can contribute to the area from which we derive so much. We came here primarily to reduce the cost of shipping finished product many thousands of miles. We believe it will be much cheaper to import some key electronic components and produce other parts and do final assembly here. Even though, at present, our unit production cost is almost one hundred percent higher than in Japan, our savings on transportation offset much of this. Certainly we hope, as we learn more about American methods and styles, to reduce our production costs. Your people are willing to work hard and are so very clever, even if they have some trouble understanding some of our peculiar methods.

"At present, we are completing negotiations with a large U.S. distributor to handle domestic sales and we soon shall ship from this plant to Canada and Latin America as well. While all has not gone as smoothly as was hoped, we see great opportunities for future success in this great country."

Tanaka explained that all hourly workers and most supervisors and technical personnel were recruited locally. Three senior technical people, two marketing staff, and the controller are Japanese nationals but Tanaka indicated his hope that they could be replaced by Americans someday.

Larry Stahl, one of three superintendents and probably the highest-ranking American in the plant, expressed his ambivalence when asked how it felt to work at Netsuki.

"Like the Scarecrow among the Munchkins," he said. "I am not complaining, mind you, but I feel like such a big dummy much of the time. I have had sixteen years of experience in this business and I'm sure I have a lot of both technical and supervisory knowledge to offer Tanaka but during the six months I worked with him prior to start-up and for fourteen months since, I'm not sure whether I have contributed anything he didn't already know.

"Tanaka and his technical staff are always asking me questions and politely write down all my answers or get me to write them up in a report. Then they go away and days, if not weeks, later come back and ask more questions about my earlier answers and have a new set of questions. They often ask six or seven of my people the same questions or related ones. Whenever I ask whether they like my ideas or suggestions they always bow and say, 'Very helpful! Very, very helpful' but I am so frustrated I'm ready to quit.

"Months after I look into something for them or make suggestions, they institute changes. If I examine the changes closely enough I can actually find some of my inputs. I am due for my second yearly appraisal soon—the first one went well but we had hardly gotten the plant started—and I really don't know where I stand.

"Tanaka has indicated that I might make assistant general manager next year and someday even replace him, but I can't pin him down on performance standards. Every time I ask him what he expects from me, he goes back to a list of six or seven 'Mickey Mouse' production standards which we agreed to last year. Hell, I may or may not meet them but I will come very close. Clearly, though, these are very short-term standards limited in scope by the narrow constraints of my supervisory authority and our start-up status. None of these standards reflect my efforts to contribute to overall technical and top-management decisions.

"I left a very good job with a U.S. firm because I felt I could help Netsuki get set up, and then have a chance to run the plant. While they made no promises, they indicated this might work out. If it does, great; if not, no hard feelings. I can get another job. I just don't want to invest three to five more years here and end up as a production supervisor."

Stahl indicated that he liked the Japanese personnel, with one exception, and felt that they treated him well but he repeated, "I just can't pin them down on anything. I don't expect a commitment, I just want Tanaka to be more explicit about what I have to do to earn one of the top two jobs in the next four years. If he would just spell it out, I would know what to shoot for."

The one Japanese manager Stahl feels he cannot work with effectively is Murio Saito who reports to Tanaka as controller and handles local bank loans and intermediate term financing.

"Saito drives me bananas," Stahl said. "To begin with, he is a has-been. He was a senior financial officer for one of Kono's largest subsidiaries and they forced him to retire two years ago at fifty-five. Now he is back over here and only works four days a week. While he is supposed to be fifty-seven, I'd swear he was ninety-seven the way he squeaks around bowing and grunting like something out of an old movie.

"If you think Tanaka is hard to pin down, he is absolutely gregarious compared to Saito. I just don't trust the guy. He has set more detailed standards for this plant than any place I have ever worked. What's worse is that he is always changing them. He'll soon have a standard for how long you should take on a toilet break—complete with acceptable variance margins. The man is a real kook. He bothers everyone with his questions, questions, questions. Then come new controls or new standards for existing controls. He has become a joke. Nobody takes him seriously anymore. We all figure as long as we hit the bottom line on volume, unit cost, quality, and safety, no one will worry about variances plus or minus on twelve hundred or so substandards."

Tanaka feels Stahl is a fine manager but somewhat impatient.

"He has great potential," Tanaka indicated, "but needs to relax and trust us. At thirty-eight, he has many years ahead of him. He has helped us greatly and I wonder why, bright as he is, he needs so much reassurance. I have much to learn about such people but have been startled to see how even the best require so much—what is your lovely expression?—'stroking.' He will in time realize how much we value his contributions.

"I have only one concern and that is his lack of respect for Mr. Saito. Mr. Saito is a brilliant man who has left much that is precious to him to be of help here. He will be a key to reducing our unit costs. His knowledge and control systems are already beginning to give us needed insight into how to reproduce what is good and improve what is not good. Mr. Stahl should try longer to understand Mr. Saito and learn his methods and he must pay more attention to Mr. Saito's suggestions."

When asked whether he had communicated this concern to Stahl, Tanaka indicated he had not. "Such a sensitive man," he said, "might be offended. Also, one cannot order respect; it must be earned by one and discovered by the other. Saito will earn and Stahl will discover."

Recently, a professor from a leading U.S. business school visited the Hartung plant. He had been studying Japanese management methods and was interested in seeing them applied in a U.S. setting. When Stahl expressed his views on the situation, the professor suggested that he look at an article on Japanese management published by a colleague who had just completed a major research project on this topic.

The following passages were particularly interesting to Stahl.

"Both productivity and quality control of the TV assembly line result from joint effort. Suggestions may come from engineers, supervisors, or workers. These are fully discussed, especially if a proposed change involves modification of either equipment or component design. Sooner or later everybody gets into the act. Even minor ideas are given respectful consideration.

"Many informal meetings are involved. And these discussions move slowly because of the politeness with which each viewpoint is expressed and the need to avoid offending anyone with a different idea. Restatement and refinement of the problem takes the place of direct confrontation, and this requires time. . . . However, because of this prolonged discussion, any emerging decisions are well understood, have few bad side effects, and are acted upon with commitment.

". . . Several features of Japanese business culture contribute to the effectiveness of this joint approach. (1) Group responsibility is stressed much more than individual accountability. Group success is an important source of social esteem. An individual gains stature by the success of his group and by his being a constructive group (team) member. (2) 'Life-time employment' and promotion (within categories) based largely on seniority provide job security. Individuals don't job-hop; instead, their future is very closely tied to the growth of their company. (3) Job duties are not sharply defined; assigned tasks depend on the current work to be done, and are subject to change. Young engineers frequently work right on the shop floor where they can respond to the total work situation. . .

". . .Normal retirement age is 55. Lump-sum pensions are paid at this time but are very small. However, good people may be rehired to fill temporary needs for their skills. This adds flexibility to the selection of the senior workforce and tends to reduce resistance to change at upper levels of management."

Stahl comments, "That may be great for Japan. But I'm glad Tanaka has not asked me to run my shop that way. And I hope he hasn't ideas of shifting too far or too fast in that direction. After all, we have a very different culture and history here. Our values and what we expect from each other just don't support their approach."

## FOR DISCUSSION AND REPORT-WRITING

**part I: planning: the execution of strategy**

1. How might you deal with Stahl's concern that his objectives are all short term and do not reflect his efforts to contribute to overall technical and top-management decisions?

2. How do you reconcile Saito's establishing many detailed standards (standing plans?) with Tanaka's use of six or seven broad objectives when asked by Stahl for feedback?

3. Stahl apparently does not participate in the development of Netsuki's U.S. strategy. How is this likely to affect his ability to develop or contribute to short-term functional planning?

4.  For which elements of decision-making does Tanaka appear to seek participation?

5.  Why do you think he limits his quest for inputs on decisions in the way he does and apparently gives little feedback on what was done with suggestions?

6.  Which methods of testing his choice for a large, difficult decision do you feel would appeal to Tanaka most?

part II: planning: elements of rational decision-making

7.  Given the proposed mission for Netsuki (USA), how should its activities be coordinated with headquarters in Japan?

8.  Do you feel Tanaka should change his methods of appraisal and feedback with Stahl? Should he discuss Stahl's long-term career plans in more detail?

9.  How applicable do you feel Japanese concepts such as lifetime employment, early retirement, etc. would be in the U.S.?

part III: organizing: strategy to structure

10.  What appear to be major differences in motivating Japanese vs. U.S. employees? Similarities?

11.  Japanese concepts of participation seem to differ from those in the U.S. What effect do you feel Tanaka's brand of participation will have on Stahl's motivation if Stahl is rewarded for performances sufficiently to stay with Netsuki another year?

12.  How do you feel Tanaka would deal with even constructive conflict among U.S. employees?

part IV: motivating: human factors in the organization

13.  Evaluate Tanaka's relationship to Stahl using "Elements of Personal Leadership" as your criteria.

14.  How relevant to this case are the concepts presented in the sections on "Contingency Approach to Leadership Style"?

15.  How important in this case is leadership as a means of "closing the gap between decisions and actions"? Why may it be more or less important than if all employees were Japanese or all were American?

16.  Do you feel political behavior is more or less likely in this situation than in an organization made up of all U.S. emloyees? Why? Is it more or less desirable?

17.  (Summary Report Question, Part V) Develop a detailed set of recommendations for (1) Tanaka, and (2) Stahl, as to specific steps (actions) they should take to improve communication between themselves and other key managers.

part V: leading

18. How helpful do you feel Saito's numerous detailed standards will be in determining how to improve performance in the plant? Explain.

19. What attributes should control systems in the plant have in order to be consistent with the prevalent leadership style and reward system?

summary question
for solution of the
case as a whole

20. Review your answers to questions Parts IV and V and prepare detailed recommendations on what actions, if any, Tanaka should take in order to improve Netsuki's long-term effectiveness in the U.S.

**CASE 5.2**
*MARATHON PLASTICS*

Marathon Plastics is a manufacturer of a wide range of plastic products with headquarters in Pittsburgh, and large plants in Houston, Chicago, and Los Angeles. Roughly sixty percent of the company's products are manufactured in these three plants. In addition, the company has a smaller, specialty-products plant in Pittsburgh, and seven more in other locations. These eight smaller facilities make up the balance of production. Over the past decade, Marathon has enjoyed steady, impressive growth with sales approaching $400 million. Profits, however, have not kept up with sales growth as a result of increased costs for fuel, raw material, and inventory.

Frank Roesch, senior vice-president of operations, has responsibility for all production, development, engineering, and transportation (see Exhibit I). A long-service executive with Marathon, he had accepted much of the blame for less-than-targeted profit.

"Not only have our fuel and raw material costs gone up," Roesch explained, "but they have bounced around in ways that are difficult to forecast. This makes pricing much tougher and leaves us unable to make long-term contracts with either suppliers or customers at what we feel will be profitable levels. In addition, even our best suppliers have been erratic with deliveries. Since many of our operations are continuous process, to avoid costly shutdowns and startups, we have had to increase inventories considerably. Even with premium prices and inventories running as much as fifty percent higher than normal, we have had to do a lot of swapping around the plants. Akron may have extra ethane and Pittsburgh may be low on ethane but has extra LPG, so they swap.

"We have even had material redirected from L.A. to Chicago, in emergencies, and I heard Norm Wherrit (petroleum manager, St. Louis) has been trading stock with several of our competitors. With all this uncertainty and wheeling and dealing, our costs fluctuated more than they should have."

Each of Marathon's eleven manufacturing facilities are considered cost centers. They are highly autonomous units whose plant managers historically have had almost total control of their plants. Manufacturing and engineering service departments, located in Pittsburgh, carry out special projects for the plants and are 'paid' on a fee basis, by the plants for work they do.

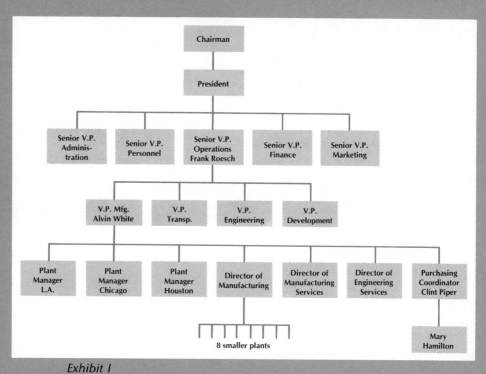

*Exhibit I*
*Partial Organization Chart*

As a result of recent problems with cost and inventory levels for fuel and raw material, Roesch requested that Alvin White, vice-president, manufacturing, hire someone to act as a special consultant and coordinator of fuel and raw material purchasing. White agreed, reluctantly, and four months ago hired Clint Piper to fill the post.

"I understand that Frank (Roesch) has taken a lot of flak on cost control, and so have I," said White. "Sooner or later, things will either smooth out or we will be able to improve our forecasting. If the product managers, particularly for industrial products, would get off their duffs, we could raise prices, or at least get more cost-plus business. Instead, they try to squeeze *us* down to unrealistic cost figures and do their pricing 'mumbo jumbo' on unsound estimates.

"I have also recommended that corporate headquarters look into acquisition of a few key suppliers. If we owned some of our most important sources of inputs, we could at least use them as hedges. Roesch says he's working on this with the president but money is tight now. He also says that he will try to help us with those s.o.b.'s in marketing, but I've heard that before. I can understand his problems and I don't mind the heat, but I wish he hadn't saddled me with this purchasing consultant/coordinator idea."

White explained his reservations by indicating that he felt the position really added little except more than $200,000 to his overhead.

"Piper's salary plus that of an assistant, their secretary, space, travel, and fringes could cost me a quarter of a million," White stated, "and I won't get a dime back from the plants. Roesch said I can't bill them for services since I am to require them to use these services. I just hope we get some benefit from Piper, though I am not optimistic. If he fails, it won't be his fault. He seems like a very smart person and has good experience in commodities but he is swimming upstream. Our plants are fiercely proud of their freedom from headquarters' interference. I have always encouraged that by keeping my staff groups small and forcing them to pay their way by selling their services to the plants. The plant managers know that as long as they produce, they run their own show. If they do well, they are rewarded personally and so are their people through a bonus pool.

"If they foul up, it comes out of their hides and I accept no excuses. Even though I understand why they have been hurt on raw material and carrying costs, I have not bailed them out. Few have gotten good personal bonuses or bonus pools for the last couple of years. They know what to do and they will fix it. I hope Piper can help them."

Piper and his assistant, Mary Hamilton, have tried very hard to be of help but thus far have made little progress.

"I know Mr. White had reservations about hiring me," Piper explained, "but he has given me as much support as he can. He sent a very good memo to all his plant people explaining that my job was to help them and that they should cooperate with me to the fullest. He also gave me veto power on contracts over $10,000 for all but the three big plants. He explained that the big plants (Houston, Chicago, and Los Angeles) have their own purchasing people and do not need my help right away. He told me not to bother about them now but to concentrate on the eight small plants. I'm sure he wants me to prove myself with them and when I do, he will give me a crack at the larger plants."

Piper and Hamilton spent many weeks going over purchasing data. They found it hard to piece together patterns in recent years, given much internal trading of material. Many of the smaller plants, it seemed, were actually using the large plants as brokers or hedges on some commodities. There were many gaps in the available data, however, and requests from Piper to plant people for records seemed to take forever to be met.

"Half the time they send me the wrong information or incomplete data," Piper said. "Their record control systems must be a mess. I asked Mr. White why we couldn't pull all these records together in one data bank. Our management information systems (MIS) people tell me they could do it. Mr. White said he thought that was a good idea but since MIS reports to someone else, he would have to run it through channels.

"Fortunately for me, Mary Hamilton was an assistant purchasing agent in the Chicago plant and she has helped me interpret what we have, and read between the lines. Several times she made a few phone calls that cleared up some of the confusion about my requests for information."

Two months ago, Piper wrote to the plant managers of the eight smaller plnts requesting that they send him copies of their most recent forecasts of materials requirements and their estimates of price and delivery information. Three plants have made no reply as yet but indicated when telephoned that they were "on their way." The other five plants sent reponses which Piper feels are far too sketchy and not at all recent.

"I think I may have to visit all eight of these plants," he said. "I have tried to do most of my work by mail or phone as I have a pretty tight travel budget. Perhaps I can visit four of the eight and have Mary see the others. We have to impress these plant people that we are here to help them but need their cooperation. I may also want to flex a little muscle here and there with my veto power and make sure they know that if they don't cooperate, I have some clout. While I have never worked in a plant, my impression is that some of the people are suspicious of staff. I hope I can allay their concerns and also show them I can be tough if I have to.

"Mary thinks the visits are a good idea but feels we should *both* go—together—to all eight plants just to introduce ourselves and let them know what we are doing. Since this would more than double the cost and time involved, I think I will do it my way."

## FOR DISCUSSION AND REPORT-WRITING

1. How might Piper's mission be made more likely to succeed by tying it more directly to the company's master strategy?
2. In what ways are Piper's objectives consistent and/or in conflict with the objectives of the managers of the eight smaller plants?
3. Should Piper be developing a good single-use plan, good standing plans, or both? Explain.

*part I: planning: the execution of strategy*

4. What do you feel are the causes of Piper's current difficulty in gaining cooperation from the plants? List at least three different causes and take one to its root.
5. For each causal element, develop either an alternative to eliminate it or a means of circumventing it by moving up the means-end chain.
6. How important are "quantitative aids" likely to be in helping Piper achieve his goals?

*part II: planning: elements of rational decision-making*

7. Is Piper's department an "auxiliary unit," a "staff unit," or what?
8. Given Piper's apparent formal and informal authority, what are his obligations?
9. How might Piper's authority be increased? Give several different ways.

*part III: organizing: strategy to structure*

10. What factors seem to be shaping group behavior in the eight plants? Can these forces be used to benefit Piper? How?

11. How may informal systems, customs, and established practices provide better solutions to purchasing problems than Piper's efforts?

12. What role(s) should Mary Hamilton play in bringing personal leadership to bear in this situation?

13. What do you think are the best media and types of communication for Piper and Hamilton to use to get vital information? To change actions in the plants?

14. What impact may internal politics be having on Piper's current situation?

15. If coalitions have formed among plant personnel, what are the probable causes?

16. For what requests should Piper seek commitment and for which accept compliance? Why?

17. What means should he use to shift response toward what you feel he needs (see question 16)?

18. (Summary Report Question, Part V) What specific actions should Piper take at the end of the case to improve his chances of success at Marathon? Be specific about both what he can do now and what other steps he might take later if his initial steps succeed.

19. What control standards and measurements should Alvin White use to evaluate Piper?

20. What changes in the control process might White and/or Roesch make if they wanted to give Piper more clout? Do you feel they should make these changes?

summary report
question for
solution of the
case as a whole

21. What would you do now if you were Frank Roesch and knew the details of what has happened since you requested White to hire someone to act as a special consultant and coordinator? Review your answer to question 18 before developing your action plan.

# CONTROLLING

Managerial control is akin to the thermostat system of a furnace. The thermostat keeps track of the actual temperature in the house, compares it with the desired temperature, and switches the heat off or on, accordingly. Many activities of an organization need to be similarly controlled.

Controlling is the counterpart to planning. Less glamorous than planning, control provides measurement and evaluation of results to ensure that plans are not mere pipedreams. No plan is complete until we have designed ways of assessing its outcome. Much more than recording history is involved. A good control system includes three kinds of controls: steering controls, yes/no checks as work progresses, and postaction evaluations.

Our thermostat analogy is over-simplified—the control of business operations cannot be reduced to a mechanistic process. Controls are effective only to the extent that they influence people's behavior. So when designing controls we must consider carefully how those affected by each control will respond to the feedback provided.

In Part VI we shall first examine the basic elements of a control system, and then explore ways of integrating controls with a company's behavioral and formal management structures.

Chapter 22—Basic Elements of Control. Here we shall discuss selecting strategic control points, setting levels of desired performance, evaluating results on the basis of various kinds of evidence, and making reports that lead to timely corrective action.

Chapter 23—Budgetary Control Techniques. Budgetary control techniques are of special interest because they are company-wide in scope. Budgets give a comprehensive view of financial plans and results. These techniques can be used in many circumstances, but we must understand their limitations as well as their advantages.

Chapter 24—Behavioral Responses to Controls. The idea of being controlled is repugnant to most people, even though they readily accept controls as a normal part of civilized living. We shall explore why people react as they do to controlling and shall consider how we can design and administer controls in order to engender a positive feeling about them.

Chapter 25—Integrating Controls with Other Management Processes. Here we explore interrelationships between controlling, on the one hand, and planning, organizing, and leading, on the other. We shall deal with a series of special problems that arise in keeping the various aspects of managerial action coordinated and integrated.

Controlling depends on, and contributes to, the other management processes—planning, decision-making, organizing, motivating, and leading. Without plans to set objectives and management decisions to specify activities, control would serve no purpose. Without organization, guidance would be lacking about who should make evaluations and who should take corrective action. Without effective motivation and leadership, a whole carload of measurement reports would have no impact on actual performance. Consequently, we must carefully fit together executive action in all these phases of management.

# basic elements of
## control

# 22

Learning Objectives

After completing this chapter you should be able to

1. Describe the three major types of controls.

2. Describe the major stages of the control process.

3. Explain how control points vary for different types of work.

4. Understand how symptoms, predictions, and sampling are used for purposes of measurement.

5. Identify who in an organization should receive control reports.

6. Describe how corrective action is carried out.

**THE CONTROL PROCESS**     Controlling is the task of every manager—from the chief executive officer to the most humble supervisor. Since its elements are the same at all levels, we will first examine simple control problems and then, in later chapters, consider controlling more elusive outcomes such as progress toward strategic targets.

The primary aim of controlling is to ensure that results of operations conform as closely as possible to established goals. A secondary aim is to provide timely information that may prompt the revision of goals. These aims are achieved by setting standards, comparing predicted and actual results against these standards, and taking corrective action.[1]

In practice, controlling is often poorly done; conflict arises about when to control and who should do it. One way to avoid part of this difficulty is to distinguish three different types of controls.

1. *Steering controls.* Results are predicted and corrective action taken before the total operation is completed. For example, flight control of the spacecraft aimed for the moon began with trajectory measurements immediately after take-off, and corrections were made days before the actual arrival.

2. *Yes/no controls.* Here, work may not proceed to the next step until it passes a screening test. Approval to continue is required. Examples are legal approval of contracts, quality checks on food, and test flights of aircraft.

3. *Postaction controls.* In this type of control, action is completed; then results are measured and compared with a standard. The typical budgetary control and school report card illustrate this approach.

All three types may be needed to control a department or major activity. But it is steering controls that offer the greatest opportunity for con-

---

[1]W. G. Ouchi and M. A. Maguire, "Organizational Control: Two Functions," *Administrative Science Quarterly,* 20 (1975), 559-69.

*Figure* **22.1**   *Three basic types of control.*

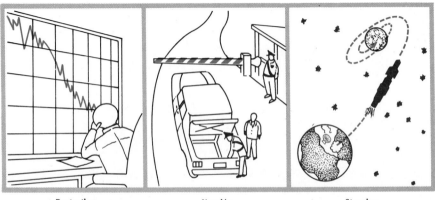

Postaction          Yes-No          Steering

structive effect. They provide a mechanism for remedial action while the actual results are still being shaped.[2]

Yes/no controls are essentially safety devices. The consequences of a faulty parachute or spoiled food are so serious that we take extra precautions to make sure that the quality is up to specifications. Avoidable expense or poor allocation of resources can also be checked by yes/no controls. If we could be confident that our steering controls were effective, the yes/no controls would be unnecessary; unfortunately, steering controls may not be fully reliable, or may be too expensive, so yes/no controls are applied.

Postaction controls, by definition, seem to be applied too late to be very effective. The work is already completed before it is measured. Actually, such controls do serve two purposes. (1) If rewards (a medal, bonus, discharge, self-esteem, etc.) based on actual results have been promised, these results must be measured and the appropriate rewards made. The aim is psychological reinforcement of the incentive scheme. The pay-off in this reinforcement lies in future behavior. (2) Postaction controls also provide planning data if similar work is undertaken in the future.

Even though controls are placed at different stages of operations, as the preceding classification suggests, three phases are always present in each control cycle.

**phases in controlling**

1. *Control standards that represent desired performance.* These standards may be tangible or intangible, vague or specific, but until everyone concerned understands what results are desired, control will create confusion.
2. *Measurement of predicted or actual results against the standards.* This evaluation must be reported to the people who can do something about it.
3. *Corrective action.* Control measurements and reports serve little purpose unless corrective action is taken.

Regardless of what is being controlled, these elements are always involved.

Expense control, from the use of electric lights to the total cost of goods; quality control, from the appearance of a typed letter to the dependability of an airplane engine; investment control, from the number of spare parts in a repairman's kit to the capital investment in a fleet of tankers—all involve standards, evaluation, and corrective action. A closer look at each of these phases will help us design controls for specific purposes.

**SETTING CONTROL STANDARDS**

The first step in setting control standards is to be clear about the results we want. What shall we accept as satisfactory performance? We must answer this question in terms of (1) the outcome characteristics that are important in a particular situation and (2) the level of achievement, or "par," for each characteristic.

---

[2]There is a close relationship between steering controls and the concept of "feedforward" control. See H. Koontz and R. W. Bradspies, "Managing Through Feedforward Control," *Business Horizons,* June 1972.

Operating objectives, already discussed in Chapter 3, serve as starting points in setting control standards. Usually, however, these must be amplified. For instance, we noted in Chapter 3 that companies with separate business-units have found that profits are an inadequate measure of success. In addition to profits, such companies often consider market position, productivity, leadership, personnel development, employee attitudes, and public responsibility. It is possible to focus on only one aspect such as profits or market position. But to do so without first thinking through *all* characteristics that contribute to good performance is to court trouble.

A furniture store, to cite another example, found that it had to think about the following factors in appraising its credit department: the attitude of customers who had dealings with the department; the total credit extended; the operating profit earned on goods sold on credit; credit losses; department operating expenses; gross income from credit charges; net expense of running the department; and departmental cooperation with the treasurer, sales manager, and other company executives. It was decided that the credit manager had to perform well on all these counts if his work was to be rated as satisfactory.

Each time a manager designs a new control, he faces this question of what characteristics to consider. An approach that could benefit some jobs would be to give thought to these three matters.

1. *Output.* What services or functions must be performed? Perhaps each of these services can be defined in terms of quantity, quality, and time.
2. *Expense.* What direct dollar expenses are reasonable to secure such an output? What should be normal indirect expenses in terms of supervision, staff assistance, interference with the work of other people, and opportunities foregone to perform other kinds of work?
3. *Resources.* Does the operation require capital investment in inventories, equipment, or other assets?[3] Are scarce human resources or company reputation being committed? If so, effective use of resources should also be considered.

Having identified the characteristics of good performance, we must then determine how high a level of achievement we desire for each characteristic. More precisely, what is a reasonable expectation, or par, for good performance? For example, pars for the credit department in the furniture store mentioned earlier might be as shown in Table 22.1.

For most performance characteristics, par is simply an ordinarily feasible achievement level. Variations beyond this level are usually desirable—such as output above par or expenses below par. But in special circumstances such as the rate of production on an assembly line, there may be only narrow tolerance limits for deviation above or below the established par.

---

[3]Although the cost of developing a well-trained corps of workers, a smooth-running organization, or a good reputation with outside groups does not appear on a company balance sheet, such assets do require investment in the same way that machinery does. Such investment is essential if future "output" is to be achieved within desired future "expenses."

TABLE 22.1

| Characteristic | Standard |
|---|---|
| Attitude of customers | 90 percent of furniture purchased on time, financed by the store |
| Total credit extended | Outstanding loans approximately equal to last 90 days' sales |
| Operating profit earned on goods sold on credit | $500,000 |
| Credit losses | 0.5 percent of credit extended ($7,000 in normal year) |
| Department operating expenses | $24,000 per year |
| Gross income from credit charges (above interest paid to bank) | $28,000 per year |

On highways, the speed limit is a single standard that is applicable to all drivers. Similarly in business, a single standard may be applicable to such things as quality of delivery service. But for many other situations we may adjust the standard for a particular individual or local circumstance. A branch manager of a national sales organization who tried this individualized approach reports as follows:

Don't compare an individual to the group average, but rather to a standard set for that person. I have tried this on quotas for growth and for new customers and during the current canvass, and the results are good. The salespeople are more quota-conscious than I have ever before known them to be. I find they will work much harder to make their own standards than they will to "beat the high person" or surpass crew average. Also—each one is much more aware of his own quota (through interest) and the total book standing than previously.

***Securing flexibility through adjustment of par*** In control, as in other phases of management, we have a legitimate need for flexibility. A firm may increase inventories if there is reason to anticipate a shortage of raw materials; it may cut its price to meet competition, knowing that dollar sales figures will be thrown out of line; during a depression it may decide not to cut employment in proportion to the drop in production; and so forth.

Unfortunately, "flexibility" is sometimes used an an excuse to disregard control entirely. Because the standards are no longer reasonable, there is a temptation to say that control is not feasible. A more sensible way of dealing with unforeseen conditions is to adjust par. The performance characteristics being watched, the measurements, and the reports continue to be useful; we need to change only the levels of expectation. As we shall note in Chapter 23, this is precisely the result of "flexible" budgets, and this concept may be adapted to many other control standards.

Both automatic and semiautomatic adjustments of par are usually based on a variation of a key external variable (that is, external to the domain of the person being controlled) such as volume, price, or wage rates. The original pars are based on a set of *planning premises;* and when these premises shift through no fault of the controllee, some offsetting revision of pars is called for. In a broader scope, this kind of adjustment suggests that when control is used for personal evaluation, the key planning premises should be identified and then *their accuracy* observed as well as the results of a person's efforts.

**relating results to individual accountability**

Control standards are most effective when they are related to the performance of a specific individual.[4] Thus both the person himself and his supervisors can know whether he should be praised or blamed. In addition, fixing accountability for a deviation helps focus the search for causes and thereby sharpens corrective action.

But accountability for a desired result is not always simply assigned. A company's investment in inventory, for example, is affected by purchases, rate of production, and sales. Each employee to whom one of these three activities is assigned looks on inventory from his own point of view, as does the treasurer, who is concerned with the financial strength of the company. In some companies, only one person, who has the task of coordinating these different viewpoints, is accountable for the level of inventories. In other companies, the task is divided. For instance, the sales manager estimates sales, the plant manager schedules production and indicates the quantities of raw materials he will need each month, and the purchasing agent decides when it will be advantageous to buy the materials specified by the plant manager. In such a situation, in which no one person is accountable for the level of inventories, standards may be set for each step. Then if there is trouble with inventories, we can ascertain where the system broke down.

An alternative to dividing complex tasks into separate steps that can be assigned to single individuals is dual accountability. When cooperative effort is crucial and contributions of each person are hard to distinguish (as in a surveying crew and in many methods-improvement studies involving both line and staff personnel), we may say that each member is accountable for the team result. The control then keeps the focus on results, with strong emphasis on cooperation.

Clearly, the establishment of standards for control purposes is heavily dependent on the previous management decisions on plans and organization. Specifically, objectives (discussed in Chapter 3) are the direct counterpart of "desired results"—the starting point in a control cycle. Similarly, the assignment of duties (discussed in Chapter 10 and 11) is the key to the assignment of accountability for achieving control standards. Theoretically, setting objectives and defining job duties need not be reconsidered when we set control standards. But in practice this is rarely so. Workable control almost always calls for refining and clarifying objectives and duties. Without fail, though, we should start with the plans that have already been developed. Then the process of developing standards for purposes of control is really a matter of refinement.

[4]G. L. Morrisey, "Without Control, MBO is a Waste of Time," *Management Review,* February 1975.

"Desired results" have been urged as a good starting point for designing managerial controls.[5] We now want to turn to several refinements of this principle.

checking at pivotal points

1. To attempt to evaluate all the results of everyone's work would be very burdensome. Instead results are usually measured only at various intervals. For instance, a dairy farmer may measure his output only in terms of pounds of butterfat produced per week. Moreover, as we shall discuss in the section on evaluation, sometimes only samples of the output are measured. The aim is to watch enough to keep track of what is happening, without going to the expense of watching everything. That is, the aim is to pick *pivotal points* that will, at least indirectly, reflect the total operation. If results at these points are off standard, a more detailed check can be made of intermediate stages to find the reasons for the deviation.

   The president of an automobile-parts manufacturing company keeps his eye on four key items that reflect operations in the plant: total output, efficiency, back orders, and inventory. By watching the ratio of standard man-hours to actual man-hours worked every month, the president believes he can detect any major difficulties with equipment or with operating personnel, and so keep track of overall efficiency. The back orders indicate whether the plant is meeting sales requirements. The inventory figures show whether good deliveries and plant efficiency are being achieved by large accumulation. There are, of course, many other local controls, but the four points are what the president watches closely.

2. Steering control is used so that a move can be made before the final results have occured. For this purpose, points which will serve as warning posts are sought. Here the aim is to *direct attention* rather than to evaluate. The Hilton Hotels, to cite an example, keep close tabs on advance bookings of conventions—one, two or even three years ahead. With this warning of the ups and downs of business volume, they can undertake special promotions to fill in valleys. On a month-to-month basis, when it is too late to change booking volume, knowledge of advance bookings is used to expand or contract staff to fit the expected level of operations.

   In safety work, control is achieved largely though training in safety methods and through maintaining safe operating conditions. In other words, management locates pivotal control points in the formative stages, and inspections are made to try to prevent trouble from ever arising.

3. Yes/no controls allow screening devices to catch serious errors. Actual results to date are measured, and work is permitted to proceed only if the results are satisfactory. Such controls may be placed anywhere in the flow of work at which safety can be checked—the earlier the better.

In many companies, requests for capital expenditures for such things as new buildings, equipment, and sources of raw materials have to be presented in writing with an explanation of why each investment will be advantageous to the company. The request then passes a yes/no hurdle. By controlling approval of the projects at this formative stage, the president or financial

[5]E. C. Schleh, "Grabbing Profits by the Roots: A Case Study in 'Results Management'," *Management Review,* July 1972.

officer can exercise an influence that would be futile after orders are placed and contracts let.

checking on
methods of work

In the preceding discussion of control standards, we have emphasized the results of work rather than the method for accomplishing it. Even strategic control points at early stages are basically devices for anticipating results. This emphasis is consistent with our stress on objectives, in the earlier discussions of planning and decentralizing. Nevertheless, there are times when control over method is more expeditious than control over results.

Sometimes controls are set on work methods simply because it is more economical to watch the methods than the results. Diamond-cutting, and quality control in the manufacture of spacecraft or parachutes, are undertakings in which control will probably be exercised over methods as well as results.

Then there are baffling situations for which it is extremely difficult to know just how good results should be. Cancer research, or negotiating with a group that is protesting ecological abuses, are examples. In these situations the manager may resort to evaluating the method by which work was done.

Whenever control is undertaken, then—from the entire company down to the work of a single employee—the manager needs to consider what kinds of results and what level of par to incorporate into company standards. And since busy executives cannot give regular attention to a complete array of standards, they must identify pivotal points to watch: summaries of overall results, results of key activities, warnings of impending trouble, and—for some jobs—*methods* of work. One of the arts of good management is setting the right standards at the right control points.

## THE TASK OF MEASURING

Once standards are set, the second basic step in control is the evaluation of performance. This step involves (1) measuring the work that is done, or predicting what will be done, in terms of the control standards, and (2) communicating the appraisal to persons who search for reasons for deviations and take corrective action. Broadly speaking, control measurements seek to answer the question, "How are we doing?"

Auditing is concerned with control, but not the type of managerial control we are discussing in this chapter. A manager focuses on achieving certain results. Financial auditing, on the other hand, is designed chiefly to ensure that no skullduggery has taken place. An auditor deals with the accuracy of financial reports—be they bearers of good tidings or bad—and especially with making sure that there has been no pilfering of cash or valuable inventory and no fraud or embezzlement.

The specific methods of measuring results are almost as diverse as the activities of business. Because at best we could give only a few suggestive examples here, it will be more useful to examine some of the common difficulties in measuring for control and to note several promising ways of dealing with these difficulties.

Engineers are far ahead of managers in their ability to measure what is going on. For one thing, managers have tended to rely on accounting far beyond its intended purpose and inherent capacity. To be sure, surveys of employee attitudes and morale, and Nielsen reports (which provide current data on the sale of goods in the grocery and drug fields by brand, region, and type of outlet) are steps in overcoming this deficiency. But great opportunity remains for improvement.

Actually, many companies have information they do not fully utilize.[6] An employment office may be able to provide a lead on labor costs long before these figures show up in accounting reports. A market-research department may be able to provide both control data and planning data. The information necessary for production scheduling can be used to measure productivity. Facts for use in control may be found in a variety of places.

Leadership in product design was set as a major control point for the engineering department of one electrical equipment company. Because product leadership is very difficult to measure, the company decided to try to summarize personal opinion systematically. Each year, a committee composed of the general manager, sales manager, chief engineer, and two outside experts try to agree on the following points:

1. The number of the company's significant "firsts" introduced each year versus competitors' "firsts."
2. A comparison of company products with competitors' products in terms of market requirements for performance, special features, attractiveness, and price.
3. The percentages of sales of products appraised to be superior to competition, equal to competition, or inferior to competition, together with corresponding market position and gross margin ratios of each category.
4. The percentage of company products in the total electrical equipment used in the plants of the twenty most efficient customers in the country.

In spite of the high degree of personal judgment involved in some of these criteria, this company has substantially better control over its product development than before it undertook such measurement; the design of managerial controls can benefit greatly from ingenuity.

Because measurement is often difficult, it is only natural to use any available figures. This is to be commended. There is the danger, however, that those characteristics of an operation that can be easily measured will receive far greater attention than their importance warrants.

An office-equipment manufacturer relied heavily on dollar-sales figures to control its ten regional sales representatives. As the sales manager was fond of saying, "The signed order tells who's on the ball." The representative in the Southern territory was an older man, and for two years before his retirement, he and the company had a clear understanding that he planned to settle down in Florida when he reached sixty-five. His sales

[6]R. L. Ackoff, "Management Misinformation Systems," *Management Science,* December 1967, pp. 147–56.

held up reasonably well. But when he was replaced, it was discovered that he had neglected to cultivate new customers. He had called only on his old accounts, and even with them he had glossed over troublesome service problems and had failed to cultivate the younger people in the customers' organizations. Several years of hard work were required before the territory again produced the volume it should. This unsatisfactory condition developed because the firm relied only on the easy measurement of results. If other, more intangible, factors had been watched, the deficiency in the representative's performance would have been noted before too much damage was done.

The danger that ease of measurement will dictate what gets attention is even more serious in operations where quantitative results are hard to pin down. The public-relations department of a pharmaceutical company kept close track of the number of letters received as a result of the news releases it issued. "Letters received" became one of the department's few quantitative measures of performance, and soon public relations was issuing news releases written expressly for the purpose of creating a flow of mail. Unfortunately, although controversial subjects and hints that a remedy was being developed for a wide-spread malady did produce a lot of letters, publicity on these topics distorted the public image of reliability that the company wished to establish.

Expense control is often characterized by an imbalance between quantitative and qualitative considerations. Zealousness in controlling, say, travel or telephone expenses, occasionally causes people to pay as much attention to these minor aspects as to the results of the work.

**using symptoms for control**

Just as the smell of smoke is an indication of fire, or bloodshot eyes and a haggard look at examination time are an indication of cramming, so in business we may use symptoms as indications of what is going on.

Employee attitudes, for example, are hard to measure directly and economically. Consequently, several companies have used such criteria as turnover, the number of absences and tardinesses, the number and content of grievances, and the number of suggestions submitted in a formal suggestion system. Under normal conditions, such factors probably do reflect employee attitudes. But we must exercise care in using symptoms as measuring devices, because (1) outside factors may cause a symptom to vary, and (2) when it becomes known that a symptom is being used as a measure, it may be possible to manipulate the measuring stick—for instance, tardiness in one office may be low because the office manager is a tyrant and not because employee attitudes are good.

**using predictions in control**

In steering controls predictions are often used as a basis for corrective action. As with the use of symptoms, actual results are not measured. But here the reason for using less-reliable criteria is a desire for prompt action. Customer inquiries may be used to predict a rise or fall in sales; a machine's vibration may be used to predict a breakdown; or grievances may be used to predict a strike. The prediction in such a case initiates corrective action; the manager doesn't wait for the predicted event to occur.

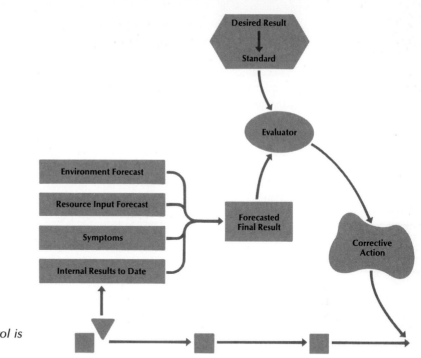

*Figure 22.2  Steering-control is based on predicted results.*

One of the large can companies has a control procedure that encourages corrective action based on predictions. A monthly profit-and-loss budget is prepared for each operating division and plant. Then, ten days before the start of the month, the various managers are asked to estimate how close they will come to the budget. Each prepares a revised estimate about ten days after the beginning of the month. A major advantage of preparing these two estimates lies in forcing the manager to predict what is likely to happen and to adjust his operations to current conditions. Because local demand for vegetable cans varies with the weather, short-run expansion or contraction of operations—and of expenses—is very important. Top executives do compare the performance of each division and branch against the original budget, but they give more emphasis to the ability of their managers to predict results accurately and take prompt corrective action.

A familiar way of simplifying the measurement task is to consider only    **sampling** a sample, which is presumably typical of the whole. For example, the quality of most food products, from kippered herring to corn meal, is tested by sampling. And students are well aware that an examination is only a sample of what they know, just as office workers realize that in his periodic visits, their supervisor samples their behavior.

Sampling is better suited to some activities than others. If a machine set to perform a particular operation turns out good-quality products both when the run is started and at the end, we can usually assume that the intervening production has also been satisfactory in quality. In a check of routine sales correspondence, if a random sample indicates that letter-writers are using good judgment and diplomacy, a supervisor will probably assume that all the work is satisfactory. On the other hand, a one-hundred percent check is desirable for some operations. A manufacturer of hearing aids, for instance, may sample at the early stages of production, but will-undoubtedly insist on a careful inspection of every finished product for performance before it is shipped.

Broadly speaking, to determine what portion of an operation should be measured, we try to balance the cost of incremental measurements against the increased value that might accrue from catching more errors. "Statistical quality control" is a special application of this general idea. When products are produced in large quantities, we can use statistical probabilities to decide when the number of errors is large enough to warrant stopping production and finding the cause. Substantial economies in inspection costs may result in situations where this technique applies. Unfortunately, the vast majority of managerial control situations do not involve the large number of similar actions that are needed for this refined statistical technique.

**personal observations and conferences**

Even with all the measurements that we have suggested in the preceding paragraphs, a supervising executive still needs to hold informal discussions with the persons whose work is being controlled; and, at least occasionally, he should visit the actual operations. Anyone who has corresponded over a period of time with another person whom he knows only by letter, and then has an opportunity to meet and talk with him, knows that there are certain impressions that can be conveyed only in face-to-face contact, personal observation, and conversation.

More importantly, personal observation has a flexibility that permits an executive to keep his eye on what is "hot" at the moment. Ability to make prompt delivery to customers may be crucial at one moment and the number of executives worthy of promotion at another. When a person is new in a job, a supervising executive will want to watch his work more closely than he would that of an experienced operator. Even if these factors could be incorporated into a formalized, continuing flow of information, to do so would probably be undesirable because of the cost and the added burden.

Discussions in other parts of this book dealing with organization, planning, and leading present compelling reasons for close personal contact between an executive and those who work with him. To those reasons we should now add this: effective measurement of results.

**CONTROL REPORTS**

Measurement of performance is of little value until the resulting appraisals are communicated to executives who can take corrective action.

The smaller the operating unit, the simpler the control reports need to be. In fact, in a small company or within a small unit, a supervising executive often evaluates results himself, and the only report is an oral discussion with the person doing the work that is being evaluated. A great many controls, perhaps the most effective ones, have this informal character. The basic steps of control are present—setting standards, evaluating results, taking corrective action—but the formal recording of results and of comparisons with standards is simple and rudimentary. Few people are involved and the facts are known to everyone, so the control deals primarily with initiating corrective action.

As more people are involved, the task of reporting and evaluation becomes more important. People work in different places, they are concerned with different parts of a total task, and there are more detailed facts than any one person can keep in his mind. A need arises, therefore, for control reports that summarize and communicate the conclusions of the measurements that have been undertaken.[7]

**who should
receive control
reports?**

Control information should be sent immediately to the person whose work is being controlled. He is the one most likely to be able to do something about it. Not that the information should go to a machine operator or a clerk who is merely carrying out specific instructions. Rather it should go to the purchasing agent who decides how much to buy, to the supervisor who decides when overtime work is necessary, to the sales representative who may be able to secure additional orders for slow-moving products, or to the foreign manager who might decide to withdraw from a market. In other words, information should reach the person who, by his own actions, can have a strong influence on final results.

Prompt feedback to the point of action encourages use of the "law of the situation," one of the means for obtaining voluntary cooperation discussed in Chapter 18. In most instances, the person on the firing line will start corrective action as soon as he knows that results are falling short of the established norm.

In addition, control information should flow, perhaps as a summary at a later date, to the controllee's boss. The person on the firing line may need help or he may need prodding; it is the duty of the supervisor to see that he gets either or both as the situation warrants.

These elementary observations about the flow of control reports are meant to emphasize that action which results from control measurements should be taken by the people who have primary responsibility for an activity being measured. Only in rare circumstances is it desirable to separate the action, or dynamic, phase of control from the duties of the one who initiates and supervises performance of the activity. But other people are often interested in these reports, to be sure: (1) executives who will use the control information to help formulate new plans, and (2) staff personnel who are expected to be familiar with, and give advice about, the particular activity under control. These people should be provided with such reports as they find

[7]M. M. Greller and D. M. Herold, "Sources of Feedback: A Preliminary Investigation," *Organization Behavior and Human Performance*, 13 (1975), 244-56.

helpful. But their claim is secondary to those of operators and immediate supervisors.

**timeliness versus accuracy**

Promptness is a great virtue in control reports. If some job is being mishandled, the sooner it is reported and corrected, the less damage will be done. Moreover, if the cause of a difficulty is not obvious, a prompt investigation is more likely to turn up true causes.

The distinction between postaction controls for overall evaluation and steering or yes/no controls affects the importance of promptness. Timeliness is especially urgent with the latter group, because they lose most of their potency if they are tardy.

Unfortunately, it is often difficult to be both prompt and accurate. An accurate evaluation may require a certain amount of investigation and double-checking. The person making an evaluation naturally wants to be sure he can justify his conclusions, especially if they draw attention to inadequacies in someone's work. In addition, delay is likely to be compounded if a report is prepared by someone who is trained to balance accounts to the last penny. A hospital administrator, for example, was having great difficulty keeping down expenses, partly because expense reports—laboriously compiled at the end of each month—did not become available until six to eight weeks following the events presumably being controlled.

Executives who use control reports should be fully aware of the kind of information they are getting. If they insist on prompt reports, they must

*Figure* 22.3   *Alternative flows of control reports.*

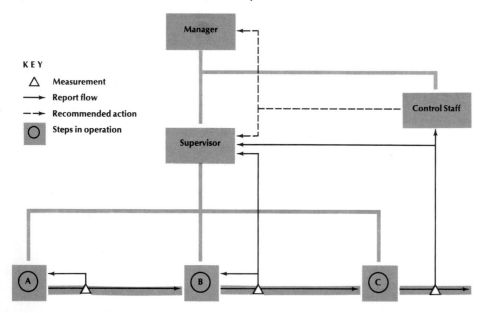

learn to disregard insignificant variations and to expect some false alarms. On the other hand, if they are interested in having the full facts and being deliberate in taking action, then they need a different kind of report.

Most control reports can be kept simple and present only key comparisons.[8] They are not intended to present a full analysis; furthermore the people using them are intimately familiar with the operations they reflect. These reports are not designed to impress the public; they are valuable if they give the operating people the facts they need quickly and understandably.

In addition to showing a comparison of performance against standard, control reports often reveal whether a situation is getting better or worse. They do so by comparing present performance with that in the recent past and with that during the same period a year ago. Such "trend" information is a helpful guide to a manager in deciding what kind of corrective action is appropriate.

**CORRECTIVE ACTION**     Control reports call attention to deviations of performance from plans, but they only signal trouble. The pay-off comes when corrective action is taken. The control information should lead to investigating difficulties, promptly deciding how to overcome them, and then adjusting operations.

Sometimes a control report will start a new management cycle: new planning and organizing, more active leadership, and another set of measurements and reports. But often, the original objectives and program are retained, and managers simply make minor adjustments at one point and push a little harder at another. These adjustments may be necessary anywhere along the line—needling a supplier; pinch-hitting for Joe Jones, who is ill; running department A overtime; and so on. In such situations a manager is like a captain who gets information on the location and bearing of his ship, and then adjusts his course in order to arrive at his planned destination.

The distinction between replanning and corrective adjustments is not sharp. For convenience, we speak of "corrective action" if plans and the final result remain the same. If an appraisal indicates that major changes in plans or goals are in order, then the manager should replan. In both kinds of action, data from measuring is fed back to executives, who modify their operation.[9]

---

[8]Computerization of management information systems does not alter this guideline. Detailed control information need not accompany the summary report. Instead, the detail will be stored in the memory bank and retrieved on request. For a comprehensive discussion of such systems, see G. A. Gorry and M. S. Scott Morton, "A Framework for Management Informations Systems," *Sloan Management Review,* 13, no. 1 (Fall 1971), 55-70.

[9]For an interesting discussion of the relationship between the "corrective action" phase of control and the "problem diagnosis" phase of decision-making, see C. H. Kepner and B. B. Tregoe, *The Rational Manager* (New York: McGraw-Hill, 1965).

That actual operations do not always turn out just as planned is not surprising when we think back over the planning process described in Parts I and II. To proceed with planning, the manager must often adopt predictions as premises—predictions of sales, competitive prices, availability of capital, research results, productivity of new machines, and a host of other things. Such premises are the best estimate at the time, although it is recognized they may not be accurate. Also, many plans involve a calculated risk; for there may be, say, about one chance in five that an assumed event will not occur.

So, when control measurements indicate that all is not well, it is necessary to investigate many possible causes to discover the one that is creating the difficulty. Perhaps some person is at fault, but it is likelier that one of the manager's premises is wrong or that he has unluckily run into the one chance that he hoped could be avoided. At this stage, he is more interested in identifying the cause than the culprit, so that necessary adjustments in operations can be made promptly.

Moreover, the control measurements themselves may lead him astray. He may deliberately watch symptoms or estimates for early warnings of trouble—sales inquiries or employee absences, for instance. But we know from our discussion of diagnosis that symptoms can be misleading (see "Finding the Root Cause" in Chapter 6). A similar situation is possible if the "exception principle" is used—that is, if watch is kept only for exceptionally high or low performance. An exception may flag serious trouble, or it may be a unique instance that probably will not recur.

In some highly routinized operations a manager can act like a servo-mechanism on a machine, automatically making a given adjustment when certain conditions are detected. Automatic pilots on airplanes and thermostats on furnaces work this way. But most managerial situations are not so simple; it is necessary to identify which of many possible causes is creating difficulty and then devise appropriate corrective action.

Once a difficulty is spotted, as a result of an investigation prompted by an unfavorable control report, the manager must move quickly to corrective adjustments. If the operating situation has shifted from what was planned—perhaps raw materials are delayed by a dock strike or the computer breaks down—he will take steps to get the working conditions back to normal. If subordinates are ineffective, he will clarify directions to them, provide additional training where necessary, consider motivational lacks, and perhaps reassign work. Or, if it is not within his power to overcome the difficulties—say, customers simply will not buy the company's product—he must then recast goals and programs. From a managerial point of view, a control is not effective until such corrective action as may be necessary has been undertaken.

### CONCLUSION: ESTABLISHING CONSTRUCTIVE CONTROL

Controlling, like many other aspects of management, is simple in its basic elements but calls for ingenuity and deftness in its application. Setting control standards at pivotal points, sampling and measuring qualitative results, balancing timeliness and accuracy in reports, translating reports into corrective action—all are examples of the many issues we must skillfully resolve for a control system to be potent.

Distinguishing between steering, yes/no, and postaction controls assists greatly in control design. The selection of pivotal control points, the use of predictions before work is completed, the balance of promptness versus accuracy in reporting, and the nature of corrective action are all affected by a choice among these control types.

Although we have seen in this chapter a range of issues a manager should consider in the controlling phase of his work, other vital factors remain to be considered. Financial control techniques will be illustrated in the following chapter. Next, we will review the responses of people to controls, and finally, the integration of controls to other areas of management. These further considerations are important in making control an integral and consistent part of the total management structure and behavior.

## FOR FURTHER DISCUSSION

1. How does an organization develop controls which indicate how well strategic plans are being implemented?

2. How are detailed objectives and standing plans likely to affect the type and effectiveness of controls?

3. List and discuss several key factors in determining *who* should be assigned the task of comparing measurement of results to standards for the purpose of determining the cause of deviations.

4. "Controls and plans are two sides of the same thing. Without good plans one cannot have good controls and vice versa." Discuss this statement and indicate in detail how you agree or disagree.

5. In most foreign countries, the Pepsi-Cola Company grants a franchise to a local bottling and distributing firm. The franchised firm must use Pepsi's secret extract shipped from the United States. All other activities are performed by local nationals. The American company provides advice on production and distribution and permits use of the well-known Pepsi-Cola trademark. The company in the United States is natu-rally concerned about both short- and long-run profits in the foreign countries and about the worldwide reputation of Pepsi-Cola. What controls should the company establish over the activities of a franchise dealer in a foreign country?

6. Are detailed controls likely to be more important (1) when an organization is following a strategy to obtain growth and profit in a new market for a new product or (2) when following a strategy of maintaining profits and market share for an established product in mature markets?

7. "Our greatest weakness in control systems is our inability to determine the reasons for failure in sufficient detail and with sufficient certainty to be able to take sharply focused corrective action." Do you feel this is the "greatest weakness"? What can be done to deal with it?

8. Who should have primary responsibility for recommending control points, (1) the person(s) who develops a plan and will carry it out or (2) independent staff experts who are more objective since they do not develop and implement the plan? Discuss.

## CASES

For cases involving issues covered in this chapter, see especially the following. Particularly relevant questions are listed after each case.

Mike Zerllini (p. 188), 16, 17, 18
Clifford Nelson (p. 192), 18, 19
Scandico (Singapore) (p. 305), 16
Marathon Plastics (p. 456), 19
Joe DiMaggio (p. 533), 14, 17, 18
Foster Promotions Inc. (p. 538), 15, 16, 19, 21

## FOR FURTHER READING

Drucker, P. F., *Management: Tasks, Responsibilities, Practices.* New York: Harper and Row, 1974, chap. 39. Concise summary of major control-system characteristics.

Flamholtz, E., "Organizational Control Systems as a Managerial Tool," *California Management Review,* XXII, no. 2 (Winter 1979), 50-59. Discusses criteria for judging the effectivenes of a control system.

Giglioni, G. B. and A. G. Bedeian, "Conspectus of Management Control Theory: 1900-1972," *Academy of Management Journal,* 17, no. 2 (1974), 292-305. Contains a complete survey of the literature and a bibliography on control.

Litterer, J. A., *The Analysis of Organizations,* 2nd ed., New York: Wiley, 1973, chap. 21. Basic elements in the design of a management-control system.

Mockler, R. J., *The Management Control Process.* New York: Appleton-Century-Crofts, 1972. Comprehensive text covering concepts and techniques related to managerial control. The frequent references provide leads into control literature.

Newman, W. H., *Constructive Control: Design and Use of Control Systems.* Englewood Cliffs, NJ: Prentice-Hall, 1975. Comprehensive analysis of managerial control including—in addition to topics in this part—chapters on control of repetitive operations, projects and programs, resources, creative activities, and strategy; and a chapter on balancing the total control structure.

# budgetary control techniques

# 23

Learning Objectives

After completing this chapter you should be able to

1. State the three essential steps in financial budgeting.
2. Understand how company size affects the budgeting process.
3. Explain the main features of a profit-and-loss budget, a cash-flow budget, and an appropriations budget.
4. Describe how to achieve flexibility in budgeting.
5. Describe the benefits and dangers of budgetary control.

ELEMENTS OF BUDGETARY
CONTROL

Financial budgeting is a widely used control technique which aids in planning and in coordination as well. By discussing budgetary control techniques here in Part VI, we underscore the interdependence between planning and control.[1]

Basically, financial budgeting involves these three steps.

1. *Expressing in dollars the results of plans anticipated in a future period.* These dollar figures are typically set up in the same way as the accounts in a company's accounting system. The budget shows how the accounts should look if present plans are carried out.

2. *Coordinating these estimates into a well-balanced program.* The figures for sales, production, advertising, and other divisions must be matched to be sure that they are mutually consistent; the financial feasibility of all plans added together must be ensured; and the combined results must be examined in terms of overall objectives. Some adjustments will probably be necessary to obtain such a balanced program.

3. *Comparing actual results with the program estimates that emerge from step 2.* Any significant differences point to the need for corrective action. In short, the budget becomes a standard for appraising operating results.

These steps will be illustrated first in an extended example of a small company. Then we shall discuss the implications of the budgeting concept for larger firms and for special situations. Finally, we shall look into ways of securing flexibility and also into some of the dangers and limitations of budgetary control. Our aim is to see how financial budgeting fits into the management processes; we are not concerned here with the details of budgetary procedure.

BUDGETING IN A NEW
ENTERPRISE

Examining budgets for a new, small company enables us to see readily how operating plans can be translated into financial figures and how budgets provide an opportunity for overall coordination. For this purpose, we shall use Belafonte Fashions, Inc., as an illustration.

general plans
of Belafonte
Fashions, Inc.

After working as a stock boy, presser, and, more recently, foreman in several apparel plants, Paul Bailey went into business for himself. He had an opportunity to buy all the equipment of a defunct ski-suit plant and to take over a lease on the space it occupied. The $64,000 price was attractive, especially since the equipment was already installed and experienced labor was available in the area. Bailey, a black himself, had a strong desire to establish an all-black enterprise in a depressed area on the Near-West side of Chicago. His new venture was made possible by an investment by High Horizons, a private urban-renewal corporation. High Horizons matched Bailey's capital contribution of $48,000, arranged for an equipment mort-

---

[1] Other management techniques also serve a dual planning/controlling function. For instance, PERT, which was discussed as a planning tool in Chapter 5, is also a control device.

gage with a bank, and made a temporary working-capital loan of $36,800. Because Bailey had little background in finance and accounting, High Horizons stipulated that he use the "MBA Consultants" from Northwestern University for help in this area; Morris Barkin is the student assigned to this client.

Bailey's strategy was to concentrate on a limited line of women's pants, which are relatively simple to manufacture and use the existing skills of the work force. Purchased fabric of polyester and cotton or wool is cut, sewn, and pressed; permanent-press finishing is subcontracted to a nearby company. Bailey started in business in the autumn, a season when the demand for pants is brisk, and by the end of the year he had a going concern. The balance sheet at that time is shown in Table 23.1.

Morris Barkin, after a careful industry survey, urged Bailey to prepare a profit-and-loss budget for his new company. At the beginning of the new year, Bailey had the following plans in mind:

1. The company would first establish itself by making four fairly standard pants at low cost. With this operation as a base, more highly styled and novelty items could be added later to provide wider profit margins. But to attempt to operate a business on novelty items alone was too risky.

2. The four types of pants Bailey had in mind usually sold to retailers at an average price of $72.80 per dozen. Even with allowances and markdowns, Bailey hoped his average selling price would be at least $67.20 per dozen.

3. Selling would be done through manufacturers' agents, one in New York, covering the territory east of the Mississippi, except for Illinois and Wisconsin, and one in Chicago, covering the remainder of the United States. In the plant, Bailey figured, he needed an experienced cutter and a sewing foreman, each of whom would be paid $400 a week. He expected to take care of designing, buying, marketing, and general administrative work himself. However, he had hired

TABLE 23.1
BELAFONTE
FASHIONS, INC.:
Balance
Sheet—
January 1

| | | | | | |
|---|---|---|---|---|---|
| Cash | | $ 13,920 | Accounts payable | | $ 27,520 |
| | | | Accrued taxes, etc. | | 4,320 |
| Accounts receivable | | 53,760 | Current liabilities | | 31,846 |
| | | | | | |
| | | | Mortgage on | | |
| Inventories: | | | equipment | | 25,600 |
| | | | Loan from | | |
| Raw material | $32,800 | | High Horizons | | 36,800 |
| Finished goods | 26,880 | 59,680 | | | |
| | | | Total liabilities | | 94,240 |
| Current assets | | 127,360 | Equity | | |
| | | | Common stock | $96,000 | |
| Equipment | 64,000 | | Loss for first three months | 1,280 | 94,720 |
| Less depreciation | 2,400 | 61,600 | | | |
| | | | Total liabilities | | |
| Total assets | | $188,960 | and equity | | $188,960 |

someone to act as bookkeeper and general office assistant at $16,000 per year. All other employees were to be paid on an hourly or piece-rate basis. While the business was getting on its feet, Bailey planned to pay himself only $1,120 per month.

4.  Experience during the fall had indicated that fabric, zippers, and other materials would cost about $34.40 per dozen finished pants. Provided the work was well planned, direct labor amounted to $16.00 per dozen.

5.  Every apparel company is torn between being able to make prompt deliveries and avoiding a large obsolete inventory. Bailey sought to meet this problem (1) by keeping well stocked with fabric (each month he would purchase the fabric needed for producing the pants he expected to sell during the next 30 to 60 days) and (2) by restricting his stock of finished goods to expected shipments during the following two weeks. This plan was intended to permit him to adapt the sizes and styles of pants being produced to the orders being received (assuming the right kinds of fabric were on hand).

**profit-and-loss budget for the new year**

After talking with his sales agents, Bailey estimated he could sell 10,000 dozen pants during his first full year of operations. In fact, the New York agent talked of large sales to chain-store buyers, but this would have involved making price concessions and maintaining a large inventory that Bailey wanted to avoid at this time.

By translating his plans and estimates into dollar values, Bailey and Barkin came up with an estimated profit-and-loss statement, which is shown in Table 23.2. The young proprietor was pleased about two features of this budget: it indicated that he should be able to earn a modest profit, and it showed that a large part of total expenses could be adjusted downward if

TABLE 23.2
BELAFONTE FASHIONS, INC.: Profit-and-Loss Budget for the Year

| | |
|---|---|
| Net Sales (10,000 dozen @ $67.20) | $672,000 |
| Expenses: | |
| Materials ($34.40 per dozen) | 344,000 |
| Labor ($16.00 per dozen) | 160,000 |
| Plant supervisors' salaries | 41,600 |
| Repairs | 11,520 |
| Heat, light, janitor | 11,520 |
| Rent | 13,120 |
| Depreciation | 9,600 |
| Office salaries | 29,440 |
| Travel expenses | 3,200 |
| Office miscellaneous | 1,920 |
| Sales commissions (2.5 percent) | 16,800 |
| Shipping (1 percent) | 6,720 |
| Interest and financing charges | 7,552 |
| Total expenses | 656,992 |
| Operating profit | 15,008 |
| Income tax | 2,208 |
| Net profit | $ 12,800 |

sales volume did not develop. Thus, through close control of "variable expenses" he should be able to avoid large losses, even if sales were smaller than anticipated. He now saw more clearly the financial results he might expect, and he had a standard to guide him while attempting to achieve these results.

**monthly cash budget**

Morris Barkin was dubious. He did not challenge the annual-profit budget, but he was worried that the company might go bankrupt before the end of the year. He pointed out (1) that wide seasonal fluctuations in sales would cause temporary demands for larger inventory and accounts receivable; (2) that High Horizons hoped to get back $16,000 of its loan by the middle of the year; and (3) that the company might have to make additional investments in equipment. An examination of this last point revealed that Bailey was using his personal car for company business and that a company car ($6,400) would be needed before the end of the year. Additionally, a different kind of fabric was needed for the autumn lines, and this would require the purchase of second-hand sewing machines for a total of $7,680.

Faced with these facts, Bailey and Barkin undertook to prepare a monthly budget of cash receipts and disbursements. For this purpose Bailey assumed that customers would pay for merchandise within thirty days after shipment and that he would pay for his purchases within a similar period. But it was more difficult to estimate how his annual sales volume would be distributed by months throughout the year. Industry figures supplied by the local sales agent indicated that the distribution would probably be as shown in Table 23.3.

With the data he already had and with his inventory policy, Bailey was now able to budget his monthly flow of cash. This analysis indicated that he might just squeeze by the March sales peak and that cash would accumulate rapidly in April and May, as he collected from customers and reduced his inventories. May and June, then, appeared to be the best time to buy the new equipment and reduce the loan to High Horizons.

Serious trouble would arise in August and September, however, as inventories and accounts receivable would rise to an autumn peak. Without financial aid, Belafonte Fashions, Inc., could not possibly meet its budgeted annual sales.

The crucial assistance was found in a finance company. An agreement was made for Belafonte Fashions, Inc., to borrow whatever it needed up to eighty percent of its accounts receivable. The accounts were pledged as

| Month | Sales (dozens) | Month | Sales (dozens) |
|---|---|---|---|
| January | 800 | July | 400 |
| February | 800 | August | 500 |
| March | 1,100 | September | 1,200 |
| April | 900 | October | 1,300 |
| May | 600 | November | 1,200 |
| June | 400 | December | 800 |

TABLE 23.3
BELAFONTE
FASHIONS, INC.:
Estimated Monthly
Sales

collateral, and special records and collection procedures were established. For its services, the finance company would be paid both a flat annual fee of $1,600 to set up the arrangement and also interest on any money borrowed, at the rate of sixteen percent per annum. With this assistance, the estimates indicated, Paul Bailey would be able to weather the financial crisis forecast for the autumn.

The budget that reflects all these plans is shown in Table 23.4. Note that the preparation of this budget required some adjustment in financial plans in order to arrive at a feasible balanced program.

**comparison of actual results with the budget**

During the first six months of the year, the operating results of Belafonte Fashions, Inc., were surprisingly close to the budget. Sales during March, April, and May were 400 dozen below the budget, but the comfortable accumulation of cash tended to obscure the influence of this drop. More serious trouble arose in November and December when business failed to meet expectations. Mild weather in the fall left retailers well stocked with the type of pants Belafonte made, so reorders did not come in as anticipated. This in turn left Bailey with a high inventory of raw materials; also Bailey could not pay off the finance company in December because of inadequate receipts. Price-cutting was necessary in order to move the finished stock, and even with this action sales were 800 dozen below the budget forecast for the

TABLE 23.4
BELAFONTE
FASHIONS, INC.:
Budget of Monthly
Cash Receipts and
Disbursements

| | Jan. | Feb. | Mar. | Apr. |
|---|---|---|---|---|
| Sales (dollars) | 53,760 | 53,760 | 73,920 | 60,480 |
| Sales (dozens) | 800 | 800 | 1,100 | 900 |
| Goods produced (dozens) | 800 | 950 | 1,000 | 750 |
| Cash received from sales | 53,760 | 53,760 | 53,760 | 73,920 |
| Disbursements: | | | | |
|   Materials | 27,520 | 32,680 | 34,400 | 25,800 |
|   Direct labor | 12,800 | 15,200 | 16,000 | 12,000 |
|   Plant supervision ) | | | | |
|   Repairs     ) | 6,480 | 6,480 | 6,480 | 6,480 |
|   Heat, light, janitor) | | | | |
|   Rent | 0 | 0 | 0 | 0 |
|   Depreciation | | | | |
|   Office salaries    ) | | | | |
|   Travel expenses  ) | 2,880 | 2,880 | 2,880 | 2,880 |
|   Office miscellaneous) | | | | |
|   Sales commissions) | | | | |
|   Shipping      ) | 1,872 | 1,872 | 2,592 | 2,120 |
|   Interest and financing charges | 0 | 0 | 1,248 | 0 |
| Disbursements for operations | 51,552 | 59,112 | 63,600 | 49,280 |
| Cash gain or loss from operations | 2,208 | −5,352 | −9,840 | 24,640 |
| Loans received or paid | | | | |
| Investment in equipment | | | | |
| Cash balance at end of month | 16,128 | 10,776 | 936 | 25,576 |

last two months. The final profit-and-loss figures for the year compared with the budget are shown in Table 23.5.

A first glance at actual results compared with the budget indicates that virtually all the unsatisfactory showing can be ascribed to the drop in sales. This is somewhat misleading. Price-cutting to an average of $66.40 explains over $7,000 lost in revenue even on the 8,800-dozen volume. In addition, direct-labor cost was $1.00 per dozen higher than the budget, which points to an inefficiency here; the total labor cost went down, but not as much as it should have. Fortunately, material costs dropped even more than might be expected from the shrinkage in volume. Variations in other expenses were minor: sales commissions and shipping naturally went down, and tighter control of other expenses would have made only a minor difference in the final outcome. In short, this comparison points directly to sales volume, price, and direct labor costs as the areas where improvement must be made if the company is to become profitable.

The revised budgets that proved suitable for the first year of operation of Belafonte Fashions, Inc., provide a simple example of the three basic steps in budgeting. Plans were translated into accounting results, plans were adjusted where the combined picture proved to be unworkable, and the resulting budgets served as a useful standard in highlighting places that need corrective action. For Paul Bailey, planning became more comprehen-

| May | June | July | Aug. | Sept. | Oct. | Nov. | Dec. |
|---|---|---|---|---|---|---|---|
| 40,320 | 26,880 | 26,880 | 33,600 | 80,640 | 87,360 | 80,640 | 53,760 |
| 600 | 400 | 400 | 500 | 1,200 | 1,300 | 1,200 | 800 |
| 500 | 400 | 450 | 850 | 1,250 | 1,250 | 1,000 | 800 |
| 60,480 | 40,320 | 26,880 | 26,880 | 33,600 | 80,640 | 87,360 | 80,640 |
| | | | | | | | |
| 17,200 | 13,760 | 15,480 | 29,240 | 43,000 | 43,000 | 34,400 | 27,520 |
| 6,000 | 6,400 | 7,200 | 13,600 | 20,000 | 20,000 | 16,000 | 12,800 |
| | | | | | | | |
| 6,480 | 6,480 | 6,480 | 6,480 | 6,480 | 6,480 | 6,480 | 6,480 |
| | | | | | | | |
| 0 | 0 | 0 | 0 | 0 | 0 | 0 | 0 |
| | | | | | | | |
| 2,880 | 2,880 | 2,880 | 2,880 | 2,880 | 2,880 | 2,880 | 2,880 |
| | | | | | | | |
| 1,408 | 944 | 944 | 1,176 | 2,832 | 3,056 | 2,832 | 1,972 |
| 0 | 1,248 | 0 | 1,600 | 928 | 0 | 0 | 2,528 |
| 35,968 | 31,712 | 32,984 | 54,976 | 76,120 | 75,416 | 62,592 | 54,080 |
| 24,512 | 8,608 | −6,104 | −28,096 | −42,520 | 5,224 | 24,768 | 26,560 |
| | −16,000 | | 16,000 | 48,000 | | −16,000 | −48,000 |
| −6,400 | −7,680 | | | | | | |
| 43,688 | 28,616 | 22,512 | 10,416 | 15,896 | 21,120 | 29,888 | 8,448 |

TABLE 23.5

BELAFONTE
FASHIONS, INC.:
Comparison of
Actual Profit and
Loss with Budget for
Year

| | Budget | Actual | Difference |
|---|---|---|---|
| Net sales | $672,000 | $ 584,320 | $−87,680 |
| Expenses: | | | |
| Materials | 344,000 | 297,280 | −46,720 |
| Direct labor | 160,000 | 151,200 | − 8,800 |
| Plant supervisors' salaries | 41,600 | 41,600 | 0 |
| Repairs | 11,520 | 9,440 | − 2,080 |
| Heat, light, janitor | 11,520 | 11,680 | 160 |
| Rent | 13,120 | 13,120 | 0 |
| Depreciation | 9,600 | 10,240 | 640 |
| Office salaries | 29,440 | 29,440 | 0 |
| Travel expenses | 3,200 | 4,000 | 800 |
| Office miscellaneous | 1,920 | 2,560 | 640 |
| Sales commissions | 16,800 | 14,608 | − 2,192 |
| Shipping | 6,720 | 5,920 | − 800 |
| Interest and financing charges | 7,552 | 7,552 | 0 |
| Total expenses | 656,992 | 598,640 | −58,352 |
| Operating profit | 15,008 | −14,320 | −29,328 |
| Income tax | 2,208 | 0 | − 2,208 |
| Net profit | $ 12,800 | $−14,320 | $−27,120 |

sive and rigorous, and postaction control became a reality. Clearly, budgets need not be elaborate to be a useful management tool.[2]

**BUDGETING IN A LARGE FIRM**     Company size does not affect the essentials of budgeting, but it does influence the complexity of the budgetary system. As a company grows, several things are likely to happen to the budgeting process.

1.  Separate budgets are prepared for each department or division of the company. Because each operating unit is somewhat independent, standards to measure its particular performance are needed. Moreover, detailed budget information is often helpful for control within the division. In a large company there may be literally hundreds of subsidiary budgets dealing with the sales, expenses, or other appropriate items of many different operating centers.

2.  Communication of "planning premises" is important if these numerous subsidiary budgets are to be prepared consistently. Each person who prepares or interprets a budget needs to know what assumptions to make about, for instance, wage increases during the budgeting period. The plant manager is dependent on the sales department for information on volume of activity. Are prices and the availability of raw materials going to change? How soon will a new product be ready for the market? Such matters will affect the budgets of several departments. Therefore, someone must provide a forecast that can be used consistently in all subsidiary budgets.

[2] A. Sweeny and J. N. Wisner, Jr., *Budgeting Fundamentals for Nonfinancial Executives,* (New York: AMACOM, 1975).

3. Coordinating the many subsidiary budgets into a balanced program becomes complicated. A big company tends to have a large number of specialized units, and a good deal of effort is needed to synchronize their activities. Even in highly decentralized companies, the total activities of the business-units, as reflected in their budgets, must not exceed the company's resources. Moreover, all business-unit and service division budgets should be reconciled with their respective strategies and with corporate strategy. Only a balanced program that supports strategy will be in the best interest of the corporation as a whole.

4. A special unit that concentrates only on budgeting may be desirable. Such a unit can help design the budgetary emphases and procedures that are best adapted to the particular needs of its company. A budgeting unit may provide routine clerical services in processing figures and in compiling and circulating reports; perhaps it will also make substantive analyses of both proposed budgets and actual experience, with recommendations for action. This staff unit, however, should neither prepare the budgets nor try to enforce them; budgeting is a tool for operating executives to use and not a device for usurping their duties.[3]

**securing flexibility**

A budget is a prediction. Using the language of accounting, it tells how the financial accounts should look at some future date. Like any prediction, it is subject to error because of unanticipated events. Strikes may occur, competitors may introduce a new product, prices may skyrocket, or some other *unmanageable* influence may prevent the prediction from coming true.

A budget is also used as a standard in the control process. Insofar as the budget is in error, because of these unmanageable influences, it loses its validity as a standard. A district sales manager, for example, cannot be held accountable for a drop in sales if a truckers' strike prevents delivery of merchandise to his customers. Obviously, we need some means of adjusting budgets if we are to use them as standards of performance.[4]

**variable budgets**

One way of introducing flexibility into budget standards is to compute in advance any adjustments for shifts in volume of work. If a plant superintendent is asked to step up output above the budgeted figure, his material and labor costs will also probably be over the budget. The question is, how much increase in expenses is justified? We need a revised par to serve as a control standard.

Variable budgets are a device for computing such expense standards for any volume of work within a broad range. The underlying approach is simple. A budgeted expense is set for both a high volume and a low volume, and a plan is prepared for interpolating between these figures. Then, at the end of the budget period, when the actual volume is known, it is possible to compute the appropriate expense for this particular volume. The variable budget approach is illustrated in Table 23.6 and Figure 23.1. Either the

---

[3] J. Bacon, *Managing the Budget Function* (New York: National Industrial Conference Board, 1970).

[4] A more comprehensive discussion of these techniques for securing flexibility is contained in G. Shillinglaw, *Managerial Cost Accounting,* 4th ed. (Homewood: Irwin, 1977).

| | Low Volume | High Volume |
|---|---|---|
| **TABLE 23.6** *THE VARIABLE BUDGET APPROACH* | | |
| Guest-days | 200 | 500 |
| Labor costs | $460 | $730 |
| Increase in labor costs | $270 | |
| Average increase per guest-day | | |
| (270 ÷ 300) | | $.90 |
| Variable portion of total | | |
| ($.90 × 200) | $180 | |
| ($.90 × 500) | | $450 |
| Fixed portion of total: | | |
| ($460 − $180) | $280 | |
| ($730 − $450) | | $280 |

Budgeted cost if volume is 275 guest-days:
  $280 + ($.90 × 275) = $527.50
Budgeted cost if volume is 437 guest-days:
  $280 + ($.90 × 437) = $673.30

figures developed in the table or the chart may be used to set a standard for labor costs in the housekeeping department of the hotel at occupancy rates varying from 200 to 500 guest-days. A similar analysis could be made for all of the expenses of the hotel, and by adding these elements the manager could obtain a budget standard for the entire operation or any of its subdivisions for the actual level of occupancy for any day or week.

This brief explanation of variable budgets suggests their limitations as well as their benefits. They deal only with changes in volume; no adjustment is made for other unmanageable variables. Adjusting costs at a steady rate, as the straight line on the graph implies, may be unrealistic; hotel maids, for

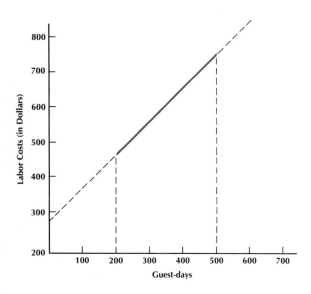

Figure 23.1 Variable budget for labor costs in the housekeeping department of a hotel.

example, may have to be hired by the week rather than by the fraction of an hour. And costs may not vary in a straight line outside of the initial volume range. Of course, more elaborate cost curves can be used but they would complicate the calculations. Finally, the flexibility achieved to improve control makes the budget less useful as a planning and coordinating device. The purchasing agent, for example, cannot wait until the end of the period to find out how much raw material will be needed. This means that variable budgets will probably be an addition to, not a replacement for, the traditional single-volume budget.

**standard costs**

Variable budgets are hard to apply when *different* products are handled. Making three television transmitters, for instance, costs R.C.A. a lot more than making a dozen radar receiving sets. For such situations, there is no simple measure of volume. Standard costs are one way to deal with this difficulty.

In a standard cost system, budgeted costs—for materials, labor, and so on—are computed per unit for *each* different product. Then, at the end of a given period, the number of units of products A, B, C, and so forth, that were processed are multiplied by their respective costs. By adding these figures, the manager can get a total for materials, a total for labor, and a total for overhead that all together reflect the specific product-mix for this period. Such totals become control standards that can be used to evaluate performance for that period.

Unfortunately, this flexibility for a product-mix carries with it some weaknesses. Most seriously, the cost per unit is assumed to be the same no matter what volume of work is processed. This assumption is not valid, especially for overhead costs. Consequently, when using control standards based on standard costs, we must still make some allowance for the level of activity. And standards lose their potency when we have to make a variety of subjective allowances about their reasonableness.

But standard costs do have additional accounting conveniences, quite aside from control, that contribute to their continuing popularity.

**periodic budget revisions**

Although variable budgets and standard costs do provide flexibility in some situations, by far the most common type of adjustment is periodic revision of the normal budget. A common practice is to prepare a budget for twelve months in advance, but to revise it for a particular month just before the beginning of that month. In this revision, we can adjust for volume, price, wage rates, or *any* other factor. Presumably, this modified budget is a realistic statement of results that can and should be achieved.

One large container company distinguishes between its "budget," which gives monthly figures for a year ahead, and "revised estimates." The budget, once adopted, is not changed, but an estimate for month X is made up ten days before the beginning of the month, and a revised estimate is made ten days after the beginning of the month. The manager of each operating division plays a leading part in preparing these estimates. Obviously, the performance of any good executive should come close to the revised estimate. The principal advantage the company finds in this system is that it puts incentive with the executive to adjust his plans to fit current conditions (for example, the effect of weather on demand for vegetable cans) and to cut expenses when volume drops. The pressure develops when there is still time to make adjustments in actual operations. The effectiveness of this system, then, depends fully as much on the way standards are set and on an executive's anticipation of being measured, as it does on the evaluation after a period closes.

Budget revisions must be held within bounds, of course. Confusion arises if changes are made too often. (Just recall how college students react if course schedules are modified even twice during a year.) One of the chief advantages of a regular, specified time for budget revisions is that people learn to expect modifications then. Desirable adjustments are "saved up" for the relatively few revision sessions, and changes do get made, yet people are not unduly upset by these changes in plans and control standards.

## APPROPRIATION BUDGETS

The budgets we have discussed thus far are concerned mainly with managerial actions that produce observable results within a given accounting period—a month, a quarter, or at most a year. Other managerial actions are taken that are not expected to yield results for two years, five years, and often longer. Such actions pose special control problems; appropriation budgets help meet this need. These budgets cover expenditures for items such as

1. land, building, and equipment;
2. research for new products and new processes;
3. institutional advertising;
4. personnel development;
5. new-market development.

Expenditures of the type just listed deserve management attention for several reasons. When wisely made, they are often crucial to the long-run success of the company. But on these items management has a wider latitude of discretion—it can expand, contract, or even discontinue them—than it has for most current expenses, which must be met in order for the company to continue operations.[5]

Typically, all large requests for new buildings and equipment are submitted once a year to top management, which examines the justifications for each project, compares prospective yields, considers the relation of each to company strategy, matches the total requests against available financial resources, and finally makes an overall appropriation. This appropriation, which usually includes an allowance for small and emergency requests,

---

[5] For some insightful case studies of how capital allocation in large corporations takes place, see J. L. Bower, *Managing the Resource Allocation Process* (Boston: Harvard Graduate School of Business Administration, 1970).

becomes the approved budget for the year. A similar procedure is often followed for research and advertising appropriations. Budgets for development expenses, however, are apt to be less formally established.

A great deal of work is devoted to preparing these appropriation budgets, and in large companies we find elaborate procedures for review and approval—especially for new equipment and buildings. In essence, these procedures provide yes/no control to proceed with—or hold back on—proposed expenditures *before* any money is spent or contracts signed.

Usually, purchasing or hiring commitments are not permitted unless they are covered by an appropriation. But note that this provides a one-sided check. It does not even attempt to measure the results—which is the original purpose of making the investment.

Unfortunately, a useful check on the results of long-term investment is extremely difficult to devise. The period from initial decision to fruition is long—extending far beyond the time when corrective action during the formative stages would be possible. During this long interval, many other events occur, making a clear chain of cause and effect difficult to establish. Such efforts as we can make to match an appropriation with specific results are more for "learning-from-experience" than for control. (One company, however, does check results of capital expenditures two years after installation "just so operating executives won't forecast all sorts of benefits they can't deliver.")

Nevertheless, appropriation budgets have some clear benefits. (1) They keep disbursements for the purposes they cover within known limits. (2) They provide an opportunity for key executives to review and compare alternative uses of limited funds. (3) They enable executives to tie major investments to strategy. (4) They provide important information for cash budgets and permit coordination of investment and financing plans.

## BENEFITS AND DANGERS OF BUDGETARY CONTROL

Budgeting is no panacea. We need to understand its strengths and weaknesses so that we may fit it into the total control structure we design for a company or subdivision.

First, the greatest strength of budgeting is probably its use of a single common denominator—dollars—for many diverse actions and things. TV advertising, tons of coal, and liability insurance can all be reflected in a budget of dollar cost and dollar result. Dollar language has its limitations, as we shall see, but it does lend itself to summaries and comparisons. The dollar, more than any other measuring device in business, government, or even military and church administration, can be applied to a wide range of work; and financial budgets capitalize on this unique feature of a monetary unit.  **unique advantages**

Second, budgeting uses records and systems already in existence. We must keep elaborate accounting records for tax returns, financial reporting, and internal management. In budgeting we utilize this system, rather than a new set of records. Figures on past experience are likely to be already prepared. Some new accounts or reports may have to be added, but the basic information system is available and easy to use.

Finally, budgeting deals *directly* with one of the central objectives of a business enterprise—making a profit. What shows up in budgets is what affects recorded profit or loss. Thus the relevance of items being controlled by a budget can be easily traced to the profit objective.

**stimulus to good management practices**

Budgeting often makes its greatest contribution as a stimulus to other good management practices. These are practices an executive might wisely use without budgets, but the adoption of budgetary control may bring them to life. For instance, here are several critical management requirements, with suggestions of how budgeting can help vitalize them.

1. Formal organization should be clear. An understanding of who is assigned to make each type of plan should be a prerequisite to the translation of such plans into budget form. Similarly, accountability for execution has to be clear if comparisons of actual performance with a budget are to have their full impact.

2. Financial accounts must be set up for each department or other unit of administration. When expenses, investments, and income are readily traceable to specific managers, they are more easily controlled. Such correspondence between accounts and departments is especially important in both the preparation and the evaluation phases of budgeting.

3. Planning must be done well in advance and should be highly specific. Without such plans, a budget for the year ahead would be little more than a guess. Precision in planning, in turn, calls for clarifying objectives and for coordinating the plans of interrelated departments.

4. Once annual budgets are well established, tentative budgets for three or five years become feasible. Experience with budgeting is also very useful in what some companies call "profit planning"—setting targets for profits and related matters and then working back through financial accounts to determine the actions that will be necessary to achieve these targets.[6]

5. When line managers use budgets as a key management tool, they at least provide an opportunity for clear directing and constructive counseling. Because budget figures are objective and tangible, everyone can avoid misunderstandings and all parties can focus on improving results.

When we dream about a "turkey dinner and all the fixin's," it is hard to tell whether the turkey itself or what goes with it is the more attractive. And so with budgeting. Budgets are useful as a financial control, but when they are accompanied by other elements of good management they can be an even more cogent force.

---

[6] G. A. Welsch, *Budgeting: Profit-Planning and Control,* 4th ed. (Englewood Cliffs, NJ: Prentice-Hall, 1976).

The most serious risk in using budgets is an *unbalanced emphasis* on factors that happen to be the easiest to observe.[7] For example, the operating expenses of the engineering or personnel department stand out clearly in budget reports, and the supervising executives are under pressure to keep expenses within prescribed limits. But the services such departments perform are of even greater importance. Inadequate service, unfortunately, is reflected only indirectly in the profit-and-loss figures—perhaps in costs or in low sales—and is difficult to trace back to the service division. In terms of budget controls, a service department can look good by keeping expenses in line even though it performs its major mission poorly.

**dangers in using budgets for control**

At the same time, a budget emphasizes the orders received by the sales department and low cost in the production department. Executives of these departments make a good budget showing by demanding more, rather than less, help from related operating and service divisions. Consequently, a budget tends to create *internal conflict* and pressures. Intangible results may not be measured at all, or they may not be properly associated with the units that produce them.

A related danger of budgetary control is that a manager may *treat symptoms* as though they were basic problems. He may become involved in a numbers game rather than probe the reality that lies behind the numbers. If total office salaries look high, for example, a manager may withhold merit increases and fill vacancies with low-salaried, inexperienced help. This remedy may make a bad situation worse. Perhaps the salary figure is a symptom of poor office organization, and a realignment of jobs is what is really needed.

To cite another example, high material costs do not necessarily mean that the supervisor in the processing department is ineffective. Such costs may be a symptom of any of the following weaknesses: unnecessarily rigid specifications, competition for limited supply of raw stock, inept purchasing, inadequate inspection of materials put into the production process, poor process engineering, or old or poorly maintained equipment. A financial budget cannot and should not be expected to reveal the real cause of difficulty. A related danger is that three-year or five-year budgeting will be *substituted for strategic planning*. Budgets and strategy differ. Strategy is more selective, probing, and innovative. Budgets should buttress strategy, but they are too detailed and finance-focused to serve the leading role of strategy.

A budget system opens the way for *dictatorial* action. The terse, objective figures of a budget make it easy for an executive to say, "Cut that expense by thirty percent." If the executive is pressed for time or does not know what else to do, he may order a change in the budget without thinking through the ramifications.

---

[7] H. Tosi, Jr., "The Human Effects of Budgeting Systems on Management," *MSU Business Topics,* 22, no. 4 (Autumn 1974), 53–63.

Finally, there is the danger that a company will go through the *form* of budgetary control *without the substance*. All too often some staff person in the controller's office merely predicts what the accounts will look like several months in the future, with little or no actual planning by operating managers. In other instances, budgets are prepared routinely and mechanically, with no thought given to how operations might be improved. Later the managers simply make excuses if performance compares unfavorably with the budget. In such circumstances, budgeting is a nuisance rather than an aid to management; it simply adds paper work and red tape to an already complex task. Budgetary control can be helpful only if key executives incorporate it as a dynamic part of their way of managing.

**CONCLUSION: PLANNING AND BUDGETARY CONTROL**    One striking aspect of budgetary control is the need for careful planning before the control feature can be effective. In fact, the pressure to refine and clarify plans when setting up budgetary controls may be a major contribution in itself. Also, although budgetary controls do not ensure corrective action at early stages, they do permit prompt identification of trouble. Both aspects provide us with a framework for making adjustments that recognize the ramifications of the actions taken.

In this review of budgeting, we have made only passing reference to the way people respond to controls. Actually, the effects of budgetary controls depend heavily on getting executives and operators to accept and use the data provided. We shall explore this subject in the next chapter.

**FOR FURTHER DISCUSSION**

1. "The key to measuring progress toward accomplishing long-range strategies is the use of short-term budgets." Comment on this statement by the controller of a steel company.

2. How will decisions on departmentation determine the quantity and specificity of budgetary controls?

3. In many companies a twelve-month budget is prepared in December for the following year, and then each month the budget for the next month is revised on the basis of more up-to-date estimates. At the end of the year, for comparing actual expenses and income to the budget, which set of budget figures for any one month should be used—the figures prepared the previous December for the entire year or the revised monthly budgets? Support your answer.

4. The sales manager of a company making electric clocks complained, "I can't draw up a sales budget until I know how much the products will cost us, so I can estimate price and sales volume." The production vice-president asked, "How can I draw up production budgets and give the sales manager the data he wants until he gives me an idea of what sales volume to plan for?" How would you resolve this apparent stalemate in the preparation of departmental budgets?

5. A number of companies now present forecasts on key variables not as single-point estimates but in terms of "best, worst, and most likely" estimates. How should these multiple-point estimates be handled when they must be recorded as budget targets?

6. "The greater the decentralization in a company, the greater the need for de-

tailed budgetary controls at the corporate level." Discuss.

7. "A company might have good plans and even good controls without good budgets, but one cannot have good budgets without first having good plans and controls." Do you agree with this comment? Discuss.

8. If a company has a formal five-year plan, would it be wise to have detailed budgetary controls developed for all five years? Consider pros and cons in your answer.

## CASES

For cases involving issues covered in this chapter, see especially the following. Particularly relevant questions are listed after each case.

Elizabeth Archer (p. 96), 18
Joe DiMaggio (p. 533), 15
Foster Promotions Inc. (p. 538), 17, 18

## FOR FURTHER READING

Anthony, R. N. and J. Dearden, *Management Control Systems,* 3rd ed. Homewood: Irwin, 1976. Text and case studies examining quantitative and management aspects of the control process.

Barrett, M. E. and L. B. Fraser III, "Conflicting Roles in Budgeting for Operations," *Harvard Business Review,* 55, no. 4 (July–August 1977), 137–46. Discusses the behavioral impacts of operational budgets.

Shillinglaw, G., *Cost Accounting.* Homewood: Irwin, 1976. Thorough explanation of budgeting, standard costs, responsibility accounting, and reporting systems; emphasis is on managerial use of data.

Sweeny, A. and J. N. Wisner, Jr., *Budgeting Fundamentals for Nonfinancial Executives.* New York: AMACOM, 1975. Explains how to understand and prepare budgets.

Welsch, G. A., *Budgeting: Profit Planning and Control,* 4th ed. Englewood Cliffs, NJ: Prentice-Hall, 1976. Comprehensive treatment of budgeting from an accounting viewpoint.

# 24

# behavioral responses to controls

Learning Objectives

After completing this chapter you should be able to

1. Understand the importance of meaningful and accepted controls.
2. Describe the type of control standards which have a positive impact on motivation.
3. Describe techniques for limiting the number of controls.
4. Explain how the proper use of feedback can aid in self-control.
5. Describe how behavioral responses differ for each major type of control.

A fire siren never put out a fire. Nor has an on-line computer printout secured a new customer. Only when some person responds to the signal or takes action in anticipation of it does a managerial control become effective. An adjustment in behavior is crucial.

In the two preceding chapters, we have considered controls primarily from an engineering, or mechanistic, point of view. Control standards derived from company strategy and operating objectives, control points selected in light of technology and administrative organization, financial budgeting made attractive by the existence of an accounting system—these are valid considerations, but they are not enough. The pay-off comes only when somebody—manager or operator—does his work better because the controls are in operation.

In fact, responses to controls may ill serve the purpose for which they were designed. The controls may be mistrusted and disregarded, with significant negative side effects. So this chapter explores ways to create positive responses to controls—and ways to minimize the negative reactions. Although people's feelings about controls vary widely, we do have some data on typical responses; behavioral scientists have described controlled behavior, and executives have reported on an even wider range of experience.[1] Our aim here is to translate these findings into guides that can be used in designing and operating a control system.

Each element in a control cycle can provoke constructive or negative responses. The standards set, the reliability of measurements and reports, and the manner of corrective action—all affect the eagerness or resistance of the people affected by the controls. So in addition to the rational, mission-focused aspects of control design discussed in the preceding chapters, we need to incorporate behavioral dimensions.

## MEANINGFUL AND ACCEPTED CONTROLS

**meaningful controls**

A desirable end-result from the viewpoint of a central manager may be regarded as vague and inapplicable by an operating supervisor. The operating vice-president of a large textile firm, for example, is deeply concerned that each company mill keeps its production costs in line with the quarterly budget; for him the financial budget provides the natural criterion for cost control. However, the mill supervisors, who are in the best position to change costs, regard budgets as a nuisance. Most of them realize the competitive necessity of keeping costs down, but in their eyes budgets merely absorb time that they could better devote to actually doing something about costs. The supervisors think—and act—in terms of machine loading, output per man-hour, spoilage or material usage, machine maintenance to avoid stoppages, and indirect labor on the mill payroll. They know what happens to these factors long before budget reports are received, and explaining budget variances is merely a chore imposed upon them by "the pencil pushers in the office." Therefore controls that have a constructive

[1]G. P. Latham, L. L. Cummings and T. R. Mitchell, "Behavioral Strategies to Improve Productivity," *Organizational Dynamics*, Winter 1981, pp. 4–23.

impact on the mill supervisors must provide prompt data on operating factors.

"Client satisfaction," to cite another example, is a poor control criterion for the printing shop superintendent of a public-relations firm. This person has unique talent for producing beautiful brochures, announcements, and reports, but takes no part in deciding what message is important or what media are most suitable. The finest creations may or may not satisfy clients. Instead of the broader goal of client satisfaction, relevant control criteria for the printing superintendent are unique and attractive publications, on-time production, and reasonable costs.

A control criterion is meaningful to a person (1) when it is expressed in operational terms—that is, in terms of actions and results within his sphere of activities; (2) when he can significantly affect the outcome being considered; and (3) especially when the outcome is clearly measurable.[2]

**accepted controls**

To spark a constructive response, a control criterion must also be *accepted* as reflecting a valuable part of the job. Psychologically, the person being influenced should feel that measuring his results in this respect is normal and legitimate.

Controls may be accepted for a variety of reasons. The person accepting them feels that they are relevant to his job, they are the way the game is scored, they are worthy, they represent "professional" conduct, they bring punishment or reward. Whatever its origin and reinforcement, psychological acceptance is a prerequisite for the success of any control. Without acceptance, the control is sure to be resented; evasion, manipulation of reports, buck-passing then become normal responses.

Acceptance is often passive. The person being controlled recognizes the objective as part of his responsibility, but beyond that he is indifferent to the outcome. The typical taxi driver, for example, conscientiously takes his passenger to the stated destination without the slightest concern with why the trip is being made. Many of us, as was pointed out in Part V, have wide "zones of acceptance" with respect to parts of our work.

Although passive acceptance permits the control to funtion adequately, active commitment is obviously superior. Psychologists speak of a goal being "internalized"—the individual includes the goal as one of his own. When an individual gains personal satisfaction from achieving a result that is also a company goal, his feeling about control shifts. Control now helps him to gain personal satisfaction. Steering controls, especially, become aids rather than irritants.

Active acceptance is common. Typically, the carpenter does take pride in the quality of his work; the teacher does want his students to learn; the gardener does like to see a flourishing flower bed. Although questions arise about levels of achievement and competing goals, a completely indifferent person is very rare.

---

[2]E. Flamholtz, "Organizational Control Systems as a Managerial Tool," *California Management Review,* XXII, no. 2 (Winter 1979), 50–59.

Control, then, is much easier and more effective when it is based on goals that are meaningful and actively accepted by the people who really shape the result.[3] So when designing a control system, it pays to seek out ways to match company objectives and personal values.

Participation in setting standards is widely advocated as a way of gaining positive commitment to control. Sales representatives in a large frozen-food company were asked to develop a picture of a first-class representative in terms of his duties and performance. Following a thorough and frank discussion of this ideal person, everyone was asked to prepare, for his use the following year, a statement of what he thought he would accomplish. The representatives were expected to cover all the functions that had been listed, but they were free to set whatever outputs they believed were reasonable. Management then used these statements as standards of performance for the following year. The only adjustments—and these were made with the concurrence of the people involved—were to scale down some of the outputs if the representatives had set too high a standard for themselves.

The success of participation in a wide variety of instances attests to its usefulness. But the way participation is employed is critical. Hypocrisy is an ever-present danger. Usually the end-result sought by a control is fixed by plans that are already settled. To pretend that these goals can be changed in participative discussions is misleading, and the participants will soon recognize this. Such discussions lead to a cynical mistrust of the whole system.[4]

Participation does help, however, (1) to develop a mutual understanding of the aims and mechanisms used, (2) to translate broad goals into criteria that are meaningful and operational for the persons whose work is being controlled, and (3) to set stimulating pars—as indicated in the following pages. These are the subjects on which the controllee can make definite contributions, and having done so, is more likely to psychologically accept—and possibly feel a commitment to—the control endeavor.

## SET TOUGH BUT ATTAINABLE PARS

Meaningful and acceptable control targets create a situation in which various control mechanisms can function. There is agreement about the aims of cooperative effort. However, further refinement of goals is necessary. The specific level of quality, amount of output, and expected degree of perfection must also be agreed upon. So we turn now to the psychological aspects of establishing pars.

Much criticism is aroused by attempts to enforce unreasonable levels of achievement. Some kind of speed limit, sales quota, or deadline, for instance, may be quite acceptable; but tempers rise if the standard is felt to be impos-

---

[3]G. Latham and G. Yukl, "A Review of the Research on the Application of Goal Setting in Organizations," *Academy of Management Journal*, 18, no. 4 (December, 1975).

[4]M. Beer, "Performance Appraisal: Dilemmas and Possibilities," *Organizational Dynamics*, Winter 1981, pp. 24–36.

sible or unnecessary. Unacceptable pars turn positive effort into all sorts of scheming to evade the pressure.

**dual purpose of pars**

Pars serve two distinct purposes, (1) a motivational target we hope to achieve, and (2) an expected result used in planning and coordination. Although actual practice varies, most evidence indicates that people generally respond to a challenging target.[5] We get more personal satisfaction and pride out of meeting a tough assignment than through exceeding an easy standard. Not everyone will meet the tough standard every time, but some will, and the overall result will be higher. Notice, however, that with such high pars, some deficiencies will occur. For planning and coordination these shortcomings must be anticipated; thus, the estimated sales volume used for coordination purposes will be lower than the total sales quotas for individual sales representatives or separate product groups.

**pars that motivate**

Tough pars will motivate people only if several conditions are met. The individuals responding must feel that the target is attainable with reasonable effort and luck. Perhaps, as with a handicap in golf, the person will privately set his aspirations a bit lower than the stated standard. But to stimulate determination and willingness to be inconvenienced, he needs a personal belief that he has a reasonable chance of success in achieving the adjusted target.

A supportive atmosphere is necessary. Supervisors and staff can provide help; they *join in the game* of meeting a challenge—like climbing a mountain or swimming the English Channel. Success is emphasized and rewarded; failure is a disappointment but is not treated as a catastrophe. If the par can be adapted to unpredictable, external variables—as with quotas tied to industry activity or cost tied to orders processed—the feeling of being supported in the venture is increased.

Motivating pars cannot flaunt social norms. Peer groups have their own ideas about acceptable behavior—output ceilings in a factory is the classic example. If a control pushes a person to take actions that are not approved by his friends, he is likely to abide by their social standards. Of course, there are plenty of instances—especially in the executive ranks—in which social pressures support controls. The attitudes that really count are those of associates whose friendship and respect the individual wants to keep. If these persons feel that a control standard and its measurement are fair and that cooperating with management is the right thing to do, they will constitute a social force supporting that standard.

Between the two extremes of direct opposition and strong support are many shades of group attitudes. Perhaps a group is indifferent to what management wants to accomplish, but it may have certain norms of its own, such as keeping the gang together or deciding who may legitimately set a

---

[5]G. P. Latham and E. A. Locke, "Goal Setting—A Motivational Technique That Works," *Organizational Dynamics,* 8, no. 2 (Autumn 1979), 68–80.

*Figure 24.1* *People usually obtain much satisfaction and pride from carrying out a tough assignment—like meeting the challenge of Wimbledon.*

standard. So exactly how peer groups affect responses to controls should be examined for each case.

**pars that breed dissension**

If a par is so difficult that controllees consider it "impossible" to achieve, a strong negative emotional response is likely. In fact, the behavioral-science literature is so full of gruesome cases of unattainable pars that naive readers assume that control always produces bad results. Sending incomplete or shoddy work to the next department, falsifying records, and transferring blame are common devices used by workers under the pressure of appearing to meet a standard.[6] If such defenses are inadequate, a person may become indifferent about his entire job, irritable to work with, and hostile to his boss. To relieve his frustration, he often joins in

[6]G. H. Hofstede, *The Game of Budget Control* (Assen, The Netherlands: Van Gorcum, 1967).

503

horseplay, slips a dead mouse into a can of soup, and takes an active part in any available protest movement.

Confronted with such behavior, a supervisor who wants to meet his commitments often increases pressure on the alienated operator. He is then faced with a vicious circle—more pressure, more resistance, the adverse response undermining the social system of which the operator is a part.

One way to avoid such a collapse is to lower performance standards to a level that the performer regards as realistic. Even if this lower par is insufficient to attain some broader output or quality objective, it is better than a standard that precipitates negative behavior of the kind just described. Fortunately, there are a variety of other steps that can be taken to reconcile gaps between what is needed and what the person responsible for the work regards as realistic; for example, redesigning the job, training, demonstrating, transferring people, and the like.

**participation in setting pars**

Since feelings about what is reasonable and unreasonable affect the response to a control so sharply, extra effort should be made to uncover those feelings. Participation in setting the pars provides this communication. Each supervisor—from the president to the foreman—can frankly discuss with his subordinates the levels of expected results that will be used in each major control.

Such participation includes fact-finding, communication, prediction, negotiation, and mutual agreement. Although the supervisor has the stronger bargaining position, sincere agreement by the subordinate is essential if the control is to induce a positive response. And this feeling cannot be ordered by the boss. The process of participation itself has beneficial side effects, but these depend on consenting to standards that the subordinate really feels are attainable.

Technical pars, such as man-hours per telephone installed or credit losses per dollar of sales, tend to be stable and must be renegotiated only when significant changes occur in the environment or technology. On the other hand, broader-output pars, such as sales quotas or budgeted profits, are reset for each period of time. Participation in setting the broader-output pars is akin to bidding in contract bridge. A player first negotiates a tough but realistic standard based on his new situation and then strives to achieve the contract.

Thus, if controls are to induce positive responses, the establishment of pars must be approached not just in terms of company needs. These standards also connote fairness, challenge, self-respect, social norm, winning, and other positive attributes for people. Consequently, the manager must perceive the attitudes and values of the people whose behavior he hopes to influence—a process explored in Parts IV and V.

**LIMITING CONTROLS**

A third cluster of behavioral considerations relates to the total load. "The straw that breaks the camel's back" must be avoided. We are all subject to an array of controls, a situation which can cause psychological problems. We may feel the controls to be so oppressive that we rebel or our responses become irrational.

Consider the controls on a purchasing agent. Quality of materials and supplies obtained must meet exacting production standards. Delivery dates must anticipate actual use. Inventory levels will be checked against capital allocations. Prices paid will be measured in terms of cost estimates. Departmental operating expenses must stay within budgets, and a wide variety of personnel and accounting procedures should be followed. No personal gifts can be accepted. In addition, there are informal controls on intangible factors, such as obtaining data on new materials, responding to normal pressures for reciprocity, and minimizing risk arising from strikes and other shutdowns of suppliers. Tight controls over all these facets add up to a great deal of pressure; the purchasing agent can justifiably feel that he is buffeted from all sides.

People differ in their desire for freedom—and in the areas in which they feel that controls are repressive. One person may feel that regular working hours and scheduled tasks infringe on his rhythm of work, whereas another welcomes specific working assignments and checks on his progress, but is irritated by controls designed to monitor how he gets the work done. To some extent, by carefully selecting people for specific jobs, we can match these individual differences in security and freedom needs with the number of controls inherent in the work assigned. However, the number of controls necessary for management is likely to seem excessive to most people.

**psychological tolerance for controls**

An emphasis on steering controls, rather than yes/no controls, will reduce feelings of constraint. Although steering controls signal a need for action, they do not restrict the action. Also, participation in selecting criteria and in setting pars—already recommended—helps to incorporate the resulting controls into the normal activities associated with the job.

The main way to make a variety of controls tolerable is to associate "satisfactory" levels of achievement with most of them. As long as a satisfactory level for personnel turnover or equipment maintenance is achieved, no one gives it much attention; there is little or no pressure to improve performance beyond a satisfactory level. In any going concern, experienced personnel carry on many activities in this fashion. Controls exist but most of them are rarely brought into play, for people have learned to do satisfactory work; and these satisfied controls do not seem oppressive.

**"satisfactory" targets for minor criteria**

Obviously, if satisfactory achievement is accepted for a particular criterion, additional improvement in that area is being sacrificed. In effect, the manager is saying that the potential benefit of a tighter control here is not worth the psychological cost and the reduced effort in other areas. So he must select carefully areas where the effects of not pushing hard are relatively minor. Experience indicates that most people can give serious attention to only four to six different objectives. This rule-of-thumb suggests that controls above this number should require merely an adequate level of performance. Even four prime controls may be too many if they deal with

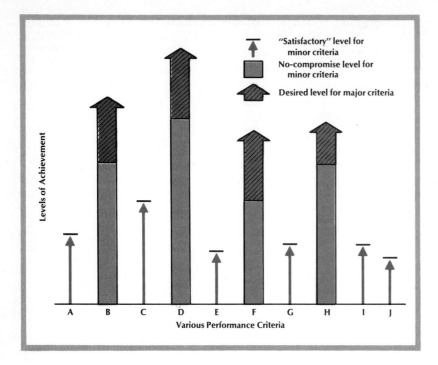

*Figure 24.2  Pars for multiple goals.*

complex and urgent matters. A simple arrangement for dealing with targets that merely need to be "satisfied" is "Management-by-Exception"—a signal is raised only on the exceptional occasions when the satisfactory level of attainment is not being met.

**reducing competition for attention**

Even a limited number of controls, each with a tough par, can place an operator in a psychological vise. For instance, the purchasing agent mentioned above may find pressures for ready availabilty of materials, high quality, low cost, and low inventories competing for his attention. He may be forced to trade off low cost for higher inventory, low cost for less quality, and so on. He feels frustrated because he recognizes that meeting one goal will hurt him on some other front.

Such compound pressures can be relieved in several ways. Simple priorities may be established—in the preceding example, instructions might be given to meet targets in the following sequence: quality, availability, cost, inventory level. A more sophisticated guide would set "no-compromise" levels below the desired pars, and then set a priority to fill the gaps between the "no-compromise" levels and pars. In financial budgeting, three levels are sometimes specified for various accounts—optimistic, expected, and minimum. More often, an implicit tolerance range is understood by people using the controls.

The key in all these arrangements is to relieve the pressure at least to the extent of providing guidance for allocating effort along competing controls. By itself each control may be desirable and acceptable, but we must also consider how that control fits into the whole.

Interference with the way a person does his work can be very annoying. A branch manager may be fully committed to training new sales representatives and have in operation his steps to meet an agreed-upon training target. But if he is then subjected to detailed control over the selection of trainees, their job assignments, and how they are supervised, he is likely to resent the control. Most experienced people—from bus drivers to atomic scientists—have a set of activities that they feel they know how to do well; they regard interference by outsiders as lack of confidence and respect for this skill.

Expense budgets are another case in point. Such budgets frequently include great detail. (The amount of detail often arises mainly from the availability of expense records.) Once specific items for telephone or overtime are in the budget, a supervisor or staff controller is tempted to watch these items closely and to insist on an explanation each time actual expense exceeds the budget. The typical manager will resent such "needling," especially if his *total* expense is in line.[7]

In behavioral terms, the person who feels that his domain is being invaded by a control is likely to be the one who can best initiate corrective action. He knows the local facts and is aware of the effect of manipulating one part of a total operation. Consequently, the control on overtime, for instance, will probably be most effective if the standard and the feedback on overtime become an integral part of *local* management.

**feedback and self-control**

In controlling detail, then, a desirable arrangement is to (1) design control mechanisms for elements worthy of systematic attention, but (2) route the feedback to the lowest level of decision-making for that element. The aim is to encourage self-control and to avoid interference by an outsider. Obviously such a scheme will work best when some evaluation of the overall results can be made, and when the local decision-maker recognizes that the detailed feedback will help him to achieve that desired overall result. In other words, for important details quick, operational feedbacks must be designed—and then the person who wants to run his own show must be encouraged to use them.

Conrad Hilton applied a variation of this arrangement in the management of his hotel chain. Each hotel, from the Waldorf-Astoria to the Shamrock, regularly computed and reported many ratios (e.g., number of meals per guest-day and coffee shop sales per guest-day). Occasionally, at an unpredictable time (one manager claimed 1 A.M. to 3 A.M. was most likely), Mr. Hilton phoned a hotel manager to ask what was being done to correct an off-target situation. If corrective action was underway, Mr. Hilton was satisfied; he relied on the hotel manager to decide what action fit the local situation. The effect of the system was that local managers retained a feeling of autonomy in operating their hotels, but they were alert to the control mechanism that central management had designed for local use.

[7]H. L. Tosi, Jr., "The Human Effects of Budgeting Systems on Management," *MSU Business Topics,* 22, no. 4 (Autumn 1974), 53–63.

This situation of considerable freedom in selecting local means to achieve an overall result is also well suited to participation in setting pars for local performance. Theoretically, the supervisor could withdraw entirely. In many cases, however, the supervisor wishes to strongly encourage the local operator to use particular controls, and periodic participation in setting pars is one way to indicate continuing respect for a control mechanism.

**control system integrity**

The human problems discussed thus far relate to the design of a control system—what criteria are acceptable, how tough standards should be, how many controls a person can tolerate, how to build on desires for self-control. We now turn to a different kind of issue, the *integrity* of the system. Can we believe what the control reports say?

Your response to the gasoline gauge on your auto or to the scale in your bathroom depends heavily on your belief in the accuracy and significance of the message the device is sending to you. Neither device is fully reliable, so

*Figure $24.3$  Prompt feedback directly to the person performing a job encourages voluntary self-adjustment and learning.*

you allow for a margin of error. But if the error is unexpectedly large, you become annoyed about the false alarm (or lack of alarm). Here, as with all controls, one's feeling about the measurement can significantly affect the response.

A prompt warning is often more useful than a tardy precise one, as we pointed out in Chapter 22. For instance, we heed flood warnings by the weather bureau even if they are "wrong" (a flood does not occur) fifty percent or more of the time. It's preferable to respond to an imprecise warning than to wait until the water is at our doorstep before starting suitable action.

**promptness versus accuracy**

Psychologically, early but unreliable measurements are a potential source of tension. The person making the measurement (or prediction) may be criticized because of his "mistakes," and the person receiving the report may become resentful if he is pushed to act on "wrong" information. Only when all persons concerned recognize the inherent limitations of such measurements (or predictions) can such friction be avoided. Some individuals are so reluctant to take risks that they are incapable of dealing with unreliable data. These people either cry "wolf" for every distant shadow they see or do nothing until they are sure the wolf is at the door. They are misfits in a dynamic-control job.

Preliminary estimates and probabilities can be used for control in a variety of ways. Perhaps they merely alert the operator, or they may set in motion a series of more elaborate measurements. If a large number of similar events are involved—as in quality control of long runs of machine-made parts or in extending credit to customers of mail-order retailers—statistical ranges of normal variability help distinguish between random and significant deviations. In all such uses, a clear awareness that the measurement itself may be misleading is coupled with precautionary action. Everyone knows that uncertainty exists. They are prepared to shrug off the false alarms.

Uncertainty arising from a small, early sample (as just discussed) is fairly easy to understand and to accept psychologically. A different sort of problem arises from the use of symptoms and subjective measurements. Here the significance of the measurement is open to question. For instance, how valid a control instrument is the number of laughs at a Broadway play or the number of lunch dates scheduled by an aspiring young management consultant?

**credibility attached to control data**

Such information is often helpful feedback; it provides some additional "feel" about what is happening. But both the measuring and the evaluating can be challenged. And this doubt about its meaning makes such data poor input for strict controls.

Such "soft" data can be used for *self*-control, and for supplementing more objective measurements. But until such a measurement has gained credibility in the minds of both the controller and the controllee, its use for yes/no controls or for postaction evaluation is likely to evoke a negative response.

## RESPONSES TO THREE TYPES OF CONTROLS

Behavioral reactions to each control element (goals, pars, measurements, feedback, and the like) are vital parts of every control design. To ensure that these human dimensions are recognized, we can also relate normal responses to each of the three basic types of control singled out in Chapter 22. The underlying response patterns are those already described, but regrouping them by types of control shows their significance in a new light.

**positive response to steering controls**

The great virtue of steering controls is that most people regard them as helpful rather than as pressure devices. If the goal is accepted, then the various feedbacks are treated as aids in achieving the desired result. Even though a control report sometimes conveys unwelcome news and prods a person to extra effort, the warning is constructive. Coming before work is completed, the signal is seen in terms of action needed rather than personal evaluation.

Since steering controls provide inputs early enough for the principals concerned to use the data in their own decisions, their personal involvement in the control cycle is high. And this close involvement adds to the positive response.[8]

Goal acceptance is crucial. Unless the sales representative wants to increase his sales, reports of deviation from course and of potential obstacles are merely so much static. And an unreasonable par can sour the reaction of the latest word about competitors or planned shipping dates. Steering controls stimulate a positive response only when the people on the giving and receiving ends of the control effort are steering in the same direction.

Who steers is also an issue. As already mentioned, outside regulation of detailed operations annoys those who see themselves as experts in that area; consequently, self-regulation is more welcome. This suggests that steering controls should be translated into action as close to the actual operation as possible. The positive response to the control activity then spreads among operating personnel.

Too many reports can swamp the system.[9] Unimportant information diverts attention from the main goals; frequent needling is irritating. So for many dimensions, "satisfactory" conditions should not be reported. Feedback should center on key variables and on major shifts in the work environment. Steering can then focus on goals we wish to maximize and on serious obstacles.

**behavioral impact of yes/no controls**

Yes/no controls set hurdles to be crossed. They ensure that quality standards are met, that a proposed action is within budgetary restraints, and the like. For the "professional" who takes pride in his work, being able to clear such hurdles easily may provide reassurance. But the check is only whether work is good enough to pass. If it is better than standard, little or

---

[8]D. A. Nadler, P. Mirvis, and C. Cammann, "The Ongoing Feedback System: Experimenting with a New Management Tool," *Organizational Dynamics,* Spring 1976.

[9]R. L. Ackoff, "Management Misinformation Systems," *Management Science,* December 1967, pp. 147–56.

no praise is given; if it is below standard, the work is rejected. And rejection of work often creates delays and resentment. On the whole, when yes/no controls demand attention, they proclaim bad news.

Negative feelings about yes/no controls are often increased (1) when a person is unable to achieve other goals because his work is blocked by this hurdle; (2) when the par is felt to be unreasonable (e.g., the budget is too tight or the requirement for a salary increase is too strict); or (3) when the standard is vague and unpredictable. The legality of a contract, the impact of a public-relations release, or the qualifications required for promotion are typical examples in which standards are likely to be vague and unpredictable. Unpredictable standards are particularly troublesome, for people lack guides on how to prepare for the control. Then if the standards applied to separate cases appear to be inconsistent, charges of favoritism and politics will follow.

Such reactions to yes/no controls can be reduced, first, by making clear that the control is necessary for attainment of company or department objectives. Both the aspect being measured and the par should be directly traceable to a basic objective. Second, keep the measurements as objective as possible, and insist on consistency in their application. (Occasional exceptions will, of course, be necessary. In fact, people working under the system may strongly advocate exceptions—to achieve justice or meet an emergency. But exceptions have little meaning until we have established a stable, predictable social system as a base.) These steps will rarely make the control popular, but they will cut down frustration and foster a feeling of fair play.

**postaction controls as scorecards**

In a strict sense, measurement and evaluation after work is completed cannot alter what is already done. Like Monday-morning quarterbacking, talking about what might have been won't change matters. Nevertheless, as previously indicated, postaction controls do serve two general purposes. (1) If we are going to play another game next week, the Monday-morning review of successes and failures helps us *plan* the *next* engagement. (2) If some kind of reward is tied to how well actual results match selected goals, then the *anticipation* of that comparison and pay-off may be a strong incentive.

The influence of anticipated rewards depends upon the strength of the rewards (or punishments) and upon the perceived basis on which the rewards will be allocated. We are not here exploring the nature of rewards— they vary from bonuses and promotions to commendations and scoring well in the game. But we are directly concerned with the scorecards that determine, in fact, when a person receives a reward. Postaction control reports are such scorecards.

Control design affects what is put down on that scorecard—the factors that are watched, how they are measured, and the expected levels of performance. Their impact on behavior has several dimensions.

People in the system will be sensitive to factors measured and reported; if valued rewards are closely allied to control reports, the participants will watch the scoring like bettors at a racetrack watch the horses. Consequently, tying controls to the desired emphasis among objectives is important.

2. A lack of confidence in the reliability of measuring and reporting mechanisms will create a feeling that granting of rewards is probably inequitable.

3. In a rapidly changing environment, people may discover that their final score is affected more by their skill in renegotiating pars after-the-fact than by efforts to improve actual results.

When the purpose of a control is to produce a scorecard, several ways of automatically adjusting par after-the-fact are available. A flexible budget that is adjusted on the basis of actual volume—sales quotas adjusted for actual disposable income in each territory—illustrates an attempt to make the final standard reflect changes in the environment. Such devices usually increase the chances that the participants believe the par is fair—even though they recognize that the par may move up as well as down.

## CONCLUSION

Managerial controls are concerned with achieving results—with a balance between inputs and outputs that pushes toward the company mission. These controls, however, take effect only when they influence the behavior of people. It is behavioral response, not the mechanics of a control, that really matters. So when designing a specific control or a control system, we must consider how executives and other people involved will react. This chapter highlights conclusions drawn from behavioral-science studies that relate to the process of controlling.

Controls typically have a poor reputation, at least in terms of their popularity with persons being controlled. Fortunately, such a negative feeling need not prevail. By including behavioral aspects in the design and execution of controls, these devices can become normal aids in cooperative effort. Important in this respect are meaningful and accepted goals, challenging but attainable pars, restraint on the number of controls, means for resolving conflicting pressures, encouragement of self-adjustments, and acknowedged uncertainty in some of the measurements. Participation in designing and setting standards also helps.

All these ways to secure positive responses to controls are only parts of a total management design. Remember that the need for controls arises from managerial planning and that controls function in an organization structure. So as the manager shapes the control process, he must also be sensitive to harmony with planning and organizing. This integration of control with other concerns of management is explored in the next chapter.

## FOR FURTHER DISCUSSION

1. "Detailed control systems let people know where they stand and make reward and punishment fairer. Thus they are a key to positive motivation."

    "No matter how you develop them, controls show lack of trust and must be considered as obstacles to pos-itive motivation and thus a necessary evil."

    With which statement do you more nearly agree? Discuss.

2. "Women dislike controls less than men. They seem more ready to have their work measured and evaluated against standards." Comment on this

statement by a woman vice-president of a pharmaceutical firm.

3. List two controls that influence your actions in some significant ways. Make one of these a control that you accept as *necessary* and regard as a useful instrument to guiding your behavior. Make the other a control that you feel to be unnecessary and that you would circumvent if you could. (1) What accounts for the differences in your feelings about the two? (2) What, if anything, would you substitute for the second control?

4. "The fewer restrictions placed on *how* a job is to be done, the greater the obligation of the person who is assigned the job." Do you agree? Why? Why not? Even if true, what dangers should be watched for?

5. "People are more willing to accept controls when they are seeking to sat-

isfy their more basic needs through such things as money and job security." Discuss.

6. "One of the major advantages of using Management by Objectives (MBO) in our planning is that now my subordinates have no basis for objecting to controls. Since the controls are based on jointly set standards, they must regard them as fair." Discuss this assertion.

7. If "par" must serve two purposes, why not have two pars? The first par would be the basis for planning coordinated effort and the second par, a higher target, the basis of motivation. Comment on this approach to setting pars.

8. Can steering controls also be used as the basis for determining appropriate rewards and punishments?

## CASES

For cases involving issues covered in this chapter, see especially the following. Particularly relevant questions are listed after each case.

## FOR FURTHER READING

Dubin, R., *Human Relations in Administration,* 4th ed. Englewood Cliffs, NJ: Prentice-Hall, 1974, chap. 19. Cogent description of workers' responses to controls.

Hopwood, A. G., *An Accounting System and Managerial Behavior.* Lexington: Lexington, 1973. Reports the results of an empirical study of the behavioral effects of an accounting system.

Latham, G. P. and K. N. Wexley, *Increasing Productivity Through Performance Appraisal*. Reading, MA: Addison-Wesley, 1981. Good overview of techniques for obtaining more positive respose to measurement and evaluation systems.

Lawler, E. E. and J. G. Rhode, *Information and Control in Organizations.* Santa Monica, CA: Goodyear, 1976. Uses behavioral-science research findings to explain responses to control mechanisms in organizations.

Said, K. E., "The Human Side of the Budgetary Process," *Managerial Planning*, 26, no. 4 (January-February 1978), 1–8. Surveys the impact of budgetary control on behavior.

Scott, W. R., et al., "Organizational Evaluation and Authority," *Administrative Science Quarterly*, 12, no. 1 (1967), 93–117. Excellent survey of the literature on resistance to control.

# 25

# integrating controls with other management processes

## Learning Objectives

After completing this chapter you should be able to

1. Explain how control is linked to planning systems.
2. Describe how decentralization modifies the control system.
3. Discuss how staff should be utilized in control.
4. Explain the concept of profit center control.
5. Describe how controls should be adjusted to matrix organization.
6. Discuss how to make leadership styles compatible with the control system.

## MANAGEMENT SYNTHESIS

The intimate relationship of controls to other management processes has been indicated throughout the last three chapters. Strategy and operating objectives, for instance, underlie the selection of control standards; programs find their financial expression in budgets; decentralization and participation have a marked influence on the acceptance of controls; and so on. Many control designs can be made more effective by modifying the company's organizing, planning, or leading. Conversely, sometimes the control design should be adjusted to aid the planning, organizing, or leading. Obviously, such tradeoffs should be considered, especially if synergistic effects in the total management design are possible.

In this chapter, we shall single out several ways controls can be fitted together with other management processes. These opportunities do not begin to cover all the interrelations. Rather, they are issues that arise time and again in actual practice, and resolving them wisely can be a great aid to effective management. These issues are: linking control to planning systems, decentralizing without loss of control, using staff in control, harmonizing departmentation with controls, and enhancing controls by leadership action.

## LINKING CONTROL TO THE TOTAL PLANNING SYSTEM

Since control becomes effective only through modifying people's behavior, the broad objectives of an enterprise need to be translated into the *specific* results required from individuals. The elaboration of strategy into single-use plans and standing plans (Chapters 4 and 5) requires continuing managerial attention. Similarly, we need to be sensitive to the influence of control information on *new* planning.

**elaborating plans and specifying results**

The basic concept that planned results become the goals of control is simple enough. However, deciding to increase the ratio of women executives or to obtain more stainless steel from European sources merely states an end result. Planning must be pushed from broad objectives to successively narrower and more specific tasks, until each necessary move or component is assigned to a particular person. Then controls at the subsidiary level will contribute to the final result.[1] If the completed plans for the construction of a building are properly integrated—and then controls set up over the work of the foundation subcontractor, the structural-steel subcontractor, the electrical subcontractor, and everyone else who makes a contribution to the total structure—the final result should be a building as conceived by the architect.

Unfortunately, this sort of matching of the control structure with company objectives is hard to achieve. Often the planning is not extended to the point where we can safely rely on individual discretion to complete the task. And if a new objective is unusual, normal measuring devices may not reflect

---

[1] P. Lorange, *Corporate Planning: An Executive Viewpoint,* (Englewood Cliffs, NJ: Prentice-Hall, 1980), chap. 5.

its distinctive features. So two questions should be asked. (1) Who must achieve what results if the new objective is to be obtained? (2) How will we know that the necessary contributions to the final result are being made? *Planning is incomplete until concrete steps have been identified and provision made to control this implementation.*

The elaboration of a plan down to results required from the many individual operators or units need not be prepared by a single central-planning body. A large block of the total work may be delegated to one division, and the elaboration of plans for that block developed within the division. Such decentralization, however, does not reduce the need for full planning and subsequent control; only the location of who does the planning and control is changed by the decentralization.

**control and new
planning**

When steering controls and yes/no controls are used to adjust activities so that a predetermined objective will be achieved, corrective action may prompt action in any of the other managerial processes. Nevertheless, objectives usually remain the same, and the adjustments are like those of a ship's pilot who modifies his course with the winds and tide to reach home port. Only if there is a terrible storm or breakdown is the pilot likely to change (replan) his destination.

In contrast, postaction controls almost always lead to planning. For example, if a sales campaign is only partially successful, both the objectives and methods of the next campaign are likely to be modified; similarly, executive-development activities planned for next year will be strongly influenced by an appraisal of results achieved this year. In situations such as these, control reports serve as a basis for an entirely new cycle of managerial activity—planning, perhaps organizing, leading, and controlling the new activities.

But the concept that postaction controls rather than steering controls are of principal use in planning needs two important qualifications. First, we must often lay plans for new activities before a present cycle is completed. University budgets, for example, are often prepared in preliminary form in December and January for the following school year. This means that the results of the fall semester activities are not yet known, and the spring semester has not even begun, when the first steps of planning for new courses and size of classes have to be taken. Automobile companies have an even greater lead-time in planning for their new models; commitments on design and engineering are often made with little or no measure of the popularity of the current year's model.

When new plans must be made before the results of the old ones are known, the results must be predicted. Control information of the steering type is naturally used in making these predictions. In some situations, then, we use information on how we are doing both as a guide to current operations and as part of the data on which the outcome of present and new plans are predicted. The benefits of control to planning, however, should not be exaggerated. If we want planning to be dynamic, we must consider new ways of performing work. Operating conditions change, and future opportunities may improve or diminish; consequently, more complete, or different, information is often needed for planning than control activities provide.

Second, as objectives are changed, established controls tend not to be readjusted. Take even the simple matter of a cutback in the sales of a product line because of a change in competition or technology. It is entirely possible that although the overall income and expense objectives will be adjusted to the new conditions, the control standards for engineering and other service departments will remain unchanged. Or suppose the company president decides to increase the number of broadly trained young men and women in the organization as a reservoir for filling top management positions. If the job specifications that control the representatives who actually hire college students are not adjusted, the specific actions at the various recruiting centers will not be attuned to the new objective.

The several steps involved in translating the new company objective into new patterns of individual behavior all take time and effort. In extreme cases, inertia is so great that inconsistency between company objectives and ineffective controls continues indefinitely. So the need to link planned results to control standards arises over and again. Whenever new plans are laid, the question "What corresponding adjustments in controls must be made?" should be asked.

## DECENTRALIZING WITHOUT LOSS OF CONTROL

Each time a manager delegates work (operating or managing) to a subordinate, he creates the problem of knowing whether the work is performed satisfactorily; hence, delegating inevitably raises the question of control. Often the degree of decentralization a manager will adopt depends on how far he can decentralize without feeling that he is losing control.

modifying control

A manager need not lose control when he delegates a large measure of planning, but he should be prepared to change his controls.[2] This alteration is illustrated in Table 25.1. First, the appropriate control standard changes. When decisions are centralized, the manager himself will establish rather detailed standards for the method and output of each phase of the work. But as he delegates increasing amounts of authority to plan and decide, the manager should shift his attention away from operating details to the results that are achieved.

The frequency of appraisals also changes. Because the manager is no longer trying to keep an eye on detailed activities, most if not all daily reports can be dropped. As his attention shifts more and more toward overall results, the span of time covered by reports can typically be lengthened. For a business-unit that operates on a profit-decentralization basis, monthly profit-and-loss statements and balance sheets come as frequently as most top

[2]J. E. Ross and M. J. Kami, *Corporate Management in Crisis: Why the Mighty Fall* (Englewood Cliffs, NJ: Prentice-Hall, 1973), chap. 19.

TABLE 25.1
EFFECT OF DECEN-
TRALIZATION ON
CONTROL

| Degree of Decentralization | Nature of Control | |
|---|---|---|
| | Type of Standard | Frequency of Measurement |
| Centralization of all but routine decisions. | Detailed specifications on how work is to be done, and on output of each worker. | Daily for output; hourly to continuous for methods and for quality. |
| Action within policies, programs, standard methods; use of "exception principle." | Output at each stage of operations, expense ratios, efficency rates, turnover, and the like. | Weekly to daily for output; monthly for ratios and for other operating data. |
| Profit decentralization. | Overall results, and a few key danger signals. | Monthly for main results and for signals; quarterly or annually for other results. |

managers want reports. Other factors, such as market position or product development, may be reported only quarterly.

retaining safequards

The shift from frequent, detailed control reports to periodic, general-appraisal reports does not preclude the use of a few danger-signal controls. A common practice is to expect a subordinate to *keep his manager informed* of impending difficulties rather than bother him with control data when conditions are satisfactory. A manager may ask to be notified when deviations from standard exceed a certain norm, thus applying the "exception principle" to control. Moreover, yes/no controls can be used for certain major moves, such as large capital expenditures or the appointment of key executives. Here again, the number of proposed actions that *require confirmation* will decrease as the degree of decentralization increases.

Still another kind of safeguard is to *insist that lower levels of management use specific control devices* even though an upper executive himself neither sets the standards nor receives reports on performance. A vice-president in charge of production may be vitally concerned that a reliable quality-inspection plan is in use, but he may take no personal part in its operation. He expects sufficient control data to be handy if the need for determining the cause of any problem arises.

As more authority is delegated, *self-control* by the subordinate becomes comes crucial. Such self-control is partly a matter of attitude and habit. In a situation in which centralized control has been the traditional practice, operating personnel naturally rely on senior executives or their staff to catch errors and initiate corrective action. If authority is then passed down to them, they need to develop a new attitude. It may also be necessary to redirect the flow of information so that these people down the line have what they need to do their own controlling.

With heavier reliance on self-control by subordinates, the manager should act more as a *coach* than as the one who decides on corrective action. Ideally, the initiative for corrective action comes from the subordinate. Clearly this degree of decentralization requires the right people. Subordinates able to perform the delegated duties must be selected, trained, and properly motivated. An executive himself must be able and willing to adjust his behavior, and the two people involved in each delegation must trust each other. Remove or significantly diminish any one of these aspects of an operating situation, and there will be a corresponding reduction in the degree of decentralization possible without loss of control.

### USING STAFF IN CONTROL

Staff assists in performing managerial work. As we explained in Chapter 12, most staff assistance is concerned with planning, but it is not necessarily limited to this one process of management. To what extent, then, should staff also be used in control?

We have noted that people naturally dislike controls, and they are especially sensitive about who may legitimately exercise control. Consequently, as we think about assigning control duties to staff, we must be sure (1) that the tasks are well suited to a person in an auxiliary position, and (2) that the control duties will not make the performance of other staff work more difficult.

*Figure 25.1   Staff may take various roles in the control process. In these three examples, staff assumes the roles indicated by the darker color.*

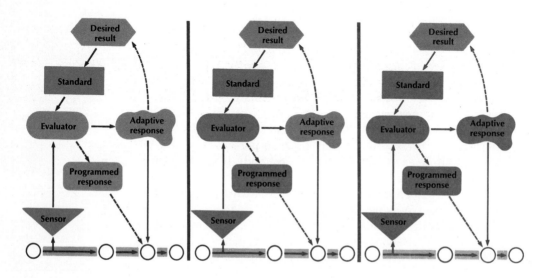

Staff is often used in setting control standards. Since the early days of Scientific Management, industrial engineers—by employing time and motion study—have set output standards; product engineers have set quality standards; and cost accountants have set detailed standards for product and process costs. Often a market researcher takes part in establishing sales quotas for individual sales representatives.

The reasons for using staff to help set standards are clear. Special skills in engineering or research methodology may be required. Besides, setting standards is often very time-consuming, and an operating manager cannot give attention to all the necessary details. Of course, when we think of the whole range of control standards a company uses, it becomes evident that many standards are established without the aid of staff. However, when controls are formalized and detailed, staff help may lead to better standards.

But the active participation of staff is also a major source of human problems with control. All too often the people being controlled feel that standards are unreasonable and that control pressure comes from illegitimate sources. The technical jargon of a staff person—his preoccupation with certain aspects of a problem, his different values, and his desire to make a good showing all contribute to a lack of confidence by workers and lower-level supervisors in the standards he sets. If, in addition, the staff person applies pressure to meet the standards and suggests corrective action, fuel is added to the flames. "Who does that graphite engineer think he is?" is likely to be the response.

The remedy appears to lie in two directions. (1) Operating managers should be instructed to give more attention to the review of standards before they are put into effect and to discuss these standards with people who will be expected to live up to them. (2) Staff people should be made to realize that their most constructive contribution lies in providing sound advice up and down the organizational hierarchy without usurping the functions that legitimately belong to the line managers.

When control standards are expressed in terms of inches or dollars, the comparison of actual performance—as in auditing—is relatively simple. But measurements are often vague, and the allowances we must make—for illness, competition, and numerous other influences—are a matter of subjective judgment. There is widespread debate about the value of staff participation in this kind of appraisal.

Operating managers, it is pointed out, often lack objectivity in making appraisals. They are committed to a program, and the drive they need to make the program succeed calls for optimism and a determination to "do the impossible." Besides, a manager must appraise the work of his friends, and he is sensitive to the effect of appraisal on their morale. On the other hand, it is argued that although a staff person has greater objectivity, he also has a less intimate knowledge of the facts. He, too, may have a bias, especially if he is looking at a situation only from the point of view of, say, personnel, engineering, or public relations.

Management needs both kinds of appraisals. The objective views of staff can be extremely valuable. But such appraisal finds its greatest use when we are formulating *new* plans rather than attempting to control activities so that they conform to *existing* plans. Corrective action is predominantly a line activity; so inevitably, an operating manager will reply primarily on his own judgment. When formulating new plans, however, an operating manager normally has more time for contemplation; and in this activity both the appraisals and proposals of staff can make their greatest contribution.[3]

**yes/no control**

In special circumstances, a staff unit, like an operating manager, may exercise yes/no control. The personnel department, for example, may have to give its approval before the sales manager can make a final commitment to hire a new representative. Similarly, capital expenditures may require the approval of the controller; changes in organization, the approval of the management-planning section; or property leases, the approval of the legal staff. When yes/no control is exercised by a staff person, we say that he has "concurring authority."

Concurring authority works best when the criteria on which a staff person can either approve or reject a particular proposal are specified. And, for those transactions where a mistake would be very serious and where time is not critical, concurring authority may be desirable as a safety measure. Serious difficulties with yes/no staff control arise when a decision to turn down a proposal is based principally on subjective judgment. It is one thing for a controller to say that an advertising appropriation has been used up, and another for him to turn down a proposal because he believes that advertising is unwise during a recession. An alternative arrangement is simply to have the staff person give advice; we may insist that a consultation take place, but specify that the operating manager's judgment prevails.

A final reason for carefully defining and restricting staff participation in control is that it undermines the constructive role staff usually plays in other areas. An unpopular assignment makes a staff person unwelcome; so his ability to be a friendly advisor is lessened if he goes too far into control.

## HARMONIZING DEPARTMENTATION WITH CONTROLS

The ease of control is significantly affected by the way the company is grouped into departments and divisions.[4] Important here are the concepts of clean breaks, deadly parallel, and direct interaction.

The simplest way departmentation can aid control is by separating departments or sections where a clean break in work occurs. Thus, a farmers' buying co-op will separate bulk fertilizer, seeds, fuel oil and gasoline, and

[3]E. K. Warren, *Long-Range Planning: The Executive Viewpoint* (Englewood Cliffs, NJ: Prentice-Hall, 1966), chaps. 5 and 6.

[4]W. G. Ouchi, "The Relationship Between Organizational Structure and Organizational Control," *Administrative Science Quarterly,* 22 (March 1977), pp. 95-113.

garden supplies; each requires distinct storage and delivery equipment. Likewise, a well-run ski resort will have separate divisions for its ski run, its ski shop, and its housing and food; to separate control of its restaurant from its bar, however, becomes more difficult because the service is so interrelated. Control is easier when either the physical separation of operations or distinct stages of work make it simple for everyone to understand the organization structure.

A second suggestion is to set up two or more operating units in deadly parallel. A telephone company may create a series of nearly identical divisions; or finance companies may organize each of many offices on the same general pattern. Control is enchanced because the results from any one office may be compared with performance in the others. This deadly-parallel arrangement removes a great deal of personal opinion in setting standards. As we noted in the last chapter, it is important that employees accept standards as reasonable; if one branch meets a given standard, an aura of reasonableness is created for that standard, and a wholesome attitude toward it tends to develop throughout all branches.

A proper grouping of activities can aid control in still another way. By placing together activities that are closely interdependent, we can reduce the amount of "overhead" control. When interrelated work is done in several different departments, we have to control with precision the quality and flow of work as it moves from one department to another. Even with the best of controls a mistake is likely to result in arguments and buck-passing. So a

*Figure 25.2* *Establishing a series of virtually identical operating units introduces a deadly parallel and enhances control by making it easy to identify any unit that is out of line.*

Holiday Inns, Inc.

more satisfactory arrangement is to assign the interrelated work to a single department or "project team," or to an individual. Two of the best examples of this basic idea are "profit centers" and "project teams" in a matrix organization.

**creating profit centers**

"Profit centers" are a valuable control device if organization and controls are well matched. A business-unit with its own engineering, production, and marketing can be judged in terms of the profit it earns. Since the profit figure shows the *net* result of all unit activities, its use as a control standard encourages coordinated and balanced effort. Also, executives within the unit must keep their activities in tune with the external environment in order to sustain profits. Although insensitive and slow to reflect intangibles, the profit standard is the best comprehensive measurement that we have.

The temptation is to over-use the idea of the profit center. Some companies try to make each plant, each branch office, each warehouse, and even service units (such as purchasing) a so-called profit center. A profit is calculated for each unit. In effect, each unit buys its materials (often from other units), hires its own labor, and sells its products or services (perhaps to other units). Then, after charges for overhead, a profit for the unit is computed. But how suitable is this resulting profit figure as a control standard?

*Figure* $25.3$  *Matching controls with alternative approaches to product management and organization. Product divisions, shown on the far right, serve as clear-cut "profit centers."*

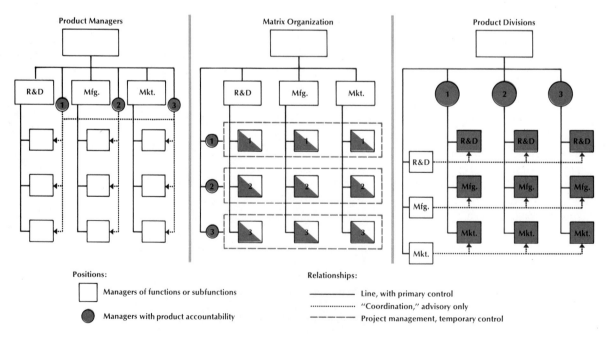

Many profit-center managers devote more energy to negotiating the artificial prices used to transfer goods in and out of their units and the amount of overhead charged to them than they give to improving the activities they can actually improve. Because of the profit control, they spend a lot of unproductive time playing games with transfer prices. The trouble arises because the control measurement—profit—is much more comprehensive than the activities assigned to the unit they direct. Most plant managers, for instance, do not decide the specifications of what they make, how much to produce, nor whom to sell it to at selected prices. Consequently, control standards focusing on cost, quality, and delivery are more appropriate for such a plant manager than total profit.

Profit-center control makes sense when (1) semi-autonomous, self-contained business-units are part of the organization structure, and (2) the primary objective of such a unit is profit. Managers of the semi-autonomous unit are free to adjust to new opportunities, and their initiative must be encouraged but controls must direct that initiative to the desired result. If the main purpose of a district office is to build sales volume, it would confuse matters to call it a profit center. The control selected should reinforce the intent of the organization.[5]

Distinct control issues arise when a matrix form of organization is used.[6] As noted in Chapter 13, a matrix organization has two types of units—resource departments which develop pools of specialized talent, and project teams to which talent is assigned to work on specific projects.

**adjusting controls to matrix organization**

In a matrix organization, scheduling and control is carried out primarily within each project team. The program scheduling and control tools normally will be those described in our discussion of adaptive programming in Chapter 5. And the director of each project team—the interim line boss—will be the person to balance the impact of the diverse controls so that the major mission of the team can be achieved. Selected reports on progress will be made to senior executives in charge of the respective teams. In all these respects the control design represents the straightforward application of the guidelines examined in Chapters 22–24.

The troublesome issue is what role the resource departments should play in controlling. For instance, in a shipbuilding company, should an engineering department (or marketing, legal, purchasing, finance, or the appropriate resource department) actively participate in controlling the quality and amount of engineering work done on a new container cargo vessel? Or in a large legal firm, should the criminal law department control the briefs prepared by a young criminal lawyer assigned to a major antitrust case? Having provided the needed personnel and perhaps other services, the resource departments take on the role of staff. The question then

[5]R. F. Vancil, "What Kind of Management Control Do You Need?" *Harvard Business Review,* March 1973.
[6]S. M. Davis and P. R. Lawrence, *Matrix* (Reading, MA: Addison-Wesley, 1977), p. 52.

arises, while in this staff posture what control, if any, should the resource departments exercise?

Three control designs indicate the array of possible relationships.

*1. **Full delegation to project teams*** In a decentralized matrix design each project team has virtually full independence in the action it takes. The presumption is that the uniqueness of the project, the need for prompt and coordinated action, and/or the high competence of the various specialists assigned to the team make localized control preferable. The team is on the field and it is up to the players to win the game.

Such independence relates to the running of specific projects. Post-action review by the resource department will, indeed, be carried out so that improvements in training for future projects can be made. These postaction reviews also seek to evaluate the effectiveness of persons assigned to the teams (insofar as this can be unscrambled from the group effort). Future assignments as well as advice on bonuses or other rewards will be influenced by this evaluation. Obviously, this postaction review is of personal concern to team members, so they are unlikely to disregard the training, suggestions, and values of their resource "home" department.

*2. **Periodic concurrence*** A second arrangement is for the resource department to participate in milestone reviews. These milestone reviews are typically yes/no control points when the progress-to-date is used as a basis for authorizing continuation of the project as planned. Resource departments may join in such assessments and their concurrence may be necessary for the work to proceed.

All yes/no controls are introduced to improve safety, and adding an evaluation by resource departments increases the chances of catching serious errors. The chances for delay are also increased. So the desirability of requiring concurrence of resource departments at milestones depends on the relative weight attached to safety vs. speed and some expense. Much depends upon how provincial the resource department is in its standards; it is possible, though by no means common, for the resource department to be as customer-oriented and results-oriented as the project manager himself.

Naturally, the people on the operating teams will try to anticipate possible objections by the resource departments (and whose views will be sustained if a difference of opinion is appealed to higher authority). This anticipation of control at the review points will temper actions in advance because prompt clearance simplifies the operating task. So, even though reviews are occasional, any resource department whose consensus is required exercises substantial influence.

*3. **Continuous monitoring*** A highly centralized control by resource departments is possible, usually by making the departmental representative on the project team merely a communicator of reactions and decisions made by the control staff group. This arrangement will undermine the project team concept. It can be tolerated only for those functions which make minor and intermittent inputs to the team's action—as may be true of, for example, a legal or real estate department. In effect, these fringe functions are withheld from the matrix. They perform an occasional service and exercise yes/no control at a few points when their specialty is involved.

Control in a matrix organization, then, does involve more or less double-checking by the project teams and their line supervisors, and by the resource groups. The scope and frequency of the double-checking calls for a careful balancing of greater freedom for the project team and closer scrutiny by the control staff group.

Since leadership style is intertwined with the application of control standards, there should be a compatibility between leadership style and control design.[7] For instance, to couple a control system predicated on close observance of standards with a permissive leadership style invites trouble.

**matching leadership styles and rewards with controls**

Our previous analysis of control design clearly indicates that some situations call for tight control whereas loose control is preferable in others. The same situational factors bear upon the choice of leadership style. Some trade-offs of benefits may be involved in the final selection of controls and leadership style, but it is vital that the controls support the leadership style, and vice versa.

Leadership style is not established by public announcement; it is based on executive behavior. Regardless of what a boss or a manual may say, those controls that are enforced are to the persons being controlled an unembellished guide to what they must do well and what they can do indifferently. They soon learn, for example, whether a "no smoking" rule means what it says or is merely a suggestion of desirable behavior. It is the action of the supervisor in disregarding or insisting that the standard be maintained that gives meaning to the control. Enforced standards communicate.

The permissive leader obviously faces a tough decision on which control standards he will seek to enforce. If he does not follow up on, say, established quotas, antipollution standards, or routine matters of attendance, his subordinates will infer that he is indifferent to their actions in such areas. This kind of permissiveness results in no control. On the other hand, if he consistently checks up on deviations of actual performance from standard but then confines his response to mild suggestions for improvement, the amount of control will be a function of the motivation of the subordinate. Of course, even a permissive leader may single out a few subjects on which no permissiveness is tolerated; the key here is to pick these subjects carefully.

*Consistent rewards and controls* The company reward system, like leadership style, should reinforce the controls. Every production worker knows that a bonus based on volume alone leads to neglect of quality. Similarly, if professors get promoted on the basis of publications, their teach-

---

[7]C. Cammann and D. A. Nadler, "Fit Control Systems to Your Managerial Style," *Harvard Business Review,* January 1976.

ing suffers. Perhaps the most common error in management practice is to reward people for short-run results while urging them to take a long-run viewpoint; such short-run pay-off is particularly insidious because long-run results are hard to measure and control. With a recognized reward (or penalty) associated with one kind of result, even the best designed controls on other results will receive secondary attention.

Individuals respond to many kinds of rewards, tangible and intangible, on the job and off the job. Tying these rewards to controls is not simple. Only part of the rewards can be granted or withheld by management. Often persons who take actions which lead to rewards—for instance, make promotions or provide challenging assignments—differ from the persons exercising control. The timing and occasion for rewarding action is often separated from evaluation of results, sometimes by several years. Actions viewed partly as a reward may be subject to other considerations—e.g., promotions.

Consequently, a careful review of the reward system should be made along with any major redesign of the control system. Insofar as flexibility permits, the granting of rewards should be clearly and explicitly related to desired performance as reflected by the controls. Usually the line supervisor will carry the primary part in this mating of rewards and controls. The interconnection is so important, however, that an occasional independent check by someone with an objective viewpoint is desirable.

### CONCLUSION

Like the nervous system in the human body, control is only one of the vital subsystems in effective management. Planning, organizing, and leading are also essential; and all these subsystems interact. If one is changed, the others may need to be redesigned also.

This interaction is a potential source of strength. By designing an organization suited to company plans, and by reinforcing both with compatible leadership styles and controls, we can create a highly synergistic force.

Several ways to obtain such an integrated management design have been flagged in this chapter: linking controls to the total planning system, decentralizing without loss of control, creating departments and profit centers that aid control, using staff properly, and enhancing control with consistent leadership styles and rewards.

The design of good controls is an intriguing task. Fitting them neatly into a balanced management structure is even more challenging—and rewarding.

### FOR FURTHER DISCUSSION

1. "A plan is no more than a rough roadmap until it is translated into a control system. Only then does an organization have a useful plan!" Do you agree with this comment by the president of a small paper company?

2. "The most critical controls for strategic plans are steering controls."
"Strategic plans require the most de-

tailed controls so that people can be encouraged to carry them out by knowing they will be monitored closely."

With which statement do you more fully agree? Discuss.

3. In relating controls to the hierarchy of plans should one attempt to evaluate the results of programs that are the means of achieving higher-order ends, or should the controls be tied to the ends themselves?

4. A major reason for removing a group of activities from an operating unit and turning them over to an auxiliary division is to ensure that these activities receive adequate attention. Would it not be as effective and less expensive to stress that these activities will be subject to close scrutiny in the evaluation of the operating unit? Discuss the pros and cons of this viewpoint.

5. "Essentially the results of staff work overlap the results of line executives' work. Therefore, you must define results you expect of staff people so that they will be harmonious with the results of line people. Both the line and staff should get full credit for whatever is accomplished, just as though either had done it himself." Do you agree? What difficulties might arise in applying this concept?

6. How does one develop good control systems for a matrix management structure?

7. Make a list, without referring to the text, of what you regard as key factors that must be considered in designing and using a sound control system. Ask yourself where else in the book, besides Part VI, each item has been discussed. You will probably find that virtually all of the items were considered in Parts I to V. What does this tell you about the design and use of control systems?

8. Discuss the relationship between control and the decision on whether to seek commitment from a group or settle for compliance.

## CASES

For cases involving issues covered in this chapter, see especially the following. Particularly relevant questions are listed after each case.

## FOR FURTHER READING

Anthony, R. N. and R. E. Herzlinger, *Management Control in Nonprofit Organizations.* Homewood: Irwin, 1975. Text and case studies explaining how the control process is applied in nonprofit organizations.

Cammann, C. and D. A. Nadler, "Fit Control Systems to Your Managerial Style," *Harvard Business Review,* January 1976. Relates selection and design of controls to leadership style and internal motivation of subordinates.

Corey, E. R. and S. H. Star, *Organization Strategy: A Marketing Approach.* Boston: Harvard Graduate School of Business Administration, 1971. A recurring theme is the inherent conflict between resource controls and product divisions.

Newman, W. H. and J. P. Logan, *Strategy, Policy, and Central Management,* 8th ed. Cincinnati: South-Western, 1981, chaps. 24 and 25. Discussion of central management's use of controls to secure united action, and the role of control in managing multinational enterprises.

Ross, J. E. and M. J. Kami, *Corporate Management in Crisis: Why the Mighty Fall.* Englewood Cliffs, NJ: Prentice-Hall, 1973, chap. 19. Penetrating discussion of how control systems should be modified as decentralization increases.

Vancil, R. F., "What Kind of Management Control Do You Need?" *Harvard Business Review,* March 1973. Selecting financial controls that fit objectives and organization design; cautions against indiscriminate use of profit centers.

## CONTROLLING IN NOT-FOR-PROFIT ENTERPRISES

The application of control concepts within not-for-profit enterprises poses special problems. Unclear standards and difficulties in measurement, coupled with sharp restraints on the use of rewards (discussed in Note Five), undermine the effectiveness of control processes, which in profit-seeking firms have widespread and successful use. Several characteristics often present in not-for-profit ventures contribute to such lame control.

The intangible output of museums, orchestras, schools, and retirement homes is *hard to measure* in terms of objective standards. Because quality of the service is often judged subjectively by persons with varying expectations, pars lack consistent definition. Of course, some aspects of the activity can be measured—such as the number of people served and direct financial expenses—but these aspects tend to receive disproportionate attention merely because they can be measured.

In profit-seeking concerns the adequacy of their service relative to its cost is repeatedly appraised by consumers. But such a *market test is unclear* for those not-for-profit enterprises that rely on gifts or subsidies. Especially when the enterprise has a local monopoly, as is often true for schools, hospitals, and other service establishments, patronage alone does not give a full evaluation of service rendered. For sensitive control, additional measures of quality of service and consumer response are needed.

One source of standards for a local service establishment is a comparable unit in another locality. Schools, hospitals, and even zoos, for example, can be compared with neighboring institutions or with "industry" averages. Such comparisons always need to be adjusted for differences in size, service objectives, existing facilities, and the like; nevertheless, they do provide some control benchmarks where standards of performance are hard to set. Unfortunately, these *cross-comparisons* usually focus on expenses, activity, and other easy-to-measure aspects; they are of limited help where qualitative judgment is required.

If an enterprise has not just one but several hard-to-measure objectives, control is further complicated. As we observed in Note One, *priority* among these objectives—for instance the relative weight to be given in a school to the 3 R's, social development, character, creativity, culture, and vocational training—is often ill defined and left to the teacher. And if the operating objectives are fuzzy, then control standards and corrective action lack their necessary base. In such circumstances, systematic control systems focused on results are rarely attempted.

Because of these limitations of output controls, many not-for-profit enterprises emphasize the *control of inputs*—expenses and use of personnel—and of the volume of activities. Such controls on the use of resources and on rates of activity are typically treated as restraints, and there is little or no positive reward for meeting the control standards. Quite understandably, the personal response of people affected by these restraining controls is usually negative.

Of course, managers do give attention to the quality and quantity of output. Certainly orchestra conductors evaluate results and take corrective action. However, this kind of control is necessarily individualistic and subjective; especially in medium- and large-size enterprises, it lacks the *consistency and predictability* that is so important in developing widely accepted norms of behavior. And if busy managers are "hit and miss" in their exercise of these controls, employees are likely to feel that corrective action is arbitrary and unwarranted.

All too often, then, controlling in not-for-profit ventures is still in an elementary and uninspiring stage. The most prevalent controls are merely postaction checks on expenses. Steering control, as described in Chapter 22, is rarely used. The concept of a balanced control structure cannot be applied where so many key areas lack acceptable measurement.

In summarizing these six notes on managing not-for-profit enterprises, four broad conclusions emerge.

1. The basic processes, concepts, and techniques of management that work well in profit-seeking ventures fit not-for-profit enterprises almost as well.
2. The profit motive itself does not lead us to the chief differences that are likely to exist.
3. The chief differences lie in intangible characteristics. What is more, multiple objectives, strong employee commitment to professions, intrusion of resource contributors into internal operations, restraints on use of rewards and punishments, and reliance on charismatic leaders—alone or in combination—call for modification of managerial techniques.
4. Since great diversity exists among not-for-profit enterprises, we must look carefully for characteristics like those just listed and then tailor the managerial design to suit each specific situation.

To try to manage either profit or not-for-profit firms without sophisticated use of successful concepts and techniques is to turn one's back on accumulated wisdom. To presume that judicious selection and fitting of these concepts to each situation can be avoided is to court disaster.

CASE 6.1
*JOE DI MAGGIO*

Joe DiMaggio pushed back from his desk and fired his pencil at the chart taped to his far wall. He hit the wall but missed the chart even though it was four-foot square. Unlike his namesake, the Yankee Clipper, Joe didn't have a good arm but like the Hall of Fame outfielder, he was a very proud man.

While he had never met the "other" Joe DiMaggio, he had come to admire him greatly. It hadn't been easy. As a child, he had borne the brunt of many jokes because of his name. As he matured, however, he thought less of invidious comparisons to his rather average athletic ability.

"From what I have heard about him, he was a winner. Even when hurt, he always gave 110 percent. He was a leader and wanted to be part of a winning team. There was no way he would have wanted to be part of a minor league or second division team which had no prospects for getting better. I'd like to think that in those respects I am like him even though I never could hit a curve ball. Yet it seems as though that is exactly what Robinson [Glenn Robinson, Group Vice-President, Agricultural Chemicals] is asking me to do."

Intercontinental Chemicals is a large international company which produces and markets a wide variety of chemical products throughout the world. Its growth in sales volume, in recent years, has been steady if not great, but its profits, adjusting for inflation, have been unimpressive. Several weeks ago, the top officers of ICC concluded a major strategic planning effort. Beginning nine months ago, each of the company's seventeen operating divisions had been asked to develop a comprehensive, strategic plan for the next decade. Individual division plans were reviewed and modified in separate meetings with their group vice-presidents. The four group vice-presidents and their staffs had then developed strategic plans for each of their operating divisions and presented their recommendations to the top officers of the corporation. After much discussion, and studies conducted by corporate staff, a final series of meetings brought the group vice-presidents and their staffs back together with the corporate officers. At these meetings, an overall strategic plan for the corporation was developed and the four group vice-presidents were instructed to meet with the division heads reporting to them in order to adjust division strategies and plans.

Among the most significant results of the corporate strategy meetings were decisions to shift emphasis and resources away from certain large volume, low profit, and/or cyclical markets. Several products and/or markets were to be abandoned as rapidly as possible through phase-out and divestiture programs. Others were viewed as slow-growth businesses which could be expected to produce low profit margins on high sales volumes and thus generate large amounts of cash. Most of the cash so generated would not be plowed back into the divisions which provided it but would be shifted to other divisions which were seen to have greater growth and profit potential. These cash-generating divisions, as long as they were not affected by wide cyclical swings, would remain a part of the corporation as long as they could contribute excess funds. If they could not continue as stable sources of "excess" cash, they would then join the businesses which had been phased out or sold.

The nitrogen-based fertilizer division had been placed in this cash-generator category. Glenn Robinson explains, "Our corporate officers concluded, and I concur, that the fertilizer market, while very large, is a mature one in which growth will be slow and profit margins will remain cyclical and on the average low. It is largely a commodity business in which acquiring additional market share has become increasingly expensive.

"For many decades," Robinson went on, "the fertilizer market has followed a pattern of ups and downs. After a few bad years, demand tended to pick up rapidly, catching the industry in short supply. Prices went up, profits soared, and we all raced to bring even marginal capacity back into production. At about this time someone would decide, during one of these strong markets, to build new capacity which would come on-stream, typically just about the time the growth in demand slowed. With low operating costs but high fixed costs to write off, the new production would be sold by discounting or other forms of price reductions to buy market share. The older facilities, while costly to operate, were usually fully depreciated and the illusion of low costs encouraged further price-cutting. Inevitably, but unpredictably, demand would drop as a result of changes in agricultural conditions. Then prices would be cut further and the industry which had enjoyed several boom years now took a beating.

"When we looked at our average growth and profit over these cycles, we decided to stop playing this game. Our cash flow from fertilizer has been good, overall, but it is too erratic. While we know the cyclical nature of this market, it is very difficult to predict the turning points and if we continue to follow past industry practices, even if we guess right, we may be locked into a disagreeable sequence of price and profit shifts."

Robinson explained that corporate management felt a new strategy for this business was necessary. They indicated they would settle for slow growth or even a decline in sales if Robinson could stabilize the division's cash flows and have it become a reliable net generator of funds which could be used in more attractive markets.

Robinson and his group staff developed a strategy for the fertilizer division that was based on the following policies:

1.   The division will not actively seek additional market share.

2.   During that portion of the cycle when industry demand is high, the division will not seek absolute growth in sales. Rather, it should seek to shift its customer mix to those who are not only *then* in need of supply, but with whom the division can develop a lasting competitive advantage which will *hold* their business when total demand slackens.

3.   Old, high-cost facilities are to be closed or sold unless it can be shown that through location they have a unique opportunity to attract or hold non-cyclical sales.

4.   No new capital will be provided the division for expansion unless a very strong case can be made to show stable, long-term returns at a rate equal to or higher than new product ventures in other divisions.

5.   Selectivity, in choice of customers and facilities, is to be emphasized. Capital, to modernize or create new low-cost facilities, will be considered only if reduction of capacity elsewhere in the division offsets projected new volumes. Projections for a high, stable return must be supported by evidence that new or modernized facilities will enjoy enduring competitive advantages.

6.   Reduction in head-count is to become a major objective as part of the overall goal of reducing costs.

7.   The division will develop strategies and programs within these parameters and translate them into a financial plan which will generate a net cash flow in one year of $8.5 million. This cash flow, for the next five years, should not fluctuate by more than ten percent in any year and should grow at a compound rate, adjusted for inflation, of two percent per year.

"I have gone over these points," Robinson explained, "with the division head and I'm sure he understands them even though he doesn't like them. We put Joe in that post about two years ago with instructions to waken what we felt then was a sleeping giant. Joe has a fine record, is very ambitious and energetic. We hoped at that time (two years ago) that he could revitalize the division and give us greater growth and profits.

"Considering the industry and what he had to work with, he had made a good start. He brought in a number of very bright young men and women, revamped our sales and distribution programs and improved efficiency in several plants. He was working on planning, control, and appraisal systems which stressed the need for more imagination and growth. Naturally, when we had to change directions on him in midstream, he was disappointed. He has been around long enough to know these things happen and he is high enough on the pyramid to realize this is necessary for the health of the total company. At forty-six, he still has plenty of time to get back into a 'go-go' business. Now, he has an opportunity to show us whether he can handle a contracting, tough, cost-conscious business.

"A week ago, he told me he was considering resigning if I couldn't offer him another post. I can't, not now; I just do not have an equal job for him, and I think I have him convinced that this is a real challenge and will show whether he is tough enough, smart enough, and team-player enough to pull it off."

Joe indeed has considered resigning.

"I have just begun to get some momentum going and they pulled the rug out from under me. I brought in some very bright, ambitious people and moved them rapidly into key technical and managerial spots. We have been developing some imaginative, innovative, aggressive plans. Even some of the old-timers had begun to get charged up again. Now, what can I do? If I stay, I will have to pull them back. We will have to adjust not only our thinking and our plans but, I would guess, our planning and control procedures. We will also have to come up with different appraisal, reward, and penalty systems. We will probably have to close several facilities in order to get any new money to modernize or build. This means layoffs, transfers, hiring freezes and, with little if any growth, few opportunities for promotions.

"How do I hold and motivate the team I have been building? Should I? Will I have to go after different kinds of people? Can I still find or use really sharp, ambitious people or will this become a dumping ground for has-beens and second-raters?

Joe indicated that he planned to raise these and other questions when he meets with Jim Kelly, president of Management Analysis Center, a small, prestigious consulting firm.

"Jim has had experience with businesses that need help working out means of implementing new strategies," Joe said. "Apparently I'm not the first one to have people dream up a new strategy for him and then say, 'You figure out how to implement it.' I hope that Jim will not only help me answer my questions, but will tell me whether they are the right questions. I would also like his advice on whether I should stick around. After all, they brought me into this job to build a winner, not manage a 'farm team' that merely feeds the other divisions. Robinson said I wouldn't be here forever and that if I could handle the assignment, he would find something bigger and better. But, how will he evaluate me? How will he or I know if I have done well? Surely that single, arbitrary $8.5 million cash-flow goal is not enough.

"Perhaps I ought to start with these last questions because if Jim can't help me on these, he can help my successor on the others. The way I feel right now I might be better off looking for a job with a bank or a coffee-maker."

FOR DISCUSSION AND
REPORT-WRITING

part I: planning:
the execution of
strategy

1. What do you think of the process used to develop strategy for Intercontinental Chemicals? What were the best elements? Which could (should) have been changed or improved?

2. Each of the seven "policies" developed by Robinson and his group staff can be viewed as objectives for DiMaggio to achieve. How useful do you feel they will be in establishing a hierarchy of plans and serving as a means of achieving long-range goals? Where are they deficient?

3. How *should* the change in direction of the Fertilizer Division affect the number and types of standing plans required?

4. Are aggressive, imaginative single-use plans appropriate to the new strategy for the division?

5. How may the seven policies or objectives set by Robinson for DiMaggio affect the need for and likelihood of generating creative alternatives at the division level? How will they affect "testing the choice"?

6. Should the number and types of quantitative aids to decision-making change with the proposed change in division strategy?

7. What would be major staffing considerations for DiMaggio if he stays and seeks to implement the new division strategy?

8. Should his appraisal, reward, and penalty systems change or remain much the same under the new strategy?

9. How important is long- and short-range personnel planning to the *total company* in supporting strategic changes in direction?

10. As Robinson, how would you seek to motivate DiMaggio? To which of his personal needs would you appeal?

11. How much and what kinds of participation should DiMaggio use in arriving at decisions on which plants to close and which customers to shed?

12. What are the major *similarities* and *differences* in the leadership required to implement DiMaggio's current vs. his original divisional mission?

13. What should DiMaggio watch for in seeking to avoid divisional politics detrimental to the new mission? What forms of politics should he seek to encourage?

14. Will measuring results against standards be more or less difficult under the new divisional mission than the old? Explain.

15. What changes in corporate and divisional budget procedures should take place as a result of the new divisional mission?

16. Review your answer to question 11 and based on it, assess its impact on key concepts presented in Chapter 24 (Behavioral Responses to Controls).

17. How should Robinson evaluate DiMaggio's performance over the next two years (assuming he stays)?

18. (Summary Report Question, Part Six) Develop a list of the key considerations for DiMaggio in building a divisional control system which is (1) consistent with the divisional strategy and (2) allows Robinson (as well as DiMaggio) to judge how good a job the division has done.

summary question
for solution of the
case as a whole

19.   As Jim Kelly, what advice would you give DiMaggio to encourage him to stay and help him succeed? Be sure to reflect, in your answer, key concepts from Chapters 26 and 27.

CASE 6.2
*FOSTER PROMOTIONS INC.*

Ron Foster, founder and president of Foster Promotions Inc., had been voted "most likely to succeed" by the senior class at Ames Business College. Within five years, he was well on his way to justifying that judgment. During his college years, he had managed a group of student agencies. These agencies sold T-shirts, magazines, newspapers, and a variety of novelty products. Under his leadership, sales and profit records were set, and procedures developed by him contributed to continued success after he graduated.

Based on this experience, Ron began his own business which grew very quickly in its first four years. At first, he made arrangements with a number of manufacturers to act as their sales agents for the university market in several midwestern states. By plowing his profits back into the business, and arranging several bank loans, he first expanded his sales efforts geographically and then began to add new lines as he established his company in the states between the Rockies and the Appalachians.

A year ago, Ron incorporated and began to revise his corporate strategy. The company still continues to act as sales representative for a number of manufacturers but has also begun to purchase products for resale. In addition, for a fee and exclusive distribution rights, it works for a number of manufacturers in developing products for the college market. While at present the company has no manufacturing capacity, Foster does not rule this out as a future possibility; however, he has shifted his attention to seeking growth by penetrating new markets.

"For the next few years," Foster said, "I would prefer to limit my selling efforts to the states in which we now market. I want to sell to other customers in those states before we go nationwide or international. We know the university market and should keep growing in it. There is another market for many of our products which I thought we could tap, however.

"Many corporations buy large quantities of our novelty products as awards for their employees and for promotional giveaways to customers and vendors. I'm sure we can capture a big chunk of this market. If we can, we not only start a new area for growth but spread our risks as well. We have good relations with our suppliers and understand the products, but I don't really know this new market and I have more than enough on my hands building this organization and tending to our existing market and suppliers. After a very difficult and at times disheartening search, a few months ago I found someone who seemed made to order to get us started in the corporate market."

Herbert Shepperd is the person Foster found and hired seven months ago. Shepperd is fifty-six years old with a wide variety of past experiences.

Beginning his work life in retailing, he moved into the travel business and twenty years ago joined a large corporation handling travel plans for senior executives. During the past twenty years, he has worked for seven corporations handling a variety of travel, convention, and conference activities. Prior to joining Foster, he had served for three years in the public relations department of a large, heavy industrial corporation. An executive search firm put him in touch with Foster and after several discussions, he accepted a one-year contract.

"Herb indicated that he was looking for a new set of challenges," said Ron Foster. "He strikes me as a lively, innovative guy who in recent years has had to hold back to stay within a big company's policies. He said that he wanted a chance to do something really different, in which he could take pride, and make enough to retire at sixty. While I was unwilling to give him a four-year commitment, I told him that at the end of one year we would review the situation. If we were both happy, then we could firm up a three-year contract.

"For this year, we are guaranteeing him a good salary and small bonus if his sales reach certain milestones. If we go with the three-year contract, I proposed that we would not increase his salary but would set up a bonus program which could add fifty percent to his base in the first year, seventy-five percent in the second, and one hundred percent in the third and final year. I feel this would give him the incentive to build this market. If he succeeds, over a four-year period we will have a large new market that may not require a 'builder' as much as a real manager. Lots of new ventures don't make it past the entrepreneurial stage because the founder can't let go. Frankly, I work very hard to make sure I'm not guilty of this with the entire company. But with it clearly understood that Herb will retire at sixty, I thought we had the best of all worlds—a frustrated tiger who wants to go out with a roar; who will build something and then turn it loose."

Foster has recently had second thoughts. Shepperd has indeed thrown himself into his work. During his first seven months, he has often put in sixty to seventy hours a week. He achieved his first year sales targets in less than six months and received Foster's approval to hire three agents who are paid solely on a commission basis. Profits from his work are also much higher than expected.

"Given his salary and expenses," Foster said, "I figured we would be happy to break even the first year. Instead, we will make good money and Herb feels he could do even better if I give him a free hand. The problem is, even though he reports to me, I don't really know what he is doing or how. He is driving my purchasing people crazy. He consistently ignores the procedures we have established in purchasing and inventory control. On several occasions, Herb made promises we couldn't keep. He offered discounts and delivery dates that my people said were impossible. We had to shift orders, pay premiums to suppliers, and we still came in late with deliveries. My legal people tell me that he has signed letters of agreement without their checking them and could easily get us in trouble with the law if competitors or even customers 'blow the whistle.'

"On one tight delivery question, Herb suggested that he explain the need to our supplier. But purchasing got a better promise so Herb's call wasn't necessary.

"Herb's travel expenses are way over budget, but his ratio of expenses to revenue is o.k. The controller is upset and I hope he has enough sense not to let information about Herb's expenses get out to other salesmen.

"Still, we are making more money than I anticipated and Herb promises that next year he will set up and follow procedures but that first he has to get us into the market."

After three months, Foster asked Shepperd to hire someone to serve as his administrative assistant.

"I hoped," Foster said, "he would get someone who could handle his paper work and act as a buffer between him and my purchasing, inventory, and controller departments so that I would not constantly be drawn into resolving disputes with his peers. He agreed, but the person he hired lasted less than a month and resigned. As a result, I hired a bright young MBA with five years' experience with a CPA firm. Herb seemed glad to have me find someone for him but last week, after only three months, he told me she left to go back to a public accounting firm. I interviewed her before she left and she said that she simply could not pass up the offer she had received, but she also indicated that she was not happy working for Herb.

"We still have some time before I have to decide on Herb's three-year contract but I am worried. Herb is very likable, and is far more capable than anyone I interviewed to fill that position. However, no one, including me, knows what he is doing in any detail. He tells me he didn't take this job to be 'suffocated by bureaucracy' and that I have to trust him. Frankly, I trust his integrity but wonder sometimes about his judgment and what makes him tick."

1. How sound does Foster's current strategy for growth appear to you? What questions should he answer to test its appropriateness?

part I: planning:
the execution of
strategy

2. What do you think of Foster's comment that if the division succeeds, in four years it "may not require a 'builder' as much as a real manager"?

3. What are the pluses and minuses associated with Foster attempting to set up an MBO system with Shepperd?

4. How might Foster get Shepperd to help him understand how to deal with the risk and uncertainty associated with decisions affecting the corporate market?

5. Is Foster wise to have Shepperd reporting directly to him? What other reporting relationship might work in this situation?

6. Has Foster delegated well to Shepperd? Discuss in the context of duties, authority, and obligation.

7. Does Shepperd appear to be a good match for the job Foster wants done?

8. Critique Foster Promotions' current organizational structure in light of "Stages of Company Growth" considerations.

part III:
organizing:
strategy to
structure

9. How should Foster seek to motivate Shepperd? To which of his personal needs should he appeal?

10. To what degree may the conflict between Shepperd and other departments be constructive? Destructive?

part IV:
motivating: human
factors in the
organization

11. To what degree should Foster try to lead Shepperd? Can Foster permit Shepperd to lead him?

12. For what aspects of Shepperd's job should Foster accept compliance? Where should he seek commitment?

13. If Shepperd chooses to use political power to deal with other departments, what are the sources of his power?

14. What role might communications play in improving the situation? To what degree may poor communications be of benefit to the company in this situation?

part V: leading

15. What types of controls are most appropriate to Foster's needs for evaluating Shepperd's efforts?

16. Is it more important for Foster to know *what* Shepperd is doing or *how* he is doing it? Discuss both sides of the question.

17. Would it be wise to give the corporate controller functional authority for budgetary controls on Shepperd?

18. If Foster decides not to insist on tight controls on Shepperd's operation, can he depend on semi-annual audits to help him evaluate what is going on?

19. How does Foster go about developing realistic standards for Shepperd's operations and maintain control-system integrity?

20. How important are controls today in preparing for longer-term needs after Shepperd's retirement?

21. (Summary Report Quesion, Part VI) Develop a detailed description of the control system Foster should develop for use with Shepperd.

part VI:
controlling

22. What steps should Foster take now to develop the best long-term approach to the corporate market? Prepare a detailed plan which matches a total management system with strategy.

summary question
for solution of the
case as a whole

# conclusion:
# need for synthesis

Thinking of management in terms of planning, organizing, motivating, leading, and controlling sharpens our analysis; it helps us sort out issues and then concentrate on a particular opportunity for improvement. But like any analytical device, it leaves us with parts. However much we refine these parts of the management process, they become operative only when we fit them back into the total management system. We may be especially pleased with a new scheme for motivating executives or with an operations-research model, but unless our new creation is compatible with the overall management design, it will be of little value. Achieving a *synthesis* of various management parts is the central theme in this concluding part.

In addition to achieving internal synthesis, the manager must keep his management design adjusted to external needs. In Chapter 2 we described master strategy as the evolving formulation of a company's plans for dealing with its environment. Now we shall give specific attention to the interrelationships between that master strategy and the overall management design. In other words, as stressed in Chapter 1, full synthesis involves both internal and external integration.

Two popular concepts are embraced in the kind of synthesis we are discussing. (1) The total *system* of management must be considered. Each phase fits in with other phases; working together they provide mutual support. (2) Each company designs a system that should be suited to its particular needs. The specific features of that design are *contingent upon* the company's individual aims and resources.

We discuss these synthesis issues in our two concluding chapters.

Chapter 26—Matching the Total Management System with Strategy. In this chapter we suggest that we can best link strategic needs and management design by focusing on technology. The character of the technology—stable, regulated flexibility, adaptive—provides a clue (along with size, complexity, uncertainty, and need for speed) to the most appropriate kind of management system.

Chapter 27—Managing Change. Fitting the total management system to strategy is complicated by constant environmental change. A system that performs well today may need revamping tomorrow. Because a neatly integrated management system cannot remain static, we turn to the complexities of managing organizational change in this chapter.

In an era of continuing environmental turbulence, management is a vital social resource. To be fully effective, however, the practice of management demands great skill in fusing many elements into a total design suited to each specific opportunity.

# 26

# matching the total management system with strategy

Learning Objectives

After completing this chapter you should be able to

1. List the five ways strategy acts as an integrating mechanism.
2. Describe the three major categories of technology.
3. Identify the management system required for each major technology type.
4. Describe the features of a management system which vary with technology.
5. Explain the difference between a composite management system and a blended management system.

## FRAMEWORK FOR INTEGRATION

Each player in an orchestra or on a football team must perform his part with skill. But real achievement comes only when all the parts are blended together in a unified effort. Similar integration of diverse efforts is just as important, and more difficult to achieve, in a business enterprise.

We have focused, in this book, on managerial tasks one part at a time. This analytical approach adds depth to our understanding of planning, controlling, and the like; and it aids in the development of skills. The supreme task of a manager, however, is to put all the pieces together into a harmonious whole—not just any whole, but rather one that performs a particular mission. Integration is essential. So this chapter picks up the suggestions, scattered throughout the book, that deal with integration.

Three basic concepts are especially useful to a manager in building integrated action: strategy, contingency design, and the management system as a whole.

**central role of strategy**

Strategy defines the mission of a company or one of its functional departments. As explained in Chapter 2, for a business-unit, strategy selects the domain of action, picks differential advantages to be sought, singles out strategic thrusts, and sets target results. With such guidance, the manager of, say, a gift shop in Niagara Falls or a coal mine in Kentucky has a clear sense of direction.

Strategy is a powerful integrating device because it unifies five elements of integration.

(1) The key to *external integration* is stated; the primary contributions of the company to society are flagged. These may be service or product, employment of minorities, dividends for misers and widows, or some other vital contribution. In addition, as explained in Chapter 1, the strategic differential advantage which the company seeks is often based on a unique relationship with government, material suppliers, or membership in a coalition. Thus, the strategy sets the dominant pattern of the company's interaction with its environment. Not all external relationships are covered by strategy but rather the ones that are central to the company's mission. These are the particular relationships which must be carefully integrated with internal operations.

(2) A basis is provided for *consistent, harmonious action* by specialists throughout the organization. The strategy sets up overriding operating goals. These goals are known to all major decision-makers, who are expected to direct their specialized input toward these shared objectives. In terms of the means-end analysis used in decision-making (stressed in Part II), strategy provides the approved higher-level goals. Integration is encouraged because the higher-level goals of all departments and divisions are the same. There is a single, common mission. At Crown Cork & Seal Company, for instance, everyone knows that strategy frowns on making aluminum cans.

So engineering, production, and marketing people all focus on building volume in steel cans.[1]

Moreover, strategy helps to establish priorities. Strategic thrusts explicitly indicate which moves to make now and which to defer. Conflicts over allocation of resources (money, skilled people, plant capacity, etc.) can be judged in terms of incremental and timely contribution to strategic targets. In any vigorous company, specialized units will seek more resources to do their job better. Strategy provides the basic direction, and thus the rationale for responding to these requests consistently in terms of integrated action.

(3) Strategy also encourages *persistent action*. Because a strategy takes time to establish and is usually long-run in its impact, it has momentum over several years. This persistence makes possible the integration of actions in several time periods. Thus, a manager can gain the cumulative effect of a whole series of moves aimed in the same direction. Rarely can, say, a dominant market position or low costs relative to competitors be achieved without persistent efforts year after year. A whole array of specific moves must be focused on such a major target, and actions which tend to undercut it must be screened out. Clear, recognized strategy is a great help in securing such integration over time.

(4) Strategy can, and should, become a *mission* to which managers and other employees are *personally committed*. Not all actions can be rationally planned, and many situations call for voluntary coordination, especially in informal and permissive organizations. The people directly involved decide for themselves how their work will be dovetailed. This flexibility can be tolerated provided the self-coordinators are all working toward common objectives. If strategy expresses the objectives being sought in this voluntary action, integrated behavior tends to arise spontaneously.

Commitment to a mission cannot be commanded; it is a personal response. However, a clearcut strategy, consistently advocated by leaders of a company, will usually be accepted as a worthy cause. The reasearch aims of Bell Laboratories, like the sales-growth aims of Procter & Gamble, are internalized by many members of those organizations. Mission achievement is undertaken in the same spirit as winning a game. That sort of commitment contributes greatly to integrated action.

(5) Finally, strategy aids integration by providing the *raison d'etre for the company's management system*. Each management system should be designed for a purpose. As we stress later in this chapter, the characteristics of a "good system" do vary; they depend primarily on the purpose the designer wants to achieve. And in a company that purpose should be execution of company strategy. Without clear strategy, the management system will merely reflect historical accident and strong personalities. With strategy,

---

[1]For a description of the tightly integrated strategy and structure of Crown Cork & Seal Company, see W. H. Newman and J. P. Logan, *Strategy, Policy, and Central Management,* 8th ed. (Cincinnati: South-Western, 1981), pp. 679–96.

the management system reinforces the selected mission and harnesses resources to a common purpose.

Note that the integrative power of strategy arises from the use of the *same* driving force for all the five elements just listed—external integration, consistent action, persistent action, committed behavior, and a dedicated management system. Synthesis and harmony come from this unity of purpose. Having a clear strategy does not automatically assure a manager that these five elements will be present in his company, but it makes them much more likely.

**a contingency approach**

Throughout this book we have explored alternative ways of planning, of organizing, of motivating and leading, and of controlling. Which alternative a manager selects or adapts depends on his purposes and his particular situation. To provide practical guidance, we suggested factors to consider in selecting an alternative. Among academicians the fashionable term for this selective way of dealing with management problems is the "contingency approach."[2] The term merely means that what is wise to do is contingent on (depends on) the practical needs in the local situation.

The contingency approach is especially valuable when we seek total integration. Customary practice, while suited to a majority of settings, may not give the best integrated results in a particular context. For example, promotion from within is typically the best way to fill a management post, but when a company embarks on a new strategy a person with the desired experience may be unavailable. To obtain an executive who fully reinforces change may require outside recruitment. Or, to return to Crown Cork & Seal, fast customer service is a major way the company seeks a differential advantage over competitors. To assure responsiveness, *both* the salesperson and the plant manager supplying a given customer are held accountable for good service to that customer. Both earn bonuses on the basis of profitable sales to that customer. Clearly, this dual responsibility is an unorthodox form of organization. But in this circumstance the arrangement supports integrated action in a vital area.

**management systems concept**

A third aid managers can use to secure integrated behavior is a systems viewpoint. The modern "systems" concept applies to a wide range of phenomena. We speak of a water-supply system, political system, transportation system, medical-care system, and ignition system. Every system includes (1) several specialized parts that perform specific activities. These parts are connected so that one part feeds or supports another; thus the output of the system relies on dependable interaction between the parts. And each system has (2) regular ways of responding to environmental stimuli.

[2]For examples of books with contingency themes, see H. L. Tosi and W. C. Hamner, *Organizational Behavior and Management: A Contingency Viewpoint* (Chicago: St. Clair Press, 1974) and G. Dessler, *Organization and Management: A Contingency Approach* (Englewood Cliffs, NJ: Prentice-Hall, 1976).

The systems concept does not add any activities or hardware; it merely focuses on the way parts are fitted together into an integrated arrangement, and on the interaction of the total system to its environment.[3]

Company management is such a system. It has parts—planning devices, organizational arrangements, leadership styles, and control mechanisms; and these parts must support each other to achieve the purposes of the company. Also, this internal management-system has established ways of keeping watch on the company environment and responding to external opportunities and threats.

The main benefit of thinking of management as a system is the emphasis on interrelations—for example, in the way a change in organization must be tied to corresponding adjustments in leading and controlling. For instance, a North Atlantic shipping company introduced container ships. The new technology calls for steel containers, the size of a large truck, to be filled by the original shipper and handled as a single, sealed unit all the way to the doorstep of the receiver. Each major port served by the company now has a company branch engaged in overland transportation to dockside. In addition to setting up these new organization units, more authority has been delegated to the local branches; the planning and scheduling procedures have been greatly modified; headquarters control is now confined largely to post-action reports; and local commitment to the new way of handling cargo is crucial. To take full advantage of the container ships, the entire management system has had to be revised.

Strategy does not remain fixed forever. The business environment is turbulent, so new hurdles have to be crossed or the action in one arena slowed down. Internal successes or failures—in, say, R & D or cost reduction—permit refinement of the strategy. In fact, many of the management issues discussed in this book arise because of necessary modifications in strategy.

Most changes in a management system are small adjustments in existing patterns of behavior. A new opportunity arises or something is not working quite right, so a policy is added or the organization modified. Such refinements leave the basic system intact. Nevertheless, *reinforcing the adjustments in several parts of the system is often necessary to make the initial change effective.*

## GROWTH AND MANAGEMENT SYSTEMS

Company growth affects the kind of management system that is needed.[4] We have already seen, in Chapter 13, how growth leads to changes in the form of organization. But a revision of the organization structure is not sufficient, by itself, to adapt the company. The planning

---

[3]F. E. Kast and J. E. Rosenzweig, *Organization and Management: A Systems Approach,* 2nd ed. (New York: McGraw-Hill, 1978).

[4]M. Leontiades, *Strategies for Diversification and Change* (Boston: Little Brown, 1980), chap. 2.

system must be recast, leadership styles need to be modified, and new controls have to be established.

When a motel grows from a single to multiple locations (as in the examples cited in Chapter 13), more than a shift from the single entrepreneur stage to a departmentalized organization will be required. Because senior managers are more remote, standing operating procedures for many activities from bookkeeping to bedmaking may be adopted. Departmental targets will also become more explicit and detailed. With the activities thus prescribed by detailed plans, the manager of each location can efficiently direct the day-to-day operations with a consistency of service for guests. Control in the expanded organization will shift to a policy of occasional "audits," to ensure that standing procedures are being followed, to monthly postaction review of departmental results versus targets, and to yes/no controls on capital expenditures, appointment of key supervisors, and increased sales-promotion efforts.

This kind of management system suits a medium-size motel chain. But other departmentalized companies will need more adaptability in their planning and control—as we shall see in the next section, on the matching of technology and management systems.

Planning and control mechanisms change sharply when a company moves from the departmentalized stage to a multiple-mission organization. In the larger multiple-mission organization, each of the operating divisions has its own internal management design. Planning in the headquarters therefore focuses on new strategic opportunities and long-run programming. Aside from accounting and perhaps labor relations, where consistency becomes the ruling virtue, there will be few company-wide standing operating procedures. Controlling will be largely concerned with having effective systems within each division, a few warning signals for steering control, and postaction reviews. In the leading by central executives, commitment on the part of division managers will be a sine qua non; in the typical multiple-mission company the degree of decentralization and remoteness is so high that central executives must rely on strongly committed subordinates.

When growth forces a company to shift to a new stage, the total management system—not just one part—is subject to redesign.

## STRATEGY AND STRUCTURE

A new company strategy can have a more profound effect on the management system than can growth.[5] A change in strategy often alters the kind of activities performed, the degree of uncertainty, frequency of change, and other characteristics of company operations. And to achieve integration the management system should be suited to these new characteristics.

But there is no simple process for moving from a new strategy to a system for executing that strategy.

[5]A. D. Chandler, Jr., *Strategy and Structure* (Cambridge: MIT Press, 1962).

The best bridge between strategy and system design is "technology." We use technology in a very broad sense to include numerous methods for converting resource inputs into products and services for consumers. The inputs can be labor, knowledge, and capital, as well as raw materials.[6] Thus an insurance company has its technology for converting money, ideas, and labor into insurance service, just as an oil company has its technology for converting crude oil and other resources into petroleum products. By extending our thinking from strategy to the technology necessary to execute that strategy, we move to *work to be done*. Once we comprehend the work to be done—both managerial and operating work—we are on familiar ground. Most of our management concepts relate directly to getting work done, so preparing a management system to fit a particular task falls within the recognized "state of the art."

The use of technology as an intervening variable produces the arrangement shown in Figure 26.1. To maintain perspective and to highlight key influences, strategy should focus on only a few basic ideas. Its formulation is by necessity in broad terms. We cannot jump directly from strategy to management design, for we have not yet classified the array of actions necessary to execute the strategy. Thinking of technology helps us to elaborate the implications of the strategy and thereby provides us with the inputs for shaping an effective management system.

Technology deals with all sorts of situations and methods. For purposes of relating it to management, however, we can concentrate on only a few of its characteristics. For instance, the way a technology deals with *change* is very significant for our purpose.

In a company with a given strategy and technology, the need for change will fall somewhere along a continuum of infrequent to frequent. Similarly, the kinds of changes the company typically faces will fall somewhere along

*technology: the intervening variable*

*types of technology*

---

[6]For an expansion of this concept of technology, see C. Perrow, *Organizational Analysis: A Sociological View* (Belmont, California: Wadsworth Publishing Co., 1970); D. F. Gillespie and D. S. Mileti, "Technology and the Study of Organizations: An Overview and an Appraisal," *Academy of Management Review*, 2, no. 1 (January 1977), pp. 7–16; and B. C. Reimann, "Organization Structure and Technology in Manufacturing: System versus Work Flow Level Perspectives," *Academy of Management Journal*, 23, no. 1 (March 1980), 61–76.

*Figure 26.1* A simple flow diagram with technology as an intervening variable.

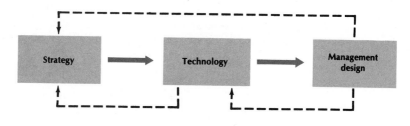

another continuum ranging from unprecedented problems to familiar, precedented ones; in the case of the latter, the company will have a well-established pattern for resolving them.

Using these two characteristics, we can set up the matrix shown in Figure 26.2. Many technologies will fit in the middle of these dimensions, but by thinking about technologies toward the end of the scales, we arrive at three well-known types of business.

Enterprises confronted only with familiar problems—and even these not very frequently—are basically *stable*. Paper mills and other firms processing large volumes of raw material fall into this category. When the need for change moves from infrequent to frequent, and the problems remain precedented, we encounter businesses that display *regulated flexibility*. Job shops—used by management writers since Frederick Taylor to illustrate

*Figure* **26.2** *Viewing businesses in terms of need for, and nature of, change.*

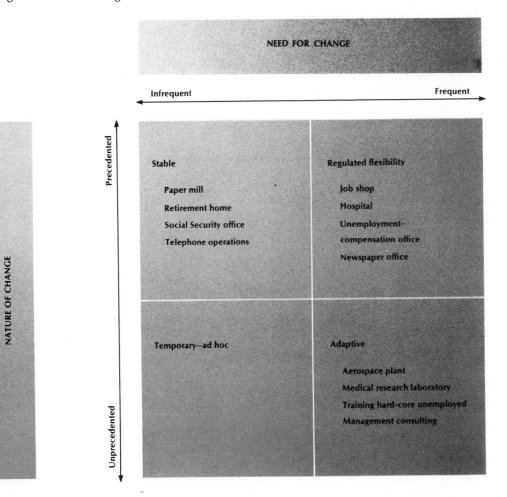

management concepts—fit this category. But when the need for change is frequent and the problems are unprecedented, we face a sharply different situation. Here—for instance, in the aerospace industry—technology requires an *adaptive* structure.

As Figure 26.2 shows, these three technology types—stable, regulated flexibility, and adaptive—are found in many lines of endeavor. In contrast, the fourth division in the change matrix does not point to a clear type of technology or management design. Unprecedented problems that arise only infrequently are handled by some temporary arrangement. This *ad hoc* setup does not exist long enough to modify the underlying structure.

An intriguing aspect of the first three technology types is that each leads to a well-known management system. The usual relationships between technology and system are presented in Table 26.1. To sharpen the analysis, the four major phases of managing have been subdivided; the features of each phase most likely to be affected by strategy are listed separately in the left column. Then the rest of the table shows, for each of these features, the typical response by a stable technology, a regulated-flexibility technology, and an adaptive technology.

**from technology to management systems**

Within each type of technology, the primary features of each system remain substantially the same even though the companies come from different industries. For instance, when the work situation is stable (as it usually is in a paper mill, retirement home, Social-Security office, and telephone exchange), planning tends to be comprehensive and detailed, intermediate goals are sharply defined, decision-making is centralized, and central staff is strong. In addition, we find limited participation and low job commitment. Controls are focused on dependability and efficiency, checks are made frequently, and few mistakes are tolerated.

Today regulated flexibility is actually much more common than the stable technology just described. A job shop, hospital, unemployment-compensation office, and newspaper all face a continuing procession of new situations, most of which can be handled by well-developed techniques for resolving such problems. For this kind of technology, the typical management system introduces flexibility by the use of craftsmen and professionals, separate scheduling units, careful programming of workloads, close control of work passing from one stage to the next, prompt information on the status of work at each stage, and so on. The kind of flexibility needed is anticipated, and provisions for dealing with it are built into the system. Each person understands the limits of his discretion, and other conditions are fully planned and controlled so that reliability of the total system is not lost.

Adaptive technology calls for quite a different management system. The research lab, consulting firm, and training project for the hard-core unemployed all face unprecedented problems frequently. Here operating units become smaller, greater reliance is placed on face-to-face contacts, authority is decentralized, planning tends to focus on objectives and broad programs, managers use participation and expect high personal commitment, control checks are less frequent and concern results rather than meth-

TABLE 26.1 TYPICAL FEATURES OF MANAGEMENT STRUCTURES
FOR THREE TYPES OF TECHNOLOGY

| | Primary Features That Distinguish Management Systems[1] | Nature of Technology | | |
| --- | --- | --- | --- | --- |
| | | Stable | Regulated Flexibility | Adaptive |
| Planning | Use of standing plans: | | | |
| | Comprehensiveness of coverage | Broad coverage | All main areas covered | Mostly "local," self-imposed |
| | Specificity | Detail specified | Detail in interlocking activities | Main points only |
| | Use of single-use plans: | | | |
| | Comprehensiveness of coverage | Fully planned | Fully planned | Main steps covered |
| | Specificity | Detail specified | Schedules and specs detailed | Adjusted to feedback |
| | Planning horizon | Weekly to quarterly | Weekly to annually | Monthly to three years or more |
| | Intermediate versus final objectives | Intermediate goals sharp | Intermediate goals sharp | Emphasis on objectives |
| | "How" versus results | "How" is specified | Results at each step specified | End results stressed |
| Organizing | Centralization versus decentralization | Centralized | Mostly centralized | Decentralized |
| | Degree of division of labor | Narrow specialization | Specialized, or crafts | Scope may vary |
| | Size of self-sufficient operating units | Large | Medium | Small, if equipment permits |
| | Mechanisms for coordination | Built-in programmed | Separate planning unit | Face-to-face, within unit |
| | Nature and location of staff | Narrow functions; headquarters | Narrow functions; headquarters and operating unit | Generalists at headquarters; specialists in operating units |
| | Management information system | Heavy upward flow | Flow to headquarters and to operating unit | Flow mostly to, and within, operating unit |
| | Characteristics of key personnel | Strong operators | Functional experts in line and staff | Analytical, adaptive |

[1]In any single system only a few of these features will dominate, and others may be insignificant. In unusual circumstances a feature not listed here may be critical. Nevertheless, careful consideration of the features listed will enable us to comprehend and to deal with the management systems of most enterprises.

554

| | Primary Features That Distinguish Management Systems [1] | Nature of Technology | | |
|---|---|---|---|---|
| | | Stable | Regulated Flexibility | Adaptive |
| Leading | Participation in planning | Very limited | Restricted to own tasks | High participation |
| | Permissiveness | Stick to instructions | Variation in own tasks only | High permissiveness, if results OK |
| | Closeness of supervision | Follow operations closely | Output and quality closely watched | General supervision |
| | Sharing of information | Circumspect | Job information shared | Full project information shared |
| | Emphasis on on-the-job satisfactions | Limited scope | Craftsmanship and professionalism encouraged | Opportunity for involvement |
| Controlling | Performance criteria emphasized | Efficiency, dependability | Quality, punctuality, efficiency | Results, within resource limits |
| | Location of control points | Within process; intermediate stages | Focus on each processing unit | Overall "milestones" |
| | Frequency of checks | Frequent | Frequent | Infrequent |
| | Who initiates corrective action | Often central managers | "Production control" and other staff | Manager's operating unit |
| | Stress on reliability versus learning | Reliability stressed | Reliability stressed | Learning stressed |
| | Punitive versus reward motivation | Few mistakes tolerated | Few mistakes tolerated | High reward for success |

ods. These and other features listed in Table 26.1 are often called "organic" or sometimes "democratic."

This adaptive type of situation is the dream of many human-relations advocates. It provides ample opportunity for employee participation and self-actualization. However, the fact that only a small portion of all work involves frequent, unprecedented problems explains why a lot of human-relations training has failed to find practical application.

Of course, no company will fit exactly into any one of the technology–management-system types we have described. But the examples do suggest how thoughtful analysis of technology provides a basis for designing a suitable structure.

**the pervasive influence of strategy**

Although it is fruitful to analyze technology in terms of the frequency and uniqueness of the problems it faces, we should not overlook other influences.[7] For instance, technology will also be affected by complexity and the need for speed. When several interrelated variables affect the work, as in building a communications satellite, more thorough planning and control will be necessary. The need for speedy action usually has an opposite effect. Here the urgency to get prompt action reduces the opportunity for thorough planning and control; quick results now may have a higher value than somewhat improved results that are available a month later.

Uncertainty permeates many activities. Because of an unknown environment or unpredictable responses to our own actions, we are confronted with uncertainty. If time permits we may try to reduce this uncertainty by further tests and experiments; and this will probably add staff to our organization and reduce the permissiveness of the structure. On the other hand, if such attempts are impractical, we may hire people with the best intuitive judgment we can find, get rid of our staff, and decentralize authority to the experts. This latter response to uncertainty, which is favored by the managers of most conglomerates, creates a simple, lean management system.

Management systems, then, must be developed in light of a variety of influences. However, the added dimensions just cited still fit into our basic proposal of moving first from strategy to character of work, then from work to management systems.

**COMPOUND SYSTEMS WITHIN A COMPANY**

Thus far we have discussed the management system for a whole company. We have assumed that one technology and one system predominates; and for a single-function company this holds true. Most enterprises, however, are more complex. Within the company, quite different activities may take place. So if we are correct in urging that the management system reflect technology, the concepts should also be applied to the parts of a complex company.

[7]R. Dewar and J. Hage, "Size, Technology, Complexity and Structural Differentiation: Toward a Theoretical Analysis," *Administrative Science Quarterly,* 1977, 22, pp. 177–202.

Consider the Greenfield Company, which has a strategy of performing the complete job of providing new, low-cost housing, from land aquisition to planting shrubbery in the play yard. Separate departments deal with architecture, real estate and finance, component manufacture, and building. The architects are the planners who conceive of types of construction, space utilization, layouts, and specifications that will create good housing at low cost; their work ranges from the highly unique and creative to the painstaking preparation of specifications for actual construction. The real-estate and finance people spend much time negotiating with government agencies and other outsiders; their problems are technical and often unique. In contrast, manufacture of components (standard wall-sections, bathroom and kitchen modules, and the like) is standardized, routinized, and mechanized as much as possible. Actual construction is necessarily "job order" in character, and requires the synchronization of various craftsmen.

In this one company, two of the major departments—architecture, and real estate and finance—come close to the adaptive type described in the preceding section. The building department clearly displays regulated flexibility, and the component-manufacturing department is moving as close to the stable type as volume permits.

This diversity has serious implications for management systems. Many executives who have had successful careers in one type of system believe their style of managing should be extended to all parts of the company. Such consistency in managerial methods does have benefits, but the astute manager will at least consider the possibility of using more than one administrative style.

Generally, when a department is both large and strategically vital, it should be managed with a system suited to its own activity. In other words, companies embracing diverse technologies should use several different managerial styles. The justification for this mixture of managerial designs lies, of course, in the improved performance of the individual departments.

Such diversity also has its costs.

1. *Cooperation between departments becomes increasingly difficult.* Voluntary cooperation between groups with different values, time orientations, and willingness to take risks is inevitably strained (as we saw in Chapter 17). Divergent management systems add to this "cultural barrier." Because the departments are so different, we may even separate them geographically—remove research labs from the plants, separate mills designed for long production runs from those for short runs, and so on.

   When management systems differ sharply, a special liaison staff or other formal means for coordination is often needed. Having deliberately accentuated the difference between departments, we then add a "diplomatic corps" to serve as a communication link between them.[8]

[8]For a discussion of the appropriate use of "integrative" devices, see P. R. Lawrence and J. W. Lorsch, *Organization and Environment* (Boston: Graduate School of Business Administration, Harvard University, 1967).

2. *Companywide services drop in value.* With a composite system, the rotation of key personnel is impeded, budgeting is complicated, training programs fit only parts of the company, capital-allocation procedures must be tailored to different inputs and criteria. In other words, synergy arising from pooled services and the reinforcing features of a management system is lacking for the company as a whole.

3. *The task of central managers is complicated.* Understanding the subtleties of the several management systems, and personally adjusting one's leadership style to each, calls for unusual skill and sophistication. Most managers, often unconsciously, favor departments whose management system they find congenial.

**blended systems**

Because of the drawbacks of a composite system and because dissimilar departments may be too small to support a distinct management structure, we often try to blend two or more systems.

Some types of systems are compatible. For instance, both the stable and the regulated-flexibility systems (used as examples earlier) call for a high degree of central planning, strong staff, limited permissiveness, and control at intermediate points. The chief difference lies in frequent adjustment by the latter to variations in client requirements; nevertheless, these adjustments normally occur within anticipated limits and often follow rules. Consequently, a combined arrangement that accommodates both technologies (for example, the component manufacturer and building construction in the Greenfield Company) can be devised. The blended system is not what each department would do for its own purposes, but the modification can be tolerated.

Another common arrangement is to build one strong structure and then recognize that exception must be made for certain segments. For instance, accounting usually gets special treatment in a research laboratory, just as members of the advertising group are accepted as "oddballs" in a manufacturing firm. If the people in the exceptional spots have enough zeal for their specialty to withstand the normal pressure to conform, the mismatch can function reasonably well.

A variation on making exceptions from the major pattern within the enterprise is to use outsiders for the deviant activity. Thus consultants may be called in to a "stable" company to provide creative ideas. Brokerage firms subcontract janitorial and equipment-maintenance work. Dress manufacturers often obtain designs from freelance designers. Although volume of work and flexibility are also factors in such subcontracting, simplification of the management design is a prime benefit.

The fact that many companies need a composite, or blended, management system does not detract from the major theme of this chapter. Integration of each management system is vital whether the system be simple or complex. Diversity of work and the resulting complexity of systems only multiply the components that we must take into account.

A final check, after arranging the many parts, involves going back to the master strategy of the enterprise, identifying the key elements to success, and asking whether the management system promises to emphasize these elements. In thinking through the necessary refinements of a system, we are always in danger of losing perspective on the major mission.

## CONCLUSION: FROM ANALYSIS TO SYNTHESIS

The study of any complex subject like management must be divided into parts, and each must be examined carefully. We have followed this pattern by devoting separate parts of the book to planning, organizing, motivating, leading, and controlling. In this chapter we turned our attention to the task of integrating management processes.

We emphasize the importance of developing a consistent management system and carefully tailoring the total system to the specific situation. Strategy plays a central role in the design of an integrated management system. In addition to establishing the basis of the company's interaction with its environment, strategy provides for harmonious and persistent action throughout the organization.

The contingency approach and the systems concept both aid managers in obtaining integrated behavior. Managerial sensitivity to local contingencies is needed in order to adapt to local needs. By taking a systems view, the impact of a change in one management process is more easily recognized, and adjustments can be made in other management processes to bring about a new balance.

A useful way to explore the impact of strategy on the management system is to consider technology as an intervening variable. By thinking in terms of technology, we move from strategy to the work to be done. For each of the key features of a management system there is a typical response to a stable technology, a regulated-fexibility technology, and an adaptive technology.

The rapid pace of political, social, and economic events creates an inevitable need for change in a company's strategy, and shifts in strategy precipitate changes in the management system. Because the management of change is such a complex and challenging task, we devote the concluding chapter of the book to this important topic.

## FOR FURTHER DISCUSSION

1. "While a clearly understood strategy has many advantages, it also takes time to communicate it throughout the organization. Some employees may not like aspects of it, others may even leak it to competitors. Thus, I communicate as few of our strategic decisions as possible to my subordinates." Comment on this statement by the president of a large, multinational company.

2. Many corporations are diversifying to the point where the differences in product/market mix within a single firm may be great. Would it be possible for one company to have some divisions that are in the stable category, while others are in the regulated-flexibility and adaptive categories? When would such a situation prove most troublesome to central management?

3. To what extent may serious personnel problems arise as a company grows and finds it necessary to shift its strategy from skimming new products and markets to profitably servicing more

mature products and markets? How might these problems be dealt with?

4. What effect do you feel participation by middle managers in strategic planning is likely to have on (1) the quality of the plans developed and (2) their motivation to carry plans out? Which is more important?

5. Is conflict likely to be constructive or destructive when it arises from differences of opinion on strategic directions?

6. Which of the various courses offered at your university (economics, history, psychology, sociology, anthropology, mathematics, engineering, law, and the like) have the highest potential for providing new ideas which will be useful to future managers? That is, where do you think new, useful ideas are likely to come from? Why?

7. The text states "strategy does not remain fixed for ever." If the proper management system must be tied to strategy, does this mean management systems must change frequently? Discuss.

8. From the enterprises you encounter in your daily life, pick an example of each of the technology types described in this chapter—stable, regulated flexibility, and adaptive. For each of these examples, check what you know of their management design against Table 26-1. What reasons do you think explain any differences between the features listed there and those in your examples?

## CASES

For cases involving issues covered in this chapter, see especially the following. Particularly relevant questions are listed after each case.

Benjo Associates (p. 92), 20
Elizabeth Archer (p. 96), 21
Camden Chemical (p. 298), 24
Delphi Insurance (p. 369), 22
Joe DiMaggio (p. 533), 19
Foster Promotions Inc. (p. 538), 22

## FOR FURTHER READING

Kantrow, A., "The Strategy-Technology Connection," *Harvard Business Review,* July 1980. Valuable review of the literature concerning the linkage between company strategy and technology.

Leontiades, M., *Strategies for Diversification and Change.* Boston: Little, Brown, 1980. Describes how diversification strategies produce changes in a corporation's management system.

Lorsch, J. W. and S. A. Allen, *Managing Diversity and Interdependence.* Boston: Harvard Graduate School of Business Administration, 1973. Research study of the organization of multidivisional companies. Chapter 9 summarizes broad guides to organizing and controlling companies with varying degrees of diversity in their activities.

Lorange, P., *Corporate Planning: An Executive Viewpoint.* Englewood Cliffs, NJ: Prentice-Hall, 1980, chap. 6. Emphasizes the need for consistency between strategy and the major dimensions of the management system.

Osborn, R. N., J. G. Hunt, and L. R. Jauch, *Organization Theory*. New York: Wiley, 1980, pts II and III. Comprehensive review of contingency approaches to management.

Rumelt, R. P., *Strategy, Structure and Economic Performance in Large American Industrial Corporations*. Boston: Harvard University Press, 1974. A study of the relationship between diversification strategies and organization designs in over 200 companies, with the unique feature of using profitability to assess the soundness of various combinations of the two variables.

# 27

# managing change

Learning Objectives

After completing this chapter you should be able to

1. Describe the two major approaches to changing organizations.
2. Explain the key elements of a management process change approach.
3. Discuss the limitations of a management process change approach.
4. Describe the central features of organization development (O.D.)
5. Describe alternative confrontation modes which can be used to implement change.
6. Identify the factors which influence the choice of a confrontation mode.

A successful, well-integrated company—like a winning football team—cannot rest on its laurels; next year the game will be new and

somewhat different. At least part of the finely tuned policies and programs that worked so well in the past will have to be adjusted to new challenges.

To emphasize this relentless, dynamic quality of management, this final chapter focuses on managing change. In today's world especially, a manager's task never stays finished.

Strategy cannot remain fixed. With the swirl of technical, political, social, and economic events, a company's niche is sure to change. We see this clearly in a product's life cycle. When a product is new, the key strategic variables are usually technical and educational. During expansion, market position is crucial; profits can be earned but initial capital investment is high. In maturity, the spotlight shifts to low cost; capital now flows in. Adjustment of strategy to these shifting key variables will typically move a company through all three types of structure that we discussed in the preceding chapter.

**external and internal pressures for new managerial systems**

Success also breeds change. Growth itself leads to system modifications. And as a company's position in the industry improves, its strategy has to be adjusted. Doubling from two to four percent can be achieved with little external reaction, but doubling from fifty to one-hundred percent will precipitate price wars, antitrust suits, and vastly different social responsibilities. Here again the necessary shifts in strategy call for modification in the management system.

Few enterprises offer the identical service over a long period. Success prompts diversification. A decline in demand leads to a search for new opportunities. When the revised strategy pushes the firm into new lines of endeavor, rarely will the old management system be best suited for the new venture. In fact, a very difficult design problem arises when a company is working with several lines in various stages of their development.

The values of key managers also change. Attitudes concerning the acceptance of government subsidies, the willingness to take personal risks, the importance attached to family happiness, the thirst for power—for example—do shift from year to year. Such value changes affect company decisions, company politics, and the capability of individuals to fill important positions.

Every manager, then, should be prepared to assist in, and adapt himself to, changes in the management system.

The process of changing to a new management system requires both adjustment of the social structure and modification of personal values.

**what change requires**

An enterprise is productive as a joint endeavor only when it has its own social structure. To work together effectively, people need to know what to expect of others, what their own role is, where they can get help, who has power, and what sources of information are available—as we have noted especially in Chapters 9 and 16. A revised management system upsets many of these established relationships.

Assume, for example, that you are a branch manager confronted with the following changes:

Bob Brown, whose actions after ten years in the treasurer's spot could be predicted, is now in Los Angeles; a young banker has the title of treasurer, but central budgeting work has been tansferred to a new assistant controller. Meanwwhile, all scheduling is to be done in regional offices, and data from the computer memory is available to everyone. Your boss reports that the president has revived his campaign for management-by-results.

You will not know what these changes really mean until you and others have had actual experience with the new relationships, have carefully observed the behavior of new people, and have tested the strength of the central staff. The new social structure—the way of working together—takes time to form.

Individual values and behavior must also change to fit the new system. When one of the most prestigious New York banks changed its strategy to include active solicitation of small accounts, a host of modifications were made in procedures, branch-office organization, lending authority, and the like. The basic problem, however, was to modify the attitudes of employees toward the blue-collar depositor. Genuine interest in such people had to replace crisp politeness.

Comparable adjustments in attitudes are usually necessary to achieve significant change in leadership styles. So difficult are some of these value shifts that a new setup is ineffective until persons compatible with the new way of life are put in key posts. For example, federal programs for aid to local education have been significantly hampered because people administering them could not quickly adjust their personal values regarding local autonomy, desegregation, religious instruction, role of parent groups, importance of professional training and other issues.

**deciding on scope of change**

Of course, the extent of change occurring in a firm at any one time varies. In Chapter 2 we identified three levels of strategy—corporate, business-unit, and functional. Rarely will all three be in flux at the same moment; more likely change at one level will lead to change on another level. We need to have one foot on the ground while stepping with the other.

New corporate strategy typically focuses on expansion or contraction of a few operating divisions, while remaining divisions pursue previously established objectives. The more diversified the corporation becomes, the less likely it is that the same strategic thrusts will fit all operating divisions. And even energetic managers can give careful attention to only a limited number of major changes at the same time. Consequently, priorities must be set at the corporate level.

Another consideration in deciding where and when to make a change is that the upsetting of a social structure should, if at all possible, be followed by a period of stability. Just as it is impractical to reshuffle the curriculum and degree requirements of a university every term, so too it is unwise to redesign the management structure of a division or department too often. Once a new organization pattern and a revised planning and control procedure have been learned, they should be retained while a "return on the investment" is achieved. Both morale and efficiency are at stake.

Small changes, especially within a functional area, can be absorbed more frequently; in an "adaptive" management system they will even be accepted as normal. But, as we have noted throughout this book, many of the external pressures that inevitably arise will require more than minor adjustments. So a first step in managing change is to decide where and how much to rock the boat; the potential benefits must be balanced against the inertia and cost.

**MANAGERIAL PROCESS APPROACHES TO PRODUCING CHANGE**  Assuming that management has decided what change is desirable in the external actions of their company, how can they make it happen?[1]

Broadly speaking, a manager can modify the way an organization actually works (a) by reforming the prescribed management processes, and/or (b) by altering the behavior of the people in that system.[2] We have already discussed both of these approaches in earlier chapters. Here we merely emphasize the applicability of these familiar concepts to managing change.

To carry out a new strategy, some changes in the explicit (formal) management design are usually desirable. For example, the merging of American Motors into the giant French automobile concern, Renault, resulted in a modification of American Motors' strategy. Consider just two features of the strategy. In the future, American Motors will rely heavily on Renault for engineering improvements—lighter engines, reliable front-wheel drives, and the like. And, American Motors' distribution system will be used to sell French-built cars in the United States as well as the improved American Motors' products. Here is just a sample of the management process changes that the managers of American Motors might make to carry out these new strategic thrusts.

**management process response to a new strategy**

*Organization structure*  In engineering, a new international coordination unit could be created, and the U.S. innovation engineering sections dissolved. Such a change would encourage, and indeed force, reliance on Renault engineering. In marketing, a Renault sales division parallel to the domestic car sales division could be established directly under the marketing executive vice-president. This would assure concentrated attention on Renault cars at U.S. headquarters, but would leave coordination of action in the field to be negotiated.

---

[1]To simplify this discussion, we focus on changing the behavior of a "company" or business-unit. However, the same approach can be used by department, section, or corporate managers with respect to activities under their direction.

[2]Alternative conceptual frameworks for organizational change approaches are contained in L. Porter, E. E. Lawler, and J. R. Hackman, *Behavior in Organizations* (New York: McGraw-Hill, 1975), chap. 15; and H. J. Leavitt, "Applied Organizational Change in Industry: Structural, Technological and Humanistic Approaches," in J. G. March, ed., *Handbook of Organizations* (Chicago: Rand McNally, 1965).

*Figure 27.1* The merger of American Motors into Renault demonstrates how formal management design changes in response to a new strategy.

***Planning mechanisms*** The new strategy could be supported by revised planning procedures as well as by changes in organization. For instance, market analyses and sales quotas could reflect the dual line. Similarly, in designing new American Motors cars, provision could be made for early data inputs about the performance and dimension specifications of French equipment. In other words, the new strategy would be put into practice by systematically revising plans for many of the day-to-day activities. Incidentally, such a revision is a laborious and time-consuming task, but it cannot be sidestepped.

***Control measurements*** To ensure that the new strategy is indeed being carried out, and to check on actual results, revised control standards and reports could be devised. In addition to broad postaction controls—on car sales, market position, production costs, and the like—a variety of steering controls could be established. These might cover, for example, an independent review of proposed new car designs, field tests of combined American Motors—Renault engineering, and spot analyses of dealer problems in selling Renault cars. The aim of these controls—in addition to flagging trouble early—would be to communicate to people throughout American Motors' organization that the new strategy has to be taken very seriously.

This example clearly implies that strategic change is unlikely to occur by modifying the management design in only one respect. Instead, as stressed in the preceding chapter, reinforcing adjustments are usually necessary in planning, organizing, leading, and controlling.

**modifying the design to change attention and values**

Managers often wish to make changes that are less sweeping than a shift in strategy. Process modification is a normal, useful approach here, also. For instance, the president of a Michigan university wants to reduce the $600,000 energy bills, but deans, faculty members, and operating personnel think they have more important things to do than bother about heat and electricity. General appeals to save energy have little effect.

One approach is to appoint a "conservation director" of the university. After study, the conservation director would issue instructions about closing buildings on weekends and evenings, about when air-conditioning may be turned on, the use of lights and elevators, and even the temperature of the gym. Then to overcome indifference, a couple of students would be hired part-time to check compliance, and a weekly report of violations sent to the president (and the violators). People would grumble, but energy consumption would go down.

Similar measures have been used at universities and elsewhere to promote "fair employment practices." Note that if and when people affected by such a bureaucratic approach adjust their values and actions so that the desired results become normal behavior, the formal apparatus could be scrapped.

Management design may be used to liberate action, as well as to constrain it as is suggested in the preceding examples. Thus, when Johnson & Johnson decided to enter the pharmaceutical business, half a dozen employees were separated from the hospital supply division and charged with building the new business. This separation had several advantages. It ensured concentrated attention and incentive for the pioneers whose personal future depended upon the success of the new venture. It permitted these people to develop an integrated structure of policies, procedures, organization, and controls which suited the pharmaceutical industry; the technology and management structure of the hospital supplies business would have been a drag, whereas the new structure expedited growth.

These examples show that one way to produce a change is to reshape the organization and the rules of the game.[3] Such reshaping can be done anywhere in the management system. An improved (computer-based) information system, a revised budget procedure, a new bonus plan, an expansion program, are all possibilities. Managers can alter the general process or a specific guide within the process. And most managers like this approach to making changes because the official rules of the game are within their power to manipulate.

**limitations of changes in management processes**

Designing a well-integrated management structure, carefully fitted to some new objective, does not guarantee that the desired change will take place. A neat system, however rational, cannot be simply ordered into place. Two kinds of limitations often arise.

[3]For an overview of structural approaches to change, see M. Beer, *Organization Change and Development: A Systems View* (Santa Monica: Goodyear, 1980), chap. 10.

First, any new design lacks social fiber. The new plans have yet to take on full meaning from varied experience. The stated organization relationships have to become mutual understandings between specific persons. The use of power has to be tested. Controls usually have to be felt before they are anticipated normally in behavior. Numerous little gaps in the formal prescriptions have to be filled in by the "doers" themselves, and interpretations tested. Only over time do group cohesion (teamwork) and confidence emerge.

During this period when structural concepts are being converted into behavior patterns, slippage occurs. Uncertainty saps energy. Political jockeying alters the structure. Interpretation of words twists their meaning. Often persons external to the organization are expected to fit into the new scheme (distributors, suppliers, and the like), and their conformance deviates even more than that of insiders. So to breathe life into the new structure managers must patiently and persistently explain, reinterpret, prod, and inspire. And the living structure that gradually arises is never quite like "the book" says.

Second, the new structure as initially designed may fit poorly the needs of the individuals and groups who are to be the actors. Typically, a manager designs a new structure to achieve new goals. The reason for embarking upon the change is to attain objectives of the enterprise. But, as we noted especially in Part IV, employees have their personal desires which only partly match those of the enterprise. Similarly, groups within and contributing to the enterprise have their own norms. Thus, in actual operations several sets of needs are interacting.

If a manager expects to get commitment, or even compliance, from employees to the new structure it must meet their needs reasonably well.[4] Some adjustment in the initial design may be necessary to achieve this degree of fit. Possibly, refinements in the structure that suit everyone better can be devised. More likely, concessions will be made to win better motivation. Because both company goals and individual needs shift with the passage of time, the optimum structure also evolves. One of the benefits of a clear strategy is the guidance it provides to a manager in deciding where and how much modification of structure to allow.

## PEOPLE APPROACHES TO PRODUCING CHANGE

Instead of relying entirely on the redesign of managerial systems, a manager who wishes to change activities can concentrate on the behavior of the individuals who perform those activities. People take center stage, rather than goals and guides for work.

---

[4]Of course, the new structure must also meet the needs of other resource contributors reasonably well (see Chapter 1). The discussion here focuses on employees because they are more likely to be intimately affected by managerial changes. However, a comparable pressure to accommodate to the needs of creditors, government regulators, suppliers, distributors, etc., may arise. The scope of managing change depends upon what is necessary to achieve the desired result.

The simplest way to redirect the actions of an individual is to use some variation of MBO (see discussion of management-by-objectives on pages 44–48).[5] Suppose, for example, that Motorola is just adding a home video-tape machine to its line of TV sets. The sales manager discusses with each branch manager how the addition will affect his work. They explore the who-what-when-how necessary to introduce and build volume in the territory. At the end, agreement is reached on what the branch manager will do, when specific goals will be reached, what resources will be provided, and how results will be measured. Other Motorola executives will have comparable discussions with their subordinates.

modifying individual behavior

Note that the MBO procedure assumes that the subordinate accepts the new objective and the conditions (e.g., advertising help) surrounding his added task. Often such acceptance is forthcoming, but not always. If instead of adding a new product Motorola were closing a plant in Chicago and consolidating production in Phoenix, Chicago managers would probably be less than enthusiastic. So a second phase of changing individual behavior is careful thought about the likely response of that individual and selection of an appropriate motivation plan—as described in Chapters 15 and 20. Skill and time are required in this phase, because the motivation plan should be fitted to the specific subordinate and his feeling about the particular change.[6] But such is the price of bringing about change.

We have noted repeatedly that effective action by a company or department requires integrated group behavior in addition to competent, committed individuals. The managerial system—already discussed—is one way to secure this integration. Another approach to integration flies under the banner of "organization development," or "O.D."[7]

"organization development"

O.D. grows directly out of behavioral science research. Its techniques and values are those of a wide group of behavioral researchers.[8] The aim is to improve organizational effectiveness by enhancing the functioning of key groups in the enterprise. This is accomplished by treating all group members as self-fulfilling individuals; encouraging open, candid and revealing communications; becoming very aware of group processes and norms, and the impact of these on each member—mutually seeking new attitudes, values, and ways of relating to others; gathering data and measurements on shifts in group behavior; and using an outside "change agent" (behavioral scientist) to actively promote a different group cohesiveness.

[5]For description of a change effort based on company-wide use of MBO, see S. Carroll and H. Tosi, *Management by Objectives* (New York: Macmillan, 1973).

[6]R. Likert and S. M. Fisher, "MBGO: Putting Some Team Spirit into MBO," *Personnel,* January-February 1977.

[7]For an overview of organization development, see R. Beckhard, *Organization Development: Strategies and Models* (Reading, MA,: Addison-Wesley, 1969), and W. G. Bennis, *Organization Development: Its Nature, Origins, and Prospects* (Reading, MA,: Addison-Wesley, 1969).

[8]See N. M. Tichy, "Agents of Planned Social Change: Congruence of Values, Cognitions and Actions," *Administrative Science Quarterly,* 14, (1974) 164-82; and N. Margulies and A. P. Raia, *Conceptual Foundations of Organizational Development* (New York: McGraw-Hill, 1978).

Under favorable conditions, O.D. does, indeed, lead to a friendly, participative group. However, managers sometimes question the heavy and protracted effort of many people that O.D. entails—because the linking of O.D. to company objectives is weak. Company targets such as increasing output or meeting deadlines may get lost amid indulgence in self-assessment.

Nevertheless, managers can use the O.D. approach in some change situations. When a company or department is under external pressure, but its managers can't agree on who should do what, a device is needed to develop consensus. Two stages are important. First, the group in open discussion should agree on the need for action; this establishes the urgency of setting aside individual wishes and confronting the overriding challenge. Second, with agreement on the broad target, the group can then explore what needs to be done and who should do it.

Working as a group has several benefits at both stages. Social pressure helps push aside selfish considerations; and diverse viewpoints openly expressed encourage a broad perspective. With a group it is easier to (a) unfreeze one's beliefs, then (b) objectively explore new approaches, and (c) finally, when consensus is reached, re-freeze in a way that enlists group commitment. An external change agent (preferably someone who understands the business and technology being discussed) can be helpful in keeping the process on the track.[9]

In such a managerial group process, several O.D. techniques can be employed, but the basic goal must be identifying and accomplishing an external mission. To the extent that group self-analysis occurs, it is only a means, not an end in itself.

**personnel shifts**
Individual and group adjustments affect people already in the organization who are expected to adjust to the new tasks. An alternative is to replace a few key people with "new blood."

The issue, to cite two examples, is whether a manager who has worked hard to construct a petrochemical plant in Mexico will be the best person to run the plant at half the planned capacity while a nationalistic government threatens expropriation; or whether the founder of a drug rehabilitation clinic should continue to direct it after it is merged with a local hospital. The question of retraining vs. replacement applies to everyone whose work is significantly altered by the new direction the company or department is taking.

Retraining present personnel has distinct advantages. They already know local facts and what to expect of each other. Numerous interactions have become routine, so they work efficiently as a team and readjust with minimum effort. The manager can predict responses to new instructions, and thus select his leadership style appropriately. Morale based on a sense of security about job and status is maintained.

---

[9]An innovative treatment of the role of the change agent is described in I. Adizes, *How to Solve the Mismanagement Crisis* (Homewood: Dow Jones-Irwin, 1979).

The reasons for bringing in at least a few new people may also be strong. It is easier for a new manager to make an objective diagnosis. He is not defensive about past decisions. Moreover, he is unencumbered by social obligations growing out of past deals. The slate is clean. In addition, the fresh energy that arises when tackling a new job can be focused on the change process. And, as pointed out in Chapter 14, a new appointee can be selected for skills and knowledge particularly important for the new thrust. Often most important of all, a new executive brings enthusiasm and commitment—in contrast to nostalgia for "the good old days" felt by existing personnel. New managers symbolize and energize a new thrust.

Obviously, in each change situation the pros and cons of shifting personnel must be weighed. The magnitude of the change, the adaptability and values of present personnel, the availability of new appointees, the urgency—all affect the decision.[10] The final choice will depend partly upon the confrontation mode—another facet of managing change which is considered in the next section.

## TACTICS FOR IMPLEMENTING CHANGE

We have just reviewed a variety of actions—some dealing with management processes and some with people—that a manager may take to produce a desired change. Another vital consideration is how aggressive must he be, and how can he win continuing support.

By "confrontation mode" we refer to the speed, directness, and offensive effort that characterize an attempt to bring about a change. The following illustrations suggest a range of possibilities.[11]

**confrontation mode**

*Mass, concentrated offensive* Occasionally, an executive will decide to push through a plan despite opposition and obstacles. Ralph Cordiner did so when he decided to decentralize the management of the General Electric Company. Orders were given, positions were abolished, the gospel was preached, new organization plans were carefully prepared, the most elaborate management education program ever tried in industry was launched, and a few recalcitrants were fired. Within a mere three years, thousands of executives had changed their way of thinking, and the company was prepared to handle the largest volume of business in its history. Rarely has such a large company been changed so drastically so fast.

*Fabianism—avoiding decisive engagement* This mode seeks gradual changes rather than revolutionary ones. The head of an industrial-equipment company chose this approach in the engineering department.

[10]For a discussion of how personnel shifts may be matched to strategic changes see M. A. Devanna, C. Fombrun, and N. Tichy, "Human Resources Management: A Strategic Perspective," *Organizational Dynamics* (Winter 1981), pp. 51-67.

[11]For additional examples of confrontation modes, see W. H. Newman, *Administrative Action,* 2nd ed. (Englewood Cliffs, NJ: Prentice-Hall, 1963), pages 86-98.

*Figure* $27.2$   *When there is a need for prompt results, mass, concentrated offensive may be the most appropriate confrontation mode.*

The engineers, the president felt, were too professional in their outlook and not sufficiently oriented to customer needs. Drastic action would have upset morale and probably caused valuable people to resign. So the president made arrangements to have the engineers visit customers' plants; they were invited to sit in with the salespeople when bids on important jobs were being prepared; those engineers who helped meet tough problems posed by a customer were given public commendation; the chief engineer counseled with his people about how they could make their work more valuable to the company. Thus, although management ventured no single dramatic action, the point of view of the engineers changed substantially over a period of time.

***Making a quick showing***   When there is skepticism, though not necessarily opposition, to a change, a prompt and favorable showing on a minor problem may open the way for more extended study of a knotty problem. For instance, proponents of electronic computers often are able to justify an initial installation on the basis of economies in handling payroll or accounts receivable records. Then, having demonstrated merit on routine operations, they can gain acceptance of more elaborate programming tactics which may take as much as two years of preparatory work.

Industrial engineers, both consultant and company-employed, have long recognized this srategy: "First find some savings that will cover your salary (or fee), then go to work on the tough problems." Frederick W. Taylor would probably not have been permitted to continue his years of study on "the art of cutting metals" if he had not also developed patents and other changes which provided more immediate benefits.

*Boring from within*  Here, people already within the organization initiate the change. The potency of this mode in the hands of Communists is well known, but a similar approach may be used in many different situations. One company used it to get its executives to take an active part in community affairs. No general program was announced. Instead, management identified managers sympathetic to community involvement throughout the branches of the company, and used them to spread the point of view. Occasionally these people would have dinner with one of the vice-presidents, at which time they talked over progress and problems; more often, however, just two or three would meet together for a discussion. All shared a missionary zeal for "having businessmen live up to civic responsibilities." Although top management let its endorsement of this type of activity be known, the effective ferment really started with these dedicated people—and it took hold in several branches in which the local manager was far from enthusiastic.

*Letting things get worse before they get better*  The treasurer of a family-owned company with a five-million-dollar sales volume was convinced that companywide budgets should be installed. Other members of top management were ambivalent toward this "big company device." In view of their position, the treasurer might have prepared some estimates simply for her own use. Instead, she waited until the company had a poor six months during which expenses went up while sales went down. There was a good deal of grumbling about who should have done what. At this point, the treasurer again suggested budgetary control. The potential benefits were now clear, and all the executives took an active part in operating the new system.

*Striking while the iron is hot*  This mode calls for prompt action while a situation is propitious. When the sales manager of a chemical company decided to retire because of ill health three years before the normal retirement age, simply replacing him would have been relatively easy. But because several readjustments in the whole sales-management organization were due, the president seized this opportunity to push through other modifications that would have been resisted if they had been initiated as separate, conspicuous moves.

*Keeping one jump ahead*  In some circumstances, being the leader is a decided advantage. The management of IBM followed this strategy when the company received orders from the Army for two electronic computers of advanced design. Although the engineering was incomplete and several tough production problems remained to be solved, the company decided to go ahead with the production of twenty such machines in order to lead its competitors in marketing this type of computer. It was a big gamble for two reasons. (1) Several million dollars were poured into the project, and (2) by seeking commercial orders, the company risked damaging its reputation if the machines could not be successfully produced. Fortunately for IBM, the gamble paid off handsomely.

The selection of a confrontation mode depends upon the following factors:

**1.  nature of objectives**

*Urgency*   The need for prompt results precludes the use of a Fabian or boring-from-within mode, suggesting rather a mass-concentrated-offensive. Contrariwise, when immediate results are not so vital, a manager may decide on letting-things-get-worse-before-they-get-better.

*Agreement on objectives*   When people affected by a proposed plan agree on desired results, it is feasible to strike-while-the-iron-is-hot. Quite another situation exists when the persons affected want different results. Then boring-from-within to change objectives is more appropriate.

*Desire for continuing cooperation*   In most business relationships we expect to deal with the same people over and over again. Consequently, today's actions become part of tomorrow's experience. Thus, mass-concentrated-offensive may haunt us, whereas stability and consistency may facilitate subsequent actions. Clearly, the time-span that needs to be considered affects the choice of confrontation mode.

**2.  present situation**

*Resources available*   A firm with relatively strong reserves of manpower and capital can give serious attention to mass-concentrated-offensive, whereas a weaker firm may find boring-from-within more suitable. And even the strong firm—or individual—may not try to keep-one-jump-ahead if committed to other, more attractive uses of resources.

*Temperament of managers*   Any manager can better carry out a mode suited to his temperament. Some people, for example, are short on patience and find a Fabian or a letting-things-get-worse-before-they-get-better mode hard to live with. Other managers are uncomfortable with aggressive, roughshod tactics. Of course, we all do things that do not exactly fit our temperament, but the chances of success are better if the action comes naturally.

*Accepted mores*   The acceptance of, or resentment to, a particular mode depends partly on the prevailing mores of the company, industry, and country where it is used. Boring-from-within is expected in some situations and frowned upon in others. Marked differences will also be found in responses to other modes. Typically, a manager should operate within accepted mores; at least any decision to break with tradition should be a conscious choice.

*Future environment*   A manager's prediction about future conditions may indicate that a plan will be easier—or more difficult—to put into effect as time passes. When events are running in his favor, he may adopt a Fabian mode. But when he faces a now-or-never situation, strike-while-the-iron-is-hot or mass-concentrated-offensive are more appropriate.

3.  chances of success

*Disruption*   Modes vary in their disruptive effect on the companies' established routines, on informal social relationships, and on personal habits and self-concepts. Perhaps industry and other external behavior will be upset. Some disruption is inevitable, but generally it is wise to keep disruption low.

4.  costs

*Incentives dissipated*   Some modes call for large expenditures of energy, out-of-pocket expenses, or even loyalty and goodwill. These are scarce resources, useful for many purposes. So one consideration in selecting a particular mode is dissipating resources only to the degree necessary to achieve the desired result.

*Side effects*   Sometimes a mode will accomplish its main objective but have undesirable side effects. For example, a textile company—using a mass, concentrated offensive—closed down its New England mill over the protests of both workers and community. The immediate objective was accomplished, but because of the way the action was taken the cost included union trouble in other plants and the reluctance of several financial institutions to extend long-term credit.

Most of the considerations for choosing a confrontation mode in the preceding list cannot be measured accurately; the manager's judgment is the main source of data. Analytical, perceptive thinking about the suitability of alternative modes can inform his judgment and thus pay high dividends in achieving change.

Conversion to a new management system takes time. Social structure and personal belief cannot be altered overnight. Managers can assist in the transition, however, by dealing with three psychological factors; learning, anxiety, and confidence (see Figure 27.3).

building a new stability

Learning new relationships and attitudes—like any other learning—is aided by clear explanations, opportunity to try the new way, further questions and explanations, more trials and adjustments, and then practice. If a manager helps everyone involved in change to recognize that the process may be tedious at first but will reduce confusion later, the total transformation will be expedited. But the need for learning will not always be willingly accepted.

Any change that alters a person's primary source of satisfaction for his security, social, and self-expression needs is sure to create anxiety. Just the uncertainty about how the new system will affect him personally is unsettling. Such anxiety often causes odd behavior—irritability, resistance, lack

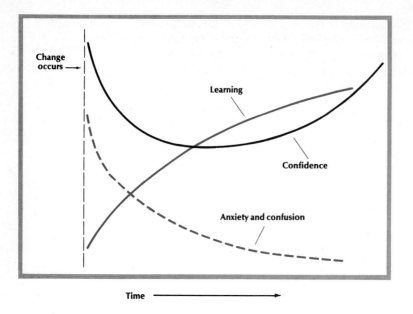

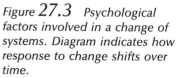

Figure 27.3 *Psychological factors involved in a change of systems. Diagram indicates how response to change shifts over time.*

of enthusiasm. A manager should do all he can to relieve anxiety during a transition period. Stating facts, explaining future plans, stressing future benefits, having people meet new associates, scotching rumors, showing awareness of personal problems—all help allay anxiety. With rare exceptions, bad news faced promptly is better than extended worry. If answers to specific questions cannot be given, assurance of when and how the information will become available is helpful.

Both learning and relief of anxiety help to rebuild confidence. In addition, a manager can bolster confidence by reinforcing desired behavior. Public recognition and reward to persons who successfully use the new design will transfer attention from old ways to the new pattern; and continuing acknowledgment of success will restore a sense of competence that had been placed in doubt when familiar behavior had to be altered.

These personal and social adjustments take time. Experience indicates that major reorganizations require at least a year to digest, even with strenuous efforts to speed the conversion. Because of this required investment in time and energy, it is naturally hoped that a new system can be used for several years. A company needs a period of stability during which it can recoup its investment. Similarly, most people need a spell of stable productivity to regain their confidence. Although we anticipate recurring need for change in the management system, the wise manager knows that there are personal and economic tolerance limits to the frequency of change.

*Participation* in the formulation of strategy and design of the new structure will speed up learning. On the other hand, participation may extend the period of anxiety, unless the participant sees clearly that he will fare well in any alternative being seriously considered.

576

# CONCLUSION: STRATEGY AND CHANGE

Whenever a manager wishes to change the activities under his guidance—and in the present world the need for change arises often—he faces the question of how to proceed. Several elements which are critical in every change program have been outlined in this chapter. Readjustment of the managerial processes—the planning, organizing, motivating and leading, and controlling—often provide direct leverage. People are also central. Either existing personnel must modify their values and behavior, or new individuals have to be introduced into the system. Overlaying these elements is the choice of confrontation mode—how fast to move with how much disruptive force. All these elements must be considered and blended together to form a mix which varies with each situation.

The magnitude of the change desired, the urgency, the human and other resources available and their fit into the new thrust, tolerance for risk and for frequent change—all affect the blend of change elements that suits a specific occasion. Because so many diverse considerations are involved, some overriding objective or mission is needed to clarify priorities and values. Strategy serves that purpose. The local situation determines which change programs are feasible, but it is strategy that establishes which ones are desirable.

The interdependence of the parts of this book has been frequently stressed. In the first chapter we singled out a manager's role in external and internal integration. The present chapter goes even further. Company strategy, which expresses a firm's attempt to integrate with its environment, has been related to management systems, which express primarily the firm's internal integration. We have focused especially on how a manager can design structures that are internally coherent and also suited to the company's strategy. Thus we have turned from analysis to synthesis, a process which calls for management of a high order of sophistication and competence.

## FOR FURTHER DISCUSSION

1. "Too many people expend enormous amounts of energy (1) worrying about, (2) protecting themselves from and (3) trying to stop change. I find change exhilarating and the basis for many opportunities rather than threats." What do you think of this observation by the president of a successful corporation? How might he encourage his subordinates to share his views?

2. "Change creates uncertainty. Uncertainty creates stress. Stress blocks rapid adaptation to change." How would you deal with this statement by a leading authority on stress?

3. To what degree may detailed standing plans actually encourage intelligent change?

4. The thrust of this chapter is directed toward maintaining effective management in the face of growth and change. Though this question may sound heretical, why not build a system that resists growth and change, an organization that seeks not to grow and to maintain stability wherever possible?

5. In what ways may an organization which practices high degrees of decentralization find change (1) easier, or (2) more difficult to manage than a more centralized organization?

6. The text emphasizes the importance of recognizing the potential impact of a change in one managerial process (e.g., planning or organizing) on other elements of the process (e.g., leadership or control). Who should be given the responsibility for considering these potential impacts and for seeking a coherent whole management design?

7. Are O.D. approaches to change likely to be more or less successful in an or-ganization whose top management has been very autocratic for years than one where participative management has been more common?

8. How does a manager decide when to use a "confrontation mode" for implementing a key change in strategy?

## CASES

For cases involving issues covered in this chapter, see especially the following. Particularly relevant questions are listed after each case.

Benjo Associates (p. 92), 20
Clifford Nelson (p. 192), 22
Delphi Insurance (p. 369), 22
Netsuki Novelty Products Inc. (p. 451), 20
Joe DiMaggio (p. 533), 19

## FOR FURTHER READING

Beckhard, R. and R. Harris, *Organizational Transitions: Managing Complex Change*. Reading, MA: Addison-Wesley, 1978. Series of practical guidelines along with case examples of how to manage complex organizational change succesfully.

Beer, M., *Organization Change and Development: A Systems View*. Santa Monica: Goodyear, 1980. Comprehensive treatment of the major approaches to organizational change with particular emphasis on conceptual foundations and empirical research.

French, W. L. and C. H. Bell, *Organization Development: Behavioral Science Interventions for Organization Improvement*. Englewood Cliffs, NJ: Prentice-Hall, 1978. Good overview of the techniques and approaches used by organization development practitioners.

Galbraith, J. and D. Nathanson, *Strategy Implementation: The Role of Structure and Process*. St. Paul: West Publishing, 1979. Analyzes the structural and management process changes needed to implement new strategies.

Hackman, J. R. and J. L. Suttle, *Improving Life at Work: Behavioral Science Approaches to Organizational Change*. Santa Monica: Goodyear, 1977. Collection of articles dealing with alternative approaches to organization change.

Miles, R. E. and C. Snow, *Organization Strategy, Structure, and Process*. New York: McGraw-Hill, 1978. Develops a conceptual framework for linking strategy, structure, and process in both stable and adaptive environments.

# INDEX

# A

# B

# C

# Q

# R

# S

# Y

# Z